Building Your Own Home

Eighteenth edition

THE NO.1 BIBLE FOR SELF-BUILDERS EVERYWHERE

David Snell

EBURY
PRESS

Originally published in the United Kingdom in 1978 by Prism Press

Updated editions: 1980, 1981, 1982, 1984, 1985, 1986, 1987
Revised editions: 1983, 1988, 1989, 1990, 1991, 1993, 1996, 1999, 2002

This eighteenth revised edition published in 2006 by Ebury Publishing

Random House UK Ltd, Random House, Vauxhall Bridge Road, London SW1V 2SA

Random House Australia (Pty) Limited
20 Alfred Street, Milsons Point, Sydney,
New South Wales 2061, Australia

Random House New Zealand Limited
18 Poland Road, Glenfield, Auckland 10, New Zealand

Random House South Africa (Pty) Limited
Isle of Houghton Corner Boundary Road & Carse O'Gowrie, Houghton, 2198, South Africa

Random House UK Limited Reg. No. 954009
www.randomhouse.co.uk

A CIP catalogue record for this book is available from the British Library

Editor: Anne Newman
Designer: Jerry Goldie Graphic Design

ISBN: 0 09191083 8
ISBN: 9780091910839 from January 2007

Copies are available at special rates for bulk orders. Contact the sales development team on 020 7840 8487 or visit www.booksforpromotions.co.uk for more information.

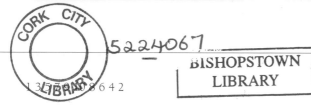

byoh-david-snell.com

Regular news updates and details of changes that occur

- Details of other books by me on related subjects
- How to obtain poster-sized copies of the Project Planner
- Details of up-and-coming exhibitions at which I will be giving seminars
- Information on residential courses and open weekends

Picture credits

Most of the images in this book are my own efforts but I would like to thank Potton Ltd. and Design & Materials ltd for the majority of the house images used.

Thanks also to Peter Harris, The Publisher, *Homebuilding & Renovating* magazine for permission to use material that has previously appeared in the magazine.

Particular thanks though go to Nigel Rigden for his superb shots.

CONTENTS

FOREWORD

This is the third edition of *Building Your Own Home* that I've written and the first that has been published entirely in my own name. But I would not want the fact that Murray Armor's name is no longer on the cover to detract from the value that he gave to this book and the services that he gave to self-building in general. His words may have been superseded by my own but the sentiment and even the phraseology remain. We did, after all, know each other for an awfully long time.

Murray is one of three men who have been hugely influential in my working life. I am not an educated man, in the formal sense. In 1962, aged just 16, I left school, and was taken on as an office boy to Peter Brownfield Pope, one of the senior partners of a London, West End estate agent, and the second of the three influential men. Mr Peter, as he was referred to, taught me the work ethic. He taught me about property, how to value it as it was and how to appreciate and grow its value. I stayed with him until I was 21, when I had to leave London because of a serious illness.

For a while I worked in a local estate agency in Hertfordshire. But it was boring and I eventually drifted into house-building. In 1970 I teamed up with two other guys and we built four houses, one of which was mine and which became Mrs Snell's and my first marital home. It was, I suppose, my first experience of self-building. I got loads of things wrong and I learned by my mistakes. But I knew, there and then, that this was for me. It was fun. Happily, I have that same sense of excitement on a building site to this day.

It hasn't all been plain sailing. In 1974, following the three-day week and the miners' strike, I, like many others, was on my uppers and I'd taken a sabbatical from gainful employment to study for the Direct Final of the Incorporated Society of Valuers and Auctioneers, which I passed. In 1975, I met Murray Armor, then the owner of a package-deal company called Design & Materials Limited, and he invited me to become a field sales representative. But he also did a lot more than that. He helped us to find a home and he generally put me back on my feet. I rose to the position of Sales Director before Murray retired, selling out his interest in the company, and I went back into self-employment.

In 1994 I had a disastrous company failure and we lost everything we had including our home in Kent. Within half an hour of him hearing of my predicament, Murray was on the telephone. He persuaded us to put the last £30 we had into petrol for a car I'd borrowed from my mother and to go up and stay with him and Jeanne for the weekend. Once we were there he informed me that, in his opinion, he'd never paid me what I was worth in the 1970s and '80s and it was about time he started. From then on, until we were back on track, he and Jeanne kept the two of us going financially.

I got a job with Design & Materials again but, to be honest, I must have been a nightmare. I'd been my own man for so long it was never going to work, and within a year I was technically unemployed.

Enter the third of these influential men: Michael Holmes, then editor of *Homebuilding & Renovating* magazine, now editor-in-chief and a rising television presenter.

I'd written a series of articles about building with subcontractors and I sent them up to Michael to see if he'd take them. He did. He commissioned 15 at a sum for each one, approaching almost half the

Right: **A modern home harking back to traditional East-Anglian roots.** © Potton

monthly wage I was then on. He also persuaded me to come out of hiding and speak at seminars at the major exhibitions. I'd felt that my failure would prohibit me from pontificating to others but he insisted that nothing that had happened detracted from the knowledge I had gained over the years. He was right, and the more I wrote, and the more I spoke, the more my confidence grew. He believed in me. He taught me to write. He taught me how to phrase things, how never to repeat the same word in a sentence and how brevity and concise text could tell more than reams of words and countless adjectives.

But it was tough going, as I would only get paid when and if an article was published, and money was tight.

Then in 1998 Murray died. I, along with most of the self-build industry he had created, went to his funeral. Three months later I was doing the seminars at the *Homebuilding & Renovating* exhibition at the NEC when Jeanne Armor came up to me and gave me Murray's watch, which I wear to this day. She told me that the 15th edition of *Building Your Own Home* was running out of steam and needed rewriting. Would I do it? It was a lifeline. I was so grateful to Jeanne and I felt that Murray was once again helping me, this time from beyond the grave.

The rest is history, as they say. I wrote the 16th edition and a new book called the *Home Plans Book*. Then I wrote the 17th edition and another book called *The New Home Plans Book*. In the meantime, the property editor of the *Daily Telegraph,* Angela Pertusini, had invited me to become a regular columnist and contributor, on the recommendation of Michael Holmes. One position seems predicated on another as over the years, various television companies, the BBC and BuildStore have taken me on as a consultant.

So now to this book.

My favourite review of *Building Your Own Home* was by Martyn Hocking, then editor of *Build It*. In it he said, 'reading this book is like having a conversation with an older and wiser friend.' His sentiments were repeated recently by a reader who rang to tell me that reading my book was like having me sitting beside him on the couch telling him all about things. Great! That's why I write in the first person – I always

wanted to write as I speak.

In previous editions I never dared to expose my personal life in self-building to public scrutiny. But now I see that was wrong. All that I write about or talk about is based upon my own experiences. So this time, having built two houses in the period between this edition and the last, I've decided to include a lot of what's happened to me and to chronicle those self-builds in detail, including all the costs.

I thought long and hard about holding myself hostage to fortune by publishing lists and tables of costs. It means, as Mark Brinkley (author of *The Housebuilder's Bible*) has warned me, that I'm always going to have to keep these figures under constant review. Those for my own houses are retrospective and will, therefore, always be right. Those for the example house are theoretical, even though they are based on the labour and material costs experienced with the other two.

So why is there such a difference between them all? Well, as you'll read, specification, method of building and design all play their part. Theoretical costs are based on strict measurement. But building's not like that. Foundation trenches will grow. Concrete requirements will spiral. Timber will get lost, burnt or broken. Nails and fixings will be ground into the mud. You'll see when you do it and, if you've remembered to put in a contingency, you'll find out pretty soon what it's for.

In this edition I've also gone into quite a bit more detail on things like the Building Regulations (or Standards as they are known in Scotland). If there is one person amongst all of those whom I have thanked and acknowledged, who deserves to be picked out, it is Ian Childs, Building Control Manager for the Forest of Dean District Council. He has been tireless in his advice and in forwarding me snippets of information on the various changes as they were heralded and even as they were withdrawn.

Writing a book with the coverage that this one has is not easy at the best of times. Writing one in such a dynamic period, particularly where the Building Regulations/Standards are concerned, has been a nightmare. I've tried to reflect what's there now. I've also tried to explain the changes that may be imminent. The trouble is that the Government has signed up to various obligations under the Kyoto and European Union treaties, requiring the introduction and enforcement of new regulations and standards. But the practicalities of doing just that and the lack of basic infrastructure to carry out the changes means that there may be delays. It's estimated that some 60% of current new buildings do not fully comply with the existing regulations and there simply isn't the manpower to oversee yet more.

I've also paid more than lip service to renovating, converting and extending, with a whole new chapter devoted to them. Oh, and one other thing. I'm proud of the fact that this is the first, and so far the only book on self-building, that recognises that there is more than just England and Wales in the British Isles; I have attempted, wherever possible, to relate things to Scotland, Northern Ireland, the Isle of Man and indeed, the Republic of Ireland (Eire).

If I've repeated myself in various passages in the book I apologise. I thought about editing repetitions out. But self-building is not one to 50. There are sequences but they overlap. If you did list all that happens then number 26 could very well be going on while number 49 was in play. And I'm aware that there are many who won't read this book from cover to cover and may just dip in and out of various subjects. So I've left those repetitions in because, if they're relevant to what I'm writing about, they need to be there.

I hope you enjoy this book and I hope that it helps you to achieve your goals.

David Snell

Acknowledgements

Jeanne, Charles and Katie Armor

Bob Bennett – the Lime Centre

Mark Brinkley – author of *The Housebuilder's Bible*

Ian Childs BSc (Hons), MRICS – Building Control Manager

Raymond Connor – BuildStore Limited

Kevin Cooper – architectural draftsman

Ken Dijksman BA (Hons), Dip TP, MRTPI – author and planning consultant

Fred Entwistle – rtrd solicitor

Peter Ferguson – Trianco Redfyre Limited

Michael J. Flint – VAT specialist

Peter Harris – Ascent Publishing Limited

Michael Holmes – Editor-in-chief, *Homebuilding & Renovating* magazine

John Horsfield – Design & Materials Ltd

John Hughes – Connor Malcolm Solicitors

Nick Jones – BRECSU

Keith, Ken & Paul @ Jewsons

Bruce MacDonald – Design & Materials Ltd

Terry Mahoney – Potton Limited

Sam Malcolm

Joe Martoccia – Potton Limited

Dante Mutti – Design & Materials Ltd

Mark Neeter – Ovolo Publishing

Tim Newman – Chumleigh Hardware

Mayur Odedra

Jason Orme – Editor, *Homebuilding & Renovating* magazine

Julian Owen RIBA, MBE – architect

Beverley Pemberton – Design & Materials Ltd

Ian Pitts – gardening contractor

David Ransley – Accountancy Services

Nigel Rigden – photographer

Linda Snell

Alan Tovey – Basement Development Group

Terry Troth – plumbing and heating consultant

James Warry – James Warry & Co. Solicitors

Most of all, to my mentor, Murray Armor and, as usual, all of the people who have put up with telephone calls from me, whilst I sucked their brains dry for information, often without them realising what I was doing.

INTRODUCTION

It is gratifying to see that the self-build industry – for an industry is what it has become – has moved into the mainstream, and that pure self-building, or new build, is embracing the already huge market of those who renovate, convert or extend their homes.

It is thought that some twenty to thirty thousand people self-build each year. Add to this all those who 'do up' or extend their homes and the figures must be enormous. Some people in the media still express complete amazement that anyone would build their own home rather than buying one 'off the peg', but they are becoming a minority and most of the national newspapers now regularly feature self-building.

But what is self-building? Many people still believe that it is all about picking up a trowel or a saw and physically working on site yourself. My definition of a self-builder, however, is someone who originates their own home: they choose the land, they decide on the design and specifications, how it is going to be built and who is going to build it. And, in the main, they do it all for their own occupation, at least in the first instance.

Some self-builders do work on site. And some, particularly those who are also involved in the building industry, undertake a great deal of the work. Others may limit themselves to clearing up or being a general dogsbody, or they may just concentrate on the management of the site, employing tradesmen to carry out the various tasks. Many choose to use a builder for the whole job whilst others might use one for certain parts of the work and either subcontractors or their own labour for the rest. Some choose to buy all their own materials, others buy selected items, and quite a few opt for package-deal schemes. Whatever their level of involvement, they are all self-builders.

The media encourage the belief that the only reason for embarking on a self-build project is financial. Headlines such as 'I saved tens of thousands', or 'I built this home for just …', do sell copies after all. And whilst it is true to say that many self-builders do make equity gains of between 15 and 50%, sometimes more, for the majority this is not why they do it. Self-building – including renovating, converting and extending – means getting exactly what you want and how you want it for the money you have.

Many self-builders go on to do it again, some of them, over and over. A self-builder friend remarked to me that he has never felt so alive as when he was self-building. Nobody can hide the fact that it is hard work, and that it can also be quite worrying, especially the first time. But it's also exhilarating. So, when it's all over and the trauma, if there was any, has died down, people miss that feeling of empowerment. They sit in their lovely new homes and they contemplate the equity they have gained and the mortgage they have. And then they realise that if they do it again they can halve or even eliminate that mortgage. At the very least they can get even more home for their money. So they do it again.

Self-builders come from all walks of life. Some are more successful than others but any measure of success must also take into account an almost

Above: **A modern home using the principle of 'additive development' for the forward projecting garage with accommodation above.** © Potton

complete lack of failure. Some self-builders may have advantages such as a work schedule that allows them to spend more time on site, or a job that provides accommodation during the build period. Some have skills that can be utilised in the context of a self-build, whilst others possess little or no knowledge of building. What all the most successful self-builders do undoubtedly have in common, however, is a capacity to get things done, to see beyond the immediate problem and to seek out the solution.

Self-building begins and ends with management, from the management of your own ideals and tailoring them to your needs and resources, to the management of your skills and the husbandry of other people's. All of this needs to be carefully evaluated and thought through.

David Snell and Murray Armor

THE NEW HOME PLANS BOOK

Over 330 inspiring plans for building the home of your dreams

'Do you need a lot of technical knowledge to self-build?' is an almost constant refrain from would-be self-builders. The answer? Not at all. Of course, any grounding you might have in the general sequence of events is all to the good, but you are going to be employing people for their skills and your job, therefore, is the management and co-ordination of those skills and of all their ancillary requirements. No lay person can learn all there is to know about self-building in the limited time available. The self-builder should aim to learn just enough to know what to ask, when to ask it, and how to understand the answer. If you are unhappy with an answer or feel that you are heading in the wrong direction, you should stop and seek another opinion or consider another choice. Any knowledge gained should be tempered with the ultimate skill in self-building: the ability to manage people and situations. Learning about bricklaying to the point where you can discuss the type of sand to be used or the additives required is fine. But if that knowledge means that you are standing over the bricklayers barking instructions, the relationship is likely to break down. Management is the key.

So, how *do* you increase your knowledge? Well, you're at the very beginning of a book that will, by its end, have given you much of what you need to know about self-building. Nevertheless, there's a lot more that you can do and what follows is a short list of suggestions. What I would warn against is taking single-interest or narrow-perspective advice too much to heart. Remember that every salesperson has a vested interest, so always keep the bigger picture in mind and remember to weigh up all advice (some of which may be conflicting) with one objective – your new home.

Books

This is by no means the only book on the market worth reading on the subject of self-building. There are many other books that will sit beside and complement this one, amongst them *The Housebuilder's Bible* by Mark Brinkley and others by Michael Holmes, Ken Dijksman, Bob Matthews and Speer & Dade (see Further Information, page 456). If you can't find them in your local bookshop look for their advertisements in the self-build magazines or visit the bookstalls at exhibitions.

If you are using a library to source books, avoid anything that's more than five years old, as well as any American books (unless you propose to build in America).

Useful books in a different category are the Building Regulations and the NHBC and Zurich Custombuild handbooks, all of which are considered invaluable by some self-builders yet ignored by others. The Building Regulations are published in sections. You may find the various illustrated commentaries on them easier to read than the regulations themselves. All are on display at the Building Bookshop at the London Building Centre in Store Street, WC1, or you can view them by logging on to the Government websites www.odpm.org.uk or www.sbsa.gov.uk.

Magazines

There are two major publications, *Homebuilding & Renovating* and *Build It,* and one lesser-known one, *Self-build & Design.* All are available at most newsagents or by subscription. Detailed case histories of other self-builders as well as a whole host of information and features make them essential reading. Most importantly, they also carry a great deal of advertising which, together with brochures you can send off for, will keep you abreast of what's available and what's going on in the self-build scene.

The magazines each have their own website. *Homebuilding & Renovating* can be found at www.homebuilding.co.uk. From the home page you can find out all about the magazine, read articles from current or back issues and get information on forthcoming shows and exhibitions. As well as its 'Plotfinder.Net' service, which has over 4,000 land and development opportunities listed at any one time, *Homebuilding & Renovating* also has a 'Products and Services Directory', which provides comprehensive listings in alphabetical order covering every aspect of self-build. There is also a discussion forum through which potential and actual self-builders can air concerns and ideas, often joined by acknowledged experts from within the industry. *Build It* can be found on www.self-build.co.uk where, again, you can view issues of the magazine, together with features on readers' homes and the latest news and information on self-build. There are also sections on finding land, finance and house design and, as you would expect, it too has a 'Products and Suppliers Directory' to help you turn your dream of self-building into reality.

Exhibitions

The exhibitions, sponsored by *Homebuilding & Renovating* magazine (*H&R*), are not to be missed by the serious self-builder as they feature hundreds of firms from manufacturers and package-deal companies through to architects and financial agencies. In addition there is a rolling programme of seminars, with advice centres on hand to help with any queries. Exhibitions are normally held at the National Exhibition Centre (NEC) in early spring, Glasgow Scottish Exhibition and Conference Centre (SECC) in late spring, East of England Showground in the summer ExCeL in London docklands in the autumn, Harrogate in early autumn and the Bath & West Showground in late autumn. Details and precise dates are widely publicised within the magazine itself.

Grand Designs (from the eponymous television programme) have started holding exhibitions at the London docklands ExCeL complex. In terms of attendance, they are certainly successful. However, I have my doubts as to how they compare with the success of the *H&R* shows in business terms as (from my observations) people attending them are far more interested in the design aspects and aspirational nature of what is on show in the context of their existing homes. Nevertheless that brings them into the category of renovators and refurbishers and, as I've already said, they are welcome to the camp.

It is remarkable just how many self-build projects can trace their origins to a visit to a show. Some visits happen almost by chance, whilst others are planned long in advance, but, in so many instances, a show seems to have been the catalyst for the eventual self-build and the forum within which many self-builders make their choices.

Show houses

Potton have a show village of three houses available for inspection, by appointment, with regular seminars. None of the other package-deal companies has show houses but most can arrange for you to visit the finished homes of some of their clients.

The Association of Self-builders

I can probably do no better than to paraphrase the association's own words. 'The association was founded in 1992 to bring together a potentially disparate group of people who have an immense amount in common. It aims to encourage an exchange of ideas, experiences and knowledge through a national newsletter, occasional national gatherings and regular meetings of regional groups.'

This is an association formed by ordinary self-builders. It's not everybody's cup of tea but it does publish a lot of useful information and it has arranged discount facilities with national builders' merchants. If you want to talk with and meet other self-builders in order to exchange ideas and knowledge (something that I continually advise), then it is worthwhile considering joining this association. They often take a stand at the major exhibitions.

BuildStore and National Self-build & Renovation centres

Why does one company get its own mention here? Some will say it's because I've taken their shilling. And I have. I'm a consultant to BuildStore and I have put in a lot of work with them to develop their range of products within self-build and, in particular, their visitor centres. However, most who know me will say that I would write what follows in any event. For I believe in what they do and I'm proud to have played a part in helping them to promote growth in the industry that I love and, in so doing, allowing more people to realise the dream of building their own home.

To contact BuildStore telephone 0870 870 9991 or visit www.buildstore.co.uk.

One of the many services that BuildStore has to offer is 'Plotsearch', which, at any one time, has over 6,000 land and development opportunities on its database. But undoubtedly the most important innovation and one which, despite its familiarity, is still deserving of an accolade is the Accelerator mortgage scheme, discussed in greater detail in Chapter 1.

The Internet is often the first and best place to look for plots or other development opportunities.

This all came about when Raymond Connor, their chief executive, visited an exhibition in Glasgow. He listened to the various lenders describing their self-build mortgage schemes, all of which, at that time, were based on stage payments in arrears and wondered, 'Why give the money after it's needed, not before?' And so the Accelerator mortgage, based on payments given in advance of each stage of the build, was born.

Connor and his colleagues also thought up the BuildStore Trade Card. Why, he felt, if self-builders, taken together, form the largest single group of builders, should they not get discounts the same as or better than those enjoyed by major developers. With the help of Jewsons and then Wolsey UK self-builders can now displaying a card giving them the same financial clout as big house-builders. Next came the question, 'Why, if most self-builders are building in large amounts of extra equity and their finances are more or less assured, can they not have decent credit limits?' The answer was that Trade Card holders can

now expect credit limits of £15,000, rising to £25,000 if they're also getting their finance through BuildStore. Plans are also in place to expand into project management and other on-site services and these will roll out over the next year or so.

But perhaps the biggest single innovation is the

advent of the Self-build & Renovation centres, one in Livingston, near Edinburgh, and one, to open in late 2006, in Swindon. These centres, permanently staffed, provide a journey through self-build with cut-away and explanatory displays showing each stage of the construction process. Visitors are greeted at the reception area and, once their details are noted, given a hand-held bar code scanner, which they can use to register interest in all or any of the products. Their details and profile are then fed through to the various companies.

These permanent facilities are worth more than just one visit and the experience of Livingston is that self-builders come back time after time over the course of their project for reassurance and advice. Open weekends and special events are scheduled to take place throughout the year together with practical and hands-on demonstrations in bricklaying, carpentry, plumbing and electrics. Residential courses dealing with both the theory and the practical side of self-building are also planned for the future.

Self-build courses

Developing Skills Limited, in association with *Homebuilding & Renovating* magazine, run two-, three- and four-day courses in the autumn and spring, covering all aspects of self-building. Although the shorter courses are largely classroom-based, the four-day courses are highly interactive, incorporating a visit to a plot, as well as a renovation or conversion opportunity, together with a tour around a timber frame factory. Subjects covered include finance, finding and assessing development opportunities, legal issues, building regulations, planning and home design. With no more than 25 people on each course and lectures from many of the magazine contributors (myself included), they provide an ideal opportunity to gain essential knowledge. Call 01480 893833 or visit www.selfbuildcourses.co.uk for further information.

Constructive Individuals (telephone 020 7515 9299, www.constructiveindividuals.com) run weekend courses in self-build project management, looking at the building process with particular ref-

BuildStore National Self Build & Renovation Centre

Above: **BuildStore National Self-Build & Renovation Centre in Swindon.**

erence to building with subcontractors. They also run three-week residential courses where up to 20 students can gain hands-on experience of building a house from empty foundations to a weathertight and carcassed shell, including making and erecting the timber frame on site and first- and second-fix plumbing and electrics.

The Centre for Alternative Technology (CAT, telephone 01654 705981, www.cat.org.uk) run various courses, concerned mainly with building in an eco-friendly fashion.

Courses on how to work with lime plasters and renders are run on one day in every summer month by the Lime Centre (telephone 01962 713636, www.thelimecentre.co.uk) and the Society for the Protection of Ancient Buildings (SPAB, telephone 020 7377 1644, www.spab.org.uk) also run courses and events throughout the year.

Chapter 1

MONEY MATTERS

Some may wonder why the first substantive chapter of this book is about finance, when for most people considering self-building it seems as if the availability of land is the most important thing. Well, important as land may be, finance comes first, and setting the budget, working out how much you can pay for the land and just how much the project as a whole is going to cost is where it all starts. In some cases, if budgets do not work out, it can also be where it all finishes or, at the very least, it can mean putting the project on the back burner until the finances are right and available.

Building for yourself is about spending money – huge amounts of money in comparison to the average person's normal expenditure. It's about spending that money so that you get exactly what you want, and spending it in such a way that you end up with a bigger or better house than you would get for the same money on the open market. How you manage this money is as important as your management of the project as a whole.

No self-build venture is entirely risk-free but if you use the information in this book, alongside common sense and professional advice (as opposed to ill-informed pub talk), you are most unlikely to experience any major problems. It is a fact that self-build disaster stories are few and far between.

Getting the money together

There is no point in going out to find your ideal plot of land if you can't afford to buy it, or if your house does not sell as quickly as you'd hoped and you lose the site after considerable expense. You need to assess all of your financial resources and establish definitively just what you can afford to spend.

The budget is always going to be made up from the cash that you have available to put into the project, plus any equity in your existing property, should you decide to sell, plus the amount you are able or prepared to borrow. The first two are simple to establish and the third has become progressively easier over the last few years.

The history of self-build finance is a fairly chequered one with building societies dipping into the market, often without fully understanding it, and then pulling out again when the going got rough. Previous editions of this book have outlined this history but the industry has been transformed in recent years, so that this is no longer relevant.

In many respects banks are perhaps the unsung heroes of the self-build market. Whilst they have never entered it amid the publicity blazes that characterised the various building societies' involvement over the years, they have quietly worked away at providing all sorts of financial assistance to those creating their own homes.

Unfortunately with many banks you can't get beyond talking to a machine or a succession of clerks, none of whom understand what you're trying to achieve. You need to be with a bank that has proper managers, and you need your manager to be sympathetic to you and what you're trying to do.

Banks are, of course, concerned at the exposure of cost to value. But in general they are able to look at the bigger picture; to consider the application and the applicant in the round and base their decisions on proven track record or demonstrated ability. If you have a good relationship with a bank manager you might find that they are quite prepared to let you open a separate 'business' account with an overdraft facility. Nothing could be simpler. As the land purchase proceeds and eventually as the build progresses, cheques drawn on this business account are covered and 'paid off' by a 'business loan'. Then, when the project is complete, this business loan is converted into a mortgage, provided either by the bank or by a completely separate lending institution.

That's the way that I've always done it, but I accept that as many banks have replaced the personal approach with an automated corporate vision, most would-be self-builders will find them impenetrable. I also recognise that many people prefer to keep their day-to-day financial affairs completely separate from their principal house finance source.

Those responsible building societies that now promote themselves within the self-build movement make many and varied offers. Most will lend a proportion of the cost of the land, plus a further proportion of the building finance required, up to a maximum of 95% of completed value. But none of them allows you to expose yourself to mortgages that you cannot afford to service. So unless you can afford the repayments for two mortgages you will end up having to sell your existing home and move into temporary accommodation. This sounds draconian and it frightens the societies as much as it does you that potential customers might be put off the whole idea of self-building. In practice, however, it's not that bad. The first objective is to secure the land. That means that only a small proportion of the eventual mortgage is required at the beginning and many people can afford to service a relatively small additional mortgage, at least in the short term.

So the building societies trumpet the fact that they have no objection to the provision of a self-build mortgage for the new house in tandem with the mortgage on the existing house, so long as the potential borrowers can demonstrate their ability to service

both mortgages. The way it works is that they deduct from the applicant's income the cost of the existing mortgage and then treat the remainder as the total gross income. They'll then lend up to the applicant's ability to pay.

This is important because it means that once an approval in principle is given the potential self-builder effectively has the money available to buy the land and won't have to risk losing it because their house won't sell. It does, however, mean that many people, despite being able to secure the land with this additional finance, will not be able to start building until such time as they have sold their existing home,

Building for yourself is about spending money … in such a way that you end up with a bigger or better house than you would get for the same money on the open market.

released the equity and freed up their income in order to take on the new mortgage.

This may sound strict, and banks may not be quite as prescriptive, but they do have a track record to look at and even they will be very choosy about who they will allow to enter into the situation of two houses and two mortgages. Building societies will remember the fiasco of the 1989 housing market collapse when they and many self-builders lost money and they are, quite rightly, concerned to see that it does not happen again.

The essential difference between a self-build mortgage and any other is the existence and distribution of stage payments. If there are no stage payments, if the land cost and building costs are not divided within the stage payments, or if the stage payments offered don't kick in until very late in the project, it is not a self-build mortgage.

Apart from stage payments the remaining mortgage criteria are the same in that your borrowing capability is based on an income multiplier, governed by a maximum ratio of loan to eventual value (usually no greater than 95%).

The standard income multiplier used to calculate the amount that a single earner can borrow is 3.5 times their income. For joint incomes, the maximum amount is 3.5 times the main income plus the second annual income or 2.75 times the joint annual income, whichever is the higher.

Regular commitments such as mortgage payments on other properties will be deducted from the gross income used in these multipliers. On the other hand, those with additional income in the form of bonuses, commission or net income from buy-to-let properties can often negotiate to borrow slightly more.

Many of the societies working within the self-build industry are prepared to advance monies against the land purchase of between 75% and 95%. This means that if you already own the land they will give that percentage of the valuation in order for you to get started on the build. On the other hand, if you're borrowing to buy the land, you will need to demonstrate that you have the necessary deposit and the building society will then release the remaining monies to coincide with the purchase of the land.

Building societies normally offer stage payments for the construction in between four and six stages. Unless you are using an Accelerator mortgage, of which more later, these are issued in arrears and monies will not usually be released until the relevant stage has been reached. This is where problems can occur for those on a tight budget, for the lenders will require that the building is inspected, usually by a surveyor appointed by them, and that the certificate is received before any funds are actually authorised for release.

Even if they agree to accept the Stage Completion Certificates given by the warranty company or the Architects' Progress Certificates, this can take an inordinately long time, which can seem even longer if you're being hassled every day for money by a bricklayer or if an intransigent package-deal company will not release materials until such time as they have the money in their hands.

However hard you try to jump the gun and pre-arrange the surveyor's visit this never seems to go to plan and the 'stop/start' that this creates is often a feature of those self-builds where stage payments are being used up to the hilt and there is no cushion of money available to carry things forward. Try to ensure that your lender knows just how crucial the timing of receipt of monies is and, above all, make your builders and subcontractors aware of particular problems before they arise rather than afterwards. You'd be surprised just how helpful a tradesman can be if they know not only that the money *is* going to be there but also that its *getting* there is reliant on them reaching a particular stage in the construction.

Many of the package-deal companies and, in particular, those where there is a bespoke or manufacturing element require money either upfront or in stages in advance of any deliveries. In addition, stage payments are often front-loaded to the point where the company can take their margin and leave a 'cost to complete' in their books. None of this need be problematic just as long as you've allowed for it all in your cashflow.

If you're making large payments in advance of deliveries, make sure either that the payments are made into a client's deposit account or that you have established the existence of an insurance-backed bond. Certain of the larger and more reputable companies have long recognised that the self-builder does

Mortgage cost calculator

Monthly payment per £1,000 of borrowing at various rates of interest

% Rate	25 Yr Repayment	Interest only	% Rate	25 Yr Repayment	Interest only
0.75	£ 3.67	£ 0.63	3.75	£ 5.19	£ 3.13
1.00	£ 3.78	£ 0.83	4.00	£ 5.33	£ 3.33
1.25	£ 3.90	£ 1.04	4.25	£ 5.48	£ 3.54
1.50	£ 4.02	£ 1.25	4.50	£ 5.62	£ 3.75
1.75	£ 4.14	£ 1.46	4.75	£ 5.77	£ 3.96
2.00	£ 4.27	£ 1.67	5.00	£ 5.91	£ 4.17
2.25	£ 4.39	£ 1.88	5.25	£ 6.06	£ 4.38
2.50	£ 4.52	£ 2.08	5.50	£ 6.21	£ 4.58
2.75	£ 4.65	£ 2.29	5.75	£ 6.36	£ 4.79
3.00	£ 4.79	£ 2.50	6.00	£ 6.52	£ 5.00
3.25	£ 4.92	£ 2.71	6.25	£ 6.67	£ 5.21
3.50	£ 5.06	£ 2.92	6.50	£ 6.83	£ 5.42

Above: **The 'Mortgage Cost Calculator' from *H&R* magazine**

sometimes need a bit of help over the financial hurdles and, also, that it's a question of *when* monies will arrive rather than *if*. These companies offer various schemes which can help you and, at the same time, guarantee their payment when the money finally comes through.

Accelerator mortgages

Introduced by BuildStore, the Accelerator mortgage schemes offer stage payments (including the one relating to the land purchase) in advance, for a fee that while significant, is nevertheless a tiny percentage in the scheme of most self-build budgets. Undoubtedly the advent of this scheme, operated through several building societies, has come to the aid of many a self-builder, enabling those with limited funds of their own to self-build and easing the cashflow of others. Undoubtedly too, the existence of BuildStore with their large panel of mortgage partners has had a profound effect on the marketplace as a whole. Even those societies, which are not within their stable, have to an extent, been influenced and educated by their example.

The scheme allows for the payment of up to 95% of the land costs plus up to 95% of the build costs to a maximum of 95% of the end value of the home that you are planning to build.

The immediate advantage is that, with funds being released in advance, you can secure your plot without having to release equity in your existing home, so long as you can raise the necessary 5% deposit and demonstrate an ability to service the additional mortgage. Even if you decide that you cannot stay in your own home during the build process this then gives you the freedom to sell your home in the intervening period whilst you are waiting for the legal and

Below: **Deal with people who understand what you're trying to achieve.**

planning necessities to be sorted out. Once building is commenced your cashflow is always going to be positive, enabling you to pay bills for labour and materials as they fall due.

Of course this type of availability of money has always been there for those using bank finance. But there is no doubt that the Accelerator scheme has enabled many more people to self-build who perhaps do not have the clout and the track record with a bank or who simply don't have a bank that they can approach with ease.

Two cautions. First of all, do not be tempted to borrow further from any other source without disclosing it to the principal lender. Secondly, do not be tempted to exaggerate the cost of the land so as to gain an advantage. In other words, if you are buying a plot for £60,000, do not tell the lender it is costing £80,000 in the hope that you will get a 75% loan, which will be equal to the whole of the real cost. This is sometimes advocated by those who should know better or who will even offer to arrange it for you. It is dishonest, and a recipe for potential disaster.

Homebuilding & Renovating magazine publish a schedule showing which lenders are offering what each month and a copy of one is reproduced on page 22 with their kind permission.

How to approach a lender

Despite all the leaflets outlining just what a building society or other lender is able to offer you and just how their product is tailored to the needs of self-builders, there is no doubt that when you sit in front of a manager, they are assessing you to decide whether you are capable of doing all that you say you are planning to do. Of course they'll look at your finances, your borrowing capacity and any track record. But more than that, they'll be weighing up whether you can actually pull the thing off.

Their decision may unfortunately be influenced or prejudiced by their own lack of understanding. Despite strenuous efforts by the head offices of banks and building societies alike, news of the benefits of self-building does not always seem to filter down to branch level. Managers earn their reputation with head office by arranging mortgages that are simple, straightforward, and generate no problems of any sort. Normally these are ordinary mortgages on ordinary homes bought on the open market. A proposal linked to a house which has yet to be built, and which may be being built on what they regard as a DIY basis may well fall into a category that they are not used to handling. You have to persuade them that your proposals carry no risk of any sort, and that you are very well equipped to handle everything in a completely risk-free way. How do you do this?

One way is to deal with your mortgage application through specialist companies who know the self-build market. The other way is to treat your application in just the same way as you would if you were applying for a job. Set out your CV or project plan clearly and concisely, detailing all of the cost elements discussed above. Allow for contingencies. Back up any cost assertions with additional information and/or brochures. Make sure that you have detailed the warranty arrangements you will be taking out, that you have listed the costs of site insurances and that you have allowed, within your budget, for the finance costs that you will be incurring. That last one is bound to impress them, by the way.

If you know that you will only be able to borrow a certain percentage of the project cost, explain where the rest is coming from. Produce a tentative programme for the work, and once more, if you need to, back this up with additional information, maybe in the form of magazine articles, particularly those chronicling the success of others, or by reference to this book.

The normal stage payments, given in advance of each stage, are:

Traditional (brick and block) build
- Purchase of land
- Foundation level
- Wall plate level
- Wind and watertight
- First fix and external render (if appropriate)
- Final completion

Timber frame construction
- Purchase of land
- Foundation level
- Kit erection
- Wind and watertight
- First fix and external rendering (if appropriate)
- Final completion

Types of mortgage

There is a bewildering array of mortgages on the market and you can do no better than read magazines such as *What Mortgage?* for more information on the subject. Self-build mortgages are, as I've said, no different from any other mortgage once the new home is built and all of the various forms can be accommodated.

Repayment mortgages

A repayment mortgage is one where the interest and principal are paid off over the period of the loan, leading to a demonstrable reduction in the outstanding balance on each annual statement. They exist in several forms:

- **Discounted mortgages** offer you a discount off the Standard Variable Rate or Bank of England Base Rate for a set period of time at the start of the mortgage, after which it reverts to whatever the Standard Variable Rate is at the time. They are very good for those on a low income with expectations of higher earnings in the future and they have helped many people get on to the housing ladder. However, they can store up trouble for those whose outgoings are rising but whose income remains static.

- **A tracker mortgage**, sometimes called a Base Rate Tracker. The interest tracks the Bank of England base rate by a set percentage with the monthly payments changing as the base rate changes.

- **Flexible mortgages** allow you to vary your monthly payments according to your circumstances. Increasing your payments means the loan will be paid off quicker with a corresponding saving in interest. Decreasing the payments or even opting for a payment holiday will extend the mortgage but may free up your financial resources when you need them most.

- **The standard variable rate** mortgage is the conventional mortgage repayment system whereby monthly payments increase or decrease as the economic cycle progresses. In times of low or medium interest rates this is usually favourable but in times of high interest rates considerable hardship can be caused.

- **Fixed rate mortgages**, as the name suggests, fix the interest rate for a set period. They have the advantage that you always know what you have got to pay each month but they can be a disadvantage if you choose a rate that is too high to start with and a period of low interest rates ensues.

- **Capped rate mortgages** offer a fixed maximum rate but allow that if the lender's standard variable rate falls below this level, your monthly payments can be reduced accordingly.

Interest-only mortgages

Mortgages are also available on an interest-only basis where you do not pay back any of the capital until the end of the loan period and instead you pay only the interest on the mortgage at the standard variable rate. This is fine for anyone who is expecting an inheritance or cash bonus to pay off the loan or for those who are planning to live in the property for a short time before self-building once again.

Alternatively, you can choose to pay additional fixed premiums into an investment option that pays off the principal at the end of the term. The most usual form of interest-only mortgage is the endowment mortgage where an endowment insurance policy is taken out with automatic life insurance to clear the debt in the event of prior death. The advantage of this type of mortgage is that it is more portable but the disadvantages have been demonstrated in recent years by the failure of some endowment policy options to generate sufficient funds to clear the mortgage.

Pension mortgages

Pension mortgages link payments to a pension plan that, at the end of the term, pays off the principal and leaves sufficient funds for a subsequent pension. The advantages are that tax relief is given on the basis of the payments being part of a pension plan but the disadvantages are that, once the mortgage is repaid, there may be insufficient capital to provide an adequate pension income.

The advice must be to examine all of the options available at the time of taking out the mortgage and to discuss them with an accountant, who will be able to relate each product to your specific or expected circumstances.

Short-term finance

Not all those who build an individual home need a mortgage and a great many people are able to finance their project from cash resources or from the proceeds of the sale of their existing homes. For those whose equity in their current home is sufficient to cover the costs of their project, essentially what they need is short- rather than long-term finance.

The H&R Guide to Stage Payment Mortgages for Self-builders

Lender	Contact no.	Web address	Advance on land	Advance for building	Stage payment details for a two-storey house	Maximum loan on completion
Amber Homeloans (Self-cert)	0870 872 0908	buildstore.co.uk	Max 95%	Max 95%	Flexible stages, released in advance	Max 90%
Bank of Ireland (N.Ireland only)	02890 241155	bank-of-ireland.co.uk	Max 100%	Max 100%	Flexible stages, released in arrears	Max 95%
Barclays Bank - via branches	0800 000929	barclays.co.uk	Max 80%	Max 80%	Five flexible stages, in arrears	Max 95%
Britannia BS (Accelerator)	0800 526350	britannia.co.uk	Max 95%	Max 95%	Flexible stages, released in advance	Max 95%
Capital Bank	0845 7253 253	bankofscotland.co.uk	Max 75%	Max 80%	Flexible stages, released in arrears	Max 95%
Cheshire BS	0800 243278	cheshirebs.co.uk	Max 60%	Max 75%	Four set stages, released in arrears	Max 95%
Clay Cross BS (England and Wales)	0800 834497	claycrossbs.co.uk	Max 75%	Max 75%	Four flexible stages, released in arrears	Max 95%
Ecology BS (Eco projects only)	0845 6745566	ecology.co.uk	Max 90%	Max 90%	Flexible stages, released in arrears	Max 90%
Ecology BS (Accelerator)	0800 018 5740	buildstore.co.uk	Max 95%	Max 95%	Flexible, released in advance	Max 95%
Furness BS	0800 834312	furnessbs.co.uk	Max 75%	Max 75%	Five set stages, released in arrears	Max 95%
Ipswich BS	01473 211021	ipswich-bs.co.uk	Max 75%	Max 75%	Four flexible stages, released in arrears	Max 75%
Kent Reliance BS	01634 848944	krbs.co.uk	Max 25%	Max 75%	Four set stages, released in arrears	Max 95%
Leeds & Holbeck BS	0800 072 5726	leeds-holbeck.co.uk	Max 85%	Max 90%	Four set stages, released in arrears	Max 90%
Lloyds TSB Scotland (Scotland only)	via branches	lloydstsb.com	Max 95%	Max 95%	Flexible, released in arrears	Max 95%
Lloyds TSB Scotland (all of UK)	01259 726650	rileyassociates.co.uk	Max 95%	Max 95%	Flexible stages, released in advance	Max 90%
Lloyds TSB Scotland (Accelerator)	0870 872 0908	buildstore.co.uk	Max 95%	Max 95%	Flexible stages, released in advance	Max 90%
Monmouthshire BS	01633 840454	monbsoc.co.uk	Max 75%	Max 75%	Four stages released in arrears	Max 85%
Nationwide BS	0800 302010	nationwide.co.uk	Max 75%	Max 75%	Four set stages released in arrears	Max 95%
Newcastle BS	0191 244 2468	newcastle.co.uk	Max 75%	Negotiable	Negotiable, released in arrears	Max 85%
Norwich and Peterborough BS	0800 883322	npbs.co.uk	Max 85%	Max 85%	Four stages released in arrears	Max 95%
Progressive BS (N.Ireland only)	02890 244926	theprogressive.com	Max 80%	Max 75%	Four stages of 25%, in arrears	Max 90%
Saffron Walden BS	01799 522211	swhebs.co.uk	Max 70%	Max 70%	Min. £5,000 a time, in arrears	Max 90%
Shepshed BS	01509 822000	theshepshed.co.uk	Max 66%	Max 80%	Negotiable, released in arrears	Max 80%
Skipton BS (Accelerator)	0870 872 0908	buildstore.co.uk	Max 95%	Max 95%	Flexible stages, released in advance	Max 95%
Stroud and Swindon BS	0800 616112	stroudandswindon.co.uk	Max 50%	Max 65%	Four stages released in arrears	Max 65%
The Woolwich	0208 3386020	woolwich.co.uk	Max 80%	Max 80%	Negotiable, released in arrears	Max 95%
TMB (self-certification)	0870 872 0908	buildstore.co.uk	Max 95%	Max 95%	Flexible stages, released in advance	Max 85%
Yorkshire BS	08451 200100	ybs.co.uk	Max 75%	Max 75%	Three stages released in arrears	Max 75%

Mortgage Guarantee Company (01744 886 884) offer specialist short term development finance. Riley Associates (01259 761456) and WWB (0800 068 7796) are independent mortgage brokers that specialise in self-build. Information supplied with the help of Moneyfacts Online. Correct as of going to press 8 August 2005

Perhaps the first port of call for this kind of help should be your own bank, assuming that you have a good relationship with them. Where this is not the case, however, BuildStore have a scheme called 'Advance'. This provides short-term finance, issued in advance stage payments, to self-builders who do not require long-term borrowing and who are prepared to repay the loan in full as soon as their new home is finished. The borrowing is based on your ability to pay the monthly premiums, as evidenced by income plus savings and investments, with the interest calculated at whatever is the standard variable building society rate in force at the time.

Slicing up the cake

Once you've got your mortgage approval in principle you'll need to start juggling the total amounts that you can afford to spend on this project between the various component parts of your new home.

The land

The price that you'll have to pay for your plot is likely to be the least movable object. Finding the plot is the first hurdle in the race and it's the one at which most self-builders fall, which is why the next three chapters are devoted to its finding, assessment and acquisition.

BUILDSTORE
ADVANCE

Short Term Bridging Finance for
Self Build, Renovations and
Conversions

easy

If you don't need a long term
mortgage but just need short term
finance to get your new home built –
you need Advance

In association with: SKIPTON BUILDING SOCIETY

Above: **Those building
in the garden of
their existing home
may only need
short-term finance.**
© Potton

For over six years I have written a monthly article for *Homebuilding & Renovating* magazine called 'Plotfinder Challenge' where I attach myself to a would-be self-building person or couple and spend an enjoyable weekend looking at plots which I have sourced. I then write about our experiences on at least three of those plots and detail the one they have chosen along with my recommendations for what they should build.

For the purposes of this book it would not make sense to state definitive figures on land costs, which can vary hugely from area to area. In the examples that follow, therefore, I have had to make assumptions. To check their relevance to your personal circumstances or area, I suggest that you look through the back pages of the major magazines catering for the self-build industry such as *Homebuilding & Renovating* and *Build It*, where plots are often advertised. Alternatively, and for much more up-to-the-minute information, log on to the landfinding agencies using the information listed in the previous chapter and in Further Information on page 456.

In days gone by, when plots were more plentiful, there was a simple rule, often quoted and still relevant in parts, called the third, third, third rule. This supposed that the plot price would form roughly one third of the *value* of the eventual house with the build costs accounting for another third and finally the increase in equity or profit making up the last third. It was an ideal, and even in the best of times it was only a starting point with regional variations in build costs and factors such as scarcity of plots in particular areas distorting it. But it still holds some relevance.

That the third, third, third rule remains at all useful is by very careful reference to its extremes of distortion and their appropriateness to your chosen area. In areas where land is readily available, and property prices are relatively low, the principal reduces the average plot price to something like a quarter of the market value of the finished property. In areas that enjoy high retail values with low plot availability, the plot price can equal or exceed half the eventual value.

But when building costs are added to the land price, the profit margins in terms of a percentage yield, or profit related to expenditure, are remarkably similar, holding at or around the 30% mark. In large part this is caused by the fact that the huge discrepancy in the ratio of land costs is balanced by the relatively small differences in build costs between the

regions and the high market value of the finished property.

Thus, if you were to buy a plot in Gloucestershire for £100,000 and spend £200,000 building a new home, you could expect the finished house to be worth around £400,000. That's a 33% increase in equity where the land formed 25% of the final market value. But in Surrey you could expect to pay as much as £500,000 for a similar-sized plot, and you would also expect to pay a little more for building costs. So if you budgeted an extra £20,000 the total outlay would be £720,000. But the final value of the home could be as much as £960,000 and that still represents an increase in equity of 33%, despite that fact that the land cost represented over half of the eventual market value of the home.

Of course I have doctored those figures a little to prove a point. But they're not that far out and what I want to stress is that this is the kind of calculation I make whenever I'm on a site for the first time, whether for the 'Plotfinder Challenge' or for myself. It enables me to decide on the economic viability of a plot, taking into account what can or should be built, how much that will cost and its eventual market value.

It's the starting point. It's not the finishing point and there are many extraneous factors that can influence the final figures. I've built two new homes in a period of two and a bit years between this book and the previous edition. The first house that I built gave me a yield on equity of 60%. In major part, for reasons that I shall explain later, that was because the price paid for the land was only 19% of the eventual resale value. The second one realised a yield on equity of 31% with the land cost representing 26% of the final market value. Again there are reasons, primarily that I managed to get a lot more on the plot than anybody else had envisaged, and once again I'll explain all that in the last chapter. Either way these figures do not contradict my assertions above or below but instead flag up the fact that careful negotiation and eye-catching design can make a big difference. And we'll talk about that later but for now, let's stick to the basics.

Once you've got your mortgage approval in principle you'll need to start juggling the total amounts that you can afford to spend on this project between the various component parts of your new home.

Build costs

Two self-builders building identical houses ten miles apart, unknown to each other but building in exactly the same way and with the same specifications, will have entirely different costs. You can tell any self-builder what they *may* build for but you can never accurately predict what they *will* build for.

'Fat lot of good that is,' I hear you say. Well yes, but the fact remains that in any self-build project there are going to be different stresses and strains. Each and every self-builder has different priorities. Some are under pressure to finish at any cost, whilst others may have all the time in the world. And in building terms, time is always money.

But you've got to start somewhere and really at the earliest stages, before you've perhaps bought the land, before you've got a design, when you're trying to convince yourself, as well as family and friends who think you've gone mad, that this is a good idea, you need to have a valid starting point.

I think that that should be the 'Average Build Cost Guide' published each month in the back of *Homebuilding & Renovating* magazine, a copy of which is reproduced on page 26 with their kind permission. But it is only a starting point. Never forget that tables reproduced in a magazine are compiled from the costs of people who have already finished building. Magazines only want to publish stories about self-builders and their homes once the house is photogenic which, in many cases, is when the garden has started to mature. This means that the figures may be quite old by the time they come to their attention. In addition, the magazines are not terribly interested in the 'bread-and-butter' or less attractive homes. They want the 'wow' factor to sell copies which means that many of the features – and therefore the cost data input – relate to homes that are expensive in terms of both design and specification. Notwithstanding this, I can still assert that the tables are pretty accurate.

In the last chapter of this book I have reproduced my costs for each of the last two homes that I have built, as they were spent. The figures are neither embellished nor are they manipulated and they were only really analysed properly when it came to the writing of this book. What is apparent in retrospect is the remarkable closeness of these figures to those in the *Homebuilding & Renovating* tables, which of course formed part of my judgement when I was originally evaluating the projects.

A closer look at build cost tables

These tables show that the specification can have a profound effect on costs with swings of 40–70% between the 'Standard' and the 'Excellent'. So it's perhaps best to concentrate on the 'Good' when assessing your initial budget. And when you do that it throws up some other interesting variations.

The first of these is that where you build has an important effect on cost but not as much as you would think, the average difference being 15%, excluding London and the inner cities. What causes these distortions? Bricks, blocks, timber? In fact most materials cost virtually the same wherever you buy them. Well, the clue is in the figures given for London, where the rise above the country in general is 25%. It's the labour costs that inflate these figures, varying from region to region and going through the roof in London and other big cities.

The second interesting variation lies in the way in which you manage your arrangements for getting the house built. If you follow the tables then the differences between those building with subcontractors plus some DIY and those using a main contractor are in the order of 18%. Now that might not seem a very large figure in comparison to the differentials brought about by specification but it does nevertheless represent a possible saving of nearly £16,000 on a fairly standard 140-square-metre house and, for many, that's not to be sniffed at.

The first home that I built in this two-year period was a fairly standard four-bedroom detached house on an infill plot. I built to a 'good' specification using subcontracted labour, some of which was lumped together into one contract, with no labour input from myself. All I put in was the management. It cost me £706 per square metre to build, which is almost smack on the figure in the tables.

The second home that I built was a bungalow. This was built to a very high specification with an innovative design and, because I was fairly busy at the time, I chose to use a builder for the weathertight shell and then made a separate contract with him for the finishing trades. The costs came out at £1,063 per square metre. Once again that figure is almost exactly the same as the corresponding figure in the tables.

Again, this is not a case of me doctoring the figures. As contributing editor to *Homebuilding & Renovating* magazine, I obviously had a hand in the preparation of these tables. But I was as pleasantly surprised as anyone and did feel almost a sense of vindication when I discovered just how close I'd got to them with my own projects.

But in order to show how the figures were made up, I asked a friend of mine, Beverley Pemberton, chief designer for Design & Materials Ltd, to draw me up a bog-standard 140-square-metre rectangular house with no protrusions or embellishments.

I have used this house and the costs that I have worked out from it to illustrate various chapters and points within this book and I have collated them all in Chapter 12. Now it is not a house that any self-

The H&R Average Build Cost Guide (£/m² for gross internal floor area)

BUILD QUALITY	BUILD ROUTE A (DIY&SUBCONTRACTORS) Standard Good Excellent			BUILD ROUTE B (SUBCONTRACTORS) Standard Good Excellent			BUILD ROUTE C (BUILDER&SUBBIES) Standard Good Excellent			BUILD ROUTE D (MAIN CONTRACTOR) Standard Good Excellent		
SINGLE-STOREY HOUSES												
Small 59m²–90m² Greater London												
South East	880	1019	1225	932	1079	1297	984	1138	1369	1036	1198	1441
NW, SW, East & Scotland	772	894	1075	817	946	1138	863	999	1201	908	1051	1264
Mids, Yorks, NE & Wales	702	813	978	743	861	1035	785	909	1093	826	957	1150
	672	777	935	711	823	990	751	869	1045	790	914	1100
Medium 91m²–160m² Greater London												
South East	806	978	1271	854	1036	1346	901	1094	1421	948	1151	1496
NW, SW, East & Scotland	707	858	1115	749	908	1180	791	959	1246	832	1009	1312
Mids, Yorks, NE & Wales	644	781	1015	681	827	1075	719	873	1135	757	919	1194
	616	747	971	652	791	1028	688	835	1085	724	878	1142
Large 161m²+ Greater London												
South East	718	942	1181	760	997	1251	802	1052	1320	845	1108	1390
NW, SW, East & Scotland	630	825	1036	667	874	1097	704	923	1158	741	971	1219
Mids, Yorks, NE & Wales	573	751	943	606	795	999	640	839	1054	674	884	1110
	547	719	901	580	761	955	612	803	1008	644	846	1061
TWO-STOREY HOUSES												
Small 90m²–130m² Greater London												
South East	847	980	1204	897	1038	1275	947	1095	1346	997	1153	1416
NW, SW, East & Scotland	743	860	1056	787	910	1118	831	961	1181	874	1011	1243
Mids, Yorks, NE & Wales	676	783	962	716	829	1018	755	875	1075	795	921	1132
	646	748	919	684	792	973	722	837	1027	760	881	1081
Medium 131m²–220m² Greater London												
South East	713	864	1096	755	915	1160	797	966	1224	839	1016	1289
NW, SW, East & Scotland	626	758	961	663	803	1017	700	847	1074	737	892	1131
Mids, Yorks, NE & Wales	569	690	874	603	730	926	636	771	977	670	812	1029
	545	659	836	577	698	885	609	737	934	641	776	983
Large 221m²+ Greater London												
South East	658	843	1058	697	892	1120	736	942	1182	775	992	1245
NW, SW, East & Scotland	578	739	929	612	782	983	646	826	1038	680	869	1092
Mids, Yorks, NE & Wales	525	672	845	556	712	894	587	751	944	618	791	994
	503	643	808	532	680	855	562	718	903	591	756	950

These figures were updated on August 8th 2005. They are for estimating purposes only. If you live in Northern Ireland, the cost of building work is considerably lower than in the rest of the UK and you should seek local advice. As an indication, use the figures for Mids, Yorks, NE & Wales and deduct 10%. If you live in the Channel Islands, London is the most appropriate comparison but local conditions affect building costs and you should seek local advice.

Above: **As the garden matures it will be difficult to tell this home from an old vicarage.** © Potton

respecting self-builder would want to build (a friend described it as a 'playschool house') but, by its very simplicity, it demonstrates just how the costs are made up and illustrates possible material and labour costs. I shall refer to it as the 'example house'. The total costs per square metre for this example house come out at £515 which, for the 'Standard' specification, is below the figure given in the magazine. Why?

The figure of £515 was arrived at by strict measurement. The labour and material costs are precisely the same as or extrapolated from the figures for my last two houses. But the calculations are made *before* the event, making no allowance for contingency, and if you're costing on a strict measurement and rate basis you need to add a contingency of at least 10%. Once that is done, the figures come out at £566 per square metre, which is much more in line with the tables.

Contrary to popular opinion, a contingency is usually used up not in some drastic single event but instead on a drip-feed basis with each element costing that little bit more than strictly measured: three days' digger hire stretching to four, four lorry loads stretching to five, 36 cubic metres of concrete increasing to 40. This creep is a feature of all building and is why all self-builds cost more than originally planned, unless, of course, they contain a contingency figure to soak up each eventuality. The only costs that are absolutely − and in the initial stages unattainably − accurate are the ones you add up when it's all over.

Before I go any further, I should explain that when I refer to the size of a house, I am talking about the net floor area, measured inside the outside walls for each usable floor. I also prefer to include the garage if it is an integral one and sometimes even if it is detached. If it is integral it is really just another room in the home. It shares the same foundations, the same walling and roofing material. Every trade is usually

The Example House

A basic rectangle of a house with few, if any, embellishments. It nevertheless manages to provide most of the accommodation that many will aspire to and is probably not that different from many of the homes on offer from developers.

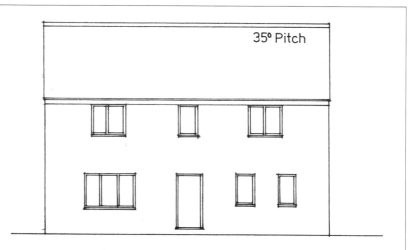

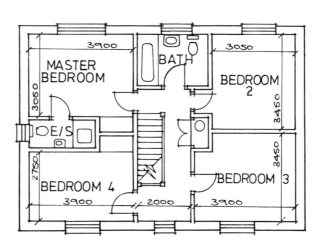

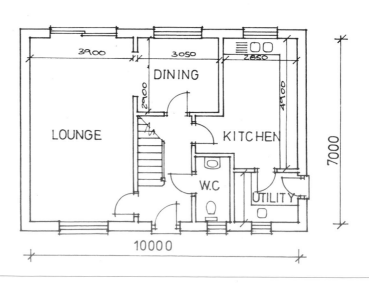

represented within it and it may indeed have features such as garage doors that are more expensive per square metre than any windows. If it is detached it is theoretically possible to build it more cheaply but in many cases, including my own example, it ends up as a small bungalow, sharing all of the materials of the main house, once again with every trade represented and, in my case, fairly expensive features. So I choose to include it in the cost analysis.

Some companies who provide plans, either in their own right or as part of a package deal, deduct in their literature as a matter of course the garage from the stated overall size of the building. They may have good reason for doing this but it can mean that people forget to include the costs for the garage, or that they think this area comes for free, which it most certainly does not. It is all the more ludicrous when the removal of the garage would render the house unbuildable without sky hooks and I have to admit a suspicion that in some cases, the deduction of the garage from the overall area is designed to make their costs look better.

So, the veracity of the tables is pretty well borne out by my own experiences and I have no hesitation in recommending them as a starting point for any costings. However, pounds per square metre is a very rough-and-ready way of costing a potential building. It can never be used as the final basis for determining the actual costs, except in retrospect. Nevertheless, I repeat that at this juncture, when you are trying to assess viability, without the benefit of detailed plans or perhaps even before you've gone out and bought the plot, you have to start somewhere.

There are, of course, factors that are always going to influence the costs and which may need taking into account at the very beginning. I have already referred to the level of specification having a profound effect on costs and this is never more true than when it comes to the choice of external materials. But there are other factors, not least the topography of the land.

Walling materials

Blockwork is often thought of as being at the cheaper end of the scale and indeed the cost of materials and labour for the external leaf of a wall in solid concrete blocks is only around £16 per square metre. But it has

Typical areas of houses and bungalows

● **Up to 65 sq. metres**

Holiday chalets, tiny 1- or 2-bedroom bungalows. Granny annexes.

● **65–75 sq. metres**

Very small 2- and 3-bedroom semi-detached houses. Small 2-bedroom bungalows.

● **75–85 sq. metres**

Small 3-bedroom bungalows with integral lounge/dining-room.

● **90–100 sq. metres**

Large older semi-detached houses. Pokey 4-bedroom modern estate houses. 4-bedroom bungalows with very small bedrooms. 3-bedroom bungalows with separate dining-room. Luxury 2-bedroom bungalows.

● **Around 120 sq. metres**

Many modern 4-bedroom estate houses. Detached houses and bungalows with the possibility of a small study, a utility room and/or a second bathroom.

● **Around 150 sq. metres**

Comfortable 4-bedroom family houses or bungalows, often with en-suite facilities to master bedrooms, studies or family rooms and a utility room.

● **Around 185 sq. metres**

Large 4- and perhaps 5-bedroom houses and bunga-lows with the possibility of en-suite facilities to more than 1 bedroom and with a separate family room.

All of these sizes exclude garaging accommodation, which can have the effect of adding 30–40 sq. metres.

CORK CITY

to be rendered, which costs another £13 per square metre. And then it has to be painted, adding yet another £6 to give a total cost per square metre of £35. And that's without taking into account that the scaffolding will have to stay up longer.

Bricks can cost as little as £130 per thousand for sand-faced Flettons (the type that many of the high-volume house-builders use). Most self-builders would, however, tend to use a slightly better brick costing around £250 per thousand the assumption in the 'Standard' category in the tables. But they can cost as much as £650 per thousand for the handmade stock bricks favoured by planners and those wanting something very special. These are assumed in the 'Excellent' category.

An expensive brick, however, requires just the same amount of mortar and time to lay, so the labour costs are not significantly different. The overall costs per square metre for brickwork should be around £29 per square metre for the very cheapest, £45 per square metre for the middle ranges and £60–65 for the top of the range.

If you choose stone, or if the planners insist that you use natural stone, then the costs of both labour and materials are going to rise quite considerably to around £75–100 per square metre. On top of that, much of the stone available today needs to be laid with a backing block, effectively meaning that the wall ends up as three leaves with a corresponding increase in lintel and other costs. And if you choose to augment the walling with stone cills or heads, then on the average home you could be looking at an additional £2–3,000.

Roofing materials

The choice of roof covering will have an effect on the costs of both labour and material. At the bottom end of the market, concrete interlocking roof tiles can be laid for as little as £28 per square metre (£30 in my example house and in the first of the two homes I have recently built). At the upper end of the spectrum natural slates, as used in the last house I built, or plain clay tiles will cost between £60 and £65 per square metre.

Special foundations

These are discussed in later sections of the book but, in general, if the example house had to switch to deep trenchfill foundations the extra cost on the groundworks would be around £5,000. And if it had to go to a piled and ringbeam foundation, that would add a further £2,000. These are large figures but still only represent an increase of 7 and 10% respectively on the total budget – certainly not enough to compromise the whole project and recoverable from savings elsewhere.

Beam-and-block flooring

On a site with a slope the warranty and the Building Inspector will be keen to see a suspended concrete floor in lieu of a solid concrete oversite. And if they start talking about thickening up the concrete, adding reinforcement and suspending the slab, then it's cheaper to switch to a beam-and-block floor immediately. Many self-builders, myself included, feel that it is well worth paying the extra cost of around £500 for a ground floor of about 70 square metres for peace of mind and the fact that you then have a stable platform to work from almost immediately.

Sloping sites

Slight slopes, i.e. up to 10 degrees, should not add very much to the costs. Almost certainly when the topsoil is skimmed from the oversite and stacked for future use, a level plinth will be created, bringing most homes back to the status quo. More severe slopes probably do begin to increase costs but not to any great degree as these days many homes utilise a beam and block suspended concrete floor and therefore all that's really changing is the amount of underbuilding. On a slope of 1 metre from back to front on the example house, that really only represents a cost increase of something like £750. Or, to put it another way, 1% up on the original total budget, or 8% on the original groundwork cost, excluding drainage, which, of course, remains constant.

Basements

There is a school of thought that given that you have to dig into the ground to build foundations, you

Above: **Rooms in the roof make this house look interesting, as well as providing additional accommodation.** © Potton

might just as well go that extra bit further to make a basement without it costing you that much more. If extra space is wanted without increasing the footprint, then a basement is ideal. But they do not come cheap. In many cases a basement is going to cost at least as much per square metre as the rest of the house. In bad ground or where there is a high water table, it could cost half as much again. Look at the costs that I've worked out for partial and full basements in Chapter 12 on the example house and also the costs relating to a retaining wall.

Rooms in the roof

The roof offers really useful and cost-effective space. For around £2,000 you could up the pitch a little and change the ordinary trusses on a house the size of the example house into attic trusses, allowing you to occupy the roof. All else remains the same unless and until you decide to do so. There may be a tiny bit more tiling but apart from that, the costs really relate to the second fix elements plus rooflights or dormers, an extra staircase and fire doors, which you'd be required to fit in lieu of ordinary doors to all rooms opening on to the staircases and landings. Even so, for close on half of the cost per square metre that you're budgeting for the rest of the house, you can have extra space without increasing the footprint or radically altering the overall appearance of the building.

Optional and elective extras

It's difficult to quantify these. When people first come to the self-build table they have very few opinions about things like bricks and tiles. They soon learn the differences and begin to appreciate their relative qualities, and it becomes imperative that such-and-such a brick or tile is used. And of course the costs go up, but the value of the home may well stay the same. If you're planning to build with a red brick costing £300 per thousand and you swap it for one costing £650, the estate agent who values your new home is simply going to describe it as being built in red brick. They won't understand the cost differential and neither will a prospective buyer. And you will have lost money.

The same with kitchens. Obviously everyone hankers after the best. But the 'best' kitchen for a 140-square-metre house could be a whopping £25,000 – ten times more than the 'worst'! This does not make economic sense and there's really no need for it, when for £3,000–13,500 it's possible to achieve all that you'd want to.

Sanitaryware is another case in point. There's no need to spend fortunes. Don't go for the bottom of the range but equally, leave the top of the range alone. Stick with the middle range. Or mix and match expensive with cheap and remember that it's the accoutrements and bits and pieces that stand out in a bathroom as much as the units.

This is not a building manual and I cannot hope to list all of the design and material cost influences. What I can do, however, is to make you aware of the need to cost things as they happen and then relate them back to your budget so that, if necessary, you can make compensatory changes. As well as this, you need to know that there are always going to be choices, that expensive is not necessarily the best and that flair and imagination can count for much more than just money.

Above all you need to understand that simple changes can have cost implications beyond their immediacy. Changing a gable to a hip will mean a more complicated roof structure and therefore considerable extra costs. But on the other hand there will be a saving in brick and blockwork, and whilst there will be the extra cost of two hip ridges, the tiling area will remain the same, so that the final bill is likely to be around £1,000. Changing from the Pvc-u joinery on our example house to softwood could save £2,000. But the need to paint them would add £1,000, extend the build time and create an ongoing maintenance cost. Internal doors can cost

as little as £19 each or as much as £300–400. But you don't need to compromise completely on quality or appearance as middle-of-the-range pine panel doors can cost around £30 each and the labour costs for fitting all three examples are likely to be the same.

Setting (and changing) the budget

We've looked at the cost of the plot and the cost of building. But these are two variables that you need to set against an invariable – namely your total budget – and you have to learn to juggle these factors.

Let's take an example and use the cost tables to see how this works. We'll stick with 140 square metres but instead of the example house let's go one better on the design, using the 'Good' specification rather than 'Standard'. Let's assume, as well, that we'll be building in Gloucestershire, not only because I know the area and many of my costs relate to it, but also because it probably represents a typical county, in cost terms.

If you elect to build with subcontractors, and without DIY, the tables tell you to budget for £678 per square metre, which works out at just under £95,000. If you decide that you want your house to be built by a single builder then the figure in the tables is £753 per square metre, which works out at £105,420. For now, though, let's assume that you are going to use subcontracted labour and that you have a budget of £180,000. This figure is based on adding together the money you think you'll have left when your house is sold, some savings that you and your wife have decided to invest in your new home, and the mortgage the two of you expect to receive. The 140-square-metre house that you're hoping to build is going to cost roughly £95,000, leaving £85,500 from the total budget to spend on the land.

Initial budget

Total funds available £180,000

Hoped-for house size 140 sq. metres @ £678 per
   sq. metre . . . . (£95,000)

Amount left in the budget for land purchase £85,000

Next, you go looking for plots, only to discover that the plots you can find are on the market at £95,000. What should you do? There's not a lot else about but you're at the limit with your budget. Something's got to give. If the vendor of the land won't come down in price then you've got to revise your ideas on the size of your new house. Working backwards that means that you've now got only £85,000 to spend on the actual construction. If you divide that figure by the £678 per square metre, your new home will now have to be around 125 square metres instead of the 140 you were hoping for.

First budget amendment

Total funds available £180,000

Land cost . . . . (£95,000)

Left for building £85,000

Divided by build cost of £678 per sq. metre
= suggested reduction to 125 sq. metres

Disappointed, you go out looking at land again, and let's assume that you now have better luck, finding a plot for £75,000. However, on further investigation you find out that whilst it is a lovely plot, it was once the site of the village pond, which means that the foundations will have to be piled at an extra cost of roughly £7,000. Again we work the figures backwards, leaving £98,000 for building. This is even better than you had originally hoped and it means that you can now choose either to build a house of 145 square metres in size, or to up the specification.

Second budget amendment

Total funds available £180,000

Land cost . . . . (£75,000)

Anticipated extra costs for foundations . . . . . (£7,000)

Left for building £98,000

Divided by build cost of £678 per sq. metre
= suggested size of 145 sq. metres

This is a very simple demonstration of how you can juggle the figures to suit the circumstances. In practice it would not be as easy as this, and, as I said earlier, pounds per square metre is only ever a rough-and -

ready reckoner and can't really be used for such exactitudes as five square metres. However, as I have also said, you've got to start somewhere and this is how you do so. These are the figures that you present to your lenders and these, especially the one relating to the total funds available, should be the figures that initiate and dictate the eventual design.

It won't always run to plan. All sorts of things can crop up, forcing you to change tack fairly radically, such as a new job, for example. This could mean that you are going to be away for much of the time, putting the mockers on the idea of building with sub-contractors. It could also mean that unless you're earning more money, allowing you to increase the overall budget, you might have to trim your ideas. You could opt to have the weathertight shell built by a small builder, then hope that you and your wife could manage subcontractors for the second fix and supply and fix finishing trades, something that might not be too difficult, as I shall discuss later. It would mean reducing the size of your building on paper to 137 square metres, but in reality, as I've said, pounds per square metre can't be used for the minutiae and you're now effectively back to the size of house that you had originally hoped for.

Third budget amendment

Total funds available. £180,000

Land cost . . . . (£75,000)

Additional ground work costs . . . . (£7,000)

Available for building £98,000

Costs using a shell builder plus subcontractors
£716 per sq. metre

Suggested size of new house 137 sq. metres

Or

Costs using a main contractor £753 per sq. metre

Suggested size of new house 130 sq. metres

On the other hand, if your new job meant that you couldn't even stomach the thought of managing the second fix trades and you had no alternative but to put the contract out to a builder or main contractor, then the figures suggest that your new house should not be much bigger than 130 square metres.

Cost versus value – is it worth doing?

Above: **Note the cantilevered upper part to this traditional home.** © Potton

The third financial element in a self-build project after the land and building costs is of course the increase in equity, otherwise known as the margin or the profit. Whilst for most people this is not the principal reason for self-building it is, nevertheless, important and it is not unreasonable to hope for some 'payback' for all the hard work that self-building undoubtedly involves.

Builders or developers assessing a piece of land make the calculation of just how much they stand to make on the project in their head, in many cases without consciously analysing or questioning their assumptions. But the lay person coming to the self-build table needs to go through all of the essential stages of valuation very carefully.

Starting off with the piece of land, imagine, possibly but not necessarily by reference to the planning permission, the finished dwelling on it and then investigate the market value for such a property in the region and in similar locations.

That might seem difficult but it's the type of calculation that most homeowners repeatedly make in the comfort of their own homes or around tables at dinner parties. It's called 'Comparative Value' and there's no real mystery to it. It's the way estate agents value homes, only they do it more often and they have a larger mental database to draw on. It might help to look in the windows of estate agents for similar properties and make a note of their values. Alternatively HM Land Registry can provide you with details of recent property transactions and average prices of the various types of house in each postal area.

You will then need to calculate the average size of these properties and relate that to what you're intending to build or to what you realistically believe your potential plot could support. Using the information on costs above plus the tables published in *Homebuilding & Renovating* magazine you can then work out the probable build costs. By deducting that figure from the assumed market value you get to the maximum amount that can be allocated to the land purchase.

Of course, you've immediately realised that this does not allow for any gain in equity and if that were the norm in any given area there would be no incentive for builders or developers to remain in business. So this is where the self-builder has to make some realistic assumptions. A developer might hope to make around 30% gross profit. But even they have to take a long-term view and there are times when they will be prepared to take less. Realistically, the self-builder is probably more interested in getting what they want for the money they have than in making an immediate profit. This is where they should have the edge on the developer.

If the plot is exactly what you want you could choose to shrink the margin to squeeze out builders who have to demonstrate an immediate profit to themselves and their bank managers. In extreme circumstances, where you are planning, in any case, to live in the property for some time, you could decide to spend right up to the finished value of the property or trust to inflation to make sure that you stay on the right side of the cost/value equation.

Self-builders must also be aware of what are known as 'ceiling values'. In any given street, even where there is a mix of properties, there is a maximum price that people will pay before they move on and search elsewhere. In a row of houses, all with three bedrooms, that regularly achieve prices of say £150,000, whilst there may well be physical scope for a five-bedroom house with a theoretical or desired value of £250,000, would someone with that kind of money to spend want to live there? The chances are that they would concentrate their property search

in a slightly better street. To think in terms of putting such a house on that site would, therefore, be exceeding the plot's carrying capacity and the ceiling value of the area.

Similarly, if a plot comes up in a street full of large, five-bedroom Victorian houses, it might not make sense to contemplate building a small two-bedroom bungalow. Not only would it look lost and incongruous, you would not achieve the plot's potential (which would, almost certainly, have been indicated by its high price in the first place).

That is, unless that's what you planned for in the first place – this is your decision and to hell with the values! After all, informed choice is what self-building is all about.

In reality much of this can be academic, as nowadays the planners will be very concerned to see that what you're proposing fits in, in proper planning terms. But there are times when it breaks down and the controls are a little lax.

All of this may seem complicated at first, but it is absolutely essential that anyone who is buying a building plot must learn how to juggle the figures. You should also bear in mind that if you are reading this book some time after the time of writing, although the figures might change, the principles

… anyone who is buying a building plot must learn how to juggle the figures.

remain. First-class and constantly updated information is always available in the national monthly self-build magazines, not just in the tables, but also in their case histories, which are packed with information on costs that can help you with your budget projections. Information of this sort is invaluable, as is that gleaned at first-hand from other self-builders who are further along in their projects and are probably more than happy to share their experiences with like-minded individuals. Bear in mind that their costs reflect only that one job and that you need to take extraneous costs and peculiar circumstances into account. But bear in mind also that it all adds up to your essential store of information.

Family money and Inheritance Tax (IHT)

Most 'ordinary' people believe that Inheritance Tax has got nothing whatsoever to do with them and that it only applies to the seriously wealthy or landed aristocracy. Well, this may have been the intention when 'death duties' were first conceived; however, in the majority of cases, these are the very last people to be affected by them. Landed families have a very different understanding of the meaning of property ownership, thinking in terms of their having a 'life tenancy' rather than absolute possession. Consequently, they have devised all sorts of ways, schemes and trusts to ensure that property and chattels pass seamlessly down the generations.

On the other hand, with property values rising so that many standard homes are far higher in value than the Inheritance Tax threshold, ordinary people are the ones who are now being caught out by this tax. Add to that the increasing impact of the property-owning democracy, with more and more people inheriting from parents, and you can see how many more are being pushed into the taxman's arms.

Inheritance Tax is often described as a voluntary tax, because, provided you make the appropriate arrangements at the right time, nothing at all needs to be paid. However, this involves giving money away in one way or the other, and just try discussing this with Aunt Lucy who, after a lifetime of being careful with money, is now worth a cool million pounds. If she is able to take a realistic view of things, she should be able to continue to enjoy her present standard of living indefinitely and ensure that her favourite niece and nephew use her money for a new house so as to avoid Inheritance Tax. This all depends on her seeing her capital as a family asset. If she does, there are various ways of going about it. If very large sums are involved, it is appropriate to make specialist arrangements, which will cost money but can be cheap at the price. Finding the right professionals to handle this may not be easy, since they should be totally independent and not people who are wanting to sell you some sort of financial service. A large firm of accountants is probably best.

The simple way of obtaining help with the cost of your new home from, say, an elderly relative, is for them to just give you the money that they intend you to have some day. Gifts given during a person's lifetime are known as Potentially Exempt Transfers (PETs) and if the donor lives for a total of seven years following the gift, there is no IHT liability. However, if a donor dies before the seven-year cut-off point, tax will become payable on the total value of the estate on death, including gifts made within the seven-year period prior to death, for anything above the threshold, currently set at £275,000 per person but, rising to £280,000 in April 2006, and £300,000 in April 2007.

If tax is payable on gifts made within the seven-year period, because they exceed the threshold, they may be subject to what is known as 'Taper relief'. This has the effect of reducing the tax payable on a sliding scale for gifts made between three and seven years prior to the donor's death. Additionally, gifts made by an individual, so long as they do not exceed £3,000 in any one year, are exempt (although if Aunt Lucy didn't give away anything in the year before, she can backdate her gift and give you £6,000). In addition, outright gifts, which can be classed as normal expenditure 'out of income', are also allowable, as are some gifts made on the occasion of a marriage. Here, parents can each give a further £5,000, grandparents £2,500 and anybody else can give up to £1,000, all of which could make a very useful contribution to a budget for a new home. These figures haven't changed for donkey's years but they are a movable feast and could come to the attention of the Chancellor at any time.

Inheritance Tax liability usually comes into effect and is payable only upon death, although with certain discretionary trusts, the liability can be immediate.

Transfers between husband and wife are exempt, so if one partner dies there is no Inheritance Tax liability for the surviving spouse. However, long-term partnerships do not enjoy this exemption and therefore a couple living and owning a home together as joint tenants, or indeed as tenants in common where they had left their share of the home to each other, could attract a tax liability upon the death of one of them for amounts or property in excess of the total personal thresholds given above. The Government is now moving to bring registered same-sex partnerships into line with married couples but there is, as yet, no movement on the plight of long-term heterosexual partnerships.

Even with a married couple, unless the right precautions are taken, there is the danger of a tax liability upon the death of a surviving spouse. Although when the first one dies, the transfer between husband and wife is exempt, when the second one dies, if the value of the home exceeds the individual threshold, then tax is payable. Unless, that is, during either of their lifetimes, and seven years before their death, they had the foresight to use up their individual threshold allowances by giving their part of the home to someone else, such as a child. If the amount exceeds the threshold and they unfortunately die within the seven years there will be a tax liability, although as mentioned above if they manage to live at least three years beyond the date of the gift, Taper relief will be available.

In general Inheritance Tax is payable at the top rate of 40%.

One way of giving money that might appeal to an elderly person who has capital invested to earn interest is for them to give you a mortgage. Anyone can provide a mortgage, not just a bank or building society, so long as it is clearly evidenced in writing, signed by all the parties and registered as a charge on the land. Any solicitor should be able to arrange this.

This really is a most useful approach. Suppose Aunt Lucy has £100,000 invested, currently earning her interest on which she pays tax. If she uses it to give you a mortgage at 1% under the current mortgage rate she will get a better return (on which she will still pay tax), you will have a cheap mortgage from an understanding source and the money stays in the family. Aunt Lucy's will may have to be rewritten to avoid complications in the future, but this is not a difficult undertaking. If both parties are interested in Aunt Lucy living in a granny flat in the new home, a whole new range of possibilities is opened up that I shall discuss in Chapter 6.

Capital Gains Tax (CGT)

Many self-builders achieve a 20% cost value differential by building their own home, and some do even better. Provided that the new property is your principal private residence, there is normally no tax to pay on any gain in equity. Private Residence Relief states that 'any gain from the disposal of your home will be fully exempt, if your disposal was of some or all of a house and its grounds, which has been your principal private residence throughout the period you have owned it (ignoring the last three years of ownership), and which in total, did not exceed half a hectare [one and a quarter acres].' Relief is not available if all or part of your home has been let or used for business but that is not meant to catch out those who work from home or have a home office, such as company representatives.

There is no set time limit for having to live in the new home in order for it to qualify as your principal private residence, although the figure of 12 months is often bandied about – probably because this is the figure that appears in the legislation in regard to certain other concessions. Normally, however, so long as you live in the property for at least one year, nobody will ask any awkward questions, although if

… before any transfers or gifts are made, professional advice should be sought as to the most tax-efficient way of going about things.

you made a habit of self-building time and time again, especially with little or no other demonstrable form of income, the taxman could deem that you were trading and tax you accordingly. On the other hand, if there is a genuine need for you to move within the normally recognised 12 months, and so long as you, once again, didn't make a habit of it, the taxman is likely to use his discretion.

Even if you have difficulty in selling your old home once the new one is built, there is a concession available whereby both properties can be considered as exempt for CGT purposes for up to 12 months, with the taxman having discretion to extend this period for another 12 months, to a maximum of two years, so long as a good reason is demonstrated. There is no facility to extend this concession period beyond the two years. If this situation is likely to occur, then it is perhaps better to retain the old house as your principal private residence until such time as it is sold, and then once that's happened, the exemption will transfer to your new house. Be aware, though, that any gain made on the new house, beyond the concession period and the date when the house becomes your principal private residence, could be taxable, subject to my comments below.

All of this is important and it could affect a great many people who buy land and, for one reason or another, take some time to get around to building on it. Let's say, for example, a couple own a paddock in a nearby village but do nothing with it for several years, and then decide to try for planning permission. Their application is successful, they build themselves a new house on the land and move in. From that moment, the new house becomes their principal private residence. But when they sell it, under the concession ruling, they are liable for CGT on any gain made in the period of ownership before the property became their main home, including the uplift in value due to the granting of planning permission.

I can recall many cases where this two-year concession has been breached for one reason or another. In truth, however, I don't know of anybody who has fallen foul of this tax in this way upon subsequently selling their home. The only mechanism I can find for this all coming to light is if the seller of a house ticks 'Yes' on their Tax Return in answer to the question, 'If you have disposed of your only or main residence, do you need the Capital Gains pages?'

It is not unusual for properties to come on to the market in tandem with a plot, formed from part of the garden. If you decide to sell off your old home and live in the existing property until such time as your new home is ready to occupy then, so long as you are moving from one home to another in the course of the project, in normal circumstances no CGT should be payable. However, if you do decide to make alternative arrangements, then consideration has to be

Above: **Try to get hold of all of the tax leaflets and read them carefully.**

given as to how you dispose of the unwanted property and your possible involvement with CGT. If you decide to do it up and sell it off, then technically you could be liable for capital gains on any increase in value, although you would be able to offset the costs of any refurbishment, together with the costs involved in the separation of the two properties. If you decide to let the house, then when you eventually sell it there could also be a CGT liability and, in addition, you will be liable for Income Tax on the rental received.

But what of the situation when you own the land? If you apply for planning permission on part of your garden and then, assuming you are successful, you sell it off as a plot, then, so long as it was part of your main home and the whole was not larger than half a hectare, there will normally be no liability for CGT. If you retain the plot for yourself, build on it and move into the new home, there will, just as in the example above, not normally be a tax liability. However, if you sell the house and move elsewhere, retaining the plot, which you then sell off at a later date then, despite the fact that it was once part of your principal private residence, there will be a CGT liability.

If you decide to build the new house and then sell it off, in an attempt to make the developer's profit as well as profiting from the increase in value of the land, you could be in trouble. The taxman might rule that you are trading and it is not CGT that you will be liable for but Income Tax. Furthermore, you will be deemed to have commenced trading at the time of the application for planning permission. The land at its pre-planning value will be your capital introduction to the project and the tax you pay will include not only the normal developer's profit but the uplift in value of the land. As if that's not bad enough, if you switch to Income Tax rather than Capital Gains Tax, the annual exemptions will not be available and you'll probably already have used up your normal allowances.

Capital gains and self-building is a very tricky area. There are some self-builders who go on to build again and again, each time living in the latest home for a year whilst they are building the next one. The tax inspector will only tolerate this for a limited period, after which he will claim that you are in business as a developer and will ask for a Tax Return to be submitted on this basis.

Let's now return to Aunt Lucy. If instead of giving you money, she gives you land or property, then there is the possibility that she could be liable for CGT on her gift, unless it falls within the rules for Private Residence Relief. Even if it's an outright gift and no money changes hands, the transfer is deemed to have taken place at full market value.

If the donor pays the CGT on a gift, the payment is ignored for IHT valuation purposes. If the recipient pays the tax, it is deducted from the value transferred.

There are annual exemptions, which at the time of writing amount to £8,200 per person per year. There are also a number of reliefs, including Roll-over, which allows for gains to be deferred if replacement assets are required. Indexation allowance adjusts gains for the effects of inflation up to April 1998 by means of tables setting out multipliers that can be applied to the original acquisition costs to reduce the tax liability. Taper relief was introduced in the Finance Act 1998 to replace Indexation allowance for gains made after 5 April 1998. This reduces the amount of gain chargeable to tax by a sliding scale of percentage points according to the whole number of years the asset has been in your ownership. None of these reliefs is exclusive and one or more may apply to any gain.

Whether any or all of this applies to your circumstances, I cannot tell. The important point, in this book, which is not after all meant to be about tax but rather about self-building, is that before any transfers or gifts are made, professional advice should be sought as to the most tax-efficient way of going about things. But I suspect that if you're in the happy position of having to worry about these things, you are either aware of the dangers or are able to provide for the eventualities.

The rate at which CGT is paid is dependent upon your income. If you have no income then you can use the 10% band for the first £1,960 of any taxable gain after exemptions. If your income does not breach the 22% income tax band then any gains that bring it up to the £30,500 threshold will be charged at 20%. Above this threshold any taxable gains, as with income, are charged at 40%.

I have decided that it would not be appropriate to include details of personal tax liabilities for the Republic of Ireland (Eire) and I shall confine my references within this book to those taxes that are broadly considered to be 'property' taxes, such as Stamp Duty and VAT.

Stamp Duty

Buying a property in any part of the United Kingdom at any figure over £120,000 will involve you in the payment of Stamp Duty at the rate of 1% of the total sum paid and you will find this tacked on to your solicitor's bill as part of the conveyancing costs. The cut-off point is absolutely precise which means that a plot sold at £120,000 won't attract any tax whilst a plot sold at £120,001 will attract a tax bill of £1200.01 – surely a spur for negotiation. Above £250,001 the rate rises to 3% and it rises again at £500,001 to 4%, a figure that may well affect prospective self-builders in the south-east corner of the country.

Stamp Duty rates in the Republic of Ireland (Eire)

In the Republic of Ireland (Eire), Stamp Duty is a vastly more complicated affair, with differing rates according to whether you are a first-time buyer or owner occupier. At the time of writing the rates are as follows:

	First-timebuyers	**Owner occupiers**
Up to 127,000 Euros	0%	0%
127,001–190,460 Euros	0%	3%
190,461–254,000 Euros	3%	4%
254,001–317,434 Euros	3.75%	5%
317,435–380,921 Euros	4.5%	6%
380,922–634,869 Euros	7.5%	7.5%
634,870 Euros upwards	9%	9%

Stamp Duty is paid on the land or property purchase only and whatever you then spend on construction or renovation does not come into it.

As if that's not complicated enough, there are differing rates for investors and for non-residential buildings, but happily these need not concern us here.

Value Added Tax (VAT)

Those who buy a new house from a builder or developer do not have to pay VAT on top of their purchase price. The VAT authorities in the United Kingdom, in recognition of this fact, have made special arrangements for self-builders, and for those converting an existing structure into a dwelling or renovating former dwellings that have fallen into disuse and remained unoccupied for certain periods.

Most of the arrangements for reclaiming VAT paid out during the construction are set out in VAT Notice 719 which has the simple title, *VAT Refunds for DIY Builders and Converters.* The regulations themselves are equally simple and straightforward, and all the details are obtainable from local VAT offices, from which you can get a claim pack containing leaflets and the claim forms that you will require.

The scheme allows self-builders in the United Kingdom to recover most of the VAT paid out during the construction of a new dwelling or the conversion of a non-residential building into a dwelling thus:

New build

With new build, a VAT-registered builder or subcontractor must zero-rate their services, i.e. you pay no VAT on any labour or upon a supply and fix contract. You do have to pay 17.5% VAT for any material purchases that you make but you can then recover this at the end of the project.

Conversions

With conversions, VAT has to be paid out on any VAT-registered labour or supply and fix builders or subcontractors at the rate of 5% only. Any material purchases that you make will attract VAT at the standard rate of 17.5%. At the end of the project all the eligible VAT paid out on labour and materials can then be recovered.

Renovations

Renovation of existing dwellings does not fall within the scheme and those doing up an existing dwelling, using VAT-registered builders or contractors, must therefore calculate that they will have to pay VAT at the standard rate of 17.5% for both the labour and material elements. This is not recoverable and, if at all possible, it therefore makes sense to use non-VAT-registered labour, thus restricting the VAT paid to just the materials. However, if a dwelling has been unoccupied for more than ten years the project is then considered to be a 'conversion' and a self-builder can, therefore, recover VAT paid out as detailed above.

If a former dwelling has been unoccupied for more than three years then, although not covered by the 719 scheme, there is a concession that allows a VAT-registered builder to charge a reduced rate of 5% for a supply and fix contract.

Additionally, although technically beyond the scope of this book, certain measures have been put in place for the benefit of builders and property developers, reducing the rate of VAT to 5% for certain classes of development. These are: renovation of dwellings that have been unoccupied for three years or more; conversion of a non-residential property into a dwelling or a number of different dwellings; conversion of a residential property into a number of dwellings (flats); and conversion of a dwelling into a care home (or other qualifying 'relevant residential' use) or into a house in multiple occupation (e.g. bedsit accommodation).

Listed buildings

Although not covered by the 719 notice, it is possible to avoid paying VAT on alterations or extensions to Listed buildings so long as they fall within the criteria laid down in a questionnaire included in the *Guide to VAT-Free Works to your Listed Home*, available from HM Customs and Excise. This relief is not by way of a refund and, instead, is given by allowing the builder to zero-rate his services. You cannot claim relief if you carry out the works yourself or on materials that you purchase for a builder to do the work for you.

Strangely enough, there is no relief for any works to a Listed building that are considered refurbishment or repair.

Administration

The revenue and excise arms of government have merged to form HM Revenue and Customs (HMRC), and it is this body that will now administer the VAT regulations. Whether or not this will provoke many changes, I can't tell. Perhaps the Excise will pass on its more efficient ways of working to the Revenue. Perhaps, also, the Revenue will now enjoy exercising the draconian rights of entry and forfeiture that belonged to the Excise. Either way, be sure to be honest in all of your dealings with them.

The VAT leaflet Notice 719 sets things out quite clearly and it would not make sense to reproduce everything in it here, although there are some comments to make. If you are unsure about anything at all you should contact your local VAT office or the national helpline for advice.

If you stick to the procedures, submit your claim on time with all your invoices properly listed, and answer any questions promptly, you should receive your refund within six to twelve weeks. Typically it will pay for all the carpets and curtains in the new home.

Points to which you should pay particular attention are:

• If you use a package company, ask them for an itemised invoice in the form acceptable to the VAT authorities. Ensure that any last-minute extras are included. The package companies know all about doing this, but as it involves a lot of typing they may wait to be asked.

• New buildings intended for occupation by the self-builder are covered by the scheme but if you are constructing the house with the intention of selling it or letting it out, or for some other business reason, you cannot use the scheme. That does not affect the self-builder's right to work from home or any subsequent sale or letting of the property – it is the first use that is the governing factor.

• Extensions to existing dwellings, renovation of existing dwellings or the creation of additional self-contained accommodation do not qualify.

• Although garages are included within the scheme, other outbuildings and ancillary structures are excluded. It is a fairly grey area but, strictly speaking, a workshop or office at the end of a garage would not attract relief. So too with a detached swimming pool house, although a swimming pool within the home, say in the basement, would be eligible for relief.

• Fencing, hard landscaping and planting are eligible for relief so long as they are included within or required by the planning permission.

• Beware of paying VAT in error, as it cannot then be reclaimed. VAT is not payable on labour only or supply and fix contracts for new build (apart from professional services). Nevertheless, I have seen bricklayers add the VAT to their bill (they were not even VAT-registered and therefore the money would have gone into their pocket). If you pay out VAT to a non-registered contractor then the only way of recovering it is to ask them nicely for its return.

- If you are converting, make sure that you only pay VAT at the rate of 5% on the labour or supply and fix contracts. Many builders are unsure of how this procedure works and you might have to persuade them or get a ruling from the VAT authorities beforehand.

You cannot reclaim the VAT on some quite unexpected materials and services. Among these are professional fees such as those for architects and surveyors as well as for management, design and planning consultants. The purchase or hire of tools and equipment, including skip hire and scaffolding, are excluded, as are fuel and transport costs and temporary fencing.

In addition you cannot claim the VAT back on things like carpets, underlay and carpet tiles, hobs, white goods such as cookers, washing machines, refrigerators and dishwashers, even if they are built-in. Fitted wardrobes bought in kit form or even the basic materials if you buy them yourself are excluded from any reclaim, although if the wardrobes are built in as permanent structures to 'dog legs' within the walls they are eligible. Doorbells, electrically operated doors or gates, aerials and satellite dishes must also be excluded from your VAT reclaim. There are other examples but these are perhaps the ones whose exclusion from the scheme might surprise you the most.

Above: **The leaflets and forms from the VAT authorities are surprisingly helpful and easy to follow.**

Purchasing materials from abroad

The 719 scheme allows for the relief and recovery of VAT paid out for material purchases made anywhere in the European Union so long as they are imported and used solely for the construction/conversion project. Most importantly the VAT is recoverable at the rate paid, whether this is higher or lower than the rate pertaining in the UK.

Most continental builders' merchants display prices inclusive of VAT and it's therefore important that you retain the invoice and that it establishes quite clearly the rate at which VAT has been paid. You need to establish the exchange rate at the time of acquisition and you must then convert the invoice and the VAT paid to sterling.

Those importing materials from outside the EU will have to pay VAT at the standard rate at the port of entry; effectively therefore paying VAT within the UK. As with imports from within the EU, if your project is eligible for VAT recovery or relief then you will need proof of purchase together with proof that the imported materials have been used on your project.

Making the claim

You make one claim only, and it must be made within three months of receiving a certificate that the building is completed. As I've already mentioned, it can include VAT paid in respect of boundary walls, drives, patios, a garage, etc, but if any of this ancillary work is left until after you move in, then any VAT paid out after the date of your reclaim is not recoverable. This should always be taken into account when you are drawing up your programme.

To make your claim, you need to get together all the invoices that you have collected so carefully, and either take them yourself to the VAT office and get a receipt for them there and then, or send them off by registered post and make enquiries if you do not receive an acknowledgement within 14 days.

It took the Excise 12 weeks to process and send me the refund on my last project – twice as long as it took them the previous time. I can't see things getting any better, so if you're relying on the refund to finish the project, you might have to make the claim a little earlier than you would have wished and swallow the VAT paid out on the last few items.

The Republic of Ireland (Eire)

For those building in the Republic of Ireland (Eire), I'm afraid that there is no provision for the recovery of VAT. Materials are split between 'prime' materials such as bricks, blocks, timber and tiles, upon which VAT is paid at the rate of 13.5%, and second-fix or fitments materials, such as sanitaryware, kitchen units and paint, upon which the rate is 21%. Labour is subject to a rate of 13.5%. A VAT-registered builder offering a labour-and-materials or full-build contract will add 13.5% to his total bill but he can then recover the 7.5% extra VAT paid out on some of the materials.

unhappy few who either took a chance or completely forgot about insurance and who then have to face the consequences not only of their own losses but also of those suffered by third parties. Ignore insurances at your peril!

If you're placing a single contract with a builder and you are absolutely confident that they carry all of the relevant and necessary insurances, then there's probably no need for you to take out additional cover. But you do need to discuss this with them. Make sure that they're aware that you are relying on them and that they understand that your reliance is an integral part of your contract with them. Having said that, even if you receive their assurances, can you be absolutely certain that your dependence is well founded and what indeed will happen if your builder simply disappears or goes bust?

Leaving aside this worst-case scenario it can still be sensible to consider taking out your own self-build insurance policy, even if there is a single contract with a properly insured builder. With things such as kitchen furniture and fittings, there is a distinct pos-

For all self-builders, renovators and converters, having the right insurance policy to suit their project and personal circumstances is as important as any other element in the creation of a new home.

Insurances

For all self-builders, renovators and converters, having the right insurance policy to suit their project and personal circumstances is as important as any other element in the creation of a new home.

It is still possible to build without insurance, but increasingly building societies (and especially those who consistently deal within the self-build sector or are in the BuildStore stable) are insisting on some form of cover. Every year there is a happy band of people who are glad that they took out adequate self-build insurance when they wake up to the aftermath of floods or storms, or to the consequences of a visit from thieves or vandals. Equally, there are always an

sibility that you might choose to arrange their purchase yourself. It's also possible that the suppliers will undertake the fitting as part of their contract with you. If there's a theft or an accident on site resulting in injury to someone, you might feel that a claim on the main contractor's insurances is justified and your builder, being a good chap, may well agree with you. But the chances are that in such circumstances his insurers will turn around and disclaim all liability if the invoices and contracts were not in his name. Such a situation, which is not at all unusual, would make the relatively small saving on the outlay of an insurance premium seem very much like a false economy. There is a strong argument in favour of 'better safe than sorry'.

However, beware of the builder who tries to avoid cover of any sort and who, instead, tries to persuade you that all that is necessary is your self-build site insurance. The builders still need to have their own insurance policies in place.

I have removed many of the references to premiums and excesses for this edition of the book because the industry is in a state of almost constant flux. Underwriters seem to come and go and many companies are forced to either pull out or hold off from writing new policies from time to time whilst they sort out new cover. Part of the reason why premiums keep going up is also the increasingly popular habit of builders trying to obtain self-build insurance in lieu of their proper, but progressively more expensive, contractor's cover.

Of course, for those building using either their own labour or through the management of subcontracted labour, a self-build insurance policy is absolutely essential. It does help, however, if one understands the full nature and extent of the different parts of a policy and how they apply to your circumstances.

The first element of a self-build policy is public liability insurance, which, most importantly, covers you for any claim made against you by a third party who suffers loss or injury as a result of your self-building operations. If you are tempted to think that this is unlikely to happen to you, consider the fact that nearly a quarter of the claims made in a given year can fall into this category. If the fence panels that you have just fixed are hurled into your neighbour's car by the wind, or if the bricklayers inadvertently spill mortar over the same vehicle, then your neighbour will have a legitimate claim against you and you need to know that you are covered. Similarly this element of the insurance covers you against injury suffered by persons visiting your site or anyone who is hurt outside the site as a direct result of your building activities. That includes persons who are trespassing on your site and you might be surprised to learn that if a child or any other person unlawfully enters your site and suffers injury you are not absolved from liability. The same rule applies to

materials removed from your site, with or without authorisation, which then cause an accident, injury or damage elsewhere.

Most household insurance policies have some sort of public liability cover attached to them covering the householder for accidents that happen to others within the house or garden but this will almost certainly not apply to any building works, even if the new property is being constructed within the grounds.

It is possible and advisable to arrange public liability cover only on a plot of land that you have bought but have no intention of building on for some time. Usually this policy will convert to a full self-build policy, on payment of the extra premium, when it is decided to start building.

The next important element of self-build insurance is known as employer's liability and there are those who make the mistake of not realising that this is important for the self-builder. Even though you might be persuaded that you are not directly employing someone in the sense that you will be 'stamping their cards' or collecting their PAYE contributions, you are still deemed to have a contract of employment with those whom you engage to carry out work on your site on your behalf. This is important. However many times the subcontractor and others assure you that they are self-employed, when push comes to shove, if they have an accident on your site, it is to you that they will turn for compensation. Self-employed subcontractors do not get unemployment or sickness benefits in the same way as others do and if they are laid off because of something that happens on your site then they or their solicitors or advisors may well see you and your insurance policy as a means of financial rescue. Perhaps this is best illustrated by the fact that nearly eight out of every hundred claims involve injuries or accidents on site.

The last element of a self-build policy is known as contractors' all-risk insurance or contract works cover and this really is the element that will cover you for the more usual problems associated with theft and vandalism together with storm, flood or fire damage. Claims against this element of self-build site insurance account for well over half of all those made.

Don't risk it

Self-build sites are not a Mecca for thieves and the incidences of a visit by thieves or vandals are perhaps less than on some of the larger more commercial sites. Nevertheless the consequences can have dire repercussions for the self-builder. The favourite targets of theft, as far as materials are concerned, are timber, copper piping and insulation as well as the more obvious high-value kitchen units, appliances and sanitaryware. As if the loss and the subsequent disruption to the self-build programme aren't enough, the main problems when these items are stolen revolve around the fact that little or no thought is given by the thieves to the consequential damage. If they can get the basin off the wall quickly with a hacksaw rather than by turning off the water supply and dismantling the connection then they will and to hell with the mayhem that a resultant flood causes.

Storm damage is something against which there is very little protection although there are some obvious precautions that any prudent person would take. In the storms of recent memory and over the last decade the insurance policies held by many self-builders were all that stood between them and ruin in respect of both the rebuilding of property and the damage inflicted on third parties.

Always choose an insurance policy that is underwritten by a household name and one that has a proven track record of meeting claims. Ensure also that you are dealing with people who can answer your questions and who understand all about the self-build market and your particular needs. Premiums are based on the reinstatement value of the building – that is to say, what it would cost to rebuild if it were destroyed just before moving in; the value of the plot and indeed, the value of the completed home, are irrelevant.

Most self-build policies involve a single premium giving cover either until the new home is finished or for a fixed period, whichever is the sooner. Most can usually be extended upon payment of an extra premium and most provide bolt-on extras if and when required. Remember that self-building usually takes longer than planned so allow a little leeway when you take out any policy; it will save you money in the end.

Caravans used as site huts or as accommodation by the self-builder and their family can usually be added to the self-build policy. You will also need to discuss with your insurance provider whether or not you need to take out cover for plant and tools or whether this is automatically included. Excesses often mean that it is not economic to provide cover for small items, whilst large items of plant are often already covered if they are hired in. Unless you own or intend owning plant to a considerable value, it might be better to take tools or things like a mobile generator home at night. If you are hiring plant then it might be best to pay a surcharge on the hire charge for the short periods tools and plant are on site. Remember, you are insuring to protect yourself from the major disasters that can occur on site, not to protect your favourite set of socket spanners!

Self-build insurance policies do not give cover for personal possessions, furniture and effects and as soon as possible you will need to take out normal household insurance cover. If you move into the new home before it's actually finished then that does nothing to invalidate your self-build policy and indeed recognition is often given to the fact that, by being on site, everything is more secure. Several policies on the market offer the opportunity to convert unused time from a self-build policy to a Household Buildings Only cover. This is not always an attractive offer as the self-builder would lose his loyalty discounts with his existing insurer and still needs Household Contents cover, something that is not always easily or advantageously available on its own.

A self-build policy will cease to give cover on completion of the building works and if you are not able or intending to occupy the property immediately you will need to arrange unoccupied property insurance. Do not assume that your normal householder's policy will extend to the second house.

Self-builders, renovators and converters may also come across the need for legal contingency insurance, sometimes known and referred to as single-premium indemnity policies. The likelihood of this necessity arising is discussed in detail in the chapters on how to evaluate and how to buy a site. But for now, suffice it to say that they can be

Above: **I hope that this self-builder in Ireland was fully insured!**

suggested in a situation where there is a restrictive covenant on the land or where all or part of a title is defective. In these cases the insurance company will assess the risk and the likelihood of any challenge to your rights of ownership or access and give cover for a single premium.

Some of the insurance providers include self-build legal protection. This gives cover, including legal expenses and costs incurred in pursuing an action taken on your behalf, against any third parties in relation to disputes arising directly from the construction or complete restoration of a policyholder's principal private residence.

As with all matters concerned with insurance and health and safety, prevention is better than cure. First of all, do not advertise the availability and attractions of your site to either casual or detailed inspection. Keep all tools and materials in a locked site hut or container and make strenuous efforts to programme

materials to arrive when they are required rather than before. This applies particularly to the high-risk items such as roof insulation, plumbing materials and electrical fittings. Be especially careful just after the delivery of things like kitchen units and sanitaryware and bear in mind that they are much more valuable to a potential thief when they are still in their packaging and therefore more readily moved and sold off. As far as plant is concerned the most obvious target is the cement mixer and it might be as well to consider removing one of the wheels so as to make it that little bit more difficult to move. As I've said, other tools should either be taken home at night or locked up securely.

There is a need to deter trespassers and that means that consideration should be given towards fencing at an early stage in the construction process. The determined and professional thief will not be put off but you will probably dissuade the more casual or opportunistic ones. If electricity is on site consider the use of proximity lighting. A 1,000-watt light coming on suddenly in the dark will unnerve the most experienced interloper and, more importantly, it will alert neighbours and others to their unwanted presence. Which brings us to perhaps the most valuable thing that you can do, and that is to make contact with your soon-to-be next-door neighbours and leave with them details of where and how you can be contacted in cases of emergency.

If you do have losses, remember to collect all the evidence that you will require to support your insurance claim. Advise the police as soon as possible, asking for the name of the officer to whom you are making your report as this will be required to support the insurance claim. Take a series of photographs of any damage, and then contact the insurers with a coherent story. You will want to hear from them whether they are going to send an assessor along to visit your site, and whether you can start putting things right before he comes. The insurers can only help you if you give them appropriate information.

This can be in a phone call when you will:

- quote your policy number
- explain that it is a contractor's risk loss, and that there are no others involved, or that it is an employer's liability incident, or involves a third party
- state simply the extent of your loss ('Vandals have broken my patio window' or 'Someone has stolen £2,000-worth of bathroom suites)
- tell them you are taking action to make the place secure again
- ask them if they are sending an assessor
- confirm the address to which they should send the claim form.

Dealing with all of this in an efficient way will help to get you back on an even keel, although you will still be concerned to tell everyone about your new-found enthusiasm for the restoration of village stocks.

Building warranties

We are all familiar with the fact that all new speculatively built houses are offered with a warranty scheme in place and that banks, building societies and other lending institutions will often not consider offering a mortgage unless an approved scheme is in place. Well, in similar vein, most self-builders needing to borrow money for their project will have to provide details of an approved warranty scheme on the new home if they are to get a mortgage. Even if they are members of that happy band who don't need a mortgage then they are strongly advised to have a warranty scheme in place, not only for their own peace of mind but to cover them for the eventuality of selling to someone who requires finance.

A warranty is designed to first of all ensure and secondly insure against faulty workmanship involved in the design and construction of your new home. It is not a substitute for the site insurance discussed above, nor does it take the place of normal householder's insurance of the buildings and property, although to some degree, and in specific circumstances, the cover can overlap. Before exploring the options on warranties and, in order to briefly explain the important distinctions between these various covers and liabilities, let us take the simple example of a wall falling down.

If a wall blows down in a storm during the building process then the cost of repairing the damage will be covered under the 'all risk' section of your self-build site insurance. If a person working on the site is injured by the falling masonry then you will be covered under the 'employer's liability' section of the self-build site insurance and if a member of the public is injured then cover will be available under the 'public liability' section of the same policy.

If this hypothetical wall blows down in a storm *after* the building is completed then you will seek to recover the cost of the damage from your normal householder's insurance policy and any injuries caused will similarly be covered under the personal accident or public liability sections of that policy.

If, on the other hand, the wall falls down within the warranty period because it was wrongly designed or constructed, then cover to put things right will be available from or through the warranty scheme without you having to necessarily seek recompense from the responsible contractors. However, and this is the important point, the structural warranty will make no provision for public or employer's liability. Therefore cover and liability for injuries or collateral damage would have to come from the relevant sections of either your self-build site insurance or your householder's insurance, whichever was in force and effective at the time.

You can see from this example why just having either a warranty or a self-build site insurance policy is not enough. Both are needed and all serious self-builders should have these in place, whatever their circumstances.

Long ago, when I first started self-building, warranties were very difficult to come by and all sorts of hoops had to be jumped through to get one. The usual way out was to use Architect's Certification, but that meant that you either had to engage an architect on a 'full supervision' basis or else you had to find another architect who was prepared to inspect for a fee. Sometimes that would work out but at other times, the second architect, perhaps with sour grapes because he/she wasn't engaged in the first instance, would make life very difficult.

An alternative, perhaps not entirely kosher, but much used all the same, was to pay a backhander to an NHBC builder to register the property and get it inspected under their name, as if they were building it. All of which was often very expensive and far from satisfactory.

Then, joy of joys, Zurich Municipal came along with their self-build warranty known as 'Custombuild'. Of course that changed things for the better almost overnight and in the years that have followed several new names, including the NHBC with their 'Solo' scheme, have come on to the scene.

I have a few fears about warranties. In the months leading up to the writing of this book big names have pulled out of the market as they have lost their underwriters and Zurich Municipal have put up their fees quite considerably.

Premier Guarantee, operating through companies such as Project Builder and Self-build Zone, have stipulated that they will not accept proposals from anyone who has built within the last ten years. You would think that someone who has built before and therefore has knowledge of the building process would be more welcome to a warranty company. However, it seems that the opposite is true and that they have identified the serial self-builder, who knows that they will be selling on in short order, as someone who does not take as much care as someone who intends to live in the home for the foreseeable future. As a serial self-builder, I think that this is pure balderdash but they make the rules and they're sticking to them.

As a consequence of all this, the NHBC are flooded with applications. Their response is to instruct their inspectors to vet all applicants very strictly and to discard those who they feel are not really capable or who are planning to use contractors or subcontractors who do not have their full approval. If they can talk a prospective self-builder into using an NHBC registered builder instead, at least for the shell of the building, then as far as they're concerned that's the best thing.

Also, if you've self-built before they might require you to register as a builder. For my part I've been told that if I do it again within the next three years, I'll have to register as a probationary member, so as I'm already looking for a plot, it looks as if that's what I'll be doing.

Some or all of the companies must have taken a few hits. If they conclude that lay people building their own homes are more likely to make or allow mistakes then they may rethink their place in self-building. My fear is that if one or more of the major players pull out of the market we'll be back to the tactics of the 1970s. My expectation is that premiums will rise quite dramatically.

One other disappointing fact is the dearth of true self-build warranties in the Republic of Ireland (Eire) where the only real warranties are those offered by builders who are either members of, or approved by, a warranty provider such as Homebond. This may change as Premier Guarantee may well extend its cover to those self-builders building with subcontractors or carrying out their own work in the southern part of Ireland.

The principal arrangements for warranties are:

- the NHBC 'Buildmark' Warranty
- the NHBC 'Solo' Warranty
- the Zurich Self-build Building Guarantee
- the Premier Guarantee
- the NHBG 'Homebond' Guarantee (Eire)
- the Premier Guarantee (Eire)
- Architect's Certification.

The NHBC 'Buildmark' Warranty

This is available to self-builders who are using an NHBC-registered builder in just the same way as any developer or house-builder offers it to his purchasers. A builder who is registered with the NHBC has to pass certain basic tests of financial probity and building knowledge and, until they can demonstrate a clean track record, they are only allowed on the register as a probationer, prohibited from advertising themselves as members.

Before any work commences on site, and in cases where there is bad ground or where there are trees on site, at least 21 days in advance of a start, the builder must apply to register the proposed dwelling and send in the appropriate fee. The NHBC will check out the drawings with care, particularly in relation to any peculiar circumstances, and then, in due course, they will allocate a registration number of which the builder's customer is advised. The self-builder will usually have to tell his bank or building society of this registration and separate documentation is issued for the attention of the 'purchaser's' solicitor (they insist on referring to you as purchaser). As the work progresses but, in particular, at certain crucial stages before the work is irrevocably covered up, the inspector will come along to the site and check the work for compliance with regulations and accepted standards of workmanship. This is his total concern at this stage; your arrangements or relationships with the builder are not his responsibility (unless the builder dies or becomes bankrupt, in which case the NHBC will step in with limited and defined assistance). The only other time that the inspector becomes involved in the nature of your contract with a builder is when an agreement has been reached whereby the builder is responsible only for construction of the weathertight shell of the building. In this case they will require written evidence and understanding of the limitations of the work and responsibilities.

It is not generally understood, but the NHBC, like all other warranty providers, is principally an insurance company. They take on responsibility for the warranty for the structural shell and integrity of the building and, in so doing, require that their registered members, the builders, take on responsibility for the other areas of the building and that they stick to those obligations on pain of being struck off the register. Even the structural warranty requires that the builder takes on full liability for the first two years so, in effect, with 'Buildmark' the NHBC is only exposed for the last eight years of its ten-year warranty, so long as the builder remains in viable business.

Brief mention should also be made here of the fact that the NHBC is an Approved Inspector, authorised to approve and inspect under the Building Regulations. This means that a registered builder can opt to have all of his Building Regulations approval and inspections carried out under the auspices of the NHBC, negating the need for a separate application to the Building Control section of the local authority.

The NHBC 'Solo' Warranty

'Solo' is specifically designed for individuals who are building their own homes on their own land, either using subcontracted labour or doing all or part of the work themselves. It is available for those building in the United Kingdom, including Northern Ireland, but not available in the Republic of Ireland (Eire). It notably excludes people who are not intending the home for their own or their immediate family's occupation, requiring a declaration to that effect within the original proposal form.

At the time of writing the premium quoted for a 150-square-metre home is £1,200. On application, the NHBC inspector will arrange a meeting, on site, at which he will make a full appraisal of your proposals, explain the scheme to you and discuss the complimentary copy of the NHBC Standards, which will have been sent to you. There is no requirement for technical qualifications or specific knowledge of the building industry or process, but there is also no

NHBC Guarantee

The NHBC divide their description of their 'product', for that is what it is, into two phases. Phase 1 covers the period during the actual building works. The inspector will come along at various stages, which are:

For a brick and block house

- Excavations
- Substructure
- Ground-floor preparation and visual drainage
- Walls to first floor
- Walls to plate height
- Roof framing and masonry complete
- First fix complete
- Completion and drains tested

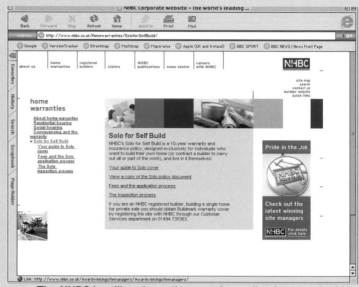

Above: **The NHBC is still perhaps the most immediately recognisable of the warranty schemes.**

For a timber frame house

- Excavations
- Substructure
- Ground-floor preparation and visual drainage
- Timber frame erected
- External leaf
- First fix complete
- Completion and drains tested

doubt that the inspector will be making an assessment of your ability to carry through what you're planning as discussed above. If it is decided at that meeting, or as a result of it, that you are not going to go ahead and that you will not be proceeding further with the NHBC, then your initial payment will be refunded in full.

Essentially the core cover that is provided is the same as for the 'Buildmark' scheme with the obvious exception that, with no builder involved, the cover for the structural shell and integrity of the building is the sole responsibility of the NHBC for the full ten-year period. Under the 'Buildmark' scheme the builder would also have been responsible

for the finishing trades for a period of two years and, therefore, under the 'Solo' scheme there is an optional damage limitation period cover available which will insure you for minor damage caused by latent defects for a period of six months. There is an additional premium for this extra cover and there is also a requirement that the work is carried out by *bona fide* subcontractors and that you enter into a formal contract with them requiring them to put right any faulty work within, at least, the six-month period. Once again, therefore, the NHBC are only really at risk if the subcontractor fails to honour his obligations or goes out of business.

At each stage they will either approve the work and issue a Stage Completion Certificate or, if the work is not up to scratch, they will require that any faulty work is put right. Then, when it's done to their satisfaction, they'll issue the certificate. The important and exclusive thing is that once a certificate is issued then all of the work up to and including that stage is covered by the NHBC and you can go ahead and use the certificate as a tool to obtain any draw-down of finance.

Phase 2 is when the building is finished and the full ten-year warranty is issued, covering the main structure of the building, any defect or damage to flues and chimneys, and defects to the drains and to the roof and tiling. It's worthwhile mentioning that the NHBC also offer a service giving help with Standard Assessment Procedure (SAP) ratings (of which more later) and, in the same way as they do under the 'Buildmark' scheme, they can also take on the responsibility for the Building Regulations approval and inspection, on payment of extra fees as required. This last service is not available in Scotland, the Isle of Man and Northern Ireland and the entire 'Solo' scheme is not available for conversions.

The Zurich Self-build Building Guarantee

Zurich, under the name Zurich Municipal, is the company that pioneered the idea and the actuality of self-build warranties under the original product name of 'Custombuild', which helped so many self-builders to achieve their dream of a new home. In no small way, it is this scheme, now known as the

Above: **Homebond takes the place of the NHBC in the Republic of Ireland (Eire).**

Zurich Self-build Building Guarantee, that enabled the self-build industry to shift up a gear, and it stood alone in the market for many years. It is, therefore, unfortunate that they now seem to be pricing themselves out of the market and are giving all of the indications that their complete withdrawal is not too far away. At the time of writing their fees for a 150-square-metre home have risen to £2,900 and I have heard of self-builders who have been quoted figures of twice that amount.

Whilst there are similarities between the Zurich scheme and 'Solo', there are also several major differences. First and foremost, the Zurich is not authorised by the Government to perform the work or undertake the role of Statutory Building Control and Inspections. In practice that's not a drawback because, in any case, this scheme works by a tie-up with the Building Control department of the local authority. This means that the Building Inspector always visits their sites with additional quality control inspections made by their own or appointed surveyors as the work progresses.

In any event, a strong argument can be made for the separation of these responsibilities and, for some, myself included, the very fact that two or more sets of inspections are being made by differing bodies can give added reassurance. Especially when linked to the perception that the local authority Building Inspector has little or no commercial axe to grind.

The track record built up by Zurich over the years is enviable and bears fruit in the many testaments by self-builders to the help and assistance given by their staff and inspectors. Although not possessing the instant recognition that the NHBC are favoured with, the Zurich Self-build Building Guarantee is equally acceptable to most building societies and banks; so much so, that many house-builders and developers now offer their products with the benefit of this cover.

As with any scheme, Zurich starts with the application form which has to be sent off with, in their case, a non-returnable deposit. You will then receive their *Technical Manual and Builders' Guidance Notes*, which is, undoubtedly, an excellent reference book in its own right. They do make a few more stipulations than the NHBC currently appear to require in that they demand that the house is designed by a qualified

architect (or other professional), that the work is carried out by professional contractors or tradesmen, and that full Building Regulations consent is sought and obtained. There is also an additional expectation that the self-builder should have a source of technical advice, a 'professional friend'. This would obviously come in the form of the architect or the package-deal company, if they were using one, but, equally, the role could be filled by a suitable friend or somebody with the relevant knowledge of building. Whilst all of these requirements may, at first, seem a trifle pedantic, they are the result of years of experience and all the indications are that the NHBC 'Solo' scheme will soon adopt similar requirements.

In common with any other warranty scheme, if bad ground or unusual ground conditions are suspected or known, then they will require a copy of a site investigation, soil report and/or foundation design. On completion of the project a ten-year structural warranty will be issued. There is also a scheme up and running for conversions and re-builds where the offer of insurance is subject to an initial survey report and the cover offered is for six years.

Unfortunately, these schemes are not available in Northern Ireland or the Republic of Ireland (Eire).

Premier Guarantee

This scheme, operated through companies such as Project Builder and Self-build Zone, covers mainland England and Wales and Scotland. It is available to self-builders whether they use a builder or subcontractors, or even if they undertake the entire project on a DIY basis. You still need to have Building Regulations approval with the normal inspections carried out by the Building Inspector. Project Builder will arrange for their own inspections to be carried out by approved surveyors. The inspection stages are footings prior to any concrete being poured, followed by one at pre-plastered out but, if they deem it necessary and on difficult or special sites, they will come out and inspect at other times. Self-build Zone advertise that no inspections are needed, presumably relying on those carried out by the local authority Building Inspector.

At the time of writing their fees are the same as for the NHBC, i.e. £1,200 for a 150-square-metre home. Cover is for ten years (extendable upon payment of a higher premium to twelve years), and runs from the date of the final inspection, although it is not issued until the property is finished and a completion certificate has been issued. Project Builder also provide self-build site insurance policies and offer a 20% discount to those clients who take up the warranty scheme.

The Premier Guarantee will issue a retrospective warranty for those who have either forgotten to arrange one or have been let down by 'architects' who turn out to be nothing of the sort and cannot give a meaningful certificate. It is not cheap or easy to get and relies on you having a full structural survey carried out. They also don't cover anything that wasn't originally built for human habitation so that rules out barn and other conversions.

The NHBG 'Homebond' Guarantee – the Republic of Ireland (Eire)

This is available only in the Republic of Ireland (Eire). The National House Building Guarantee mirrors what the NHBC offers in the UK with its 'Buildmark' scheme, which means that it is not a true self-build scheme. Builders have to register with the company and pass basic tests of ability and financial probity and, unlike the NHBC scheme, they are liable for any structural defects for the whole of the ten-year guarantee period, with the NHBG only stepping in, in effect, if the builder fails in his obligations.

'Homebond' works in three ways:

- **The stage payment bond.** For a period of two years from the date of registration, this will repay lost deposits or contract payments in the event of the builder's bankruptcy or liquidation, up to a maximum of 15% of the purchase price or 25,000 Euros, whichever is the lower. From the date of Final Notice, after the main structural inspection, to the completion and the handover, for a maximum period of six months, this indemnity rises to 65,000 Euros, or 50% of the purchase price, whichever is the lower. At the time of writing I am told that these figures are about to be changed in line with inflation but that no decision has been made as to what the new ones will be. Check with

the company before you start.

- **Two-year defects warranty**. This gives cover for water and smoke penetration for a period of two years following completion.
- **Ten-year structural defects warranty**. This protects against major structural defects within a period of ten years following certification of the home.

A home-builder must first of all write to the builder, asking them to put any defect right and then if the builder fails to carry out the work, Homebond will step in and get another builder to effect the repairs, at no expense to the homeowner, so long as they fall within their cover. At present there is no scheme for those building with subcontractors.

The Premier Guarantee – the Republic of Ireland (Eire)

At present Coyle Hamilton provide this insurance product, which provides a ten-year structural defects insurance policy, in the Republic of Ireland (Eire). It is only available to builders and developers and the application must be taken out by the builder on behalf of the owner. There are, however, plans to launch Premier Guarantee Self-Build throughout the Republic. This product will be specifically aimed at one-off self-build projects and should be up and running by the time this book goes to print.

Architect's Certification

In the years before the advent of the Zurich Municipal 'Custombuild' scheme, now known as Zurich Self-build Building Guarantee, if a self-builder wanted to build with subcontractors or their own labour then, unless they could persuade a friendly NHBC builder to take them under their wing, the only other way of achieving the necessary certification to satisfy the bank or building society was to go for what is known as Architect's Progress Certificates. This was an entirely different procedure to Architectural Supervision but there was, and still is, endless confusion between the two, exacerbated by what appears to be a blurring of the distinctions by some of the building societies.

Architect's Progress Certificates are where an architect comes out to the site, at recognised, agreed and specified times, for an agreed fee of anywhere between £50 and £250 and certifies that, at the time of their visit, the building has reached a particular stage in its construction and that the work appears to have been carried out in accordance with the plans and specification. It is not necessary for the architect carrying out the certification to be the same architect who was responsible for the design. Differing architects will place different emphasis on their responsibilities under this arrangement. Some will want to be as certain as they can that the work has been carried out satisfactorily and some will merely be concerned that the correct stage in the construction of the building has been reached.

Some building societies and banks leave the question of the architect's actual responsibilities and obligations open for the architect to define, whilst others try to tie down the architect to a warranty which they clearly cannot give under this scheme and which would override, completely, any legal limitation by reference to reasonable skill and care. For this reason the current advice to architects is that they should not accept the wording or documentation provided by these institutions and that they confine their responsibilities and legal obligations to certifying that they have visited the property to inspect the progress and quality of the work to check, as far as they are reasonably able to do so on a visual basis, that the works are being executed generally in accordance with the approved drawings and contract documents.

Architectural Supervision, on the other hand, involves the architect being responsible for every detail of the work, necessitating his visiting the site frequently and being involved in every aspect of the construction. It is relatively expensive and is usually carried out by the same architect who formulated the design, probably as part and parcel of his original arrangement with you.

Building societies and banks will accept Architect's Progress Certificates. They do not carry any warranty, as such, and the only way a claim can be established is for the self-builder to sue the architect, who will then fall back on their professional indemnity insurance. In order to practise as an architect, a person or practice has to be qualified and registered with the Architect's Registration Board (ARB) and must have a professional indemnity policy. Nevertheless, if you do go along this route it's a good idea to make absolutely certain that the amount of cover is sufficient for your needs.

The interesting fact is that these Progress Certificates and the liability of the architect extend only to the original party to the contract, namely the self-builder. The burden of the contract is not passed to any successor in title, so anybody buying the house from the original self-builder would not be able to pursue a claim against the architect. Perhaps the banks and building societies have turned a blind eye to this point in the past. It has always been open for them to insist on a collateral contract but instances where this has been the case are few and far between.

Below: **A typical Architect's Certificate.**

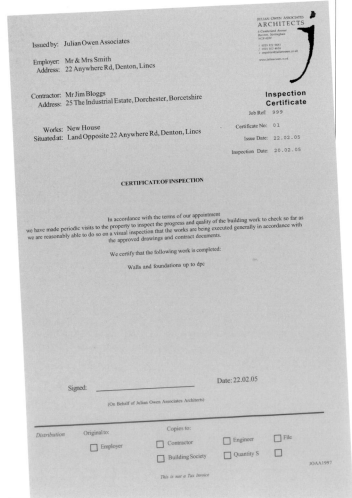

Above: **An architect with flair and imagination can bring something special to the interior of your new home as well as to the outside.**

Right: **Light from above and from the end wall will compensate for the restricted headroom in this useful room in the roof.**

© Potton

I think that if you are using Architect's Progress Certificates, it is a good idea to use them in conjunction with one of the other warranty schemes, even though there is probably no requirement from your lender that you should do so. If, for example, the builder goes bust then that would not necessarily be attributable to any fault or wrongdoing on the part of the architect and you might not be able to make a claim against them.

Before I leave this subject, just a word of warning about your choice of architect, should you decide to opt for Architect's Progress Certificates using a different architect from the one who was your original designer. Architects who work consistently in the self-build field, or are members of Associated Self-build Architects (ASBA), are more likely to be amenable to your requirements and your aims. Others, however, might not be quite so sympathetic to your needs, and may be put out by the fact that you did not go to them for their services in the first place, and, if you've used a package-deal company, they may have a marked aversion to the whole concept of everything you're trying to achieve.

Where do you live, whilst it's all happening?

I have attended seminars at countless exhibitions where the representative from a building society has outlined the main choices of where to live whilst your new home is under construction: in a caravan on site, in rented accommodation or (to the sound of embarrassed laughter) with the in-laws. This is then followed up with an assertion that, as far as their society is concerned, just so long as you can demonstrate that you can service the mortgage on two properties, they are quite happy for you to stay in your own home. There is generally a palpable sense of relief in the room at this point, but I know that when the figures are actually worked out, for most people with a mortgage covering a large percentage of their borrowing capacity and a significant amount of

the value of their existing home, there is going to be little or no choice but to sell up and move into temporary accommodation.

The introduction of 'shorthold tenancies' in 1988 breathed new life into a rental sector that, up until then, had almost ceased to exist under draconian legislation that made it nigh on impossible for landlords to be certain of recovering their property. Nowadays, there is usually a considerable choice of furnished and unfurnished accommodation available at rents that do not differ significantly from the monthly mortgage payments that most people would be expecting to pay. Of course, it does mean moving twice and it may well mean that all or part of your furniture has to go into storage. But it is a way of freeing up capital whilst continuing to live in relative comfort. A drawback can often be that you might need accommodation for longer than the six months that these tenancies usually run for and that, in turn, might mean either having to move again or choosing a property that is likely to be available for the longer period. By the way, unless notice is served in the proper way (at least two months before the expiry date of the tenancy), the tenancy automatically reverts to a monthly one, terminated by either party with one month's notice in writing.

Staying with in-laws or friends can have many advantages. Not least of these is the fact that not only is the capital in your old home released for use in your new home, you are also spared the outgoing of the monthly rent. It's nearly impossible to predict or advise on this course of action as each family is different, and whilst for some it is an entirely successful arrangement, for others it is a nightmare experience. Remember that, for those you are moving in with, this is not their project, it is not the most important thing in their lives and their only motivation is to help you. Fitting two families into one home is not easy and it's important to allow 'space' and arrange breaks for both parties – after all, when the relatively short period of your build is over, you will still have to maintain the long-term relationships you started out with.

Living on site can have huge advantages. Being on the spot means that you always know what's happening on your

Living on site can have huge advantages.

site, who has been there and for how long. You are there for deliveries and, if you're working on the site, you have not got too far to travel when you're working late or just getting the odd few hours in. You're also hugely increasing the security on your site, a fact that is often recognised in a consequent insurance discount. If you're building a replacement dwelling, and the existing structure is habitable, or capable of being camped out in, consider whether it's possible to position the new home, so that the existing property can remain until such time as it's no longer needed.

It's not at all unusual for plots to come on to the market encumbered by an existing house. Whilst this can sometimes put a strain on finances because you have to buy an element of property that you don't really want, it can also provide you with suitable accommodation right next door to your plot. If you don't need it, or if finances dictate that you must sell it off as quickly as possible without moving into it, remember to allocate the relevant costs of any separation and refurbishment against any gain for Capital Gains purposes. If you do live in it, then, under normal circumstances, the Revenue will consider that your double move is all part of the business of moving from one home to another.

Living in a mobile home on site is often considered the least favourable option. However, I feel this is a misconception since once again, there are distinct advantages to living on site and there are obvious financial incentives in the savings you can make on your monthly outgoings. It is a false economy to think in terms of buying too cheaply. For the period of your self-build, you are going to be living virtually rent and mortgage free apart from the cost of the mobile home purchase and it really does not make sense to make what is after all a trying time even more difficult. At the end of the project, if you look after it, it's a pound to a penny that you're going to get most of your money back, so why stint on what is always going to be a relatively modest proportion of your total budget? Don't forget services. Spending money on getting the electricity and water connected and in putting in drains will pay off in the end as, in nearly all cases, the services can be used as the site supply and, when the new home is finished,

easily re-routed. Living in a mobile home on site is never going to be an entirely pleasant experience. (I know, I've done it!) But it is a means to an end, and it is certainly worthwhile putting as much thought in as possible to making it comfortable. It's also a fair bet that you'll buy it from a self-builder and sell it on to another.

Various companies have spotted opportunities in the self-build market and now advertise caravans and mobile homes for sale or for rent in the monthly magazines with delivery to site and basic set-up costs all included.

Local authorities do not like caravans but so long as you explain in your negotiations with the planners that you intend to live on site whilst you are building, a formal consent is not usually required. However, if are going to put the caravan on site long before you actually apply for planning permission for your new home you will need formal consent for its siting. If you experience problems with the council, remember that it will take a very long time to get an order requiring you to move it or cease occupation, by which time you will hopefully be well on the way with your project.

Council Tax

The question often arises as to when you are deemed to have fully occupied the new home, as opposed to just camping out there for security purposes. Many authorities will deem that full occupation takes place when the furniture is placed in the home. Others have inspectors who keep a watching brief on the home, tipped off no doubt by the Building Inspectors, to determine when proper occupation commences.

Once the property is completed the local authority will arrange to inspect and assess it for Council Tax purposes. If you do not agree with the assessment, you may appeal against the new entry and/or the effective date. Most councils issue completion or habitation certificates for Building Regulations purposes, which you can quote if necessary or appropriate. If you have been living in a caravan on the site and have paid Council Tax, make sure that you are not being billed twice when you move into your new home.

Chapter 2

FINDING THE SITE FOR YOUR NEW HOME

Buying a building plot does require some knowledge, particularly about planning permission. If a parcel of land has neither planning permission nor the certainty of getting it, then it isn't a building plot at all, it is simply the corner of a field or just part of somebody's garden. For a better understanding of this go on to Chapter 3, and then come back to this one.

It is a belief commonly held by those seeking a plot that there are no plots out there, or that those that are available get snapped up by builders or developers before they even reach the market. Regarding the former point they are quite definitely wrong, and as for the latter, they are, in part, right. However, the idea that self-builders stand no chance is quite incorrect. If it were true, the self-build magazines would not be filled with success stories, and neither would this book now be in its 18th edition!

Another myth is that although there may be plots available in the outlying reaches of the country, they are never available in your particular area (often the south-eastern corner of England). Again, this is not the case. If all of the plots on the land-finding agencies' books were marked on the map, the whole of the UK would be covered. Even in the home counties there are plots for sale on a regular basis. They may be expensive, but so they should be, for the properties built upon them will have high values and very few plots are sold at figures which make the project untenable.

The message about plot finding comes down to diligence, vigilance, perseverance and some luck. Plus, of course, a knowledge of some of the tricks of the trade and an understanding of just what you are up against – just as a general going into battle knows that in order to win you must put yourself into the mind of the enemy. Above all, be prepared to compromise. People who spend years looking for a plot before finally giving up have usually failed to do so. And I bet they're the ones who drive past brand-new self-build houses and regret that they couldn't, didn't or wouldn't see the possibilities that others have clearly realised. That site may not be the self-builder's final dream home. But, on the other hand, it might well be an important step on the way to it and the extra equity that it represents plus the experience gained will probably give them the financial clout and inside knowledge to achieve their goal.

I can't pretend that it's going to be easy. Finding the land is the first hurdle and the one at which most would-be self-builders fall. But as I've said before, it is possible. I've found a plot and self-built ten times in my lifetime and I expect to do it a few more times before I settle down. As well as my own first-hand experiences, I have, as I mentioned in Chapter 1, been writing a feature in *Homebuilding & Renovating* magazine called 'Plotfinder Challenge' for six years. Every month I search a completely different part of the country and usually find at least ten, sometimes more, plots to look at. So it really can be done.

But where do you start?
Estate agents
Estate agents sell land. Most of the land that is sold goes through an agent, sometimes because the agent

Above: **Most self-builders can only ever dream of the greenfield site with stunning views.**

Right: **Registering with the plotfinding agencies is an essential first step in finding a plot.**

was instrumental in getting the planning permission in the first place.

In any town there are two distinct types of estate agent. Firstly there are the long-established traditional agents who sell houses as part and parcel of their general business, which can include activities as diverse as furniture sales and livestock auctions. These are the types of agent who are also more likely to have a professional department and it is this department which is often used by prospective vendors to obtain planning on their land. They will be cagey about what they've got coming up, preferring to maintain the anonymity of their clients and the potential plots until such time as they have consent and specific instructions. Once they have those instructions they will act in the way that is best suited to their client, the vendor.

These more traditional agents will often want to sell land by auction or tender and whilst that can benefit the self-builder insofar as it brings the land on to the open market there are several draw-backs. Auctions are distinctly uneasy places for lay people, who sit there nervously trying not to scratch that itch that inescapably comes up on their eyebrow whilst at the same time trying to keep track of the stream of indecipherable words coming from the rostrum. Similarly tenders, with their inherent lack of any proper legal framework, are extremely unpopular with purchasers. Both of these methods of buying land are explored in greater detail in Chapter 4.

The second sort of estate agent is fairly familiar to us all. They very rarely get involved in actual applications for planning and instead simply take on properties and land at face value. They have a much more brash way of dealing with things and won't always see the full potential in any particular property, existing through high turnover rather than long-term investment. They're much more likely to discuss what's up and coming and you'll come out of their offices, even if empty handed, with a feeling of greater hope, albeit one which may dissipate fairly quickly when nothing further happens.

Estate agents do tend to come in for a pretty bad press, sometimes deservedly so. However, they are not just in business for the relatively short time frame of a self-build and they rely on sowing the seeds for future deals in the course of their normal trading activities. Small wonder then that when a plot comes up, their first thought is to sell to a builder or developer who will, in return, engage them for the sale of whatever is built on the land. Popular opinion amongst agents is that if somebody takes the time and trouble to build their own home, they are going to build exactly what they want and then live in it happily ever after. Of course, this is not the case and most self-builders do, in fact, self-build again at some stage, some more frequently than most other people buy and sell their

> ### Questions you should ask yourself:
>
> **If you find that you're always missing out on plots, what are you doing wrong? Ask yourself the following questions:**
>
> - Am I being too fussy?
>
> - Am I looking for an ideal that will never really happen?
>
> - Am I looking at things only as they are and not as they will be? Many plots are parts of gardens or covered in old sheds, tangled undergrowth and rusting cars, hardly appealing and a far cry from anybody's dream plot. But you have to cut through all that. Close your eyes and imagine how things are going to be when you've finished.
>
> - Am I making sure that I'm in the right place at the right time? Plots don't hang about on the market for very long and if the person selling it can't get hold of you or you don't respond to the call about a plot, they'll simply move on to the next interested party.
>
> - Could I extend my parameters? Maybe go that little bit further out or one junction on down the motorway?
>
> - Am I being proactive enough in my search and keeping an open mind to all options?

houses. Whether driven by finance and the need to reduce or pay off a mortgage, or simply because they get the building bug or want to improve upon what they've already achieved, the serial self-builder falls into the same category as the small local house-builder or developer. All of which means that if you identify yourself as such to an estate agent and discuss resale prospects in an informed way, you might find that they treat you very differently.

Estate agents do, of course, have a duty to their clients – the vendors of the land. Many now realise that the self-builder can perhaps give that little bit more for the plot than the builder or developer. More importantly, many vendors also recognise this. The days of self-building existing in a parallel universe, undiscovered and misunderstood, are long gone. Most estate agents will know of the land-finding agencies and the market they serve and some vendors are beginning to cut out the agents altogether and advertise their land directly.

Just putting your name and requirements down with an agent is unlikely to produce very much. Make yourself known to them – try to visit their offices regularly, even if you feel they are fed up with seeing you. Make small talk and ask what's come in during the week. You need to ensure that when that plot comes up, your name is almost the first one they think of. If you can't visit, phone in on a regular basis. Get to know names and establish relationships.

An estate agent selling a piece of land gets a relatively small fee for doing so. What interests them of course is the much higher fee for selling any resulting house – that and the thought that their advertising board will be on a prestigious site for months to come. Try representing yourself as a 'private housebuilder'. Give the impression that you're going to sell the house when it's finished. Talk about values and the best way of selling. After all, as we've already identified above, the likelihood is that, in any event, you'll be selling and moving on again.

So when you do find a plot and you go into the agent to make an offer, start talking immediately about your 'next plot'. If they see you as 'repeat business' then maybe they'll do what they can to make sure you get that plot rather than, at best, just sitting on the offer or, at worst, advising their preferred buyers of the strength of yours so that they can top it.

Another idea is to visit the agent's offices at the weekend. Some firms employ weekend staff whose only job is to 'mind the shop'. Tell them that you're looking for land and that you're on the land list. Ask them to check their files for any land may have come in. You might see files or details of land that the principal staff have neglected to tell you about, and on the Monday morning, when proper business resumes, you might be able to get further information. In turn they might wonder how you heard of the land and they might well have something to say to their weekend staff.

Does any of this seem underhand? Well, it shouldn't. You want a plot. The vendor wants to sell the plot to the highest bidder and it's the agent's job to do just that. All you've done is to assist them in that task. I don't want to sound anti-estate agent. In fact, many years ago, but don't tell anyone, I was one. I saw what went on and I know the tricks and all I'm trying to do is to even out the game.

Finding a plot before the agents get involved and being proactive

The maxim, which needs repeating, is that as a self-builder rather than a property speculator, you should not buy land if it does not have planning permission or at least the certainty of it. But that should not mean that you have to wait for all of that to happen before you register your interest or come to an agreement with a landowner.

You don't have to own land in order to make a planning application. All that is required is that you serve notice on the owners. But to go around making planning applications on land that you do not own might be extremely costly unless you have made a prior agreement with the owners. You do need to tie up some sort of legal agreement if you want to avoid doing a load of work at the end of which the vendor says, 'Thank you very much for all of the work you've done in getting planning on my land, but I'm selling it to somebody else.'

In England and Wales it is possible to buy the land and exchange contracts 'subject to receipt of satisfactory planning consent'. This means that if you get the planning permission everything proceeds smoothly to completion but that if you do not, the contract is voided. The Scottish legal system requires the offer to be made and accepted on condition that satisfactory planning is received within a certain time.

The other way of tying things up is to enter into a legally binding option to purchase the land in the event that you get planning permission. This would normally be prepared by a solicitor and might include a non-returnable payment of anything between £1 and £1,000. It might also set a time limit, such as six months, and it should certainly detail either the precise payment to be made in the event of the purchase going ahead or else the method by which that is to be calculated. If there is uncertainty over the value of the land then the easiest way is to appoint a valuer, acceptable to both parties, to determine the price. Either way, in the event of planning being granted such an option would make it legally binding that you purchase and that the vendor sells. So do

Above: **Your plot is probably part of somebody else's garden at the moment.**

not enter into such things lightly or without the funds to see things through.

Study the Ordnance Survey (OS) maps of your local or chosen area. Look out for obvious plots such as gaps in the street scene. Look out for streets where infill has already taken place but where certain properties have not taken advantage of this opportunity. In particular, look for houses that are set to one side of their plots or where the size of the plot is disproportionate to the size of the house. It might sound unlikely. It might sound as if I'm sending you on a fool's errand. But if I tell you that the first of the two houses that I feature in this book was built on what was originally someone's side garden, it should prove to you that this is a really useful way of identifying and buying a plot.

Look out for signs of previous backland development, where properties have been built in the rear gardens of houses with either shared access or a new access down the side. Even if there are no signs of this type of development having already taken place, see if you can identify those houses where lopping off part of the rear garden with access down the side

would or should be possible. Some local authorities are dead against the idea, believing that backland development will change the character of an area, alter the street scene and lead to overlooking. Nothing could be further from the truth. The street scene remains largely unaltered. The character of the area doesn't change because in most cases the new house at the rear shares the driveway to the existing house. And the overlooking is a lot less with a long and mature garden than it is on many new housing estates.

Watch out for houses with long back gardens that front on to a side road. When studying the maps one normally looks out for the obvious plot that either exists in its own right or can be subdivided from a larger property. However, if there is a row of houses, all with relatively narrow but longer than average gardens, and one of the houses is on a corner plot with access to the road, then it might be possible to join up the rear portions of several gardens to make

Sow's ear to silk purse

Look at things as they're going to be – not as they are. These three photographs are taken from the same camera position and show a run-down workshop dragging down a pleasant street scene – and the house that replaced it.

up a plot with separate access. The trick is to devise the scheme and tie it all up with legally binding options from each of the owners, allowing you to purchase in the event of satisfactory planning permission. Beware of trying to go too far without such an option as, once you've got planning consent, a single owner, maybe with landlocked land that has no intrinsic value other than as part of your plot, could hold you to ransom. Remember that it's important to demonstrate to prospective vendors that the scheme can be realised with little or no detriment to their continued occupation and that it is unlikely to adversely affect their values.

When you've identified possible plots, get out there and check them on site. Sometimes the maps might be out of date. Sometimes there are physical reasons why plots can't be developed.

Identifying the land is one thing but finding the owner for some vacant plots is quite another. If your enquiries at the village pub or at the local post office don't bring results, you could do no better than look on the Land Registry. Not all land is registered but quite a bit of it is, especially if it's changed hands in the recent past. The register is open for anyone to inspect. A registered title is the legal evidence of ownership of or title to land. It contains details of the address, the owners and any charges, covenants or easements affecting it. The information supplied is in the form of a Property Register containing all the details in three succinct sections together with a plan upon which the land is outlined. If you find a piece of land and you want to trace its ownership, then you need to apply to the Land Registry with full details of the address and, if at all possible, a map or copy of the OS sheet to identify it. If you cannot identify the land in this way then you can send off for, or inspect, the Index maps held by the Registry. These Index maps have all registered land marked and numbered and, if the plot you're interested in appears on them then you should be able to find out just who owns it.

I repeat, not all land is registered, and it is the empty parcel of land that has lain fallow and unused for donkey's years that is the most likely not to have been. Nevertheless, if you're unsure of the ownership of a piece of land that's caught your eye, and local enquiries have been unsuccessful or would stir up a hornet's nest, you could do no better than to apply. There is a modest

Above: **Study any OS map of any town or village and you will spot potential plots. Some of these have recently been built on.**

scale of fees payable and I would suggest that, in the first instance, you write to HM Land Registry at Lincoln's Inn Fields, London, WC2A 3PH, or telephone them on 020 7917 8888, asking them for their explanatory leaflet 15.

Before you get too far with all this you'll need to visit the planning office and ascertain what the likelihood is that these 'plots' would obtain consent. Maybe the planners will be negative. If so perhaps it's best to move on to another possibility. Maybe they'll be non-committal, but maybe, and especially in the light of recent government directives to utilise land more intensively, they'll accept the fact that this is a potential building plot. Much has been made in the past few years of the need to utilise 'brownfield' land, i.e. land that has had a previous use, instead of 'greenfield' land, where the countryside is gobbled up. Well, brownfield land is not all factories and dark satanic mills and the definition extends to existing dwellings and their gardens. Couple that with directives to intensify the use of land and you effectively have the Government on your side for many such applications.

If the planners do give you a positive response, ask them if they would prefer a 'Full' application, rolling the Outline and Detailed stages into one. If they would, this will save time and money and, whilst not a certainty, probably means that the project stands a pretty good chance of success.

Subject to my comments above, don't waste too much time on possible plots where the planning officer has indicated that the authority would be dead against the principle of development, especially if it would conflict with their adopted and ratified local planning policy. Always remember that you are a prospective self-builder, not a property speculator, and in all probability you have neither the time nor the resources to go on a crusade against planning policy or laws. That doesn't mean that you can't learn to work within them to your advantage and I will explain that further in Chapter 8.

The hardest part, of course, is to convince the landowner that they should sell to you. Don't be afraid to knock on doors and ask. They may welcome your approach, especially if you represent yourself to them as a private individual looking to build your new home. They may well tell you to get lost – but nothing ventured, nothing gained. And remember they're not allowed to shoot you!

When I'm out doing the 'Plotfinder Challenge' I knock on doors all the time. I knock on the neighbours' doors to find out all I can about the plot, where the sewers are, what the ground conditions are like. Sometimes – very occasionally – I get the brush off. Mostly, however, I find out loads of useful information that either stands me in good stead for that plot or points me towards another.

Whilst you're talking to the planners, ask to see the Planning Register. This is not a secret document. It is open for public inspection, as indeed are all of the files on applications. Study this register and you will see that it is a list of all of the planning applications currently under consideration. Some of them will be for things like extensions. Ignore those. Some will be for 'Approval of Reserved Matters' pursuant to an original Outline consent. Maybe they're not worth that much attention as they probably indicate that whoever owns the land has already decided what to do with it. But don't discount them if they're exactly what you're looking for. And don't forget that if land has detailed planning permission for one house and it's not what you'd like to build, in most cases, it's possible to change that by making either a new Full application or an additional application for Approval of Reserved Matters, all of which I'll explain in greater detail in the next chapter.

But for now pay the most attention to the Outline applications. Make a note of each applicant's name and address, especially if it's clear that they live next door to the proposed plot. You'll also notice that there is often an applicant's agent. And guess what? That'll probably be one of those estate agents who's already told you that they don't have any land for sale and that they don't know of any coming up!

So it's no good writing to them. They've already decided that they don't want to deal with you on this project. Write instead to the owners. Tell them that you're a potential self-builder hoping to build your own home and that if they ever want to talk to you about you buying their land, you'd be delighted to hear from them. You may hear nothing. But you might just get a call from them one day.

Above: **Talking to vendors or neighbours about the plot can yield valuable information.**

Left: **Why not join in with others to buy that multiple plot?**

When people get planning for part of their garden they're delighted at the cash windfall that this usually represents. The agents, in competition with each other, will, in all probability, and to gain the business in the first place, have inflated the value, and the prospective vendors automatically allocate the money with plans to pay off the mortgage or buy that longed-for villa in Spain.

But once they've had a chance to think about things they start to worry. What will it be like? What effect will it have on their enjoyment of their home? What effect will it have on the value? If the agent has 'sold' the land to local developers, what sort of house will they be building? Will they be building the biggest house they can and to hell with the consequences or the effect on their existing home? Are they getting the right price?

Well, maybe. But many a time the offer that comes in, as a result of the cosy relationship between agent and builder, is a lot less than the figure that was first quoted. They stomach that with a little sense of disappointment but the agent assures them that it's a good offer and that it's 'all they can expect in the circumstances'. Then the sale starts to drag on with the builders not wanting to commit financially until they have either sold the previous house they've built or actually got detailed planning permission for what they want to build.

It is at this point that the owner may well go to the

file, turn up your letter and contact you. For what you are offering is not only to buy the land but also to be their neighbour. And you can sit down and talk to them as potential neighbours about all of their fears and empathise with the mutual need to preserve values and enjoyment. And most importantly you can offer them the right price.

And if you think that sounds far fetched, I have to tell you that that has happened to me in exactly the way I have described. It's also apparently quite common, for when I was relating that scenario to an audience at a self-build show, a chap in the audience stood up and told us all that he'd got a quarter-acre plot in the middle of York about which he'd seen nobody but builders. He'd finally received an offer substantially below the asking price and yet here he was in a room full of 300 people who wouldn't let him out of the door without finding out all about it!

Studying the Ordnance Survey maps, looking around your chosen town or village, scanning the Planning Register and generally getting to know the people and the area intimately are probably the most important things that you can do proactively. However, there is more.

Try having a haircut, or visit the local pub. And when you've eliminated all the horror stories which invariably happened to someone who knew someone, and got over trying to explain that you're not completely mad, you may come out with a few pointers that could lead you to a plot. Seek out the oldest person or the local village busybody to identify land that might lie hidden behind hedges or walls. Get some flyers printed and deliver them door to door in chosen villages or streets, making it clear that you are a private individual seeking to self-build and not a developer. Put notice cards in shop windows, again making it clear that the land is for your own use and family occupation rather than as a pure profit-making venture.

If you do visit an advertised plot in a town or village make a point of talking to local people. Ask for directions at the post office, even if you know exactly where the plot is. You'll be surprised at just how much the postmaster or mistress knows about not only the plot you've come to see but other plots or potential plots in the area. Talk to neighbours. They may be keen to put you off and you might well have to read between the lines of their animosity to it being a building site in the first place. But you may also pick up bits of information and history on the plot that'll stand you in good stead when you make an offer or start negotiations with the authorities.

If you spot any building taking place in the area, stop off and talk to the workers on site. From them you'll glean what the authority's attitude and requirements are, what sort of design they like and what sort of ground conditions you're likely to experience. Not only that, but once again you'll probably come away with information that could lead you to another plot or plots in the area.

Incidentally, it's sometimes well worthwhile visiting a plot that you know has already gone and doing all of the above and perhaps a little bit more. Ask the vendors if it really has been sold. Leave your details

Seek out the oldest person or the local village busybody to identify land that might lie hidden behind hedges or walls.

so that if anything goes wrong, they can contact you. Impress upon them your disappointment at missing out yet again. You never know, maybe the fears and doubts that I've outlined above will be coming to the fore. And, if they like you and feel that you might make a better neighbour or give them the price they had originally hoped for, they might well get back in touch. You might also find that they know of other plots in the area, some of which might not yet be on the market. They could well have had to fight quite hard to get their planning consent and, in so doing, they might well have made contact with others who were in the process of, or contemplating doing the same as them.

There are a number of other headings that I'd like to include in this chapter but bear in mind that none of them is mutually exclusive and that much of what I've said already will apply equally to these categories.

The land-finding agencies

Whenever I start a 'Plotfinder Challenge' my first ports of call are the land-finding agencies who are not only heavily featured in the magazines but also have large stands at most of the major self-build exhibitions.

Studying these lists can be very helpful. Firstly, you should be able to glean from them just what sort of price you're going to have to pay for the plot of your dreams. That will help you to establish your budget. It might, on the other hand, persuade you that if you are ever going to self-build you're going to have to change tack somewhat or think about doing it in a different area.

It will tell you which plots are on the market at the time, but more importantly it will tell you which agents you should concentrate on. They will be those who, by virtue of their being on the register, are demonstrating that they are prepared to deal with the general public. It will also help you to see those who obviously pick up most of the land that's going in a particular area.

If you telephone any of the agents who have plots listed and find that the plot you are after has been sold, you should then go on to ask for details of other plots of a similar nature, or whether they know of anything that will shortly be coming on to the market. Keep in touch with them so that you can short-circuit the grapevine as it were, giving you a head-start on everybody else looking in the area.

The principle land-finding agenices are:

Plotfinder

Plotfinder.net, which is part of *Homebuilding & Renovating* magazine, publishes lists of over 4,000 plots or renovation opportunities at any one time. You can call them on their hotline, 0906 557 5400, for a one-off listing for one county or you can visit their website on www.plotfinder.net. A five-county subscription costs £40 per annum, or else you can get a trial of three months at just £15. Renewals are half price and they frequently have special show offers at the self-build exhibitions held around the country. There is a free plot-alert service, which tells you if any new listings have come up within your chosen area. They also publish about a quarter of their database in *Homebuilding & Renovating* magazine each month but remember that this may have gone to print months before publication so the listings are liable to be out of date. Nevertheless they are still very useful for research purposes.

Plotsearch

BuildStore have their Plotsearch service, which lists around 6,000 plots and renovation or conversion opportunities on the register at any one time. They can be accessed on www.buildstore.co.uk/plotsearch. A subscription to their online service for three counties costs £44 for a lifetime or £29 for three months. You can add counties to your subscription at £10 per county, or else a £100 per annum professional subscription will give you access to all counties. There is also a monthly mailing service available on 0870 870 9991 for those with no Internet access. Whilst they do also publish lists of plots for sale in *Build It* magazine every month, these are, once again, often out of date by the time the magazine is published and are therefore principally of use to those who are exploring and assessing the market.

Plotsearch also have some very useful bolt-on extras. The first, and perhaps most important, of these is PlotAlert. This costs just £15 extra and for this, if a plot comes in within your stated cost and regional parameters, the details will be e-mailed to you instantly.

As I have said above, speed is of the essence in plot hunting and the quicker you hear of the plot and the faster you get there and start talking about buying it, the better.

One thing that you will have to learn to put up with is the number of wasted journeys that you'll make. My advice is to go to everything. When doing 'Plotfinder Challenge', I have to write about three plots. In order to do that I have to source many more and might indeed set up around ten prospects. Inevitably one or more of the plots becomes the favourite with the most hopes pinned upon it and the rest are slipped down in the pack. But you'd be amazed at the number of times the favourite turns out to be a non-starter and a makeweight turns out to be an absolute humdinger. Plotsearch have an extra service called Aerial Images that might save some wasted journeys. For £15 for the quarterly, £20 for the lifetime and £30 for the annual all-counties subscription you can receive aerial photographs of the site, allowing you to view it within its surroundings and warning you of any proximity to gas holders, railways, motorways or the like.

Professional developers might also be interested in Plots4Developers, and those interested in looking for a new home for refurbishment might be interested in Homes4Refurbishment.

Replacement dwellings

A large proportion of self-build projects are not greenfield plots and, instead, are one-for-one replacements. Large numbers of houses built since the war, even as late as the 1970s, have run their course: they are structurally unsound, cannot be brought up to modern requirements for thermal insulation and energy efficiency and do not provide the sort of accommodation that we all now require.

Pictures of various replacement dwellings are dotted through this section.

Most self-build projects in the south-eastern corner of the realm are built as replacement dwellings rather than on greenfield plots. Estate agents, however, do not always recognise this. Sometimes they take a property at its face value and they might try for ages to sell a substandard bungalow or house, with a string of disappointed mortgage applications, little realising that this should more properly be a plot. A prime example of this occurred when I was doing a 'Plotfinder Challenge' in Kent. As we were driving to one of the sites I'd identified, I suddenly spotted a bungalow for sale in open country on a plot of at least half an acre. But to me it wasn't a bungalow – it was a plot. The couple I was with did not buy it as they found something else that day and they're happily building as I write. However, they did pass on the information to friends of theirs who have since bought it, and have planning permission to knock it down and build a new 180-square-metre house plus a detached double garage!

So when you're putting your name down for plots,

consider also asking for details of properties in need of refurbishment. Consider, if you're at a distance, whether you might want to separate the two issues and register this other interest under a different name or with a different address. Why that subterfuge? So as not to alert the agents to your real intentions and the actual possibilities.

Replacement dwellings often have huge advantages over greenfield plots. Whilst there may be demolition costs, in most cases these are insignificant or unlikely to detract from the value of the site. Even if the dreaded asbestos is present it's not the end of the world. Some lagging or loose-fibre asbestos may well require specialist removal, but even then it's unlikely to make the plot non-viable. What's much more likely is that the asbestos is in the form of cement fibreboard or as roofing slates, all of which can usually be removed to a council tip by the self-builder with the minimum of sensible precautions.

But to offset all of this, in all probability the driveway and entrance are already in. The drains and services may well be connected. The fencing and hedging may be sound and the garden will probably

Most self-build projects in the south-eastern corner of the realm are built as replacement dwellings rather than on greenfield plots.

be laid out and established, if a little overgrown. All of which could represent savings of at least £10,000. And it does not stop there because there may well be another benefit that I've already referred to in Chapter 1, namely that the planning consent will often allow the old building to remain until such time as the new one is complete. Now that could solve your accommodation problems for the duration of the building.

Speaking from personal experience, I once bought a timber bungalow with a corrugated iron roof and got planning permission to knock it down and build two new four-bedroom chalet bungalows on the site. One was sold off and one became our home.

I should mention one word of caution on replacement dwellings. Many local authorities have policies

Above and right: **It's not only timber bungalows that make ideal replacement sites; some brick-built dwellings are also past their 'sell-by' date.**

whereby they will allow replacement, so long as the new home is not bigger than the original by a certain percentage. This percentage varies from one authority to the next. In some cases there is no allowed increase in floor space whilst in others it can be half as much again. The reason for this is a reluctance to see the continual erosion of small homes in favour of larger ones. As a social policy that does of course have some merit but there are times when it's just plain silly. I remember a leafy road in Sussex where the large plots all had large four- and five-bedroom houses on them with swimming pools and multiple garages. In the middle of this there was a 1-acre plot with a 65-square-metre bungalow on it and the authority were insisting that any replacement should not exceed its size by more than 10%. This was enshrined in their development plan and in most cases one would be on a hiding to nothing trying to

overturn such an adopted policy. But someone did. For when I drove past eighteen months later a large house, commensurate with the area, was being built. I imagine that they successfully appealed against a refusal by the local authority. I will cover the appeals process in a later chapter but suffice it to say that appeals are notoriously unreliable and there are other ways of getting that little bit more, which I will explore in Chapter 8 with particular reference to 'Permitted Development Rights'.

Local authorities, English Partnerships (formerly the Commission for New Towns or CNT) and plot-creating companies

Many local authorities sell land and some of them are well known for doing so. But as many authorities get to the end of their land bank and have sold off land on which they would previously have built council housing, the supply is beginning to dry up. That does not mean, however, that it's not worthwhile getting on to them because things do change and at any one time either a complete site can be in the offing or the odd spare parcel of land can be identified as suitable.

English Partnerships sell fully serviced plots in and around Milton Keynes. Whilst there is no doubt that this is also a diminishing resource they are hoping to put serviced plots on the market over the next few years. The plots are much sought after and often heavily oversubscribed upon release. So they usually choose to sell the plots by informal tender, which means that a date is set by which all offers have to be received and they then accept the highest bid.

In America and the former dominions it's not at all unusual to find plot-creating agencies and the principle has now arrived in this country. Several companies have arisen which seek out and purchase larger plots of land that either already have planning consent or where they perceive that there is a good chance of getting it. They then prepare a full development brief and agree it with the planning authorities, setting out the development criteria, including acceptable house types, with the result that detailed planning, so long as it's within those parameters, is either unnecessary or a mere formality. Finally, having put in all the roads and services, they offer the plots for sale. Unfortunately many of these companies have tended to exist only for the duration of the scheme, but there are names that are beginning to be established. BuildStore have indicated that within the shelf life of this edition they hope to actively enter the market to buy up land and sell it on as serviced plots for individual self-builders.

The media

Newspapers, national, local and classified, self-build magazines and some well-known sales magazines are a good source of land. Subscribe to the local papers in your chosen area and don't forget that there's quite

Adverts for plots in magazines may be old by the time they go to print but they still give useful information on prices and on which estate agents to concentrate your efforts.

a bit of overlap, so buy the papers in the adjoining areas. If you see a plot advertised, then get on to it immediately and don't wait for the weekend. The last home that I built which is featured in this book, was the product of just such an occurrence. I saw a plot in the local newspaper, was on to it within 20 minutes, had made an offer ten minutes later, and this was accepted within the hour.

If you are dealing with a private advertiser, be aware that they will be bombarded with offers from estate agents and others and that you, as a private individual, might well have to fight hard for their attention. Play up the fact that you're looking to self-build as an individual or a family. Vendors, especially those who will continue to live next door, are, as I've said, often apprehensive about any loss of control over what happens on the plot and you might well be able to put their minds at ease in this respect.

Both Michael Holmes, editor-in-chief of *Homebuilding & Renovating* magazine, and another senior member of staff found their plots by scanning the local papers. Both moved fast to see and secure the land and both built successfully.

And of course newspapers work both ways in that you can advertise for a plot. You may get time wasters and you may get a string of no-hope plots that would never get planning consent. You may get the chap who's just fed up with mowing his large lawn. But, you may get the plot of your dreams. You may even get someone who's been trying to sell his plot through your friendly local estate agent who has been unable to interest any of his builder chums but still didn't tell you about it!

Do you already own the plot or part of it, without realising it?

Plots aren't created by divine intervention. They already exist – they just need to be identified. Most plots are or were part of somebody's garden. So, before you go out bothering prospective plot owners with offers to convert their garden into your dream plot, take a close look at your own home. Is your house in a street where the density of dwellings is rising due to large gardens being divided off as plots? If not, could you start the trend?

Maybe your garden backs on to or is side-on to

another road where a new access could be formed. Maybe the rear garden is so long that it's possible to create a new driveway down the side of your house and build at the bottom with very little detriment to your existing home either in amenity or financial terms?

A visit to your local planning department will either confirm or deny your hopes and it will cost nothing to investigate unless or until you decide to go for an application. Prepare the ground first, though, and make certain of your facts; look out for precedents that you can quote if necessary. And if you live in a semi-detached or end-of-terrace house on a corner or between blocks in a high-density location, consider whether or not there's room to extend the terrace with another similar house attached to yours.

If your plans are a little more long term, and you've been knocked back by the planners because, for example, the proposed plot is outside the village envelope or development boundary, remember that these are the subject of almost constant review. Planning policies change all the time. Backland development, which I've talked about, used to be the eighth deadly sin but now it's the latest virtue. Putting up two houses where there used to be one would once have given planners the vapours but now they're falling over themselves to satisfy the density requirements demanded by the Government. Buying land and then arguing for its inclusion within a development boundary might be a trifle too risky, but if you already own the land, and you've got the time, there's nothing to lose. Give it a go.

And don't forget what I've said about making up a plot from smaller sections of land (see page 62). Maybe one of those smaller sections is your own and maybe, just maybe, you can convince your neighbours to let you stitch the pieces together to form a plot.

Self-build jungle drums

Self-build sites are often quite easy to identify by the mobile home on site and self-builders can be a surprisingly excellent source of land. Nearly all of them will have had a long hard search for a plot but invariably, having found it, they then continue to hear of others. Maybe they can tell you about plots that they had had under consideration and maybe they know of situations where other would-be self-builders have had to give up on their hopes. Speak to them, tell them what you're hoping to do and ask them what they know. I have done this several times when out plot finding and have been tipped off about plots that I might not otherwise have got to hear about. The other thing, of course, is that these guys are ahead of you in the game: they can tell you who the best bricklayer is and which one turned up on the Monday and then never showed his face again, who to use and who to avoid at all costs. They are a mine of information.

Joining in with others

Sometimes self-builders have double plots or obtain planning for more than one dwelling and want to sell off the spare plot. The chances are that when they do they'll try to sell to another self-builder through the self-build media or discussion forums that the major magazines host rather than through estate agents. Sometimes prospective self-builders will want to bid for a multiple site and will advertise for other self-builders to join in with them. BuildStore have recognised this with 'PlotShare' where, as a subscriber to PlotSearch, for an extra £10 you can register your interest in joining with others to buy land.

In previous issues of this book the advice would have been to consider forming a private self-build group. This still happens from time to time and I have come across situations in which groups of like-minded individuals have built homes on a community basis. But in most cases the 1998/99 crash brought an end to all that and group self-build, in many of the forms it took before those dates, is no longer really around. That's not to say that it does not exist on a small scale or that it won't be back, but it is no longer a cogent force other than where it fulfils a specific social need and comes under the auspices of community self-build.

Nevertheless, the idea of being involved with others, perhaps developing a site together, sharing work on common services and co-operating in hiring plant and employing tradesmen, can seem attractive. In order to do this you would have to become one

Plots aren't created by divine intervention. They already exist – they just need to be identified.

body, either in the form of a limited company or a self-build group, and be warned that the financial institutions really don't want to know about private self-build groups, tending to view them in much the same light as the Pharaohs did the plagues.

So, if a larger site does come up it is probably better to devise some way of building on it with others whereby you are all acting as individuals. The ease or difficulty of doing this will depend on the nature of any road or drainage works, so the smaller the number of actual plots, the simpler the task of sorting it all out will be.

All of this presupposes that a vendor of a site for two or more homes is willing to sell it to multiple purchasers. Ignoring situations in which an individual or a company has set out to sell serviced plots, what happens when an enthusiastic would be self-builder sees a site for three units and thinks how nice it would be to build one of them, with two other people building the others? There are two options: either the first self-builder buys the whole of the site and immediately sells off the other plots, or else all three parties persuade the vendor to sell the site in three parts. In either case all the contracts will be signed at once, either with everyone using the same firm of solicitors or else with a gaggle of solicitors sitting around the negotiating table. The contracts should include appropriate arrangements for any shared drive or services, or else take into account any requirement for an adoptable road, in which case a separate agreement for this should be signed by all the purchasers at the same time. I'll discuss the arrangements for the entrance and driveway in the next chapter.

The self-build industry

Whilst they cannot always seek to provide a comprehensive and up-to-date list of plots, many of the package-deal companies and their local representatives might know of land that is available. Quite often prospective vendors contact well-known companies asking if they have clients looking for land. Do not expect the companies to tell you about plots that other clients are contemplating buying or building upon because that would be anarchic. However, clients do sometimes have to drop out or are unable to proceed for reasons that have little or nothing to do with the suitability of the plot. In those cases, if you're in touch with the staff it might well be possible to 'take over' the contract and plot.

Architects and surveyors, being more local, often have a far greater knowledge of the plot situation in their area and many of those working exclusively within the self-build industry keep their own registers of plots for sale in their catchment area. In addition, just like the package-deal companies, there may also be a 'wastage factor' in that, from time to time clients might drop out of a project. If you as a prospective customer can impress them with your keenness, then at a point where they are fearful that a lot of work could have been to no avail, you could well be the answer to their problem.

Local builders and developers

When the housing market is buoyant, developers buy up land and form their own land bank. When the market is sluggish and sales of their houses are down they might be persuaded to offload surplus plots just to keep some sort of cashflow going. However, it's always worth contacting them as they might well have plots upon which they're prepared to enter into a 'turnkey' arrangement, whereby they'll build the house to your design. It's not strictly self-building and there is unlikely to be a significant saving over buying a house 'off the peg' but it can get you what you want. Occasionally developers have plots to sell on partially finished estates. Large estates of houses need areas set aside for site huts and compounds that are required almost up to the end of a project. At times, a new and more attractive proposition can come up and the smaller developer might well be persuaded to cut his losses on the old site in order to make a clean start on the new one. The beauty of these plots is that they are serviced but the drawback is that you might be limited in design expression.

Farming and rural enterprise plots

Development of agricultural land is usually only allowed if it can be proven that it is necessary for the proper maintenance and running of a viable agricultural enterprise or an approved rural industry. That does not mean that if you've got couple of horses in the field you can build to be near them but if, on the other hand, you run a successful livery or riding stables with a proven track record of economic viability, you might just get consent. It's often easier to demonstrate necessity on larger farms but it is also possible to prove a need for a dwelling on smaller enterprises such as nurseries, intensive units and specialist growers. The important thing to realise is that the land and its use, rather than the house, is paramount. As such, many new enterprises are required to demonstrate that they have been successfully up and running for some time before a dwelling is finally approved and that it's really necessary for someone to actually live on site. That means that the applicants might well have to contemplate living in a mobile home for some time and any consent that is granted might well limit the occupation of the dwelling to those engaged in running the enterprise.

It's not at all unusual for land or property to come on to the market with an agricultural consent where, by means of a planning condition, the occupation of the dwelling is limited to someone wholly or mainly engaged in agriculture, last engaged in agriculture or the widow or widower thereof. Sometimes the drawbacks are reflected in the asking price but not always. Sometimes, the importance of the restriction is belittled or played down and you might be told that nobody will find out and that the planning authorities are not really bothered. Don't accept this. Although many breaches of planning permission can be authorised if, after four years, no action has been taken, breaches of conditions can be enforced up to ten years. In many cases, if money is being borrowed against the property, the lenders will flag up the problem and refuse to lend on it, because they know full well that in the event of them having to foreclose, they would have difficulty in selling it on. But a cash purchaser will not have this safeguard. Be wary of buying land like this, unless you are pretty sure that you fulfil the criteria for occupation.

Above: **An old wreck in a fairytale setting makes for a dream plot, as long as the planners see it that way.**

Right: **What used to happen in large telephone exchanges such as this one, now takes place in a small box, so that this is now ripe for development.**

It is possible to apply to the planning authorities to have the restriction lifted. You may need to prove that there is no longer a necessity for agricultural dwellings and you may be required to market the property as an agricultural dwelling for one year to prove that no farming enterprise or person engaged in agriculture wants to buy it. As an agricultural dwelling the price should be heavily discounted and there is always the possibility that during that year, some bright spark will come along and spoil all of your plans by putting in an offer. But if that does not happen, the committee may remove the stipulation.

As already stated, breaches of planning conditions

might be a considerable amount of equipment and pipework to remove. Additionally, provision for access to any replacement equipment might be needed and there may well be sterile zones. Railtrack own many parcels of land, not all of which are close to railway lines. They, like many of the other service providers, have an estates department that actively seeks to develop and dispose of surplus land. Try writing to the various companies, explaining what you want to do and asking if they've got any surplus and suitable land for sale. Better still, get out there and identify these things yourself and then write or call in to ask them directly about a specific property.

The UK is dotted with countless redundant and unoccupied buildings … many of which, with flair and imagination, could be converted to residential use if only the planners would allow it.

can be enforced within a period of ten years. However, if you or your predecessors in title can prove, beyond doubt, that the breach has gone unnoticed and unchallenged, with no attempt at secrecy, for ten years or more, then it is mandatory for the local authority to issue what is known as a 'Certificate of Lawful Use'. This has the effect of granting planning permission for the property to be de-restricted.

The public utilities (telephone and gas companies, electricity and water boards and Railtrack)

Telephone relay stations, gas regulators, pumping stations and electricity transformers used to take up large areas of land in the middle of residential areas. In some cases the buildings used to house these things were the size of small bungalows. Today this land and these buildings are redundant and the planners are often more than happy to see the street scene tidied up by replacement of these anachronisms. The drawback with these plots is that the land might well be contaminated in some way or that there

Change of use/conversions

The UK is dotted with countless redundant and unoccupied buildings from old barns to shops, factories, water towers and churches, many of which, with flair and imagination, could be converted to residential use if only the planners would allow it. The situation varies from area to area in that some local authorities enthusiastically welcome the renewal and regeneration of these buildings whilst others actually state that they'd prefer to see them fall down rather than contemplate them becoming homes. Check out your local authority's standpoint on this one but even so it's often well worth making a case for a change of use or conversion. Take out an option before taking things too far so as not to see your efforts, if successful, enjoyed by others. Remember that what the planners and conservation officers are often afraid of is that buildings might be developed in an unsympathetic way and if you can demonstrate that you really want to preserve the essential aspects and historical relevance of the building, your case will be considerably strengthened.

Renovations or extensions

The land agency lists are full of renovation opportunities that vary from almost complete re-builds to properties that really just need a makeover, say a new kitchen and bathroom. However, unless the change envisaged is fundamental there is unlikely to be the equity gain that is available with new build.

Look for the house that is really the missed opportunity. For example the 1960s house that's too small or of a design that is out of character with the local vernacular, yet enjoys an enviable plot. We've all seen them – the blots on the landscape or the street scene, in styles and of materials that bear no relationship to the rest of an attractive village. But rendering or cladding, new windows, new roofing materials and maybe even re-modelling with judicious use of extensions can totally transform the external appearance of a house. And modern heating systems, thermal insulation, new kitchens and bathrooms can make them into the kind of homes that we expect in this day and age, without compromising the re-vamped external look.

It's sometimes even possible to enthuse the planning and/or conservation officer with your proposals. There's nothing they can do to force the alteration of properties that are detracting from the street scene. They are hostages to their predecessor's mistakes and if you come along with proposals that will improve the area, they might well support your endeavours.

Find out, before doing any work, whether the Permitted Development Rights have been curtailed or removed and if not, utilise them to the full before making any planning application. This might be very important in a situation where an extension's acceptability might well be related the size of the dwelling. You might need to read up about this in Chapter 8 to understand fully what I mean here, but suffice it to say, there are certain classes of development that do not always need express planning approval. If the authority has a policy that restricts the extension of buildings to, say, 50% larger than the original, then if you have the right to enlarge the building beforehand, the calculation will be more in your favour.

Renovating and converting are sufficiently different in many respects for them to be given their own chapter later on in this book (Chapter 7). Additionally, in Chapter 10, I have made separate references to building practices and working with tradesmen on older buildings.

Plotfinding checklist

Look at everything ☐

See things as they're going to be ☐

Be prepared to compromise ☐

Get to know estate agents and visit them frequently ☐

Register with the plotfinding agencies ☐

Be proactive ☐

Study Ordnance Survey maps ☐

Study the local development plan/framework ☐

Look out for obvious plots ☐

Watch out for infill plots ☐

Investigate whether backland development is possible ☐

Don't be afraid to knock on doors ☐

Check ownership with HM Land Registry ☐

Talk to local people ☐

Get to know the area ☐

Put out flyers ☐

Watch out for brownfield sites ☐

Study the planning register ☐

Look out for properties suitable for replacement ☐

Keep a watch in the local media ☐

Consider advertising yourself ☐

Check you don't already own a suitable plot ☐

See if a suitable plot is already in the family ☐

Consider joining forces with others to go for a multiple site ☐

Befriend local builders and developers ☐

Watch out for that conversion or renovation opportunity ☐

See if judicious extension could take a property into a different league ☐

Contact public bodies for spare or vacant land ☐

Chapter 3

ASSESSING AND UNDERSTANDING THE POTENTIAL

What you can afford to pay for a suitable building plot, and the probable size of the house that you will be able to afford to build, have been discussed in Chapter 1. But having identified a plot there is still a lot more that you need to consider before you actually buy it. This chapter is concerned with evaluating the plot and the issues which may affect your costs, what you can build and, in the final analysis, whether or not the site can be developed at all.

Remember that just because a piece of land is described as a 'building plot' does not necessarily mean that it is a practicable place to build a house. It only means that the vendor has chosen the words to attract prospective purchasers. Much has been made of the 'seller's pack' or log book that the Government would like all homeowners to keep and, having gone through trials in certain areas, it is now to be rolled out across the country. But I very much doubt that the information contained within it will have any greater significance than the bland answers to questions that any purchaser or their solicitor would normally be asking and receiving. And I'm pretty sure that it will never have real relevance to building plots other than to bring together all of the planning documentation. It might have some greater significance when it comes to conversions or renovations, especially with Building Regulations approvals, but even here, most vendors of such properties would leave that up to the purchasers. Remember the words, and legal terminology, *caveat*

emptor, meaning 'let the buyer beware'. What follows is about what you must aware of.

You should start by wondering just why nobody has built on the plot before or done something with that redundant building. Really first-class individual building plots and development opportunities have been in very short supply for ages. Why is this still a building plot? Why is this building still empty? Why didn't anyone do something with it twenty years ago? There may be a simple answer. The site may have been part of the garden of a large house and only split off from it a short while ago. Planning consent may have been granted very recently following a change in a local development plan. Or, with old buildings, they've just always been there as ruins and nobody ever thought of restoring them to proper use.

What you find out may or may not prevent you from building on it and the pages that follow will guide you through the solutions as well as the problems, bringing to your attention the things you need to know about before, rather than after you have committed yourself.

Planning permission

There are various types of consent, and in any consideration of a plot or development opportunity, it

Right: **The dream cottage that looks as if it has always been there.** © Potton

is important to appreciate the differences between them and their relationships to each other. They are:

- Outline planning consent
- Approval of reserved matters
- Full planning permission.

Outline planning consent gives permission, in principle, for the development of land. It means that some sort of building or development may take place and it is what confers the value on the plot. Outline consent does not, in itself, allow you to commence work but, rather, it allows you to move on to the next stage of the planning process. It is always given subject to conditions, some of which are standard. Up until recently most permissions have been valid for a period of five years with a condition that within a period of three years, from the date of granting, application will be made for Approval of Reserved Matters (see below). These reserved matters are usually the siting, design and access arrangements, which are not normally dealt with at the Outline stage. There may well be other conditions and, at the next stage in the planning process, these conditions will have to be satisfied.

Legislation brought into being in the autumn of 2004, but only enacted as this book went to press, introduces a standard time limit of three years for all planning consents, but at the same time, gives local authorities the power to impose their own time limits. In future, Outline consents will require that application is made for Approval of Reserved Matters within three years of granting of the consent and that work is commenced within two years of the Detailed approval. On the face of it you might think that nothing has really changed. Except that, and this is important, if your application for Approval of Reserved Matters runs over the three-year period and then fails, the original Outline consent will have expired.

Happily, this latest legislation is not retrospective and for the time being things will remain largely unaltered. But it does make it even more important that anyone considering a plot should study the consent very carefully to determine whether or not it is current and whether conditions within it have been satisfied or are capable of being satisfied within a laid-down timescale.

Approval of Reserved Matters is the next stage in the normal planning process. It is sometimes referred to as 'Detailed permission' and it concerns itself with the actual design, siting and access arrangements for the development. In normal circumstances, it does not confer any extra value to the plot, over and above that already given to it by the outline consent. Within this application any conditions imposed by the Outline consent have to be satisfied and it is possible that fresh conditions will also be imposed. An Approval of Reserved Matters never stands alone; it is always related back to and is a part of the original Outline consent. As an example, if there is a condition on the Outline consent that the development is for a single-storey dwelling, and the planning officer agrees that you may, in fact, make application for a two-storey dwelling, then you cannot do so as an Approval of Reserved Matters pursuant to the original Outline consent. A fresh application will have to be made.

It is necessary to understand, however, that even though the Approval of Reserved Matters cannot stand alone, it does not follow that it is a mere formality. Additionally, the granting of an Approval of Reserved Matters does not preclude further applications for quite different schemes relating back to the original Outline consent, and the refusal of an application for Approval of Reserved Matters does nothing to negate the original Outline consent so long as it remains in time.

Full planning permission is really nothing more than a rolling up together of the Outline and Detailed stages of an application into one consent. It grants permission in principle and at the same time considers and approves the full details of the proposed development. As such, it confers value to the plot in just the same way as an Outline consent does. Full consents granted up to the spring of 2005 last for five years. The new legislation means that Full consents will now last for three years, making it all the more important to check all dates.

Where the issues of whether or not the land

should be developed are not in contention and it's more a question of establishing what will be built, then a Full application is wholly relevant. On the other hand, any attempt to confuse or obscure the issue of principle by making a Full application, rather than an Outline application, is likely to backfire.

The words 'permission' and 'consent' are interchangeable in all that you read here (or anywhere else) about planning matters. It is important to realise that planning permission says that you *may* develop land. It does not say that you *can* develop land and it confers no other rights or obligations. If you get a consent and, for physical or legal reasons, that consent cannot be acted upon, then there is no liability on the local authority. Once work has commenced on site, the planning permission is perpetuated.

Planning permission normally 'runs to the benefit of the land'. That means that the consent relates to the plot, regardless of who the applicant or previous owner was. Exceptions to this are rare and relate more to things like the siting of mobile homes for prospective farm enterprises and the occupation of an annex. In these cases the exclusivity is normally achieved by the wording on a condition on the consent.

Consents for Approval of Reserved Matters and Full consents can still have conditions attached to them which have to be satisfied before any commencement of work. An example of these may be that before any work commences on site, the approval of the local authority shall be obtained, in writing, for a landscaping and tree-planting scheme. Or that before any work commences on site, the approval of the local authority will have been sought and obtained in writing for the use of any external materials such as bricks or tiles. In these cases the approval of these items is delegated to the officers and in the latter example they may wish to see samples of the intended materials. The condition may go on to say that this approval shall be sought, notwithstanding the materials mentioned or stated on the plans, but whether or not it does, these words are implied and you cannot rely on the fact that another material was specified.

Make no mistake, these conditions and their sat-

isfaction are vital to the continuance and viability of a planning permission. I remember the case of a man who bought a plot of land in the Green Belt, where there is a presumption against planning. Work had already commenced on the site and he, and unfortunately his solicitor, assumed that as the building had reached oversite, the planning was therefore perpetuated. What they didn't check was whether the condition requiring the authority's approval of the external materials *before commencement of work* had been cleared. It hadn't and the planners maintained that any work that had taken place, despite the fact that it had been inspected by the Building Control department, was in contravention of the conditions of the consent and therefore illegal. Because of the passage of time, the consent had lapsed. A subsequent application to obtain retrospective approval was then refused on the grounds that development in the Green Belt was contrary to planning policy!

There are many other conditions which can be attached to any consent and which have the effect of making it inoperable until such time as they are satisfied. Most of these will be flagged up in this chapter and in the Site Details Checklist on page 130. But beware! It is possible, as in the case outlined above, to commence work on a project and even to get to the stage of a practically finished dwelling without addressing a condition, and occupation and full operation of the consent will be illegal until such time as the formalities are sorted out.

In the normal course of events the advice must be to buy only those plots that have an express planning consent, either Outline, Detailed or Full. To every rule there must be an exception. I have discussed this partially in the preceding chapter and will discuss it further in Chapter 8. However, for the purposes of this section of the book we will assume, in the main, that you are buying a plot with planning permission.

It's surprising to some, but the number of times a plot is offered on the market on the basis of it having planning consent when the reverse is in fact true are legion. This generally happens not through any deliberate attempt to mislead, but often because of the naivety of the people selling the plot which can, as I have demonstrated above, include solicitors.

The first thing you need to check when buying a plot with planning permission is that the consent has not lapsed. Most planning permissions at the time of writing last for five years from the date of the consent. If it's a Full permission then it will simply state this fact, but if it's an Outline consent, it will go on to say that within a period of three years an application for Approval of Reserved Matters must be made. In effect, therefore, if your prospective plot has Outline consent and you are being offered the land more than three years after it was granted, with no Detailed application ever having been made, then the Outline consent is out of time. In such cases, either a fresh Outline application has to be made or else your prospective Detailed application has to be changed to a Full application. Either way you are at risk in that, if the policy of the local authority has changed in the intervening period, your new application could fail, leaving that parcel of land with no valid consent. It is therefore vital in these circumstances that you identify the problem quickly, and only agree to purchase the plot 'subject to receipt of satisfactory planning consent'. When the new shorter time frames are introduced this problem will become even more acute.

It's not unusual for land to be offered with either a Full consent which has expired or else with the benefit of a Detailed consent which has itself expired when related back to the original Outline permission – always *check the dates on all planning documents*. If the expiry date is fast approaching then the best course of action is for the vendors to apply for an extension of time. But the chances are that they will fail to see your concern. In their minds the land has got planning and they are unlikely to see that the plot they've thought of for so long as money in the bank could be anything other than that. Your only option then is to insist on buying 'subject to receipt of satisfactory planning approval'. If they won't play ball on that, then really you have three options: you take an enormous gamble and buy the land anyway, you pull out altogether, or you try to string out the purchase whilst processing your own application.

The land I built my last home on had a planning permission that was fast approaching its expiry date. It had Outline consent reached on appeal but no application for Approval of Reserved Matters had ever been made. For reasons that I will go into later, although the local authority indicated that they would accept a fresh Full application and they conceded the principle that the land could be developed, I did not want to rely on this assurance. I therefore made a spoof application for Approval of Reserved Matters, using any old plan in order to stay in time. At a later date I withdrew this application and substituted it with a fresh application for what I actually wanted.

It may seem strange to some people but you don't have to own a plot of land in order to make a planning application on it. In fact you don't even really need the consent of the owner. All you must do is inform them, by means of a form in the planning application documents, that you are making the application. This means that if you come across a plot where the planning is suspect, it is open to you (preferably by agreement) to make your own application in order to clarify matters. In similar vein if the plot you're interested in has no consent, but you feel that it stands a good chance of getting it, then it's open to you to make an application before you actually buy the land.

Beware, though! The owners could very well let you get on with all this and then, when you've sorted it all out and enhanced the value of their land by tens of thousands of pounds, turn around and sell it to somebody else. To avoid this, either tie things up beforehand with a formal legally binding option or else, as I've said before, buy the land 'subject to receipt of satisfactory planning permission', in which case, if it fails, the contract is voided.

Does the consent relate to the property on offer? Well, in fact, it's not unusual to come across situations where a vendor gets planning permission for a part of their garden and then when it comes to selling decides that they really can't stomach the thought of the loss of a particular tree or area of garden, and that they just don't want the new house so close to theirs. The plot which was outlined in red on the plan, which got planning permission and which was shown as being 18 metres wide and stopping 3 metres from their house wall, suddenly becomes 12 metres wide and a long way from their wall. The area of land is still contained within the original outlined site, but it manifestly is not the same site and it is

When planning does not go to plan ...

Perhaps the most blatant example of a vendor moving the goal posts that I know of occurred when a young couple I met bought a plot that was originally the side garden of a house. The land was not fenced and the boundaries were marked out by pegs in the ground with the boundary between the two properties as a dogleg. They got planning permission and had already started building when their builder telephoned them to say that he couldn't get the house on the plot. It simply did not fit. They rushed up to the site and he was right. A site meeting was arranged with the vendor, the solicitors for both sides and the planning officer. The vendor shrugged his shoulders and said that it wasn't his problem. The couple, in tears by now, walked away from the group to comfort each other. They walked across to a bush that they had previously thought was in their plot but which was now a couple of metres beyond the boundary. They fished around beneath the bush and found a perfect square hole where the peg had been. At the bottom boundary there was similar hole. The vendor blustered and protested but happily his own solicitor advised him to concede and the building work was able to continue.

that way. To them the area outside the original red line does not have the benefit of any planning consent and whilst they may be amenable to this 'new' plot being developed, it nevertheless does not have consent and your application will have to be a Full one rather than an Approval of Reserved Matters. Again, in any and all of these instances, you need to buy 'subject to receipt of satisfactory planning permission'.

Sometimes planning is granted conditional upon something else happening. An example of this would be where planning consent is granted on a plot, or plots, conditional upon, say, an old building being demolished. You're only buying the plot and the condemned building is outside your jurisdiction. If that part of the site is sold to another party who fails to demolish the old building then, although your vendor, and/or the other purchaser, is technically in breach of contract, you might find it very difficult to fully satisfy the conditions on your consent. It probably won't come to the point of totally invalidating your planning but it could well lead to some sticky moments and the exchange of more than a few letters. So, it's best to point all this out to your solicitor at an early stage (unless of course they've already picked up on it) and also to make sure that some sort of timetable and undertaking is given for the work to be done. Multi-plot sites are often given planning on the condition that certain works will be undertaken to improve or create an access and it needs to be established, right at the outset, that this work will and can be carried out. I shall touch on this subject again under access, roads and driveways and visibility splays on pages 84–5.

Special conditions on a planning consent can impact on whether or not the plot is suitable for your purposes in the first place. It has become common for

open to the planners to rule that the consent is consequently invalid on this smaller plot.

A way around this, if the smaller site is acceptable to you, is for the Detailed planning application to go in on the basis of the larger plot whilst at the same time you proceed to purchase the smaller plot. But be very careful. Although there's nothing to stop this from happening, the planners won't necessarily go along with your new home being situated to one side of the plot, as they see it, and any explanation that you're only buying a portion of the original consent will have no influence on their opinions.

Similarly, vendors can often simply move the original-sized plot to one side so that it either partially or wholly slips out of the original area shown on the consent. They won't see that they've done anything wrong but planners don't see it

Special conditions on a planning consent can impact on whether or not the plot is suitable for your purposes in the first place.

local authorities to stipulate the maximum, and very occasionally the minimum, size that a dwelling can be. And they mean what they say. If they say that the dwelling must not exceed 180 square metres plus a garage then, as far as the planners are concerned, that's what you're going to get and no more. If the building is to be single storey then a bungalow is what you're going to be able to build under that consent. In some cases the limitation may go further to curtail or remove what are known as 'Permitted Development Rights'. That's the second time that these rights have cropped up and, therefore, before I move on I'd better explain briefly just what they are, although I will be covering them in greater detail in Chapter 8.

Within the Planning Acts there are certain classes of development that can be carried out without the need for express or specific planning consent. These are known as Permitted Development Rights. You may still need Building Regulations approval but you don't have to apply for planning permission to carry out certain classes of development, including extensions up to a certain size, garages where none exists, and development within the curtilage of the building. They can be varied or negated within a consent and are usually excluded in conservation areas and in sensitive planning situations.

There has been some talk lately of these rights being curtailed. To date nothing has happened and it's possible that, like many of these 'flyers', nothing will ever happen – but do always check before doing any work under Permitted Development Rights.

Brief mention needs to be made about planning on neighbouring land and 'planning blight'. In any consideration of a plot it's necessary for you, your solicitor or both to investigate what planning applications have been granted or are up for consideration in the locality that could possibly affect you. If you are buying a site for a sea view and then discover that a large hotel is going to be built that would completely block that view, you would probably want to know about it before committing to the land. In similar vein, if a major public undertaking such as a by-pass or an airport is being mooted, then, although it might be at the stage where no formal application or plans have been formulated, it could still have a dramatic

effect on the property. Indeed, the possibility of it coming to fruition could well blight your property and render it virtually unmarketable. Now, although there may well be compensation available for such blight or indeed for any diminution of value or enjoyment if the scheme is ever enacted, I wonder whether, in most circumstances, a property such as this is a suitable one to take on. I fear as well that if someone purchased in the knowledge of the blight, the compensation could be limited by the assumption that they had paid a price which reflected its effects.

It's not at all unusual in certain areas to come across conditions on a planning consent relating to some sort of archaeological interest. Sometimes an archaeological survey is required, either before consent is granted or before any work is commenced. These are not cheap and, if anything of particular or peculiar interest is found, there could be an almost indefinite delay on any development of the land or property.

Occasionally development will be allowed with special foundations that allow access beneath the dwelling at some future date. Usually, however, the authorities limit their involvement to a watching brief, in which case all that needs to be done is to notify the relevant department and/or local archaeological society and allow them time to come out and inspect your foundation trenches.

If the plot is in a Conservation Area, Area of Outstanding Natural Beauty, National Park or the Broads, then there may be particular planning restrictions that you will need to be aware of. The same applies if you are planning to convert or renovate a Listed building or if your site is in what is known as a Site of Special Scientific Interest (SSSI). These issues are dealt with in Chapter 8, but once again, you should be aware of the implications at the evaluation stages.

Access, roads and driveways

Unless there are peculiar circumstances such as off-site parking or, in certain towns or cities, on-road parking, a plot is not a plot unless it can demonstrate that there is a viable vehicular access.

Direct access to a public highway

This would always appear to be the best option. However, whenever a new access is proposed to the public highway, the opinion and recommendations of the Highways Agency, or the local authority department responsible for administering the roads, will be sought. And they may well wish to impose some fairly stringent conditions.

Highway requirements vary in different parts of the country, and the rules in East Anglia are obviously going to be very different from those in parts of Wales or the North. If you are considering a plot with access from a highway, you must get hold of the Highways Agency's requirements at a very early stage and consider whether the development that you propose for the plot will be practicable.

In general terms, the higher the category of the road – A, B, unclassified, etc. – the stricter the requirements, and whatever the classification there will be a concern for road safety. At the very least this will involve an absolute ban on vehicles joining or leaving the road at a sharp corner or at a blind spot. At the very worst there will be an absolute ban of any access – but that, of course, would mean that this wasn't really a plot. More usually the requirements will involve being able to enter and leave in a forward gear, setting back any gate a fixed distance from the carriageway, and providing a visibility splay, of which more later.

The actual junction may be required to be level or at a gentle gradient for a certain distance inside your property. They may go on to stipulate the maximum gradient for the rest of your drive, usually 1:10, and in turn that might mean that your driveway, instead of being straight, might have to be curved around the site. In turn that will take up more land and might even restrict the area where you can build.

In most cases, you will also be expected to make sure that surface water from your drive cannot spill on to the road and that can mean having to install drainage, which may or may not be allowed to discharge into the surface water drains in the road.

The minute an application is received by the planning authorities, they send it out for what is known as 'Consultations' and, almost the first one is to the highways authorities who will in turn make certain recommendations, which can vary between outright rejection and qualified approval. The planning authority is bound to consider any objections from Highways, even though in many cases they do have the power to overrule them.

A prime example of this occurred with the last house I built. The Highways Agency recommended that the entrance should be situated centrally on the plot and that I should provide a passing place within the curtilage of my land as this was a narrow lane. The planners were horrified at the thought that if these requirements were enacted, most of the natural hedge and bank to the frontage would be lost and they overruled the Agency in favour of an entrance to one side, which combined the bellmouth with the necessary passing place and preserved most of the hedge.

If you're buying a plot where planning has already been granted, have a good look at the proposals for the entrance on to the highway. It's also no good assuming that if the access is shown in a particular way you can simply change it. If the entrance to your plot is shown on the right-hand side of the road frontage then you cannot automatically assume that it can be moved to the middle or the left-hand side of the plot without exciting attention from the planners and/or the Highways Agency. If you're making a fresh planning application on a plot that you've identified, consult the Highways Agency beforehand and if necessary have a meeting on site to discuss what they want so that you can incorporate their recommendations within the application.

One thing that does seem to be cropping up in certain areas, particularly in Wales, and is certain to spread, is the requirement for some sort of off-site trade-off in return for planning permission. This may mean that whoever builds the house has to pay for the construction of a passing place or lay-by further up the road, possibly on land that has been 'gifted' by the original applicants for the purpose.

Visibility splays

These cause endless problems for both single- and multiple-use accesses. It probably starts with a simple condition on the planning consent that says, 'The access shall be formed in accordance with the requirements of the Highways Agency.' All perfectly

Visibility splays

The local authority will want an access like this ...

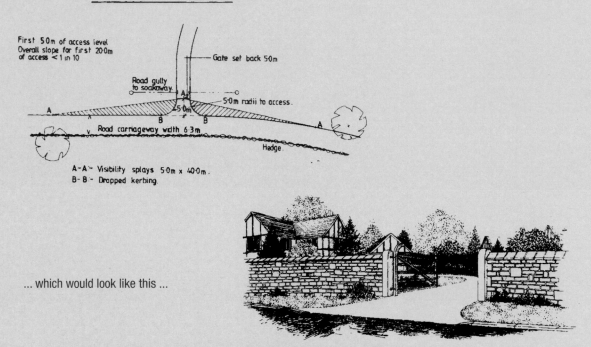

Proposed Drive Access.

First 5·0m of access level
Overall slope for first 20·0m
of access < 1 in 10

Gate set back 5·0m

Road gully
to soakaway

5·0m radii to access.

5·0m

A

B   B

Road carriageway width 6·3m

Hedge.

A~A :- Visibility splays 5·0m x 40·0m.
B~B :- Dropped kerbing.

... which would look like this ...

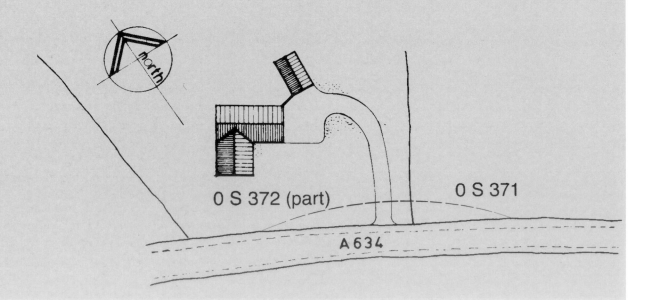

... but if your plot is field no. OS 372 and this is how you want to site your new house, you will have to negotiate with the owner of field no. OS 371 to provide your visibility splay.

north

0 S 372 (part)   0 S 371

A 634

harmless, you may think, and many people take no further notice, assuming that everything that was relevant was sorted out at the initial planning stage. Well, it may well have been discussed but all that has resulted is the condition on the consent. So how can you know if that condition can be satisfied unless you know what the requirements are?

The need for a visibility splay is one of the most common conditions imposed by the Highways Agency and, in general, the busier the road, the more stringent the requirements for its provision. But what does it actually mean when the wording calls for, say, visibility splays 2.4 metres by 120 metres east and 2.4 metres by 90 metres west. Almost certainly that means that your plot is on the southern side of an east–west road with the frontage facing roughly north. The longer visibility splay will relate to the traffic approaching on your side of the road and is calculated by measuring to a point 2.4 metres back from the carriageway edge along the centre line of your proposed driveway. From that point you then take a line eastwards 120 metres until it meets the carriageway and a similar line from the same point but to the west this time, and for only 90 metres, until it again meets the edge of the carriageway. These are your visibility splays. Now, if everything within those two triangles is within your plot you have nothing to worry about except for the fact that, at all times, you'll have to keep those areas clear of any obstruction higher than 1,005mm (eye-level for a person seated in a car), and that includes shrubs and trees.

But what if the triangles you arrive at extend beyond your boundaries and cross the neighbour's land? The planners aren't particularly concerned about the legalities of this. As I shall say many times in this book, planning permission says that you *may* build on the land; it does not say that you *can*. In their eyes it's up to the developer of the land to sort out any necessary easements or covenants, and all they're concerned with is that the requirements are demonstrated. So, if you're offered a plot with such a requirement and the vendors cannot give you assurance that they have secured a legal arrangement with their neighbours to keep their land free from obstruction in perpetuity, you need to steer clear of that plot.

You could, of course, try negotiating directly with the neighbours yourself, but be prepared that the person you're dealing with may either see this an opportunity to afford a holiday home in Spain, or be determined that the plot next door will never be developed, even to the point of deliberately planting tress and shrubs within the visibility splays.

However, it's not always as hopeless as this may sound. In many cases the requirements are limited or even non-existent and in others you'll find that the visibility splays cross the grass verge of the highway, which is fine. The thing is to check it both on site and on plan before you move on to buying a site. And, once again, if any money has got to change hands in order to secure any necessary agreements, then it is the vendor and not you who should be paying it.

The crossover

The planning requirements for the entrance and the visibility splays to the road have been discussed, but there may well be additional requirements concerning the construction of the crossover or bellmouth to the road. Most general contractors can carry out works within your plot up to the point where it meets the public highway. Beyond that point, however, works to and within the public highway may well have to be carried out by an Approved Contractor.

This may even include works to the footpath and/or works within the grass verge if it is part of the highway. An Approved Contractor will be on a list that the local authority will provide to you and they are never cheap.

In some cases the bellmouth immediately adjoining the carriageway can be constructed to driveway standards but in others, even if it's on your land, there may be a requirement for it to be constructed to adoption standards, even if there is no intention to adopt. Works to create a new footpath or to lower curbs may also have to be undertaken by approved contractors and the local authority will want to stipulate the level and nature of the construction, once again, to adoption standards.

Gates

Although many modern houses do not seem to employ gates and the drive is usually open to the road, in rural and forest areas a gate is essential, if only to keep sheep and other animals from consuming your garden. Where gates are employed, there will usually be a requirement for a 45-degree splay from each side of the gate and for the gates to be set back at least 5.5 metres from the edge of the carriageway, so as to enable a car to pull off the road completely whilst the gates are opened inwards. If the slope of the land makes this impossible then your gates will have to move even further back.

Parking and turning

In many cases there is a planning requirement, usually at the instigation of the highways authorities, for all cars to be able to enter and leave the site in a forward gear. This is not universal. It will obviously be necessary if the access is off a busy road but might not be required at all if the access is from a side or estate road. If the requirement does appear on the planning document then you need to make a note of it because such a requirement, including that of minimum radii on bends, can take up a large amount of land. Almost certainly that will, in turn, affect the positioning and indeed the size of your proposed new home. One innovation that might help is a turntable, set into the driveway and often operated by hand.

Most local authorities will want to see a minimum of two car parking spaces per property. In most cases there is no particular requirement for garaging and these can often be provided as part of the driveway and turning area. In urban areas on-street parking may well be acceptable. Generally the busier the road the greater the requirements for off-road parking and turning will be, and the Highways Agency and local authority assess each case on its individual merits with regard to visibility and safety.

Access on to an unadopted road

There are many sorts of unadopted roads, but those most usually found by self-builders came about in the first 40 years of the 20th century. At that time developers often sold plots leading off a private road with no intention that the road would ever be taken over, or adopted, by the local authority. This was considered to be a way of guaranteeing that the development would always be suitably exclusive in the

days before the planning acts. The plots and houses built on them were often very large, although sometimes this way of doing things was used in low-cost bungalow towns, known locally as 'Plotlands'.

Sixty years later these unadopted roads are often in a sorry condition and the residents owning the road would usually dearly like the authority to take it over and put it in good order. The council will not do this unless all the residents pay 'road charges', which may amount to tens of thousands of pounds per property. As it is most unlikely that they all can or want to pay this, the road remains unadopted with only the most urgent repair work paid for by some form of residents' association, usually only when they find that the cost of filling the potholes is less than the cost of replacing their broken exhausts.

Houses on the more up-market of these developments often have large gardens, and high land values. This means that it is likely that they will be subdivided and sold as building plots if planning consent to do this can be obtained. The bungalows on Plotlands also have large gardens by modern standards and they are coming up for sale as sites for a replacement dwelling. Both of these types of plot are becoming predominant, especially in the light of Government antipathy towards the continued development of greenfield sites. But there are aspects that need very careful consideration.

What are the arrangements for the ownership and maintenance of the road? What road charges are likely to be levied if it is ever adopted? (Road charges are levied on the basis of a rate per metre of road frontage and that, if you're on a corner, could be quite considerable.) Above all, what is the long-term future for property values when the 1930s vintage road in terminal decay deteriorates further?

In the case of Plotlands, there is an element of them existing outside the normal confines of society. Residents who have grown up and grown old in stigmatised situations may resist changes that either highlight the eventual demise of their beloved homes or threaten to involve them in expenditure that is way beyond their means. In the case of the estates of larger houses, the affluence of their occupants might well mean that, in the intervening period, some form of legal framework or documentation listing each owner's rights and responsibilities will have been set down. This may well be in the form of a residents' association or a company in which each party has shares, rights and obligations. In turn that can be problematic for the potential self-builder because when the original agreements were drafted, they may well have contained a list of the properties able to enjoy the facilities. Effectively therefore, a new property, created by subdivision, may not have the automatic right to either access or services, giving a ransom or veto to all the other members.

Once again, if any payment is to be made to secure access or services, then it is the vendor who should be making it, not the purchaser or self-builder.

Sharing an existing access

Infill plots may well receive planning on the basis that the new house shares the existing access, and that may well mean that part of the driveway to your new home could be in somebody else's property and ownership. The same will often occur with backland development where the local authority will be concerned to ensure that the street scene remains largely unaltered and that a new access is not made to the carriageway.

If you are buying a plot where the access is over another landowner's property and that landowner is the vendor, it is important to make sure that your right of access is enshrined in any and all of the legal documentation. It will also be necessary to establish who is liable for any upkeep and how the need for maintenance is to be established.

Where a new driveway is to be brought across intervening land, it is important to establish whether ownership of the driveway will run with the plot or whether a right of way will be granted over land which will remain in another's ownership. In most cases, just so long as the proper arrangements are in place governing usage and maintenance there is little to choose between the two.

In Northern Ireland it is not unusual to come across plots sold off by farmers, which are two fields back from the road. In many cases the farmers undertake to construct the new lane to the base course

and then leave it to the self-builders to 'finish off' the driveway when the house is completed. That's all very good if ownership of the new driveway passes to the plot owner for their exclusive use. But if the farmer retains ownership or the right to use the driveway without agreement for future maintenance, the self-builder could be at a significant disadvantage.

Creating a new shared access or driveway

In most local authority areas three or four houses can be built with access off a private drive. The drive will not be adopted by the local authority and the home owners will have to maintain it themselves. This makes it simple for each of them to buy a plot with the usual reciprocal liabilities to be responsible for the drive and drains, which are built either by the vendor of the land or by the purchasers sharing the costs. Private driveways with multiple use do have their drawbacks, in that it can sometimes prove difficult to get everyone to live up to and pay for their responsibilities. That's why it's important that the details are worked out and fully understood in advance.

The basis on which you may be sharing a drive with other people requires very careful consideration. A very basic requirement is an arrangement that there is no parking of any sort under any circumstances on the shared part of the drive, especially if this would have the effect of restricting normal access. It is also very desirable that the shared length should be constructed to a high standard with proper kerbing and a surface that is up to the wear and tear to which it will be subjected. Future maintenance arrange-

Pros and cons of a shared drive

Shared drives have short-term advantages and long-term problems. Solicitors will elaborate on their disadvantages to prospective purchasers and some estate agents might well confirm that the property value could be lessened by such an arrangement. On the other hand, there is a particular benefit in being able to control just who parks on or uses a private driveway and, unlike the cost of a proper road, it's unlikely to be a major proportion of the development costs of any one plot.

ments need to be put in place and there must be a legal framework and pre-arranged formula to divide the costs fairly between all of the users.

If four or more homes require a new access, it is quite likely that the authorities will call for the road and the drains under it to be constructed to highway standards, with a bond leading to formal adoption. This costs a great deal more money and is complicated, as either a single person or a formal body of some sort has to take legal responsibility for the bond.

The actual arrangements to build a drive, road or drains to adoption standards have to be made very carefully. Avoid any joint responsibility for this work; it is preferable that it should be the responsibility of one person or body. This could be one of the self-builders but, more often than not, as only approved contractors can carry out works to or abutting the highway, will be a contractor or civil engineer. This person or firm should provide a guarantee that the work will be done, preferably with a bank bond, so that if they default the bank will step in and get the work done. In return they will look for a guarantee of payment from all of the plot owners, often with the money deposited with a solicitor, or with a second charge over the plots. In this way there are mutual obligations all round that will ensure that the work is done, without any one participant's special circumstances jeapordising the whole job.

Ransom strips

Whatever sort of road there is you need to check that it directly abuts the property and that there is no intervening strip of land. If there is, either visible on the ground or apparent in the documentation or the plans, then there is a distinct possibility that a ransom strip exists.

Ransom strips are narrow strips of land (often as tiny as 150mm wide) between your plot and the access, which prevent the site from being developed. They are not there by accident. Someone has arranged for them, and the purpose is either to stop anyone building on the plot at all, or to make them pay for the privilege. This may sound like some sort of sharp practice, but in fact it is rarely anything of the sort. What has happened is best understood by looking at the background history to the situation, which will

be different in all cases but will follow the same basic principles.

The story probably starts when all the land, including both the strip and the plot, were part of the garden of a large country house. This may well have been a hundred years ago. Someone who wanted to buy part of the land for some purpose or other, but who had no intention of building on it, probably approached the landowner. The owner of the big house might well have been amenable to a sale but was concerned that no development took place that would impair their privacy or their views. Now, the land could have been sold with a covenant to the title to prevent anyone from ever building there. However, to make it even more certain that no one could do so, it was sold with just a pedestrian access and no way of getting a vehicle to it at all. As the purchaser did not want to build on it anyway, everyone was happy with this arrangement.

A hundred years later the big house has been demolished and the site where it stood is covered with modern homes at ten to an acre. At the time when they were built, it would have been sensible for our plot to have been developed as part of the same estate, but, for one reason or another, it lay dormant.

Now the plot comes on to the market. The vendor either knows nothing about the ransom strip or, if they do, says nothing about it. The plans aren't that clear and in any event those used to obtain planning permission make no mention of the existence of the strip. But the company that developed the larger site and which may well have gone to huge expense to put in roads, sewers and drains, all of which might now benefit the plot, might well just be waiting for all of this to happen. With their ears close to the ground and a general watch on what goes for planning, they are waiting for their chance. It matters not that all of this dates back hundreds of years, nor that the roads and sewers have been adopted and that the houses on the estate have all been sold off. The ransom strip will, almost certainly, have been withheld and is still in the legal ownership of the developer.

And the courts have generally held that the value of such a ransom strip is around one third of the uplift in value of the plot from being just a piece of

Above: **This old house is in a lovely position but getting vehicular access could prove problematic.**

land to becoming a viable building site. Which in most cases is virtually the same as saying one third of the value.

Make sure you don't get caught by this one. If any monies are going to change hands then this should be before you buy the plot and it is the vendor who should be paying. What you don't want is to buy the land and then have to pay the ransom. If it can be proved that the vendor was aware of it all along then you might get compensation. But on the other hand that might be very difficult to prove.

So what can you do to guard against finding you have a ransom strip situation? They are sometimes quite apparent on the ground but, at other times, can only really be established by careful measurement and by detailed cross-checking of all plans. They can go unnoticed by solicitors if there is no reference to them in the title documents or in the Land Registry

Whenever you are buying land you should:

● Ask yourself why no one has built here before

● Measure every part of the boundary on the ground and compare it with the plan on the title deeds – and this means the title deeds and not the plan in the estate agent's particulars or the one used to gain planning permission! And find out why the plot is the shape that it is. If there seems to be a discrepancy, go to the public library and look at the 19th-century Ordnance Survey maps of the area. They often provide clues as to what has happened.

● Drop in at the local pub, strike up an acquaintance with the local busybody and ask his opinion of your prospective purchase. You may be told that the soil is full of eelworm and won't grow brassicas, or that it was once the scene of a horrible murder, or that 'There's a ransom strip'!

details, which, as they are outside the boundaries of the land, is quite possible.

If the owner or beneficiary of the ransom is known then you have no real alternative but to negotiate for its release or purchase. They of course do not have to play ball. They might not want to see the land developed or they might see their strip as a lever to gain ownership of the entire plot. Either way you might find that the negotiations are best conducted at arm's length by a solicitor or agent.

And if you cannot trace the owner of the ransom strip? Well, then you are in a slightly better situation, because in many situations it is possible to take out a single-premium indemnity policy to cover against the possibility of an owner turning up.

By the way, it's no good just pretending that you don't know the owner if their existence and identity has already been established. In order to write such a policy, the insurance company will want statutory declarations from the previous owners/vendors and possibly from neighbours. They may also make their own enquiries. The premium will be set according to the risk and if that risk becomes a certainty, then they'll decline to quote.

Construction traffic

A major consideration when assessing a plot or development opportunity is just how you're going to get the materials on site, and indeed, in many cases, how you're going to get considerable quantities of spoil off site.

Nothing is, of course, impossible but if you're going to have to offload materials at the bottom of an unmade lane, half a mile from your plot, and either manhandle or carry them to site on dumper trucks, it's going to cost time and money.

If a lorry can't get to you and has to turn back, and you haven't advised them of the difficulties, you could find yourself liable for abortive delivery charges on top of the inconvenience of not having the materials when you want them. Trusses, for example, come on very long articulated lorries and if there are any low bridges, wires or other obstructions within

the vicinity of your site you will be expected to inform them before they set off. Readymix concrete lorries are prodigiously heavy and if you crack a neighbour's drains or a local authority culvert, or tear up the surface of the road, it could cost you a great deal of money.

Consider the site itself as well. Concrete lorries are not only heavy but very unstable too, and excess gradients or cambers on the immediate approach to your foundation could well tip them over. I can tell you from experience (although happily not on one of my own sites), that one of these turned on its side is a frightening and expensive occurrence. If you think that this could happen, arrange a dumper truck to take the stuff on to the site itself whilst the concrete lorry stays safely off site discharging into it. Better still, arrange a pump to which each concrete lorry simply backs up and the concrete is jetted to where it is needed.

If you feel that there's any likelihood of vehicles getting stuck in soft ground, at the very least make sure that there is a digger on site to pull them out. Even better, make it a priority to construct a proper hardcore driveway and hard standing for material offloading.

Establishing or acquiring a legal right of access (Prescriptive Easement) where none exists or can be traced

There are instances where no legal ownership or rights of access can be established. Yet, clearly, several houses enjoy joint and uninterrupted access from a road, which they all maintain to one standard or another. In the Plotlands that sprang up in the immediate aftermath of the Second World War with bombed-out people moving to the countryside to construct wooden and asbestos bungalows on plots of land sold off by local farmers, the bungalows are now fast disappearing, demolished to make way for modern country homes, but the roadway still remains in its old state, both legally and physically. When whole communities originally bought their individual parcels of land nobody thought that the access would be anything other than just used by them all. Nobody thought that 50 years on each house

Ask yourself why no one has built here before.

would have two to four cars coming and going daily and certainly not that one day people would need to demonstrate legal rights of way to get to their houses.

Your solicitor will want to, nonetheless, and may face an uphill struggle, with no party having exclusive ownership and all parties unable to show collective responsibility. It doesn't mean that you can't buy the land. Quite clearly the other residents are enjoying their access and it would be in none of their interests to block or frustrate the use of the road. The older residents probably won't see what the fuss is all about with these newcomers wanting all this legal mumbo jumbo.

The law comes to the rescue here in that it is generally accepted that if you can prove that a property has enjoyed unencumbered and uninterrupted access over land for a period of 20 years or more, a legal right of way is capable of being established. These are known as 'Prescriptive Easements'. They allow the acquisition of a right through long use or enjoyment, provided that the right was lawfully granted or obtained either at common law, by lost modern grant or under an 1832 Act of Parliament.

As you would expect, there are a number of caveats:

- The right must have been obtained without force, without secrecy and without permission.

- The right must attach to a freeholder – if it is established by a tenant of the land, then it may still stand but it will attach to the land it benefits and not to the tenant.

- The use must be continuous, although the Prescription Act of 1832 allows a break of up to one year.

- Most importantly, the right of access must not be illegal and since the passing of the British Transport Commission Act 1949 it has not been possible to acquire rights over railway land or land owned by the British Waterways Board. Crown and Public Highways land is also exempt and in any event, as Highways land is expressly there for the purpose of public access there is, therefore, no need to acquire further rights.

One problem that previously occurred was where a right to an access by long usage was sought over common land. It is illegal to drive over such land without the owner's consent and the law could not countenance the sanctioning of an illegal act. However, in an effort to address this situation, the Countryside and Rights of Way Act 2000 gave users of an access over common land, in England only, the ability to acquire rights of access. It laid down that if an owner of property could prove that they had driven over common land for a period of 20 years or more, they could apply to the owners for an easement or legal right of vehicular access. This had to be accompanied by a valuation of the house that the easement was proposed to serve, and compensation or payment at the rate of 2% of the house value. This was reduced to 0.5% for houses built before 31 December 1930 and 0.25% for houses built before 31 December 1905.

All of which seemed to satisfactorily clear things up, until in mid-2004 the House of Lords decided that Prescriptive rights could, after all, be acquired over common land. They didn't actually rule against the Act but the effect of their decision rendered this section of it redundant. That cleared up the situation for all future applicants but it also left a large number of highly aggrieved people who had paid out quite considerable amounts of money to acquire rights that they were now entitled to for free. Happily, for many of them, as this is a mistake in law, they should be able to recover their money from whoever they paid it to. But for a significant number who have either paid out and sold on or made payments to companies that may no longer be in existence, there may be no recompense.

Application for Prescriptive Easements must be made to the Land Registry using their forms. This is fairly complicated and the burden of proof is on the applicant at all times. The application must therefore be accompanied by a proper description detailing how the right has arisen, together with Statutory Declarations backing up the claim. If the owner of the land registers an objection then the claimant has three options.

They can obviously withdraw the application or they can seek to negotiate a settlement. However, the Land Registry will not want these negotiations to go on indefinitely and if this looks to be the case they

Above: **Could the trees that set off this home so beautifully actually cause problems?** © Potton

will refer the matter to the Adjudicator to HM Land Registry.

The Adjudicator will either hold a formal hearing and give a binding ruling that has the same force as a court judgement, or the Land Registry will require one of the parties to commence legal proceedings to have the dispute resolved.

If no owner can be traced and you or your lenders cannot just accept things as they are, the simple solution may be a single-premium indemnity policy to guard against the extremely unlikely event of a chap arriving back from Australia and claiming the road as his own. Most competent solicitors can arrange these quite easily although it is a sad fact that many do not think of doing so unless prompted.

Trees

Trees make houses and bungalows look good. They make plots look good. But trees have to be very carefully thought out because there are several downsides. They may complicate your plans, limit the size, the shape and the siting of your new house and, make it considerably more expensive to build.

There are many angles to this which are best considered under the following headings:

- Trees and planners
- Trees and foundations
- Trees and your design
- Trees and neighbours

Trees and planners

This is where the trouble really starts and is of such importance that it needs consideration in full at the evaluation stage of any project. Planners and people who serve on planning committees like trees and they have ways in which they can protect them (see box right).

Any application for planning consent that involves felling trees always receives special consideration. If the trees are not subject to a Tree Preservation Order (TPO), you may decide to fell any tree which is in the way straight away, although due thought must be given to the possible future effect on foundations (see page 96). If the removal of the tree or trees is likely to create a rumpus, you might well decide to do it very quickly and at a weekend so as to prevent a provisional TPO being issued whilst you're busy sharpening your chain saw. This does happen. But be aware that action of this kind and the furore it might cause may have the effect of putting people's backs up which might, in turn, delay or complicate any subsequent planning application.

If you do have a problem tree which is the subject of a TPO it might be worthwhile getting a tree specialist to carry out an inspection and provide you with a report. Hopefully they will write 'the specimen is over-mature and should be replaced' or at least 'an unremarkable specimen which can be replaced without affecting the character of the local arboreal environment'. For every tree that you plan to remove you should show on your plan at least three replacement trees elsewhere in the garden, and make sure that the species are from the recommended list in the local design guide.

Sometimes this will do the trick. However, during the course of your negotiations with the planners you may develop the suspicion that they care far more for trees than they do for people. As a last resort you can of course appeal but that could set your project back six months and it might be better to alter your plans. Whatever you do, this is one area where the guidance of someone with local experience is invaluable.

One other thing that may occur is where the planning permission requires that precautions are taken to protect trees during the construction process.

How planners protect trees

- A Tree Preservation Order (TPO) can be placed on an individual tree or group of trees that the planners think worth protecting. This prevents any felling of a tree or trees subject to the order and limits any pruning to authorised work that will not harm their health or appearance. If the authorities feel that any worthwhile trees are in danger, they can place a provisional TPO on them in very short order and this remains effective for six months whilst the council considers whether or not to make it permanent.

- Removal of, or damage to, a tree that is the subject of a TPO can result in prosecution leading to an unlimited fine plus a requirement that the tree is replaced. The exceptions to this are where specific planning consent has been granted within which the removal of the trees is specified, where the tree has to be cut down or pruned by statutory undertakers such as the water and electricity boards, and where the tree or trees are dead, dying or dangerous. Additionally trees on Crown land, and fruit trees grown for the commercial production of fruit, are exempt from these orders. Although that doesn't mean that simply putting a bucket of apples for sale outside your gate would qualify you to call your tree 'commercial'.

- You can obtain details of TPOs in your area from the local authority and, in common with most areas of planning, there is the right of appeal.

- Trees in Conservation Areas are subject to special protection. Any work to fell, lop or prune a tree in a Conservation Area requires six weeks' notice in writing to be given to the local authority. If they then consider that the tree is of importance to the area, they can issue a TPO in the normal way.

- In just the same way that planning conditions can be used to permit the felling of a tree that would otherwise be the subject of a TPO, they can also be used to protect them. Additionally, conditions within a planning consent can require the planting of further trees and it is therefore possible for a TPO to be placed on a tree that has not yet been planted.

This will usually take the form of a fence erected either half the height of the tree away from the trunk or at the limit of the canopy spread, whichever is the greater distance. The fencing can be the orange plastic mesh type or chestnut paling. I remember one site where I was required to erect a chestnut paling fence in a 6-metre radius from two trees at the front corners of my plot. The trouble was that the site was only 12 metres wide! Luckily the planners saw reason and were able to take a pragmatic approach.

Trees and foundations

Trees can affect the foundations of houses in many ways:

- The roots may simply push into or invade the foundations and crack them.
- Roots can rot, leaving voids under the foundations, leading to subsidence.
- In periods of drought, trees can take large amounts of water from the soil, leading to shrinkage and, again, subsidence.
- In clay soils, when a tree is felled and no longer takes hundreds of gallons of water out of the subsoil, the ground may heave, causing upward movement and cracking.
- The roots of trees can invade and block drains.

All of these potential difficulties are dealt with by a combination of special foundation designs examined later on in this chapter but, in general, any foundation design to meet problems caused by trees is a matter for your architect and structural engineer to address together. Your plans will not receive Building Regulations approval unless they are satisfactory and all of the relevant authorities and warranty undertakers will want to ensure that things are done properly.

One thing to be very careful of is a vendor who removes trees and covers up the evidence. It might be because they feel that the planners would object to a consent that required the removal of the tree or trees, or that they know that the presence of trees might put off potential purchasers. It's unlikely that they appreciate the full structural implications of what they've done. But you, as a reader of this book, must know. Sometimes they will have carefully filled in

the hole and there may be unexplained patches of newly seeded grass. If the subsoil is clay the work involved in solving the problems they are trying to hide can be considerable. But any avoidance of the problem, to save money in the short term, can prove a false economy.

I saw a site in Kent quite recently where there were signs of a very large tree having been removed and I shall never forget one chap, building in Berkshire, who thought he was so clever at hiding the previous existence of several large oak trees. He got Building Regulations approval and built his house with normal foundations. Two years later there was a crack running right up the side of his home that widened to 50mm at the top. He was culpable in his own misfortune and it was a costly subterfuge.

The minimum distance between a new house and a tree depends on the tree's species and potential height and the nature of the ground (whether it has a high or low shrinkage capability). There are strict rules for this and they are, most conveniently, set out in the NHBC handbook. Whoever is designing your house and its foundations will deal with these problems, probably on the basis of, and as a result of, a soil investigation survey. If there are mature trees present on your site this soil investigation is an almost certain requirement and a good idea in any event.

As a rule of thumb, I don't think that it's sensible to build closer to any tree than 4 metres or one third of its mature height, whichever is the greater. This is not only because of the effect on foundations but also for the pure aesthetics and the health of the tree itself. On some soils this distance may be increased and with some species that are particularly harmful to buildings, such as poplar, elm and willow, the distances may be quite considerable. It does not, however, mean that if your site has trees on it, it can't be developed. The tables in the NHBC handbook show the distances between trees and houses where normal foundations or foundations not exceeding 2.5 metres in depth can be employed. After that you will, it is true, need an engineered solution but although that might cost more, it is unlikely to jeopardise the project as a whole. Later on in this chapter, I will cover the special foundation types that may be needed to counter these problems.

Tree roots can also cause problems with driveways, which will be a nuisance but not specifically expensive to deal with. What is more likely is that the planners will be concerned that any driveway should not adversely affect the tree by compaction of the ground beneath them or by interference with the soil's access to air and water. Once again there are solutions with driveway surfaces that allow the passage of water into the ground such as grasscrete blocks, of which more later.

Tree roots can also quite dramatically affect drains. The small young and beautiful weeping willow that you plant when you first move in may grow into a very large tree indeed and a joy to behold. However, one day, the toilet may refuse to flush and you might find out that your prized tree's sustenance and vigour was gained from its root's invasion of your drains!

Trees and your design

A large tree or a group of trees within 100 feet of any house or bungalow is going to enhance the appearance of the property, but must be taken into consideration at the design stage:

- Will part of the building be in shade at certain times of the day?
- What about views from key rooms and should rooms be arranged accordingly?
- An attractive green woodland scene in June can become a dank, dark miserable outlook in January.
- Big trees need their own sort of garden: bear in mind that they affect everything growing beneath them, produce huge quantities of leaves, and usually rule out having a swimming pool.

Living with trees means letting them dominate your garden and whilst you, like many people, might like that very much indeed, this should not come as a surprise. Many planning consents contain a condition that a tree-planting and landscaping scheme be agreed either before work commences or before occupation of the dwelling. This is important and is not something that can just be swept under the carpet and

forgotten about. Of course you might feel that you are being asked to put the cart before the horse, and there is some truth in this, in that it's awfully difficult to get things right at the early design stages. What looks fine on plan might, when translated into reality, be quite wrong. All you can do is to specify the minimum and to try to imagine each tree and its possible effect on your future home, its outlook and enjoyment. That said, you might still come away with the impression, once again, that trees are sometimes more important to the planners than homes.

One thing that I have noticed is that people often plant trees to create a garden and then sit back and watch the trees grow out of all proportion, to the point where they begin to ruin the very thing they were designed to enhance. If they are not protected then don't be afraid to chop them down and start again at some point, possibly with a new or more exciting species.

Trees and neighbours

If your neighbour has a tree which overhangs your boundary and which will interfere with the house that you want to build, you must clear the situation with your solicitor before you commit yourself to buying the plot. In most circumstances you can cut the branches overhanging your fence, and you can cut roots that encroach on your land and will affect the foundations of the house that you want to build. But this can be a complex issue. It is particularly difficult if the outcome of your activities means that the tree becomes unsafe. Perhaps it is already unsafe? If it falls on to your house, you hope that your neighbour is properly insured or else very rich. He may be neither, and almost certainly he is unlikely to tell you, which is why you have to take out a self-builder's insurance policy to cover you until the house is built and your domestic insurance takes over.

Also remember that a neighbour may choose to fell their own trees, seriously affecting your view and risking changes in the subsoil that could have a

One thing to be very careful of is a vendor who removes trees and covers up the evidence.

Points to bear in mind when planting trees

- If you are planting trees for planning reasons or possibly to replace those cleared to make way for a house, keep in mind that they will be there for a century at least.

- If your garden is big enough to split off a building plot in the future, try not to cause problems by putting a tree in the middle of the potential plot.

- If you are planting a tree at the corner of your vegetable garden, make sure that it is on the north corner so that it does not shade your vegetables in the years to come.

- Choose the species carefully, and consider whether you want to invest in something really worthwhile that will grace your home and its surroundings for many years to come.

Below: **Don't forget that the small sapling will one day be a huge tree.** © Potton

detrimental effect on your foundations. In some cases such action, especially if it involves excavation close to a boundary or to your buildings, could be deemed to come under the Party Walls Act 1996, at least in England and Wales. However, there is often, in fact, little you can do about this, short of resorting to a court injunction or other legal redress.

Your tree or theirs

Everything is simpler if the trees are on the land that you want to buy, but you must still consider the implications at an early stage. First of all, your tree may fall across the boundary and damage your neighbour's property. This risk is covered by your self-builder's insurance policy whilst you are building and by your householder's insurance when you have finished, but the policies will require that you exercise normal prudence in this matter. This definitely includes being aware of dangerous trees and those that present a special hazard, and then doing something about it. If there is a potential problem, you should get the tree inspected by a qualified tree surgeon, who can either give you a report saying that there is no hazard or advise on sorting things out. If you are buying a plot with potentially dangerous trees you might be able to negotiate for such a report to be a condition of your purchase.

Neighbours have a habit of stirring up trouble with the planning authorities. Everybody lives in houses but the minute someone else wants to build one, all hell breaks loose. Most planning applications receive objections from adjoining occupiers or from those who perceive that in some way or another, their enjoyment of and privacy within their home is going to be ruined by another dwelling. In many cases this 'Pull the ladder up, Jack, I'm firmly in the dinghy' approach to any new development contains little or nothing that is of any consequence in planning terms. Except where they mention trees. That's when the planners sit up and take notice. If you start cutting down trees on your property, it won't be the local authority who initiate action, even though they will be the ones taking it – it will be your neighbours.

Ground conditions

Ideally you are hoping to build on good bearing ground, which will support the weight of your new house using simple and cost-effective foundations. Sadly, this is not always possible and you must be conversant with other options. Incidentally, the cost of dealing with difficult foundation situations as a proportion of the total cost of the whole house has dropped dramatically in recent years with the result that most sites can now be economically developed.

The first potential problem is that there may have been mining activities in the area and that there is consequently some danger of ground subsidence. This is normally detailed in a mining report attached to either the planning consent, the searches or both. It usually just means that you will be building on a reinforced raft instead of on orthodox strip footings and the additional cost is unlikely to be more than 5% of the total cost of the new home. Occasionally, in areas such as Cornwall, there is a more serious problem caused by old bell mines. These were or are holes in the ground that opened up as they went deeper. Unfortunately they were not always plotted and the fact that the hole at the top was relatively small means that it can be covered over or lost. It makes considerable sense to commission a full survey in such areas. If a bell mine is found it can get expensive as it is sometimes necessary to fill the hole with lean mix concrete. But it's still unlikely to ruin the whole scheme.

Geological problems are more complicated. The principal hazards are that there is a spring on the land, a slip plane between two types of rock that outcrop on the land, or that you have a pocket of greensand under the turf. Fortunately all of these hazards are easily detected by someone with a practised eye, and in areas where they are likely to occur you will find plenty of people to point them out to you, not least the local authority Building Inspector.

A serious foundation problem can arise if you are building on filled land. This is not always detectable, although there may be signs if you dig just beneath the surface. Watch out for broken bricks or tiles in freshly dug flowerbeds or in the soil that was disturbed for new fencing. If there is or was an old building on the site, check to see if it had any cellars or a basement. Once again consider the question, 'Why hasn't this land been developed before?' And once again, ask around. Perhaps it was the site of a brick pit where the locals fired their own bricks for their homes. Perhaps it was the charnel pit used by the local butcher. Now it's just a gap between the houses that outwardly appears to be an ideal building plot. So it still might be – provided that you understand the need for special care in designing the foundations.

When you visit a new site, don't confine your inspection to just the plot. Look at the surrounding houses. As you approach, from ten miles away, study the architecture because that is going to help you in the design of your new home and, particularly with new houses, it's going to tell you what the planners like or accept. But more importantly, for the purposes of this chapter, look out for signs of damage caused by subsidence or heave. Cracks through brickwork that may have been re-pointed. Cracks in the render of older houses. Maybe it's because they were badly built. Maybe it's because they have foundations that couldn't cope with the droughts we've been having. But maybe it's the indicator of a general problem in the area.

You need not rush immediately to employ the services of a soil investigation engineer, although it may well come to that in the end. First off, try having a chat with the local Building Inspector and tell him what you're planning to do and where. He'll have seen and inspected nearly everything in the area and, even if he wasn't directly involved with the project next door to yours, he is probably still aware of what went on. He won't only have had dealings with new properties, he'll also have inspected any extensions that have been built, and if he's from the old school, there will be very little he doesn't know about ground conditions in your area. If he thinks that there's a possibility of bad ground then he'll say so and in that case you really need to get hold of a soil investigation company who will come along and dig or bore some trial holes to establish just what you've got. Another

How Nature reflects ground conditions

What grows naturally on the land is often an indicator of what lies below. Oak trees often favour clay soils. Beech trees tend to prefer underlying chalk. Willows signal the presence of streams and high water tables. Watch out for badly draining ground. The usual warning is an area of grass that is unnaturally green in the summer and marshy in the winter, perhaps with indicator soft rushes or sedge (spiky dark green clumps). At the worst, this can involve you building on piled foundations. Even here, the additional cost is unlikely to be more than 10% of the overall building costs for an average house. More likely, all that will be needed is a few hundred pounds' worth of land drains.

thing to do is to seek out the oldest local inhabitant (in the pub?) and ask about the history of the plot. They may remember that it was the site of the old village pond.

In the event that soil investigation proves either advisable or necessary, normally everything is fine and dandy but there are a few things you need to understand. The engineer will dig or bore holes in three, possibly four, positions on the site and will evaluate the contents of each bore, reaching conclusions and recommendations based on those trial holes. What you will hear is what they've discovered from those holes, not what would have been in a hole a few metres away (although from the holes they've dug certain conditions may be extrapolated and assumed). So, this report, useful as it is, important as it is, is nevertheless, a report based on four trial holes and the only real survey that is 100% accurate is, in the end, your actual construction work. That makes it all the more vital that you get out and about and ask around, because that's the only way you're going to find out that an old air-raid shelter used to be right in the centre of where you're going to build and in the middle of all these trial holes. And if all this fails to turn up a problem and you go on to buy the plot? Well, chances are that it's not going to be that serious anyway and you'll know that you did all you could but the rest was in the lap of the gods. In the end, that's what your contingency fund is there for.

Foundations

What can seem like a foundation problem to one party can, by dint of the fact that its solution has become common practice, seem like the norm for another. In certain areas of north Nottinghamshire and South Yorkshire, to build without using an edge beam raft would almost be unthinkable. Yet, if the same system of foundation was suggested on a site in Essex, there would be much scratching of heads and sucking of teeth, and the price would escalate out of all proportion. In similar vein, the Essex builder is probably quite used to digging trenches 3 metres deep and lining the sides with compressible material surrounding amounts of concrete to rival the Berlin bunker, in what the Yorkshire builder would prefer to think of as civil engineering.

Special foundations need specialist engineers to design them following a site investigation and soil survey. The need for all of this should be flagged up during your initial site investigations and from asking local builders, neighbours and the Building Inspector. However, it's surprising just how many arrive at the point of actually starting work, only to discover that something different has got to happen. At that point it can get expensive, not least because, in all probability, everything that has gone before has either got to be scrapped or may even make the solution more costly. Read this book. Check every line in the Site Details Checklist on page 130 and keep asking questions.

If you do discover that you need the services of any of the experts in this field then the first port of call should always be the local Building Inspector. They won't directly recommend anyone in particular, but they will probably be able to give you three or more names of suitable people and by implication and by reading between the lines, you should be able to deduce which one is the most favourable. Free and very good advice is available from piling contractors but they may be seen to have an axe to grind. You'll find them in Yellow Pages. Alternatively, your architect might be able to recommend someone with whom he can work to come up with the foundation solution that will suit both your site and the design proposed. That might seem like the perfect solution, and it often is, but all of this might be happening when you are still in the process of considering the plot or property and you might not want to commit to a particular architect, practice or package-deal company at that point.

To give you some sort of understanding of the possible foundation solutions and the reasons behind their employment, perhaps a brief run through the main methods of providing a foundation will help:

- Deep strip foundation
- Trenchfill
- Piled foundations
- Raft foundation

Deep strip foundation

This is the standard form of foundation, and the one that many builders will quote for in the absence of any other information. This consists of a trench, usually 600mm wide by between 1 and 1.2 metres deep underneath all external and load-bearing walls. In the bottom of this trench a minimum of 225mm of concrete is placed and levelled. The two skins of foundation blockwork or brickwork are then built off this to damp proof course or oversite level and the cavity subsequently infilled with lean-mix concrete to at least 225mm below damp-proof course (dpc) level.

In most cases this is sufficient but if there are any soft spots it might be necessary to introduce reinforcement to beef things up a little. This often involves putting either reinforcing bar or mesh, usually 50mm

Remember, above all, when considering special foundation situations, that you are unlikely to be alone and that others in the area will have experienced similar problems and invariably worked out the best and most cost-effective solutions.

from the top and the same from the bottom, in the concrete, which is sometimes also thickened up a little. It's relatively easy but care has to be taken in the placing of the reinforcement and in keeping it in place during the pour. This should be done with little metal tripods but you will often see it wrongly done with bricks, blocks or even paving slabs.

Trenchfill

Trenchfill foundations are advisable in certain cases, where the concrete, instead of just being at the bottom of the trench, is brought nearly all the way up to the top. This method of creating the footing can be particularly useful in wet or waterlogged ground where it would be difficult for bricklayers to work successfully below ground. It is also useful where even though the bearing ground is fine the top layers are unstable and the trenches are liable to fall in if they are left open for any period. In these conditions it can often be the best choice as, by definition, one is out of the ground in a day. Obviously there is quite an increase in the amount of concrete needed and

on paper this form of foundation can appear to cost more. But if you consider that the below-dpc blockwork is often reduced to just one or two courses and the time saved, you can see why it is a very popular option (and the one I favour whenever I build).

In many cases, however, the use of trenchfill is dictated by the presence of clay and trees. I've already talked about the problems that this combination can cause, so now let's look at cause, effect and solution.

Trees take huge amounts of water from the subsoil and even in the depths of winter the ground beneath a tree can be quite dry and friable to a considerable depth. When the tree is removed the ground becomes waterlogged again. Clay has a propensity to expand when it is wet, causing the problem known as 'heave' where the ground literally rises up. Even if the tree is not to be removed, which, as you can appreciate, is often the worst solution to the problem, account has to be taken of the effects of the living tree on your

Below: **A pond in the garden might be an indication of a high water table.** © Potton

proposed home and the possibility of its dying.

The solution in these cases is often a refinement of the trenchfill principle. Firstly the trench is taken deeper, in accordance with the tables published by the NHBC, but in general to a depth where the soil ceases to be affected by the presence or removal of the tree. Next the trench is lined with a compressible material, usually just to the inside edge and within 500mm of the bottom, but sometimes to both faces. This absorbs any sideways ground movement with any upward, frictional pressure being relieved by a slip membrane of sometimes one, but usually two layers of thick polythene. With the example house (see page 412) having a ground-floor area of 70 square metres, such a solution to a manageable depth of say 2.5 metres would add around £5,000 to the costs.

The constructional limitations are, however, obvious. If there is 50mm, and sometimes 100mm, of compressible material on each edge of the trench, then that trench has to be dug considerably wider to accommodate both this material and the concrete it will sandwich. Additionally it might be necessary to go down to depths of up to 3 metres in order to seek out ground with a consistent moisture content or where the effects of the tree's demands are reduced. Not only does all of this mean that there is considerably more spoil to dispose of, but the deeper one goes, the more unstable and dangerous the foundation itself becomes. Add to that the huge amounts of concrete (sometimes up to 100 cubic metres for a single house) and the high cost of the compressible material, and you can easily see that at some stage this solution becomes uneconomical. There comes a time, therefore, when it's easier to go down another route.

Piled foundations

These would, in the old days, strike terror into the heart of any self-builder. But things have changed quite dramatically and the rig that comes is no longer like a mobile version of the Eiffel Tower and instead, a whole range of more user-friendly mini pile rigs have been devised. Costs will, of course, vary but in general on the example house (see page 412), switching to a pile and ringbeam type foundation would add around £7,000.

Special foundations

Reinforced strips
A simple solution to minor problems. If you are pouring your concrete yourself take expert advice on how to keep the mesh in position.

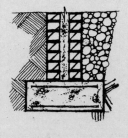

Trenchfill
Expensive in concrete but minimal labour costs. Popular with self-builders.

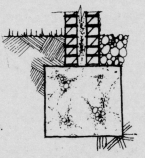

Edge beam raft
Commonly used but a job for an experienced tradesman.

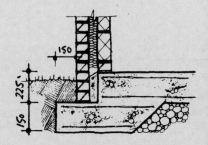

Piled foundation
A specialist solution to difficult problems. Consultants and piling contractors will add significantly to your costs.

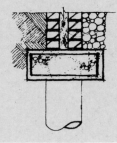

It is unnecessary to describe all of the variants here but essentially they boil down to three types:

Driven piles, which can be a shell of concrete or steel that is then filled with concrete or pre-cast reinforced concrete. These are driven into the ground. They are noisy and the vibration that they cause might well upset your neighbours and result in you having to replace an expensive set of antique plates that have fallen from their Welsh dresser.

Bored piles are a little more friendly and mini pile boring rigs are often mounted on a small lorry or Land Rover-type vehicle which will, of course, need access on to the oversite area (something that should be considered before it arrives rather than afterwards). They come in many different forms. Some are just drilled straight down and filled whilst others balloon out at the bottom to give extra bearing.

Dug piles are sometimes carried out by specialist contractors but can just as easily be undertaken by your normal groundworker as long as they have the correct digger with the appropriate reach.

The reinforcement bars within the piles are usually, but not always, left sticking out of the top for incorporation into the concrete ringbeam or groundbeam that is then built from pile to pile to provide the actual foundation for the house. It is at this point that the most recent and welcome advances have been made. One of the most difficult things after the completion of the piles, as far as the self-builder is concerned, is the ringbeam itself. If it is to be cast *in situ*, then not only might it need to be isolated from the ground by the compressible materials I have described under trenchfill foundations (page 102), but, almost certainly, the reinforcement is more likely to be in the form of cages rather than simple mesh top and bottom. These cages have to be fabricated by specialists to a bending schedule prepared by the engineer and their installation is a daunting task. They need to be positioned perfectly within the

eventual concrete and they need to be wired up and connected to a schedule. Now, along comes the great idea of having prefabricated pile caps with similarly prefabricated ringbeams that are simply lowered into place to span between the piles, thus achieving in hours what can take days if not weeks to realise.

Incidentally, I mentioned the fact that the reinforcement is not always left sticking out of the top of the pile for incorporation into the ringbeam. This occurs when there is the possibility of lateral ground movement. Here it's possible to use wide dug piles with the narrower ground beam spanning from pile to pile, yet separated from them by a slip membrane that allows the building to move, imperceptibly, across the top.

Raft foundation

A raft is employed where there is likely to be significant movement in the ground but the ground itself has good bearing capacity. In coal-mining areas one can see a field with a tiny depression running across it and, as the days go by, this will move across the land. It happens when the roof is allowed to fall in as the coalface moves forward half a mile or more below ground. Any structure which is to withstand that kind of movement has to be able to float over the 'wave' whilst, at the same time, maintaining its integrity. The solution is a reinforced raft. This is created by excavating an area a little larger than the footprint of the house and filling this with layers of suitably compacted hardcore. Upon this a slab or raft foundation is cast in reinforced concrete, often with a thickened and stepped section at the rim, leading to the common name of 'edge beam raft'. As I've said before, in the areas where these need to be used the builders are completely familiar with them and what looks suspiciously like a swimming pool in the course of construction turns out, in the end, to be a raft foundation which should not cost any more, in real terms, than those foundations considered standard in other parts of the country.

Remember, above all, when considering special foundation situations, that you are unlikely to be alone and that others in the area will have experienced similar problems and invariably worked out the best and most cost-effective solutions. Perhaps, once again, the best place to start is at the council offices with a chat with your local Building Inspector. He'll have seen it all and I'm sure that he'll be pleased to point you in the right direction.

Radon gas

A special foundation situation in some parts of the country results from the presence of a naturally occurring radioactive gas called radon, which seeps from the ground. Radon is present everywhere in the atmosphere, and accounts for 50% of natural background radiation. (Less than 1% of background radiation comes from Sellafield or Chernobyl or any other human activity.) Modern houses with good draught proofing can build up concentrations of radon which seep up through the foundations, and in some areas this health hazard is now recognised as making a significant contribution to the statistics for deaths from lung cancer.

As a result there are special design requirements for houses built in areas where there is a high level of radon seepage, and Building Inspectors will advise on this as a matter of course. The precautions involve making foundation slabs gas tight, and in some areas of high risk also providing ways for the radon to be discharged into the atmosphere. This is not complex, difficult or expensive but it has to be done. The Government's Radiological Protection Board has a range of free leaflets about this, and even offers test kits to indicate radon levels. You can contact them on 01235 831600 or fax 01235 833891 in the UK. In Eire the telephone number for the Radiological Protection Institute of Ireland is, from Ireland, 1800 300 600 and their website is www.rpii.ie.

Radon has been part of everyday living for the human race since the dawn of time, and until very recently our draughty houses meant only cave dwellers were at any risk from it. Modern Building Regulations completely remove the risk, which is very small anyway, and if you build in Devon there really is very little risk that you will end up glowing in the dark.

Contaminated land

District authorities have a duty, under the Contaminated Land Regime, Part 2A of the Environment Protection Act 1990, to inspect their area for land considered to be 'contaminated land'. In consequence, landowners are also required to notify the authorities if their land is contaminated. Contaminated land is deemed to be land where the contamination is likely to affect an underground watercourse, humans, livestock or the natural environment.

The onus is therefore on a vendor to advise all interested parties of the possibility of land being contaminated and their failure to do so could result in not only prosecution by the authorities but the possibility of civil action for damages from an unhappy purchaser.

Wherever possible the authorities will try to enter into a dialogue with owners leading to voluntary remedial action being taken. However, they do have enforcement powers and, if all else fails a Remediation Notice may be served requiring a landowner to take certain steps to clear up or prevent further contamination. If that fails or if the problem is so serious that the council has no alternative but to step in and clear up the problem itself, they can do so and will seek to recover the costs of such work through the courts. Planning applications are also referred to the Environmental Protection section of the Environmental Health department of the district authority in the form of consultations, and they may make recommendations regarding the application and any remedial action they consider necessary.

All of this might seem a million miles away from most people's idea of a dream site but the fact is that as land and suitable property for conversion becomes ever more difficult to find, things like filling stations as well as previous industrial sites are now being considered for housing. With a modern filling station there's usually no problem but older and pre-war stations often had concrete tanks that leaked like sieves, leaving the subsoil contaminated with hydrocarbons. Sometimes this means digging out the contaminated soil, carting it to an approved dumping site and replacing it with fresh soil. This is the expensive option in cash and environmental terms with costs ranging from £20,000 to £30,000. Another way of doing things is to cap the site with an impermeable layer or to treat the soil *in situ* with processes referred to as 'bio-remediation' where microbes are cultured or encouraged to proliferate on site to break down the long hydro-carbon chains and neutralise the problem. A buzz phrase that has grown up in recent years is 'human health risk assessment' whereby, if it can be proved that a hazard, though present, is manageable, then the authorities can be persuaded that no intrusive action is necessary, especially if it can be proven that the amounts that anyone would need to ingest make a problem unlikely.

The term coined in recent times for sites, usually in urban areas, which have already been developed in the past but whose use has now lapsed, is brownfield sites. This conjures up visions of broken factories, contaminated land and disused waterways. In the years since the end of the Second World War, many of these sites have been left to decay in favour of the development of the greenfield site. Now, however, political pressure is being applied in an attempt to stop the wholesale destruction of the countryside and attention is being focused back on to the redevelopment and regeneration of inner-city and town areas.

Many of these sites are more suitable for multiple development. The problems experienced with their development are manifest but, of most interest to the individual self-builder, are probably those associated with existing foundations. That's not something that is entirely confined to an inner-city site, as any who have developed an old farmyard will know. But what's more likely in the town is that these old footings may well be heavily reinforced, sometimes still having the steel girders protruding from them. New foundations may have to be constructed to go below previously disturbed ground and avoid 'hard spots'. Contaminated or previously consolidated subsoils and topsoils may well have to be removed and replaced entirely with fresh new earth and almost certainly you will need a full soil investigation and survey followed by an engineer's report.

However, the definition of brownfield land also encompasses gardens of existing houses and the intensification of land use by an increase in the density of housing. This suits the proactive self-builder who takes the advice in Chapter 2 on finding land, and the problems associated with such land are not of any greater significance or incidence than with any greenfield plot. Incidentally, whilst many unused buildings or ground come into the definition of brownfield land, agricultural or redundant agricultural buildings, including barns, are specifically excluded. That doesn't mean that they can't be developed: it simply means that they are not classed as such. Whether they are capable of being developed therefore depends on normal planning criteria, including where they are, what the land is zoned as and whether or not they have suitable access or facilities.

A hidden contamination problem can occur where the plot was previously used for intensive agriculture or horticulture. Our forebears weren't as fussy or as careful with their use of pest control substances and it's not unusual to find high concentrations of things like arsenic. If you have any fears in this sphere have a soil sample analysed. It will probably not stop you building, nor will it prevent you from enjoying your garden, but it might make you think twice about growing food on it.

Sloping sites

If you're lucky, a sloping site will come with a levels survey or contour map, but if it doesn't, this is, perhaps, the first thing you should commission before any serious work is done on possible designs. A levels survey may, at first, appear to be an indecipherable jumble of lines and figures, but is, actually, quite easy to understand. The figures all represent a height relative to a particular datum point, which is often the cover of a manhole or some other immovable object on or near site. The figures therefore have to be read in relation to each other and if, for example, the figure on the front left-hand corner of the site reads 100.500 and the figure on the front right-hand corner reads 101.500, there is a rise of 1 metre from left to right. Similarly, if contour lines are drawn, the figure against each one is the level along that line and you can extrapolate the relativity of any other point on your site by reference to its proximity to each line.

In parts of Wales, or in the West Riding of Yorkshire, homes are commonly built on sites with 1:5 slopes, and local styles and local building practices are geared to this factor. In other parts of the country even the most insignificant gradient is deemed to merit special consideration. Wherever you are going to build, the first thing to do is to have a careful look at how other people choose to build on slopes in the local area, and try to analyse the basis for the regional practice.

This may depend on the ease with which excavations can be made. If there is rock just below the surface, it will probably determine that buildings are built out from the slope because of the high cost of quarrying into it. If the subsoil is easily excavated, there are many more options. It may be that local cottages nestle into the hillside because in earlier centuries they had to do so to escape strong winds which would have had an adverse effect on poor local building materials. This may have given the area a particular style which the planners will expect you to accept.

Below: **A severe slope such as this one might lend itself to a split-level design, to take advantage of the views.**

Wherever you build, there are two approaches to be considered: should you arrange to remove the slope, or should you design a home to make use of the slope?

If the site permits, it is invariably cheaper to excavate a level plinth for a new home, adjusting the levels and spreading the surplus soil as part of your landscaping. This involves either just digging into the slope, or else digging out part of the plinth and using the excavated material to raise the level of the other part. This is called 'cut and fill' and the sketch on page 108 more than adequately illustrates it.

Digging out a level plinth is not always possible, sometimes because the site is too steep or the ground too rocky, but usually because the plot is too small to allow for the necessary changes of level. Remember that you might not be able to excavate close up to your neighbour's fence as in law his land is entitled to support from your land and in turn, that might mean construction of expensive retaining walls. All of which will be of enormous interest to your neighbour and which, in their eyes, will be the cause of every ill that their property suffers from that day forward. In this case you may well have to consider a design to make use of the slope, which will usually mean a multi-level home.

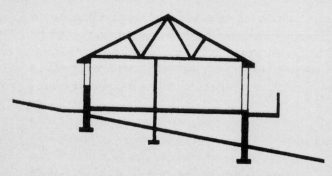

Building on a slope

Option one

Build up above the slope. Involves suspended floors, some additional foundation costs, and the need for very careful landscaping to conceal the large area of brickwork below floor level. Will improve the view, especially from the balcony.

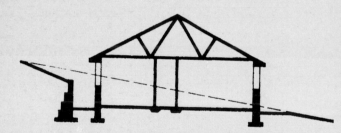

Option two

Build into the slope. Permits a cost-effective solid floor on natural ground, but may require a retaining wall or steep garden to the rear. Excavated material will have to be carted away unless it can be used for landscaping on stand.

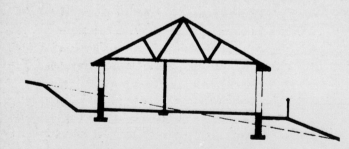

Option three

'Cut and fill'. This is the usual approach, combining the minimum foundation costs with the look of being built into the hillside. Care required with landscaping.

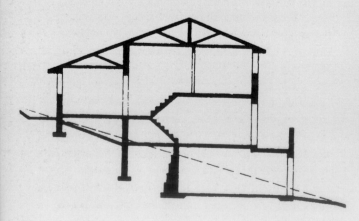

Option four

Multi-level. Garage below with living accommodation above, following the slope. Gives interesting layouts with opportunities for balconies to take advantage of views, but construction costs will be high. Inevitable steps outside and changes of level inside may limit resale potential.

A property of this sort may be slightly more expensive to construct than one that provides the same living accommodation on a level plinth. In simple terms, your designer has to make sure that the whole building will not slide down the slope. The cost of such foundations is one reason why many sloping sites have not been developed in the past, and are only now coming on to the market as rising property values make the costs acceptable. On the other hand, on many sites, split- or multi-level solutions that run with rather than fight the contours of the land are often the cheapest way of developing the plot.

The very problems associated with a sloping site can and should mean that your architects or designers are forced to think outside the box and the exciting nature of the resulting designs means that in many cases there is a premium value to the finished home. It does, however, depend to some extent on what is known as 'kerb appeal' and I shall expand on that further in Chapter 5.

One advantage of a sloping site is that it usually comes with an interesting view. If you are deciding whether or not to buy a plot on a hillside, remember that the view that you have from your ground level is not going to be the same view that you will enjoy through the windows of the finished house. If the outlook is very important to you, do not hesitate to take a couple of step ladders to the site and make some sort of platform that will enable you to stand at the level from which you can see the view as it would be from the windows of a finished home. You may look rather ridiculous at the time, but if the view is a key factor in making your decision, make sure that you see what you will really be getting!

River frontages and flooding

After years of drought, in which hosepipe bans became part of the pattern of summer life, we now have to put up with intermittent flooding. We're told that this too could become an annual event and it does seem clear that climate change has brought with it wildly variant and unsettled weather. In previous editions of this book and articles I talked about using unwanted cesspools as aquifers. Less than a decade later the emphasis had shifted in favour of flood pre-

cautions. What the floods of 2000 and 2001 brought about is a greater awareness amongst the house-buying public and the people who insure houses. The Environment Agency has produced maps showing areas that are likely to flood. Some arms of central government are cautioning local government about the granting of planning on flood plains. Some authorities are indicating that unused planning permissions in areas liable to flooding will not be renewed. There are calls for land that is needed as flood plain, in order to soak up, hold back and gradually disperse floodwater, to be given a new designation, 'bluefield' land, and that development should be discouraged in much the same way as it is with greenfield land.

Other arms of government are demanding an increase in the housing stock and virtually requiring local authorities to allocate land that up to now has been flood plain for development.

The maps that the Environment Agency uses are sometimes wildly inaccurate. Nevertheless they can stop people from wanting to buy houses and can severely affect the insurance premiums of those that continue to live in them. There's no doubt that there is a serious problem in some areas. Flood levels and the incidence of flooding have to be re-assessed all over the country but to my mind the solutions should not be beyond the wit of man. The Iceni successfully populated the marshes of East Anglia by building on stilts and having roadways that floated on the boggy ground. It seems to me that building methods could be devised to allow development whilst still leaving the ground available to act as a flood plain.

For those localities where the river has been a consistent and desirable feature, these are indeed the kind of solutions that have stood the test of time. In the Thames area of Surrey, houses by the river are built with an oversite above the highest known flood level and foundations that allow the floodwater to pass freely beneath the floor, a bit like houses on brick stilts or piers. It might sound dramatic but, in fact, this lower covered level often proves very useful for storing boats and canoes, and even for parking.

Properties that are liable to intermittent flash flooding can be protected, to a degree, by earth bunds or barriers plus a sump-and-pump disposal system.

Above: **Building off the ground on stilts can solve problems in areas that are likely to flood as well as providing useful storage.** © D&M

This works by having a series of perforated pipes set in the ground leading to a sump with a dual pump to send any water back outside the barrier. The pumps are designed to cope with up to 75mm of rainfall per hour but they have to have somewhere to dump the water, and if the flood gets above the barrier it will cease to have any effect. The biggest problems with flooding are either the mixing of sewage with the floodwater or the backing up of the drains into the house. The first of these problems can be mitigated by positioning any private sewage systems, such as septic tanks, outside the bund. The second can be solved, except in the case of a flood breaching the bund, by the installation of non-return valves in the foul drains.

Insurance is, as I have hinted, the biggest problem. And the fact remains that once flooding has occurred or in areas where the risk of flooding is identified, some properties might become uninsurable and therefore, ultimately, may never sell.

On the other hand, plots with river frontages are always in demand, offering the prospect of interesting gardens and possibly fishing rights or even a boathouse and river picnics. If you have a chance to build a riverside home you will have already considered flood levels and any special foundations requirements. But it is also important to know about the rights and obligations of a 'riparian' landowner, as someone who owns a riverbank is called.

You may be obliged to leave an unobstructed route along the bank for Environment Agency plant and vehicles, and they may have the right to dump mud dredged from the river on to your land. You certainly cannot assume that you will be able to build a boat-house or tidy up the banks without permission. On the other hand it may be a condition of your consent that the riverbank is shored up and that could involve you in some fairly expensive sheet piling. Nevertheless, if you've managed to secure a river frontage plot then you're probably not short of a bob or two and, particularly in the Thames area, you'll not have flinched from paying as much for your plot as most would only dream of their finished house being worth.

Plot details and site dimensions

Estate agents details are remarkably frothy about dimensions: 'The site has a frontage of approximately 14 metres and a depth of around 45 metres' are words which might well persuade you to have a look at a plot. But when you get there, you do need much more than that to progress in your assessment of it.

With a large overgrown plot, you may have little or no option but to consider commissioning a full survey, possibly in tandem with a levels survey. But with a small plot, there's no reason why you can't do things yourself, so long as you go about it in the right way. Start by measuring the frontage, the two sides and the rear width. Then take the measurement from the back right-hand corner to the front left-hand corner. When you've got that, take the measurement from the back left-hand corner to the front right-hand.

These last two dimensions are the triangulations. Very few plots are going to be perfect rectangles or even parallelograms and by using these measurements you can determine the actual shape of your potential plot. On a large piece of paper, measure out the frontage. Then, using a pair of compasses, with the point at the extreme of the left frontage, make an arc the length of the left-hand boundary. Place the point of the compasses on the extreme of the right-hand frontage and make an arc the length of the relevant triangulation measurement. Where they cross should be the proper position of the junction of the left boundary and the rear boundary. Repeat the process, in reverse, for the other boundaries. You might have to jiggle things about a bit, and you might

find that you need to take some measurements again, but you should, by this method, get a fairly good idea of the proper shape and dimensions of your plot.

If the boundaries are curved or uneven, use the same procedure to create a theoretical straight line shape from point to point and then measure off those straight lines to mark the actual boundaries. If the lines of measurement are interrupted by buildings it might be necessary to leave it to a professional, but you could still produce a fairly good representation by means of breaking the site up into a series of triangulated shapes.

Measure out the distance that any adjoining properties are set back from the road, making a note of double- and single-storey projections. This is the building line. Measure the rear building lines as well. Although strict adherence to building lines has largely fallen into disuse and most authorities recognise that they were a bizarre invention of the recent past, where there is a definite one, it is usually necessary to conform. In any event, any building that you propose should bear a proper relation to its neighbours to prevent any excess overlooking in either direction. Make a note also of each neighbour's distance from the boundary, as you will be expected to conform to what is usual in the area. If possible, and especially where the boundaries are defined by hedging, try to establish the ownership of each boundary. This might not be possible without reference to the deeds and neighbours might seize the opportunity to establish that the fence that's badly in need of repair is your responsibility whilst the hedge that is 1.5 metres thick is completely within their property and was never planted on the actual boundary!

If disputes over the boundaries seem to be in the offing, attempt to settle them before actually buying the plot, putting the onus on the vendors to establish exactly what they are entitled to sell you. Now, that's the ideal, but the fact is that these things sometimes don't crop up until the land has changed hands and the neighbour with designs on enlargement thinks that, as the new boy, you'll be an easier touch. Don't be. Get some stakes and some wire and, in consultation with your solicitor, clearly mark out the boundaries and send a letter by recorded delivery to your neighbours, telling them that you've established the boundaries and marked them out accordingly. The onus is then on your neighbour to get in touch with their solicitor to try to establish any claim on *your* land, and not vice versa. You have the initiative and, possession being nine-tenths of the law, it will be your neighbour who faces the uphill struggle.

Orientation and exposure

Make a note of the north–south axis. If you're a sun lover and the motivation for self-building is, in part, the desire for a sunroom or conservatory, this is something you'll need to know right from the start and could mean that some plots are not going to be suitable for your purposes.

Certain regions have what is known as high exposure ratings where wind-driven rain can cause problems. Check with the local Building Control department to see if you're in one of these areas. In some regions you will not be allowed to use full-fill cavity insulation for brick and block construction and, instead, will have to employ one of the partial-fill solutions, at a slightly higher overall cost. In areas that suffer from high exposure, the architecture has evolved to cope with it and you may have to incorporate features such as tabled verges and position the house in such a way as to minimise wind damage. Living close to the sea can be wonderful but the effects of wind-blown salt on your windows and joinery can be devastating. Almost certainly you'll have to shelve any ideas of painted timber or raw aluminium and even the more up-market galvanised steel, powder-coated metal or Pvc-u joinery will need special attention and washing down on a monthly basis.

Drains and sewers

Any consideration of a plot must include drainage from three points of view:

- foul drainage
- surface water drainage
- land drainage.

Foul drainage

Foul drainage are the drains that take and dispose of the waste water from kitchens, bathrooms and toilets. You will need to consider:

- Is mains drainage available and, if so, is it at the right level in the ground to enable you to connect to it by a normal gravity connection or will you have to employ a pump?
- Is the connection available within your plot or on the highway directly adjoining your plot and, if not, do you have the necessary easements and consents to cross other people's land in order to make the connection?
- If mains drainage is not available will you be able to use a septic tank or a mini treatment system?
- If the ground is capable of accepting percolation, will the Environment Agency and/or the local authority delegated to act on their behalf accept such a system in that location or will they insist on a cesspool? Septic tanks are not normally acceptable in urban or built-up locations and they cannot be used in situations where a mains foul sewer is available, but the cost of connection makes that a less attractive option.

The best of all worlds is obviously a private foul sewer crossing your land to which you can make a gravity connection in the run of the drain. As easy is the situation where the run of the drain is in the grass verge or on unmetalled land over which you have the right to pass for a connection. More usual, however, is where the sewer is in either the footpath or the highway. Here, you're faced with an entirely different ball game. It's no use thinking that you can just dig holes in the Queen's highway. As with alterations to the carriageway and new access arrangements, any work in relation to new drainage connections will require various licences and consents being issued by both the Highways Agency and the relevant water board or sewage authority, although in most cases the local authority will act as their agents. This work can only be carried out by approved or accredited contractors and for that, read 'expensive'. The mechanics of how it all works is discussed in Chapter 10.

If the mains drain is too far away to be reached

by gravity or is at a higher level than that of your proposed house, then the answer could well be a pumped system. A pump can be used in two ways. It can either lift the effluent from the level of one run of drains to a run at a higher level, after which it can then continue as a gravity drain to the connection with the main sewer, or else it can be employed to pump the effluent all the way to the sewer connection. It involves a small holding tank which is usually fitted with twin electrically powered pumps and macerators operated by a float control. These units break up the sewage and then pump it up and along a flexible pipe to its destination. If this is to be a drain at a higher level then it normally discharges into a manhole at the start of the next run of gravity drains. Alternatively, the flexible pipe can be laid, possibly by an agricultural contractor using mole drain equipment but, more usually, by a mini digger or the narrow bucket of an ordinary digger, to the discharge point.

Some of these pumps can move the effluent for half a mile or raise the level by as much as 20 metres but the chances are that on a single dwelling or even on a small group of dwellings, nothing like this ability is needed. The pumps obviously cost money and they do need proper installation, maintenance and a power supply, but they are efficient and reliable and the costs can often be offset by the savings of having to lay a flexible pipe in soil rather than proper drains surrounded in pea shingle.

In some cases where connection to a main drain is expensive by reason of it, say, being a very busy main road, the choice of a pump to take the sewage to a different discharge point, even if an easement has to be purchased, can prove cost effective. Incidentally, as a footnote to pumps, whilst we're not talking here about surface water drainage, there are specific cases where the levels may dictate that the only way to get surface water away is to utilise a pump. In these cases a similar system is employed but there is no need for the macerator.

And then there is the plot where mains drainage is neither available nor achievable. This is not the end of the world. Far from it, for the solutions that are available are often cheaper than a normal road connection and much cheaper when compared to a

sewage connection on a busy main road. It is, however, important to understand clearly what is involved. First of all, in many cases it does mean that you are going to need space to accommodate not only the main system but also any ancillary percolation drainage. That will not mean a loss of land, for most systems can work quite happily underneath what will be your garden or indeed driveway. It may mean, however, that on a small plot you have to acquire additional land or, at the very least, come to a legal arrangement with an adjoining owner for parts of your drainage to be constructed beneath their land.

Modern sewage treatment tanks arrive as prefabricated units, which are simply dropped into place in a suitable hole and connected up. On the other hand, concern about environmental pollution means that everything to do with the discharge of sewage effluent is extremely carefully controlled and monitored. You may think, therefore, that the best thing to do is to contact the Environment Agency first of all to get their advice on what steps to take. Well, getting the various leaflets and guidelines may well be a good idea but contacting them about your specific problems at too early a stage, before you've taken the best advice and allowed the professionals working on your behalf to devise a system, may not be the best plan. Far better to 'keep your powder dry' until such time as you have the answers and can present these as an effective solution to your drainage problems as well as the Agency's concerns.

If there is an existing drainage arrangement on site, perhaps an old brick-built septic tank, and it has been discharging the treated effluent for at least 20 years, and is still working, it may seem an attractive option to carry on using it (and one that, on paper, could save you a considerable amount of money, time and effort). On the other hand, this is a very uncertain area in the law and the Environment Agency now have the power to regulate and prevent any discharge that fails to conform to their requirements. Nevertheless, you may well decide that, as there is an existing system, you should use it and that your drawings should show the drainage going down a pipe which is marked on the drawings 'discharge to existing septic tank'. If the authorities accept that, then fine. Chances are, however, that they'll require full details and dimensions of the existing system. At this stage, your professional advisors will show a marked aversion to dank, dark, smelly places or the donning of diving gear and, in the absence of specific information, all parties will suggest a new system.

If the existing system is working well, and you know this for a fact, then you're doing nothing wrong in using it. If, on the other hand, you know that, at times, the effluent flows across open ground or that there's a secret discharge to a nearby ditch or stream then it's open for you to question whether you really want to be responsible for a local typhoid outbreak at worst, or at best, a country stream flowing grey instead of clear. Don't imagine that such activity will remain forever undetected, especially if attention is drawn to the system's existence by the presence of your new home. And don't imagine that the Environment Agency is a toothless organisation – far from it. It has tremendous powers and, once these are employed, the solution imposed could well prove to be far more costly that anything you would previously have envisaged.

If your plot and your proposals involve the creation of a completely new drainage system then it all comes down to three major options with a few variations and a couple of other interesting, more than practical, ideas. The Environment Agency, through the Building Control system, will be the final arbiters of which system you do actually employ. They will take into account the type of soil and subsoil on both your plot and the

surrounding land and whether you are in the catchment area of a water supply. Almost certainly a percolation test will be required, to establish exactly what sort of system is to be employed, and once more, although we're talking principally here about foul drainage, some local authorities will also require a similar test to establish what type of surface water drainage is employed. A percolation test, which is usually carried out by the applicant or his agent with the details being given to the authorities, involves digging a hole in the ground, filling it with water and timing how long it takes for that water to go away. Obviously any old hole won't do and in general what is required is a 300mm cube with its bottom 600mm from the surface. This cube is then filled with water and allowed to soak away for 24 hours, after which it is refilled and the time taken for the water to disperse is noted. These figures are then used to calculate what system of drainage is applicable or workable on your land and the nature and quantity of any weeper drainage that will be needed. The best possible solution, and the one that is likely to prove the cheapest to install, is a septic tank.

A septic tank is a miniature sewage works that requires no external power and usually involves no pumps. They are quite small, requiring a hole about 4.5 metres across and 3 metres deep, and they can cost under £500. They are easily installed. They need to be pumped out by a small sludge tanker once or twice a year, at a cost of just under £100 a time, and all that you see of them, above ground, is the manhole, which gives access to the interior.

This interior is divided into two by a baffle. The raw effluent comes into the tank and is allowed to settle out, with the sludges falling to the bottom. The relatively clear liquid at the top then passes over the baffle and settles further on the other side. During this process millions of friendly little anaerobic bacteria break down the sewage into a semi-sterile effluent which can then be discharged into the subsoil via a system of weeper or land drains. If they are working they don't smell at all. In fact a crust can develop on the top, virtually sealing in all that is going on below. It is important to realise, however, that you may need to make a slight adjustment to

Above: **Lowering a standard septic tank into the prepared excavation.**

Right: **Chalk is usually a good medium for sub-strata drainage solutions, so there must be a planning reason for this site to employ a cesspool.**

Far left: **Solutions to the treatment of sewage continue to evolve with hybrids between the various methods and specialised extras for individual conditions.**

your lifestyle if you are going to have a septic tank (see box right).

New and innovative septic tanks that increase aeration and speed up the bacteriological process are coming on to the market all the time. The prices are obviously higher but the principles remain essentially the same.

A septic tank relies on the fact that its final effluent will be discharged into the subsoil. That's why the percolation test is so important. If the subsoil is of an impermeable nature, such as heavy clay, or the water table is too high, then the effluent will not be able to get away and it will back up into the tank and stop the entire process.

If the ground conditions are not quite right or there is a requirement for extra refinement of the effluent because of, say, proximity to a watercourse, then the authorities may require that your septic tank discharges into a filter bed of some sort before the effluent is then passed on down the weeper drains. In some cases these extra requirements for land drainage may mean that a self-builder building on a restricted plot has to seek and obtain easements allowing the installation of drains on adjoining land. In other cases the requirements for the quality of the effluent discharge may mean that an entirely different system has to be employed, known as a mini treatment plant.

A mini treatment plant works like a septic tank insofar as it receives raw effluent and then processes it into a sterile effluent that can again be passed into the ground. Where it differs considerably is the fact that it is electrically powered and that the quality of the effluent is such that, whilst it's not exactly drinking water, it's often good enough to be discharged into a ditch, stream or other watercourse. In certain circumstances this can happen as a direct discharge but, more often, it is effected through either weeper drains or a filter bed of some sort. Whereas a septic tank utilises mainly anaerobic bacteria (those which live without air), the mini treatment plant utilises both these and aerobic bacteria (those which live in air)

To live successfully with a septic tank:

- Do not put things like sanitary towels down the loo (you shouldn't anyway).

- Do not use excessive detergents; use soap powders instead.

- Be careful about putting salts down the drains from, say, water softeners. (These could kill the bacteria upon which the system relies.)

- Avoid putting fats down which could solidify and block up the system.

It always causes a snigger when I say that if your septic tank doesn't work or is smelly, you can restart the bacteriological process by borrowing a bucket of effluent from a friend's tank. Do drive carefully, though!

---

to break down and neutralise the sewage. This is effected either by a paddle or turbine system alternatively exposing the effluent to air and water, whilst all the time passing it through towards the outlet, or by the introduction of a stream of air to the settling effluent. The merits of each type of machine will be trumpeted by the various manufacturers but the essential factor is not how they work but the quality of the treated effluent. The prime cost of one of these units for a single house is in the region of £3,000 and they may also have to have the sludge pumped out more often. In addition they do require a power source and regular maintenance. That said, they are a significant advance on the sewage disposal systems of previous generations, and as we all become more and more aware of the need to restrict contamination of our ground water, rivers and streams, they have an increasingly important role to play.

I mentioned, when discussing the three main off-site sewage disposal options, that there were some interesting variations and these have much to do with the use of reeds. These can soak up and neutralise an extraordinary amount of effluent and, space permitting, a reed bed can often solve a problem with effluent quality. In some cases a septic tank can discharge, probably with the aid of a pump, on to a series of flat reed beds and in others an even more satisfactory system can be devised using floating beds of reeds growing on mats. With a series of baffles such a system can return perfectly good water to the environment and at the same time provide a magnificent habitat for all forms of waterlife. The drawback is that most self-build plots simply don't have the space for such enterprise.

And what if the authorities won't allow any of these solutions and all the tests in the world prove to you and everybody else that your ground just isn't suitable? What if the plot is in a built-up area where mains drainage is either not available at all or available but any further connections are banned until such time as either the drains themselves have been upgraded or the local sewage treatment plant has extra capacity? Well, then you're on to the third option, the one involving a cesspool. A cesspool is bad news in one sense but, if that's the option that you're left with, then it's no good dwelling on it and the best thing is to try to see it as the way forward in the development of the site of your new home. Cesspools are simply great big tanks, which hold your sewage until a vehicle comes to pump it out and take it away. The normal size of a tank for a single dwelling is 18,000 litres, and it has to be emptied quite frequently at a cost of up to £250.

A modern fibreglass cesspool will cost about £2,000 and the cost of the excavation and installation may be significant. It goes without saying that a cesspool is the solution of last choice. It also goes without saying that many of the factors which make the use of a cesspool necessary, such as waterlogged or rocky ground, are also the factors which tend to increase the cost of its installation. There may also be latent problems in that possible buyers may be put off by it and, where a cesspool is employed because the mains drains are not yet ready to accept additional burden, the planning consent may well require that once the sewers have been upgraded, the house is then connected. That means that one day, maybe only a few years after the occupation of your new home, this large piece of expensive below-ground equipment will become redundant. Once again, you have to look at the bigger picture and consider all of this as an incidental but necessary expenditure in the achievement of your new home. It does, however, make sense to spend that little bit more, whilst you're building, putting in the by-pass drains and the road connection as far as the boundary.

Thought also needs to be given to the siting of any such tanks. Modern tankers can often pump sewage from tanks up to 100 metres away but if the route is convoluted, with your house in the way, that distance can very soon be eaten up. Balance your obvious wish to hide them at the very bottom of the garden with the need to get access to them.

Grey-water systems separate the less harmful wastewater from baths and wash basins, and recycle them for use in flushing toilets. Whilst that may not seem much, there are estimates that up to one third of domestic water usage is involved in flushing toilets. The water is of course filtered and does require chemical dosage from time to time and there is, therefore, no question of nasty soapy water coming out of the cistern. The tanks used for grey-water recycling are fairly small as they are constantly being

When you install a septic tank, mini treatment plant, cesspool or some other system that negates the need to connect to the sewers, you can apply for your water and sewage rates to be reduced.

topped up. Water for these purposes can also be acquired by harvesting the rainwater from the roofs and guttering. It will need larger tanks at ground or below ground level and the water will have to be pumped up to a header tank for use. But it can still provide a saving on water charges. Having said all that, I still have my doubts that these systems, worthy as they are in terms of saving the planet, are fully cost effective from most self-builder's point of view. Although it wouldn't take much of an increase in water or sewage rates to alter my view.

If mains drainage is available you'll be required to

connect. But if it's not available, then there are some interesting variations, which can be used in tandem with the off-site sewage disposal methods mentioned above. Composting toilets in one form or another have been around for some time, amazing and revolting people in equal measure. Modern versions employ a centrifugal principle where, when the toilet is flushed, the effluent descends through a special downpipe that whirls it around in such a way that the water and the solids are separated. The grey water runs to a soakaway and the solids fall into a composting bin in the basement that is shovelled out and put on the garden every so often. Not everyone's cup of tea, I admit, but interesting nonetheless, and useful, I've no doubt, in certain circumstances.

Finally some good news. When you install a septic tank, mini treatment plant, cesspool or some other system that negates the need to connect to the sewers, you can apply for your water and sewage rates to be reduced, and the savings can go a long way towards emptying and servicing costs.

Surface water drainage

Surface water drainage is another form of drainage that you will have to evaluate. This is the water that is collected by the rainwater guttering systems on your house, from its outbuildings, driveways and pathways. It all still has to be got rid of and except in a few, ever-diminishing locations where there are combined drains, most local authorities will not allow it to discharge through the foul sewers. In some areas the local authority will insist on surface water being connected to their surface water drainage system. In others they prohibit any private connections, even from driveways directly abutting the highway.

Usually surface water drainage is discharged through gullies and pipework to a series of soakaways on the plot. These soakaways can, in acceptable ground, be quite simple rubble-filled holes. But in other areas where the ground is less amenable to accepting water you might be required to construct quite elaborate soakaways from perforated concrete rings or purpose-built brickwork. A refinement on these, if a percolation test proves that the subsoil is incapable of accepting any run off, is the employment of a pump to lift the water into the vegetable

Above: **An 'Aquatron' centrifugal toilet in the basement with the handle of the shovel just visible so that the contents can be emptied and used in the garden!**

zone. A lawn constructed on a gravel or stone bed can then be used to soak up the water. Alternatively or in tandem with these ideas the use of a rainwater harvesting system will mean that a large amount of water, once used within the home, can be disposed of through the foul drains.

Land drainage

Land drainage is the one aspect of drainage that everybody forgets. If a site is waterlogged then it's an absolute certainty that your construction work will exacerbate the problem unless specific measures are taken to get the water away. Sometimes it's enough to lay land drains in the foundation trenches of the new home, before they're backfilled, in order to conduct the water around the house and away. At other times it may be necessary to lay individual land drains across the site to take water coming on to it from the surrounding land. What you don't want is to live in a swamp. When looking at the plot for the first time, make a note of the kinds of vegetation. Crack willow and alder prefer damp conditions and sedge and soft rush growing on the land is an indicator of bad drainage.

One way of draining land quite well can be the foul drains themselves. You can't, as I've said above, directly connect any surface water or land drains to the foul drains. But the drains are, nonetheless, surrounded by clean pea shingle and the lie of that medium will follow the drains away from your site, creating a form of 'French drain'.

Services

Most estate agents' details state that as far as they're aware all mains services are available, but then go on to say that any prospective purchaser should satisfy themselves as to their availability. Chances are that the agents haven't even bothered to really investigate. We've already discussed drains, so what we're talking about here is gas, water, telephone and electricity. You may not wish to make formal applications for all of these before you have actually bought the land, if only because you wish to avoid paying the application fees, but you should satisfy yourself that they are readily available at a reasonable charge. Contact each of the suppliers and ask them for a quotation for the supply of their services together with a map of just where they are.

Following privatisation and the splitting of responsibilities, all of the service providers, including those concerned with the supply of gas, now make a charge for a new service. For an average house in a suburban street or a large village, you will need to allocate around £2,000 for the services and where the services are not close by, considerably more. If mains gas isn't available it's not the end of the world as there's always the option of liquid petroleum gas (lpg) or oil as the firing source.

If mains electricity isn't available then things get a little more tricky. But there are alternatives. Small modern generators have made huge efficiency strides in recent years. They work with a battery back-up so that when a light switch or appliance comes on, the generator automatically starts up. There's a small delay but nothing you can't get used to. Generators are fairly expensive to buy and maintain but if the only other alternative is not building your home where you want it, then this is a small price to pay. And there are other ways of generating electricity.

Technology, gained in part from space exploration, has come up with the option of photovoltaic cells on the roof. These work by converting sunlight rather than heat into DC electricity, which can be converted

into AC current. If you think that you've never seen them, just look at your light-powered calculator – same principle but bigger. They are, however, frightfully expensive and that's despite the fact that there are often grants available of up to 50%. A full array will typically cost between £12,000 and £20,000 for an average house. They need expensive battery back-up and/or a generator for the hours of darkness but, when working, they can provide all or most of a normal household's needs. Nevertheless, at their current level of development, they cannot to be considered as true alternatives.

So too with solar panels. Quite apart from the cost and the sheer ugliness of these things, they can, at best, only hope to augment other heating sources. I have heard claims of savings in fuel costs of 80%. I'm more inclined to believe that it's half as much as that in the most favourable circumstances and half as much again in most instances.

But every little helps. If combinations of wind turbine power, generators, photovoltaic cells and solar panels, backed up by batteries, can, in theory, provide all of a normal household's needs, then there is an argument for every new house to include at least one of these elements and in so doing reduce our national dependence on fossil fuels. But that's one for the politicians. Self-builders need to look to their own finances and, whilst many might want to save the planet, most will be concerned that the capital cost for most alternative technologies far outweighs any financial saving in running costs and adds absolutely nothing to the final valuation of the home.

The non-availability of mains water can be a problem but in some most areas can be got around by the use of bore holes. Yellow Pages lists drilling companies under 'Water Engineers' and there are likely to be quite a few in each area. The cost will vary between £5,000 and £20,000 depending on the depth and the ground conditions but, in general, a bore hole will work in most areas of the UK, with the water from them being 99% likely to be potable, or capable of being made so. It is, however, necessary to satisfy the Environmental Health department of your local authority that the water you will be drinking is safe. Once again, in Yellow Pages the companies that analyse and test water are listed under

'Water Treatment'. These same companies will, if necessary, supply and install treatment systems using either chemical, mechanical or ultraviolet treatment designed to screen out or remove most pollutants. They will also provide the householder with a home test kit to make sure that the water remains safe.

I have already alluded to rainwater harvesting for things like flushing toilets and for washing machines, in order to save on water charges. Rainwater harvesting to provide drinking water is not quite so common but it is eminently possible. It relies on having a large enough roof collection area with the water being stored in an above- or below-ground tank before being pumped up to a header tank. It may still need filtration or treatment to satisfy the authorities but it is no more, and perhaps less, prone to contamination than ground water sources.

If you're in any of these situations then you are probably thinking of building in an extremely rural location. In which case you're either a farmer or a seeker of things from another age and much of this will be old or welcome news for you.

Diverting drains and services/sterile zones

In this book, I repeatedly urge anyone considering buying a building plot or other development opportunity to find out why it has not been developed in the past. One reason may be that there is a sewer, gas line or electricity cable across the site, and that the authority that installed it took an easement to do so from the previous owner of the land and, in so doing, prohibited anything being built on top of the service, or within a certain distance either side of it. This creates what is known as 'sterile zone'.

On all but the largest of plots the existence of a sterile zone usually means that the plot is not capable of being developed. Certain things such as high-pressure mains cannot be tampered with. However, in some cases, this is a situation which can be exploited by the resourceful self-builder. Unlike builders and developers, they often have time to arrange the diversion, and the patience to cope with the huge correspondence that is likely to be involved.

If you do decide to involve yourself in such a situation it is important to arrange an option or conditional contract on the land before you research the problem, otherwise you may get everything sorted out only to find that the vendor puts up the price or decides to build on the land himself! The price should reflect the cost of the diversion, which can be significant, and so you have to establish this before committing yourself in any way.

Make a start by obtaining a photocopy of the actual easement granted to the service provider, which should be with the title deeds. If it is not in intelligible language you will have to seek the help of an expert to work out exactly what it says. If it is a very old easement, particularly a 19th-century one, you may find that there is a clause which requires the authority to move their service at their own expense if the landowner wants to build his dwelling on top of it. This is often a feature of old electricity cable easements. Do not celebrate too soon: in the 1950s the electricity boards offered sums to all the land-owners who owned such rights to extinguish this part of the easement, and many of them accepted. If they did, the documentation involved may never have been with the title deeds. However, the board will not have lost their copy!

Usually you can expect to be quoted a most unreasonable sum for moving a service and it may take a lot of patience to get a quotation at all. However, if you do get a quotation, it is an admission that it is technically possible to move the service and you can then start to negotiate. Try to reach the engineers concerned, rather than the legal department of the services authority. The engineer may permit you to seek tenders for this work to be done from a list of approved contractors, which will probably be cheaper. It may also be possible for you to open the trench involved, lay the gravel bed and back fill after the drains, pipe or cable have been laid by the contractor. This will probably save a lot of money.

Read any quotation carefully to see that it's strictly relevant to your site. If there is an overhead line crossing your plot, and that line also crosses the line of houses on either side, the board might well seek to get the whole line buried underground, whereas all you're interested in paying for is the bit that crosses your land. Whilst that might still mean that a pole has to remain at each boundary, the costs of taking the service underground on your plot only will be significantly cheaper – unless of course you can persuade your neighbours that burying the whole thing will benefit their properties and that they really should join in with you to get it all done.

If you are successful in negotiating some arrangement for the diversion, and the arrangement to buy the land reflects the cost of the diversion, make sure that the legal arrangement with the authority refers to you *or your successor in title*, so that if you buy the land but have to sell it on for any reason a potential purchaser does not have to renegotiate the whole business.

If a private drain or sewer crosses your land, probably linked to the houses on either side, then this is often a cause for celebration rather than dismay – even if it crosses your plot under the planned position of your new home. You're not going to have to go to the expense of having to create a new road connection for a start. In all probability the drains are laid at 1:40 when modern 100mm drains can run at 1:80 or, if they're 150mm, 1:150. So levels are probably not going to be a problem (1:40 means that the drains fall 1 metre for every 40 metres run).

Your designer will probably show the drains diverted around your house with your drains connected to them. But the reality is that you would have had to build the drains anyway, and what actually happens is that you build your drains and then the other drains are diverted into yours. Usually the existing drains are allowed to continue running through the site until the last moment with your foundations built around them and then, when the diversion is made, they become redundant and can either be removed or left in the ground.

A word of warning on this point, about a situation which does not crop up very often but is not unknown. Sometimes on a private estate the deeds allow for the use of a private drain by named houses with no provision for the splitting off of plots and the creation of extra houses. In these cases it is often necessary to get the agreement of the other houses on the estate for the fresh connection and this is something that your solicitor needs to check out and

which is really the responsibility of the vendor in the first place. On the other hand, as I've said repeatedly, vendors have a habit of failing to understand your concerns and you might find yourself having to make the running on this one. Make sure, therefore, that you do have things tied up by some sort of option or contract before you go about enhancing the value of a vendor's land. If ransoms are payable to the other occupiers then this really should come off the asking price of the plot.

Covenants (Burdens)

Covenants (or burdens, as they are known in Scotland) are clauses in the contract for the sale of land which limit or modify how that land shall be used. A covenant is usually put there by the previous owners or sellers but can arrive by mutual negotiation between two landowners. They attach to the title of the land and they are binding on all future owners. Some covenants may be very old indeed, and may have passed with the title to the land at any time since the middle of the last century with the reason for their existence lost in the mists of time.

The covenant that causes the most consternation is one that prohibits any development of the land, normally referred to as a 'restrictive covenant'. Others typically require that any property to be constructed shall be of only one storey, shall be set back a certain distance from one of the boundaries, or shall not have any windows facing in a certain direction. With modern plots it's not at all unusual to have a covenant put into the deeds by the adjoining vendor, stating that 'no development shall take place without their prior approval of the proposals'. However, in these cases it has been held that the words 'such consent not to be unreasonably withheld' are implied, even if they are not actually expressed.

The deeds of my present home contain a covenant, imposed by the vendors, specifying that if I, or my successors in title, ever develop the land as more than one dwelling, an amount equivalent to one third of the uplift in the plot's value must be paid to my vendor or his successors in title. He tried for ages to get planning for two dwellings rather than one and he obviously felt that, having sold it as a single plot, if I or anyone else managed to get what he'd tried so hard for, he should have some benefit. It's not unfair. It's not taking liberties. He only got the price for a single plot and imposing a covenant was the sensible option. He won't ever get anything as I've built in such a way as to make a second dwelling impossible. But that does not mean that the covenant doesn't exist and if in 50 years' time this house gets knocked down and the then owner tries to build two houses, they'll have to cough up.

In like manner, it is not at all unusual for a covenant to be put in place for the benefit of the owners or occupiers of a particular house, often to preserve a view. Years later the house could long since have been demolished, and the original owners either died or gone away. The covenant, however, will remain and as long as it exists there is the chance that somebody will come along with the power to enforce it.

It is possible to have restrictive covenants removed but this is, undoubtedly, a job for a suitably experienced solicitor. It is an extremely lengthy business involving application to the Lands Tribunal who have discretionary powers to modify or remove covenants if they see fit. The outcome is never certain and, as

with all lengthy legal procedures, the costs can escalate quite alarmingly. In addition, even if you do succeed in having the covenant removed or modified, it might be at the expense of some sort of compensatory payment to the owner or beneficiary.

If the owner or beneficiaries of the covenant are unknown or untraceable it is usually quicker and easier to take out indemnity insurance against the possibility of anyone claiming rights under the covenant and the mechanics of this are discussed in the next chapter.

Easements and wayleaves

Easements are very similar to covenants except that they tend to grant specific rights of passage over land, rather than modify how the land is used. A wayleave is slightly different in that it grants a third party or body the right to run services over land. Both easements and wayleaves will attach to the title of any land or property that they affect in just the same way

Below: **The deed of covenant on my present home.**

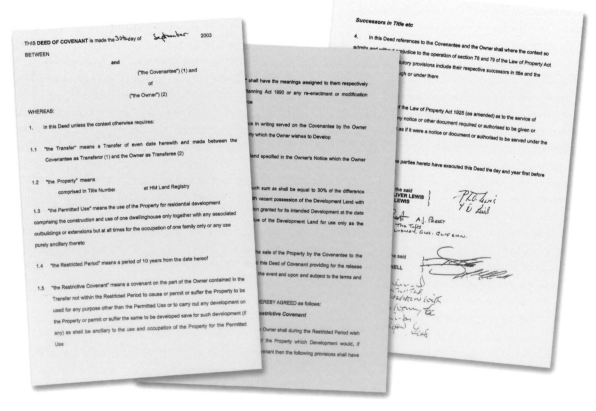

Above: **The more land you have around you, the more likely it is that there will be footpaths or rights of way to consider.** © D&M

as covenants do. Statutory undertakers take out easements or wayleaves to enable them to cross land with, say, electricity cables or gas mains. Such services can benefit the land but they can also blight it. A high-pressure water main or sewer can sterilise land up to 6 metres either side of the run. Easements can also give others access or the right to pass over your land for the purposes of access to another parcel of land and their importance needs to be properly examined when you are evaluating your possible purchase.

That's the negative side of things, but easements can also run to the benefit of your land in granting you, say, the right to use a driveway or access or in giving you the right to connect drains or services over an adjoining piece of land. Just as with covenants, they can be altered or modified and there are the same rights of application to the Lands Tribunal and the same warnings.

Footpaths

In rural areas a common difficulty is that there is a public footpath running over the land, possibly coming over fields and joining the village street through the land where you would like to build your new home. It does not matter that the footpath is disused: if it has been gazetted and appears on the local authority's footpaths map, then it is as firmly there as if it was a public road.

It is possible to have a footpath moved, but usually only if the realignment is going to be more convenient, in every way, for those using the path. This

Not only are footpaths protected in law and jealously guarded by local authorities, but there are also footpath preservation associations with members who make it their business to try to make sure that they are never, ever moved.

usually means that the new alignment has to be shorter, less muddy and more easily maintained, and provide a nicer view and a more pleasant walk. It is absolutely no use thinking that the footpath can be shifted to run round the edge of your site, which will not bother anyone because hardly anyone uses the path anyway. Not only are footpaths protected in law and jealously guarded by local authorities, but there are also footpath preservation associations with members who make it their business to try to make sure that they are never, ever moved. Probably the best advice on moving a particular footpath will be obtained from a local solicitor, who may know what applications to do so have been made in the past, and why they failed.

Unknown owners, Adverse Possession and Prescription

Sometimes you'll come across a dream site but nobody knows who owns the land. Now, you could try the Land Registry but not all land is registered. Sometimes an owner may live close by but simply doesn't want anyone to know that he owns the land. Sometimes the land has 'slipped out of ownership' because an owner went abroad or was killed in the war. Other times an elderly person has simply forgotten all about it. Your first enquiries should be discreet ones with neighbours and particularly with older inhabitants of the area. Ask in the pub or study the details on the Land Registry for the properties on either side to see if they shared a common ownership. Look in the parish records for details of anyone who might have lived there.

If all these discreet enquiries draw a blank, what can you do about it? Well, very little really except possibly put a notice on the site or take out advertisements in the local papers. All of which may alert other prospective self-builders in the area to the existence of the plot, meaning that, when an owner does surface, you could find yourself in a long queue.

But there is one other way of gaining title to land. And this is often referred to and is best known as 'squatter's rights'. This method, known as 'Adverse Possession', dates back to the very earliest times when all land was vested in the Crown and the kings and queens saw land as always having to serve a useful purpose, with the primary purpose being to benefit them; the thought of land just lying vacant and unused was therefore a complete anathema. In England and Wales, where land is occupied 'without let or hindrance' for a period of at least 12 years, the occupier can register what is known as a 'Possessory Title' and, with the passage of a further 12 years, an 'Absolute Title'.

If anyone comes along within the first 12 years and either allows you to continue your occupation upon payment of rent (a let) or tells you to get off their land (a hindrance), then the clock stops and the adverse possession has failed. If someone comes along during the period of the possessory title then the matter may well have to go to court. Providing the squatter has done things properly, they, or their successors in title, may well be granted the absolute title. But there may also be some element of recompense for the original owner.

In Scotland things work slightly differently and the process is known as 'Prescription'. A prospective occupier of vacant and unregistered land is required to create and register their own title and then after a period of ten years of uninterrupted and unchallenged occupation this interim title can then be converted to an absolute title. If during the ten-year period an owner comes along and disputes the occupation, then it has failed.

All land has to be registered with the Land Registry whenever it is sold or mortgaged or if a lease of more than seven years is granted. However, there is no requirement for land to be registered unless one of these transactions takes place and it is this unregistered land, with untraceable owners, that is most likely to be the subject of a claim for squatter's rights. An Adverse Possession is most unlikely to succeed if the land is registered and the registration has been kept up to date, with the owner's current address listed. Under the Land Registration Act 2002, anyone contemplating an Adverse Possession must give the Registry two years' clear notice of their intention to register a possessory or interim title. The Registry will then make their own efforts to contact or establish an owner and give them due warning.

The most common occurrence of a possessory title being offered is where a vendor has moved the fence over to take in some overgrown or unused land at the side. The main plot will then be offered with an absolute title and the acquired bit with a possessory title. If you are offered land with a possessory or incomplete title you should make certain that there is a single-premium indemnity policy in place to cover the eventuality of an absent owner turning up to dispute your occupation. The premium for this policy is usually arrived at through the insurance company making its own enquiries backed up by statutory declarations from the 'owners', neighbours or other relevant parties. It is unlikely to exceed three figures and is usually the responsibility of the vendor.

If you visit a prospective plot and there appear to be signs of occupation, you need to move fast and inform your solicitors and/or the vendors. Unfortunately the vendors of this, presumably previously unregistered land, may fail to see the significance, especially if they live remotely from it. They may feel that the land is theirs and they may have a bundle of dusty old title deeds to prove it. But as I have said, if the neighbours have in the meantime registered a possessory title then all or part of the land may not be available for you to purchase. I repeat, any let or hindrance within the first 12 years in England and Wales or ten years in Scotland negates the adverse possession. If an owner tells the occupiers to clear off their land, then for the squatter, the clock goes back to zero.

Incomplete or defective title

As I've already said, whenever land is sold the transaction and the land has to be registered with the Land Registry. This first became compulsory in parts of London in 1899 but did not extend to the whole country until December 1990. By its very nature, vacant land most often falls into the category of unregistered land. The most common problem that can occur is where the deeds have been lost and, whilst it might be perfectly obvious who owns and occupies the land, the proof is not there. Another fairly common occurrence is where a family has occupied property through many generations. As each one succeeded the other, no one thought to register the

change of ownership so that the title deeds, if they can be found, show the land as being the property of a father or grandfather, long since deceased.

On the face of it this might seem like an impossible situation to overcome and indeed, I know of solicitors who have baulked at the prospect of their clients buying such land. However, as with Adverse Possession, much property law reflects the principles that land should always serve a useful purpose and that is only served if there are the mechanisms in place to establish ownership or lawful possession. The solution to this and related problems is to obtain Statutory Declarations from the would-be vendors and from associated parties and neighbours. Once these have been obtained then it is quite likely that the Land Registry will agree to register a title. In any event, and as well, it should be possible to obtain defective title indemnity, which usually costs no more than a couple of hundred pounds and is, once again, normally paid by the vendor.

Wildlife

Most of us are concerned in some way to preserve our wildlife and flora but sometimes our concerns come into conflict with the wish to build a new home. It is illegal to disturb a badger set and it is also illegal to dig up or disturb some extremely rare plants or reptiles, especially the great crested newt. Some houses, and particularly the type of old barn that's suitable for conversion, may hold roosts of bats or provide a refuge for other protected species, such as barn owls. There are various societies and organisations who make it their business to see that no disturbance takes place and to initiate prosecutions where necessary. The Royal Society for the Protection of Birds (RSPB) is particularly and rightly active in this respect. Bats also have special friends in the form of the Bat Conservation Trust. In the UK it is illegal to disturb bats at any time. Many species of bat use the lofts of houses or outbuildings for their summer roosts and breeding, leaving in the autumn to hibernate in nearby caves or hollow trees. It is illegal to stop up the holes in a house, preventing the bats from returning in the spring; and there are people who make it their business to stand in streets counting bats in and out and taking note of any obstruction.

The thought of sharing your home with these creatures may be repugnant to you. All I can say is that the diet of those species living in and around our homes is exclusively insectivorous and that they therefore do a lot of good. The droppings are dry and crumbly, consisting mainly of the indigestible parts of their prey such as wing casings. They do not

Wherever possible, try to talk to the immediate and surrounding occupants of any property you're going to buy.

normally smell, unless they are allowed to get damp, in which case you have an even bigger problem. There is, however, one species, the Soprano Pipistrelle, that does have a musty body odour problem that can prove irritating. In rare cases, if the statutory agencies in the UK (English Nature, Scottish Natural Heritage, Countryside Council for Wales or Environmental and Heritage Service of Northern Ireland) agree that the bats' continued occupation makes human habitation untenable, they may permit their removal and re-housing under controlled conditions.

If you are contemplating any works which might mean that wildlife fauna or flora would be disturbed then these named agencies must be notified of any action. Such work would include remedial timber treatment, renovation, demolition or extensions and the agencies must be given time to consider and advise on the best course of action.

There is an imperative on government and authorities to identify and maintain Sites of Special Scientific Interest (SSSIs). In addition there are international conventions such as the Ramsar Convention on Wetlands. These impose restrictions on the development and use of land that are often tantamount to the prohibition of any building. It is very unlikely that you will be dealing with a project within their boundaries. However, if you are developing land or buildings adjoining such a site you might well be subject to restrictions imposed for the benefit of, for example, nesting or roosting birds.

Neighbours

The subject of neighbours has cropped up several times so far. Neighbours are important, not only because you're going to have to live next door to them, but also because they can have considerable influence over whether or what you're going to build.

Wherever possible, try to talk to the immediate and surrounding occupants of any property you're going to buy. If there has been hostility to the idea of the property being developed, it's as well to find out about it right from the off. Whether that hostility is transferred to you or whether it is confined to the original applicant depends on many factors, not least of which is that you might be the one instigating the project in the first place. Sometimes it's possible to mollify an objector. Sometimes it is impossible but at the very least you'll know what to expect and you can either modify your plans or move to head off their argument before it achieves significance with the planners.

I always advocate talking to anyone and everyone who could possibly know anything that might affect a site. In doing so I've discovered drains that even vendors didn't know were there and learnt things about the planning history that no amount of reading up would have given me. When you're looking at a plot, I bet you a pound to a penny that someone somewhere is watching you and itching to ask you what's going on and what your intentions are. When you march up to their door, therefore, they'll almost be pleased and if you can combine the obtaining of vital information with a chance to build bridges for the future, it's a worthwhile exercise.

Property for conversion or renovation

I have devoted an entire new chapter to the renovation, conversion and extension of existing properties later on in this book (Chapter 7) and in the chapter about working with subcontractors (Chapter 10) there are separate sections dealing with the techniques of working on older buildings.

Above: **Michael and Emma Holmes turned this 1960s 'mistake'**(right) **into an Arts and Crafts home that improved the whole street scene.**

There is sometimes confusion over the words 'conversion' and 'renovation'. Converting is what happens when a property or structure that was not previously a dwelling is converted to a home. Renovation is where an existing or previously occupied dwelling is brought back into use or altered or modified in some way. There are, as has been discussed in Chapter 1, important VAT implications.

Assessment of a conversion or renovation opportunity follows the same guidelines as for assessment of a greenfield plot, in that the acquisition costs, plus the building costs, taken away from the final market value, should leave a profit margin. I think it fair to warn, however, that increases in equity are often on the low side, and don't usually match up to those available with new build. Of course it's also not at all easy to predict costs on a general basis, and each individual project will have to have its costs assessed by means of a survey. A tumbledown wreck might in fact have to be practically demolished and put back up again whereas a structurally sound barn might need next to nothing doing to the main shell.

I will probably be taken to task, but many a time, when I first investigate conversion or renovation opportunities, with the exception of those where all that's needed is a bit of TLC and titivation, I apply the cost multipliers for new build, as if the existing structure isn't there. In fact, crude as that may seem, my initial assessments are often correct, as benefits gained from the existing structure are usually cancelled out by increased costs arising from unforeseen problems.

House renovation grants are sometimes available from your local authority to cover basic improvements such as defective walls and foundations, roofs, damp proof courses and wiring. There are also grants to cover things such as loft insulation, cavity wall insulation, draught proofing, gas or oil central heating systems repairs or replacement heating, dual immersion hot-water tanks and jackets and low-energy light bulbs. In the main they are means tested and discretionary, which means that they are probably not available to most self-builders. In particular, if you have recently purchased the property with the intention of renovating or converting, the various bodies will assume that the purchase price reflected the need for the work to be carried out. This does not apply to those grants that are available from the Energy Saving Trust and Clear Skies described in Chapter 6.

In England, Historic Buildings grants are sometimes available for Listed buildings of Grades I and II that are also on the Buildings at Risk Register, compiled by English Heritage. These are discretionary, with money available in one local authority and not in another; they can provide up to 25% of the costs, but with a fairly low ceiling that differs from county to county. They are also means tested and, in addition, there is often a residency requirement that, for example, you have lived in the property for at least three years and that you will continue to do so for a further five. Once again this is variable. In Scotland, Building Repair grants, covering the inside as well as the outside, and Conservation Area grants for necessary external work that will enhance or preserve the character of an area, might be available through Historic Scotland. Once again these are discretionary and means tested. In Wales these things are

handled by Cadw, which means 'keep'. Lastly, many of the Government organisations are able to give lists of charities and societies prepared to give grants for specific purposes.

If you are interested in restoring or renovating old buildings, then my friend and colleague Michael Holmes, who is well known as the editor-in-chief of *Homebuilding & Renovating* magazine and for his many television appearances on property-connected programmes, is in the course of writing a book to be called *Renovating for Profit*. I have no doubt that this will be a must for those thinking of undertaking such a project and will have a well-deserved place on the bookshelf alongside this book and all of the others that I mention from time to time. Additionally you could contact the help and advice line of the Society for the Preservation of Ancient Buildings (SPAB) on 020 7377 1644. They publish regular pamphlets on specific subjects to do with the restoration and maintenance of historic or ancient buildings and hold courses around the country at which you can learn the ancient crafts of building. The SPAB is consulted on Listed building applications affecting pre-1720 buildings.

Adjoining sites and surrounding land
In any assessment of a potential project it's important to look beyond the boundaries of the property you've come to see. As you enter the village or area, start to look at other properties. Study the architectural vernacular. Look for details that are consistent and for the types of materials, particularly walling and roofing materials that have been used or are traditional. If you are planning to build a new house or bungalow, keep a sharp eye out for recently built properties or those under construction. These will give you a pretty good indication of what is required in design terms as far as the local authority are concerned and what types of bricks, roof tiles, etc. they are prepared to accept.

Study the immediate street scene. I've already mentioned the inadvisability of trying to put a house in a long line of bungalows and vice versa but it goes much further than that. You, as a self-builder, will be learning all about bricks. You'll be finding out the differences between a stock brick and a sand-faced

Fletton brick, a plain tile and a concrete interlocking tile. You may, as a result, have definite ideas about just what you want to incorporate in your new home. But will it all be worthwhile? After all, you can't make a silk purse out of a sow's ear, as they say. If the adjoining houses are all built with relatively cheap bricks and concrete roof tiles, spending twice as much on the bricks and three times as much on plain clay roof tiles might not make a pennyworth of difference to the eventual value.

Another reason for studying the neighbouring houses is to see if they have any signs of damage. Whilst cracks in one house might well mean that it was badly built, cracks in a number of them might well be an indicator of something wrong below ground.

It has to be said, but one of the most distressing factors regarding neighbouring properties is the extent to which their appearance and general upkeep can impact on your site. I have often seen lovely plots ruined by untidy neighbours. Old rusty cars on your site are something you can do something about. On your neighbour's land if they think that their garden looks better with lines of disused vehicles or if their hobby is doing up old bangers, there's little or nothing you can do about it. It really brings it home to you just how much we rely on our neighbours sharing our values in life in order to keep up our values in property. And whilst I admit that noisy or untidy neighbours might not stay for ever, there could well be no time limit on it and their activities will blight any project.

Values

I've already referred to the dangers of over- or under-developing a plot – something that's often referred to as the 'carrying capacity' or 'ceiling value'. These are the value of the most appropriate house or bungalow that your plot will take and the maximum that anybody would pay for anything in that street. They are brought about by income levels in the general area and the expectations of anybody coming to live there. In other words if most of the houses in your street sell for £150,000 and you want to build something a lot better, would it be attractive to somebody with £200,000 plus to spend or would a person with that amount of money prefer to live elsewhere?

It is vital for any self-builder to know and understand local house prices. There is no better way to find out than to browse the windows of the local estate agents to see just what the type of property you're envisaging might fetch in the area. Build up a dossier of relative prices. Start with the common three-bedroom semi-detached house and work up to the larger properties so that you can get a feel for the middle ranges. There are no precise formulae for valuation. It's all comparative and when an estate agent puts a value on any property he is simply comparing it to others that he's dealt with and assessing its value relative to them.

But for anyone interested in property, and to be reading this book you must be one of them, this is merely dinner-party stuff and something we all talk and think about in our daily lives.

Preliminary budget

At the start of the book we set an initial budget for the purposes of evaluating just what you'd got to spend, just how much you were going to borrow and where from. Having read further you can now set the preliminary budget on the last page of the Site Details Checklist that follows. This may or may not be different to your first thoughts, as it will be arrived at by reference to what you have discovered in the previous chapters. It's still not the final budget by any means – there are many factors that are going to alter that, not least, design, materials, the requirements of the planning authorities and, of course, your own aspirations. This is an ongoing process and it will only finish when you finally move in and add up just what it all did actually cost you.

But if it starts off right, it has a better chance of finishing up right. If you have a baseline cost then when you fall in love with that kitchen that's going to cost £5,000 extra, you'll have something to add it to and a list of figures that you can scan for savings to pay for it. And if that means that you have to sit down every night for the duration of your project and relate costs to your original projections, then that's fine; for the alternative could be a nasty shock.

SITE DETAILS CHECKLIST   1

PLANNING

● Outline planning permission?   Yes | No

● Detailed/Full planning permission?   Yes | No

● Expiry date of planning permission?

● Was planning permission gained at appeal?   Yes | No

● If so was this because of local opposition or local authority (LA) planning department opposition?

● Has this died down?   Yes | No

● If the land has no planning permission, what are the realistic chances of getting it?   %

● Is this the view of the planning officer?   Yes | No

● Have you studied the local authority's Local Development Plan or Framework?   Yes | No

● Is what you are proposing in accordance with this/these policies?   Yes | No

● In particular is the land within an area where the planners will accept development?   Yes | No

● Planning conditions (other than standard)?   Yes | No

● Are they satisfied?   Yes | No

  If no, what needs to be done?

● Are Permitted Development Rights restricted or removed?   Yes | No

● Any planning permission on neighbouring land?   Yes | No

● Any planning blight?   Yes | No

  If yes, what?

● Planning authority

SITE DETAILS CHECKLIST	2

● Name of officer

● Conservation Area/AONB/National Park/Listed building/SSSI or higher?   Yes | No

● Archaeological interest?   Yes | No

● Archaeological survey required?   Yes | No

● Special foundations to facilitate future surveys required?   Yes | No

● Watching brief if necessary?   Yes | No

ACCESS

● Public highway/private access?

● Is there a right of access?   Yes | No

If not, what arrangements have to be made?

● Any sign of a ransom strip?   Yes | No

● Does the driveway need making up?   Yes | No

● Is it suitable for construction traffic?   Yes | No

● If not, is there an alternative/temporary site access?   Yes | No

● Visibility splays required?   Yes | No

● Obtainable within site curtilage?   Yes | No

● If not, are the necessary easements in place?   Yes | No

● Levels right for gates/bellmouth?   Yes | No

● Crossover made?   Yes | No

● Pavement?   Yes | No

● Grass verge?   Yes | No

● Is this part of the highway?   Yes | No

SITE DETAILS CHECKLIST	3

● Parking space requirements

● Turning circles/need to enter and leave in forward gear?   Yes | No

● Highways Agency local office

● Name of officer

TREES

● Are there any significant trees on site?   Yes | No

● Are there any on adjoining land?   Yes | No

● Location plotted?   Yes | No

● Species and sizes?   Yes | No

● Any Tree Preservation Orders in force?   Yes | No

   If so, on which trees?

● Any sign of trees having been removed lately?   Yes | No

GROUND CONDITIONS/SUBSOIL

● What is the natural vegetation?

● Any signs of sedge or rush?   Yes | No

● Ground water or signs of high water table?   Yes | No

● Has there been any flooding?   Yes | No

SITE DETAILS CHECKLIST	4

If so, what level did the water reach and is it possible to build above that level or take other precautions?

● Is the plot shewn on any floodplain maps?   Yes | No

● In the flowerbeds or disturbed ground, is there an indication of subsoil?   Yes | No

If yes, what do you see?

● Any trial pits dug?   Yes | No

Findings?

● Rock?   Yes | No

● Streams/watercourses?   Yes | No

● Radon gas precautions necessary?   Yes | No

● Heavy clay?   Yes | No

● With trees?   Yes | No

● Any sign of local buildings employing special foundations?   Yes | No

If so, what type?

● Locals consulted?   Yes | No

Findings/rumours?

● Evidence of filled ground?   Yes | No

SITE DETAILS CHECKLIST	5

● Any contamination?   Yes | No

● Any existing foundations?   Yes | No

● Local Building Control department

● Building Inspector

● Any comments by him?

PHYSICAL CHARACTERISTICS/SITE DETAILS/SERVICES

● Level site/slight slope/severe slope?

● Levels survey available?   Yes | No

● Datum point?

● Key dimensions:

    Width at building line (front)

    Width at building line (back)

    Triangulation measurements

● Ownership of boundaries:

    North

    South

    East

    West

SITE DETAILS CHECKLIST	6
● Sun/shade noted?	Yes | No
● Exposure – none/moderate/severe?	
● Overhead cables/power lines?	Yes | No
● If significant, are they movable?	Yes | No
● Drains on site?	Yes | No
● Foul drains?	Yes | No
Available?	Yes | No
Location plotted?	Yes | No
Invert	Yes | No
Cover	Yes | No
● Surface water drains?	Yes | No
Location plotted?	Yes | No
Invert	Yes | No
Cover	Yes | No
● Public/private?	
● Legal right to connect?	Yes | No
● Easements in place if necessary?	Yes | No
● If no mains drains available, what system is acceptable/workable?	
Cesspit	Yes | No
Septic tank	Yes | No
Sewage treatment plant	Yes | No
Other	Yes | No
● Environment Agency consulted and approvals given?	Yes | No
● Is there space on site for these works or do you need to negotiate for it?	Yes | No
● If no surface water drains available, what system is acceptable/workable?	
Standard soakaway	Yes | No
Sophisticated soakaway	Yes | No

SITE DETAILS CHECKLIST		7
Aquifer		Yes | No
Stream or ditch		Yes | No
● Any sterile zones?		Yes | No
● If yes, are they plotted?		Yes | No
● Electricity available?		Yes | No
Overhead/underground?		
Connection charge	£	
● Gas available?		
Connection charge	£	Yes | No
● If not available, will you want to install an LPG system?		Yes | No
● If so, is there space for the tank or can it go underground?		Yes | No
● Or will you want oil?		Yes | No
● If so, is there space for the tank?		Yes | No
● Telephone available?		Yes | No
Connection charge	£	
● Mains water available?		Yes | No
Connection charge	£	
● If not, is a bore hole possible?		Yes | No
Estimated costs	£	
Comments		

LEGAL

● Rights of way established to plot's benefit?		Yes | No
● Rights of way to benefit of others?		Yes | No
● Covenants and easements to plot's benefit?		Yes | No
● Covenants and easements to others' benefit?		Yes | No
● Footpaths		Yes | No

SITE DETAILS CHECKLIST   8

● Any sign of adverse possession?   Yes | No

   If so, how long has it been established?

● Does any loss of land through adverse possession question the viability of the plot?   Yes | No

● Land being sold with full title?   Yes | No

● All or any part of the land being sold subject to a defective/incomplete/possessory title?   Yes | No

● Any protected wildlife, fauna or flora on site?   Yes | No

NEIGHBOURS

● Did the neighbours object to the granting of planning?   Yes | No

● Is there a legacy of hostility or has it calmed down?   Yes | No

● Will neighbours be able to obstruct site works?   Yes | No

● Is there anything you can do to resolve the situation?

ADJOINING SITES/SURROUNDING LAND

● What type of buildings are in the street scene?

● Are there any new dwellings in the area that give an indication of the planners' likes and dislikes?

   If so, describe.

SITE DETAILS CHECKLIST	9

● Is there a building line?　　　　　　　　　　　　　　　　　　Yes | No

● General characteristics of local architecture/design – mixed/uniform

● General architectural features on nearby buildings:

Sizes

Complex/simple shapes

Brick/render/stone/black and white/tile hung/timbered/other

Features, e.g. mullions/quoins/corbels/keystones/cills/heads

Roof pitches

Roof coverings, e.g. plain tile/profiled tile/slates/thatch/stone slate/other

Roof treatment, e.g. gabled/hipped/barn ended/tabled verges/clipped verges/

Barge boarded verge/dry verges

Soffit overhangs/soffits/exposed rafter feet/exposed purlins

Window types, e.g. softwood painted or stained/hardwood/upvc/metal

Glazing, e.g. clear/all bar/leaded square or diamond

● Any sign of structural damage to adjoining buildings?　　　　Yes | No

● Any pollution/noise/smell/light from neighbouring properties?　Yes | No

VALUES

● What are the general property values within the area?

Semi-detached houses	£
Bungalows 3 bedrooms	£
Bungalows 4 bedrooms	£
Detached houses medium 4 bedrooms	£
Larger detached houses/bungalows	£

SITE DETAILS CHECKLIST   10

- What sort of property directly joins the plot?

    Houses/bungalows

    Detached/semi-detached

    Mixed

- What is the most appropriate type of dwelling for this plot?

- What is the carrying capacity(£)/ceiling value?   £

- Are there things in the offing that could affect local values e.g. new roads, motorways, industry moving in or out, major infrastructure works

METHOD OF BUILDING/PRELIMINARY BUDGET

- Timber frame/brick-and-block/other?
- Builder/subcontractors/shell building plus subcontractors/own labour?
- £s per sq. metre assumed
- Preliminary building budget   £
- Site costs   £
- Fees   £
- Finance costs   £
- Other costs   £
- Total costs (A)   £

- Value of finished house (B)   £

- Equity gain (B minus A)   £

Chapter 4

BUYING THE PROPERTY (the legal bits)

Buying land is not the same as buying other goods or services. By long-established law the purchase of land has to be evidenced in writing, and by long-established practice the legal profession has gone out of its way to make that evidencing as complicated and as obscure as possible, with its own unique vocabulary and sets of procedures. Solicitors, land agents and estate agents make their living by operating within this system and they make very little effort to explain it in any sort of plain English to their clients. If you are going to buy land then it is important that you familiarise yourself with the terminology and the procedures. It is also important that you employ professionals who know where the pitfalls are and can help you look out for them.

When you buy a property in England, you in effect buy the land with whatever's on it at the time. The concept of landownership in England and Wales goes right back to William the Conqueror who, when he stepped on to the beach at Hastings, threw his arms out wide and claimed the kingdom for his own and for his heirs and successors. He got his feet wet, which is why the title of any coastal land extends to the median high-water mark! As time went by the Crown then parcelled out the land under various forms of tenure, which normally required payment or favours of some kind. One of the most important, from the Crown's point of view, was the requirement for the grateful recipients to build castles to defend the realm – making them early self-builders. Other payments could vary from the provision of goods and foodstuffs right through to the supply of soldiers for the army and wenches for . . . well, for whatever they used wenches for at that time.

That basic tenet of land occupation in England and Wales stems from that early appropriation, in that all land law endeavours to ensure that land is occupied and that it serves some useful function. Great pains were always taken to make sure that land could not, in the natural course of its division and subdivision, become landlocked, for instance. As time went by crafty people got around that by the use of ransom strips and covenants, as I have already discussed (see Chapter 3), but they were always against the driving spirit of land serving a useful function.

In Scotland the Crown similarly parcelled out land on a grace-and-favour system under various forms of tender. The legal system is different, as I explain later, but it does have many similarities and the increasing use of forms of tender south of the border is tending to blur the distinctions.

The most important form of tenure which has come down to us through the ages is that of 'freehold', and when you own land in this way it basically means that you hold the land free of any payment. Most land outside that still retained by the Crown is now freehold and in turn it is open for the freeholder to consider letting off all or part of their land on lease-

When you buy a property in England, you in effect buy the land with whatever's on it at the time.

hold. Worthy of mention, at this point, is the 'commonhold' form of tenure that has been introduced over the past few years. It is unlikely to feature in many self-build projects and is more for situations such as blocks of flats or properties with common rights and parts.

There are various methods of buying land and there are, as one would expect, different procedures in place within the individual parts of the United Kingdom and in the Republic of Ireland.

England and Wales

If you are buying through an estate agent then the details might well include reference to the price. But not always, as there are three recognised and distinct ways of selling land.

Private treaty

Most land in England and Wales is sold by private treaty. This is the familiar way whereby details are prepared and the property is offered for sale at an advertised price. Agents will try to vary this somewhat by adding words such as 'Offers in the region of' or 'Offers over' but essentially the details are 'an invitation to treat' and it is open to any interested party to make an offer on the land.

This offer is made 'subject to contract' and at this point, if the vendor is minded to accept, solicitors are instructed. The purchaser's solicitor obtains a Contract of Purchase from the vendor's solicitor and raises enquiries on it, which they send through to the vendor's solicitor. If they wish, but there is no compulsion, the purchaser can arrange for a survey. They will also, if finance is required, make application for a mortgage and pay for the lender's survey and valuation, which they are entitled to have sight of. In most cases the purchaser's solicitor will also act for the lender to protect their interests and oversee the preparation and signing of any mortgage or the repayments of any outstanding balances.

The solicitors continue to exchange letters and enquiries and the purchaser's solicitor arranges for and receive local searches, including details held by HM Land Registry, if the land is registered. They check that the vendor has good title to the property and is entitled to sell and in most cases they will also obtain details and copies of any planning permissions related to the land or the surrounding land. In many cases they will also obtain a mining report and more information on anything that the searches throw up that is likely to affect the property either adversely or beneficially. This would include details of road-widening proposals or street orders, requiring, for

Below: **A conditional offer to purchase land in Scotland.**

CONNOR MALCOLM SCHEDULE OF TERMS AND CONDITIONS (as at 1ˢᵗ August 2003)
Referred to in the foregoing offer to purchase the subjects at

1. Throughout this offer:-

(a) "the purchaser" means

(b) "the subjects" means pertaining thereto, all and pertinents thereof;

(c) where the context so re masculine gender will i

(d) where the seller com obligations undertake given jointly and sever

2. Entry and vacant possessi given no later than 12 no agreed when the purchas shall be left clean and tid removed.

3. If the seller us unable t under the missives on th on the part of our client or at any time thereaft bargain and our client v said period of fourteen under the missives at th without prejudice to hi incurred by our client storage charges, loss of to implement his oblig any such loss or expens

with the Building Wa prior to, and delivered extensions requiring t necessary documentati the relevant document documentation to be settlement.

24. Notwithstanding the g had the benefit of w purchaser, and that pr with all current buildi prior to or at settlemen

25. The seller warrants tha

26. The seller warrants tha rot, woodworm or risi which the subjects of eradicate any of the sai settlement, the Survey to the purchaser's satis validity of the Guara warrants that nothing l

27. The seller will be respo the purchase price in a tear excepted, and will settlement. In the even date of actual settlemen be entitled to resile fro

1ˢᵗ April, 2004

FAX NO: 0131 557 6712

Messrs Colin Blaikie & Co
DX ED 232
EDINBURGH

Dear Sirs,

On behalf of and as instructed by our clients, ███████████, residing at █ ██████████, we hereby offer to purchase from your clients, ALL and WHOLE the subjects known as and forming ██████████ at a price of One Hundred and ████████ Thousand Nine Hundred and Ninety Five Pounds (£██████) Sterling but that subject to the terms and conditions contained in our Schedule of Conditions annexed and signed as relative hereto and also on the following terms and conditions:-

1. The date of entry shall be as at 25ᵗʰ June, 2004 or such other date as may be mutually agreed between our clients.

2. The price shall include all items as detailed in your Sales Particulars, a copy of which shall be annexed and executed as relative to any acceptance following hereon.

3. This offer is open for verbal acceptance by 11am today with

instance, that any development should make provision for a footpath to be constructed to Highways Agency standards and subsequently adopted. An optional extra, but one that it is advisable to take, is an environmental search, which will throw up any suspicion of land contamination or natural hazards such as noxious ground gases or risk of flooding. When all is in place, the purchaser's solicitor will usually prepare a 'Report on Title' and arrange to discuss their findings with their client. If, as a result of these enquiries, it is decided to proceed, then each party's solicitor will arrange for their client to sign identical contracts and will then hold them until such time as they are given instructions to 'exchange contracts'.

This exchange of contracts, should it happen, is the first time that either party is bound to the sale and purchase and is effected by a simple telephone conversation between solicitors, noting the time and date of the exchange. Once this has happened there is no going back unless you are prepared to be in breach of contract and liable for damages. A deposit, usually 10% of the purchase price, is payable upon exchange of contracts, and each solicitor receives the copy of the contract that has been signed by the other party. This contract details the completion date, usually 21 or 28 days thereafter.

The 'Conveyance', 'Transfer' or addition to the title deeds, noting the sale and purchase, is prepared by the vendor's solicitor and signed by the vendor. Upon the completion date, the final monies are paid over in return for the keys and the purchaser is free to take up occupation. Within three months the title must be registered and any Stamp Duty that is payable, which will almost certainly have been taken from the purchaser upon completion, must be paid over.

Auctions

Auction rooms are daunting places for self-builders. They are supposed to be accessible to the public but everything that happens within them often seems designed to exclude the ordinary man in favour of the professional and those in the know. I watched in horror recently as an auctioneer pointedly refused to look in the direction of a lady waving her wish to bid and instead concentrated on a chap at the front whom he obviously knew. You've got to be quite brave and assertive. Shout out your bid if necessary and position yourself so that you can see the silent winks, nods and grimaces that the auctioneer is accepting. Incidentally, for those not wishing to bid, it's hell trying to keep still. At an auction in Wales not so long ago, I inadvertently scratched my eyebrow and suddenly found to my horror that I'd just made a bid of £55,000 for the fishing rights on a stretch of the local river!

It used to be thought that the price a property fetched in an auction room was the ultimate valuation: a proper and final demonstration of the market price. Whilst that is still true to some extent, it was always a flawed supposition because it could never take into account the individual who just had to have a property, come what may, or the failure of an auctioneer to properly market the property.

Buying land at auction is a highly legal process whereby at the fall of the hammer, the highest bidder is deemed to have accepted all of the terms and conditions of sale and to have exchanged contracts at that point, legally binding themselves to purchase and the sellers to sell. Failure to complete means that the purchaser will be charged interest at a predetermined rate, usually 4–5% above bank rate, and that if they back out altogether, they can be sued for any re-marketing costs and any discrepancy in value.

It's not quite clear what would happen if a successful bidder got 'cold feet' in an auction room because, following the fall of the hammer, the purchaser is required to sign the contract. If they refused to do so, then although they might well be liable for misrepresentation and could be sued on the promise, it is probable that they could not actually be made to buy, as the law requires that any sale of land is evidenced in writing. In reality, in an auction room where others had been bidding, the chances are that the auctioneer would take a pragmatic view and re-offer the property there and then.

This legal framework is the reason why most reputable auction particulars contain within their terms and conditions all or most of the questions that a proposed purchaser's solicitor would wish or need to ask, and a good few also provide copies of the searches. Nevertheless sole reliance on these partic-

RESIDENTIAL PLOT
FOR SALE

HASSETT
ESTATE AGENTS

TEL. 01909-501338

Left and below: **Two typical plots: one is a mature orchard, the other is part of somebody's garden split off by a new fence. If these were for sale at auction your solicitor would need to do most, if not all, of their work before you bid. You might also need a survey and all of this could end up being money wasted. But don't be tempted to leave things to chance or to take statements from vendors or agents at face value.**

ulars is not to be recommended and if you are proposing to bid at an auction you should give your own solicitor time to study the detail and to make what enquiries they feel necessary or appropriate.

Of late many auction details have tended to put forward a guideline price, but experience shows that this is often wildly misleading and is employed simply to attract interest. I have attended quite a few auctions over the past few years with hopeful would-be self-building couples and in most of them the guideline prices were set at about two thirds of the eventually realised figure. Most auctions are subject to a reserve price, which does not have to be advised to interested parties, and unless the bids reach that figure, the auctioneer can choose to withdraw the property. It is all too easy to get carried away in an auction room. You look across at your rival bidder and convince yourself that they are at their limit and that just one more bid will see them drop out. That is the way to come out of the room having paid far too much and it really is important that you go into an auction with a set ceiling beyond which you cannot or will not go – and stick to it!

Tenders

There are various forms of tender. Open tender, closed tender, formal and informal tender are all words that are used to describe the process but they are all variations on the theme whereby offers are solicited in writing for a property. The conditions of sale, dictated by the agent or the seller, are the rules by which the sale will be governed.

The details for a tender often take on a similar

form to auction particulars, save the fact that they normally require that all bids are received in writing by a certain date. Closer inspection, however, will reveal that in most cases, the vendor reserves the right not to accept the highest offer, or indeed any offer at all. One solicitor described the process of selling land by tender as a system whereby the estate agent gets to write his own rules. In fact, unlike an auction, where the fall of the gavel has distinct legal connotations and is binding on both parties, success by virtue of being the highest bidder in a tender does not guarantee that you'll be able to buy the property.

The problem with tenders is the lack of legal framework to an otherwise highly legal process.

Sometimes the conditions of sale will require that offers are submitted together with a cheque for the deposit and go on to insist that acceptance of the tender will constitute an exchange of contracts. With no legal requirement for the vendor to accept the highest offer, this really is a one-way street and the system is either actually open to abuse or manipulation or, just as damagingly, the suspicion that that is the case. Buying land by tender has been likened to entering an auction room blindfolded and with earplugs. It is hugely unpopular with purchasers because, whatever they bid, they never really know if they've missed it by £1 or obtained the land for well over the odds.

Below: **Your solicitor will want to discuss the results of their searches with you before you buy.**

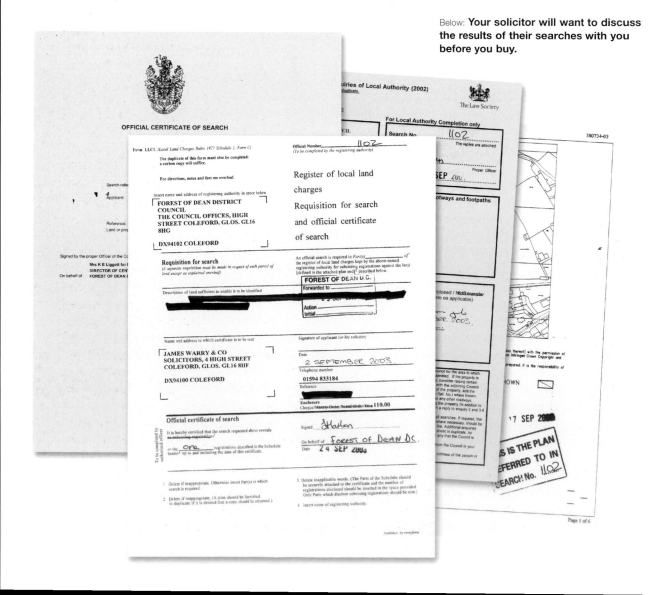

As to what to bid, that can only be arrived at by doing all of the sums and setting a figure in much the same way as for an auction, before trusting it to luck. But if there is any advice it is to always add that little bit extra on to your calculations. Whilst there is no requirement that any particular offer must be accepted, if all other things are equal, the highest offer, even by a few pounds, still stands a better chance of success.

Scotland

Opponents of the process of buying land in England and Wales often point to the Scottish system, on the grounds that it would avoid costly delays and stop the incidences of gazumping and gazundering – the practice of a vendor suddenly asking for more money or a purchaser suddenly demanding a reduction in the price. The problem is that most proponents of this argument don't actually know or understand the Scottish system.

In England and Wales, all land was originally held by the Crown, before being disposed of piecemeal in the various forms of tender that have principally boiled down to 'freehold'. In Scotland, where huge areas are still held by the Crown, land was similarly parcelled and then re-parcelled out on the basis of patronage and the 'feu' was the tenure, or form of payment that allowed continued occupation. Over time these payments in kind have largely fallen away and the feu has come to mean the larger holding from which sales of land by division and subdivision are made. 'Feu disposition' therefore means the sale or alienation of land.

You will also come across several words that might at first seem strange. 'Feudal Superior' doesn't mean that you're going to be faced with some plaid-clad baron demanding *droit de seigneur* and to help understand what it does mean I'll introduce another word, 'burdens'. Burdens, or to give them their proper title, 'Real Burdens', are essentially the same as covenants in England and Wales and the Feudal Superiors, often the original owners of the land, are the ones benefiting from them. These burdens take all of the usual forms plus one other that is not often come across in the rest of the UK, namely the 'right of pre-

emption'. This gives the seller (vendor) the right to buy back the property if you ever decide to sell, usually limited to a right to buy at the level of the highest offer within 21 days or at valuation.

Another word that you might come across is 'servitude'. But despite the obvious medieval connotations, this is merely the Scottish equivalent of an easement or wayleave.

The procedure for the sale of land or property usually goes like this. Property is advertised for sale, often by solicitors who, in the main, take the place of and combine the roles played by estate agents and solicitors south of the border. The details they issue and the price that is quoted are really just the same as details offering land for sale by private treaty in England and Wales. If you like a property then you have to decide what price you are prepared to pay, obviously taking your lead from the figure quoted on the details and by using comparative values.

Where the procedures in Scotland do begin to differ from those in England and Wales is that if there are indications that your price is acceptable, you then ask your solicitor to register an interest in the property. Following this, the seller's solicitor or agent should not sell to another party without telling you first. You then get a survey and valuation and, if necessary, approach your finance source, as your solicitor will not proceed further until they are satisfied that you have the full purchase monies sorted out and available.

Your solicitor then makes a written offer with an expiry date and a long list of other conditions and enquiries to which the purchase is subject. These are known as the 'Missives' and they are basically the same as the conditions and preliminary enquiries that go to and fro between solicitors in England and Wales. If the other side accept this written offer, then it is binding on both parties, unless something turns up or goes wrong in the Missives negotiations.

At some point in this process, your solicitor will obtain, quite often from the seller's solicitor, the Property Enquiry Certificates, which once again are basically the same as the searches that are done south of the border. Following 'Conclusion of the Missives', the purchaser's solicitor will receive a 'Draft Disposition' and there is sometimes, but not always, a deposit required at this stage. When all is agreed between the parties, the 'Disposition' is signed and the 'Date of Entry', or completion date is agreed. With the monies paid over on the due date, the purchaser is free to take up occupation and the solicitor's last job is to register the transaction and property and pay over the Stamp Duty.

I have previously sat firmly on the fence over which method is better – that in Scotland or the one used in England and Wales. But I am now beginning to doubt the ability of the Scottish system to deal with the high inflation of prices that is perhaps being

imposed by buyers from south of the border. The ways of coping with this phenomenon seem to have many of the ills that are attributed to the English system but have the effect of introducing much more uncertainty. Property is often put on the market with the price being 'offers over …', and whilst this price may at first seem like a guideline I have experienced many plots being sold at figures twice and even three times the original figure. This creates a blind auction where no closing date is set and the bids just keep coming in ever higher. What therefore do you offer? The suspicion is always that any offer will be used

Summary of the different procedures for buying a property

England and Wales
- You see a property for sale through estate agents or others.
- You make an offer, 'subject to contract'.
- The vendors accept the offer 'subject to contract'.
- Solicitors are instructed and the purchaser's solicitor prepares a draft contract and a list of preliminary enquiries.
- You arrange for a survey (optional).
- You make an application for a mortgage and pay for the survey and valuation.
- The solicitors exchange letters and enquiries and your solicitor arranges for and receives the local searches.
- Your solicitor prepares a report on title.
- Each party's solicitor arranges for their client to sign copies of identical contracts and holds them until such time as their respective client gives them the go-ahead to proceed to exchange.
- Exchange of contracts takes place with a 10% deposit payable by you and the completion date is set.
- The conveyance is signed by the vendor.
- Upon the completion date, the final monies are paid over and the purchaser takes up occupation.

Scotland
- You see a property that's advertised for sale.
- You decide what price you'd be prepared to pay for it.
- You ask your solicitor to note an interest in the property.
- You get a survey and valuation.
- You approach your finance source.
- Your solicitor makes a written offer with conditions.
- Once the written conditional offer is accepted it is binding on both parties, unless something goes wrong on the Missives negotiations.
- Your solicitor obtains the Property Enquiry Certificates.
- Following the 'Conclusion of the Missives', the purchaser's solicitor receives a 'Draft Disposition'.
- The Date of Entry or completion date is agreed and noted in the Missives.
- When all is agreed between the parties, the Disposition is signed.
- With the monies paid over on the Date of Entry or completion date, the purchaser takes up occupation.

Above and right: **Two distinct styles of home, one harking back to the Regency period, the other to traditional Essex longhouses or barn conversions.**
© Potton

to prompt more offers and that eventually, when the vendor feels that enough parties have registered an interest, a closing date will be fixed; all of which simply changes the process to a tender with final and best offers. When an offer is formally accepted there is a quasi-contract which comes into existence and prevents the gazumping and chain breakdowns that plague the market in England and Wales. But on the other hand most offers are conditional and many do not contain an entry date, which tends to introduce the same uncertainties.

Northern Ireland

As you would expect, the Northern Irish system of land tenure and the buying and selling of land broadly follows that of England and Wales. There are, however, minor differences and there are elements and language that are reminiscent of the Scottish legal system.

There is no 'exchange of contracts' as such. An offer is made to buy land and if accepted, when the various parties' solicitors have made all the necessary enquiries, the purchaser signs the contract and it is sent off to the vendor. When and if the vendor signs his part and returns it to the purchaser's side, a contract is deemed to be in existence. Thereafter the route to completion is virtually the same as for England and Wales with a similar legal requirement for the registration of the land and transaction, and the payment of Stamp Duty.

The Republic of Ireland (Eire)

Southern Ireland was, of course, once part of the United Kingdom and it is hardly surprising, therefore, that much of its legal system harks back to that time and has been retained. The system for the sale and purchase of residential and domestic land in the Republic of Ireland is substantially the same as for England and Wales, but with a couple of minor variations that are reminiscent of parts of the Scottish system.

One of the first differences that a buyer from England or Wales will notice is that a booking or holding deposit of 5% is often payable with the balance of the 10% paid over on contract. Another main difference is that title is not investigated until after contract – something that is similar to with the way the Missives are conducted in Scotland. If something turns up that goes to the root of the title then the contract is voided but otherwise, if everything is as it should be, the transaction proceeds to completion in the normal way.

Solicitors and conveyancers

All of the above should tell you that the buying and selling of land is no easy matter and that whatever and wherever you are buying, you do need a good solicitor or conveyancer. If you already have, or know, one whom you wish to act for you, that is fine. Otherwise you will probably entrust your affairs to the person whose office you first contact and it is largely true that there is little if anything to choose between the overall competence with which different firms of solicitors or conveyancers will deal with the purchase. But there may be a big difference in how long they take to do the job and it is important that you impress upon whichever company you employ that 'speed is of the essence'.

Many of the forms of contract and procedures that solicitors use are designed for the sale of houses and many of the questions on standard enquiry forms have no real relevance to the sale or purchase of vacant land. However, the buying of land is a special task and one that is best handled by an expert in the problems that can occur with a potential building plot. Do be careful that, when the job is allocated in the office, it is done so on the basis of relevant experience and knowledge and not merely on the basis of the purchase price. You do not want to entrust your plot purchase to the office junior.

Your solicitor will be concerned to advise you on just how to make your offer and they will want to make sure that you are not irrevocably committed before they've had a chance to properly examine the title. This normally means that you should never sign any papers or make any written offer unless it is qualified by the words 'subject to contract'. If you pay a deposit on the land then you must also make sure that your payment is made subject to contract and that the deposit is fully returnable in the event that you do not proceed. If you intend to buy at auction, effectively exchanging contracts at that point, it is crucial that your solicitor must be given the chance to do all of their work before you do so.

It is also part of the solicitor's job to evaluate and verify the planning situation on the land. From reading the previous chapters, and those to come, your knowledge of planning matters could well equal or exceed that of your solicitor. However, if there are problems or inconsistencies with things such as visibility splays or the ability to satisfy planning conditions in order to make a consent operable, it is to them that you will have to turn to get them resolved.

Along with all the documents which the solicitor receives there will be the title deed plans and these may well be the first time that you have anything to compare with the badly copied fragment of the local Ordnance Survey that was reproduced on the estate agent's details. The title deed plans will, in effect, form a record of plans

down through time and will show the history of the plot and how it was arrived at by subdivision of larger segments of land or by addition of others. As I've warned before, there is a chance that none of them necessarily represents the site that has been pointed out to you and that possibly none of them represents the plan that the planning authorities have. Your solicitor can notice and point out any apparent discrepancies in the plans but what they can't do is verify them on the ground. You need to be able to get out there with a 30-metre tape and measure up your plot to make certain that what you are buying is the same as that being offered on paper. If you can't do it, or there's any doubt at all in your mind, then engage a surveyor for the purpose. Often the discrepancies are immaterial but there are times when they are vital,

Right: **If any land is sold or let for longer than seven years, it must be registered with the Land Registry. This makes it a most useful tool with which to find out all you can about the land, its owners and any charges that there might be against it.**

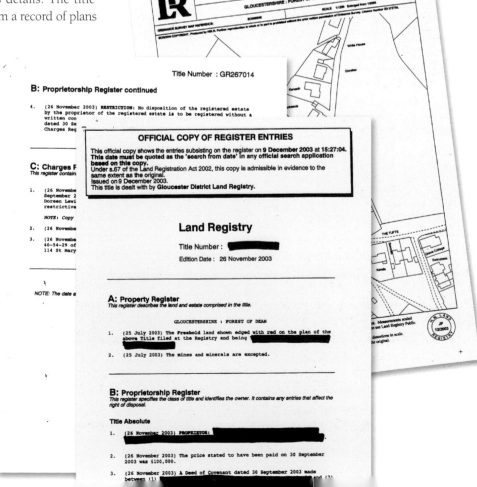

such as with visibility splays and accesses. These things need to be sorted before, and not after, you've signed the contract.

Try also to get a copy of the title deed plans that you can keep. You never know when it'll come in handy for settling things like boundary disputes or arguments over repairs to fences, without expensive recourse to solicitors.

Legal options and conditional contracts

The advice for anyone buying land without express planning consent in England and Wales is that they should only do so *'subject to receipt of satisfactory planning permission'*. This means that all of the normal procedures for buying the land are gone through, right up to and including the exchange of contracts but that, in the event of planning permission being refused, the contract is voided and any deposits returned. Conversely, of course, it also means that with the granting of planning consent, the contract is irrevocable and binding on both parties. In Scotland the receipt of planning permission must be one of the accepted conditions of purchase and the vendor will usually want to impose some sort of time limit.

Another way of reserving land so that in the event of successful planning application you can ensure that the vendor sells to you, and does not retain the land for his own use or sell to someone else, is to enter into a legally binding option to purchase. Normally this has to be prepared by solicitors because this is a highly legal document that must detail the length of time that the option will run for and the amount that is to be paid for it. It must also specify whether the money paid counts as part of an agreed purchase price or is additional to it.

Prospective vendors often prefer the legal option because, if the planning application fails, they still get some money. They might also be worried that a conditional contract could drag on for ages whilst you try for a contentious scheme and they might, therefore, try to impose an unrealistic time limit.

The Party Wall etc Act 1996

This Act seeks to provide a framework for the prevention and resolution of disputes in relation to party walls, boundary walls and excavations that are close to neighbouring buildings. It requires that whenever such work is proposed, those intending to carry it out must give the adjoining owners notice in writing. There is no penalty within the Act for non-compliance but it recognises that if the proper notices and procedures are not followed, then legal redress or an injunction might be sought in the courts. The implication is that non-compliance would count against any offending party.

Work on existing party walls

The Act lists works that may be done to existing party walls, even though they go beyond ordinary common law rights. These include:

- cutting into a wall to take a bearing beam or inserting a damp-proof course all the way through a party wall
- raising a party wall, whilst, if necessary, cutting off any projections that might prevent you from doing so
- demolishing and rebuilding a party wall
- underpinning a party wall
- protecting two adjoining walls by putting a flashing from the higher to the lower.

The advice for anyone buying land without express planning consent in England and Wales is that they should only do so 'subject to receipt of satisfactory planning permission'.

At least two months' notice in writing must be given of any intention to carry out these works and the recipient of the notice has 14 days to respond or issue a counter notice, after which a dispute is said to have arisen.

Party Wall extensions

In many urban situations, any extension to the home or work to the garden might lead to involvement with a party wall.

Here the property was extended to the full width of the plot on the ground floor and in the dormer conversion to the roof.

To maximise the inside space of the glass-roof extension it was neccessary to build on to the boundary wall, requiring the neighbours' consent. This was gained by building a new load-bearing wall on to which both parties are entitled to build.

New building on the boundary line

The Act does not confer any right to build any new walls or structures that bestride or intrude upon a neighbour's land, without their prior consent. However, and this is important, where a new wall or structure is to be built up to a boundary, the Act does confer the right for the footings for that wall or structure to intrude under the neighbouring land, subject to the payment of any compensation for damage caused during the construction.

One month's notice in writing is required and once again, if the adjoining owner responds or issues a counter notice within 14 days, a dispute is said to have arisen.

Excavations close to neighbouring buildings

You must inform an adjoining owner in writing, at least two months before work commences, if:

- you plan to excavate or construct foundations for a new building or structure within 3 metres of a neighbouring building or structure, where the excavations will go deeper than the foundations of those structures, or
- you plan to excavate or construct foundations for a new building or structure within 6 metres of a neighbouring building or structure, where that work would cut a line drawn downwards at 45 degrees from the bottom of the neighbour's foundations.

If a dispute arises over this, or any of the other works listed above, then an independent surveyor is appointed, their fees being paid by the person wishing to carry out the work. The surveyor will make an 'award' setting out what work can be carried out. They will also dictate how and when the work is to be done and they will record the conditions prior to the commencement of work, so that any damages can be properly attributed and made good. Either side has 14 days to appeal to the county court but this should be done only if an owner believes that the surveyor has acted beyond their powers.

Most importantly, where work is being carried out that is expressly authorised by the Act, and where the proper procedures have been followed, the Act gives the right of entry in order to carry out those works, provided that 14 days' notice of the intention to enter is given. It is an offence for an adjoining owner to refuse entry to someone who is entitled to enter premises under the Act, if the offender knows that the Act entitles the person to be there. If the adjoining premises are vacant then a police officer must accompany the workmen, surveyor or architect, as they enter.

The Act applies in England and Wales only. It doesn't override many common law rights such as the right of natural support. For example, you never could carry out excavations that destabilised your neighbour's land or property, and in Scotland they continue to rely solely on the established tenets of common law and have not seen the need to introduce similar legislation.

Undisclosed problems and final checks

In the previous edition of this book I referred to the introduction, in test areas, of the 'Seller's pack' and speculated that it would soon become universal. It hasn't happened yet, although the Government is still talking about it and much of their recent legislation refers to a 'Home Information Pack'. They hope that it will make a lot of difference but the chances are that it will make very little at all. It may make it more difficult to cover up a particular fact or to forget conveniently about some previously documented thing that has affected the land, but it will probably still not deter the person determined to hide the truth. All vendors have to answer, through their solicitors, a list of what are known as preliminary enquiries. These include questions like, 'Do you know of anything adversely affecting the property?' The honest vendor will answer just as honestly. But proving that a less honest vendor gave the wrong answer might be frightfully difficult.

That is why, to avoid unpleasant surprises, it is so important to make the right enquiries. Just to make sure, ask yourself, one more time, 'Why hasn't this plot been built on before, or why hasn't anyone else done something with this building?' There may be a very good reason and maybe, if you've done your homework, by following the guidelines and the checklist in previous chapters, you will know what that reason is. And if not? Well, ask around just one more time, just to make sure.

Insurances and legal contingency insurance

Once you've contracted on land, even though you might not have full title to it, you nevertheless have a beneficial interest in it. It is therefore possible that you could find yourself with shared liability for any mishaps that occur on the land and, on exchange, you will need to make sure that you have the necessary insurance and, in particular, public liability insurance.

Defects in titles can take many forms, and many can be dealt with through special, single-payment insurance policies, known as legal contingency insurance or single-premium indemnity policies. As far as restrictive covenants are concerned, these policies protect the insured and their successors in title against enforcement or attempted enforcement of the covenant. It includes the costs, expenses and any damages in connection with a court action or lands tribunal action, the cost of alteration or demolition following an injunction, the loss of market value of land as a result of development being prevented and abortive capital expenditure.

Legal contingency insurance can also cover situations where title deeds are lost, problems over uncertain rights of way, possessory or incomplete titles and services indemnities where the right to use drains or other services is uncertain or unknown.

The premiums payable are assessed and evaluated according to the risk factors determined by the underwriters. It is surprising, but many solicitors seem either not to have heard of these policies, or to have forgotten about their existence. I can recall many a time when a solicitor very nearly persuaded a prospective self-builder to withdraw from a plot where the title was mildly defective or rights of way could not be proven over an access. In nearly all of these cases, when the suggestion of a single-premium indemnity insurance was put to the solicitor it was very speedily arranged and the purchase was able to proceed, usually with the premium being paid by the vendor!

Fees, disbursements and registration of land

Upon completion the solicitors will want to make sure that they are in funds in order to finalise the transaction and they will take their fees out of the monies they hold. For the sale and purchase of an average house and plot in the provinces, these can be around £1,000. To this must be added various extraneous charges such as local search fees (£110), Mining search fees (£45), (optional) environmental search fee (£30), Land Registry search fee (£4) and Land Charges search fee (£2).

It is also usual for the solicitors to defray certain other costs and fees on your behalf. These include the Stamp Duty, the rates for which are set down in the tax section of Chapter 1, and the estate agent's fees which, for a sole agency, usually amount to 1.5% of the sale price. Additionally, any purchase of land or property transaction has to be registered with HM Land Registry within three months and it is therefore normal for your solicitor to arrange this and to tack the charges on to their final account, by reference to the land or property cost.

Charges for registering a purchase of land or property transaction with HM Land Registry:

£40 for transactions up to £40,000

£60 for transactions between £40,001 and £70,000

£100 for transactions between £70,001 and £100,000

£200 for transactions between £100,001 and £200,000

£300 for transactions between £200,001 and £500,000

£500 for transactions between £500,001 and £1m

£800 for transactions in excess of £1m

Chapter 5

DESIGN AND CONSTRUCTION OPTIONS

I do not flatter myself that this is the only book that you'll be reading about self-building and, indeed, I sincerely hope that you are looking and asking around for as much information as you can get. Discounting the late-night advice at the bar, over which one should be a trifle circumspect, there are a whole host of people out there ready and willing to help, and perhaps the best of these will be other self-builders. It's like a club, and if you come across another self-builder, I'd lay odds that you'll be welcomed within it and that you'll go home with your ears ringing with new-found knowledge. The people who work within the industry know this and reputations and company successes are built upon this premise. Read any brochure and you'll find that it spends as much, if not more, time, relating how happy their clients are as it does explaining just what it is they do. Read any of the monthly magazines, such as *Homebuilding & Renovating* or *Build It,* and you'll very quickly realise that, business though it is and industry though it is, it is predicated upon ordinary people realising their dreams.

So, the purpose of this chapter is to help you find your way through the minefield of conflicting advice, much of which, whilst true, has, nevertheless, a financial axe to grind:

- Who do you run with?
- Which company should you go to and should that be a package-deal company or an architectural practice?
- Should you be building in timber frame or should you build in brick-and-block?

- Why does construction of your new home have to be restricted to one method or another and why can't elements of each of the various methods be utilised where they are most applicable or most likely to enable you to achieve what you want in design terms?
- Should you think about dumping all of the advice, all of the companies, to make your own way forward?

These are the vital questions facing the self-builder who has already jumped the first hurdle of getting hold of a plot. And they are choices, which have to be made. In many ways the choices you make at this stage will colour the whole outcome of your self-build project so it's important that you understand the range of options and that you feel your way through to the eventual decision with as much information as possible. When you've read this book, when you've read all the magazines and brochures, when you've met and talked to the people you think you might like to deal with, stand back and think. Don't be rushed; don't be pushed into anything. Make sure that you're comfortable with what's on offer. Make sure that you're comfortable with the people who are offering it. Does it sit with what you're planning? Does it feel right? If you need more information or more time then take it and don't be hassled. Remember that to a successful company you're another client and that they don't stand or fall by your business alone. For you, however, this project is

Right: **The entrance hall provides the first clues as to the character of your new home.** © Potton

the project and it stands or falls by your decisions.

It is important that any professionals you engage should report back to you at specific intervals or stages. Planning a self-build project can be very worrying, and you will want to know how things are getting on. That doesn't mean that you should necessarily ring your architect or the package-deal company representative every evening, but it certainly is appropriate for them to let you know just how things are progressing on a regular basis. Keep in contact and don't be afraid to ask what's happening – after all you're the one paying for everything.

Reading the self-build literature, one could be forgiven for believing that there is a battle raging between brick-and-block and timber frame and that most self-builders choose the timber frame option for their new homes. In fact only about a quarter of self-builders choose the timber frame route in the United Kingdom as a whole, which is substantially

In many ways the choices you make at this stage will colour the whole outcome of your self-build project ...

more than the national average for the house-building sector where, in 2002, timber frame accounted for around 15% of the market. In Scotland, timber frame is far more prevalent and gets up beyond 70%, wherea in Northern Ireland, brick-and-block is once again the dominant approach.

How do you square this with the heavy promotion of the timber frame option in much of what you'll read about self-building? In part, it's because of the historical fact that it was, until relatively recently, quite difficult to build a timber-frame house without using the services of a package-deal company or timber frame manufacturer whilst at the same time there was, and is, nothing like the imperative to use a package-deal company for brick-and-block construction. In part, also, it's because all of the many timber frame package-deal companies have to compete for that small section of the market that's available to them and, in order to do this, they have

to keep their profiles up. That said, it does not mean that there aren't package-deal companies that either concentrate or specialise in brick-and-block forms of construction, because there are, and some of them have been going strong for many years.

Despite the differing claims, most of the reputable package-deal companies do not go out of their way to promote or denigrate either main method of construction. It's generally accepted that clients can be put off by too much negative campaigning and in any event, most of the chaps who have been in the industry for some time know full well that, on the whole, the level of advice from all sides is good. Most of them meet their competitors at exhibitions on a regular basis, staying in the same hotels, eating and drinking, sometimes to excess, with each other. The successful ones are far too busy running their businesses to spend too much time running down their 'friends'. Conflict, however, makes good media copy and that's where the blame for any contrived argument rests.

The fact is that there is no real argument about which method is best and the reality is that both methods are equally valid ways of achieving your new home. Many people, in any case, don't even know or care about the construction of their home and a significant number who have antipathy towards timber frame, brought about by slanted media coverage, might be quite surprised to find that they already live in one. Now, before you all go off chuckling at these people, stop and think for a moment. The finished homes of either timber-frame or brick-and-block construction can, and mostly do, look exactly the same. A further blurring of the distinctions, as far as the lay person's living experience is concerned, comes about by the increasing use of dry lining for masonry constructed homes, which means that if you didn't see the house built, it's not that easy to know its make-up. In days gone by the estate agent would knowingly tap the walls, nod and studiously write down something on his memo board. If he did the same thing nowadays, the chances are he'd probably get things wrong.

In terms of time scales, from all of the case histories I have written up for previous editions of this book and magazines, the pattern is that a remarkably similar time is taken from turning the first sod to moving in. Of late, however, the switching back to timber frame by some of the high-volume developers has soaked up the manufacturing capacity with the result that lead times have increased to three and, in one case I came across, five months.

Now with the best will in the world nobody's groundworks will take that long. You can't or shouldn't order the frame until you get planning permission and Building Regulations approval in case the authorities require some change of design or specification. So either you get to ground-floor level and wait or you delay your start. If you do manage to iron out this particular problem and organise everything on site to the day then there's no doubt that the actual time taken on site in the construction process is quicker with timber frame. It is also less dependent on the weather and the fact that much of the construction process can be moved from the site to a controlled factory environment is probably a major reason for its success in Scottish and other northern climes.

As far as costs are concerned it's the similarity that's the startling fact if like is compared with like. Any cost movement either way has much more to do with the level of fitting out and the expectations brought about by the design itself, than it does with the method of construction. Bad ground or difficult foundations have the same consequences with either main method of construction, as will any requirement for expensive roof coverings or walling materials. The levels of thermal and sound insulation can vary but, again, nothing very much is unattainable with either method, if that is what your requirements are, and if they're thought out in advance. As I've said many times, informed choice is what self-building is all about and what I seek to do, in this chapter, is explore the options and point you on the road to discovery, rather than draw lines in the sand and form up on one side or the other.

So, let's look at some of the options available and evaluate each one.

Architects

When I first came into the self-build industry, many architects had virtually thrown away their right to any place within it through their arrogant denial of the self-builder's right to expression. Indeed, I often tell the story of the time I timorously suggested to one architect that perhaps a few changes might be advisable to a plan he'd drawn and the set square embedded itself in the door, behind which I had rapidly retreated! Happily architects like that are now slipping into a minority and the vision of the poor self-builder having to go in and see a crusty architect who demands as much respect and fear as the headmaster in his study is fast receding.

In no small way, this has to do with the advent of Associated Self-build Architects (ASBA) who entered upon the self-build stage like a breath of fresh air in 1992. Conceived by chartered architects Julian Owen and Adrian Spawforth, ASBA set out to show just how much the profession has to offer self-builders and to instil and promote, through a like-minded membership, the principles of architects working *for* and *with* their clients in order to realise their dreams. All ASBA architects are expected to fulfil certain basic conditions and, whilst this book is not a promotion vehicle for any one group or interest, those conditions do bear publication because their criteria could very well be applied to any architect, whether a member of that association or not, that you may be thinking of engaging.

All practices must have a registered architect taking responsibility for self-build projects. The title 'architect' can only be used by someone who has undergone a thorough training course lasting seven years, and passed a tough set of exams that ensure a base level of knowledge and experience has been achieved.

The practices themselves must be members of the Royal Institute of British Architects (RIBA), the Royal Incorporation of Architects in Scotland (RIAS) or the Royal Society of Ulster Architects (RSUA). At the moment ASBA are not represented in Eire but they have plans to be so, in which case their members will be affiliated to the Royal Institute of Architects in Ireland (RIAI). Each of these organisations operates a strict code of conduct laying down rules regarding impartiality and the need to provide a professional service. Some manufacturers or suppliers do offer incentives for consultants or companies to use their services but architects must be independent in the advice they offer, or declare any vested interest. ASBA itself does carry sponsorship but the architects themselves do not receive any incentives or commissions and their practices are not under any obligation to those sponsors. All ASBA architects must offer truly independent advice to their clients.

ASBA architects must have no more than six professional staff. The idea behind this is that smaller practices are able to offer the flexible service that is applicable to the self-builder and to tailor their fees to suit the situation. Quite often clients will find themselves dealing directly with the partner or director who runs the business. The larger architectural practices do find it difficult to offer a personal service and, generally, are only really interested in expensive commissions that will cover their considerable overheads.

Architects must carry professional indemnity insurance because of its great significance to the self-builder. Most banks and building societies will, in any case, insist on this before they will accept any payment or progress certificates.

ASBA architects also agree that they will provide an initial consultation free of charge and that they will provide as much free advice and assistance to self-builders as possible, recognising that the earlier advice is sought, the more likely the project is to succeed.

Finally, and perhaps most importantly, ASBA requires its members to have appropriate design skills and a general commitment to one-off house design as well as an approachable, unpretentious attitude to their work and to their clients.

Well, just a quick scan through those conditions shows that these guys are a long way away from my old set-square-chucking chum. Now, whilst that all may sound like a promotion pack for ASBA, it isn't meant to be, however it comes across. What I do hope to promote is that these ideals are the ones that should distinguish the sort of architects that you may wish to employ and I see nothing wrong in you taxing a prospective architect with questions

of a similar nature to those on this list.

The key stages of building an architect-designed house using the full services right through the project from beginning to end can be described in the following list. Some of these points are exclusive to ASBA architects but, again, there is no reason why they have to be and your search for a suitable architect could well start with an enquiry as to how much or how little of this they can or will provide, and for how much.

Finding a plot

Technically this isn't part of most architects' brief but, nevertheless, try asking a prospective architect whether they know of any land for sale in your area. Don't expect them to tell you about plots where they are already involved with another client, but there is always the possibility that they know of one where a client has had to drop out. Certainly if you do identify a plot then the architect should be called upon at the earliest possible stage to advise on its suitability.

Above: **Planting will provide shelter and soften the stark architectural outlines of this new home.** © Potton

Making an offer on the plot

We've gone into this in a fairly detailed manner in previous chapters but, nevertheless, your architect's input may well be beneficial. Hopefully the land has Outline planning consent and possibly your architect can help you negotiate the terms upon which you can buy, maybe subject to receipt of satisfactory Detailed planning consent. If there isn't any kind of consent and you're weighing up the pros and cons of whether to do anything with the land or whether or not planning is at all likely, then your architect may be able to advise.

Site analysis. This involves an assessment of your plot to check it for hidden problems and to highlight its features. A professional can tell an awful lot about a plot just by looking at it, seeing what sort of vegetation grows on it and what sort of ground conditions are likely. If the architect feels that a more thorough site investigation is necessary, including a soil investigation, then they're almost certain to be able to put you on to the right people to carry out this work for you.

Developing your brief

The architect will want to talk to you in fairly intimate detail about what you hope to achieve and just what features you want your new home to have. The headings under which this discussion will probably progress may be: budget analysis, accommodation requirements, room-by-room analysis of your proposed occupation and construction and materials preferences.

Sketch design

Using the brief prepared, the architect will draw up a sketch design illustrating the floor layouts together with elevations showing the external appearance of your new home, and any possible or suggested alternatives. This will be used to make sure that they are

JULIAN OWEN ASSOCIATES
ARCHITECTS

Job: Chelston, Coxmoor Rd
Sutton in Ashfield
Title: Site Plan
Date: May 03   *Scale:* 1:200
Drawing No: 605/06

on the right lines to provide you with what you're looking for and at the same time make sure that the developing house designs are likely to find favour with the planners. At this stage you should also make sure that the architect can verify that the project is capable of being completed within your budget.

Purchasing the plot

Again this is not strictly within the province of the architect but they will want to be involved and will certainly want to assist with advice, in any way they can.

Detailed design

From the sketch design, the architect will move on to the preparation of detailed plans that will be suitable for an application for planning permission. It is at

Above: **A design for a sloping site.** © Julian Owen

this stage that the all-important issues regarding window details, brick colours, roofing tiles, driveways and a myriad other topics, many of which we've already explored in other chapters, are decided. For most self-builders this stage, which is discussed in detail in the next chapter, is, perhaps, the most exciting.

Planning permission

The architect will submit the planning application and prosecute it with the authorities. He will discuss any matters arising from the application with the planning officers, conservation officers and highways authorities. If any amendments are suggested or required following meetings and/or letters, then the architect will discuss these with you before agreeing to them.

Building Regulations

The architect will prepare and submit plans for Building Regulations approval. These will include any necessary structural calculations and specifications describing the basic construction of your new home, a range of health and safety standards and energy conservation issues. If any special foundation details or designs are required as the result of either the soil investigation or in consequence of the application being made, then the architect will usually arrange for these to be carried out by other professionals on your behalf. The fees for these additional professionals will normally be charged to you direct as they are outside the architect's normal scope of activities and you will be concerned that any warranties and liabilities given will devolve directly to you.

Drawings and specification for tender

The architect will draw up a detailed specification to accompany the plans, in order to obtain tenders from suitable builders or contractors. Quotations can vary quite considerably (up to 100% in some cases!) so this is the stage at which an architect doing their job properly can save you considerable sums of money. A properly drawn-up specification can make all the difference and easily cover an architect's fees for the entire project.

Finding and appointing a contractor

The architect will suggest suitable contractors for the tender list and when the quotations are received, and the builder is chosen, he will assist in the preparation of the contract documents.

Monitoring the construction

The architect will visit the site and make spot checks to see that the construction is being carried out in accordance with the approved and contract drawings. If any form of 'certification' is required, as discussed in detail in Chapter 1, he will undertake this and liaise with the necessary lending institution.

Snagging

Once the building work is complete, you and your architect will inspect your new home together to check for defects. If there are any present or if work has not been completed to a satisfactory standard, your builder will be required to put this right prior to you accepting the property.

Handing over and moving in

This is what it's all been about and once your new home is completed it will be handed over in return for the final stage payment to the builder. Normally a retention of 2.5% is made out of the total tender price. This is withheld for a period of six months to ensure that the builder will put right anything that may go wrong and, once again, the architect may be involved in the final decision to release this money.

Where clashes can occur when working with an architect

I repeat that the list above details the full services that can be expected from an architect. You may or may not want to take advantage of all or any of this. What is important is that things start off correctly and in order to understand how that can and should happen, perhaps the best thing is to examine the areas where the relationship between client and architect is most likely to go wrong:

- **No meeting of minds.** Warning the self-builder against the architect who will insist on drawing what he thinks you should have rather than what you want to live in is easy. The slightly anarchic nature of most self-builders will recognise that danger immediately. More difficult to guard against, perhaps, is getting sucked into a glossy make-believe world that will spiral out of control or relevance to your budget. The architect whose principal practice is engaged in grandiose schemes for the redevelopment of town centres and has no experience of one-off housing will never really come down to your level of costing or expectations. Either what gets drawn will be way beyond your budget or you'll be made to feel that you're somehow trying to 'do things on the cheap'. Talk to your architect and don't just hear what you want to hear. Part of being a successful self-builder is the ability to sift and assimilate information to your own advantage.

- **Lack of detail in the original brief.** The success or failure of a design is in the original brief. Most architects have a fairly detailed and comprehensive checklist that they go through on the first meeting. Even so, if you've got a wish list of your own design requirements then make certain that your architect is aware of it and that each point is discussed. Planning and design are all about compromise and some things might have to give way. But they should only be lost as the result of a conscious decision rather than an oversight.

- **Failure to set the budget.** Stories abound of people who've spent thousands with architects having a house designed that could never be built within their budget. All the more incredible therefore that in equally large measure, one can still hear of contracts between self-builders and architects where the subject of money has never even been raised! If your architect won't talk about the budget and is either not capable, or not prepared, to constantly relate it to the plans that are being drawn, don't employ them. Move on to another one who will.

- **Rows about the costs.** You'd think that all architects would be aware of building costs – but you'd be very wrong. Whilst there is no doubt that the reputable ones amongst them, and especially those specialising in one-off self-builds, are *au fait* with current costs of labour

Above: **The symmetry of this home is maintained, despite the fact that the door is to one side.** © D&M

and materials, there is a significant minority who simply don't have a clue. As I've discussed in previous chapters, it is relatively easy to find out about rough build costs in various regions by reading the magazines and by reference to the build cost tables in the back. Make sure that the architect or designer you are talking to also understands those costs and, above all, make sure that they believe them. Some have become so used to unquestioning clients and the acceptance of extortionate costs that they have simply left reality. They don't often trespass into the self-build world but when they do, they cause much grief. Deal with the person or practice who is willing to talk prices from the very start of the project and who demonstrates a shared desire with you that whatever is drawn is built within budget.

• **Rows about fees.** If everything goes smoothly, the design is just what you want, and it is all built within budget, then it's highly unlikely that there'll be much of a row about fees. It's where the self-builder perceives that they have had a bad deal that rows about money abound. Certainly it can be argued that in some cases fees can have a disproportionate impact on an already stretched budget. Ten per cent might sound quite reasonable but it's worthwhile extrapolating that to an actual amount. There are architects who would consider any move to negotiate fees as an attempt at vulgarity but don't let that put you off finding out just what you're letting yourself in for and what you're getting for your money.

• **Slow responses and lack of competence.** It's all too easy to imagine that you're the only client that your architect has and if that's how you feel, then perhaps in some way that's a measure of success in your relationship. The facts are, however, that in all probability you're not and that anything that's done for you has to be done in proper order. Even so that's no excuse for things taking inordinately long times, particularly when delays can affect planning applications or building progress, and there are times when you should expect priority. Pressure of work is one thing, but if your architect is out of his depth, you need to know, rather than let things drift on. Flair and imagination in the original concept drawings might not be translated into an ability at other levels and it is important to ensure that design innovation is matched by the perhaps more pedestrian skills needed for working drawings and specifications.

• **Confusion over responsibilities and liabilities.** In law you cannot pass on the burden of a contract and unless there is a specific collateral arrangement, the self-builder using a design and build contractor might not have any comeback on the architect in the event of the builder ceasing to trade or behaving fraudulently. Wherever possible insist on a direct contract with the architect and make sure that you know just what responsibilities your architect has to you.

• **Jobs for the boys.** Part of the attraction in using an architect must be that they will be able to pass you on to, recommend or introduce you to other professionals you might need and builders with whom they've worked before. But it's a double-edged sword. A strong relationship between professionals can be beneficial but they should still outsource from time to time. Despite the fact that using someone they've known for a long time might make the architect's job easier, a longstanding relationship might get a little too cosy with little or no thought for checking whether more competitive prices are available. Bad ground conditions might well require the input of soil investigation companies and engineered solutions for the foundations. Complicated structures might need structural calculations. All of these have to be paid for by the self-builder, if for no other reason than to take advantage of their professional indemnity. However, none of them should be engaged without your prior knowledge and consent. The question also arises as to whether the average self-builder really needs the input of some professionals. Large projects will almost certainly require a full bill of quantities but if they're using a builder, the average self-build project probably doesn't.

• **Poor definition of service.** An architect's service is divided up into a number of disciplines and phases, all of which are readily understandable to those in the professions but few of which might be apparent to a self-builder. Sketch plans prepared at the earliest stages of an association, in order to establish a relationship, might not actually be capable of being built from in their presented form. Drawings that might be perfectly acceptable for the obtaining of planning permission might not be sufficient for the approval of Building Regulations. Drawings that are used to obtain Building Regulations might not be detailed enough for use as constructional or working drawings. Unless there is an overarching fee structure agreed, the charges for these various elements will have to be negotiated separately, particularly bearing in mind that copyright might make it difficult or impossible to split the responsibility between different practices or companies. Establish exactly how far your relationship with an architect is to go and discuss fees for every stage.

•**Lack of or insufficiency of professional indemnity.** This really shouldn't happen nowadays but, where it does, it's because of confusion over the very term 'architect' or as a result of misleading information. In order to practise in the UK, an architect has to be a member of the RIBA in England or the RIAS in Scotland but most importantly they have to be registered with the Architects' Registration Board (ARB). If they are not registered with that body then although they can, of course, work, they cannot call themselves an architect. It is a requirement of these bodies that all practising architects carry professional indemnity insurance cover of at least £250,000, but this might not be sufficient for some self-build projects. Always check that your architect is registered and carries the correct professional indemnity. For example, retired architects can use 'RIBA' after their names for social reasons but nobody can practise as an architect unless registered with the ARB.

• **Rows over extras.** In any self-build project, things will change as the building progresses. If these are requests after the event by the self-builder that require fresh drawings to be prepared, then they should be prepared to pay for them at a rate that is agreed on each and every occasion. If they are required because the drawings are unclear or ambiguous, then the self-builder should certainly question whether or not they should be considered as extras. By the way, watch out for the situation where an inspecting architect, perhaps one who has not been responsible for the preparation of the principal drawings or design, seeks to enhance their take from the job by offering to prepare drawings detailing changes or explanations on queries received during their visits. If they're necessary, great. If all that happens is that they arrive after the event then why bother?

• **Are they really 'architects'?** Problems can arise when a person represents themselves as an 'architect', either directly or indirectly and it turns out that they are nothing of the sort. Only an architect who has passed all the relevant exams after a long training period is entitled to call themselves by that title and that is something that is protected by law. Inspections during the construction period by an unqualified person are not recognised by the banks or building societies. If, therefore, you do decide to use the services of an unqualified designer, as discussed below, you should make absolutely certain that you do have an approved warranty scheme in place, as outlined in Chapter 1. None of which is meant to denigrate the service designers provide, but merely to ensure that you are aware of just what you're getting when you employ them and just how far their responsibilities and liabilities go.

If a dispute does arise with your architect, it goes without saying that one should attempt to settle any differences by amicable discussion. Having said that, it's not always that easy and it can get to the point where there's no other recourse but to bring in some outside agency to resolve the dispute.

The last resort is always the courts but that really is a last resort and it's unwise to consider them unless all other avenues have already been exhausted. RIBA have systems in place to settle disputes and the first of these is mediation. Here a mediator is appointed and it is their job to examine all the facts and to see if they can effect reconciliation. They usually do this by written representation and their decision is not binding on the parties unless they wish it to be. If agreement cannot be reached then the next step up the ladder is adjudication. This normally arises out of a contractual dispute or in consequence of the use of a JCT contract. The process varies and the adjudicator, appointed by RIBA, can choose to accept either written representation or oral submissions. They may also arrange site visits and their decision must be given within 28 days. The decision of the adjudicator is binding and it can only be overturned by arbitration or by the courts. If it is decided that the dispute has to go to arbitration then once again the arbitrator is appointed by RIBA. Effectively this is as far as one can go under their auspices. There is no time scale for the reaching of any decision but once it is made, it is binding and can only be overturned by the courts.

Make sure that you are comfortable with the architect or practice you engage for this, probably the most

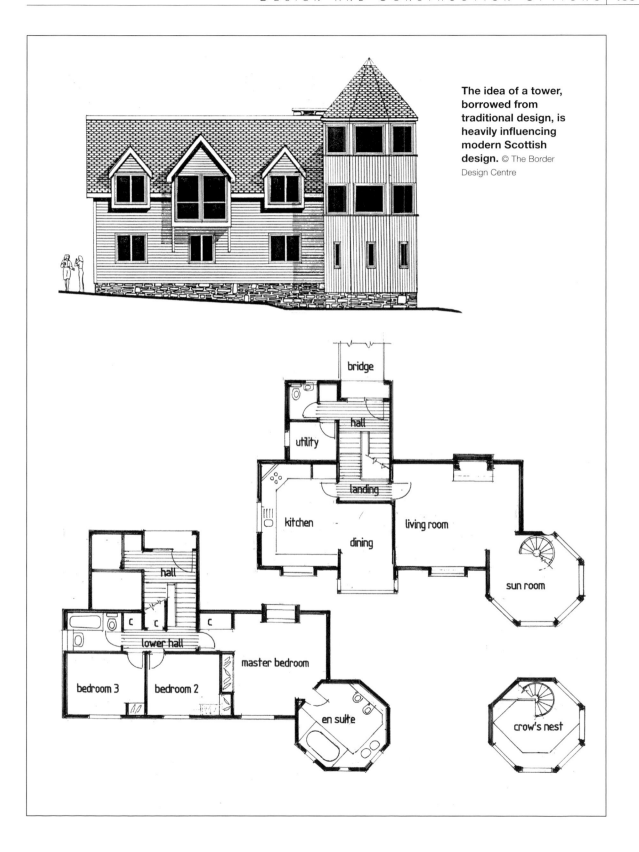

The idea of a tower, borrowed from traditional design, is heavily influencing modern Scottish design. © The Border Design Centre

important project of your life. Fortunately architects are becoming more accessible and approachable as market pressures force them out of their offices and into the real world where the client calls the shots. Their role should be that of enabler, transforming a series of wishes and aspirations into a finished new home. That doesn't mean that they shouldn't have a meaningful input of their own but it does mean that in the end it's their client's new home and it should reflect the decisions made by you, the self-builder.

Designers

It is easy to get the idea from publications that the great majority of individual homes are either built to architects' designs, or come from the package companies. If you go to the town hall and ask to see the planning register you will quickly discover that the overwhelming majority of applications are made by designers who are not architects, many of them working on a part-time basis in the evenings when they have finished their other jobs. Many of them are council Building Inspectors and the like who will only design for the next-door council's area, not the one that they work in. Some of them are listed in Yellow Pages, but all of them get most of their business by personal recommendation. If they have been providing this service for any length of time they are pretty good at it, although of course they might not have professional indemnity insurances. What they are very good at is gaining the confidence of clients, who happily put their trust in them.

Registered architects can get quite sniffy about designers, complaining that they haven't had the years of training that they've had and implying that they are, therefore, not as good at designing houses. Nonsense! Flair and imagination is something you're born with and no amount of training can produce it if the spark is simply not there.

Architectural technicians, or technologists as they now prefer to call themselves, have their own professional body, the British Institute of Architectural Technologists (BIAT). They publish lists of members who have achieved the approved levels of training, currently three years of supervised experience in addition to a first degree, resulting in a total of six years of training. There is a code of conduct, members are required to have professional indemnity insurance and the Institute's qualification is recognised and accepted by banks and building societies for the issuing of certificates and the release of stage payments. Architectural technologists are not principally designers although many of them are extremely competent in this field. Their main skills revolve around the technical aspects of house design, which is why many architectural practices also have technologists working within them.

The package-deal companies

In large part, package-deal companies evolved as a response to, and in consequence of, the lack of understanding previously given to self-builders by architects and builders' merchants. In the early 1970s there were no books such as this one, no *The New Home Plans Book* and no monthly magazines devoted to the ideals and the concept of self-building. If a self-builder was brave or lucky enough to get a design done for him by an architect or designer then when he went along to a builders' merchants he was in

Part of being a successful self-builder is the ability to sift and assimilate information to your own advantage.

Right: **This double-fronted home reduces the visual impact of being on a sloping site by having the forward gables partially hipped.** © Potton

Below: **A very large country home with a relatively simple footprint, broken up by complex and varying roof planes.** © D&M

for an even worse time. I can remember self-builders having to get proper printed headed paper, describing themselves as 'Private House Builders' before they could get any sort of an account and, even then, the credit limits were set so low as to render the account 'cash on delivery'.

The package-deal companies moved in to fill the gap in the market, many of them starting off as poor brethren offshoots of either timber companies or major block manufacturers. In the early days their plans, published in the form of their brochures, showed houses and bungalows of mind-boggling simplicity and an utter lack of imagination. But, as the industry grew, so did the aspirations of the self-builder and, inevitably, the package-deal companies shifted their positions to give the market what it wanted. For a while many companies held out and continued to run with the times by constantly updating their range of 'standard' designs. Inevitably the more successful ones soon came to the conclusion that they would have to become completely flexible in their approach to design. Either the 'standards' would have to be capable of alteration or they would have to be able to accommodate 'specials'.

Design is the key, of course, and the package-deal companies recognised that this was the bait with which they could attract their self-building clients. What the self-builder has to realise is that, although many of the package-deal companies advertise and promote themselves through their designs, in truth, their real business revolves around the supply and/or manufacture of kits and materials. They do all of this in a very highly polished and effective way, as any recipient of their literature can see and as any visitor to the exhibitions will note. The expertise they have gained over the years is apparent within the breadth of their information and there is no doubt that most, if not all of them, successfully fulfil the role of specialist designers and builders' merchants for the self-builder.

From all of this you may get the impression that the majority of self-builders now use the services of the various package-deal companies. In fact nothing could be further from the truth and there is much scratching of heads in the boardrooms of these companies as they agonise over why, and whether anything can be done about it. Perhaps the reason why only around 8% of self-builders do so lies with the mental makeup of the self-builders themselves. By opting not to conform, by choosing not to just go out and buy a developer's house, the self-builder steps, quite deliberately, outside the normal pattern of behaviour. Perhaps, for the vast majority, the desire to 'do their own thing' extends to not wanting to fit in with anyone else's concept of how things should be done and, almost, a determination not to seek the help of others. Perhaps as well, a great many self-builders are people from within the building industry itself, with skills in one or more of the trades involved and opinions which lead them down the 'go it alone' path. Be that as it may, for those who do choose to use a package-deal company, there is no doubt that the comfort they get from having a 'friend' or mentor to guide them through the process is an important factor in getting them beyond the dream stage and on to the realisation of their hopes.

An interesting by-line on all of this is that whilst many self-builders actually go on to do it all again, only a relatively small proportion choose to use the package-deal company the second and third time around, even if they have been completely happy with the service they received. Perhaps by then they fall into the same category and have the same opinions as the experienced self-builder who originally disdained the use of a package-deal company.

You cannot cherry pick the design ideas of the package-deal companies and then run off and build the house without using the main part of their service. The plans in their brochures, those they publish in *The New Home Plans Book,* and the ones they may prepare for you, are their copyright. That also extends to any design that could be considered to have been derived from one of their plans. This is why you may see the words 'or within the design concept' used in connection with their claim to copyright. If you commission a design study or feasibility study from a package-deal company and then, for any reason, you do not proceed with that company, you are almost certainly going to have to think in terms of a completely different design.

Most of the larger package-deal companies have an 'in-house' drawing office with staff architects, but others successfully employ a panel of outside architects or designers. There are arguments for and against both ways of working but, in truth, much of the competency of their drawing-office service relies on the abilities of either their field staff or the sales staff that you actually deal with. If you're dealing with a sales force who are demonstrating a chosen product and making notes of your specific and individual requirements and alterations then, in many cases, and in particular in those cases where the product can be demonstrated in the form of a show home, it is easy to get across what you're trying to achieve. There may well be an element of shoehorning your requirements into a format but in most cases the compromise is well thought out and realises everybody's ambitions. If the product, for that indeed is what it is, didn't appeal to you, then you wouldn't be there in the first place and the companies are well aware that, for some, the idea of living in a particular design can be akin to a new-found religion.

Working with the representative

Where a completely fresh design is proposed then, whether it is drawn 'in house' or by a panel architect, the translation of your requirements depends entirely on the representative you are dealing with. These individuals are a remarkable lot, with most of them having been in the industry for many years and many of them having either come into it as a result of building their own homes or having done so since they started. In many cases they will stand between you and the architect, with the architect preparing the initial drawings on the basis of, and as a direct result of, a brief prepared by that representative. Architects and designers who work outside the package-deal companies always express amazement that such a system can work. Clients of the package-deal companies themselves are often sceptical at first and sometimes feel that they should be visiting the offices of the company or that the drawing-office staff themselves should be visiting them, not realising that in the time taken for such a person to travel to and from them, their drawings could well be done. The amazing reality is that in the vast majority of cases the drawings that are produced from this arm's-length way of doing things conform, almost exactly, to the client's wishes. In almost all cases this is due to the company representative's skill at interpreting what the client wants, his ability to balance that with what he knows is achievable in design terms, his knowledge of the planning criteria and his ability to translate all of that into a brief for his drawing-office staff, with whom he is likely to have an uncanny rapport. If you add to that the fact that he, as much as you, will be concerned to make sure that the project remains on budget then you'll appreciate that he really has to draw a lot of strings together. Happily these guys usually do just that and, in most cases they do it jolly well.

The stages concerned with the planning and Building Regulations applications are also handled in two ways. Either the head office of the package-deal company makes the application with the local representative progress-chasing it, or else the local panel architect makes the application supported by the head office of the company. Once more, the suspicion is that a company based in one part of the country will not be able to properly process an application in a different part of the land. Nothing could actually be further from the truth. The package-deal companies have always set out to provide a service on a nationwide basis and their thought processes tend to consider the whole country in much the same terms as most think of their county. They are aware of regional variations in styles. They are aware of variations even within the larger regions and they have long since adapted to the provision of houses in styles that carry the local vernacular, even if, in some cases, the floor plans remain almost consistent.

Perhaps then, to the chagrin of many local architects, it is this very ability of the package-deal companies to look at architecture on a nationwide basis that enables them to understand fully the local and regional variations that make up the delightful diversification of styles and detail. Perhaps, also, this is demonstrated in the remarkably high success rate that most companies have with planning applications, although to be fair, the more discerning and successful companies will always choose which applications they make and ensure that they control, as far as is possible, the quality of those applications.

Many of the package-deal companies specialise in

Above: **Stone mullions and window surrounds add a feeling of quality to this home.** © D&M

Below: **An imposing suburban home that borrows from many periods and styles.** © D&M

timber frame construction of some sort and their literature and advertising is concerned to extol the virtues of their own particular way of building. Not all of the companies, however, are concerned with timber frame. Some concentrate exclusively on brick-and-block construction, whilst others, recognising that the service element of their operation is of the foremost interest, do not really mind which method of construction is employed as long as there remains an element of supply.

Historically the reason why there is such a preponderance of timber frame companies has been the fact that until fairly recently, the contention was that to build timber frame automatically meant that you would need to use a timber frame company. This idea came about because of the very real problems that the average self-builder would have had in the provision of the necessary design calculations for the frames. What's changed here is, in fact, a spin-off from the very success of the package-deal companies, in that they created a whole new genre of professionals working as timber engineers and designers and, inevitably, they found their way into the freelance market. Nowadays, it is fairly easy for architects to either design a timber-frame house themselves or else to draw one up and then get the relevant details and calculations checked out by other professionals. This has given impetus to the 'go-it-aloners' who want to 'stick build', of which more later.

But back to the package-deal companies. The services they offer, whether timber frame or brick-and-block, can be divided into yet more sub-categories. Some offer a design service based on standard designs. Some offer a service based on the variation or modification of standard designs within carefully defined parameters. Some offer a bespoke design service, with each house or bungalow being individually tailored to the client's and the site's dictates. Some offer a planning service whilst others will want to provide you with the plans for you to prosecute your own application.

The package-deal company will be concerned to supply a recognisable package deal of materials to the specification set out in their literature and confirmed to you in their quotations. All of them, therefore, will be concerned that you are able to put

their kits or packages together and, therefore, most of them will ensure this by helping you obtain or evaluate labour. None of them will go so far as to actually recommend any subcontractor or builder to you but, instead, they will introduce them and then stand by to ensure that you make the correct arrangements with them. Quite obviously, a recommendation, as such, would make them a party to the contract that you make with the builders and they will want to avoid that. Nevertheless, if the package-deal companies do introduce you to a builder or subcontractor, you can be pretty sure that they've vetted them in some way, in the knowledge that if things go right on site, their job is made all the easier. The package companies often provide advice, again with the same motives, on many other aspects of building a new home, from recommending the right people to design any special foundations that may be needed, through to helping with VAT claims. But, once again, you will find that the package-deal company will not be a party to any ensuing contract.

Of course, none of these reservations applies to the 'design and build' or 'turnkey' packages that are available, where the package-deal company is actually going to be responsible for the construction of the new house, probably also providing an NHBC warranty at the end. In essence these companies are really building companies who have adapted their business to be able to work and promote themselves within the self-build market, sometimes on a nationwide basis, but often, in a limited regional area. They really replace the builders of old who often provided a design and build service in their local areas but did not have the forums to promote themselves in the professional way that is possible for their successors. Oft-times these arrangements involve the self-builder in little or no work and take the project right up to completion, handover and moving in. Sometimes, however, the contract can be for the weathertight shell only and, in those cases, the self-builder becomes responsible for the fitting out and second fix trades.

The kits sold by package companies are specific to a particular house or bungalow, and the elements like the roof, walling panels, etc. have to be made weeks before they are delivered. For this reason companies expect to be paid a substantial deposit when an order is placed, and usually require the balance of the contract sum in advance of delivery of materials. These sums may represent a substantial percentage of the total build costs of the new home, and self-builders are naturally concerned that this arrangement is 100% safe. Before any order is signed the self-builder will undoubtedly have taken up references for the company or asked their bank to do so on their behalf. It is important, especially in light of the very different services and level of service that the companies provide, that the self-builder makes absolutely sure that they understand exactly what they're getting for their money. It's also important to know just when those monies will be required and to allow for this in any cashflow projections. Most of the larger and more reputable companies are either able to offer an insurance-backed bond scheme or else operate 'client accounts' into which the monies that are, quite naturally, required in advance of delivery are placed. The money then remains in the legal ownership of the

manufactured will meet the requirements of the Building Regulations as well as the relevant British Standards. However, if the work is to be inspected by the NHBC or by an architect, then it is possible for there to be some variation in their requirements and in these cases, unless it is already there, when accepting the quotation of the package-deal company, you should confirm that everything should also comply with their standards. If necessary write it on the acceptance or authorisation above your signature.

You pay for the services of a package-deal company. There is a fairly hefty mark-up on most materials and manufactured items, over and above the price that you would pay at the builders' merchants or if you went straight to a timber frame manufacturing company. But that would be an extremely unfair comparison, as that would exclude all of the other services that the package-deal companies provide, such as architectural services and help with labour. You don't get 'owt for nowt' in this world. If you feel that you need someone to hold your hand through all of the processes, or that you have a limited time that you can devote to your self-build and that such time would be better employed on site, rather than off site chasing materials, then that's the role the package-deal company fulfils. And the simple truth is that when they are involved, they make it happen.

All the methods of building new homes promoted by the major companies are equally valid and, in the end, the selection of method you employ comes down to personal choice.

Package-deal companies provide excellent services to thousands of self-builders, but in the natural way of things there are sometimes problems or disagreements. If you meet difficulties that cannot be resolved at a local level you should take pains to deal with them promptly, but in a way that demonstrates that you are a most reasonable client. Avoid letters that are written in anger. If appropriate, arrange to call in at the head office by appointment and explain the difficulty in a friendly but firm way to someone at director level. No company can afford to ignore a customer who has a five-figure contract, and you should be treated accordingly.

client until such time as a trustee of the account gives authority to pay it across to the company. This has advantages to the company because they can raise money against the sums in the client accounts that they operate. If you accept this arrangement, make sure you ask your solicitor or bank to check out the status of this client account, always make out cheques to the client account and not simply to the company, and if the money is going to stay in the client account for any length of time enquire who gets the interest. Finally, there is a legally implied assumption that the package-deal service and the goods supplied and/or

Timber frame

One of the most common misconceptions is that all timber-frame houses are alike. In fact, nothing could be further from the truth and there are many differing methods of construction which, for the sake of convenience, usually get lumped together under this heading. All the methods of building new homes promoted by the major companies are equally valid and, in the end, which method you select comes down to personal choice. In all probability the impetus for this choice has much more to do with the self-builder being comfortable with the people they're dealing with, the level of service they are providing and the cost they are providing it at, than it does with any construction method. Once the choice is made, however, it is usual for the customer to become a devotee of the construction method and the zeal with which they defend their choice has to be seen to be believed.

The word 'traditional' got bandied about and fought over, for some time, by the various competing interests. Proponents of building in brick and block claimed that theirs was the traditional way of building, in an attempt to brand timber frame as, somehow, 'new' and therefore untried. The timber frame exponents immediately hit back with the assertion that timber frame was an old and well-tested method of building, tracing its roots right back to the Middle Ages. In fact, and in the end, all of them realised that they were on a hiding to nothing and, whilst the brick and block enthusiasts now prefer to describe themselves as such, the timber frame interests now prefer to promote themselves as 'timber and brick'.

The principal method of building with timber frame is the open-panel system and when most people describe or think about timber frame, this is what they're talking about. It is the inner skin of a cavity wall that supports the roof and gives the building its structural strength. In a timber-frame house this is formed by panels that are usually pre-fabricated and then raised up into position and fixed together to form a rigid structure. The panels are manufactured from softwood timber framing over which a structural sheet material, such as plywood or Sterling board, is fixed, known as the sheathing. It is this boarding that gives the frame its lateral stability, known as racking. A vapour-permeable, but water-proof, breather membrane is then fixed to the outside face of this sheathing.

Of course it's a lot more complicated than that and if this were a technical manual I would move on to descriptions of noggings, cripple studs, headbinders et al. But it's not, so I won't. The insulation which fills the space between the studs is normally put in on site, once the house is weathertight and the electrical and plumbing carcassing have been done. The wall is then finished off to the interior, and a vapour barrier and the internal boarding trap the insulation. Standard 89mm x 39mm walling panels with high-performance mineral wool insulation gives a 'U' value of around 0.35. Increasing the studs to 140mm, allowing thicker insulation to be packed in, takes this down to 0.29.

It's perhaps worth explaining just what a 'U' value is as it will be referred to many more times throughout this book. A 'U' value is a measurement, in watts, of the heat flow through a square metre of any building material for every one degree Celsius temperature difference between the inside and the outside. The lower the figure, the more thermally efficient the material or element is. As you'll read in Chapter 6, 'U' values, as a method of showing compliance with the Building Regulations, are going to be largely replaced from April 2006. They remain, however, a useful way of comparing different materials and building methods and I, along with, I suspect, the rest of the building industry, will continue to use them for some time to come.

It is no longer strictly true to say that all of the insulation is between the studs as there are now insulated breather membranes on the market. But it still remains true that, with timber and brick cavity wall construction, the cavity is always left clear and is never filled or interrupted other than by fire stops and cavity barriers, which have to be inserted at certain points, as required by the regulations. Now, although most of the literature you'll pick up referring to timber and brick assumes the use of a cavity wall, there are instances where this is not so. It is possible that the outside leaf can be done away with altogether

A timber-frame panel

A typical timber-frame panel showing load-bearing studs and noggins. The racking, indicated by the dotted lines, will be provided by the sheathing board.

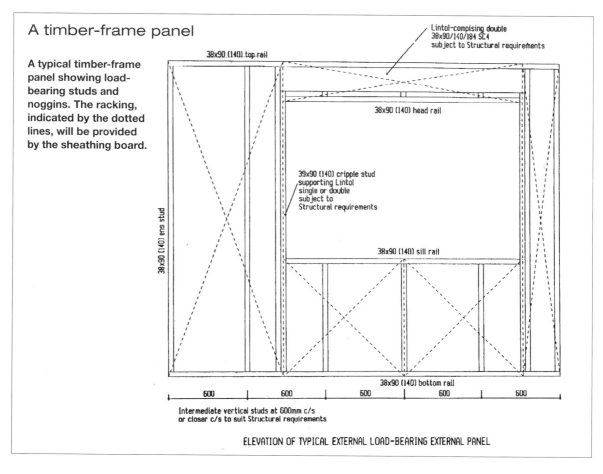

Lintol-compising double 38x90/140/184 SC4 subject to Structural requirements

38x90 (140) top rail

38x90 (140) head rail

39x90 (140) cripple stud supporting Lintol single or double subject to Structural requirements

38x90 (140) sill rail

38x90 (140) ens stud

38x90 (140) bottom rail

600   600   600   600   600

Intermediate vertical studs at 600mm c/s or closer c/s to suit Structural requirements

ELEVATION OF TYPICAL EXTERNAL LOAD-BEARING EXTERNAL PANEL

by the use of a vertical counter batten, creating a cavity, to which either expanded metal wire mesh is fixed for rendering or an external timber finish, such as shiplap boarding, can be fixed. Tile hanging can also be fixed against a single skin of timber frame. Again, the vertical batten is used to bring the horizontal battens away from the breather membrane, and the tiles are then hung from these battens in the normal way. Many of the houses from the Potton 'Heritage' range use this 'single leaf' construction and many others may use it in combination with timber and brick cavity wall construction to the ground floors. Custom Homes, Scandia-Hus and Potton are amongst those who use the open-panel system.

The Scandinavian timber-frame houses, whilst generically similar, utilise a slightly different form of timber framing, known as the closed-panel system, where the panels are designed to be 'airtight'. By the very nature of the beast this means that each panel

has to be manufactured in carefully controlled factory conditions with each one being assembled, complete with the insulation and vapour barrier installed, the internal boarding fixed and all windows (usually triple glazed) and door linings fitted. The vapour barrier is installed in such a way as to create a seal not only at any abutment to an adjoining panel but also at the roof level, where it is also tucked into and joined with the roof felting and boarding. Building a home that is insulated to these degrees, with achieved 'U' values for the walling of around 0.20 or less, means that thought has to be given to ventilation and it's normal for a mechanical ventilation, and heat recovery system to be employed. The arctic weather aside, there was another imperative which inspired the creation of these systems. Daylight is at a premium in northern climes and, quite simply, the more that could be done under controlled factory conditions and the less that needed to be done on

Above: **A substantial timber-frame house by Taylor Lane Ltd pictured just a few days after the erectors arrived on site. Once it's felted, battened and tiled it'll be all but weathertight.**

site the better. This feeds through into the ethos behind the level of fixtures and fittings included by most of the 'Hus' manufacturers and suppliers. Daylight and the need to husband as much sunlight into the house as possible are also reflected in many of the designs and layouts. In the early days of the marketing of Scandinavian houses, the designs, with their timber external cladding and 'A' frames, found little favour with planners conscious and protective of the 'local vernacular'. What the companies marketing these products managed to do, and to do successfully, was combine all of the design ideals and construction imperatives of these homes with the traditions of British architecture.

But there was and is a big drawback. If these panels are to be made up in the

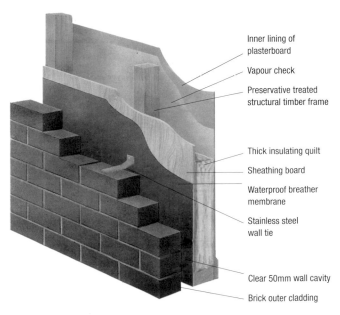

Inner lining of plasterboard

Vapour check

Preservative treated structural timber frame

Thick insulating quilt

Sheathing board

Waterproof breather membrane

Stainless steel wall tie

Clear 50mm wall cavity

Brick outer cladding

Above: **Schematic showing a section through a typical brick and timber wall.**

Aisle frame construction

Pioneered in this country by Potton Ltd, this form of construction puts the loadings on the massive internal framework rather than the external studs, allowing clear space as pictured below.

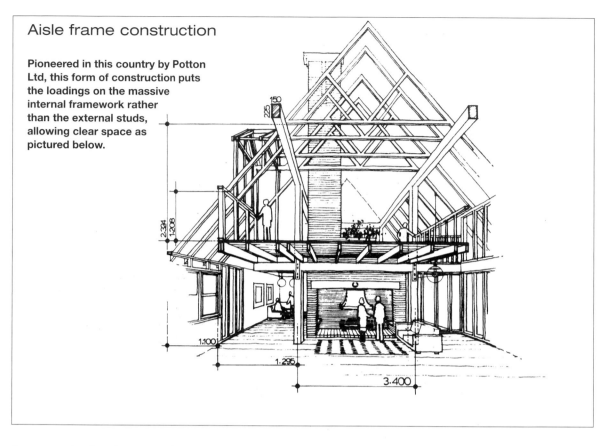

factory to be fitted together on site and provide finished walling then minds need to be made up as to where all of the electrical and other fittings are going to go at the very earliest design stage. Once the panel is made up there's no room for alteration. And what many companies found was that their British customers wanted to be able to change things around at the last moment. The original proponents of the closed-panel airtight system were Scandia-Hus and they battled against our collective indecision for decades until they finally gave up and switched to the open-panel system. The principal company operating this closed-panel system in the UK at present is the Swedish House Company.

Aisle-framed buildings are another form of timber-frame construction where the major loadings, instead of being borne solely by the walling panels, are taken by massive timber uprights supporting a skeleton frame. Potton are the major exponents of this system of building and many of their well-known designs

utilise it. Design apart, the essential features of these houses and, in particular, the walling panels follow the same patterns as for the open-panel systems described above.

Structural Insulated Panels (SIPs) comprise two outer skins of orientated strand or MDF board sandwiching a polystyrene or polyurethane centre. As their name suggests, they can be used in structural situations for both walling and roofing where they replace the traditional stud panels and the trusses. Either they can be delivered whole to the site and then have the window and door openings cut into them, or alternatively, and more usually, they are manufactured off site to specific requirements. Relatively few houses in the United Kingdom have actually been wholly built with these panels but they are, nevertheless, very useful in certain situations, especially where clear space is required within a roof void. If the manufacturers can get the costs down then they could even start to give traditional timber frame a run for its money.

Oak-framed housing

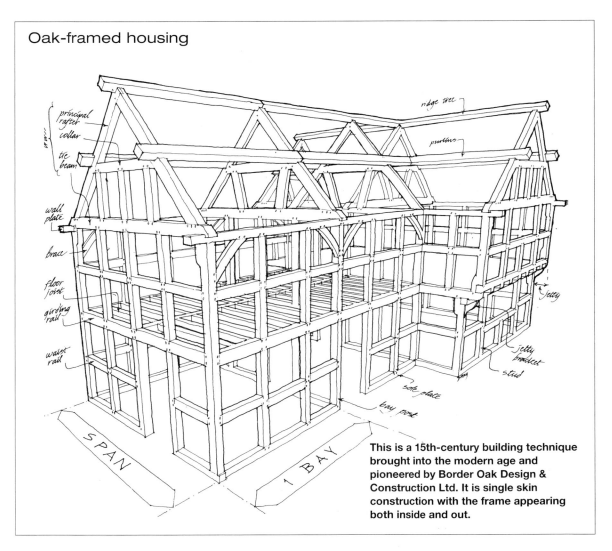

principal rafter
collar
tie beam
wall plate
brace
floor joist
girding rail
water rail
SPAN
1 BAY

ridge tree
purlins
jetty
jetty bracket
stud
sole plate
bay post

This is a 15th-century building technique brought into the modern age and pioneered by Border Oak Design & Construction Ltd. It is single skin construction with the frame appearing both inside and out.

Traditional oak-framed houses are, perhaps, so unique as to warrant consideration under a heading all of their own. This is fifteenth-century building technique brought into the modern age with a massive skeleton of heavy oak timbers forming the frame. The important difference, with the purest form of this system, is that this frame is visible internally and externally and that the building is of single skin construction. The spaces between the oak timbers on the external walls are filled in with urethane infill panels with galvanised perimeter trims and mesh reinforcement. A sophisticated system of trims, water bars, weather seals and drainage channels then ensures that the building meets the proper standards and can deal with the worst that the British climate

can provide. Hybrid forms using the oak frame as an internal leaf and then cladding it with timber, brick or even SIPs are also seen from time to time.

To sit in one of these oak houses is to go back in time. They are not cheap and those that sell them, buy them and live in them are embarking on a love affair. If you want a modern home with no cracks, creaks or strains then this is not for you. These are homes of character and each one will develop its own. To listen to Tim Crump of T. J. Crump OAK-WRIGHTS talking about his homes, and to see the way in which he lovingly strokes the wood and extols its virtues, is an experience in itself. Needless to say, each one has to be manufactured individually and is normally put together on a test run at the works

before each part is carefully marked and shipped out to site.

Although many of the timber frame companies will provide you with their services based on your own plans and designs, there is no doubt that for most of them, design is the baited hook. However, whether or not they get involved in the preparation of the plans and the planning process itself is immaterial to the fact that all of them will, if you accept their quotation, have to be involved with the preparation of the detailed and working drawings.

Developers and builders often take the timber frame supply and arrange their own erection but it is more usual for the self-builder to use the erection services provided by the company. The specification for the supply and erection will vary from company to company, according to the method of timber frame

they employ. Some companies can properly be described as 'kit' suppliers in that they supply a large proportion of the component parts for the houses, including second fix materials. Some would probably be best described as 'panel manufacturers', whilst others fall somewhere between these two stools. In many cases, but not always, the supply and fixing of windows and door frames will also be within the package-deal company's remit, as will the supply and fixing of the prefabricated roof trusses. Some companies will go on to felt and batten the roof, and fix the insulation material, the vapour check and the internal plasterboard but most times these are quoted as extras. The important thing, as ever, is that everyone, and especially you, knows just what you're getting and just what your contract with the timber frame company comprises. Almost certainly the

Left, above & right: **Transferring the main loads to a massive timber skeleton releases the walling systems from the task of supporting the roof, allowing greater design freedom and utilisation of the roof voids. It does, again, mean that these support timbers become visible, but, in turn, they become an essential part of the interior design ethos.** © Potton

external cladding will be down to you and in most cases this will take the form of an external leaf of the cavity wall, constructed in brick or stone although, in some cases, as I have previewed above, the external finish will be render or tile hanging.

In any consideration of timber frame, the same hoary old chestnuts keep coming up. Why should this book be different? It's not, except that I can answer those questions with no axe to grind and any answers given can be read in conjunction with all of the other choices facing you and which are outlined in this chapter.

I don't want this section to turn into a puff for any company in particular and the mention of any company name is a reflection of the help they have given in the preparation of this book as well as for *The New Home Plans Book*. In certain cases, it is also as a result of their having a unique product or service. All of the major timber frame companies working within the self-build industry, many of whom are household names, have a wealth of experience, which they can draw on to your benefit (see Further Information, page 456). All of them provide a slightly different service in terms of both design and specification. My task is to make you aware of the choices, as they apply, and to lead you into your further discoveries. Your job is to sift through their brochures and decide which ones you feel can best help you to express and realise your dreams of a new home. The only guidance I can give is that with the diversity of levels of service, you must make sure that, when comparing between any of them, you are comparing like with like.

Frequently asked questions about timber-frame construction

● **What is the main difference between a timber-and-brick house and a brick-and-block house?**

Visually very little, internally as well as externally. Structurally, the inner leaf of the cavity wall is built out of prefabricated, engineer-designed and insulated panels instead of blocks.

● **Can a timber-frame house be built quicker than a brick-and-block house?**

Yes, it can, although new large-block, thin-joint systems are coming on stream that claim to be as fast. However, the speed of the build has as much to do with the self-builder's ability to organise and finance things, both on and off site. If there's a long wait for the delivery of the frame after the groundworks, you'll lose any advantage.

● **Is a timber-frame house as strong as a brick-and-block house?**

Yes, just as strong and structurally just as sound. Each house has the benefit of computer-aided calculations to prove that the frame will not only support the structure and the roof, but also withstand windforce and all other exposure factors.

● **Will a timber-frame house last as long as a brick-and-block one?**

Of course it will. Some of the oldest houses in the land are timber framed and with modern technology and precision-engineered stress-graded timber, many modern houses will do as well.

● **Is a timber-frame house more susceptible to damp?**

Not at all. All of the building practices in this country have always been concerned to prevent the ingress of damp. With a timber and brick construction the cavity, which was first invented to prevent the transference of damp, is always maintained as a clear cavity. Leaking pipes or incorrectly fitted flashings and trays are not peculiar to timber frame and can cause just as much damage to other methods of construction.

● **What happens about fire and in the event of a major fire how does timber frame compare?**

Timber frame is as safe as any other form of construction, with death or injury no more likely to occur. Even if the frame did catch fire, much of its integral stability would be retained.

● **What about bad workmanship on site?**

What about it? Bad workmanship does not confine itself to any one method of building. However, with a large part of the construction and manufacture usually carried out under controlled factory conditions the chances of anything going wrong are reduced. In any event, the inspectors from the Building Control departments and the warranty inspectors will watch out to make sure that everything is done properly and I bet you, as a self-builder, will as well.

● **What about hanging things like cupboards on the walls?**

This isn't really a problem and in any event not one that's confined to timber and brick as many brick-and-block houses are now dry lined. As long as the proprietary fixings are used for normal loads such as kitchen cupboards, shelves, pictures and the like there will be no problem. For very heavy bookshelves, you might need to locate the studs and fix through to them or to fix a batten on the wall. Alternatively, if this problem really worries you, then you could always switch from plasterboard to a gypsum fibreboard such as Fermacel or, in specific locations, change to plywood.

● **Can you extend a timber-frame house?**

Of course you can. In fact in many instances extension is even easier than with a brick-and-block house and not half as messy. You do obviously need to check things out with either the original frame manufacturer or with a timber engineer. But there's nothing different about that and one would hope that whatever the method of construction is, professional advice is sought before anybody goes around hacking holes in a structure.

● **What levels of thermal insulation can one expect?**

How long is a piece of string? The fact is that the sky's almost the limit and it really is down to you to evaluate your own requirements and to weigh up the competing claims from the various manufacturing companies. The thermal insulating properties of timber and brick are well known and usually exceed the regulation requirements. Timber and brick houses heat up very quickly and their level of insulation means that they then stay warm for longer. In addition, with no 'cold spots', they are not prone to condensation.

● **What about sound transmission?**

Most sound from outside the house comes through the windows rather than the walls. Internal sound transmission is the biggest bugbear and there's no doubt that this is the one area where timber frame has to fight hard to beat brick-and-block. Internal sound transmission between rooms can be improved quite dramatically by making sure that there are no air gaps at the top or bottom of any partition. Filling the void in the wall with insulating or sound-deadening material can help, as can additional layers of plasterboard. Alternatively you could change from plasterboard to a gypsum fibreboard such as Fermacel. There are also laminated plasterboards, which sandwich single, double or triple layers of a rubberised material, pioneered by Noise Stop Systems. Sound transmission through floors can be alleviated by filling the void with mineral wool, by the use of specialist screeds or by laminated flooring panels, again made by Noise Stop Systems.

● **Do you have to use a package-deal company or timber frame manufacturer?**

Not nowadays. Most timber-frame houses in the UK are probably built with the aid of one of the companies, even if it's only for the manufacture of the panels rather than the full service. Stick building is, however, gaining in popularity and I'll go into that in the section on page 186, entitled 'Going it alone'.

● **Will a timber-frame house be as valuable as a brick-and-block house and will it be just as easy to get a mortgage or take out insurance?**

There's no difference at all.

● **Are there environmental benefits from building timber frame?**

Trees are the earth's lungs. They absorb and lock up carbon dioxide and they give out oxygen. Renewable forests are an undoubted benefit not only in the fight against global warming but also for their pure beauty and wildlife habitat. Thermally- and energy-efficient housing means less use of non-renewable fuel sources and the effects of that go far beyond the undoubted benefit to one's pocket. Although these qualities are not the sole province of timber-frame houses, they undoubtedly lead the way and their very existence has provided the spur for environmental consciousness in the housing sector.

Brick-and-block

Most new houses built in the UK are constructed in brick and block and, because of its universality, there doesn't seem to be the need to defend it or extol its virtues in the same way one has to with timber frame. Equally, this familiarity means that many a discussion will hinge on the advisability of its use and the foolhardiness of departing for another system. From what you've just read, you'll realise that these opinions are very often invalid and that brick and block is just one of the choices that you have to make, rather than being the only option. Nevertheless, it has to be admitted that most people feel themselves instinctively drawn to the idea of building in brick and block and for those that do so, the choice is justified with as much zeal as any proponent of another method can muster.

With a modern brick-and-block, cavity-wall construction, it is the inner leaf of the cavity wall that takes the load and provides the structural stability for the house or bungalow. Whilst this block may well provide part of the thermal insulation, it is the cavity, and the insulation that is built into it, that provides the most. It wasn't always thus. When the cavity wall first started to replace the solid wall it went on to gain full acceptance because of its undoubted ability to prevent damp from getting from the outside face of the wall across and to the inside. This remained its principal purpose for many years and, without dating myself too much, I can still remember the tooth sucking that went on when ideas of interrupting or even filling the cavity with insulation were first mooted. That the doubters were often proved right by a whole host of cowboy operators who blew all sorts of unsuitable material into cavities which had never been designed to be anything other than clear did nothing to stop the onward march of progress and the refinement of materials and techniques in the systems we have today.

I suppose our preoccupation with the costs of heating and running our homes really began with the Six-day War in the Middle East in June 1967. Prior to that, maybe a few souls really cared but, for the majority, the words 'thermal efficiency' had no real meaning or significance. In the early 1960s many brick-and-block houses were still being built with open cavities, common brick or breeze block internal wall leafs and large areas of window, often single glazed. It's not that we were any hardier in those days or that we enjoyed being cold or sitting in draughts; rather, it's the fact that heating costs were such an insignificant part of our income and expenditure. I can still remember the 'U1' block replacing the old breeze block and I can remember too the introduction of the 'modern' idea of insulating the roof, although, to be fair, that had much more to do with the prevention of mould. The ratchet tightened inexorably from then on with the miners' strikes of the 1970s, further troubles in the Middle East in the 1980s and our '90s concern over global warming. Brick-and-block-construction couldn't stand still in the face of all this and it had to move with the times and the ever-increasing and tighter regulations on thermal efficiency. It's also had to answer the challenge from timber frame and there is no doubt in my mind that the high levels of thermal insulation found in modern brick-and-block houses owe a lot to its having to keep pace with this competition. Be that as it may, the end result is that brick-and-block construction can now equal mainstream timber-frame construction in its provision of thermal efficiency and many houses built with this method go on to exceed the level of requirements.

In much the same way as with the timber frame heading, there are quite a few ways of going about constructing a brick and block cavity wall. Although there aren't the number of companies specialising or promoting one particular method or another, there are, nevertheless, a bewildering array of different blocks to choose from and a whole host of combinations that can be used to provide you with the wall that will conform to all of the regulations. Whether you're using a package-deal company or an architect, they'll be concerned to match your aspirations with the budget and the particular or peculiar requirements of either the design or its exposure. Some blocks can cost two or even three times more than others, and some of them, whilst seemingly appropriate may not actually be suitable for your particular situation.

To match the speed of timber-frame on-site construction, H+H Celcon introduced a system of light-weight thin joint blocks, together with flooring and even roofing panels known as Jamera. With these, highly engineered and square blocks are literally glued together, meaning that the building can proceed without waiting for courses to go off. Whilst thin joint blocks have found some favour, the system as a whole hasn't really taken off. Perhaps the problem is the inherent conservatism of the building industry. Perhaps asking bricklayers who had turned their backs on other methods of building to nevertheless retrain in a different form of blocklaying, which they perceive to be designed to speed up the process and therefore do them out of work, was always going to be difficult.

Below: **Careful planting will minimise the impact of all this turning and parking space.** © D&M

One of the most common ways of building is a cavity wall with an external brick, a 100mm cavity, full filled with mineral wool insulation and a 100mm lightweight block. This will have a 'U' value of 0.25, well below the current requirements and well able to satisfy what we expect the new regulations to impose. But this requires the cavity to be filled and there are many who still prefer to maintain the clear cavity. Indeed, in certain parts of the country with high weather-exposure ratings it is a requirement of the regulations. Changing the full fill cavity to a partially filled cavity with 50mm of rigid foam insulation maintains essentially the same 'U' value at virtually the same cost.

Some of the higher insulation blocks gain much of their property by the use of a lightweight aggregate trapping air. What they gain in thermal efficiency, they can often lose in crushing strength and if there

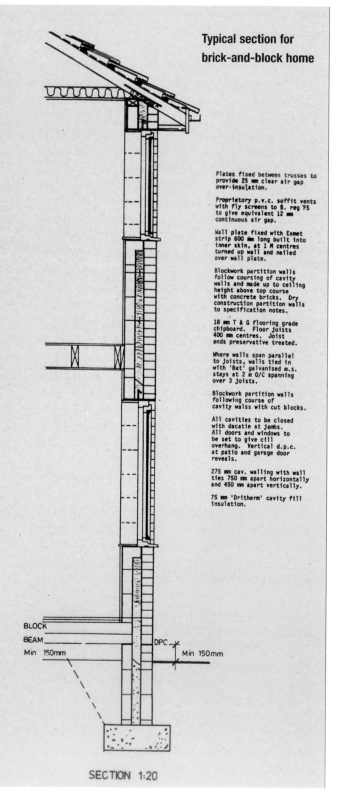

Typical section for brick-and-block home

Plates fixed between trusses to provide 25 mm clear air gap over-insulation.

Proprietory p.v.c. soffit vents with fly screens to B. reg F5 to give equivalent 12 mm continuous air gap.

Wall plate fixed with Exmet strip 600 mm long built into inner skin, at 1 M centres turned up wall and nailed over wall plate.

Blockwork partition walls follow coursing of cavity walls and made up to ceiling height above top course with concrete bricks. Dry construction partition walls to specification notes.

18 mm T & G flooring grade chipboard. Floor joists 400 mm centres. Joist ends preservative treated.

Where walls span parallel to joists, walls tied in with 'Bat' galvanised m.s. stays at 2 m O/C spanning over 3 joists.

Blockwork partition walls following course of cavity walss with cut blocks.

All cavities to be closed with dacatie at jambs. All doors and windows to be set to give cill overhang. Vertical d.p.c. at patio and garage door reveals.

275 mm cav. walling with wall ties 750 mm apart horizontally and 450 mm apart vertically.

75 mm 'Dritherm' cavity fill insulation.

BLOCK
BEAM
Min 150mm

DPC

Min 150mm

SECTION 1:20

are point loadings or even heavy floor loadings they can prove unsuitable for that situation. However, the companies have solved that problem by the introduction of special blocks with a high compressive strength together with reinforced lintel blocks. Alternatively, the simple introduction of a metal plate into the mortar bed beneath point loadings such as steel beams, in order to spread the load, will suffice.

One factor that you might like to consider is that, quite apart from the level of thermal insulation that is possible with a brick-and-block house, there is another, less well-known, but, nevertheless, obvious benefit. When a dense material is heated up, it takes a longer time to cool down. This is known as thermal mass. In a block-built house, when the heating goes off at night, the blockwork will retain the heat for longer. By contrast, in summer, the effects of a really hot day will be delayed as warm air coming into the house gets cooled by the walls. Well, that's the theory and one that is put forward by those wishing to persuade you to use brick and block. It is true, of course, but if you dry line the house instead of using a wet plaster, the effect is largely negated and if you're trying to heat up a house with cold walls, then it will take considerably longer.

Without a doubt the biggest innovation that's come about in the field of brick-and-block construction has been the introduction of solid first floors. Some time ago a large proportion of the claims the NHBC received related to failed ground-floor oversites where either the concrete and screed had cracked or the infill had failed and the whole floor had sunk. In large part this was occurring on sites where there was a slope that made it necessary for the fill material to be greater on one side or at one end of the building than it was at the other. The solution was normally to thicken up and reinforce the oversite slab which was then cast so as to be capable of suspension. It was an expensive option with several inherent problems; and it was extremely time consuming. Then the floor-beam manufacturers started to move in on the house-building market, having previously, largely, confined themselves to factories, office blocks and commercial buildings.

It very quickly became common practice for the ground floors of houses, whether timber frame or brick and block, to use floor beams, and the NHBC and Building Control departments of many of the local authorities actively encouraged this, especially in situations where there was the slightest risk of differential settlement. There was resistance at first, and there still is in some quarters, but gradually people began to realise that, although the costs of the flooring were slightly more than the equivalent in concrete, there were definite savings to be made in time and labour costs. A ground floor could be prepared and ready for the superstructure in under half the time taken for a consolidated, filled and concreted oversite and, moreover, the costs were a known rather than an indeterminate factor.

Before I go on I'd better just describe a floor beam and what is known as a 'beam-and-block floor'. The beams are shaped like railway lines in a 'T' section. They are laid, with the head of the 'T' downwards, from foundation wall to foundation wall, spaced one block apart. Blocks are then placed in the web between the beams to form a floor that is then brush grouted.

It wasn't long before people started to ask, 'If we can build the ground floors like this, why can't we do the same with the upper floors?' And, of course, the floor-beam manufacturers were only too happy to oblige. One of the main selling points with brick and block had always been the sense of solidity that it gives. Imagine the disappointment of many people when, having chosen a brick-and-block form of construction with the normal timber first floors, they discovered that they were going to have studwork or lightweight partitioning for the walls upstairs. Now with a beam-and-block first floor, most, if not all of the upper part partition walls can be in blockwork with all the advantages of sound insulation that was previously only achieved on the ground floor. There are other advantages. Solid first floors meant that transmission of sound between floors is almost eliminated and there is greater fire protection, especially where garages are integral, with rooms above them. Design & Materials, a package-deal company specialising in brick-and-block homes, say that up to 90% of their clients now choose a solid first-floor construction.

The finishing of the upper floor takes exactly the same form as it would for any of the ground floors. It can either be boarded on insulation panels, as a floating floor, or it can be screeded. The provision of services can cause some scratching of heads amongst the uninitiated but, in fact, they too find their way around in much the same way as they do for the ground floors. In addition there is a built-in 'service duct' between the bottom of the infill blocks and the bottom of each floor beam and this is increased by the battens that are put in place to hold the plasterboard ceiling on the underside.

Wet plaster is a choice that is unique to brick-and-block construction and there are many devotees of this 'hard' form of finishing off the internal walls. Without a doubt there are benefits in the very durability of hard plaster and doubtless, also, there are drawbacks in the length of time that such a finish takes to dry out and become ready for decoration. Timber-frame houses are finished off with a dry lining of plasterboard, or similar, which is then either taped and filled, or skim coated. The advantages of this system of wall finish are obvious and they will become even more obvious as the end of any self-build project approaches and the time for decorating and finally moving in gets even closer. There's no reason why brick-and-block houses can't enjoy the same benefits as their cousins by using the dry lining method. The only difference in the technique is that, instead of being fixed to the studs by nailing, the plasterboard, in a dry lined brick-and-block house, is usually fixed by either dabs of plaster or by the fixing of battens to the walls. Which is best, dry lining or wet plaster? Neither really. Both have their benefits and drawbacks and in the end, they cost about the same. Design & Materials report that about 80% of their clients choose dry lining. Whether that is more an indication of their promotion and sale of the product than it is of people's preferences, I don't know, but it has to be said that in today's world of deadlines, decorating, finishing and getting in become ever-more important.

As with timber-frame construction, there is a series of questions that constantly crops up and, as with the timber-frame section, I can answer each one without fear or favour (see page 186).

Frequently asked questions about brick-and-block construction

Do the foundations for a brick-and-block house have to be stronger?

The foundations for brick-and-block houses are almost always just the same as they are for timber-frame houses. Ground conditions are what dictates differing solutions to foundation problems although, in a very few cases, calculations can be used to prove a lighter structure which can then, for instance, find a bearing on an oversite.

Can the same level of thermal insulation be achieved?

Yes, and in fact many of the standard methods of brick-and-block construction are equal to or better than standard timber frame in terms of 'U' values.

Does brick-and-block construction have better sound insulation?

Generally, yes, especially within the house itself, and usually you don't have to do anything special to get good sound insulation. Low base notes have more power than higher-frequency sounds and solid mass absorbs them more easily. If you really want to make things soundproof then all of the products such as Fermacel or laminated plasterboards can just as easily be used.

Will it cost more to build in brick-and-block?

Not at all. The costs incurred by most self-builders, whether they build in timber frame or brick and block, are remarkably similar, although those building in brick and block are represented in greater numbers within the group that experience very low costs. It is design, external materials and the size and expectations of a house, rather than whether it's brick and block or brick and timber, which dictate its cost.

Will it be easier to find labour?

Not easier – no different really. Most labour knows all about building in brick and block but, as I've said, timber frame isn't that different in concept and if one uses a package-deal company, they'll undoubtedly help with the introduction of builders and subcontractors who understand their system.

Can it be extended?

Yes, of course it can, but always with advice and in accordance with the regulations. No building should have holes cut into it without proper thought and consideration of the consequences.

Will it take longer to build?

There's no doubt that building in brick and block usually takes longer and that this method of construction is much more susceptible to bad, and particularly wet, weather. Thin joint systems are able to rival timber frame with their speed of erection. For most self-builders, however, the time taken from starting on site to moving in is remarkably similar, whichever construction method is chosen.

Going it alone

A self-builder, by definition, is someone who has consciously decided to step outside the norm and to do their own thing. The very factors that go towards their character make-up mean that it is all the more likely that a significant proportion will eschew any 'help' which might seem to corral them into any semblance of conformity. Most self-builders choose to self-manage the site. But just how far should this quest for individuality be taken? Well, the answer to that comes down, once again, to our old friend, choice, but this time the choice has to be carefully thought out in relation to the self-builder's own abilities.

Above: **Space within the home does not always have to serve a purpose – sometimes it can exist purely for its own architectural merit.** © Photodisc

Going it alone doesn't mean that one should forgo all advice, whether given directly or indirectly. If you're a qualified architect or an extremely competent designer, then, by all means, why not do your own drawings and get your own planning permissions? If not, then to attempt to do so would be to enter a minefield. If you're a bricklayer then it makes sense to do all or most of the labour on your new home, assuming you've got the time. But, if you're in your mid-50s, have worked in an office all your life and never laid a brick, to do so would risk the success of your project and, probably your health as well.

In terms of design and the preparation of drawings, especially those for the later stages of planning and Building Regulations, I really believe that this is best left in the hands of a professional.

On the other hand, I don't see any reason why the self-builder can't be involved in the negotiations for what is, after all, their project and, as far as the Outline stages of planning are concerned, I often believe that the private individual can do a better job. Estate agents often charge £200 or more for 'handling' applications for Outline planning permission. In fact all that many of them do is take a photocopy of the Ordnance Survey (OS) sheet that they possess, fill out the forms that the local authority hand out, attach their client's cheque for the application fees and send it all off with, or without, a covering letter. Then they'll tell their clients the result some six to eight weeks later. If you turn forward to Chapter 8, you'll see that there's a lot more that can be

Going it alone doesn't mean that one should forgo all advice …

done to try to make sure that such an application is successful. Some of the lobbying I refer to can only really be done by the applicant as a council taxpayer and a potential voter. A planning officer can talk to a professional in a different way from that possible when talking directly to a member of the public. With a professional he can be quite rude or dismissive about a proposal, by hiding behind the detached relationship they both have to the application and the applicant. Faced with the applicant in person, or in writing, the answers given have to be couched in more conciliatory terms and any reasons for objections have to explained and expanded. Again, that's not to say that there aren't situations where a professional could be usefully employed, but what I'm trying to illustrate is that it isn't always so.

Employing an architect or designer to do your plans doesn't mean that you lose control of your project. If you turn back to the section in this chapter on architects you'll see that the measure of a good one is the ability to be able to translate *your* ideals, *your* requirements and *your* wishes. The same goes for anybody else or any other company. If you decide on an architect who doesn't produce initial or sketch drawings to your liking by the second or third attempt, then pay them off and move on to another choice. Do not just stick with something you're not comfortable with, just because you either don't want to admit you've made a mistake or in the vain hope that things will get better.

If a package-deal company is providing you with what you want, then there's no loss of sovereignty. If you're being forced into a straitjacket that you're not comfortable with then the only thing to do is to pull out and pull out quickly. Although this chapter is about making the choices and moving forward, that doesn't mean that, having made a decision, one shouldn't proceed through the next phases without keeping a constant enquiry going as to whether you've chosen the right route. An initial choice to run with a package-deal company may well commit you to payment for sketch drawings, design studies and/or feasibility studies. However, when that part of their service is completed, they normally won't go any further until you've committed yourself fully to them and signed up for their full package.

You do need to think carefully before going beyond those stages. Remember what I said earlier on, though, about not cherry picking. If you decide that you don't want to play with a package-deal company you cannot then run off and build the house they've designed for you – the designs remain their copyright.

All self-builders are alone to some extent whether or not they take on a mentor. The self-builder who gives the whole job over to an architect who then goes on to employ a builder still can't get away from the fact that at some stage the choices are down to him. That is, unless he's prepared to move in and only then discover that everything's just as wrong as if he'd gone out and bought a developer's house in the first place. The self-builder who uses a package-deal or timber frame company will find himself alone to some extent when it comes down to sourcing the materials that aren't included in the package.

If you're building in brick and block then the choice has always been there to 'paddle your own canoe' and source the materials from a builders' merchant, and that's just what the majority of self-builders do. What has changed over the last few years has been the attitude of the builders' merchants and the fact that the ordinary mortal rather than just the initiated can now expect all the help and advice necessary from them. If you're building in timber frame then, again, many of the merchants will arrange your frame purchase in just the same way as they always would have done with, say, an order for trusses. And, if you don't want to use a frame manufacturer then, as I've prefaced earlier, there's always the option of stick building.

So what is stick building? Well, it's building the timber frame on site from piles of lumber and plywood rather than having it done for you in the factory. In fact it's the way most homes in the United States are built. But for a long time it was difficult in this country because timber is a difficult medium to prove and it needed specialised knowledge to calculate the loadings, windforce and thermal properties. And they simply weren't available. Then the very success of the package-deal and manufacturing companies in the timber frame industry gave rise to this whole new breed of professionals, able to provide services and advice on the design and construction of a timber-frame building. Architects can now draw on this expertise to design a timber-frame building that can be completely constructed on site. In Scotland a large proportion of buildings are now built in this way and the practice is growing in England and Wales. What are the advantages apart from the fulfilment of a desire to go it alone? Well, flexibility really. Flexibility of design in that even once the drawings have been done and work has started on site, design changes such as moving windows or internal walls can be accommodated, subject of course to their being structurally feasible and to the planners agreeing.

But there is another significant benefit. Building a timber-frame house on site from lumber delivered from a local merchant or timber yard is never going to be as quick as if the panels were delivered already made up for quick assembly. And that's the point, because it means that if finance is tight, or if it's not available in fairly front-loaded stages, the purchase of materials can more or less follow the progress on site, evening up the cashflow. You don't have to be anything other than a reasonable carpenter to do this but you do need to follow recognised procedures and you'll probably need help of some sort, either in a professional or a labouring capacity.

There are a few hardy souls who are self-builders in every sense of the word, taking on all or much of the labour, as well as the management of the project. They're the true 'go-it-aloners' and I take my hat off to them. For most of us living in the modern world, our self-build aspirations have to fit in with a job of work and that means that we have to divide our time between what the boss would consider an extra-curricular hobby and what to us is, possibly, the biggest financial undertaking of our lives. If you're going to be crawling into work late and falling asleep at your desk, then the chances are that the job that pays for the mortgage that pays for the house will fall away. And when that falls away so will your house. Most self-builders choose either to use a builder for all or part of the construction or to use subcontract labour for all or some of the trades and I'll cover that in later chapters.

If you do waive the use of any other labour on site to truly go it alone, make sure that you do know what you're taking on, that you do know what you're doing, and that you keep your mind open enough to recognise when you need to back off and seek help.

Alternative construction methods

If you go to the exhibitions or read the magazines, you'll see quite a bit about alternative methods of construction. Some of them are quite interesting. Some of them may have a big part to play in the future. But all of them are represented and featured because they are different and interesting and that doesn't always translate to them being the sensible option for most self-builders. Whenever you're faced with a salesman giving you their pitch about just how good their product is and why you should choose it, stop and think. They have their own financial agenda. They may well believe with absolute certainty in the product or method they're peddling. You may find it exciting. But is it right for you?

I've talked of the zeal with which people defend their choices. Make sure that your decisions are made for the right reasons. Question whether or not you're making your choice in an effort to be different or trendy, or whether it's for sound financial reasons or from deeply held beliefs. Popular as they are with the media, alternatively built houses form a tiny propor-tion of self-built homes. I know that straw is a renewable and cheaply available resource. I know that old tyres should be recycled. Combine the two with the tyres as the damp-proof course and the bales as a tightly packed walling system that can be ren-dered inside and out and you've no doubt got a very useful and interesting structure. Log cabins, and houses made from recycled telegraph poles, hemp and the like, do have their place in this world. But if you're ever going to be moving on you may just find that they're difficult to sell, difficult to mortgage or insure and frighten the living daylights out of the estate agents and surveyors asked to value or verify them.

I am not a dinosaur; within this book, I urge self-builders to push the boat out in design terms, and in

Above: **Putting the ICF blocks together is simple; the hard part is filling them with concrete.**

order to achieve that, I recognise that new ways of achieving such innovation must be employed. But looking back over my four decades in the building and property industry, I have the perspective of having seen many bright hopes fail to live up to expectations. I remember the solutions that solved the problems of the day only to come back and haunt future occupants with problems that nobody had ever foreseen.

Of late there have been some moves to import prefabricated concrete-panel-type homes from the continent. I wish the exponents well. But I'm old enough to remember the concrete-panel local-authority homes of the 1950s and '60s and the inter-locking concrete-panel bungalows that sprang up all over the countryside in the 1970s and '80s. They were a disaster. These new ones might not be and it's perhaps unfair to compare them with what went before. But people and surveyors will. And that's always going to be the problem.

These prefabricated concrete-panel systems have been very successful in basement construction. Now they are coming out of the ground, so to speak. The panels or sections, complete with the windows and external joinery, are manufactured by a company called Danilith with lightweight concrete as a hollow construction, linked together with a web of steel with applied insulation and ready-mortared brick slips. These are hoisted into position and fixed together. It's cost effective and it could very well perform a useful function over here in high-volume housing. But, for the self-builder, system building such as this does require some conformity of design. And that, to an individualist, is an anathema.

One method of building that's not really new, but which disappears from time to time and then resurfaces, is steel frame. Essentially what has gone before was not that different in concept from timber frame in that it simply replaced the timber studs with steel. It sounds good and those that have been built are really just as good as any timber frame, only arguably even more durable. But it's never really caught on. Perhaps it's the cost. Perhaps it's the design inflexibility. It's not easy to handle or to alter and it's perhaps best suited to long production runs.

But now comes a new concept, which once more borrows from the timber industry, only this time it's emulating the SIPs I've already talked about. Jablite have introduced a structural walling system called ThermaSteel, which is, basically, insulated panels of fire-retardant polystyrene bonded to a lightweight galvanised steel frame. These can be used for walls, partitions and roofs. They are so light that each panel can be carried by one man. They fit together in steel channels fixed to the oversite as a soleplate and can be built up to three storeys high. The 140mm thickness gives a 'U' value of 0.25 and the 190mm, 0.19. Maybe they'll catch on, although they may be, once again, better suited to high-volume housing than self-build.

Where steel frame might yet catch on to a better degree is in internal stud partitioning, mainly because of championing by the major plasterboard manufacturers. Here lightweight galvanised steel sections can be easily cut and fixed together by trained tradesmen. It's by no means taking the world by storm but it does have quite a few advantages over timber, especially since the almost universal adoption of screw fixing for plasterboard rather than nailing. But here is an illustration of the building industry's reluctance to change. I've seen this system demonstrated twice. The first time was at an open weekend where all of the benefits were eagerly soaked up by an audience of potential self-builders, leaving nobody anything other than convinced that this was the way forward. The second was at my local builders' merchants' branch at an open evening, where free wine, beer and nibbles were on hand. This time the audience were local builders and tradesmen. They drank the drink. They chatted and watched as the guys demonstrated the system and they all professed to have had a great evening. But nobody ordered on the night and, as far as I know, a year later, nobody yet has.

Another method of construction that has been around fairly consistently is the use of hollow polystyrene interlocking blocks or insulated concrete formwork (ICF), as it's called. These are assembled and then filled with poured concrete and reinforcement to create an insulated walling system. It sounds a great idea and the attractions are obvious, in that the self-builder can imagine assembling his own house to a large extent. But pouring large amounts of concrete into formwork is a skill all of its own and one that is more often found in motorway bridge construction than single building sites. It can go wrong. Voids can be left, reinforcement can move and, in the worst cases, the blocks can burst open during filling. I have no doubt that this system has merit and I used to believe that much of that lay in the construction of basements. But having heard of several cases where the tanking or waterproofing has failed, I find myself dubious once again. In any event with the polystyrene blocks costing a minimum of £28–30 per square metre before you've even positioned and filled them with concrete, where's the cost incentive? For the same money and without the hassle, you can have two skins of blockwork, or one skin of blocks plus one skin of bricks, fully laid.

If you want to go for alternative technology, then please examine your reasons. If, for you, self-building is all to do with pioneering, and pushing the frontiers of technology to the limits, then by all means go ahead. If it's about housing yourself and your family in the most cost-effective way and providing the very best in accommodation and facilities, then my advice is to stick to recognised, tried-and-tested construction methods. It doesn't mean that within those methods there won't be advances, because there always will be, and you should be aware of them, but what it does mean is that you should not expose your self-build to risk.

It's a common misconception that professionals within the building industry such as bank and building society managers and estate agents and surveyors are knowledgeable about building and alternative methods. They're not. Many of them don't know one end of a brick from the other and many limit their knowledge to the ordinary. A few have detailed knowledge of ancient or local ways of building but most simply do not have a clue. When they're faced with something out of the ordinary they pull away, downvalue it or put their clients off buying it. One day you might want to build again and you might need to sell your home quite quickly. If you're having to defend a decision you made years beforehand and your defence makes a potential purchaser jittery, especially when they're waving a surveyor's report at you, then you might regret your original choice.

Chapter 6

THE DESIGN AND SPECIFICATION OF YOUR NEW HOME

This chapter is about the design of your new home. Yet there is not a single explanatory drawing or sketch contained within it; nothing except a few pretty pictures to whet your appetite. Instead, what I want to do is to try to make you aware of the design influences that you can't control, those that you can and the cost implications involved.

I have done this by means of a series of headings and by posing questions for you to ask yourself before you commission a design.

I do have fairly strident views about design and architecture. I don't like the modern formatted designs that we see so often on estate developments and which so many self-builders seem to emulate. I don't like their conformity and I hate them even more when they seek individuality by the addition of vernacular or period 'features'. Yet I recognise that there are constraints put upon the self-builder by the need to not stray too far from public taste and planner's opinions, particularly in a street scene where some continuity of design is perhaps desirable. I don't like displaced architecture, where somebody or some company has latched on to a regional or national design and transported it elsewhere. The black and white East Anglian houses that suddenly find themselves stuck between rows of stone cottages or vice versa. Or the Spanish-style bungalow in an English village street. I like old buildings of architectural merit but I don't see why we must slavishly copy them. I fail to see why we can't sympathise with them instead and I don't see why ancient can't sit beside modern and why the mundane can't just be allowed to slip away. I love bungalow living – well, I would do at my age – but I hate bungalows that look like railway carriages. They don't have to, as I think I've proved with my last home.

Well, that's got that little rant off my chest. They're my views. You'll have yours. Your designers will have theirs. In the end what I want you to do is finish up with the home that you want to build, not what I, or anybody else, thinks you should live in. That's what self-building's all about: choice made from informed opinion.

By the way, it used to be said that it was the planning authorities who had the most influence on design. But in fact, as you'll read in many of the headings below, the Building Regulations are becoming increasingly involved in the design process.

I originally wanted to divide this chapter into three basic sections: the effect of the plot on the design, the esoteric bits concerning the regulations, and the straightforward concerning the spatial elements. In the end, the host of regulations meant that there was cross-pollination between so many of the headings that, whilst I've still tried to stick to my original concept, there has been some blurring around the edges.

The first questions you need to ask yourself are the personal ones:

Why are you doing this?

Examine your own motivation for self-building:

- Is this the culmination of a long-standing desire to create something permanent that you can be proud of and which will be there long after you are gone, or is this merely a step on the ladder to your eventual dream home?

- Are you doing this in order to have a home that fits your individual needs and your family's lifestyle, or are you more interested in the possible gains in equity that are there to be made? Much of the media would have us believe that the only reason why any of us self-build is to make money. Well, for a small proportion that's probably true. But for the majority it's more about getting what they want for what they've got and the fact that they make money on it is almost incidental.

- Is it all about more accommodation, particularly more bedrooms, or is it about quality?

- Is kerb appeal and instant attraction more important than having a home that grows upon you or opens up in unexpected ways when you walk through it?

How long will you be living in this new home?

- Are you planning to go out of the door feet first eventually in a wooden box or will you be planning your next move shortly after moving in? You may think that it's going to be for ever but the pattern of all our lifestyles suggests that, for many of us, five to seven years in one house is the most we'll manage.

- If you're going to be in the same house whilst you raise your children will you need to think ahead for their accommodation requirements and the maintenance of your own sanity?

- If you opt for all of this extra accommodation, what use will it have when the family has left home? Will it be an expensive albatross around your neck at a time when your income is shrinking?

- What about visitors? Do you have family or friends who will often want to visit and, if so, do you have to design around the ability to put them up in relative comfort?

- If you are planning to live in this home right through to old age, should you make adjustments to the design to accommodate the eventual need to sleep on the ground floor or the possibility of physical disability in later life?

- Could part of the building that provided semi-detached accommodation for noisy teenagers provide either a granny annex for you to move into or else could it be accommodation for a carer?

- Could you countenance moving into the granny flat and giving the main house to your children to avoid Inheritance Tax liability?

- What about running costs? If you're only going to live there for a short while then it probably doesn't make sense to spend large amounts of money in energy-saving devices that probably add nothing to the market value of the house. On the other hand, if you are still going to be living in this house when you're a pensioner then investment in energy/money-saving equipment at this time might be very welcome in the years to come.

- If it really is going to be your home for only a short while then you'll need to keep a check on resale values. The motto must be 'least in, most out' and you must think in terms of general attractiveness within the market, rather than any peculiar or individual requirements. Never forget that the market favours conformity. Certain features might 'wow' them but if the design goes too far out on a limb, they'll back off in droves. It doesn't mean you won't sell it. It does mean that it will take that little bit longer to find the right buyers for your home – the ones who share your own aspirations but haven't thought or dared to self-build.

Are you ready for compromise?

In the first chapter I talked about costs and the effect that certain design and material changes can have. Keep those in mind. In this chapter I further explore how design changes can influence the costs and in

Above and below: **Our continental friends may have the best weather, but why can't we share their design ideals?**

Chapter10, concerning the individual trades, I show how costs are built up for the example house and for the last two homes of my own. You need to understand that in all probability, nothing is going to stay exactly the same. The authorities might well insist on changes during both the planning and Building Regulations process. Further site information or unforeseen problems in the ground might stretch your budget or even dictate a design change. Your own aspirations might change. As your knowledge of building, design and materials increases you may well develop quite firm views over what is right or wrong for you and your new home, views and opinions of which, at the very start of the project, you had no inkling.

Maybe you're not prepared to compromise on the design, the size or the material choices. If so, could you look at things another way? Is it possible that you could think in terms of a design that could be built in stages or one that could evolve as future finances permit? Could you cheapen the specification in some ways in order to gain more space on the understanding that at some time in the future you could, say, strip that cheap kitchen out and put a better one in its place? Could you think in terms of managing subcontractors for all or some of the trades rather than paying the higher price for a builder? Could you undertake one or more of the trades yourself? I can't answer these questions for you, but I can prompt you to think about them and so many more.

Starting your design wish list

Unless one has experience of designing houses with both planning and Building Regulations in mind, it is certainly not a field for do-it-yourself. Virtually all those who build for themselves use the services of architects, designers or package-deal companies. That is not to say, however, that in many cases the original ideas and conceptions cannot be arrived at by you and presented as the starting point for the eventual design solution. There's nothing wrong in giving the person who's going to draw up your new home the pointers that will indeed make it *your* new home and not the product of someone else's ideals.

Take a trip around the area you're going to build in. Photograph houses or bungalows that you like. Photograph features and details that you see on buildings, old and new. By all means, do your own sketch designs. These can be freehand or line drawings. A good trick is to cut out squares and rectangles of your ideal room sizes and fit them together before drawing around them. Don't be shy. Whoever you eventually get to do your drawings won't laugh. Anybody worth their salt in the self-build world won't take offence – quite the opposite. They'll probably be pleased that you've taken the trouble to illustrate your requirements in a cogent form and that you've given them a starting point.

Buy a scrapbook and stick all of your photographs in it. Make notes and cut out features and pictures from the magazines that take your fancy. In a separate section, collect illustrations of things that you don't like and at the end of the book start pasting in pictures and details that you've gleaned from advertisements and the like. Study house plan books and the brochures of package-deal companies and make a note, either of particular plans that appeal to you, or of individual features. Have a look at *The New Home Plans Book* that I've referred to. Maybe, just maybe, there's a design in there that completely fits the bill, in which case perhaps the best thing to do is to contact the company or practice in question, with a view to doing business with them. What is more likely, though, is that you'll get design ideas from the various plans and that these will go into your scrapbook to be incorporated in your eventual, and entirely individual, design.

When you've arrived at your design criteria and translated these into a long, illustrated wish list, set it out, leaving the first line blank; then fill in this line with the number one criterion: your budget. Whatever design is produced, it must accord with your budget and whoever does the drawing for you must understand that whatever they draw must be capable of being built within it.

And then put it all on the back burner until you've found the land. For it's only once you've found the site for your new home that you really can start to think in detail about the design.

The plot

In the chapter dealing with the assessment of land I was concerned to investigate whether the land was suitable for any kind of construction and whether, therefore, it could be called a building plot at all. In this chapter, I want to explore further how various features of the plot can affect the design of your new home, rather than the viability of the plot itself.

The land itself is probably one of the most important factors in determining the cost of your new home, with the location of the plot being the first major design influence. Other than preparing your wish list, it does not make sense to think in too much detail about the design before the plot is chosen. Let your design evolve to suit the plot, rather than the other way around. Never go looking for a plot to suit a particular design; it is putting the cart before the horse.

The large greenfield site might seem as if it has no restrictions on design. On the other hand, planners will be concerned that any new dwelling should follow the local vernacular. None of which means that you necessarily have to follow outdated design ideals or use precisely the same materials. Imaginative designers or architects can often come up with solutions that empathise with traditional architecture without slavishly copying them. I don't want you to think that I'm against all buildings that copy what's gone before – I'm not. But I do think that we have to keep moving forward in design terms. Sometimes we make mistakes, as we did in the 1960s and '70s, but, in the end, if design ideals had never advanced, most of us would still be living in turf hovels. Remember that the great houses, the Victorian or Georgian mansions, the Regency terraces, were all once new dwellings and that when they were built, chances are that there were those who referred to them as that 'modern monstrosity'.

Infill plots are more likely to have to fit in with the street scene. Indeed, it simply wouldn't make sense to build something totally incongruous and you must always be aware of values and, in particular, ceiling values as discussed in Chapter 1. The exception to that would be where there is, say, a street of small bungalows, which everybody accepts are past their sell-by date and which will eventually all be coming down to be replaced by substantial houses. What you build might look incongruous for a while, dwarfing its neighbours. It might also be difficult to sell in the short term, in which case those hoping to move on quickly might be best advised to avoid such a situation.

Sloping sites

After ground conditions, it is the topography and the orientation of the land that are likely to have the greatest effect on the design of the house and everything around it. The fact of the matter is that land is scarce and the plots that are increasingly coming on to the market are the ones that got left behind in the past. Perhaps this was because of perceived difficulties in getting a reasonable design, maybe because of ground conditions, which we've already discussed, or perhaps simply because there were easier plots available. We can't be as fussy. Nor do we need to be.

For the lay person, looking at a site with a steep slope can be a daunting experience. But sloping sites are a unique opportunity. Adversity fires imagination. The very nature of these sites and the excitement that the design solutions create mean that the resulting dwellings become flagships for the flair and imagination of their architects. Here is the chance to create a home that has stepped outside the boring conformity that most developers and many self-builders seem locked into. It may be slightly more expensive. But there are ways of mitigating that and, if you're careful and follow a few simple guidelines, then the very uniqueness of the design will provide added value.

I've already stated that I don't believe that a slight slope, and by that I mean one that's no greater than ten degrees, adds very much to the overall costs, particularly if a cut-and-fill approach is used in tandem with a pre-cast concrete or beam-and-block floor. Cut and fill describes the process of carving out a level plinth on a sloping site in order to build a home that is essentially designed for use on a level site. Any spoil cut from the bank is reserved to be brought back to make up the levels on the lower edge. It virtually negates the need to send spoil away, which with tipping charges and Land Tax represents a huge saving. You will recall that in Chapter 1, I estimated that the only additional costs would arise from the need for more underbuilding and that this would be around £750 for the example house with a 70-square metre oversite.

On the other hand many sites have limitations on the overall ridge height and in some cases, even where the planners are not insisting on keeping things down, it might be decided that the house should 'sit into the land'. This will have cost implications. If we go back to our example house (see page 412), perhaps the cheapest way of achieving this would be to employ a retaining wall at the rear and halfway down each side of the building. As long as this wall was no higher than 1.2 metres it wouldn't need designing by an engineer and could be constructed in single-skin blockwork, thickened at the base with a brick facing. Such a wall, running down to nothing halfway down both gables, would add around £2,650 to the costs.

But what if that wasn't acceptable? Well, if the back end of the house was sunk into the ground by about a metre, then effectively the rear part of the house would have to be treated as if it were a basement. It wouldn't be a full basement, which is discussed later. But the rear wall, and a part of each gable end wall, would become retaining walls. They would have to be strengthened and most importantly they would have to be 'tanked' or made waterproof. Not only that, but quite a bit more spoil would have to be got rid of and, if that wasn't possible on site, then that factor alone would bump up the costs. I've done some figures, which appear in Chapter 12 and you can see that on our simple house this way of building would mean extra costs of around £4,300.

A sloping site may involve extra costs with drainage and sewers. If your site slopes down from a road in which the sewer is fairly shallow then you may have to think of using a pumped sewage system. This can add at least £2,000 to the drainage costs but having said that, there may be a corresponding saving due to the fact that the 50mm flexible pipe may well be cheaper to lay than conventional drains. Sloping down from the road may also mean having to install a drainage channel to prevent surface water from collecting around the base of the lower floor or finding its way into the garage.

Sites, which slope up from the road and sewer, may seem more attractive so far as drainage is concerned. But if the slope is too great then it might be necessary to install tumble bays within the manholes in order to slow off the fall so that the effluent can enter the sewer at a reasonable rate. Surface and rainwater are also a consideration. Sloping up from the road may at first seem to present fewer problems with surface water. But many local authorities will not allow surface water to go into the public sewers and many require that precautions be taken to ensure that it does not flow on to the road.

One way of building on steeply sloping land is to build out from it on a series of supporting stilts or columns. This removes the need to build extensive foundations on sloping ground and it negates the

Flair and imagination can release a potential and provide levels of accommodation and comfort far beyond that which many larger sites enjoy.

need for tanking. It also leaves the ground relatively untouched, allowing planting to take place over much more of the site. In certain situations it can be a cost-effective solution and there is no reason why it cannot be employed with multiple-level designs.

A sloping site often means that there is a view and one of the best ways to obtain the full advantage is to reverse the accommodation to bring the living areas to the top with the sleeping areas on the lower floors. The garage can be a complicating factor in all of this. If the road is at the higher level then the solution is for the garage to move with the rest of the reception accommodation. If the road is at the lower level then there might be no alternative but for it to remain. However, it is likely that in those circumstances the entrance accommodation will also have to share the lower floor. As I've already hinted, you need to be aware that for every potential buyer who is excited by the individuality of the design, there are many who cannot accept departure from the norm. The house-buying public is incredibly conservative. They expect a natural progression of rooms. It may not devalue your home in real terms but it will reduce the number of potential buyers and therefore lengthen the time it takes to sell.

Level changes within the home can be visually exciting and allow for the creation of architectural

space for its own sake rather than the merely functional. Rooms can be divided by level without the need for walling. Multiple levels will mean that, unless you have the space or the inclination to install a lift, you are always going to be excluding the physically impaired from ever buying your home so there is really no sense in compromising. Use stairs to advantage. Like space they do not have to be merely functional and can be architectural features in their own right.

All too often homes built on sloping sites fall into the trap of providing purely functional accommodation and pay little heed to the need to maintain a good visual impact. Sites that slope up from the road may well use the expedient of having the garage, entrance and utility accommodation on the lower floor. This can be boring especially if the remaining storeys then tower above with little or no break in regimented windows and walling. Try to break up the hard edges. Set garage doors back or beneath overhanging balconies to reduce their visual impact. Introduce doors as well as windows to upper floors and break up the front elevation by stepping parts back and introducing forward gable projections. If there's no overlooking, consider bolt-on balconies and also whether the ground has to be level at the front and whether stairs up one side to an entrance on the middle level might not look better.

Sites that slope away from the road suffer from being unable to advertise the full extent of their accommodation. If a five-bedroom house looks like a small bungalow from the road, potential buyers might be put off coming in and even if you do get them in, they might opt

Left: **The setting of a new home is just as important as the design.**
© Nigel Rigden

Above: **It makes sense to utilise the roof space wherever possible.** © Potton

for a property with more obvious kerb appeal. There is little you can do apart from positioning the home so that even the casual observer can see from the front that it extends downwards. Alternatively hint at additional accommodation by introducing roof lights, even if all they are illuminating is the unused loft space.

Sites with a slope from side to side are probably the easiest with which to gain kerb appeal and there is often scope to create mezzanine levels that are visible from the road. But even here care has to be taken with the garage if it is not to dominate the frontage. The garden, the driveway and pathways need special attention on a sloping site and I'll discuss these under those specific headings later on in this chapter.

In Chapter 2, I talked at length about brownfield land – land that had had a previous use – and about searching for infill plots, backland development plots and parts of people's gardens that could be split off as a building plot. Whilst these can be quite large plots, in the majority of cases they tend to be a bit on the small side. Don't be put off. As with sloping sites,

small sites present the self-builder with a chance to acquire plots that many others may have foolishly bypassed. Whilst some may baulk at the restrictions, others revel in the opportunities.

Flair and imagination can release a potential and provide levels of accommodation and comfort far beyond that which many larger sites enjoy. Inventive design can create homes that look as good as they feel to live in. Clever juxtapositioning or the highlighting of different elements can impart that all-important 'kerb appeal' and it is this that gives a property its value. Whatever the accommodation, if the property is not attractive from the road, few people will bother to stop and come in when you come to sell. Slim properties that are gable end on to the road are not always attractive, although this way of doing things does help to distance the property visually from its immediate neighbours. Cheer them up by introducing a gable projection or by hipping the front plane of the roof to draw the eye backwards. If there is a garage door, try to face this across the plot rather than allowing it to become the dominant architectural feature. If this is not possible consider recessing the garage door to drag it back from the focal point. Another way is to detach the garage and incorporate it with walls and attractive gates to create an enclosed courtyard or mews effect.

The tendency with a narrow site is to go for simple rectangular shapes that maximise the width coverage of the plot and go as deep as possible. This often works quite well, although care must be taken with the front or street elevation. On the other hand, if you are building close to boundaries, the absence of windows can actually restrict the number of rooms that this form makes available. Consider, therefore, staggering the design to allow for windows to look forwards or backwards.

On very narrow sites gaining space in the rooms of as little as 150mm can make a big difference. Many of the timber-frame structures do not rely on having an outside leaf to a cavity wall and can be built as single-skin structures. The external face can be rendered or clad with timber or tile hanging.

The entrance area of any building with a restricted width is going to make usage of the front section difficult, which is why many narrow designs try to have the main entrance on the side. If you cannot avoid the entrance being at the front, try to combine it with other rooms such as the dining room to create a living or great hall. This avoids wastage of precious available natural light. Wherever possible try to combine rooms so that they can borrow light from each other and think about the use of transom lights, 'sunpipes' or roof lights.

Within planning law there is an acceptable degree of 'overlooking and overshadowing'. The question comes with the interpretation of this. Some authorities have a rule whereby, at least to the rear of a property, no building shall go back far enough so as to cross a line drawn at 45 degrees out from the edge of next door's windows. Others have no such rule and judge each application separately. Balconies can be 'red rag to a bull' as far as both neighbours and planners are concerned and it is better to avoid them if there is any question of overlooking.

Most people will want to have a pathway down at least one side of the house, although this is not always possible. Strangely enough there are no hard-and-fast planning rules on building close to boundaries. Whilst some local authorities may have minimum requirements, most will consider each application on its own merits with the deciding factors being the appearance of the building and its impact on neighbours.

The Building Regulations are equally vague on this point. Quite obviously there has to be access for drains and services but if these can be accommodated at the front or if they can safely run under the oversite, then this is perfectly acceptable. Some authorities will not allow buildings to have guttering or downpipes overhanging a neighbour's land but as walls must be built centrally on a footing, this effectively means that the closest you can actually build a detached house to a boundary is 150mm. Suitable space for refuse bins must also be demonstrated. Where restrictions under the Building Regulations do come into play is with the fire regulations. These preclude an opening of glass or timber of greater than 1 square metre adjoining the boundary and limit openings 1 metre away to 5.6 square metres.

The Access to Neighbouring Land Act 1992 gives access, upon due serving of notice, for the purposes of maintenance only. It does not confer any right to enter upon land to build and those building close to a boundary may have to consider building overhand from scaffolding that is set up inside the building.

The planning and Building Regulations are largely silent about just how much of the site can be covered by the house, although many local authorities have, within their Development Plans or Framework policy documents, rules about just how much amenity space must be allowed for, together with stipulations on distances between windows of different houses. In my area the planners require a minimum area of 80 square metres' private amenity space for every detached house.

Building lines have fixed themselves into the mindsets of much of the population, which is a pity because, to a large extent, there is no such thing. For a brief period in the 1960s and '70s they were adhered to but planners soon began to realise that they were an invention of the recent past. If it is appropriate for the property to come forward to the edge of the footpath and this can be done without detrimentally affecting the neighbouring properties or interfering with the necessary visibility of adjoining driveways, then it may well be acceptable.

Most local authorities will want to see a minimum of two car parking spaces per property. There is usually no requirement for garaging and in some cases and with smaller properties the general requirements will be eased. In urban areas on-street parking is often acceptable. Generally speaking the busier the road the greater the requirements for off-street parking and turning will be. The Highways Agency and the local authority will assess each case on its individual merits with regard to visibility and safety. Where visibility splays are required on a narrow site, it might be necessary to come to a legal arrangement with adjoining owners. Where turning space is difficult to obtain, the use of a turntable can be considered.

Going up or down

With space at a premium it makes sense to go for as many floors as possible and occupation of the roof space is likely to prove the most cost-effective way of gaining floor area. Access is important. If a completely separate staircase area is planned it will take space from the lower floor. Try to keep all the stairs in the same well. Straight flights, all running in the same direction, take up the least space. Be aware that the landing must be at the full height section of any roof space and not at the point of the roof slope, unless it is possible to take a dormer out to accommodate it. Be aware also that with three floors, you will have to have self-closing fire doors and the staircase will have to be a contained area.

Going down and forming a basement is always going to be more expensive than going up, as is discussed in greater detail on page 222. Nevertheless, on a tight site it can make sense. If at all possible, and particularly where the rooms are going to be habitable rather than utility, try to give the rooms below some sort of natural light and ventilation. This can be achieved by high-level windows or by the use of light

wells. If the planners are sticky about the overall size of the building and are insisting that the basement area be considered within the total area, indicate the lower floor as void or storage and occupy it at a later date under Permitted Development Rights. On a narrow site with adjoining properties close by, you will have to take extreme care with the construction and choose methods that are likely to cause the least disturbance, including noise and vibration, to your neighbours. Take detailed photographs of the adjoining properties before work commences to avoid arguments over any ensuing damage.

If garden space is limited or is likely to be overlooked, consider the idea of an internal courtyard. This can be open to the elements or else form a central atrium to a glazed roof or light tower. Rooms that would otherwise not have light can then use this and obtain natural ventilation.

Some sites are restricted by the presence of sterile zones either side of services. This may tax the designer and many of the tips about design mentioned in relation to smaller sites may have to be brought into play. On the other hand although the physical limits of the building may be impaired, light may be freely available to all elevations, giving greater scope for innovation. If services can be diverted, then despite the cost, this may well be a worthwhile thing to consider. Tree Preservation Orders may also restrict a site. If you cannot negotiate to replace the trees, it may be possible to design a home around them. You will have to make sure that the trees are unaffected during and by the construction and it may be necessary to employ root barriers.

Building on a tight site is never easy. Space for the storage and mixing of materials is at a premium. Even more than on any other type of site, the programming and delivery of materials must be closely co-ordinated to their requirement and use. In some cases it might even be cost-effective to negotiate for materials to be stored off site so that you can continue to take advantage of full-load prices. In others there may be no alternative but to accept that materials will have to be purchased piecemeal. If you are building close to a boundary, hang sheeting from any scaffolding to minimise or avoid damage to adjoining property.

Energy efficiency

Well, that's the design influences of the land. Now we come to the complicated bit concerning, in the main, the energy efficiency of your new home and the effects on the design and specification of the various regulations.

Passive energy efficiency

If energy efficiency is high on your priority list, you need to make sure that your designer fully under-stands this, right from the word go. Many of the factors that can make a home more energy efficient are passive ones and they start, of course, with the site that you have chosen. The orientation should, if at all possible, be south facing, plus or minus 45 degrees, ideally with shelter from prevailing winds but without shading to the house. That said, plots are fairly hard to come by, even in the best of times, so, whilst this is an ideal, don't go passing up a site just because this can't be achieved.

Using the sun to heat your house saves energy and makes it more pleasant. You don't need to increase the window area but the more of them that can face south the better, although you may need external blinds to prevent overheating in the summer months. A con-servatory can certainly help with the saving of energy, but in certain areas, such as Conservation Areas, Areas of Outstanding Natural Beauty and the National Parks, the planners will have a lot to say about their use and just how they look. In other areas they may be quite amenable but even then may baulk at having them on the front of a house. Of course, some windows may have to face north to ensure good daylight in all rooms. Any gain from any of the above is known as passive solar heating and the most impor-tant thing about it is that it is free.

A compact plan, without 'extensions', minimises the external wall area, reduces heat losses and reduces the shading of other parts of the house. A bungalow will lose more heat than a three-storey house of the same floor area. Rooms that are used most should be on the south side to take advantage of any solar gain. For rooms that are used mostly in the mornings, such as kitchens and breakfast rooms, a south-east orientation will get the best benefit from the sun. If

possible halls, landings, staircases and less frequently occupied rooms such as bathrooms and utility rooms should go on the north side. That's the ideal of course, but when thinking about energy conservation, all of this has to fit in with the street scene and what the planners require. Additionally, there may be other factors that you may want to take into account such as the specific views from a window or windows. As ever, the conflicting requirements have to be brought into balance and that's the task facing you and your designers.

Energy conservation

Part 'L' of the Building Regulations sets out standards for building work in order to conserve fuel and power and to minimise heat loss – if you like, the active or mechanical side of energy efficiency.

We live in dynamic times as far as the Building Regulations are concerned in England and Wales and the Government has announced changes to both Parts 'L' and 'F' (ventilation and fuel conservation), to take effect from April 2006. These are necessary for the implementation of the 'Energy Performance of Buildings Directive', which all EU governments have signed up to, and will therefore spill over into other parts of the United Kingdom and the Republic of Ireland (Eire). It is estimated and hoped that the new regulations will save more than 1 million tonnes of carbon per annum by the year 2010 in England and Wales alone.

Standard Assessment Procedure, or SAP, is, and will remain, the Government's standard system for home energy rating. It estimates the space and hot-water heating costs per square metre of floor area of a house (based upon such factors as its size, heating system, ventilation characteristics and standard assumptions such as occupancy and heating pattern) and converts it into a rating from 1 to 100. The higher the number, the lower the energy consumption. An SAP calculation is a requirement under Part 'L' of the Building Regulations and it is necessary for one to be provided before a Completion Certificate is issued. See also page 204.

The revisions to Part 'L' to be implemented in April 2006 will set maximum carbon emissions for whole buildings and will, in many respects, be very similar

Above: **The greatest heat loss is always most likely to occur via the windows.** ©photodisc

Right: **The regulations concerning energy conservation are under almost constant review.**

to the carbon index method described overleaf. The Government maintains that this performance-based approach will offer designers the flexibility to choose solutions that best meet their needs, and that are cost effective and practical. That may well be so but the upshot of it all is going to be that the general public, having finally got to grips with the idea of 'U' values, will be faced with a new method of calculation which they cannot hope to fully understand and which can only be demonstrated by a new breed of professionals. A senior building inspector recently remarked to me that the new rules seem to have been written by scientists for scientists and that his inspectors will now have simply to accept information at its face value rather than ensuring that each element of the building complies in its own right.

Office of the
Deputy Prime Minister
Creating sustainable communities

The Building Act 1984
The Building Regulations 2000

Proposals for amending Part L of the Building Regulations and Implementing the Energy Performance of Buildings Directive

A consultation document
July 2004

The SAP scales will be revised to a scale of 1–100 where 100 will represent a zero energy cost. Dwellings that export energy, such as those that create a positive outflow of electricity to the grid, will be able to have a score of more than 100. Each element of the building's fabric will also have to conform to minimum 'U' values with an avoidance of thermal bridging plus certain levels of air tightness. This latter requirement, by the way, may conflict with the new requirements for adequate ventilation and it's not at all clear how the Government will square this circle. The design will be required to balance window sizes with orientation and the achievement of maximum solar gain. Extensions, by the way, will have to comply with Elemental 'U' values.

Since April 2005 all gas boilers have had to achieve a SEDBUCK rating of 'A' or 'B' (of which more later) and from January 2006 for new homes and April 2007 for older homes, the same will apply to all oil boilers. Certificates will have to be signed confirming that the heating and hot-water systems have been properly commissioned and all these details, together with all operating instructions, SAP ratings and the building's energy performance certificate must be available within a Home Information Pack. External lighting will have to meet set standards with a maximum power of 150W per luminaire and either sockets that can only be used with low-energy bulbs or a passive infrared (PIR) system that automatically turns them off after a short period.

The Government will not be prescribing the use of solar panels or other 'low and zero carbon' (LZC) technologies such as wind generators, heat pumps and wood-pellet stoves. However, the revisions to

Part 'L' compliance

Prior to April 2006 there were three basic methods of demonstrating compliance with Part 'L' of the Building Regulations and all of them had to show an SAP rating:

1. Elemental This laid down maximum permissible 'U' values for walls, roofs, floors and windows.

Table of 'U' values	Floors	Walls	Standard roofs	Sloping roofs	Windows	Flat roofs
England and Wales	0.25	0.35	0.16	0.20	2.0	0.25
Scotland (still applicable)	0.25	0.30	0.16	0.20	2.0	0.25

Metal-framed windows could have an average 'U' value of 2.2. There were also limits, within the regulations, to the area of windows and doors of 22.5% of the floor area but options to increase this by the use of high-performance glazing.

2. Target 'U' value This allowed you to calculate the average 'U' value for your design using a formula based on the outside area of your building and the floor area. So long as the average 'U' value achieved a target 'U' value, the building complied. There were also allowances made for more efficient heating systems and for orientating the house and glazing southwards. This method was slightly more complicated than the elemental method but allowed for greater flexibility in design. With both this and the elemental method, the requirements became more stringent if the SAP rating was less than 60 (a poor rating for new housing).

3. Carbon index method This provided the greatest flexibility of all three but it required extensive data on the construction, location and occupation of the dwelling including the proposed heating requirements. The principal requirement was that the design achieved a set SAP rating of between 80 and 85, depending on the floor area. So long as this score was met there were very few restrictions on the design.

Part 'L' will, it is hoped, raise performance standards to a level that will provide a strong incentive to designers, taken alongside the various grants available, to consider these systems.

Apart from the issue of boilers, it looks, for the moment, as if the Government has got cold feet over the idea of bringing existing dwellings or buildings below 1,000 square metres into these new rules. However, the fact that the lobby may, for the moment, have persuaded the Government to backtrack, in part, on their obligations under the European Energy Performance of Buildings Directive to bring in these, and other, changes does not mean that they won't surface again shortly. The Sustainable and Secure Buildings Act enables the Building Regulations to be used to improve the energy performance of existing dwellings and these powers could be used at any time when it is considered politically acceptable to do so.

The requirement under the Directive for all buildings that are built, sold or rented out to have a certificate detailing their energy performance, including a summary of just how that performance could be improved, is supposed to come into force in January 2006. However, it's not at all clear that there are enough trained professionals in place to carry out the necessary inspections and reports. It's possible, therefore, that these requirements may be delayed for up to three years. When they do come into force they will undoubtedly have a major effect on the whole process of property transactions and become a bargaining tool in the negotiations over price.

I would think that if you are going to specify anything about this subject to your designer you should understand that extra insulation, in all elements of the building, is going to give you the biggest payback for the least outlay. Think about asking that the 'U' value for the walling approaches as close to 0.2 as is possible. A loft with 250mm of insulation (100mm laid between the ceiling joists with 150mm laid across them) will achieve the required elemental 'U' value of 0.16. Rooms in the roof and dormer windows need careful attention to detail but can be insulated to a high standard. If you ever intend to occupy the roof void then you might like to consider the placing of the insulation so as to provide a warm roof instead of a cold roof. With a cold roof, the insulation follows the shape of the occupied rooms below, so leaving the loft outside the insulated area. The area between the insulation and the roof structure then needs to be adequately ventilated to avoid condensation. With a warm roof, the insulation is placed between and along the route of the rafters, under the tiles. Even though the loft is not heated it still finds itself within the insulated envelope. Condensation is therefore unlikely, so there is no need for ventilation, particularly since the advent of breathable membranes or roof underlays. Neither is inherently more or less efficient than the other so if you have no plans to occupy the roof, a cold roof will be perfectly suitable and will, by virtue of the fact that the area to cover is reduced, cost less to insulate.

Ground floors are much more difficult as far as heat-loss calculations are concerned, as there are so many different types of floors. Most houses employ a solid concrete oversite laid on consolidated hardcore. In order to achieve the required 'U' values for the flooring it is necessary to introduce some form of insulation, usually in the form of 100mm of rigid foam-type insulation. This can be laid in three different ways. The first one is that all of it can go beneath the concrete, separated from the hardcore by a sand-blinded membrane with a further membrane between it and the concrete. In which case it will also be necessary to introduce perimeter insulation, usually by means of 25mm rigid foam boarding. Many lay people gasp in disbelief at the thought of a solid slab of concrete resting on expanded foam, but all I can do is assure you that I have never heard of this creating a problem. The other way is to place all of the insulation above the oversite, beneath either a floating floor of chipboard or a sand and cement screeded floor. And finally it is possible to split the insulation and put, say, half beneath and half above.

Timber-suspended floors usually have the insulation beneath the decking either as rigid foam supported by battens nailed along the sides of the joists or as mineral wool supported by netting. Beam-and-block floors usually have all of their insulation, in the form of solid foam slabs, above the infill blocks, beneath a floating or screeded floor. However, some companies have now introduced a solid foam insulating infill block which can be laid between the beams and directly overlaid with a reinforced screed to give a 'U' value of 0.25.

If you are contemplating under-floor central heating then thought must be given to which system you are going to use and what form of flooring you are having. With a solid concrete or beam-and-block floor the pipes can run through or integral with the insulation layers beneath the screed or the chipboard decking. Alternatively they can be run through and within the screed itself – arguably the most efficient method. With a timber floor, either at ground floor or intermediate level, it is usually necessary to introduce pipe channels and baffle plates to spread the heat, beneath the decking. If different floor finishes are to be employed for different rooms in the home with, say, the lounge having a floating chipboard floor to receive carpets and the kitchen having a screeded floor to receive ceramic tiles, remember to draw this to the attention of the contractors so that the floor and cill levels are set at the correct height. A screeded floor might have an overall thickness of 165mm, whereas a floating floor might have a thickness of only 122mm.

System layout comparisons

Conventional Boiler System Layout

Combi System Layout

Conventional Boiler System Layout labels: Feed and Expansion Cistern; Cold Water Storage Cistern; Hot to Baths, Showers and Basins, etc.; Hot Water Cylinder; Motorised Valve; Programmer; Pump; Boiler; Room Thermostat; Hot to Basins and Appliances, etc.

Combi System Layout labels: Hot to Baths, Showers and Basins, etc.; Room Thermostat; TriStar Optima Gas Combi Boiler; Hot to Basins and Appliances, etc.

Heating your home and the hot water

Heating your home and the hot water have to be thought of at the design stage. The choice of boiler will have a significant impact on the energy rating of your new home, its SAP rating and ultimately, therefore, the design. The method of heat delivery and the type of hot-water system, whilst having to conform to certain regulations, do not have as great an impact on the design as such. Nevertheless, most self-builders will want to consider these at the design stage and the choices will be high on their wish lists.

It is the boiler, rather than the method of delivering the heat, that is the most important determining factor, after insulation, in the overall energy efficiency of the home. All boilers are given a rating according to their efficiency at converting fuel to heat and this is expressed in percentage terms. They are then listed in the SEDBUK (Seasonal Efficiency of Domestic Boilers in the UK) tables and categorised within various bands. Starting from the lowest permissible, Band 'D' boilers have a seasonal efficiency of 78–82%, Band 'C' 82–86%, Band 'B' 86–90% and Band 'A' 90% and upwards.

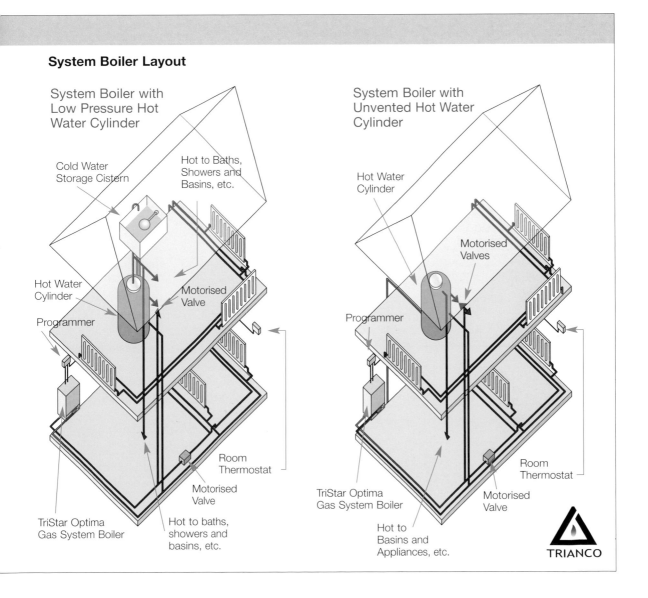

System Boiler Layout

System Boiler with Low Pressure Hot Water Cylinder

Cold Water Storage Cistern

Hot to Baths, Showers and Basins, etc.

Hot Water Cylinder

Motorised Valve

Programmer

Room Thermostat

Motorised Valve

TriStar Optima Gas System Boiler

Hot to baths, showers and basins, etc.

System Boiler with Unvented Hot Water Cylinder

Hot Water Cylinder

Motorised Valves

Programmer

Room Thermostat

TriStar Optima Gas System Boiler

Motorised Valve

Hot to Basins and Appliances, etc.

TRIANCO

As mentioned above, since April 2005 all new gas boilers must have an efficiency rating that puts them in Bands 'A' or 'B'. Oil-fired boilers get a little more time but they must still be in one of these top two bands by January 2006 for new homes and April 2007 for replacement boilers. Oh, and if you're wondering why I've even bothered to mention Bands 'D' and 'C', it's because, at the time of writing, these regulations haven't come into force in Scotland.

Many observers assume that these requirements necessarily mean that in future all boilers will be of the condensing type. That is not strictly true. Presumably, as long as the boiler is capable of satisfying the efficiency thresholds set out in the tables, it must comply. Trianco Redfyre Ltd, who opened a brand new factory in Sheffield in 2004, maintain that they are perfectly capable of producing a system boiler that could fit into Bands 'A' or 'B' and that they wouldn't need the two-year period of grace allowed for oil boilers; they were ready. Be that as it may, the assumption that all boilers must in future be of the condensing type is reinforced by leaflets and advice concerning difficulties with replacement boilers in multi-occupancy buildings. Where the installation of a condensing boiler would be uneconomical by virtue of the fact that the position of the new boiler would necessitate an extended flue or a pump to dispose of the condensate, or where any new position of the boiler would mean it having to be sited within living or sleeping accommodation, a 'non-condensing' boiler will be allowed. The Government feels, however, that this is never likely to exceed more than 15% of the total.

So what's all the fuss about and what's the difference? In a conventional boiler, the heat is transferred to the water via a heat exchanger, which is a bit like a water-filled cast-iron jacket around and above the burner. This is a tried and tested method but it does, nevertheless, waste a lot of heat in the form of exhaust gases. Condensing boilers in general have efficiency ratings of over 85%. Essentially they work in just the same way as an ordinary fan-flued boiler, except that they have a secondary heat exchanger which recovers and utilises the heat from the exhaust gases. In fact, the water passes through this 'second' heat exchanger first and then as the boiler gets going, preheated water

is therefore passing into the primary heat exchanger. Under certain conditions, when the return water temperature is low, the flue gases condense, releasing latent heat in the process, and it is from this that the boiler gets its name. The gases coming out of a conventional boiler's flue are very hot (250°C), but with a condensing boiler they are around 50–60°C, so the potential for savings are obvious. The condensate is mildly acidic and the heat exchangers have to be stainless steel rather than cast iron, so this type of boiler is generally more expensive at £1,200–1,500 rather than £600–800.

A friend of mine recently told me that up to 60% of new boilers being installed are now 'combi' or combination boilers, which, by the way, can exist in standard or condensing forms. No doubt that figure refers to the market as a whole as they are very popular with developers building higher-density and smaller dwellings. A combination boiler works in much the same way as the old 'Ascot' heaters did, in that they heat up the water as it passes through the boiler directly on its way to the tap. The obvious advantages are that there is a saving in pipework and space with no need for hot-water cylinders or any tanks in the loft. These advantages are slightly offset by the increased cost of the boiler over a conventional one – a gas-fired combi boiler will cost between £700 and £1,000 with an oil-fired one costing a further £200. Combi boilers require mains pressure of at least 1.2 bar with a flow rate capable of satisfying both the boiler and any cold-water outlets within the dwelling. They may also require a slight change of lifestyle on the part of the occupants in that if you are expecting to be able to run two baths and also have the ability to turn on a third tap or outlet at the same time, the boiler will not be able to cope. Some floor-standing appliances have a heat bank or hot-water store within the boiler. This super-hot water stays within the boiler with the cold water passing through it within a heat exchanger on its way to the taps. Flow rates of 18 litres a minute can be achieved by this method and one can draw off 180 litres of hot before it starts to cool. Recovery time is then nine to ten minutes. But once again it could not cope with a third outlet being operated simultaneously. Wall-mounted combi boilers cannot have this heat bank because of the weight and they can only usually achieve flow rates of around 16 litres per minute.

Heat pumps have recently surfaced again. The principle behind these is very like an electric refrigerator working in reverse. A loop of pipework, buried in the garden or a pond or stream, takes the latent heat from the ground and converts it into useable heat for the home. They are frighteningly expensive with figures of around £7,000 being mentioned after taking into account the various grants that are around (currently £1,200 from www.clear-skies.org plus an additional £500 in Northern Ireland only). Although they are in the 'fuel for free' category they still have running costs and I've heard of figures of around £1,000 per annum for the electricity needed to work them. So when you add in the capital costs, as with so many of these ideas, there really is little financial incentive at the moment. There might come a time when they have a proper place in self-building. Until then, without a reasonable payback time, they are really only for the dedicated planet saver. Those not planning to live for ever in the new home should also beware. Prospective purchasers and estate agents will probably not know what a heat pump is, they may well be put off by its unfamiliarity, and they will certainly be unwilling to pay any more for the house because of its installation.

Partially covered in all of the above and affecting both the design and its compliance with the regulations is the choice of fuel, although I appreciate that, for some, the choice may be limited. Mains gas is always going to be the fuel of choice. It is just about the cheapest to install and it is the cheapest to run. But mains gas is not available for many rural areas and there the principle choices boil down to either liquid petroleum gas (lpg) or oil.

Lpg has many of the advantages of gas. It can be used for the cooking and for gas coal or log-effect fires. The boilers don't cost very much more than mains gas boilers and, indeed, many can be converted with very little fuss. It doesn't smell and the boiler can therefore be sited within the kitchen or a utility room. But it is expensive to run, perhaps the most expensive over most cycles of all of the main fuel choices. It also needs a tank and the principal supply sources for these are the supply companies, who will install them for a fee of between £300 and £400. They are also unsightly, but if you opt to put them underground the costs escalate to around £1,000. The problem is that taking these subsidised tanks from the suppliers ties you to them and their tariffs.

Oil heating

Oil is the next most popular choice and the second cheapest to run. Oil boilers are efficient. I have a Trianco Redfyre Eurostar 50/90 condensing boiler and, on installation, the commissioning plumber remarked that he had measured its efficiency at 97%, despite it being listed as 92% in the SEDBUK tables. To my mind they are noisy and smelly. Although many people site them in their kitchen, I certainly wouldn't want to. I've had them in the utility room before but in my current house the boiler is in its own external cupboard on the end of the building.

The siting of oil or lpg tanks is the concern of the Building Regulations and full details of where you can put them and what you have to do to satisfy their requirements are listed in Chapter 9. As well as that, many faced with having to have oil-fired central heating but unable to contemplate having to cook with electricity might opt for a separate lpg or propane cylinder supply for the cooker, which, by the way, could also be employed for gas coal or log-effect fires. The Building Regulations also have something to say about where you can put these and the details are listed in the same section.

I'm not going to dwell on solid-fuel central heating because I don't really think it figures any more. There are, of course, those who want their coal-fired Aga/Rayburn or cooker boiler but even they usually only have it as a secondary heat source, maybe heating the water, relying on either an oil, gas or lpg boiler to deal with the central heating. The only real place for solid fuel in most modern self-builds is with the open fire or the wood-burning or multi-fuel stove. Otherwise it's medieval, dirty and labour intensive.

For many self-builders the principal choice, as far as central heating and hot water are concerned, is radiators vs under-floor central heating.

I have no doubt that the most cost-effective and efficient system for hot water and central heating is

Standard vs condensing boiler

Gas condensing boiler comparison

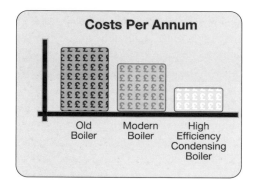

Costs Per Annum

Old Boiler

Modern Boiler

High Efficiency Condensing Boiler

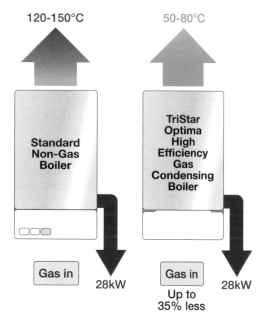

120-150°C

50-80°C

Standard Non-Gas Boiler

TriStar Optima High Efficiency Gas Condensing Boiler

Gas in   28kW

Gas in   28kW

Up to 35% less

TriStar Optima Wall-mounted Gas Condensing Boiler

1   Fan
2   Manual air valve
3   Boiler shell
4   Gas valve
5   Boiler water pressure sensor
6   Automatic air valver
7   Pump
8   Return temperature sensor
9   Safety valve
10 Pressure gauge
11 Expansion vessel
12 Drain tap
13 System filling valve
14 Domestic water pressure switch (CB ONLY)
15 Domestic water temperature sensor (CB ONLY)
16 Bypass
17 Delivery temperature sensor (CB ONLY)
18 Three-way valve
19 Condensation trap
20 Plate Heat Exchanger (CB ONLY)
21 Burner

A   Heating flow
B   Heating return
C   Domestic hot water (CB ONLY)
D   Domestic cold water inlet
G   Gas inlet

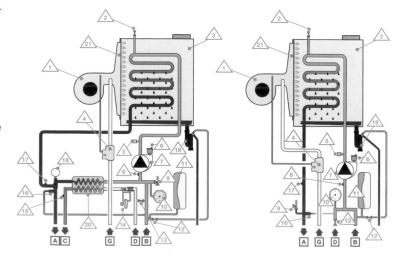

TRIANCO

the combination of a boiler and radiators with the efficiency of this partnership greatly increased by the addition of thermostatically controlled radiator valves (TRVs). These control each radiator and react to changes in temperature caused by sunshine or other extraneous factors. I have installed this kind of system in all of my homes up until the last one and have always been quite happy with both performance and installation costs, which I estimate at between £1,600 and £2,500 lower than under-floor central heating.

People get awfully worked up about the amount of wall space that radiators take up but, to my mind, this is offset by the reaction times and the inherent flexibility of the system. It's also somewhere to dry things and upstairs, in bedrooms, they are very rarely a problem. For those whose occupation of the dwelling is limited to a few short hours in the mornings and evenings this is the best option. It can come on shortly before you get up or arrive home from work and it will normally have got to temperature in under an hour.

Radiator systems work at relatively high tempera-

tures, 65–80°C, whilst under-floor heating systems typically work at temperatures as low as 45–55°C. Under-floor heating, can, therefore, combine with a condensing boiler to provide an extremely efficient system, especially if you are in the home all day and as long as your temperature expectations aren't too high. It does not suit those whose occupation is intermittent, however, as it is at its best when run on an almost continuous basis, perhaps with a night-time set-back a few degrees lower than the daytime settings.

I have under-floor central heating in my current home. I love it. I love the fact that all parts of the room are the same temperature with very few or no cold spots. But it is remarkably unresponsive. It takes at least three hours in colder weather to bring the lounge, admittedly one with a 5.5-metre vaulted ceiling, from the night-time temperature to the daytime one, just two degrees higher. If I had it on an on/off arrangement then it would take even longer. It was undoubtedly more expensive to install (probably at least £2,000) than if I'd gone for radiators and I know that

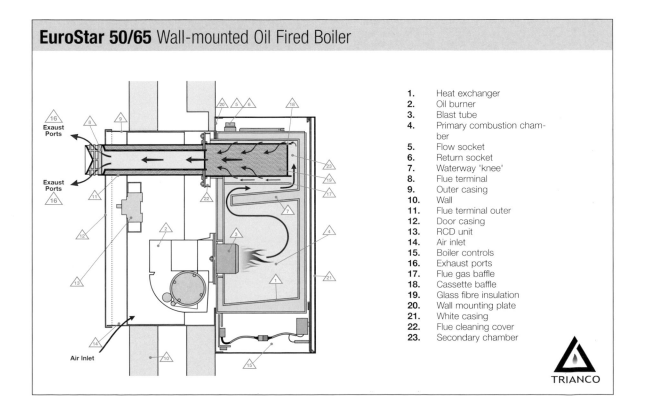

EuroStar 50/65 Wall-mounted Oil Fired Boiler

1. Heat exchanger
2. Oil burner
3. Blast tube
4. Primary combustion chamber
5. Flow socket
6. Return socket
7. Waterway 'knee'
8. Flue terminal
9. Outer casing
10. Wall
11. Flue terminal outer
12. Door casing
13. RCD unit
14. Air inlet
15. Boiler controls
16. Exhaust ports
17. Flue gas baffle
18. Cassette baffle
19. Glass fibre insulation
20. Wall mounting plate
21. White casing
22. Flue cleaning cover
23. Secondary chamber

TRIANCO

it's costing me a lot more to run – possibly 40% more.

One reason for that might be my own choice but I venture to suggest that, in this modern world, I'm not alone in expecting a shirtsleeve environment within the home. The brochures and manuals from the under-floor central-heating company refer to comfort level temperatures of 17°C in the kitchen, 15–17°C in the bedroom and 19–20°C as a sitting relaxed temperature in the lounge. I think that's too cold and I tend to want 22°C in the lounge, 18–20°C in the bedrooms and 20°C in the kitchen/dining/living room. On the other hand I'm not that out of kilter with the modern world as the NHBC minimum standards for central heating with an external temperature of -1°C are 21°C for the lounge and living areas, 18°C for bedrooms and the same for the kitchen. So these systems seem designed to achieve only or just below the bare minimum heating and if it costs you more to run, then 'that's your choice'. I'm sure they are efficient at those lower temperatures, as with a modern thermally efficient and insulated home they haven't got that much to do. And that was demonstrated when, in January, I had to have the heating off for a day in the kitchen, to allow for some re-grouting to dry naturally. The temperature didn't drop below 17.5°C during normal activities – fully half a degree above the manufacturer's suggested comfort level! Still, I'm pleased with the choice, the ambience it gives my home and the warmth of the mainly tiled floors.

And it's the popularity of those tiled floors that have perhaps had a lot to do with the corresponding popularity of under-floor central heating. Carpets went out of style for a bit, fuelled by fears about asthma and a quest for an easy-clean environment. But tiles are frightfully cold. Even with two large radiators in the kitchen of my house before this one, whilst the air temperature was warm, the cold from the floor would seep up and you wouldn't want to walk around in bare feet in the winter. There was another option, although I didn't think of it at the time – the combination of electric under-tile matting to take the chill off the floor. But I determined to have under-floor central heating in the next house.

By the way, with the pendulum swinging back in favour of carpets due, in part, to the noise problems associated with other forms of flooring, it's impor-

tant to realise that under-floor central heating is quite capable of working beneath them. The underlay has to have a relatively low tog rating and the number of pipe loops might have to be increased. That's why it's so important that when you're talking to a supplier or installer, you tell them which floor-covering medium you're having in each room.

Without doubt under-floor central heating is at its most efficient when installed within a solid screed. It can be used on a suspended timber floor with metal baffle plates and pipe clips but it loses much of its efficiency. Perhaps the best compromise therefore is to have under-floor central heating on ground and solid upper floors, and radiators with thermostatic valves on timber upper floors.

Warm-air heating

Warm-air heating is efficient but fiendishly bad to live with. However well you filter it, it distributes dust and it's practically lethal for those who suffer from asthma and can cause it in others who haven't previously suffered. I know, I've been there. It is very popular in America and I've been told about systems that purport to solve the problems by introducing humidity to the warm air. But I have no personal experience of it. Nor can I see any particular cost advantage. But I can, however, see that, once again, there might be market resistance to it and that it might affect the resale value of your home.

Electric heating has its place. The pros are undoubtedly the low cost of installation plus the facts that little or no maintenance is required and there is no need for flues, storage tanks or header tanks. All of which means that for the first ten years or so, despite high day-to-day running costs, it can keep pace with more conventional systems. The con is obviously those high running costs and the public perception of electricity as an expensive form of heating. But it does have distinct advantages in certain situations. Trianco Redfyre have a boiler called the Aztec Gold, which is ideal for garage or flat installation as well as conservatories as, with no flue or noxious gases, it can be sited anywhere. It can be used with radiators or with under-floor wet central heating and it is available in a 2kw or 4kw version. In a garage or outbuilding, where you only want hot water to say one tap, the modern version of the Ascot heater, now situated under the sink, is absolutely ideal. Ariston make a 2kw and 3kw model. And then there's under-floor electrical heating. This is usually in the form of a matting that can go under tiles or even carpet. The running costs are around 1p per hour per square metre, which makes it ideal for rooms like conservatories where the requirement is intermittent or for just warming up those cold tiled floors, as I've discussed.

The problem with electric heating for the whole house is that whilst over the long term the payback is on a par with other systems, if you ever come to sell, it's you and not your purchasers who have reaped that reward. All they're being left with is the legacy of the high running costs and the market resistance to this form of heating that will remain for many years to come.

Much of the older housing stock employs the traditional 'vented' system of hot-water supply and storage. This uses storage and header tanks in the loft to take up any expansion as an overflow and to top up and return water to the system. The header tank keeps the primary system, running through the boiler, the cylinder heat exchanger and the radiators, topped up. The storage tank keeps the secondary system, delivering hot water to the taps, topped up. For years the complaint was that this created an imbalance between the mains-pressure cold water and the hot water, which relied on the height of the header tank for any pressure at the tap or outlet.

These days, most new houses employ a sealed system where there is no requirement for tanks in the loft. Instead, the natural expansion that occurs when water is heated up is taken up by expansion vessels within the boiler and the hot-water storage cylinders, with safety valves venting to the outside in an unlikely emergency. Hot water stored under pressure is then delivered to the tap or outlet at mains pressure. This means that there is no need for expensive power showers as the hot- and cold-water pressures are evenly balanced.

Hot-water storage cylinders are also undergoing changes. Most are still the indirect type where the primary hot-water circuit passes from the boiler through a coil within the tank that heats up the main body of water within it. It is this secondary system of water that is then drawn off to the tap. A thermal store works almost in reverse. The primary circuit from the boiler heats up the main body of water within the tank. Cold, mains-pressure hot water passing through this super-heated body of water is then heated up on its way to the tap.

Electric showers have a fairly low flow rate and only heat the actual amount of water that is used. Nevertheless, if there is a store of hot water only yards away, then the cost of their purchase and installation may not be worthwhile. If you want a powerful shower then either use a sealed hot-water system or think of a power shower where the water is pumped. Of course these do use a lot more water and energy and they are not inexpensive. Perhaps in today's ethos of saving they are an expensive and unnecessary luxury.

Controlling the system

Good controls are essential to maximise the efficiency of any heating system and they are required by the Building Regulations. Most radiator systems employ TRVs in combination with a single room thermostat, usually situated in the hall, that switches the system off when a certain temperature is reached. Most decent under-floor central heating systems divide each room into a separate zone, controlled by its own adjustable room thermostat. All can be controlled by a programmer that turns the system on or off according to the time of day or night that you set it for. These programmers are becoming ever more sophisticated and can divide the week up so that you can, for example, differentiate between working days and the weekend. There are also programmers on the market that can sense the outside temperature and react to it by turning on the heating in anticipation of your previously planned heat requirements. And as I have mentioned, it is possible to have a night-time set-back control that, when and if the temperature in a particular or chosen room drops below a certain level, overrides the programmer and turns the heating on. The boiler will have its own thermal bypass and thermostat and it is always a good idea to have a frost stat that will override all controls and turn the system on if the temperature drops below a certain level.

Active solar power

This is as opposed to the passive, and therefore free, solar power I have discussed above. Setting out to harvest actively the natural heat of the sun and the question of just how far you go with your quest depends on how long you're going to be living in the new home. Be aware that many of the energy-saving devices and technologies have very high capital costs and that you might never recover these. We have already discussed heat pumps, or geothermal heating as it prefers to be known, but there are other methods of harvesting the heat from the sun and the energy from the elements.

The one that most people are familiar with, of course, is solar panels, usually used to heat the hot water. Claims of savings of 80% are frequently made but I'm more inclined to believe that it's probably close to half that figure in the most favourable circumstances and half as much again in most instances. Solar panels, in another demonstration of non-joined-up government, are distinctly unpopular with planning officers and a complete 'no no' in Conservation Areas. They also cost quite a bit, with a full array having a payback period of between 15 and 20 years, so if there's a chance that you might be moving on, it simply won't be worth it. Unless, as I've said, you decide that to invest now, when you have the money, will be advantageous in your old age, when your income has shrunk. Clear Skies renewable energy grants of £400 are available for the installation of solar-powered hot-water heating to domestic premises; contact them on www.clear-skies.org. In Northern Ireland there are additional grants from NIE Clear Skies +, www.niesmart.co.uk, of £500. Where I think solar panels can be cost effective is where heating is required for a swimming pool that is, after all, only used in good weather.

Photovoltaic cells convert sunlight into electricity and there are times when they can even put back power into the grid. They are extremely expensive and the payback time verges on the impossible. I recently shared a speaking platform with a self-builder who had spent £12,000 on his array, even after the 50% grant from the Energy Trust (40–50% grants available from the Energy Savings Trust, www.est.org). As a result he was now in receipt of a quarterly cheque for the princely sum of £20. I think I would want to invest my money a little more advantageously. But don't lose heart. Steer clear for now but this, as with all technology, is an ever- and fast-changing scene, and I look forward to the day when I can write an edition of this book that praises and recommends them.

Wind power is another way of harvesting what's out there 'for free'. Except, of course, it's not for free when you add in the capital expenditure and the fact that, in the typically non-joined-up world of

Left: **Active and passive solar gains are achieved through solar panels and a conservatory.** ©Nigel Rigden

government, the planners might object. Clear Skies grants are available at £1,000 per kWe up to a maximum of £5,000 and in Northern Ireland there are top-ups available under Clear Skies + of £200 per kWe.

Clear Skies also have grants for the installation of:

- hydro-electric water power – £1,000 per kWe up to a maximum of £5,000
- ground-source heat pumps – £1,200, regardless of system size
- biomass-fuelled (wood or timber pellet) standalone heaters – £600, regardless of system size
- biomass-fuelled boilers or stoves with a back boiler – £1,500 regardless of system size.

In Northern Ireland, under the Clear Skies + scheme, there are additional top-ups of:

- £500 for ground-source heat pumps
- £1,000 per kWe for small hydro systems
- £250 for biomass standalone room heaters
- £500 for biomass boilers/stoves with a back boiler.

Perhaps, and I'm dreaming now, the regulations may change one day and require each new home, or a home where substantial alterations are made, to install one or more of these energy-saving devices. Maybe they will not add up to the energy requirements of each home but maybe, added together, they'll make a difference. And surely, if their use becomes universal, the prices will come down and eventually we'll see the capabilities matched by the costs.

That's the theory bit and, if you like, the hidden elements of the design over with. Now we can go on to the spatial elements.

Above: **Unashamed modernity on the outside is matched on the inside by the very latest heat-saving innovations.** © Nigel Rigden

Complexity is always going to cost money but the trick is to balance those extra costs with increased value.

What do you want your home to look like externally?

The whole reason for building your own home, rather than just nipping off and buying a house from a developer, is to get what you want, rather than something that somebody else thinks you should have. What do you want it to look like externally? The answer to this question is often governed by the planners, who will be concerned to retain what they consider to be the local characteristics of their area as a whole, and individual parts of it in particular.

Do you want to push the boat out in design terms? Are you ready for the extra work and the costs that that could entail? Are you ready to face the fact that any radical departure from the norm might affect your chances of resale or the value of the finished home?

The magazines feature innovative, exciting and extremely photogenic new homes. You'd imagine that most self-builders, unwilling to accept what the building industry dictates they should have, would aspire to build homes such as these. Well, you'd be wrong. Influential as they might be, important as they are to the media, that importance is in almost inverse proportion to reality and it's a sad fact that most self-builders stick to convention when it comes to design, and almost all copy the houses of the developers that they purport to despise.

It's understandable of course. Many self-builders suffer the same constraints as the developer, and if they do succeed in avoiding standardised design, it will only be with considerable effort. All influences in modern society urge towards conformity and many features of this conformity are actually desirable, reflecting, as they do, the very best in modern living standards. But others are imposed – whether directly or indirectly – by the planners, the dictates of finance, fashion, and the need to ensure that a new home represents the best possible investment.

Complexity is always going to cost money but the trick is to balance those extra costs with increased value. Of course, the cheapest structure to build is always going to be the simple rectangle with gable ends, similar to the example house that I've referred to in Chapter 1 and in the later chapters dealing with builders and subcontractors. Take that simple shape and change the rendered blockwork to natural stone, and you've increased the walling costs fourfold and the overall costs by 10%. Change the roof tiles from concrete interlocking to plain clay tiles and you've added another 10%. If you want to make the roof shape more attractive then, without altering the overall design, you could introduce a gable projection to the roof. But although the overall tiling area would remain the same you would be adding a gable end. And this taken together with more complicated roof timbers plus the new ridge and valleys would add around £1,200.

The chances are, however, that in today's planning environment, that's exactly the sort of thing that the planners would want you to do. And what's the betting that that's what you want as well and that those features and characteristics are what attracted you to the area in the first place!

Could you go for freedom of expression, internally?

Happily the planners will play no part in the internal design and you have a far wider opportunity to employ design features that suit your own lifestyle. Once more, however, the internal arrangements of most self-built homes are little different from those built by developers, with a predictable and recognised progression of associated rooms. So ask yourself:

- Do you feel the need to stick to these conventional design formats?
- Does each area of your home have to justify its existence by reference to a particular function or could you contemplate the idea of architectural space for its own sake?
- Could you envisage a layout or mixture of rooms that defies the accepted wisdom, yet fits in with your own lifestyle?
- Do you dare to think in terms of open plan?
- Do you want a strict division between sleeping and living arrangements?

The entrance and hall

The entrance hall is the window into the rest of the home. Too pokey and it gives a first impression of a cramped and often untidy space. Too big and it begs the question 'Could this space have been better employed?'

Could it indeed have some useful function other than just as an entrance and passageway? What about all or part of the hallway becoming a dining hall or a great room? What about the idea of the hall doubling up as a sitting area? How about scrapping the idea of a hallway entirely and making the entrance through a conservatory or atrium or even directly into the living rooms or area? Does the staircase to the upper part have to run from the hall? Could you think in terms of it being enclosed, or leading up from another room, or is the staircase itself part of the statement you want to make about your home?

Do you need a downstairs toilet by the front door? For general living it might make more sense to have it closer to the utility area or easily accessible from the garden. But that would mean that casual visitors and strangers would have to enter your private areas, so would that prove impracticable? Maybe there's space for both?

The lounge, fireplaces, living areas and family life

A large lounge, after the kitchen, is probably the biggest single selling factor in a house. The magazines illustrate and feature two extremes in their case histories, both of which happen to be very photogenic. The first is the cosy old-fashioned one with the inglenook fireplace – all dreamy and with a feeling of solid dependability. That's the one that major package-deal companies have latched on to in order to sell the dream. The second predominant type is the open and airy living room with high vaulted ceilings, light streaming in and minimalist furnishings. What most people actually build is probably somewhere in the middle of these two.

What do you want? How important is light going to be in your lounge? Will you use it in daylight hours or will it be a room to which you retreat in the evenings? Do you want the lounge to take up most of the available reception area space or would that area be better employed by dividing it up into more usable rooms?

Staying with the main lounge for the moment. What other rooms must it adjoin? Does it have to be next to or interconnecting with any of them or could it stand alone with access only from the hall? Do you want easy access to the garden or is the thought of children traipsing mud all over your fashionable cream carpet too much to bear? Do you want the conservatory opening off it or would it be more useful if it came off another room?

Within most lounges the fireplace is one of the most important features. Are you sure you're not building a lounge around a fireplace rather than the other way around? Have a care. An inglenook fireplace looks right in a very large lounge but it can dominate a smaller one. It also looks right in houses of a certain style, particularly those that were derived from the East Anglian black and whites. It can look incongruous in an unashamedly modern home. Of course a chimney in a modern home is really an anathema because you go to all the trouble of making the room draught-free and then you go and stick in a pipe with a minimum size of 225mm that, when there's no fire on, allows all the heat to whistle up it! Still, it's what most people want in an up-market house. But it doesn't come for free and you've really got to think in terms of each chimney and fireplace costing you at least £1,000. Oh and by the way, if you aren't going to use the chimney but want it there just in case, put a deflated football up the flue or a ball of newspaper to stop the draught. And don't forget to take it out if you do decide to have a Christmas fire!

If you want a focal fire and you want to maximise energy efficiency, then multi-fuel stoves are a very good option, especially if you are able to take advantage of a free fuel such as wood. These are much more efficient than an open fire and won't give such high heat losses through the flue from increased ventilation when not in use. The costs can be quite horrendous with some stoves costing up to and beyond £1,000. Take a tip. Look for the same thing on the continent, where they will cost under half as much as in the UK.

What about high or vaulted ceilings? They look lovely in the photographs, but what would it do to the heating and comfort levels? I now have personal experience of living with these and I have no doubt that, in the coldest weather, most heating systems will struggle to maintain or get to temperature. Conversely, in hot weather, the fact that the hot air can rise leaves the occupied room at a comfortable temperature, especially if there are roof vents or lights, which can let the excess heat escape. Consideration also needs to be given to costs. You're effectively building a floorless room in the roof and not occupying it. There are also practical problems such as spiders and dust at heights, which most appliances cannot reach. I will discuss my experiences in the last chapters when describing and reflecting upon my recent self-builds.

If you do decide to split up the living space, how big or how small do you think your family lounge could go before you begin to seriously affect any resale value? What to do with the space? A snug could provide you with somewhere cosy to sit in the evenings without the need to heat up a large room. A study or a home office might – in an age when working from home is become ever more prevalent – almost be a necessity, but couldn't that go elsewhere – maybe in the attic, in the basement or even in the garage or an outbuilding? A music room or library would be nice but it'll have to be quite large if it's to house something like a grand piano. However, if the piano is not your instrument then the room could be quite a modest affair. It'll need careful thought, though, as to where it goes, what it adjoins and what's over it, if it's not to intrude on other activities within the home.

When children are young they want to play in their bedrooms and then sit with Mummy and Daddy in the lounge before bedtime. As they grow up, unless you can persuade them to study, they spend less time in their rooms and their tastes in music and television, and in particular, their volume levels, can cause friction. The family room was invented for this. In reality it's just a second lounge that often starts off as a playroom and then progresses to a full-blown youth centre. Careful thought has to be given to its siting. If your bedroom is directly above it, you'll get no sleep. Somewhere upstairs or a long way from the kitchen,

the toilet and the entrance, and you'll be woken by the nocturnal comings and goings. Best, perhaps, in the basement or in the garage roof.

The kitchen – cooking and eating

In many homes the dining room is the least used and most expensively furnished room in the house. Do you really need it? When you say that you couldn't have guests eating in the same area that the food is prepared in or even adjoining and open to it, are you thinking clearly? Who do you have to dinner? Do you really have total strangers to dinner or are they more likely to be friends and family? Even if you do have to entertain business clients at home, do you have staff or is the person cooking the meal to be excluded from most of the party? What about an archway between the dining area and the kitchen at the very least – that way the cook could at least take some part in the general conversation.

Kitchens are one of the biggest selling points in any house. Is yours the right kitchen for your house? Have you chosen from a brochure or for fashion's sake, without thinking how it will look in your home? Showroom lighting makes everything look different. Would a breakfast bar or an adjoining breakfast room become a useful and much-used space? Remember, as with bathrooms, flair and imagination can count for far more than money. The best-looking kitchens are often the least expensive. Consider mixing and matching expensive with cheap. Melamine-faced doors are all pretty much the same and nobody gets on their hands and knees to check on the carcasses once the cupboards are full. Changing the knobs can make an enormous difference to the look. Saving on the units but pushing the boat out on the worktops with, say, granite, can get you a better-looking kitchen for a fraction of the cost of some of the hand-made ones, especially if they are complemented by the right choice of tiles to the walls and floor.

Care also needs to be taken if you're having an Aga or Rayburn cooker, or one of their generics. Many of these need a chimney, so you've got to accommodate that going through the upper floors or else position

Above: **Plenty of island and peninsular units make the most of the available space.**

Right: **By combining the kitchen, dining area and a seating area this space is turned into a true living room.** © Potton

the cooker on an outside wall where it can possibly have a balanced flue. They take up a large space, they interrupt the run of modern units, they're extremely heavy and hugely expensive, yet they're loved with a passion that once even moved a poet laureate to wax lyrical. They should never be an afterthought.

Utility rooms and storage

What is the purpose of your proposed utility room? Is its use allied to that of the kitchen and, if not, does it have to connect to it? If it's really a laundry room, why cart clothes downstairs, wash them and cart them back up again? Couldn't the room go upstairs? If it's a mud room, somewhere for dirty dogs and wellies, could it just be a lobby and could it benefit from not only a toilet but perhaps a shower as well? Or is that going to be a great idea on paper that, in the end, just gets used as storage? If space is at a premium, how about scrapping the idea of a utility room altogether in favour of a bigger kitchen or a breakfast area?

However many advances are made with modern kitchen units and appliances, the larder still retains its affection in the housewife's mind. The trouble is that in many modern kitchens, it's expected that the units will get a clear run and there isn't always room for the larder. That's a shame because a fairly modest larder can provide the same shelf space as a lorryload of kitchen units. As it's really storage, see if it can be positioned in the utility section, so as to leave the kitchen uninterrupted. It should be positioned on a northern wall if possible with fly-proof ventilation in the traditional manner, but if this proves impossible, there are electrical larder-cooling units.

If you're having under-floor central heating, you're going to need some pretty big cupboards to hide all those pipes and manifolds. If you're having a central vacuum, do you want that to go in a cupboard in the house or would you prefer to site it out in a garage or outbuilding? They are, after all, very noisy. Will the linen cupboards be accessible to the communal areas or must they go in one of the bathrooms or a bedroom? Have you already got wardrobes as furniture or will you want built-in wardrobes or bedroom furniture in all or some of the bedrooms?

The conservatory or sunroom

In most cases conservatories can be constructed under Permitted Development Rights, after the completion of the building. Good job too, because conservatories can be hugely expensive and would break many budgets. They can be simple, single-glazed affairs in softwood or they can be elaborate double- or triple-glazed structures in either hardwood or Pvc-u. I believe, although the British Woodworking Federation understandably believes otherwise, that whatever the construction of the walls of a conservatory, the roof is better made from aluminium or Pvc-u. If they do have to be timber then it's best to have the glazing set in aluminium 'T' bars, so that it looks like wood from below. Alternatively use glazing tapes rather than compounds and make sure that the glass is held firmly in position by hooks.

A constant complaint about conservatories is that they're too hot to use in the summer and too cold in the winter. Well, that is, I'm afraid, the nature of the beast. You can mitigate the effects of the sun by the use of trellis across the outside of the roof and the planting of a deciduous creeper such as clematis or a vine. But internal blinds only really trap the heat that has already come through. Most roofs are of the poly-carbonate translucent type but Pilkingtons make a glass that reflects the sun's rays. There is also another product on the market called Heatguard, which reflects the sun's rays in the summer and retains the heat in the winter. It's not cheap and costs about £30 per square metre more, which works out at around £800 for the average conservatory. For around a quarter of that sum you could purchase a mobile air-conditioning unit that doubles up as a heater in the winter.

Conservatories can help to save energy by reducing heat loss through adjoining walls and by trapping heat from the sun. Simple fans fitted with a thermostat can expel excess heat in the summer or pass it through to the house in the winter. The savings are small but to be effective it does need to be on the south side of the building without any overshadowing. Even high-quality conservatories should not have the heating connected to the main heating system for the house, as this could lead to high fuel bills. Trianco

Redfyre have an electric boiler called an Aztec Gold, especially designed for use in a conservatory or out-building, which will run either radiators or under-floor central heating quite effectively. Another alternative is the matting type electric under-floor heating, which is laid in the adhesive of the floor tiles. I doubt that this latter idea would mean that the room could be used in the depths of winter, but it could increase the times when it could be occupied.

Which room do you want your conservatory to come off? Off the lounge is the most usual but would that fit in with your lifestyle? Might it not be better off the dining room or the family room or even the kitchen? Could it be big enough to have access to all of these rooms? It is also a Building Regulations requirement that all conservatories should have double-glazed doors to shut them off from the main house when they are not in use.

A sunroom is a different matter. That's really another room in the house, only with far more windows. Usually there is a wall up to cill height and the roof is constructed and clad in the same material as for the main roof, perhaps with roof lights as well. All of the Building Regulations will apply and the heating will almost certainly be part and parcel of the main house system, although it might be better to have some way of shutting it off in extremes of weather. At the very least the radiator should have its own thermostatic valve or any under-floor central heating should have its own zone and controls.

How many bedrooms do you want or need?

Whilst not wishing to preach conformity, I still feel the need to stress the importance of keeping a weather eye open for future sales. You might not want more than two or three bedrooms, and if that's what you decide, then that's fine. But do consider that a house with three large bedrooms compared with an identically sized house with four smaller ones could be at a disadvantage on value, even though its costs might be substantially the same. Could you plan for the larger rooms to be subdivided and if you sell, do you understand that it might be better for you to

effect the change, rather than relying on a prospective purchaser's imagination?

What about bedroom sizes? You might well consider that as it's your house and it's you that's paying for it, your bedroom suite is going to have the lion's share of any space. On the other hand you might feel that things need to be evened out a little, or you might want to head off arguments between children and make all their rooms the same size. Will you want dressing rooms? Do you need a guest suite or will one of the other main bedrooms suffice?

Bathrooms and toilets

An en-suite is considered a necessity in most larger family homes and is an important factor when it comes to resale value. Do you want it to be a shower room or a full bathroom? Many of the smaller homes that now have en-suite facilities tend to try to cram the sanitaryware into a windowless space that's not much larger than a cupboard. Would that satisfy you?

With the communal or family bathroom, do you want the toilet to be separate or would it be better to have a toilet in there as well as a completely separate one? What about en-suite accommodation for other bedrooms, or at least for one that you can then designate as a guest suite? Could the idea of one bathroom being directly accessible to and serving two bedrooms work? Have you thought through the family routines, especially in the mornings? Would it help to double up the number of wash-hand basins per bathroom? What about hand basins in some or all of the bedrooms? Care needs to be taken with the latter if you've got boys, by the way!

Later on in this book I discuss the material alternatives. But for now, at the design stage, suffice it to say that you don't necessarily have to spend a fortune to end up with a 'wow factor' bathroom. It's often the fittings, fixtures and accoutrements that make a bathroom special rather that the sanitaryware. Just the right choice of tiles, again not necessarily expensive, perhaps with attractive borders, makes all the difference. Remember, flair and imagination count for more than just money.

Basements

Basements are, after many years in the doldrums, becoming more popular. The scarcity of land and correspondingly high property values mean that the provision of a basement is now cost effective, especially in urban situations or on tight sites where to go down means that the accommodation can be increased whilst the overall footprint of the building remains the same.

In situations where the planning permission for the house sets a limit on the size, it is open to interpretation as to whether the addition of a basement would breach these requirements. The attitude of planning officers is different from region to region, with some insisting that, at all times, any such habitable space is to be included and others feeling that, perhaps, so long as it does not have an effect on the overall appearance of the house, it should be allowed. If there's any doubt on this point, then I suggest you denote the space as 'storage' or 'void' and occupy it later under Permitted Development Rights. That will usually do the trick but if the effect of a basement is to lift the house out of the ground or show windows

below ground-floor level, it might be a little difficult to deny your intentions. A planning officer could then claim that either there had been a material departure from the consent, or that the effect of your future proposals was having a detrimental effect on the overall design.

There are many different ways to build a basement. Massive blockwork, hollow blockwork, shuttered and poured concrete, pre-formed concrete sections and polystyrene blocks filled with concrete – all have their place and are suitable for differing situations. There are also schools of thought about how to make the basement waterproof. The normal way is by 'tanking' – the application of a waterproof layer either inside or outside the structure or both. However, there is a school of thought that believes that it is impossible to tank a below-ground structure infallibly and that the right way to proceed is with specialist wall and flooring panels which channel any moisture harmlessly to a sump, from which it is then pumped to a drain.

One other way of achieving a watertight structure is to create drained voids between the external ground and the basement living accommodation, negating the need for tanking. It does mean that you're con-

If I was building a basement nowadays, I'd probably opt for the prefabricated concrete type (right).

structing a structure, which you will never occupy, and rooms, which will sit there below ground as buffers. It is a particularly useful solution and effective on a sloping site where the house is above ground at the lower end and drainage can be taken to soakaways sited further on down the slope.

I have built several basements in my time. They were all fraught with worry and I never knew, when arriving at site each morning, whether next door's house had slipped into the massive hole that seemed to stay open for days on end. It's not a job for an amateur. Leave it to the specialists or to builders who have done it before. Whenever I've done it I've used hollow concrete blocks, which have reinforcement rods taken up through them and where the voids are subsequently filled with concrete. Bituthene tanking is then stuck on the inside face of this hollow blockwork and then protected by an inner skin of 100mm blockwork. The tanking is also taken across the floor and beneath a protective screed to

Above: **Sloping or skillion ceilings need not be a problem so long as there is adequate space in the room.** ©Potton

create a completely sealed basement. Outside the walls, which in certain situations may have to be thickened up, the external face of the blocks is painted with a waterproof solution to minimise any external water pressure. The void is backfilled with clean stone after land drainage is laid in the bottom to take the water away to a convenient point.

It sounds fairly simple and it is. But in ground with a high water table, or in ground where the bank of close on 3 metres doesn't stand up and keeps falling in, it's never as easy. In heavy clay, in the rain, with a wall of mud moving towards you at 50mm an hour, you might wish that you'd made other arrangements. Above all, you need to be able to act fast. You need the right equipment and materials in place. You need emergency pumps for water ingress, concrete pumps to get the concrete to the right place and shuttering to keep the hole open. Oh, and to repeat my earlier advice, make sure that you've got self-build site insurance. If things go wrong then you'll be covered. And even if they go smoothly, don't forget that all your neighbours will be convinced that every hairline crack in their walls is down to your activities, so take photographs of their houses with as much detail as you can.

I've costed out the example house as if it had been decided to incorporate a third floor in the form of a block-built basement and you can see the full tables in Chapter 12. From them you'll see that this 70-square-metre structure as a full basement is going to cost something in the region of £25,000. That's to a shell state and with a larger contingency of 15%, because of the complexity of the task, it works out at around £400 per square metre. Recent quotations received for prefabricated waterproof-concrete-type basements generally work out at around £560 per square metre. The polystyrene blocks filled with concrete work out at around £400 and the shuttered and poured concrete type come in at around £300. However, that cheaper method is really one for the professionals as the skills needed with shuttering and formwork are not often found on a single-building site and are more often used in motorway bridges.

But back to our example. Of course this £25,000 isn't just a complete extra cost. The basement that's just been built is also the foundation for the original two floors. So if we deduct the original groundworks cost, less the drainage costs, which we'll assume remain constant, it really represents an extra of £15,000. And if we spent the same again on fitting it out, then the total of £30,000 for this extra 70 square metres would represent £430 per square metre. That's good value. But this is best case and we still have to add in contingencies.

Natural light in basements adds enormously to their use and enjoyment, not just visually but by providing natural ventilation. If you cannot use light wells consider the use of high-level windows, although be aware that these can have the effect of raising the ground-floor level of the building which might, in some circumstances, be unacceptable to the planners. If no natural light or ventilation is available make sure that you have plenty of mechanical ventilation, especially if you are going to use any part of the basement as a utility or bathing area.

Mention should also be made of the fact that once the basement is part of the living accommodation and, effectively three floors are created, the Building Regulations will require that the staircase is a contained area and that all doors opening on to it must be fire doors. Additional costs might also be incurred by the need to get drainage out of the building. Obviously, even if the levels are right, it's not possible to take drains through the tanked walls. A sump-and-pump system has therefore to be employed, lifting the effluent to a higher level where it can be discharged to the drains in the normal way.

The attic

I've already discussed the use of attic or loft space when talking about designs for small sites, but of course all houses, large or small, can benefit from this extra space and, more often than not, the provision of attic trusses is one expense that is really worthwhile. If we were to change the ordinary trusses on our example house to attic trusses then the cost would be around £2,000. That's money in the bank if you ever want to expand your home into the roof.

Whilst attic space may be cheap space, its use or eventual use has to be planned for in advance. You cannot simply go around cutting up ordinary trusses and you have to think ahead and use either attic trusses or a traditional purlin and spar roof construction, of which more later. As with basements, the planners might, where there is a restriction on the size of the dwelling, want to consider attic space as part of the allowable accommodation. Once again, if this is the case, it might be better to omit any reference to occupation of the roof space and to plan for its eventuality under Permitted Development Rights.

What will you use the attic for? Will it be additional bedrooms or bathrooms? Will it be office space, play space or a gym? If so, what are the implications for the bedrooms below? How will you get heavy office machinery or furniture up there? How will you gain access? You could, for occasional use only, put up with a pull-down loft ladder or staircase, but if you're thinking of more generalised use, you'll probably want a proper staircase. And if you do, then, as with the basement, you may fall foul of the requirements for three-storey dwellings whereby the staircase has to be within a containable space and all doors opening on to it must be self-closing fire doors.

Windows, window styles and doors

The planners will have a great deal to say about the windows and doors in your house, usually referred to as 'the fenestration'. Many people like lots of glass and don't like it interrupted by lots of transoms and mullions. Planners, on the other hand, usually hate large areas of glass and have a particular aversion to horizontal transoms, preferring windows with a more vertical emphasis and often with narrow modules. In Conservation Areas, you can almost guarantee that they will not accept Pvc-u and instead will insist on painted timber, although, now into my fifth decade in the business as I am, I've yet to fathom out precisely why.

When you're making your design scrapbook (see page 195) make a particular note of the type of windows in your area, especially those that have been used on new housing of a similar ilk to the one you're planning. Departure from the normal manufacturer's ranges can be prohibitively expensive, as can the use of stone mullions, surrounds, cills and heads. Box sash windows can also be expensive, although some manufacturers are now introducing them into their standard ranges.

As for what material to choose, softwood windows are now pressure impregnated and treated so that they will last and are often guaranteed for 30 years. Hardwood windows are more expensive. I know we're always being told that they come from sustainable sources but I'm never really sure if that's true. They look best dark-stained and they often don't take to paint very well. Metal or steel windows suffer from cold bridging but have the benefit that they can provide a very thin profile. As such they are often used in conjunction with stone mullions and surrounds. Make sure they are galvanised and/or powder coated. Aluminium can suffer from many of the drawbacks that steel windows have, unless there is what's known as a thermal break in the window, prohibiting the transference of cold. They are most suitable for patio doors where a combination of strength with a relatively thin profile is required. Raw aluminium is unattractive and weathers badly, and should therefore be properly powder-coated or enamelled.

By the way, on the subject of patio doors, these are modern inventions and they do not trace their history or origins back to any architectural feature other than, perhaps, French doors. It looks nothing less than daft, therefore, if glazing bars or leading are introduced and they should always be left as clear glazed.

Pvc-u windows come in all shapes, sizes and profiles. They were meant to be the maintenance-free option but some of the cheaper ones have suffered over time with discoloration and brittleness. Avoid the cheap end of the market and opt for units where the extrusion is slower and therefore thicker, with reinforcement within the sub frames. All windows, whatever they're made of, should be washed down regularly, quite apart from normal or periodic decoration, and in seaside areas they should be thoroughly cleaned at least once a month to remove salt.

The entrance door is one of the first and most important impressions of your new home. Take care that you choose the right one for the period or style you are emulating. If you've gone for Victorian, nothing looks sillier than a six-panel Georgian type door. Stick to the four-panel door with the larger panels at the top. Pvc-u windows can look great, whilst Pvc-u doors, at least to the front door, can look cheap and nasty, whatever they cost. It doesn't look incongruous, in fact it looks right, if the front door and frame are in quality timber with the rest of the external joinery in plastic. Incidentally, it's a personal, but strongly held, opinion, but I never think that the wood-grained-effect Pvc-u joinery looks anything other than a plastic imitation of the real thing.

Garage doors have already been discussed with regard to their orientation and the effect they can have on a design, if you're not careful, with their becoming the dominant architectural feature. The doors themselves come in a variety of styles and materials. Remember that garages are a recent phenomenon. They didn't exist in earlier times or if they did it was in the form of cart sheds or stables. Up-and-over doors can look good, especially if they have vertical or chevron-type panelling. Double garage doors always look hideous and planners hate

them. If at all possible, substitute them for two single doors. Doors look even better to my mind if they're proper doors that hinge open.

Ventilation

Ventilation is important to both provide fresh air and prevent condensation. The Building Regulations require that there should be extractor fans or passive stack ventilation (PSV) in all kitchens and bathrooms. With PSV, air is drawn out of the house, without the need for electric fans, through a combination of the effects of the air flowing over the roof and the natural buoyancy of the warm moist air. In order to prevent over-ventilation, humidity-controlled dampers can be fitted which need no electrical connection. Permanent ventilation must also be provided to all other rooms using trickle vents that are fitted to all windows.

Mechanical ventilation, with or without heat recovery, may offer benefits such as filtered air and reduced noise intrusion. The systems use fans to supply fresh air and extract stale air in a very controlled manner. The heat recovery options recover much of the heat from the extracted air and add it to the returning air using a heat exchanger so that the two air streams do not mix. Filters can be fitted to the supply air to remove dust and pollen and they can, therefore, provide very good-quality air. There is no need for trickle ventilation with such a system and this may be an important factor in reducing the noise from outside in certain locations. Mechanical ventilation will not work properly unless the house is well sealed and sealing of the house can only really be done at the construction stage, involving very close attention to detail and a close watch on workmanship. Unfortunately open fireplaces are incompatible with these systems. There is of course a capital outlay, which can be anywhere between £1,500 and £2,500. The running costs are also significant and may outweigh the energy saved, so, whilst they will provide good ventilation and good-quality air, they should not generally be seen as an energy-saving or -efficient feature.

Left: **Both the fireplace and the staircase make bold design statements in this home.** © photodisc

Lighting

Maximising daylighting with the design and good lighting design, combined with use of low-energy compact or strip fluorescent lights, will save considerable amounts on running costs. Fluorescent lamps have a much longer life than ordinary light bulbs. The Building Regulations now require that one room in three has a dedicated low-energy fitting or bulb holder and that external lighting must be of the low-energy type with external lights on either a timer and/or a PIR system.

Twelve-volt downlighting has become extremely popular, either as a complete replacement for other forms of lighting in certain areas or as a supplement to it. It does need a transformer that can be hidden away in a cupboard and it can save considerably on electricity. Downlighters in bathrooms and kitchens must be of the sealed type and you should ensure that there is an intumescent cowl over each one to prevent any spread of fire.

Contents and furniture

Make a list of your favourite furniture. Most modern furniture is designed to fit through door openings as narrow as 760mm or else be capable of disassembly. But antique furniture certainly isn't. Is the dining area going to be large enough to accommodate your dining table at its full extension and is there enough room around it for chairs and circulation? Are the ceilings going to be high enough for antique wardrobes or dressers? If your snooker table is going in the loft or the basement, make sure that the access is large enough. If it's going into a room on any upper floor check that the floor can take the weight. Check also that there is a space of at least 2 metres all around it so that there's room for the cue.

The Building Regulations now require that one room in three has a dedicated low-energy fitting or bulb holder ...

Granny flats

Any consideration about whether to include a 'granny flat' in a self-build project needs as much thought given to the possible unravelling of the situation as it does to its creation. For many the idea of bringing their parents into a loving and caring home environment, to become their built-in friend, baby- and house-sitter, is a wonderful and fulfilling dream. For others, that same thought is about as welcome as the onset of bubonic plague.

But looking on the positive side, let's consider the advantages and how the objective, once decided upon, can be achieved. First of all there is the financial side of things. Will Granny simply be passing over her share of the costs of the project as cash? Will she be part-owner of the completed establishment or will she just be coming to live in your house? What security of tenure will she have and, if it all goes wrong, how will she be able to recover her share in order to be able to house herself? All of these are questions which may seem unpalatable or intrusive, but they are questions, nonetheless, which need answers before rather than after the event.

One way around things may be for Granny to give you a private mortgage, negating or limiting your need to apply for outside finance. That way she will retain a financial stake in the house and you will have security for as long as you continue to meet the agreed repayments. Granny now has an income and that is important if you project your thinking forward to the time when she is no longer able to live with you and needs to go into a nursing home. The going rate for care in a nursing home is almost as much as the average wage. Help is available, of course, but, of late, that help has only been supplied by the Government upon realisation of the older person's assets down to a fairly paltry minimum. If the bulk of an older person's assets takes the form of a properly set-up mortgage, then that puts it beyond reach. The income from your repayments plus that from state and other pensions should then ensure a more comfortable placing for the later stages of your parent's life.

The important thing with all of this is sound advice from solicitors and accountants. On the death of the parent, in the case of an arrangement such as I've described above, it is vital that any will reflects the fact that you won't want to be turfed out of your home and that, if possible, the mortgage lapses and the deceased parent's share of the home comes to you. What can complicate this is the need to accommodate the aspirations of other siblings, who may well discount the loving care you've given your parent during the latter stages of their life, and simply feel that you have purloined the bulk of their inheritance. Then again, what if you predecease your parent? Will they then be homeless and dispossessed or will there be provision for them to recover their equity in reasonable fashion with the minimum of upheaval? Nothing in life is for ever, and I repeat, as much care needs to go into the possible need for unravelling of any financial pooling of resources as it does with its original amalgamation.

And when you've taken all of the advice and decided on your course of action, surely the planners are going to welcome your proposals with open arms? Well, not necessarily. Planners are often fearful of any suggestion that the single dwelling for which they have given consent could possibly be divided and end up, effectively, as two homes. They've been caught out before, you see, and for everyone who manages to hoodwink a planning authority into giving consent for something they didn't intend, there are countless others who are forever blighted by that deception.

One way of alleviating the planners' fears is to demonstrate that the annex is an integral part of the main home and to consider whether or not it needs its own entrance. Maybe the French doors from its lounge are enough? Maybe it can share access with the secondary access to the main house or even share the utility room?

Home offices

These words can cover a multitude of applications right through from the company representative who sets aside a small space under the stairs, to plush suites with separate offices and toilet accommodation. What all of this reflects is, however, the growing trend towards working from home. In part that's due to the greater use of computers and the Internet, which obviate the need for a group of people working together to be in the same room, and in part it's due to the fact that many women with children now choose to work from home. In addition, companies find that they can expand into new geographical areas simply by employing representatives who are prepared to work from home, only meeting their colleagues in person at regular sales functions. It saves them the costs of office rentals and maintenance and it gives the employee a freedom and flexibility previously only enjoyed by the self-employed.

The office can really go anywhere in the home if it's only ever going to be occupied or used by members of the household. However, if things start to get a little more sophisticated with staff coming in and/or clients visiting, much more careful thought has to be given to its siting. You can't expect a secretary to have to go trooping up to your family bathroom and if your kids have left it in a mess, it's not going to impress your boss or a client. If this is the situation, you really need to be able to get the office accommodation somewhere where there is, firstly, a separate entrance and, secondly, dedicated toilet facilities. Maybe that could be in the utility area? Maybe it could be above or behind the garage or maybe it would be better to consider a purpose-built outbuilding?

We're talking here about working from home. What we shouldn't really be considering is running a full-blown company from home. There is a difference. If things get too big or too busy, your neighbours and the planners might well take an unhealthy interest in the goings on. You might be prepared to go the whole hog and apply for planning for change of use of part of your premises. In certain situations that could be successful but in a purely domestic setting, it's unlikely. In any event there's the tax angle. 'If part or all of your home has, at some time, not been used as your home; for example, if it has been let or used for business', it will not be exempt for Capital Gains purposes under the relief that is available for your principal private residence. Now none of that is supposed to catch out the writer or the company representative working from home, but if you've gone for formal planning permission, it would be frightfully difficult to argue against.

Designing for the disabled or inclusive access

Part 'M' of the Building Regulations seeks to make sure that there is inclusive access to the entrance storey, all habitable rooms in that storey and, most importantly, the toilet, although it no longer refers to 'disabled people'. These rules apply to all new dwellings.

The requirements for the outside of the building and the approach to the dwelling are dealt with under 'Pathways and patios' on page 235.

The threshold of the entrance door, although it can be a secondary door, should preferably be a level one with a retractable water bar, but in any event should not exceed 150mm. This entrance door should also have a minimum opening width of at least 775mm. In addition there are guidelines that set down the minimum width of internal doors in relation to the width of the corridor, dependent on whether the approach to the door is head-on or not. These are designed to allow the free passage of wheelchairs.

Access to the toilet is crucial and the regulations insist on the provision of a toilet to the main entrance storey with an outward opening door. Whilst it is recognised that it will not always be practicable for a wheelchair to be fully accommodated within the toilet compartment, thought must be given to making that access as easy as possible. The WC enclosure should provide for a clear space of at least 450mm on each

Guidelines for disabled access

Doorway clear opening	Corridor/passageway width
750mm or wider	900mm (when approached head-on)
750mm	1,200mm (when not approached head-on)
775mm	1,050mm (when not approached head-on)
800mm	900mm (when not approached head-on)

side and 750mm in front of the pan to allow a wheel-chair to approach to within 400mm of the pan from the front or within 250mm of the pan from the side. The washbasin must be positioned so that it does not impede access.

The regulations also stipulate that switches and plugs must be set at heights to assist those people whose reach is limited. In general sockets must not be lower on the wall than 450mm measured from the finished floor height and switches must not be higher than 1200mm above finished floor level. Accessible consumer units should be fitted with a childproof cover or installed in a lockable cupboard.

People still get very hot under the collar about these requirements, claiming that as they're not disabled and they know nobody who is, why should they be forced to adopt these measures. All I can say is that having lived in my last three houses with these in place, the only inconvenience I suffer is that when I go to other people's houses, I find myself reaching too far up the wall in the dark for the light switch. Remember, we are all one heartbeat away from accident or infirmity.

If you want help with the design of your new home, with particular reference to this subject, contact the Disabled Living Foundation on 020 7289 6111 or the Disability Alliance on 020 7247 8776.

Security features

These days many windows and doors have espagno-lette or multi-locking points, and even those that don't have lockable window catches and five-lever mortice locks to the doors. Couple that with double-glazing and, as far as the structural components are concerned, it's probably as much as most people will want. Nevertheless there are those for whom security is high on the agenda and for whom the building in of even greater security measures is an important incentive in the whole business of self-building. Proximity alarms, sensors, floodlighting – there is a whole wealth of equipment to satisfy even the most insecure of minds.

Right: **Having your office at the bottom of the garden can give you a sense of 'going to work'.** © Nigel Rigden

I've never got terribly excited about alarm systems, probably because I've never chosen or had to live in the kinds of areas where they're considered necessary. I would think that as a minimum, proximity external lighting on a PIR sensor is always a good idea, although where I live, it goes on and off all night due to cats and foxes. It is also a good idea to have some sort of system whereby you can arrange for lights, radios and even televisions to go on and off as if you were in occupation. The expensive way is with a complicated programmer. The cheap way is with a series of simple plug-in timers.

A feature which can be built into a new home is a secure cupboard offering protection for valuables, shotguns and the like. If this is given consideration at the design stage, it is relatively easy for an ingenious

carpenter to install a hidden door to a hidden cupboard, which will escape the notice of a burglar. Those whose work involves keeping large sums of money in the house from time to time can arrange for an under-floor safe to be set in the foundation concrete, to be reached by turning back a rug or carpet in one of the ground-floor rooms. This may be a condition of their special insurance.

Renovations and conversions

If building a new home from scratch means starting from a blank canvas in design terms, then renovating or converting is by no means painting by numbers. It may well be that; to a large extent, with renovations, the pattern of the accommodation is firmly set. However, there's a lot you can do. In villages all over the country there are bungalows and houses built in the 1960s and early '70s. These stand out like sore thumbs, bearing little or no relationship to their neighbours or to any architectural vernacular. They cry out to be replaced and, in many cases, because of the distortions in cost caused by the present rules on the recovery of VAT, that's the only viable option. But not always.

You can change their external appearance out of all recognition from the original. Take out the old land-scape joinery and replace it with more sympathetic fenestration. Render or otherwise change those horrible tiled or timber-clad panels. Re-tile the roof. All of this should be considered as a social service. In

fact, as far as most planners are concerned, it is, and a chat with them and/or the conservation officer that starts off with the premise that you want to do something to improve the street scene will go down very well.

Of course, the probability is that the accommodation might need enlarging or extending in order to bring it up to modern standards and requirements. In many village streets in sensitive areas, planners will only usually consider enlargement if it comes within the scope of Permitted Development. In Conservation Areas, the Permitted Development Rights might well have been removed. But going to the planners with ideas that will improve the street scene and offering them a trade-off between those and the need to extend the property could well pay off.

Conversions obviously depend on the type of building. If it's an old water tower, a lighthouse or a pumping station, then flair and imagination, coupled with sympathy for the original structure, can have quite startling results. Where it is all getting a bit predictable is with barn conversions. Perhaps it's because barns throughout the realm are remarkably similar: a vast open space with a very high entrance, usually, but not always, situated in the centre of one side. As such, most barn conversions simply seem to fill in this entrance area with a vast glazed screen and then create galleried landings and upper parts that look down into a largely open-plan ground floor where the only demarcation between uses is denoted by the furniture. Perhaps there's little or nothing that can be done and the fault lies with the insistence of planners that, despite the fact that the building is being converted to a residence, it must still display its agricultural origins, at least to the outside. But if one is aware of the danger of a boring conformity, and you make your architect aware of your concerns, maybe a little more excitement could be brought into the project.

Do you need a garage?

Considered almost essential by the market, yet rarely used for the housing of motor cars, do you want a garage at all and if so will you ever use it and what for? Could you think of building more house or could you envisage inclusion of the garage space within the home, on the understanding that if it ever comes to resale, it can be put back to its original purpose? Could you have a carport instead? Should the garage be attached, integral or detached? Planners feel that detached garages reflect the rural character, whilst attached and integral ones are an urban solution to the problem of what to do with the motor car.

Whatever garage you have, think carefully about its impact on the overall design of your new home. Many houses have, as their dominant architectural feature, the huge open maw of the garage doors. What to do about this and how to make them as attractive as possible has largely been left to the manufacturers, who have come up with solutions such as Tudor panelled garage doors. Well, Henry VIII did not have a Rolls Royce! Try to vary the shape of the garage, the setting and, above all, the choice of the doors. Wherever possible, get doors to face across a plot rather than straight out to the street.

If the garage is detached or attached to the side of your new home and finances are stretched, could it be left until later? That way you could concentrate all of your monies into the home. You could even bring it up to the oversite level and treat it as a hard standing or parking. Or, if money permitted, you could buy some or all of the materials at the same time as those for the house and store them carefully. Remember, however, that if you do buy materials after your VAT reclaim, you won't be getting the VAT back on them.

The garden

A garden that slopes away from the visual point within a home can be 'lost'. Think about raised decks or patios. Raised wooden decks can be attractive and they can be constructed in such a way as to allow light to filter down to the windows of lower storeys. If you want to build a patio up to a raised level, think very carefully before you do that by the use of fill. It will always settle and the slabs will become uneven. Instead, use floor beams to create a raised patio with an empty void beneath. You can then build walls at the edge with railings and steps down to the lower levels. And these walls can be made as planters so that your garden is brought to the reception level.

A garden that slopes up from the home is one that can be seen to an even greater degree than a flat site. It becomes a three-dimensional garden that can be terraced and planted so as to bring beauty to all levels of the home. However, if retaining walls are required, be careful that they are sufficiently far enough away from the house to provide suitable access and drainage. If they or any other pathways are north facing, be careful to select materials that will not become slippery when wet.

The garden should be an extension of the living space within the home, rather than a separate entity. Weather permitting, it should fit into the natural progression between rooms. Can your access be via a sunroom or conservatory? Which rooms do you want to have direct access to the garden? Are you worried about children or dogs bringing in the dirt? In bad weather, could the garden be brought into the home by the raising of flowerbeds and planting, so that the eye is led through the window and beyond? Will access to the garden be suitable for elderly or disabled people and will the paths and patios be designed so that they too can enjoy it?

Does the house design reflect the need for direct access between the garden and the street? Carrying plants, mud and other garden materials and furniture through the house can be tedious. Of course this might not be possible. You might have a very narrow site or even a terraced property. In which case could you access the garden through the garage? What do you want from your garden? Do you like weeding? Do you like mowing lawns and pruning shrubs? Or do you want a garden that's virtually an open-air room with easy-to-maintain surfaces and plants in pots?

In any building site there will be large amounts of spoil to get rid of, something that can prove extremely costly. Why not, therefore, consider retaining some or all of the excavated material, assuming your site's big enough? Why not use it to change the contours of the land with, perhaps, a raised shrubbery or mounded-up area giving either visual or sound privacy? Why not contain a heap of soil with a low brick wall to provide backache-free gardening?

Whilst you've got an excavator on site you could dig out a pond and pile the excavated material around

it to form an attractive rockery backdrop. I won't go into the methods of pond lining in this book, as there are plenty of other tomes specific to that subject. Much of course depends on your idea of a pond. Should it be formal in shape or containment? Should it be informal and look as natural as possible? Is it intended to house expensive koi or is it intended as a future residence for frogs and newts? If you're going to need lighting, either under or over the water, or if you're going to need pumps and filters, then you're going to have to think about the supply of electricity and you may even have to think in terms of a small shed or building to house all the equipment. Might this be possible as an underground structure beneath the rockery, and whilst you're running all this cable around, why not think of other areas in the garden that could benefit from lighting?

The thing to do is think about all of this at the design and pre-planning stages; certainly before machinery is on site and before you send away 'spoil' that you might need. Topsoil is very expensive to buy and extremely difficult to barrow around to a back garden. Stone for the rockery is horrendously expensive and having to pay for it would be all the more galling if you'd already sent loads away!

The driveway

Unless you have a very big garden indeed, the driveway is probably going to be one of the single most dominant features of your new home. I've already discussed access arrangements and the requirements of the authorities. What I'm talking about here, therefore, is the driveway within the curtilage of your property. To some extent this is your business, but as you'd expect, the authorities do have some say, particularly in respect of parking and turning and the need to be able to enter and leave in forward gear. They might also, in certain circumstances, have an input in the choice of surfacing, where, for example, a tree or its roots might be affected.

In many suburban streets, there is little or no alternative to a straight driveway running between the garage doors and the road, with any associated parking or turning space leading off it to one side.

The problem that this creates, quite apart from looking boring, is that there is a loss of privacy. Consider whether, if you've got the room, you could bring the entrance in on the other side of the frontage to the garage doors. That way the driveway can curve across the plot and whilst that might seem to take up more space, it will, nonetheless, afford you the opportunity of planting or banking that will give privacy to the home.

There are several choices when it comes to surfacing and once again, it pays to think carefully about which you use. A pea shingle or gravel driveway is often thought of as the cheapest, easiest and quickest surface for a new driveway, which may well be true. However, it can look incongruous in a suburban street and where there are slopes there can be a problem of migration. This can be overcome by either a series of baffles or by 'sticking' the stones down with some sort of tar emulsion to a previously prepared and hard sub base. Where most pea shingle or gravel driveways go wrong is in the preparation of the sub base and the choice of edging. Any driveway is only ever going to be as good as the foundation it is laid upon and in the case of a gravel driveway that should either be hard-rolled hoggin or well-compacted and blinded hardcore. Edging is important not only to look neat but also to contain the surfacing material.

It needn't always be concrete, although that's obviously best, and it could be tanalised timber. The gravel itself needs careful thought. Too often round stones are used to excessive depths that make walking or driving up it akin to trudging along Brighton beach. Choose a flat stone that is capable of compaction and lay it only in sufficient depth to give good cover.

Of course, if you ever get fed up with your gravel driveway, you'll probably find that it provides an excellent base for a tarmac driveway. Beware the itinerant who knocks at the door telling you that they're doing a job around the corner and they've got some tarmac left over that they can do you a good deal for. What you'll get is the heated-up scrapings from the resurfacing work down the road, and when it all comes up or fails to create a homogenous surface, they'll be long gone. Choose a company with premises and a landline rather than just a mobile number and that way your driveway can be every bit as serviceable as the Queen's highway. I question whether some of the colour choices that are available ever really look right and I have an intense dislike of coloured chippings in a rural environment, but that's really a matter of choice. Once again the sub base and the edgings are important and it's as well to insist that, before the black goes down, a good dose of weedkiller is applied.

Concrete driveways seem to have gone out of favour, at least in their traditional tamped form. Properly formed, with a good sub base and with expansion joints and bays, this can be an extremely serviceable surface that can look attractive. What seems to have taken their place, to some degree, is the imprinted and patterned concrete that purports to resemble cobbles or paving. Many people like these but what strikes me is that when they crack, they never seem to do so along the indentations, often because, in order to make them look realistic, the contractors haven't put in the necessary expansion joints.

Block pavers look right in the town but can look out of place in the country where one would, perhaps, be better advised to use proper, but much more expensive, brick pavoirs. They come in a variety of colours and, badly chosen, they do little more than imitate the petrol station forecourts that they so often grace. The costs can rival that of tarmac and properly laid, on a good sub base with kiln-dried sand into which they are tamped, they are virtually maintenance free. Some like the gaps between the blocks or bricks to get mossy. Some hate it, spending endless hours scrubbing and scraping. The choice, as with all self-building, is yours but if you are after a more natural or non-intrusive surface, you could do no better than to consider the use of grass blocks that simply blend into the lawn whilst providing a durable running surface. And, of course, although I've talked about each surfacing method in singular terms, it's open for you to think in terms of a combination of the various surfaces and textures.

Pathways and patios

The Building Regulations have a lot to say about access to the home, entrances, steps and pathways, which can have a profound effect on just how you plan the hard landscaping on a sloping site. Externally, they require that access ramps for slopes up to 1:15 should not be longer than 10 metres and those for gradients up to 1:10 no longer than 5 metres. Steeply sloping sites can, in the absence of a ramp, employ steps at least 900mm wide with a rise no greater than 150mm and a distance between landings of no more than 1800mm. Additionally, if there are more than three risers, handrails must be provided to at least one side. However, the regulations require 'reasonable provision for disabled people to gain access to a building'. Building Inspectors are usually pragmatic people and if a steeply sloping site made this interpretation impossible and threatened to render a site undevelopable, a reasonable solution can often be negotiated. This could entail the use of a lift, a spiral ramp or, in the final analysis, a complete relaxation on what would probably, and in any event, be a site that was never going to be suitable for disabled people.

The right garden path can give a special feeling to a house and garden. A winding path, moving between shrubs and raised features, will gradually reveal your new home and give it an air of mystery that a straight path or an open-plan front garden can never provide.

Paths around the garden enable you and your guests to walk around when it's wet and, properly considered, can make your garden look larger than it is. On the other hand all paths need maintenance of one sort or another and if they're not properly laid they will become uneven and dangerous. Some stone flags or brick pavoirs become lethally slippery in wet weather, particularly if they're on a side of the house that doesn't get the sun so, in these situations, it might be better to consider another paving material.

The patio or terrace is the means by which we project our living arrangements from within the confines of the house into the open air. Often it directly adjoins the house with access from one or more of the living rooms, but not necessarily. If you're after sun or perhaps even shade or a special view, then it can be divorced from the main house. But, always, thought has to be given to its primary purpose. If it's principally a feature to be admired but not regularly walked on, the gaps between the slabs can be filled with alpine plants and dwarf walls can be set at a height where they don't impede the view, with everything arranged for visual effect. If the patio is to be used for sitting out, or for parties with lots of guests, it's important that there are no gaps to trap high heels and walls are built at a convenient height for either sitting on or at the very least, resting one's drink on.

The norm used to be that patios and terraces were constructed with one material or another. But I invite you to consider whether a combination of materials and textures might not give this important feature more interest. Why not have areas within an otherwise stone-slabbed patio as large round pebbles set in concrete? What about mixing pavoirs or quarry tiles, on edge or flat? What about shingled areas planted with aromatic herb shrubs? How about areas of raised timber decking?

Walls, fences and hedges

Walls are a very special feature in a garden, and building a new one announces that you are seriously into landscaping. Walls also involve considerable expenditure. If you want to build a garden wall, it is important that you make no attempt to cut corners, as a cheap-looking wall will damage the appearance of the garden as much as an appropriate one will enhance it. If you use the wrong bricks or stone your wall will look wrong and will get worse as it weathers, whilst the right materials will look better and better as time goes by. Walls should give a feeling that they are part of the landscaping: they will not do this if they are inappropriate to the surroundings. In particular, this means that concrete blocks of all sorts, particularly the ornamental pierced walling blocks, should only be used in the sort of urban or seaside situation which suits them, and never as part of a rural scene.

Retaining walls are a different kettle of fish. The type of construction depends on the height of the land that is to be retained and whether or not any buildings are to be supported, but, as a rule of thumb, if you're retaining more than 1.2 metres, you need a specialist engineer to be involved in the design. As much care needs to be taken with the drainage of the retained land and the reduction of water pressure as it does with the actual strength of the wall itself. There are alternatives to building a wall, some of which, like the cages of stones one can see on British motorways, are singularly unattractive and some of which, like the cleverly designed interlocking planted blocks one sees on French motorways, are much more pleasing to the eye.

Prefabricated interwoven fence panels are a flimsy and temporary solution to the immediate requirement for enclosure and privacy in a new garden. They are by no means even a medium, let alone a long-term, prospect but if they are used in the proper place, as the backdrop for a growing hedge or a system of climbing plants, then they too can serve a purpose. Heaven preserve us, however, from the waving and unsteady lines of deteriorating timber that greet us on so many estates, purporting to represent permanent boundary definitions.

There are so many other choices that I can never understand why people don't give this matter more careful thought. Post and rail fencing with its solidity, its bold statement of enclosure, coupled with uninterrupted vision, serves, with the addition of mesh at the lower level, to keep animals out. The single rail fence serves to demarcate the boundary between public pathway and grass that should not be crossed. The 2-metre-high close-boarded fence serves to enclose a garden and give solid privacy at the same time whilst its cousin, the hit-and-miss slatted fence, gives a little of the privacy away yet provides an ideal backdrop for the climbing plants and shrubs that front it. However, if any of these was left in isolation and not combined with landscaping and planting, then they too would gradually fail in their role.

If you have an existing field hedge on a boundary to your land, you are very lucky, but it may need a great deal of work to put it in good order. First of all, check with your solicitor whether it belongs to you or

Remember that your house must also be what a prospective purchaser will want to buy some day.

your neighbour. If it is your neighbour's, or if it straddles the boundary and is jointly owned, try to impress upon him that it's important that it is maintained from both sides. If necessary offer to nip around to his side and trim it for him. That's not altogether altruistic as a hedge that's only cut on one side will gradually become misshapen and fall over. If he won't agree, all you can do is to keep it trimmed from your side 'in accordance with good practice', but it will never last.

Hedges undoubtedly get a bad press from time to time – even within the covers of this book – because they are at the root of so many disputes between neighbours. It shouldn't and it needn't be so. Talking with my son-in-law Ian Pitts, gardener to the Kent glitterati, made me realise that whilst a fence is immediately socially divisive, a hedge is something that can, and should, bring neighbours together. It's important that things are properly thought out. There needs to be no argument about where the boundaries are. Position durable stakes within the hedge or plant it within two lines of post and wire. The choice of the hedging plants themselves is also important with species being chosen for their ability to provide both privacy and beauty. But once made, and once made correctly, the choice of a hedge, over most of the cheaper forms of fencing, is likely to be something that will continue to evolve with the garden and provide a constant topic of social intercourse and co-operation between neighbours.

A properly laid hedge is a sight to behold and it's gratifying to see that the practice is coming back. The methods of carrying out the laying of a hedge vary slightly from county to county but in the main they involve the main uprights of the hedge being almost completely cut through and then bent down and intertwined with stakes cut from the same hedge. Such a hedge becomes thicker with each season and can present a durable and stock-proof enclosure, unlike its annually flailed compatriot, which becomes thinner year on year.

Under the Anti-Social Behaviour Act 2003 a homeowner who believes that their home is being blighted by a hedge can require, upon payment of a non-returnable fee of £600, that the local authority acts as an intermediary between them and their neighbours. If the 'guilty' party refuses to cut their hedge down to 2 metres in height, then they could face a fine of £1,000. If they still refuse to carry out the order then they will be liable to an additional fine of £200 per day. The powers, which have been long awaited, do not apply to deciduous hedges and only refer to evergreen and leylandii hedges.

Sheds, summer houses and greenhouses

All of these, as well as garages, can often be constructed or erected at a later date under Permitted Development Rights, which are discussed in detail in Chapter 8. However, you might like to include them within your initial planning permission and, that way, you will not be using up those rights.

Under other headings, I've referred or alluded to offices, hobbies rooms and play areas. If these are constructed as part of the house their costs are going to be every bit as much per square metre as they are for any other part of the home. I invite you, therefore, to consider whether these activities could best be housed in a shed or outhouse for which you would pay a tenth of the cost.

Unusual features

I've said several times that the reason most people get into self-building is so that they can have their houses just how they want them and not how anyone else thinks they should have them. I've also expressed my dismay that more self-builders don't push the boat out in design terms. They've led the way for the last three decades in pushing forward design to suit people rather than planners and architects, but I can't help feeling that we could all go that little bit further. That said, I have also stressed that an eye has to be kept on the probability that you will want to sell your new home some day. Think about peculiar or unusual features before you go ahead and, if you can, think of ways to get what you want without compromising the value of your new home. This entire chapter has been about building what you want. But remember that your house must also be what a prospective purchaser will want to buy some day.

Chapter 7

RENOVATING, CONVERTING AND EXTENDING

A lot of what follows in this brief chapter could be equally applicable to new build, especially the thoughts regarding location and valuation. However, there are significant differences in much of the approach to renovating, extending or converting an existing dwelling and enough of them to warrant this separate chapter. In addition, when it comes to discussing the role of the various tradesmen in Chapter 10, I have added separate notes about the methods and approaches necessary for this and older types of property.

By the way, renovation is the act of making an existing dwelling into a better one. Conversion turns a building that wasn't previously used as a dwelling into one. These distinctions are important, especially when it comes to being able to reclaim VAT, or not.

Almost the first thing anybody will require, having decided to embark on a renovation or conversion project, is a full survey of what's there already. This should be carried out by a competent surveyor, architect, structural engineer, or indeed a combination of any of these disciplines working together. They should have a thorough knowledge of basic architectural history and specialise in the restoration or conversion of old buildings.

There is always an element of having to put the cart before the horse. When a project such as this comes on the market, the value and therefore the price you are prepared to pay relies to a large extent on the soundness of the existing structure. A full survey is going to cost money, which you might not want to spend before the property is actually yours. At the very minimum you need an initial estimate, from a competent and knowledgeable person, sufficient to secure the property, after which you will commission the full survey, which will, hopefully confirm the initial assumptions.

Bringing a property up to date takes a person with building knowledge, flair and imagination and, above all, empathy with the architectural history of the building and the area. If the property to be 'done up' is in the local vernacular, possibly even Listed, then it becomes even more important that the person doing the design work and creating the specification, is *au fait* with what the planners want, and what is right in order for the building to retain its architectural integrity. If the building is one that has little or no architectural merit, one that is, and never was right in the street scene, then the same skills will be necessary in order to create a dwelling that does fit in with the local vernacular. You need to find the right person for this and to do so, you need to ask around and interview prospective professionals in order to assess their abilities. Perhaps, as usual, the local authority is a good place to start for names. As well as the Building Inspector, you could also try the planning officers or conservation officers, all or some of whom will undoubtedly be able to put you on to individuals or practices who have successfully completed projects in their area. If they are reluctant on

Above: **Building in flint is best done with a traditional
lime mortar.** ©The Lime Centre

this point, maybe fearful of showing favour, then try
looking out for completed or current applications
where the necessary skills are demonstrated, and get
the names from the files.

Conversion projects, and the abilities of the professionals who specialise in them, follow similar
criteria apart from the fact that with many there is
more of a blank canvas upon which to create a new
home out of something completely different. The
planners might also have a pretty big input as there is
a tendency for them to want much of the original
agricultural or industrial heritage of the building to be
preserved. 'I don't want it to look domestic' is not an
uncommon phrase used by planning officers describing what is to be your new home!

Many experienced renovators claim the ability to assess a possible renovation project by instinct. Whilst there may be some truth in that, the probability is that, through practice, they have learnt to fast forward through the various checklists and cut straight to the potential, only going back to check on the details when the decision in principle has been made. For those with less experience it is necessary to consider the detail in a step-by-step approach and to learn and understand the principles involved in a successful and profit-making renovation project.

Recognising and calculating the potential

Surely anybody investing their time and money on renovating or improving a property wants to know that their efforts are going to be rewarded, either immediately by selling on or in the long term by increased equity. To calculate the potential of any renovation project, one needs to know three things:

• the possibilities

• the costs

• the values.

The problem is that whilst all three of the above are of equal importance there is no specific sequel. You cannot make a decision on the possibilities without knowing the costs and when you know the costs you still can't make the decision until you are sure of the values.

Are you hoping to gain by simply bringing a dilapidated property back into use or are you hoping to expand the potential of the property? Thoughtful re-modelling and updating of the interior and the fittings and fixtures, including kitchens and bathrooms, may be all that is needed to bring a property up to its true potential value. In other instances it might not make sense to consider an extension or even to improve the scope of the accommodation as the costs of carrying out the work, added to the original costs, will exceed the value of the completed property, probably by taking it beyond the ceiling value that we have discussed before. Yet with another property the full potential may be waiting to be unlocked by judicious extension, by the opening up of the attic to provide additional accommodation or by bringing the basement into proper usage. Doing your homework on local values and understanding the costs will help you to identify just where your money is best spent and where it is best saved.

Pick the right location

Areas go in and out of fashion. What is now a run-down street of terraced houses may well be the next up-and-coming place to live. What is now a comfortable suburban street may, by dint of other things happening in the area, be on the way down. What you need to do is to find the areas that are on the way up, where direct improvements to the environment are going to change things or where extraneous factors such as overspill from a higher-priced area are working to increase values. Urban regeneration programmes can transform towns or inner-city areas in a few short years with old or dilapidated factory buildings and derelict sites being converted to trendy flats and apartments and overgrown towpaths and canal banks being cleaned up to create a focus of smart town life.

Find out all you can about the town, village and street you're thinking of investing in. Get to know the streets where you are going to concentrate your search. Make regular trips to note down those properties which you feel might be likely prospects. Build up a portfolio of sale details for surrounding properties in both good and bad condition until you get a real feel for values. Note the accommodation that seems to fetch the highest prices and in particular,

Renovation is the act of making an existing dwelling into a better one. Conversion turns a building that wasn't previously used as a dwelling into one.

establish for yourself what the ceiling values are or the maximum price that an area can sustain.

Talk to local estate agents. Property values often follow fashion and they'll be the first to know which areas are on the up. It's perhaps not a good idea to rely on this information coming entirely from the agent who's trying to sell you the property. Try talking to others in the area who can give you an unbiased opinion, especially if you represent yourself as a developer who may be looking to sell through the right agent in the future.

Steer clear of long-term depressed areas unless you know that something is happening or going to happen that is going to have a beneficial impact. Look out for things such as the opening of an enterprise park or the creation of a new road or rail link that might transform the economy, and therefore the values, in the area. Avoid those that these new links will blight. However, if you know that a rail line is to be discontinued or a new by-pass is to be constructed that will turn a noisy and depressed village into a quiet backwater, then the time to buy is before it becomes general knowledge and not after.

Understanding costs and construction methods

Those building completely new homes on greenfield sites can, to a large extent, accurately predict their costs at the very earliest stages of their consideration of a project. Plenty of companies working within the self-build and building industries base their whole marketing strategies on pounds per square metre. They might be a bit on the low side as far as specification is concerned and some of the wilder claims might have to be discounted. But in general, it's not that difficult to come up with reasonably accurate budget tables, many of which are regularly featured in the specialist *Homebuilding & Renovating* magazine.

However, those who are renovating or converting an existing property cannot always fall back on published tables because, by the very nature of the beast, every single project is going to be different. Some might need to be completely re-roofed. Some might just need minor attention to some tiles or slates. One

might need walls taking down and re-building whilst another might be either completely sound or just in need of a little re-pointing.

But don't let that put you off. The new-build camp may be able to judge costs at an earlier stage, maybe even before plans have been drawn. But they still have to translate those initial budgets to a final specification. Pounds per square metre may be fine at the initial stages but it is a rough-and-ready guide and those who become experienced in renovation projects can quickly learn to assess probable costs and then firm them up when a detailed specification is available. At which time, they're in exactly the same position as the person undertaking a new build.

Another problem is the fact that, unless a complete refurbishment is being undertaken, using a rate based on pounds per square metre can create distortions when compared with new build. When new buildings are costed or their final costs are broken back against their size to arrive at a figure per square metre, all of the rooms are lumped in within that figure. But it is quite obvious that various rooms are going to cost much more than others. A dining room is often the most expensively furnished and least used room in a house. Yet in most cases all it consists of is four walls, a floor and a ceiling plus any windows and doors. On the other hand kitchens, utility rooms and bathrooms contain expensive fittings and fixtures with a concentration of trades and materials within them. Renovations and extensions that focus the work on expensive rooms such as these are obviously, therefore, going to cost more per square metre in face value terms. But in real terms, against the cost of similar rooms in a new build, the costs should be more or less the same.

When it comes to the building processes, the renovator or converter may well use many of the same trades that are used for new building. But, whilst they might have the same description, and many of the tasks they undertake have the same name, the skills needed are significantly different. Plasterers on new dwellings spend ages trying to perfect a mirror finish and they might find it extremely difficult or even impossible to produce a genuine rough surface rather than a good one that has been subsequently distressed. For older buildings, the trades and skills

Above: **Many old houses have barns and stable blocks that are ideal for conversion.**

in things like horsehair, sand and lime plasters are ones that are either lost or in very short supply. Carpenters, too, can have the vapours at the thought of making something out of square and bricklayers need to be able to lay bricks and stone in such a way as to emulate what's already there and not as they might do for new work. Whichever professionals or tradesmen you employ for these projects, they should be used to working on this type of building and they should be able to show a portfolio of their previous work.

Labour rates are more or less the same for new build and renovation on a like-for-like basis. The problem with many renovations, however, is that there is always going to be a greater element of work that has to be costed on a time basis. With renovations to relatively modern buildings, it is usually the preparatory work that is the add-on factor – getting

the building to the position where the real work of renovation can start. With older buildings the biggest add-on cost factor is always going to be the skills shortage for disciplines such as working with lime or even finding someone who has an understanding of the principles behind the various different forms of construction through the ages.

Although the oft-repeated advice is that one should never take on a builder on the basis of daywork or timework, the fact of the matter is that even a lump-sum price is usually arrived at by the contractor assessing just how much time a certain job is going to take. Even if it is presented in the form of measured work, i.e. a price for each square metre of work, then those prices are established by reference to the amount of time that each metre of work will take and the amount of money that the contractor would expect to receive for it.

With new build and most extensions, I don't think that there are many times when there is an excuse for builders and subcontractors not to give a lump-sum price. If the work is easily quantifiable and is listed in a specification then perhaps the reason behind not giving one may be because they don't have enough confidence in their own abilities. The unfortunate fact is that many tradesmen will work at one rate on price work and another, much slower one, on daywork. If a bricklayer wants to earn £200 per day and his usual rate is £300 for every thousand then if he lays close to 700 bricks he'll get his money. But if he's going to get that anyway then his laying rate will drop to around 400 per day.

With renovations and conversions the situation is slightly different and builders and subcontractors may well have good reason not to translate their work into a lump-sum price. They may have determined that the nature of the work or its uncertainty makes it impossible to successfully quantify. They may feel that measured work is inappropriate because, for example, whilst some bricks can be laid to a string line at a fast rate, others, such as brick details, will take a lot longer.

Incidentally, whilst many of you might think that these rates sound extortionate in comparison with other workers' wages, do bear in mind that unlike most other industries, the weather is an important factor in building and can put paid to many days' work at a time. Most of the people working within the industry are either self-employed or paid on the basis of time. Whilst on the face of it £200 per day for five days a week adds up to close to £50,000 per annum, the reality is that rain, frost and holidays probably bring that down to much closer to the national average wage.

Many may also wonder, when reading this book, why some trades appear to earn much more than others. The answer is twofold. Firstly, there are skill shortages in some trades such as bricklaying, and secondly, trades such as plumbing tend to be supply and fix and their level of capital investment in any job is therefore reflected in their pricing.

Understanding values and the principles behind valuation

If you asked many members of the public, 'How do you value houses?' most would not know how to answer. Yet, as I've already discussed in the chapter on money and finance, the value of property in the UK is the cornerstone of many people's sense of well-being and discussion of house prices is the stuff of countless conversations. Most people do the calculations in their heads on a regular basis, assessing what the value of their home is, calculating what they owe on it and concluding their true worth. They do it by comparing their home with other similar homes that come on the market in their area. If a 'For Sale' board goes up on a house then the first calls the estate agent can expect are from the next-door neighbours, keen to find out what it's up for and ready to use the knowledge to recalculate or confirm the value of their own properties.

That's exactly how estate agents arrive at a valuation. There's no magic formula. It's simply comparative value. They use exactly the same method of arriving at the value as the ordinary person in the street, only they do it more often. From time to time agents in some areas will start relating values to square footage but they'll never agree with each other. It'll work for a time and then the natural distortions will render the method useless. A poorly presented house, set against a well-maintained one that is slightly smaller yet offers the same basic accommodation, will not fetch more in the market place. And by the time you have finished adding and deducting to compensate for the differences you are back on the principle of comparative valuation.

But what do you do when there are no immediately apparent comparisons? Estate agents can often flounder at this point and the thing that gives them away is the when they ask, 'What were you thinking of asking?' It might mean that they have arrived at a value in their heads but are unwilling to give it away in case it's much lower than the figure you were thinking of. It might be that they are aware that you're talking to other agents and they don't want to put themselves at a disadvantage against an agent who confidently predicts that they can get much more.

But it might be that they really don't know.

A word of warning to those who plan to sell on quickly. Siren voices in the shape of agents jacking up the asking price simply to get the commission and do down the other agents shouldn't be listened to. However good it makes you feel at the time, when the property goes stale on the market and you end up taking what the others said at the beginning or possibly even less, you'll realise that you have deluded yourself.

The truth is there are always comparisons. Somewhere in the area a property like yours will have sold. It may have gone some time ago or there may have to be some adjustment for subsequent inflation. In the end, the final value of anything is the price that it will fetch in the open market. In the past that final arbiter was reached at auction and to some extent that principle is still used. In periods of high inflation, when properties are rising so fast in price that it's almost impossible for an agent to put a final figure on value, properties are either put to auction or sold by tender to the highest bidder.

Apart from that, inflation should be discounted. Never build inflation into your figures other than as a hope value, which will probably be used up in contingencies. If a project doesn't stack up financially at current values, then trusting to inflation is not the answer. Unless, that is, you know that that inflation is going to be a local phenomenon caused by the improvement factors that I have spoken about above.

It is important to understand that you don't have to spend a fortune to create a good impression.

A final word of warning about values. Your remit ends at the boundaries of your property. All property values rely on your neighbours sharing those values. If you are unfortunate enough to have untidy neighbours or if the adjoining houses are likely to remain in a derelict state, no amount of money, time and effort will counteract the dragging-down effect that these houses will have on yours. Unless you know that the situation is going to change, that someone like you is going to be getting hold of those properties and bringing them up to scratch, anything within their midst is best avoided.

Creating the best impression and spending wisely

It is important to understand that you don't have to spend a fortune to create a good impression. It is possible to buy cheaper kitchen units and create the same or in some case a better effect as with much more expensive ones. The right worktops with the right tiles will be what people want to see and they'll be much more interested in what facilities the kitchen provides than the make of the units. Similarly with bathrooms. It's possible to spend a small fortune on sanitaryware yet cheaper items can be made to look just as good by the clever use of accessories. Flooring is important. Good-quality carpets can give a feeling of absolute luxury to a room. Ceramic, stone or natural wood flooring will give a feeling of solidity underfoot that cheaper vinyl flooring or laminates can never impart, transforming the ambience of a room.

Be careful about changing the windows. There's a whole industry out there simply dedicated to getting you to do so. They sell their wares on the basis of greater thermal efficiency and there's no doubt that if the old windows are rotten or draughty then replacing them can seem like the best option. But new regulations demand that replacement windows conform to certain thermal requirements and in meeting these requirements many do compromise on style. If the new windows don't look like the originals you could lose the character of a building and that in turn could have a negative effect on value. Be aware that there are specialist companies who can restore things like sash windows at a fraction of the cost of new and that there are others who can make new windows to match the originals.

Whether you're planning to sell on immediately, stay for a while or call this home for ever, it's always a good idea to think of the market. Think about the sort of person or family who is going to be attracted towards buying your renovation project when it is finished and balance the accommodation. If it is a family house with three or four bedrooms then they may well require more than one and possibly as many as four reception rooms. If it is a one- or two-bedroom townhouse then too many reception rooms might actually detract from its desirability. Think about the size of rooms. In that townhouse it might be more acceptable to have more and smaller rooms, whilst in other houses fewer and larger might find more favour. If you're planning to provide a utility room make sure that its provision does not make the kitchen too small. Consider whether the space could be better utilised as a breakfast or dining area.

En-suite facilities often exercise the mind of the renovator. Yes, it's true that an en-suite bathroom or shower room to at least the master bedroom can make a difference to the value of some properties, but not if it makes the bedroom too small or if it means that another bedroom will be lost. Remember that once again this is an expensive room and it's important to keep a careful eye on costs versus value. The market isn't stupid – en-suite facilities are not the norm in older-type dwellings and most people looking for this sort of property won't be expecting them.

There is often a temptation to imagine that each and every space within a property has to be utilised. This is simply not true. Look at any of the magazines on property and you will see that the photogenic ones, the ones that often obtain the highest values, are of homes where space has been used for its own architectural merit, enhancing a property simply by existing. Consider the provision of light wells, sun vents and/or roof lights. Combine these, if you can, with vaulted ceilings to flood light down into a room and increase the impression of size. And if none of this is practicable, consider whether a similar effect can be achieved through indirect or hidden lighting. The more you can open up rooms using lighting and the careful choice of wall colours, the better. Avoid dark finishes. In particular avoid dark wood kitchen units in all but the largest and lightest of kitchens.

If it's going to be your home for the foreseeable future then do things just as you want them. But if you're going to be selling on in the near future, be very careful about straying too far from the norm. What you're trying to achieve is quality and excitement. But if you go too far in that quest you may go beyond the tastes and expectations of any purchaser. Just because you're excited about a boiler that's as complicated as an aircraft engine and costs the earth doesn't mean that you can translate that enthusiasm to every person who comes around to view the home. Stick to tried and tested. Stay with white sanitaryware and paint walls white or magnolia. It's not just coincidence that virtually every developer in the land follows suit. And it's not just them following each other blindly or opting for the cheapest. They know that these colours present the potential purchaser with the best first impressions and the blank canvas upon which they can later put their own stamp. Keep to pastel colours with kitchen doors and drawers but then cheer things up with bolder colours for worktops and accessories.

Be careful with your choices

Wooden or stone floors are fashionable and, as I've said above, can impart quality. But they are not that popular on bedroom floors where carpet might be much more acceptable. In fact the increasing use of wooden or laminate floors in renovations has given rise to complaints of noise in multi-occupancy buildings. So, as well as thinking about increasing the thermal efficiency of a home, try to think about how you can cut down on the transference of sound from one room to another or from one dwelling to another. Laminated plasterboards, insulation within the studwork, ceilings and floor zones can all help. As can carpets and/or noise-deadening underlays. When and if you come to sell, this, as much as any other provision, will be the deciding factor.

Above all, when you're planning your renovation, try to stick to conventional layouts. Most people have a general expectation of which rooms should follow through from each other and if you muddle up that progression then you will only confuse the potential buyer and put them off.

Consider all of these points. Weigh up in your own mind just what physical possibilities there are for your chosen property and then cost these out, com-

Above: **Nothing could be more hideous than the huge flat-roofed extension to this bungalow. In contrast, the sideways extension** (right) **will finish up looking as if it belongs even though it does narrow the space between it and the adjoining house.**

paring them to the potential for increased value. If they work out then adopt and adapt them. If they don't, then you might like to think again. I don't do anything to a property that won't increase its value. You, on the other hand – if you have decided that you are going to stay in the property for a while – might think that you want things as you want them and to hell with the future value. And that's your choice.

Materials and VAT

Many of the materials used will be the same as for new build. On the other hand those doing up older places will have to source traditional or reclaimed materials. Recent revived interest in older methods of building has meant that there are many companies specialising in traditional forms of construction and building materials. Some of their names appear on pages 456–8. Others can be found by reading specialist magazines or by reference to the Society for the Preservation of Ancient Buildings (SPAB). In any event, seek out your local architectural salvage or reclamation yard, where you will probably find all or most of what you need.

Those building new properties have a distinct advantage over those who are renovating in that they can recover most of the VAT paid out during the construction and don't have to pay any VAT on labour. If you're converting a property, changing it from a non-residential to a residential use, then the rules are slightly different in that you are supposed to pay VAT at just 5% on the labour but this can, however, be recovered, along with VAT paid out on material purchases. On the other hand, if you are renovating or extending an existing residential building you will have to pay out VAT on all materials and labour at the standard rate with no facility for recovery!

This lack of a level playing field, which undoubt-edly means that most renovation work costs at least 17.5% more than a new build, often makes it more economical to demolish and re-build. Whilst in many cases, where buildings have no particular architectural or structural merit, that's a good thing; in others it really is a shame.

By the way, if you are presented with a bill that includes VAT, make sure that the presenter is actually registered with HM Customs and Excise. It is not unknown for unscrupulous workers to make an extra 17.5% by adding VAT to their prices, which never goes anywhere near the Excise. All VAT invoices should have the VAT registration number clearly printed and if you are in any doubt, ring up the authorities and check. Whilst most subcontractors are not registered for VAT the most likely exceptions are always going to be the plumbers and electricians who, as supply and fix trades, are almost always VAT registered.

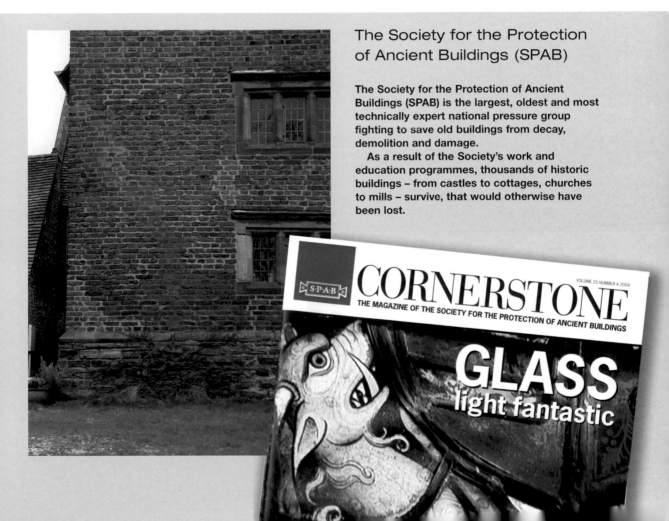

The Society for the Protection of Ancient Buildings (SPAB)

The Society for the Protection of Ancient Buildings (SPAB) is the largest, oldest and most technically expert national pressure group fighting to save old buildings from decay, demolition and damage.

As a result of the Society's work and education programmes, thousands of historic buildings – from castles to cottages, churches to mills – survive, that would otherwise have been lost.

The important stages in a renovation or conversion project

Whilst the trades involved may well be the same, the sequence of events between new build and renovations and conversions is significantly different. In effect each building or project is going to be different from the next and it's practically impossible to prepare a project planner in the same way as one would for a new build.

Nevertheless, there are recognisable stages and these are as follows:

Preliminary preparation
Secure the property

As soon as the property for conversion, renovation or refurbishment is yours, you will need to move to secure the premises to prevent vandalism or illegal occupation. Secure all doors and windows by boarding them up if necessary. Make sure that as soon as you are the beneficial owner, you have adequate insurance in place. Safety is vital during the re-building process both for people working on site and for members of the public, so you must make an assessment of the safety needs. A safety fence to keep the site and materials on and within the premises secure and the general public out is a good idea. If there is no secure storage available, a lockable store for tools and equipment is recommended.

Arrange for a full structural survey

This will be needed in order to prioritise the order of work and in order to obtain quotations for any warranty. It is also necessary to find out all you can about the method of construction that has been used so that you can arrange appropriate materials and begin discussions with contractors or tradesmen who are familiar with the type of building.

Planning, Building Regulations and Listed building consent

Make any necessary applications for planning permissionand Building Regulations/Warranty as soon as possible. If the building is Listed, make sure that you have Listed building consent before carrying out any work. If emergency work is required prior to such approvals, always check with the authorities before acting. Assure them of the necessity, and stress that it should not prejudice their decisions. Make sure warranty providers have adequate notice of commencement of works and send in 'Commencement of Works' cards to the local authority in good time.

Prevent further deterioration

Much of what will be wrong with any older building will be caused by the ingress of water. If parts of the roof are missing or leaking, cover them with a tarpaulin. Take particular care to ensure that water is prevented from entering the tops of walling particularly from broken or blocked guttering. Where walling is unstable, either arrange for early demolition or shore up using stout timber props or scaffolding supports. Make the building weathertight by covering all unglazed windows and openings with sheets of polythene fixed up by battens.

Secure or isolate the services

If electricity or gas supplies are connected to the building you should arrange for them to be either cut off or isolated if they are unsafe. Alternatively, to keep power on site, make sure that the electricity supply is secure by locking the building or taking it to a temporary consumer unit within a lockable box. If there is no electricity supply, apply for a quotation as soon as possible and make arrangements to hire a generator for use with heavy tools, together with a transformer, as many are 110 volts. Make sure that any existing water supply has a proper stopcock and that it is adequately protected from frost. If there is no water supply on site, arrange for a building supply as soon as possible and, if necessary, hire a bowser.

Strip back the building and salvage what can be re-used

Once the building has been made safe it is time to strip it back to those parts that are to be retained. Materials that are to be re-used should be carefully removed and stored. Waste materials should be disposed of off site.

Organise the site

Decide where on the site materials will be stored. Consider how deliveries will be made and whether the access is suitable. If necessary arrange to create a hard-standing or offloading point. If on-road parking is all that is available, make sure that you have notified the highways authorities, and arrange for warning signs or traffic lights in good time if required. Bear in mind that during the course of the work a number of items may be required at short notice such as scaffolding, diggers, dumpers or cranes, so ensure that there is adequate space for them. Position a skip on site for the gathering and regular removal of rubbish and, if necessary, hire a rubbish chute to take waste directly from the scaffold to the skip.

Stabilise the building

Stabilising the foundations and underbuilding

The structural survey will detail the remedial works that are the most essential and although it is the roof that may need attention first, it may also point towards necessary work to the foundations and underbuilding.

- **Underpinning:** subsidence of foundations is the most common cause of cracks to the super-structure. Older houses may have concrete strip foundations, which have been taken to an inadequate depth. Others may have no foundations other than a spreading of the brickwork. Underpinning usually involves digging down beneath the foundations to a depth of at least 1 metre and infilling with concrete. Usually this is done in alternate metre sections to avoid the collapse of the building, with each section joined by reinforcement bars. It is most often undertaken by specialist contractors who can issue a warranty for their work.

- **Underbuilding:** foundation walls to be renewed or replaced and keyed into existing ones are best built with common or engineering-quality bricks. Extra strength can be gained by the use of expanded metal brick lathe. New foundation

Basements

Planning permission is required to dig a new basement beneath an existing building. Occupation of an existing cellar can normally be carried out under Permitted Development Rights. If the basement is to be a habitable space it must be waterproofed. This is usually achieved by tanking with a waterproof material. Alternatively there are systems that effectively line the walls and floors with material that is corrugated on the backside to allow moisture to be channelled to a sump and pumped away. Thought needs to be given to ventilation of a basement and the provision of light through either high-level windows or light wells.

walls can be built from blockwork founded on concrete foundations that are at least 1 metre deep and, in any event, deeper than the existing. These may be deep-strip foundations with concrete in the bottom of the trench or trenchfill with the concrete brought close to ground level. Where new foundations abut existing ones they should underpin them at the junction. Specialist foundations for certain conditions may be required and will have to be designed by an engineer.

- **Damp-proof course:** where there is no damp-proof course, lenders may require one to be installed. This can be by silicone injection, which is best carried out by specialist contractors who will provide a guarantee. A damp-proof course can also be installed by mechanical means and the insertion of slate or non-porous brickwork. This is usually carried out in alternate sections.

- **Subfloors:** concrete oversites may need taking up and replacing with damp-proof membranes and insulation beneath them. Where there is no subfloor, excavate to a depth sufficient to lay hardcore, blinding, insulation and membrane prior to the laying of a new concrete oversite. If this subfloor is to support sleeper walls it may need thickening underneath the runs with reinforcement mesh placed within the concrete.

Stabilising the walling

As a general rule the method of repair should mirror the method that was originally used to build. If modern methods and materials are applied to some older buildings, then the act of restoration can create long-term problems that can eventually lead to the virtual destruction of some buildings.

- **New brickwork and blockwork:** if an extension is planned then it is often best to build this in modern materials, at least for the inner leaf of any cavity walling. The internal leaf can be built with either a timber frame or insulating block-work using a cementatious mortar. If reclaimed or salvaged materials are to be utilised for the external leaf to match the existing one, then these should use the same mortar as was employed when the building was first built. All walling will need to be properly founded and, where it abuts an existing wall, tied into it by crocodile ties.

- **Re-building in reclaimed brick:** try to curb any individualism that your bricklayers may wish to express and, wherever possible, follow the pattern and the gauge of the existing brickwork. Older bricks are usually in metric (larger) sizes. If you are using a modern close match, try to gauge the courses so as not to clash with the original. Never re-build or repair walling until the cause of the original movement has been eliminated.

- **Re-building in stone:** in some areas stone is laid in courses where each layer of stone has a uniform height in the face of the wall. In other areas the stone is laid in random courses where the beds of the stone are more or less horizontal but jumpers are employed from time to time to lift a course into the ones above. Stone is usually

Understand the nature of the building

Many older properties were built with solid walling, relying on the thickness of the walling to provide an acceptable degree of comfort and dryness. Walls may be brick, stone or cob (literally clay, chalk, straw, animal hair and dung). All absorb moisture from time to time and need to breathe. Lime-based mortars, renders and plasters never fully set, unlike cement-based products. They develop a more or less hard exterior veneer but always remain pliable behind the face and, most importantly, present no barrier to the wall's ability to breathe.

Left and above:
Cleaning off inappropriate render or paint from otherwise pristine brickwork is a job for specialists.
©Strippers of Sudbury

delivered to a cut size to the bed or width. In modern construction stone is laid with a backing block to prevent sagging on the bed, which makes the maintenance of a cavity difficult. In the old days when the walls were solid this problem was overcome by building the wall as two skins and then filling the centre with a rubble and mortar mix as they came up, to stabilise both leafs.

- **Re-pointing:** with the exception of granite, much of the stone used in older buildings is softer limestone based. Older bricks are also softer than their modern equivalents and were origi-

Above: **The principal rafters should be sound in this barn as they have been protected by the lightweight corrugated iron roofing.**

Left: **As long as it's kept dry, cob or rammed mud walling will maintain its integrity.**

nally laid with a lime-based mortar. Any moisture getting into the wall is able to express itself through the weaker and sacrificial mortar rather than causing damage to the principal walling medium. Re-pointing these soft facings with harder, cement-based mortars can lead to 'spalling' where the water, frost and sulphate are only able to exit the wall through the brick or stone, resulting in lamination and die back. Always re-point these walls using a lime-based mortar. Avoid both heavily recessed or proud re-pointing. Go for flush, weatherstruck or slightly recessed. Harder modern materials can, of

course, be re-pointed with a sand and cement mortar.

- **Steel purlins and RSJs**: it may be necessary to support upper walls or the roof by steel purlins or joists. The size and configuration of these will have to be determined by an engineer. Steels must be supported on solid brickwork or block-work and bedded on a concrete padstone or spreader beam.

Stabilising the roof

It is often the case that problems with walls can be traced to a leaking roof or broken guttering. If water gets into the top of a lime mortar-based construction it creates a loss of adhesion and integrity. But you cannot go on the roof until the rest of the super-structure has been stabilised and, with the exception of minor repairs, a full scaffold erected.

- **Strip back and salvage:** the roof may be covered already, in which case you have to decide whether it needs touching at all. At the very least a roof should have an underlay and, in Scotland, sarking boards. Attention must also be given to the provision of ventilation and insulation. If you are going to use a new roofing medium then the old slates or tiles can be quickly ripped off and discarded. If you intend to re-use them then they must be taken off carefully and stacked neatly on the scaffold. Some breakages will be unavoidable, so you will need to identify close matches from local reclamation or architectural salvage yards. If you cannot obtain the exact match confine the odd ones to roof planes at the rear or out of sight. Discard old or rotted under-lays and always use new treated timber battens. Pay close attention to the nailing of tiles and slates. Each slate should be nailed at least once and most tiles should be nailed every third course.

- **The roof construction:** many homes built in the last hundred years employ a roofing system based on rafters supported by purlins and braced by ceiling joists or ties. In more modern homes prefabricated trusses often replace these. Older buildings may employ various systems based on principal rafters or trusses supporting purlins, which in turn support common rafters spanning from the wallplate to the ridge. It is important to understand the principles behind the construction and I have described and illus-trated the various forms in Chapter 10, within the section on carpenters, dealing with renova-tions and conversions.

Ensure that all timber is sound and, if neces-sary, arrange to have all timbers treated against insect infestation. Some members may need replacing altogether. Others may need augment-ing with additional timber. New extensions can often employ prefabricated trusses.

- **Plates, valleys, hips and ridges:** check that all wallplates are sound and properly tied down with plate straps. Pay attention to ridges, hips and, in particular, valleys where ingress of water may have rotted the principal timbers and the lay boards. Watch out for any separation of the jack rafters from the valley board. The lower ends of the rafters were often just tosh-nailed and time and the weight of the roof may have pulled the nails free, allowing the rafters to slip sideways. Sometimes they can be jacked back into position and fixed with galvanised strap-ping without the need to strip the valley completely. At other times this may be necessary. Strip back valleys and re-lay any tired lead, dressing it up and over a batten laid down on either side of the valley. Re-bed ridge and hip tiles using hip irons.

- **Guttering and downpipes:** leaking guttering and downpipes are often the cause of problems with walling, where the water is conducted into the top resulting in loss of integrity. Remove and replace broken guttering with new. Take care to choose styles that complement the period in which the home was built. Guttering is available in Pvc-u, aluminium, cast iron and copper.

- **Lead flashings:** if lead is tired then it is best to replace it with new. Lead trays through chimneys can be re-utilised so long as they are sufficiently pliable to be dressed over new cover flashings tacked well up underneath their overhang and dressed into the masonry. Make sure that all lead soakers, valleys, cavity trays and flashings are properly fitted, dressed and pointed in, especially at chimneys and roof abutments.

- **Flat roofs:** these are frequently a source of problems and if they can be replaced with a pitched roof it is often better. If you are

Unless you are deliberately changing the character of the building, always try to stick to the original style.

going to retain a flat roof, build the decking as a 'warm' roof with the insulation above the decking (obligatory in Scotland). The traditional waterproofing is two or three layers of bitumous felt laid on to hot bitumen, finished off with a top layer of mineral felt and/or protective chippings. Modern alternatives use four layers of glass-reinforced polyester bonded to the decking and each other with no joints or seams.

- **Insulation and ventilation:** despite the fact that the Government seems to be fighting shy of new legislation to require thermal upgrading, most people will want to put the best insulation in their new home. Rigid foam or mineral wool can be placed between the rafters or the ceiling joists. If a breathable underlay is used beneath the tiles or slates, no ventilation is required. Otherwise continuous ventilation is required at the eaves and at the ridge.

Doors, windows and openings

Don't rush to change the windows. Repairing them can often be a better option. Unless an exemption can be obtained for historic buildings or those with particular architectural merit, replacement windows must conform to FENSA and Building Regulations requirements, having a 'U' value of 2.0 or, in the case of metal framed windows, 2.2.

Be careful about the style

Unless you are deliberately changing the character of the building, always try to stick to the original style. Many older buildings have box sash windows in which the top and bottom sections can slide up and down independently. Others may have casement windows that open like doors, hinged at the side. Large picture windows, often in combination with opening casements and top lights, are an invention of the recent past and do not generally sit well with older-style or traditional buildings.

Modern copies of traditional sash and casement windows do not always look the same as the thermal requirements within the regulations require that they are double glazed. This means that the glazing bars and rebates may have to be thicker in profile. One way around that, in part, is for the glazing bars to be introduced within the double-glazed unit. It works quite well at times, but with some manufacturers it really misses the point.

Sliding patio windows are a modern phenomenon. If you are building an extension, then they can look right. At other times, the traditional alternative would be French windows.

Roof lights

Considerable extra light can be brought into the home by the use of roof lights. Modern tilt-and-turn-type opening lights can look right, even on an older building. Alternatively there are 'conservation' types, with central glazing bars and a low profile, but these are often non-opening.

Doors

The front door in particular is an important feature in the home and the style should reflect the character and period of the property. Many older homes have framed, ledged and braced or solid front doors. Others have panel doors, with or without glazed sections. The garage is of course an invention of the recent past and it is almost impossible for the doors to emulate the doors and windows of older buildings. Try, wherever possible, to make the garage look like a stable block or cart barn and consider, if it's big enough, whether it really needs doors at all.

Lintels and arches

Some older homes do not have lintels above the doors or windows, relying either on the frame itself or an arch of masonry to support the superstructure above. Others may have a timber lintel, which may have deteriorated. Insertion of a new steel or pre-stressed concrete lintel must be carefully carried out, with the walling above supported by pins taken through the wall supported by adjustable steel props. Archways rely on the 'keystone' being in place. Relief can be gained for flat-topped openings by the introduction of a 'save stone', shaped like a wide wedge in the walling above.

Cold bridging

Care needs to be taken to avoid cold bridging at the reveal with a cavity wall.

Timber floors, staircases and first-fix carpentry

Many older homes have ground floors comprising timber joists with tongued-and-grooved softwood floor boarding. Intermediate floors are usually timber joists, supported either by timber beams or steels with tongued-and-grooved timber board decking.

Check the sleeper walls

Ground-floor joists will be spanning from the outside walls to sleeper walls built off the oversite. Check that these sleeper walls are in good condition and that the wallplate is sound and bedded on a damp-proof course. Do not compromise the honeycomb structure as this is designed to allow a free flow of air.

Make sure all air bricks are clear

It is vital that there is adequate ventilation below the ground floor. Check that no vents or airbricks have been covered by soil or paving.

Insulate

Insulate ground floors by slinging netting between the joists to support mineral wool insulation or by firring the sides of the joists to support rigid foam insulation board. Additional draught proofing can be obtained by laying a damp-proof membrane before replacing the decking.

Attend to faulty joists

Faulty joists should be removed or, if this is not possible, strengthened by new joists placed beside them and bolted through. If support beams to intermediate floors are suspect, consider replacing them with an RSJ and cladding this with timber. Alternatively, use oak or similar, to a thickness specified by your engineer. Joists that have suffered from insect or fungal damage but are otherwise sound may need specialist treatment. Prevent squeaking by the introduction of midspan strutting using proprietary metal strapping or by solid blocking. Use lateral restraint straps running across at least three joists at 2-metre spacings, built into or firmly fixed to the external walling. Wherever possible, and with new joists, use a joist hanger built into the wall to support the ends of joists.

Decking

Before any decking goes back down, the electricians and plumbers will have to drill through and notch out for their new services. The same rules as for new

Left: **Timber lintels will almost certainly need replacing.**

Professional stripping services

Cleaning the black paints, pitch and stains can go a long way towards restoring the original features of a building.
© Strippers of Sudbury

build, regarding the notching and drilling of joists, will apply. If you are re-using the old decking, make sure that it is sound, free from nails and treated if necessary. Sand all floorboards once they are laid. New tongued-and-grooved boards should be cramped up as they are laid, with all ends taken to a joist or supported by a nogging. If you are laying tongued-and-grooved moisture-resistant chipboard, this should be laid across the run of the joists with all short ends

Above: **Death watch beetle can render a piece of timber almost unrecognisable.**

either running to a joist or supported on noggings. All tongued-and-grooved edges must be glued.

Staircases

Existing staircases can be utilised but may need replacement parts. Knocking out the wedges before tapping them firmly back and gluing them in place can often cure creaking staircases. Make sure that new newels and balustrading match the style of the home you are creating. Cover up staircases and tack hardboard to the treads to protect them from following trades.

First-fix carpentry

This includes boxing out for soil and vent pipes, the fixing of window boards, garage door frames, the making and erecting of new internal studwork partitioning and the fixing of all door linings. Any tank stands in the loft will have to be built and the loft trap formed. Floating floors of chipboard laid on membrane over insulation come under the heading 'first-fix' but may be left until after plastering.

Drainage and services

If the supplies have been isolated or cut off during the stabilisation and major construction period, you will need to make sure that they are back on in good time and that any necessary meter boxes have been built in.

Any exposed drains should be stopped off with bungs and covered over with steel plates to prevent blockage or damage.

Existing drainage

Wherever possible, and as long as they are working properly, the existing drainage and sewage arrangements should be left in place. It may be necessary to upgrade on-site disposal systems and also to investigate existing drainage and sewer connections by means of a camera survey.

New drainage

Re-arrangement of accommodation and the provision of new facilities may require the construction of new drains and the re-routing of wastes within the property. Consider these well before new floors are laid and take care to give wastes a route through flooring to the soil and vent pipes, whilst maintaining the integrity of the joists.

Special situations

If you are trying to bring drainage to areas of the property where normal gravity flow for waste is not possible such as in a basement or in rooms where direct access to the vent pipe is impossible, consider the use of macerating and pumping systems.

Services

If there is an existing water supply to the premises, then this should be maintained and protected as far as is possible. If it is necessary to cut off the water supply, have this re-routed to a standpipe for construction purposes that is in a safe and lockable position, adequately protected from frost and with a non-return tap connection. Gas connections may need isolation during the re-building process and should be stopped off in a suitably safe environment such as a new meter box. Make sure that the suppliers are aware of the fact that

any disruption is of a temporary nature. Electricity supplies may also have to be suspended but should, if at all possible, be routed to a new meter position with a temporary consumer unit. This type of work has always to be carried out in concert with the suppliers and by qualified, registered and competent contractors.

Re-wiring and electrical

In England and Wales, and to a slightly lesser extent in Scotland, electrical work to domestic premises, including outhouses, swimming pools and gardens, now comes within the ambit of Building Control. All work must be carried out by a competent person registered under an electrical self-certification scheme or by an electrician who could be considered competent for the purposes of signing a BS7671 Electrical Installation Certificate, but is not registered with an electrical self-certification scheme.

General

This rules out most DIY work and excludes most general builders from the definition of a competent person. If an electrician who is registered under a self-certification scheme does the work, there is no need for a separate Building Regulations application. An unregistered but competent electrician must make a separate Building Regulations application and provide written evidence that the works have been designed, installed and tested to ensure that they comply with BS7671. The works must then be inspected and approved by the Building Control department who may not have the expertise. You are, therefore, strongly recommended to use only electricians who are registered with an approved self-certification scheme.

Certain limited works can be carried out outside the regulations. These include replacing socket outlets, control switches and ceiling roses. Replacement of cable for a single circuit only, and adding lighting points to an existing circuit and socket outlets to an existing ring or radial circuit, are also exempt, so long as they are not in a kitchen, bathroom or wet room.

Replacement

Premises with old-fashioned rubber- or lead-sheathed wiring should always be re-wired as this type of wiring is unsafe and will have deteriorated. Round-pin, unfused sockets and switches should also be replaced. You are also strongly advised to consider the replacement of fuse-wire-type consumer units with modern consumer units that split the light and power into separate circuits. The lighting, central heating and smoke detector circuits are then protected by MCBs (miniature circuit breakers) that detect any short circuit and cut off the power, whilst the power circuits are protected by RCDs (residual circuit devices), which detect the slightest earth leakage and cut off the power immediately.

Re-wiring should be planned so that, wherever possible, new wiring is run through the floor and ceiling zones and up and down the walls vertically to the outlet, protected by sheathing conduit. If there is no alternative to wiring being surface mounted, then it should be run in special galvanised metal channels.

Disabled access

Extensions in England and Wales must comply with Part 'M' of the regulations and have sockets no lower that 450mm from the floor and switches no higher than 1200mm from the floor. If you are completely re-wiring an old house then sockets and switches should be within this 450–1,200mm zone. If you are partially re-wiring then sockets and switches can stay as before so long as access to them is not made worse.

Contracts

Most electrical work is quoted on the basis of a supply-and-fix contract but some electricians will either agree to a labour-only arrangement or to fittings and fixtures being supplied by the client.

New plumbing and central heating

Plumbers installing and working on a gas-fired system must be CORGI (Council for Registered Gas Installers) registered. Those working on oil-fired systems should be OFTEC (Oil Firing Technical Association) registered.

Most people renovating, converting, refurbishing or extending property will choose to use the same contractor for the heating and domestic hot water. The trade is usually supply and fix although the client can supply many items.

General

Strip out all lead piping within the site and the home. If the supply is lead, contact the water board and require them to upgrade this on their side of the stopcock. Most older properties have a vented system of plumbing and domestic hot water, employing storage tanks in the loft. These take up any expansion as an overflow and top up and return water to the system. Modern systems work on mains-pressure systems, which do away with the need for tanks in the loft. Instead, any expansion is taken up by expansion vessels connected to the boiler and the hot water storage tanks, which are capable of storing hot water under pressure. Plan the plumbing layout at the earliest possible stage so that most pipework can be hidden in the floor zones and consider the use of plastic plumbing so that the routes can be more flexible.

Boilers

At the risk of being repetitive, all gas boilers installed in England and Wales must now achieve an efficiency rating of at least 86%. From April 2007 this requirement will be extended to include replacement oil-fired boilers. Most observers believe that this, of necessity, means that in future all boilers will be of the condensing type. However, with renovations and conversions, where the installation of a condensing boiler would be uneconomical by virtue of the fact that the position of the new boiler would necessitate an extended flue or a pump to dispose of the condensate, or where any new boiler position to avoid those problems would mean it having to be sited within sleeping or living accommodation, a non-condensing boiler will be allowed. Combination boilers (which can also be condensing) do away with the need for storage tanks altogether and heat up the water as it is required. They are most suitable for the smaller unit or where storage tanks would be difficult to locate. Those converting flats or smaller premises might also consider an electric boiler and water heating.

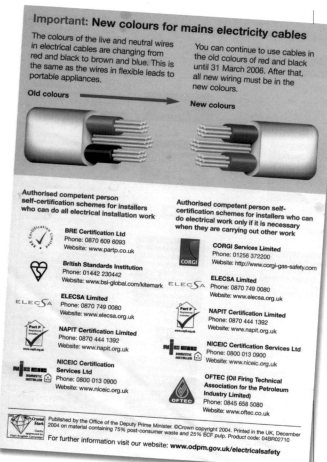

Above: **You should only ever use registered and self-certifying electricians.**

Radiators

Older radiators may need replacing if they show signs of corrosion. On the other hand, and especially if they are cast iron or decorative radiators that suit the style and age of the building, they can be refurbished and may indeed simply need de-sludging. Additional radiators may also be sourced at reclamation or architectural salvage depots. The addition of thermostatic radiator valves will add greatly to the efficiency of any system.

Under-floor central heating

Although under-floor central heating can be installed with timber-suspended floors, it is at its most efficient when employed with solid or screed floors where there is a thermal mass to take up and slowly release the heat. Solid ground floors can receive under-floor central heating in combination with radiators in other positions. If all that is required is to heat up otherwise cold tiled or stone floors, then consider electric under-floor matting on a timer and possibly also off-peak-rate electricity.

New sanitaryware

Replacing and modernising dated bathrooms and toilets is, after new kitchen units, the single most important improvement that can be made. On the other hand don't rush to discard that old bath or basin as they can be refurbished.

Re-plastering and rendering

As with the walling, the method and materials used for re-plastering and rendering should follow and reflect the original. In some cases, particularly with ceilings, it might make more sense to start again and use modern methods. In other cases, modern Gyproc or cement-based materials could actually harm the building.

Lime plasters and renders

If the external rendering of any building has broken down then it does need to be attended to fairly quickly. Cob walling, for example, is rock hard when dry but if it gets wet, it will revert to its constituent parts pretty soon. These solid walls of older buildings need to breathe. Natural moisture is evaporated mainly on the outside where the passing wind draws it out. If a cement-based external render is used, which prevents this natural balance, then any moisture may express itself either as damp patches within the home or by areas of plaster or render becoming loose. Lime-based renders and plasters allow the wall to breathe naturally. Coarse or medium-grade sand is used for external renders and fine sand for internal plasterwork. Animal hair is used to strengthen the mix.

Whilst that's the general advice, I do accept that in certain very damp, high-exposure areas, where wind-driven rain is a problem, rendering older cob-walled buildings with cement-based renders can be beneficial.

Above: **The renovated flint-and-brick facia at the Lime Centre and as it was,** right.

Below: **Repairing damage to pointing caused by masonry bees.** ©The Lime Centre

This is especially so if the internal plasterwork is maintained as a breathing medium and the natural moisture balance within the walling is maintained.

Ceilings

Lath and plaster ceilings can become loose, usually because the laths rot or detach from the joists. They can be fixed back by screws and plates or by the use of plaster of Paris and hessian. Laths can also be replaced. Many will decide that it is easier to take lath and plaster ceilings down and replace them with modern plasterboard, which is then skim coated or set with Gyproc plaster. Usually this has no deleterious effect and in many cases original decorative mouldings can be saved and re-used.

External cement render

Cement-based renders used on cavity and modern construction usually comprise one, two or occasionally three coats of a sand and cement mix. The topcoat can have a waterproof additive mixed within it and can be rubbed up smooth with a float or a trowel. Pebbledash is created by thickening the final coat and then dashing pebbles into the mixture before pushing them home with a float. Tyrolean is created by a hand-held machine that dashes a mixture of pebbles and mortar on to a base-coat render.

Internal hard plaster

Traditional hard plaster comprises one, or sometimes two, coats of sand and cement render with a finishing coat of smooth plaster. The base coats can be replaced with proprietary plasters of differing types, each one of which is formulated for use with a different substrate. It is very hard wearing but has a long drying-out time, particularly in the winter.

Dry lining

New internal studwork or stripped-down partition walling can be tacked with plasterboard. This, in turn, can be finished by taping and filling the joints or by a skim coat of gypsum plaster. External walls can be dry-lined with the plasterboard either fixed by dabs of plaster or to battens. Where solid walls are to be dry-lined any damp should be cured before the wall is battened out with treated timber and tacked with foil-backed plasterboard. Thermally bonded plasterboard can reduce heat losses considerably.

Floor screeds

The addition of a floor screed to a solid concrete floor can present an opportunity to introduce a damp-proof membrane and insulation. If the levels make this impracticable then it may be advisable to take up and relay the oversite. Timber floors that have suffered from rot or infestation can also be replaced by a solid floor with insulation, damp-proof membrane and a screed finish. A sand and cement screed that is bonded to an oversite can be 50mm thick. One that is laid over insulation must have a minimum thickness of 65mm. Screeds can be mixed on site or delivered ready mixed.

New fitting out and redecoration

With the structure of the building sorted out, it is time to get on with the second fix and re-decoration. This is when a particular mould or character can be given to the building. You may want to preserve the traditional features. On the other hand you may decide to give the property a modern makeover.

Second-fix carpentry

Although the main staircase may well have been fixed at an earlier stage together with the main newels and supports, the balustrading, handrails and any aproning are usually left until this later stage. Internal doors will have to be hung and all skirtings, architraves and any other mouldings fixed. Loft traps and ladders will be finished off and any shelving, together with fitted cupboards and wardrobes, built in. If timber floors are required these should be laid prior to the skirting if at all possible and covered over to prevent damage. The carpenter will also be responsible for the hanging of garage doors and the replacement of any temporary doors on the home with the permanent choice.

The kitchen units

The choice of kitchen units is crucial to the ambience and value of the finished home. Kitchen units come in many forms but most take the form of a chipboard carcass unit with the doors and drawers in melamine board or timber. Worktops also come in many styles and sizes with most being melamine-faced chipboard. Avoid the highly glazed finishes as they will show every scratch. A touch of class can be brought to the room by the use of granite, marble or natural timber worktops. Avoid dark finishes in all but the largest and lightest of rooms. Flat pack may seem cheaper but if you have to add the cost of labour this may bring the price up to the same as for rigid pre-assembled.

Floor and wall tiling

Ceramic, quarry or stone tiles are usually laid on a cement screeded or solid floor but they can just as easily be laid on timber or floating floors, so long as the correct flexible adhesive and grouts are used. If there is likely to be any shrinkage or movement in the floor, and especially where under-floor central heating is installed, it is best to use a flexible adhesive in any event. The choice has to be made whether to tile up to and just under the kitchen units or right through to the wall. The latter may involve using more tiles but it presents a better finish.

Walls and floors to be tiled must be smooth and free from dust and grease and it is important to use the correct spacers. Choose colours and textures with care to maximise the feeling of light and space. Buy more tiles than you need as breakages will occur and if you have to order new tiles they may be a different shade or size.

Redecoration

Preparation is two thirds of the decorator's job with lots of rubbing down, sanding and filling involved. It is the decorator who finally makes good and snags after all the other trades have finished. Make sure that all painting or staining of external timber is done whilst the scaffolding is still up. Make sure that the painters and decorators only work in a clean and dust-free environment. If timber is to be gloss painted, make sure that it is properly knotted and primed beforehand and check to see that all skirtings, architraves and timber mouldings are primed or undercoated on the back side before fixing. Allow good time for plasterwork and render to dry out before attempting to decorate. If a lime render is used you will need to decorate using a limewash with natural pigmentation in order to maintain the wall's ability to breathe.

Insulation, energy efficiency, and eco- and green issues

Possible new regulations

The Government in England and Wales seems to be backing away from the immediate introduction of new regulations requiring people carrying out works to existing dwellings with a contract value of £8,000 or more to take reasonable provision to improve the energy efficiency of the building. However, the enabling legislation to bring about these changes is in place and it's possible that they could be introduced at any time. I would think, however, that most people thinking of doing up a property would want to incorporate many of these mooted changes in any event, whether it's to improve the comfort of their prospective home or to increase its selling potential.

Thermal insulation

There is probably no better way to make your home eco-friendly than to spend the money on increased insulation. Unlike many of the other options, additional insulation is the one that is most likely to provide an immediate and worthwhile payback. Insulation comes in many different forms. Mineral wool or fibreglass can be used in suspended ground and first floors, in walls and in roofs and ceilings. Rigid foam boards made from expanded polystyrene, extruded polystyrene and polyurethane can be used above and below solid ground and first floors, in

There is probably no better way to make your home eco-friendly than to spend the money on increased insulation.

cavity walls and in pitched and flat roof situations. Cellulose fibre made from recycled newspaper and sheep's wool can also be utilised, especially blown into cavities.

By the way, before you go filling cavity walls you should always insist on a CIGA (Cavity Insulation Guarantee Agency) warranty. Any reputable installer should not only offer this as standard but, in order to do so, should follow important procedures. The cavity must be at least 50mm wide. If it is less then it should never be filled. A borescope survey should be carried out to check to see that there are no blockages and that the wall ties are free of obstruction and have not corroded. If there any areas where damp is occurring then the problem must be sorted out prior to the cavities being filled.

Radiant heat barriers, a blanket of mineral wool within shiny, reflective outer sheets, can also be used in wall and roof situations. There are also many products on the market to prevent 'cold bridging' and to close and insulate cavities around windows and door openings.

Acoustic insulation

New regulations, detailed in Chapter 9, require minimum acoustic performance for both walls and floors. There is a wide variety of rigid foam, mineral wool and laminated products used either in combination with or bonded to flooring and walling materials such as plasterboard or gypsum fibreboard.

Green ideas

It is not difficult to incorporate green ideas within a conversion or renovation project. Passive solar power is often obtainable, particularly if thought is given to opening up windows and the addition of south-facing conservatories. If accommodation is being re-arranged, consider having as many of the habitable rooms as possible to the southern side of the home with utility and bathrooms to the north.

Active solar gain can be obtained by the use of solar panels to heat the hot water and at certain times of the year this could halve your hot-water heating energy requirements. Photvoltaic cells, which convert sunlight into electricity, can provide all or most of the home's electricity requirements in daylight hours. Geothermal heating is becoming feasible with the use of heat pumps that effectively work like a refrigerator in reverse, taking the latent heat from the earth, air or water. Grey-water recycling and the use of rainwater for flushing toilets can save on water consumption. Wind turbines can also make a useful contribution to energy requirements.

All of these are available but you will have to consider that the costs, even with the various grants that are sometimes available, are unlikely to provide a reasonable payback in purely cash terms, good as they undoubtedly are for the planet. I often feel that the principal effect of all of these devices is in the sense of wellbeing that they give to their proponents rather than anything else. All of that – and my scepticism – would change if and when the Government takes a firm stand and maybe insists on greater use, leading to a reduction in the capital outlay required.

Hard and soft landscaping

The garden should never be considered in isolation from the home. Don't forget to plan the garden properly as this can have a significant effect on the value and attractiveness of any home.

Disabled access

Although there is no requirement for existing dwellings to provide disabled access and facilities in the same way as new build has to, many renovators and converters will want to emulate the requirements as far as is possible so that those with physical difficulties and elderly people can enjoy the garden to the full.

Wherever possible the requirements for external ramps, pathways and access arrangements referred to in Chapter 9 should be adopted for renovations and conversions. With increasing public awareness of these requirements, their implementation can only have a beneficial effect on the re-sale vale and desirability of the project.

Planning your garden

In many respects the rules for the garden and landscaping for a renovation or conversion are exactly the same as they are for new build. On the other hand you might not be starting with a completely blank canvas as much of the garden might already be planted. That doesn't mean that there won't be room for improvement and there are some simple points to follow:

• Large amounts of spoil may have to be taken

Above: **Below: Make sure that you choose the correct driveway materials to suit your home and its surroundings** © Potton

away from some sites. This is expensive. Consider whether this could be retained and used to landscape the garden with banks, terraces, rockeries and ponds.

- Choose the hard landscaping materials carefully to match and emulate the walling materials of the main house.

- Remember that certain surfaces such as brick paviours can get very slippery in dark or damp positions in the winter.

- If trees are past their best, and they're not subject to a Tree Preservation Order, replace them. If trees are causing problems to the structure remove them only after consultation with your engineers and/or architects.

- Soften up any bland architectural features with careful planting or screening. Blank walls can be made more attractive by the simple planting of

climbing plants such as Virginia creeper, clematis and wisteria.

- Avoid ivy (*Hedera* species) as it destroys brickwork.

- Before planting trees or shrubs make sure that you know just how big they're going to grow.

- Avoid willows and poplars anywhere near a building.

Fungal and insect depredations

Finally, with any renovation or conversion of an older building, it is perhaps a good idea to consider, even if your lenders haven't insisted upon it, having the main timbers treated against fungal and insect damage. I know some won't like the thought of noxious chemicals in the home. If that's how you feel, so be it. But when and if you come to sell an older house that's been adapted, extended or modernised, purchasers and/or their solicitors might be more than happy to receive this extra surety.

Chapter 8

THE PLANNING SCENE

To a degree, I have pre-empted some of the contents of this chapter when dealing with the important business of the evaluation and purchase of a site. However, much of what I've said bears repetition and expansion, and an understanding of the planning scene is an essential prerequisite for any successful self-build project. This applies as much to those who are going to leave their application in the hands of their chosen professional as it does to the self-builder who decides to handle the application themselves. Even if you do engage the services of a professional, you cannot divorce yourself from the process that follows, and it is important that you and your advisors act in concert and work as a team.

In the run-up to the writing of this book there was much speculation that the Government were going to re-vamp completely the planning laws and scrap many of the existing rights such as Certificates of Lawful Use and Permitted Development Rights. In fact the Planning and Compulsory Purchase Act 2004, whilst far-reaching in many ways, left much of the previous legislation intact. For many, the only real change that they might see is the length of time for which a consent is valid; something that I've already discussed when detailing the types of planning permission in Chapter 3.

What *has* changed considerably over the past few years, and which may indeed have even been the reason why no wholesale change in the legislation was eventually sought, is the level of 'interference' from national government. Up until recently each local planning authority has had to prepare a Development Plan for its area. This plan, reviewed every five years, set out the detailed planning policy that the local authority would be working to. It had to be ratified by the Secretary of State and was then referred to as the adopted local plan. Of course, as it only lasted five years, once it was ratified and adopted, preparation of the next five-year plan then commenced, which meant that by the time the plan was adopted it was often out of date. Applicants would therefore have to try to determine which Development Plan was being adhered to or referred to within any negotiations or determinations.

The new Act requires the local authority to prepare a Local Development Framework containing all of the local authority's planning policies. This is quite a detailed and lengthy document illustrated by and including an Adopted Proposals Map, which will identify areas of protection, such as nationally protected landscape and local conservation areas, Green Belt land and Conservation Areas. It will also identify locations and detail sites for particular land use and development proposals included in any adopted Development Plan document and set out the areas to which specific policies apply.

The Local Development Framework will be made up from Local Development Schemes, which in turn will be made up from Local Development Documents. These will set out the planning authority's policies for development and will include a Statement of Community Involvement specifying how the public can become involved in the preparation of the plans and decisions on planning applications. Effectively therefore, this new framework will become a kind of 'loose-leaf' plan subject to continuous review, all of which must be considered at examinations in public and approved by the Secretary of State, which at present is the Office of the Deputy Prime Minister, through their appointed inspectors.

Phew! What on earth does all that mean, I hear you ask. What it means, dear reader, is that the Government is going to be involved very much more in local planning policies and decisions. Planning Policy Guidance notices (PPGs), by which the Government indicated its preferences, are now considered too long and complicated and they are to be replaced with much stronger and more specific Planning Policy Statements. Already local authorities are bombarded with PPSs and it bears fruit in the calling in of applications and the closer adherence of local planning decisions to national government aspirations. In some ways nothing much has changed as the planners' hands were always tied by established government policies and edicts. A planning authority considering an application for a single house might spend hours arguing about it, but only a few minutes discussing an application for a thousand houses because they had little or no fundamental power over government policies as embodied in their own local plan. What may appear to change is the requirement for local consultation and involvement in all levels of the planning process. In some ways this could be disastrous as a public, largely uneducated in planning terms, unable to distinguish between their subjective opinions and the objective of planning law existing for the good of all, will do their level best to see that the status quo pertains. But here, the overarching ability and readiness of the minister to see that national government policies are the ones that are enacted will reduce this increased local democracy to a paper exercise.

Where I fear that the self-builder will see a change relates to the Government's requirements for an increased density of housing with an ideal, expressed by the Office of the Deputy Prime Minister, of 30 to the hectare. In days gone by, if in a village, somebody put in an application for 20 two-bedroom starter homes, then when the usual

furore resulted in the scheme being altered to five large detached homes the locals would consider that they had won a victory. It could not go on for ever, of course. As a society we always needed to build a mixture of house types and in certain areas we had simply stopped building homes for our kids and for those on the lower rungs of the housing ladder.

So government, quite rightly, has decided that something has to be done and that has resulted in what many would consider as strange goings on. A chap came up to me at a recent exhibition and complained that he had gone to the local authority and asked for permission to build himself a new home on his large garden. He was appalled to be told that he couldn't build one house and that they required that he built seven! In Cornwall a paddock recently came up for sale with no planning permission and a guide price of £15,000. A reader went to the local authority to ask whether they would allow a single house and the answer was that they would prefer multiple development. The land went for £305,000!

There is a reverse side to this coin. In the south and south-east of England, where the Government perceive that there is a housing shortage, the local authorities are required to identify actively suitable land for development and to strive to achieve quite high targets for new housing by other means. But in areas such as the north-west of England, where the Government believe that there is an overabundance of development, they issue orders for a virtual moratorium on new consents. This can lead to the bizarre spectacle of a perfectly obvious plot, or one that may have had planning permission that has unfortunately lapsed, being refused renewal of planning permission.

So that's the big picture: one that may impact on the self-builder, especially the last point, but one that may, just as equally, pass them by. Each local authority will interpret advice from the Department of Environment in its own way. The Planning Acts are

The golden rule is to avoid applications which may be contentious, and to present anything unusual in a non-contentious way.

concerned with whether or not a dwelling can be built at all in a particular locality, with its appearance, and with the way in which it will relate to its surroundings. In theory, and hopefully in practice, those decisions should be based upon the common good rather than any specific self-interest.

So how does it work?

In principle all planning applications are considered by a committee of councillors who are advised by the council's professional planning officers, but in practice, for run-of-the-mill applications, they often just rubber stamp the officer's recommendations. In some local authorities, applications for Approval of Reserved Matters and non-contentious applications are not even put before the committee and, instead, the planning officers themselves have the power to determine the application using 'Delegated Powers' handed down to them by the authority. Members of the public are entitled to appeal to a higher body, against any decision of the local authority in a planning matter.

One of the things many professionals hear when talking to their clients is that such and such a planning officer is very difficult to deal with or that they are always negative in their dealings with any application (actually the character descriptions can be a lot earthier that this, often consigning them to a position of authority in the Third Reich!). The professional will usually listen politely but they will know the reality, which is that the planning officer, who may well be known to them, is simply a person who is just doing their job. Planning officers can never really win. The person who *doesn't* get planning for exactly what they want will feel aggrieved, yet the next-door neighbour of the man who *does* get exactly what he wanted may also feel just as aggrieved. All planning officers can do is to try to act within their powers, in as fair and as even-handed a manner as their brief allows. Each planning officer will interpret their own role in the administration of the Planning Acts in their own way and a change of personnel can make a marked difference to the progress of an application. However, and this is important, never lose sight of the fact that every decision a planning officer makes must relate to the adopted

and ratified planning policy of the local authority. As such, the personal opinions, prejudices and preferences of the officer are not valid except and insofar as they relate to an interpretation of that planning policy. If an officer were to say, 'I don't like that,' then the next question could quite properly be, 'I understand that. But does it conflict with the planning policy of this authority?'

At meetings with planning officers, clients who are not getting their way may become extremely upset, as is evidenced by the panic buttons that you'll see in most meetings rooms. If their architect does not share their anger, some may even turn their resentment against them, failing to see that firstly, their approach won't get them very far and that secondly, and most importantly, their architect is there in a professional capacity. As such, they have to bear in mind that they may well have dealings with the planning officer on behalf of other clients and that, if they allow themselves to become as personally involved as their client, they may well disadvantage their other clients and jeopardise their future business. Having said that, the experienced professional will understand that, although for them this is just another job, for their client it is *the* experience that colours their whole existence at that time and that they are much more personally involved. It helps if each party understands everyone else's roles and starting points and, if this book can assist in that understanding, then fine.

It is always the land that acquires the planning permission, not the person who applies for it. If land with planning permission is sold, the consent is available to the new owner. You don't even have to own the land in order to make an application on it and many self-builders, as we explored in previous chapters, make applications on sites which they are in the process of buying, long before they actually have legal title. It is necessary to serve notice on the owners of the land and it is advisable to tie things up with them to make sure that if you are successful, the land is not sold to someone else. This can be in the form of a legal option to purchase in the event of a planning application being successful or, alternatively, you can buy the land, subject to the receipt of satisfactory planning permission.

Making a planning application

Planners make their recommendations in accordance with set criteria after going through set procedures. The way to obtain a planning consent quickly and easily is to ensure that it meets all the established criteria for an approval. This fact is often forgotten. A planning officer has the discretion to make recommendations at a variance with planning policy, but this is unusual The golden rule is to avoid applications which may be contentious, and to present anything unusual in a non-contentious way.

As discussed above, the Local Development Framework will include a plan of the area with the intended designation of all of the land in their area marked on it. The titles used in this allocation are probably familiar to most people. Land may be designated as being for residential, industrial or recreational use. Other land may be zoned as 'White Land' or land that, while not being designated as 'Green Belt', has not been zoned for any other specific purpose. Most agricultural land falls within this category. 'Green Belt' refers to land where the policy is that no new development shall be permitted. It should never be confused with greenfield, which is simply a term for land that has not been previously developed. District plans will clearly show the designation of land for specific purposes and village plans may indicate the 'envelope' or

Above: **A choice of external materials that reflects the local vernacular is always going to find more favour with the planners.** © Nigel Rigden

Left: **The planning authorities issue helpful booklets and guidelines that are well worth reading.**

Planning
A Guide for Householders

DETR
ENVIRONMENT
TRANSPORT
REGIONS

What you need to know about the planning system

Thinking about altering or improving your home?

Putting up a building in the garden?

Building an extension?

Department of the Environment, Transport and the Regions and The National Assembly for Wales

boundaries within which any development is expected to take place. All of these designations and the policies pertaining to them will be detailed in writing within the Local Development Framework.

Just because land falls within an area designated as being for residential use or a plot falls within the village envelope does not mean that it will necessarily get planning consent for development. It's difficult to put into words, because it relies partly on a gut feeling built up over years of practice – just why one plot of land should get planning consent whilst another most certainly will not. I say again, planning is law that, perhaps more than any other branch of the law, is translated by opinion. Prior to any consent or refusal, therefore, all opinions are equally valid, but some might be a trifle more accurate than others. Professionals working within the planning scene have, probably, long since ceased to be surprised by the outcome of many applications and many will have stories of the plot they were certain would get planning that didn't, and the one they were convinced would never get planning, yet did.

If you're employing a professional at this stage then their opinion might be the spur or the disincentive for you to take matters any further. On the other hand, many of you will want to make your own minds up on this issue and might like to obtain information first, rather than second hand. There may also be a slight suspicion that there are financial axes to grind if you agree to adopt a particular course of action or commission someone to do something for you, based on their advice alone.

I've talked about obvious plots left by circumstance and there are many of them in different situations around the country. If you either own or come across such a plot, then perhaps the first thing you should do is make general enquiries at the planning office about their attitude towards that piece of land. Keep your questions on the broad theme of whether or not the piece of land would be considered as a building plot. Listen carefully to the answers and, without badgering the officer to make statements that they would rather not make, read between the lines of what they say. Now, you may think it preferable for the officer to come out to site, and in

some cases it is certainly true that a visit to a site will serve to sway a wavering opinion one way or another. In most cases, however, and particularly at the first enquiry, it's likely that the officer can give an opinion by reference to plans and their own local knowledge. Phrases like 'Every application will be treated on its own merits' mean little or nothing in this context, and most planning officers will avoid using them when answering questions on the principle of whether land should be developed or not. 'We would resist such an application' or 'Such an application would run counter to the policies of this authority' are much more clear cut and I would invite you to consider, in such circumstances, whether or not you should pursue that particular plot any further.

Of course whether you accept such advice depends on many things, not least whether you already own the plot, but again, I invite you to consider whether a long history of planning rejections will aid your case at some future date when perhaps the authority's attitude might be slightly different. Certainly getting involved in an argument about the planning policy of the local authority is pointless. The officer will not debate the policy itself and he must, and will, confine himself to dealing with your enquiry on the basis of the implementation of that policy. Sometimes, however, the lay person will pursue the argument and may even convince themselves that the planning officer has given way and agreed with their contentions. Normally nothing is further from the truth and the reality is that the planning officer has simply extricated himself from a tricky situation by using words which seem to satisfy or partially mollify the member of the public with whom he is faced. In the end planning officers will know that, prior to any actual determination of an application, nothing they say, either verbally or in writing, is binding on the local authority, a fact that has been tested in the courts and is established in law by precedent.

Of course, the planning officer might look at your proposals and decide that an application would be acceptable or even welcome. In which case, your next question should be whether they would like to see any application made in Outline or whether they would prefer it to be a Full application. If they ask for a Full application then, in many cases, it's a pretty sure bet that, at officer level, the land is thought of in terms of being a potential plot. But beware. You are not home and dry just yet and, although rare, it is not unknown for committees to take a differing view on things. The planning officer's recommendation might also come about because they feel that it would not be possible to consider the matter in Outline, and that they therefore need more detail, in order to reflect on the issue of principle. In fact they do have the power to ask for further details with an Outline application where they feel that it cannot be properly considered without full plans.

If it is to be an Outline application then although you're a lot further forward than the chap who got brushed aside, you must not count your chickens before they're hatched. At this point you really need to consider whether you should be using a professional to handle the application or whether you could handle it yourself. It all depends on your own circumstances and abilities. Chances are, however, that if you were a complete no-hoper you would not have got to this point anyway. In any event I do believe that the potential council-tax payer and voter has the edge on many professionals. Maybe the reason the planning officer has asked for an Outline application is that he's not really sure about whether or not your particular proposal or the development of this particular plot will find favour with the planning committee. Maybe he knows that it will but, by taking it through the Outline stages of the planning process, he will then have a chance to influence the eventual outcome by the imposition of conditions. Maybe you've been advised to make this application because the planning officer felt that you were not prepared to accept his reservations and that the only way to prove them to you is for you to make an application which

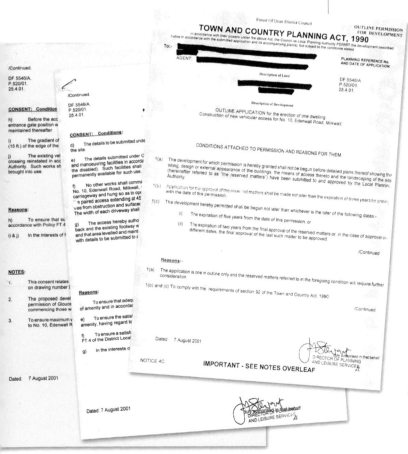

he hopes and believes will be turned down. Whatever the reason for arrival at this point, there is a lot that the lay person can do to ensure that the application stands the best chance of success, whether or not a professional is employed to prosecute it.

Most Outline applications are considered by committee and it is perfectly legal to lobby the members of that committee to vote on your behalf. In the first weeks of May, councillors will be asking for your support at the ballot box and, in turn, you are perfectly entitled to ask for theirs. They don't have to give it, of course, and if your request for their support is accompanied by a bottle of whisky, then you have stepped beyond the bounds of lobbying and into the realms of bribery.

When the local authority receives an application they will normally acknowledge it and give it a reference number. After this they should determine the

Left: **There is always more than one page to a planning approval. Make sure that you have the whole thing.**

application within a period of eight weeks unless they obtain your written consent for an extension of time. It doesn't make sense to refuse this as in that case the authority may well simply determine the application by a refusal. Sometimes there will be repeated applications for extension of time. This may be because they and you are still in active negotiation but it may also be a simple failure on the part of the authority, in which case you do have the right either to refuse the extension of time, bringing matters to a head, or to appeal against their failure to determine.

Other local authorities, with their eye on the league tables and government targets for the determination of applications, stick rigidly to the eight weeks, even to the point of disallowing further negotiation or amendment. It has to be said that dealing with these authorities is a most frustrating experience.

Assuming that all is going normally, a date will be set down at which your application will be considered by the committee and you and/or the professional working on your behalf should make sure that this date does not pass by without you knowing of it. Two weeks before the application is to be heard,

contact those members of the planning committee whom your local councillor has identified as being most likely to have influence, and ask them for their support. If you think it's necessary, present a written appraisal of why you think your application has merit and, if you think it would be helpful, offer to meet them on site to discuss the application. Don't leave it any later than this or they won't have time to do anything, and don't do it any earlier either or it will not be fresh in their minds when the meeting comes up. *Do not* take things any further and *do not* badger them in any way – having made your submission leave the rest up to them. When your application comes up at committee, you will have made sure that it will be considered by as broad a cross-section of opinion as is available and that it will not just be swept into a decision based on a single report – that is as much as you can, and should do.

By the way a few local authorities allow the applicant or their representative to address the committee for a specific and limited time, often three minutes. If you avail yourselves of this then once again the advice must be to calmly state the advantages of your application and to resist the impulse to harangue or complain about your treatment or the policies with which you disagree.

If the planning officer asks for a Full application, if you are either buying land with the benefit of an existing Outline consent or if you're seeking to amend or substitute an existing Approval of Reserved Matters, then most of the negotiations will be concerned with the actual details of your proposed new home, rather than just the principle. In this case, I earnestly believe that the application is best handled by a professional. The issues of principle are ones in which the democratic process can be brought into full play and where the lay person, by virtue of his ability to lobby, can seek to influence any outcome. An Outline application

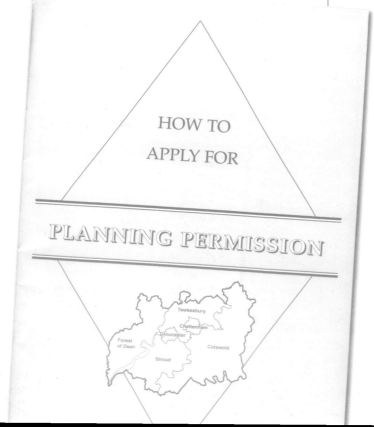

Right: **The clean lines and large glazed areas of the Art Deco periods are coming back into fashion and should last this time around, thanks to modern building materials and methods.** © Nigel Rigden

requires the minimum of plans and may indeed only require the drawing in of a red line around the perimeter of a plot on a copy of the Ordnance Survey plan sold to you by the local authority. The merits of such an application can be argued by an articulate lay person. A Detailed application needs to be properly presented and the accompanying plans need to be sufficiently attractive in order to stand the best possible chance. Whilst I advocate consultation with the planning officers by lay people at the Outline stage, I do advise caution at the Detailed stages.

Planners are anxious to influence development by advice as well as by control, and there is usually a notice at the reception desk saying just that. Unfortunately this advice is usually a council of perfection, and it may not suit you to take it. For instance, suppose you are buying an attractive site with Outline consent. As a first stage in establishing a design it may seem sensible to call at the planning office to ask for the free advice on offer. You will be well received and impressed by the trouble taken to explain how the site 'needs a house of sensitive and imaginative design to do justice to its situation'. You may be shown drawings, a sketch may be drawn for you, and it is not unknown for the planning officer to drive to the site with you. This is splendid, until you realise the ideal house being described suits neither your lifestyle nor your pocket. You will wonder what the reaction is going to be to your application for the house that you want, which is quite different as well as being the one you can afford. The simple answer is that your application will be dealt with on its merits, and that the planning officer has an obligation to approve what he thinks acceptable, and he should not insist on what he thinks is best. However, he might well be disappointed to find that all of the advice that he gave you has been ignored, and that disappointment might well colour his thinking. From this it will be seen that a preliminary discussion with the planning officer is not to be taken lightly. As a general rule, the best person to deal with the planning office is the professional whom you employ to submit your application.

Not having face-to-face contact or negotiations with the officers themselves, in order not to compromise a future application or cut the ground from beneath the feet of the professionals you have engaged, is one thing. Failing to take notice of the planning policy guidelines or to study the published information put out by the various planning and other agencies is quite another. These are important. When, and if, it ever comes to an appeal, the first thing an inspector will want to know is whether you have followed these guidelines and whether or not your proposals conflict with the adopted and ratified policy of the authority, as set out in the Local Development Framework.

Some will be buying a plot for which a Detailed consent has already been granted. If the consent is for just what you want then everything's fine and, so long as you've got a current Building Regulations approval, there's nothing to stop you starting work on site. If there are some minor changes that you'd like to the drawings then it is possible that the planners will agree to these being carried out on the basis of a 'minor amendment to the existing consent'. They will require a letter and drawings, listing and showing the amendments, but it's better to talk your ideas through with them beforehand. If they feel that they cannot accept your amendments, or if your proposals are radically different from the existing consent, then you may either have to make a fresh application for Approval of Reserved Matters, pursuant to the original Outline consent, or else make a Full application. The failure of either of these methods of application will not, of themselves, invalidate the original consents. Nevertheless they may lapse of their own accord, by virtue of being out of time, so watch out for that eventuality.

When your planning application is made you will have to pay a standard fee to the local authority and this is payable whether it refers to an Outline application, a Full application or an application for Approval of Reserved Matters. There is no refund if the application is refused and the level of fees is reviewed at frequent intervals. At the time of writing it is £265 for a single dwelling but this is always likely to be adjusted upwards.

The consideration process of any application follows a general pattern in that, once the application is registered, it will be assigned to an officer who will then send out for what are known as Statutory

Consultations. These are made to bodies such as the Highways Agency and the Environment Agency as well as, in England, the local Parish Council or the Town Council. Although the planners may discuss the application within the consultation period, nothing much will be decided until such time as they have received all of their consultations. It is better, therefore, to wait until the application has been with the local authority for about four weeks before endeavouring to enter into any meaningful discussions with the officer who has been assigned to the case. If the Parish or Town Council approve of your plans then that's fine. They cannot then be rejected under delegated powers and, if the officers do not share their opinion, the application must be taken to a full committee meeting. If the Parish or Town Council reject them then it is by no means the end of the world. Parish Councils have a long history of rejecting what is put before them and there is no way of saying it other than to say that, in many areas, they have long since 'shot their bolt'. Statutory as their consultation is, the fact is that their conclusions have little or no bearing on the decisions which the officers will reach in their recommendations, other than to reinforce an existing opinion.

It's all out in the open

When a planning application is made, letters are also sent out to neighbours and other interested parties, advising them of the application and inviting them to inspect the details of the proposals at the planning office. Anyone, not only those who have been notified, can make representation to the authorities about the application. A great many objections are invalid in planning terms but their effect is, nevertheless, to raise the profile of an application and to render it incapable of being given a delegated decision. Try to talk to your neighbours beforehand. Try to get them on your side. If possible take their reservations on board or at the very least, prepare the ground by explaining why you have discounted them.

The officer assigned to your case will prepare a report on your application, which will form the basis of the recommendation to the committee. If it is to be considered under Delegated Powers then the same report will be submitted to the senior officer or group of officers who will determine the application. In general the applicant is entitled to see and have a copy of the report and also to see any background papers or documents used in the preparation of the

It all comes down to preparation and thinking about the application and proposals long before they are committed to paper and long before they finally arrive on a planning officer's desk.

reports. If an objection is received then it is usual for any Delegated Powers to be withdrawn and for the application to then be considered by full committee. Most authorities allow members of the public to attend full committee meetings, although you are not usually allowed to talk. Others, as I've said, allow applicants or their agent to make a timed representation at the meeting, but not to question or interrupt their subsequent deliberations.

There is a fine line to walk at the consideration stage of any application, and your professional is the one to consult on this. If the application is not contentious, but the officers are, nevertheless, constantly assailed with requests to consult on it, then you may well stir them into a more detailed consideration than would previously have been the case. On the other hand, if they have reservations on any part of the application and nobody goes near them, then it is possible that they will simply report their reservations to the committee and a rejection may follow for something that could have been altered. The question most professionals will ask, when telephoning after the consultation period, is the simple one, 'Can you tell me the current situation on application reference …?' The answer will then be given in the form of a statement of just where the officer has got with the application and they will usually then go on to explain or set out any reservations or objections they may have. Hopefully, if you've followed all the rules, carefully thought out your proposals and made sure that they are non-contentious, the officers will say that everything is all right. If not, they may go on to list some changes that they would like to see and almost certainly they will then confirm this by letter.

It may well be that the reservations, if any, expressed by the planning officer do not disturb you overmuch. In which case your professional, having consulted you first, will quickly move to incorporate the suggestions within the plan and the application will then receive a favourable recommendation and proceed. On the other hand, you may have doubts about some aspects of the officer's objections, in which case a meeting needs to be convened as quickly as possible. Sometimes the planners will request an input from their own architects or conservation officers and when you attend the meeting, you and your architect may be faced with a whole group of people showing an interest in the outcome of your application and wishing to exert their influence. Whatever the attendance at the meeting, keep calm and make notes of all of the objections and requirements.

If you are able to agree things at that meeting which can later be enacted on the plans, then fine. If not, the best thing to do is simply to take away the list and discuss it privately with your advisors. If you feel that there is no compromise then you have the right to insist that your application proceeds unaltered, but it will almost certainly end in a refusal. In many cases a compromise solution can be reached that will, at the end of the day, satisfy all parties. What you have to bear in mind at all times is your objective to build a new home, and that means not only in design terms but also in budget terms. Hopefully by reading the earlier chapters of this book you will have anticipated any peculiar requirements for, say, external materials, and hopefully, their imposition will not come as too much of a surprise to you, and your budget will be able to accommodate them.

Sometimes a planning officer can be persuaded that your application has merits that they had not realised. Sometimes a conservation officer can be persuaded by a series of photographs, proving that you have taken the trouble to incorporate features that are indigenous to the area. Sometimes a planning officer can see that you have followed a particular style in an area which itself has diverse styles of architecture. It all comes down to preparation and thinking about the application and proposals long before they are committed to paper and long before they finally arrive on a planning officer's desk. And that's the path, and the point, to which this book should have led you.

What about lobbying at the Detailed stages of planning? You can try it, but it isn't nearly as effective as at the Outline stages. Local councillors may well be prepared to argue with a professional planner on the question of principle, but not nearly so ready to engage them in long discussions over architectural details or merits. What you can do by lobbying is to bring about a site meeting where the committee convenes on the site. Technically the applicant is not allowed to talk at most site meetings. In practice, when a group of disparate people have entered *your* land, they'll find it very difficult to ignore you and, in most cases I've attended, several questions have been addressed directly to the applicant or their agent. *Do* be careful to keep any answers or matters you have to raise succinct and to the point. *Don't* go off on a tirade about your application and the ills that have befallen you at the hands of the planning officer. Choose the right moment to put your point and then let the people given the power of decision come to their democratic conclusions.

If you are not satisfied with a decision made about a planning application, you do have the right of appeal. However, it is often better to make an entirely fresh application in a way which you think is more likely to be approved. If this seems a possibility, visit the planning officer and ask his advice on this in a straightforward way. If you do not get anywhere, only then should you consider an appeal. I shall elaborate on appeals and the appeals procedure a little later on in this chapter but before we get to that there are a few more headings which need to be considered.

Designated areas

Certain areas have a special planning status and these are collectively referred to as 'Designated Areas'. They comprise the National Parks, Areas of Outstanding Natural Beauty, Conservation Areas and the Broads. In these areas, either different planning rules apply or rights are modified in some way and I have referred to these within the various sections.

Getting planning permission in the National Parks, the Broads or Areas of Outstanding Natural Beauty is considerably harder, not least because there is an extra tier of bureaucracy to satisfy. Essentially, rather than the considerably looser design guides that most local authorities issue, there will be strict criteria aimed at achieving conformity in design and, in particular, the choice of external materials.

A Conservation Area is a slightly different matter. People often think that just because a site is in one, it's going to be difficult to get planning permission. It might be. But just as equally, it can sometimes make things easier. For if you can prove that what you are proposing does not detract from the surroundings and in fact could materially enhance the area, then it might be all the harder for the planners and conservation officers to mount an argument against it.

Permitted Development Rights

I've mentioned these rights several times in the book and it's perhaps time to explain just what they are and their scope, for they are of the utmost importance to the self-builder, the renovator and the converter.

So what are these wonderful things? Permitted Development Rights give consent for all sorts of development of land, without the need to apply for planning permission in the normal way. They are granted as part of the Planning Acts known as the General Development Orders. They are not a certainty; they can be varied or negated completely by the wording or conditions in a planning consent. They are severely restricted in National Parks, Conservation Areas, Areas of Outstanding Natural Beauty and the Broads and they can be removed in their entirety or varied over a whole area by the local authority, of which more later.

The Government in England and Wales had indicated that they were going to make changes to Permitted Development Rights. In the event they backed away from doing so in the 2004 Act. But they have already issued a consultation document regarding future curtailment and it's quite likely that they will revisit this 'problem' over the next few years. That makes it all the more necessary to check with the LPA that what you are intending to do falls within these rights and that, as far as your property is concerned, they are unimpaired.

Getting the planners on your side

Much of what I've written above has been directed at making life easy for you, the applicant, the planners and the passage of your application, by ensuring that it is, as far as is possible, non-contentious. I have to square that with my urgings in other sections of this book and within other forums for self-builders to 'push the boat out' in design terms and to think about whether they really want to simply emulate the developers' designs. If you want to do something different, then you have to take people, and especially the planners, along with you. Surprising as it may seem, it is not that difficult, and in many ways, the more 'way out' the design, the easier it can become.

Deracinated architecture, by which I mean styles taken from one region and imposed upon another, will always put the planners' backs up. New, innovative and even fantastic designs have a very different effect. A planner's job can be fairly humdrum. Day after day they are dealing with houses that look just the same or which their own brief requires that they shoehorn into conformity. Along comes someone with something fresh and exciting. Now, if you can enthuse the planning officers with this design, it will represent a high point in their life as well as yours and they might be very enthusiastic about it, almost to the point of wanting to see what it really looks like when it's built.

The box below outlines what you may do if your Permitted Development Rights are not curtailed.

There are other things but these are the ones that usually concern the self-builder and, in any event, it's better to check with the local planning office regarding any extension or further development that you're planning, just to make sure that you are within your rights. Building Regulations approval may also be necessary and any alterations that you make to the dwelling must not contravene the regulations or affect the stability or structural integrity of the dwelling. Incidentally the term, 'original dwelling' is important. It means what it says and it harks back to 1 July 1948 when the Planning Acts first came into force. For any dwelling constructed since that date, it refers to the original dwelling that was given planning permission. Any extensions undertaken since either 1 July 1948 or the original consent have the effect of soaking up the Permitted Development Rights. In some circumstances the volume of other buildings which belong to the house such as a garage or shed will count against the volume allowances, even if they were built at the same time as the house or before 1 July 1948. These are where an extension comes within 5 metres of another building belonging to your house and where a building has been added

If your Permitted Development Rights are not curtailed:

● You may build an extension to an original dwelling in England and Wales so long as:

- it is no bigger than 15% of the volume of the original dwelling or 70 cubic metres, whichever is the greater, up to a maximum of 110 cubic metres or, if it is a terraced house or is in a Conservation Area, National Park, Area of Outstanding Natural Beauty or the Broads, the volume is no greater than 10% of the original dwelling or 50 cubic metres, whichever is the greater.

- The extension does not protrude above the original ridgeline or is more than 4 metres high or closer to the boundary than 2 metres.

- The result of the extension does not mean that more than half of the area of land around the original house will be built upon.

- The extension does not protrude in front of the original building line, unless that would still mean that it was at least 20 metres from the highway.

● You can carry out development within the curtilage of the building, which means that you can alter walls or rearrange rooms and occupy the roof void, subject to the limits below. However, if you do live in a specially designated area, such as a Conservation Area, a National Park, an Area of Outstanding Natural Beauty or the Broads, you will need to apply for express consent for any extension to the roof or any kind of addition that would materially alter the shape of the roof. This includes roof lights or a dormer. In other areas loft conversions are allowed, so long as they do not add more than 40 cubic metres to the roof volume of a terraced house or 50 cubic metres to any other kind of house and the work does not increase the overall height of the roof. Any increase in the roof volume occasioned by the addition of dormer windows or extensions to the roof will count against the allowances for extension listed above. No planning permission is required for roof lights on any roof slope and solar panels are allowed, so long as they do not project significantly above the roof slope. Planning is, however, required for dormer windows on the roof plane facing the highway.

● You can construct a garage for a dwelling where none exists so long as it does not go closer to the highway than the nearest point of the original house, unless there would be at least 20 metres between it and the highway, and as long as it does not exceed 3 metres in total height or 4 metres to the ridge if it's got a pitched roof.

to the property which is more than 10 cubic metres and which, again, is closer than 5 metres to the house.

In addition if you live in a Conservation Area, a National Park, an Area of Outstanding Natural Beauty or the Broads, all additional buildings of more than 10 cubic metres in volume, wherever they are on the plot in relation to the house, are treated as extensions of the house and reduce the allowance for further extensions. In all these cases, the volume of the buildings concerned is deducted from the volume limits given for the extension of your house.

Normal home maintenance, including re-roofing a house, so long as the roof profile is not altered, and external painting and decoration, unless of course there is a planning condition prohibiting it, is allowed. In Conservation Areas, National Parks, Areas of Outstanding Natural Beauty and the Broads you will need planning permission to alter the external appearance of a building or to clad it in stone, plastic, tile or timber, etc., but in all other areas there is no such restriction.

You can see why I suggest that before you contemplate an extension you should consult the planning officer and get a definitive ruling on whether or not you need express planning consent. And you can see also why I urge that if you are planning to

- You do not need planning permission to convert an integral or attached garage into living accommodation, unless, of course, this is prevented by a condition in the original planning permission.

- You may erect a porch for a house, so long as it's at least 2 metres from the highway, it does not exceed 3 metres in height and is no larger than 3 square metres.

- There is no requirement to seek planning permission for the insertion of new windows or doors, even if the effect of carrying out this work is to create an overlooking situation that would otherwise be unacceptable. This is an anomaly in the planning laws that might well be addressed at some future date. You cannot carry out this work if there is, once again, a condition on the original planning, or a clause or covenant in the deeds, preventing it and of course you cannot carry out works of this sort to Listed Buildings, or in the specially designated areas.

- You can construct walls to the boundaries so long as they do not exceed 2 metres in height or 1 metre adjoining the highway. Deciduous hedges are not covered by these restrictions and you can plant and grow these to whatever height you wish, at present. Evergreen hedges are, however, controlled by separate legislation, which effectively limits their height to 2 metres (see details under 'Walls, fences and hedges' in Chapter 6).

- In most cases you can also construct sheds, greenhouses, conservatories, accommodation for pets, summerhouses, ponds, swimming pools, and tennis courts, so long as they do not cover more than half of the garden and so long as any above-ground structure does not exceed the height and size restrictions listed above.

- Satellite dishes have come in for special attention. In most areas, only one dish per house is permitted, it must not protrude above the highest part of the roof and, if fixed to a chimney, it must not exceed 450mm or stick up higher than the chimney itself. In some counties the maximum size of any dish is 900mm whilst in most others, it is 700mm. In Conservation Areas, Areas of Outstanding Natural Beauty, National Parks and the Broads, the dish must not be fixed to a chimney or positioned on a roof slope that fronts a road, public footpath or a waterway.

- In Scotland the rules are more or less the same except that the measurements for an extension are worked out on a square metre basis rather than a volumetric one. The extension for a detached or semi-detached house must not exceed 24 square metres and for a terraced house, no more than 16 square metres.

If your Permitted Development Rights are not curtailed:

build a home with an eye for future extension, you carefully think out the design and the strategy you employ. If you think that the size of the building, as you envisage it eventually becoming, will put the planners off your proposals and if you and your architect/designer feel that Permitted Development Rights are unlikely to be curtailed, then you may decide that the best course of action is to go in for the smaller dwelling with an intention to extend at a later date. If, on the other hand, you feel that the planners won't be particularly bothered about the eventual size of the dwelling, but your finances dictate that you can only carry out the development in stages, then perhaps it's better to apply for the whole thing and then build in stages as finance permits.

Whichever option you adopt there are some important things that you can do to make the eventual extension easier and less intrusive. Building in the lintels for any future door or window openings and spacing the brickwork or blockwork to create straight joints ready for cutting out can save a lot of time and trouble as long as you take care to maintain the structural integrity of the walling with ties or reinforcing mesh. It's open for you to consider whether, as long as you've got the necessary consents, you put the foundations in for any future extension, thus limiting the amount of disturbance you will experience when you eventually get around to it. Foundations needn't be left open: they can be covered over and grassed or even brought up to oversite where they can exist as a patio or parking space, until such time as their true role is realised.

Where a roof is to be occupied it makes no sense at all to use standard trusses which can never be altered to create living space so, instead, think about either a purlin and spar roof or an attic trussed roof. If dormer windows or roof lights are going to be used then you might not be able to put them in to start with but you can still 'cripple' the roof timbers for their eventual construction and, whilst we're on the subject of the roof, get your tradesmen to consider your future plans when installing any pipework, cable runs or insulation.

The local authority does have the power to restrict or remove some of your Permitted Development Rights by issuing what is known as an Article 4

Direction. This is normally issued pursuant to an area being made a Conservation Area or where the character of an area of acknowledged importance would be threatened by unauthorised or haphazard development. An Article 4 Direction remains in force for a period of six months whilst it is being confirmed, and once confirmed it is permanent. Those affected by such a proposal have the right of appeal and, in certain circumstances, compensation may be payable for the diminution in value of a property because of its imposition. Flats and maisonettes, whilst not falling within the usual self-builder's orbit, do not have Permitted Development Rights in the same way as a house does and it is necessary to apply for planning permission to build an extension or an outbuilding such as a garage, shed or greenhouse.

At seminars and courses held all around the realm, I consistently ask the question, 'Hands up those who know what Permitted Development Rights are?' And almost always there are no takers. This is a great shame as these rights are very important. To a government increasingly intent on centralisation they are an anathema. If they have their way they will be extinguished. But if nobody knows about them, who is going to make the necessary fuss?

For the renovator, converter or self-builder, knowledge of these rights is vital. Many local authorities limit the size of new dwellings by reference to square meterage. Others simply refuse to accept designs on certain plots, claiming that they are too big or that they have too great a visual impact on the street scene, for example. As I've said above, if the Permitted Development Rights are intact then these dwellings can be increased in size afterwards (technically Permitted Development Rights only come into being once the property is occupied and becomes a dwelling).

But it goes further than that. If, for example, there was a policy in place (not at all unusual) whereby a replacement dwelling should not exceed the size of the original or should not be more than a certain percentage bigger in floor area, then you may well be able to breach those limits by the use of Permitted Development Rights. If the existing dwelling has not been extended then, assuming the rights are intact, it should be possible to build an extension to it. It might be possible to occupy the roof space or to build a garage, where there wasn't one, or outhouses in the garden ancillary to the use and enjoyment of the property such as a snooker room, cinema room, playroom, etc.

Now would you want to do all that just to prove the point that in any consideration of the size all of that should be taken into account, simply to knock them down again shortly afterwards? Unlikely. But the simple fact of knowing that you have those rights and your demonstration to the planners that you know about them might well assist you in your negotiations.

And if they still won't play ball? Well, you could in certain circumstances actually build them, using up the Permitted Development Rights of the existing dwelling, prior to operating your planning consent for the new home that, on paper, fits in with the authority's size criteria but is smaller than you want. But if, when demolishing the existing property, you leave up the new extensions and outhouses and your design happens to butt up to and incorporate them, then you may well have achieved what you wanted in the first place!

Re-submissions and strategic withdrawals

If you do get a refusal on your planning application, you can make a re-submission, with no additional fee payable, within 12 months of the date of the refusal. This only applies to the first refusal and not to any subsequent or serial refusals and it must be filled by the same applicant and relate to the same site. If you choose to withdraw an application, you again get another free go but this time it must be made within 12 months of the date of the original application.

If you think that your application is going to attract a refusal, think very carefully. A refusal can blight land and prejudice any future application and it is often better to withdraw it. This can be done by fax or telephone right up to and including the short time between the decision being made in committee and the written consent being issued.

Serial applications can be successful and can be used to ratchet up what you can build on a site. The important thing, especially where there is no consent of any sort, is to get a planning permission on the land; to establish that it is a building plot. But if that planning permission isn't quite what you want, there is nothing to stop you making a series of applications. These can either be Full applications in their own right or Approvals of Reserved Matters pursuant to an original Outline consent, assuming that it is still in time. So you could get planning permission for a three-bedroom house, and, having got that, you could apply for a slightly bigger four-bedroom house. With that in the bag you could move on to extending the lounge or increasing the footprint. Sounds impossible? Well no, it's actually quite common and the thing that's in your favour is that each fresh application is considered against the consent that has already been issued. So the fact that it's an empty site, which was pertinent to the original application, is ignored for subsequent ones.

But there is another tactic, almost the reverse of the above. You can make an application for something that is much bigger than you really want. When the hullabaloo starts you then withdraw the application and substitute it with one for the house that you wish to build, which may then be bigger than the planners and others had originally hoped for. But in the euphoria of the 'defeat' of the original, and to your mind, sacrificial application, this is accepted as a reasonable compromise.

Highways

A new access driveway entering a class 1, 2 or 3 classified road will need planning consent. This is normally dealt with at the same time as your application for the proposed dwelling and there is a duty on the planning authority to consult with the relevant highways authority, although there is no requirement on them to accept their recommendations. With class 4 or 5 roads, no planning application is necessary and, instead, the approval and the consent of the highways authority is all that is needed. Trunk roads are a completely different kettle of fish in that they come under the auspices of the Highways Agency, who may well devolve their powers to other agencies or companies.

Demolition

Demolition is classed as Permitted Development, so long as the building to be demolished is not greater than 50 square metres, measured externally. If you intend to knock down an old or substandard dwelling and replace it with a new one, then you might be tempted to demolish it during the planning process, in order to save time. *Be very careful!* Once the old building is gone, there is technically nothing to replace. If the site is in the Green Belt or in any situation where the planners would prefer that a house wasn't there, they could simply refuse what would be tantamount to a new dwelling. If you find that difficult to believe, I have to tell you that I have seen it happen on several occasions. Never take the old building down until you have received all the consents, and I believe that, in almost all cases, it is better to include the demolition in the description and the wording of your application.

If the building is Listed you will need to apply for Listed building consent if you want to demolish all or part of it. If it is in a Conservation Area you will need Conservation Area consent to demolish a building with a volume exceeding 115 cubic metres, or to demolish any part of it. You will also need consent to demolish a wall, gate, fence or railing over 1 metre high adjoining a highway (including a footpath or bridlepath) and over 2 metres high elsewhere.

Agricultural consents

These usually limit the occupation of the dwelling to someone wholly, mainly or last engaged in agriculture, or the widow or widower thereof, and they do it by imposing this as a condition on the planning consent. In certain cases, for example a rural industry, such as stables or a riding school, the same procedures and similar conditions are used to encumber a new dwelling that is justified by the enterprise. Whilst these conditions exist in perpetuity, many local authorities will want to strengthen their hand and require the landowners to enter into a legally binding agreement giving extra force to their requirements. They may even insist that the agreement goes further and either ties the dwelling to a farm as a whole, or further encumbers an existing farm dwelling, or dwellings, which, up until then, had been free of any planning conditions. In such cases the consent will be issued subject to the preparation and execution of the agreement, and until such time as the documentation is signed and sealed, no work can commence on site.

Some of these agreements, which seek to tie both houses to a single farm enterprise, could possibly fall foul of European Union legislation against the restriction of trade. Who is to say that what is today a viable enterprise as a single entity could not one day need to be financially separated?

I do warn the lay person against being inveigled into buying a plot with an encumbered consent. It is not at all unusual to see plots of land offered with a few acres attached and a planning consent that contains these occupation restrictions. Quite often the prospective buyer will be told that 'Everything will be all right, so long as you keep your head down and keep a few sheep or other stock on the land.' Nothing could be further from the truth. You will effectively be in illegal occupation of the dwelling for ten years (that is if you're lucky and nobody reports you), you will find it nigh on impossible to raise money or a mortgage on the property, and the value of the finished home will be severely diminished. It is possible to apply for de-restriction. In many cases the local authority will require that the property is marketed as an encumbered dwelling, at a reduced value, for a year and a day. If the house remains unsold then they may agree but if somebody comes along and offers to buy this bargain, then all your plans could be scuppered.

The real problem with agricultural consents is that so many people have abused them. The local authority will have countless tales of farm enterprises that simply faded away once the new house was completed.

Be that as it may there are many genuine farmers who either wish to create a new home for themselves on the farm or need additional housing for farm workers. Agricultural consents cut across many of the norms in planning and if you see a new house being built in a rural position outside the village envelope the chances are that it is an agricultural consent that has allowed it there. Most Development Plans state that development in the rural area shall be resisted unless it is of proven necessity for the proper maintenance or running of agriculture. So before any agricultural dwelling will even be considered by the local authority, it is necessary for the applicant to prove the necessity for the new dwelling and the ongoing viability of the farm unit that will support it. A special form will have to filled in to accompany the application, listing the acreage of the farm, its usage and stocking, and the number of people employed. This form will also ask what other dwellings are already on the farm and whether any have been separated from the farm or sold off.

Some local authorities will evaluate the agricultural viability in house; some will ask for an agricultural appraisal from a recognised authority on farming such as an agricultural consultancy or a planning consultancy specialising in agricultural matters. In all cases, it is best to provide such a report and if, in commissioning that report, it does not come down completely in your favour, it is perhaps best to delay, and to carry out any recommendations made within it before actually making any planning application. On occasion it may be best to consider making application for the temporary siting of a mobile home on the farm until such time as financial viability can be firmly established. Local authorities will often be more amenable to this course of action; then after a few years, when your presence is firmly established on the farm, your development plans are sufficiently advanced and your finances are more secure, application can be made for a permanent new home. I write this, by the way, knowing that groans of disappointment will follow, but also that it is the best advice in many a circumstance.

Those for whom viability is not an issue and where the agricultural appraisal is full-blooded in its support for the new home can consider skipping the Outline stages of the planning process and going straight to a Full application. If no development is to be allowed in the rural area, unless it is of proven necessity for the proper running and maintenance of farming, and

you have proved beyond reasonable doubt that your requirement is necessary for the proper running and maintenance of your business, why should you bother about the issue of principle? Surely it is already established? What you need to talk about is *what* goes there, not *whether* anything goes there.

Affordable housing

The Government is extremely keen to see a greater usage of land and an increasing density of housing, with 30 to the hectare deemed to be the ideal. Some local authorities aren't doing too much about this and are tending to try to preserve the existing density ratio in their area. Others have enthusiastically taken the idea on board and are insisting that wherever there is a multiple-house site, a proportion (usually half) should be designed as 'affordable' housing. I've even heard of this happening on sites where there are more than two houses.

However, the words 'affordable housing' can be used in another context. Rural housing is in crisis and homelessness is increasing faster in the country areas than it is in the towns and cities. According to surveys 27% of rural households have annual incomes of less than £9,000. Average housing prices in the south have now well and truly breached the £150,000 barrier with even entry-level housing at figures way beyond the capacity of local people. Even in the rented sector, average rents have soared beyond the reach of those in housing need, fuelled by incomers and company lettings. Local authorities are struggling to contain this problem but even they are hampered by the pincer movement of their areas being attractive to incomers and housing allocations being set well below their own forecasts of need.

The last Tory government's directive PPG3 Annex 'A', 'Affordable Housing for Local Needs in Rural Areas', sought to address this need by providing the mechanism for local people who are in housing need to come together to build their own affordable homes. Crucially it relies on being able to buy and build on land that would otherwise not be available for development, at a fraction of the cost that would normally be paid. Annex 'A' makes it clear that provision of affordable housing should be regarded as additional to the provision in the development plan for general housing demand, that local plans should *not* seek to identify sites, and that the policy is one of limited exceptions. It goes on to require that where sites are released for affordable housing as an exception to normal policies of restraint, it will be essential that there are adequate safeguards to reserve the housing for local needs, both initially and on subsequent changes of occupant.

Whilst it can apply to single dwellings it is more often used for a group of homes. How it works is that a group of local people come together to form a self-build group. They must be people who are local to the parish with either strong family or work ties linking them to it. In addition they must be in housing need. This is defined as wishing to set up home for the first time, a need to be near to dependent relatives, being in substandard or unsuitable accommodation or having a requirement to live close to work. The land needs to be identified, but this does not have to be within the village envelope and it can indeed be within the Green Belt, so long as it is part of and adjoining the village and is, of course, suitable for development. Normally a small premium is payable as an incentive to the vendor but, in general, land can be bought at agricultural rates or close to them.

Initial funding of up to 40% of the costs of the scheme can be obtained from the housing corporation in the form of a loan that will eventually be repaid by the members taking out mortgages on the completed houses. Normally an initial contribution of up to £1,500 is made by each member and the group has to register itself as a self-build housing association under the Industrial and Provident Societies Act 1965, to the National Federation of Housing Associations, adopting its rules. What this means is that the group

Watch out for...

Where a particular need for affordable housing has been identified, some local authorities are now requiring developers to either provide substantial cash payments towards local housing or else to include affordable housing within their proposals. The value of these houses is calculated by reference to the assumed maximum rental that the proposed occupants can afford. If this is £250 per month then this would service a mortgage of £45,450 which added to a 5% deposit, makes £47,722. The house can either be sold at that price to the occupants or rented by the local authority and sublet with an option to purchase within five years.

becomes a corporate body, able to open bank accounts, purchase land, labour and materials, and negotiate overdrafts to cover any shortfalls in cashflow.

What distinguishes these self-build groups from their forebears is, firstly, that there is no requirement for all of the houses to be of the same type and specification. Secondly, there is a requirement for the self-builders to enter into a legally binding agreement that in the event of the house being re-sold, it must be to local people in housing need and at a discounted price, normally 20% below the full market value.

The planners' attitudes and interpretation of the requirements of the document vary from authority to authority. There is nothing in the documentation to require that affordable houses should only be in the rental sector. All it says is that there are wide variations in house prices and earnings between different areas and that this means that there can be no single national measure of what constitutes low-cost housing. Yet this is how many local authorities have chosen to interpret it. Others accept that such schemes are appropriate so long as the means are in place to ensure that they remain available in perpetuity to local people at affordable prices, and quite a few have accepted them with open arms.

It is a common misconception that parts of a building can be Listed. In fact, if a building is Listed, the Listing applies to the whole of the building, including its grounds.

Listed building consent

There are two grades for Listed buildings: Grade I, covering buildings of major importance, and Grade II, which comprises most of the listings that have been identified in an area as being of historical or architectural value. Listed Building consent is required for any alterations or extensions to Listed buildings including gates, walls and fences. It is also required for any significant works, internal or external, and for the erection of any structure in excess of 10 cubic metres. There are considerable restrictions on Permitted Development Rights, as detailed above, and, if you carry out works that are permitted under these rights, you will still need Listed building consent.

Any application for permission to do something to, alter or extend a Listed building is made to the local authority but they cannot consider the application in isolation and must consult with what are known as 'Statutory Consultees', such as:

• English Heritage
• Historic Scotland
• Cadw
• the Council for British Archaeology
• the Ancient Monuments Society
• the Society for the Protection of Ancient Buildings
• the Georgian Group
• the Victorian Society.

Building Preservation Notices

Local authorities can issue a Building Preservation Notice if they believe that a building of merit is being endangered, or if work that is detrimental to the character of the building (such as demolition) is proposed or imminent. The building does not have to be Listed but it does have to be worthy of listing and the effect of the notice is to give the authorities six months in which to take steps to have the building Listed. A Building Preservation Notice does have to receive ratification from the Secretary of State.

The local authority has the power to issue 'Repair Notices' on owners who are allowing Listed buildings to deteriorate but, if the owners are unable or unwilling to carry out the necessary works, and the building is unoccupied, they may carry them out themselves and charge the costs to the owners. In extreme cases, they may even consider Compulsory Purchase. There are other powers, such as Closing Orders, which can prevent anybody from living in a house until such time as repairs are carried out, and Demolition Orders, which may also require Listed building consent. The time limits that preclude action against certain classes of unauthorised development do not apply to Listed buildings and the normal enforcement procedures and powers (discussed in detail below) are available.

It is a common misconception that parts of a building can be Listed. In fact if a building is Listed, the Listing applies to the whole of the building, including its grounds. It will also affect the surrounding properties inasmuch as when any application is made for planning permission to do something to them, the effect on the Listed building must be taken into account. If a Listed building is extended, then the new extension also becomes Listed.

In England and Wales the Listing system is being devolved from central government to English Heritage and Cadw, who will notify and consult with the property owners and the local authorities. That should enable people to have much more of a say in whether their property is or should be Listed. It does, however, leave it open for anybody to approach the societies to express their view that a property is in need of Listing or may be under threat if it is not Listed.

Infrastructure charges

It is by no means universal, but some local authorities are starting to put conditions on planning consents requiring the developers to pay a sum of money towards local infrastructure (such as schools and roads, etc.).

I've seen consents with figures of £3,000 and I've read of charges as high as £18,000. It's obviously a revenue source that many more local authorities will seek to exploit. There has long been the idea that the state should have some sort of clawback for the act of giving planning consent and in my youth the Wilson Labour government succeeded in introducing the Development Land Tax, which was then repealed by an incoming Tory government. The difference between that and these new conditions is that it is the developer and not the applicant who normally has to pay. Thus the clawback is not necessarily coming from the beneficiary of the planning permission. Self-builders should try to ensure that any amount payable is knocked off the land value and therefore paid for by the vendor.

The clawback may not always be in the form of cash. Sometimes there is a requirement for work to be carried out to improve such things as access or highways. If those works are within the site, then fine. Quite often, however, they involve, for example, construction of a new lay-by or passing place at a point removed from the site, in which case it is vital that the consent of the landowner, hopefully also the vendor, is enshrined in the agreement to purchase the land.

Appeals

One other change that the Planning and Compulsory Purchase Act 2004 brought about was the demise of so-called 'twin tracking' whereby an applicant could make an appeal against a refusal whilst at the same time making a fresh application to the local authority for a slightly different scheme. Now, once an appeal is lodged, the local authority has eight weeks in which to consider their original decision, after which the appeal procedure will either go ahead or be withdrawn.

An appeal is always made against the reasons for refusal, and although other arguments can be brought into play the focus must be the reasons for refusal. You can appeal against the refusal of a planning application and you can also appeal against any conditions that are imposed within a consent. In addition, you also have the right of appeal against the local authority's failure to determine an application.

If there are conditions on an approval by the local authority that you feel are unfair or unreasonable, and the local authority refuses either to vary or remove them, then you can appeal against the imposition of those conditions. But beware – the inspector will consider the whole of the application again. They can change other conditions that you had not previously objected to and can impose new conditions. They can even reverse the local authority's decision altogether, although if they were thinking of doing so, you would be informed and given an opportunity to withdraw the appeal and stick with the local authority's original approval and conditions.

An appeal against a local authority's failure to determine is all well and good on paper but the reality is that most authorities, faced with such an appeal, will move to determine the application prior to the appeal being actually conducted.

Costs are normally borne by each party, whichever method of appeal is decided upon. It is open for either party, however, to request that the other party pay their costs either in part or in whole, and the inspector will decide the merits of such an application. He will only award costs against a party if he feels that they have acted in an unreasonable, vexatious or frivolous manner.

The first thing to do, when thinking about an appeal, is how, or whether, you can avoid one. Seek out an early meeting with the planning officer to discuss whether or not there is another way forward. At this meeting it is most important that you are not aggressive or sarcastic, and that you do not waste their time by explaining how unfair you consider the planning laws to be. You should be seen to be a most reasonable person, and take an early opportunity to say that you know they cannot commit the council in any way in their discussions with you. This will make them much more likely to be helpful, either by suggesting a way in which you can frame a further application, which they may be able to support, or by giving you a clear idea of exactly what the council thinks about the issue. And that's going to be useful when you are considering appeal tactics.

If the planning officer will not discuss the matter in a helpful way, do not assume that they are being deliberately unfriendly. It may be that your category of application is a very hot political issue locally, and that they feel obliged to deal with you in a very formal way. If this is the case, you can at least ask them to advise you about the planning history of the area and ask for a copy of the recommendation made to the council in respect of your application. Of course, you should have been aware of the planning history before you made your application, but you may find, to your surprise, that there has been a string of previous refusals on applications made by other people, and that this was a major factor in the council's decision.

Sometimes local politics come into play in such a way that the local authority does not want to be seen to be granting consent for certain types of development even though they know that they cannot sustain that argument at a higher level. It will be denied, of course, but there are cases when it appears that there is almost a deliberate policy to refuse applications, when it is known that their refusal will be overturned at appeal. What happens here, of course, is that when the applicant is finally successful, the local authority can turn around and claim that it was none of their doing, thus keeping on the right side of their local critics.

It may be that the council considered that the design, siting, materials or some other feature of the proposed dwelling was inappropriate. If this is the case, it is even more important that you establish an effective relationship with the planning officer to see if you can reach an agreement on features that they will find acceptable. All of this adds up to the advice that you should try every way of getting approval by making further applications. A planning appeal should be your last resort; it effectively closes the book if it is unsuccessful, and also takes at least nine months to get a decision. This time lag is usually critical to those building on their own.

What are your chances of success? Well, although many appeals are disallowed, quite a few are successful and all in all you've probably got a 50/50 chance. It all depends on so many things. The inspector will consider an appeal on the basis of its planning merits and any personal circumstances are unlikely to influence their decision. An important factor in any consideration is whether or not the proposal fits into the Local Development Framework. You recall that I wrote about 'zoning' earlier and that I also mentioned

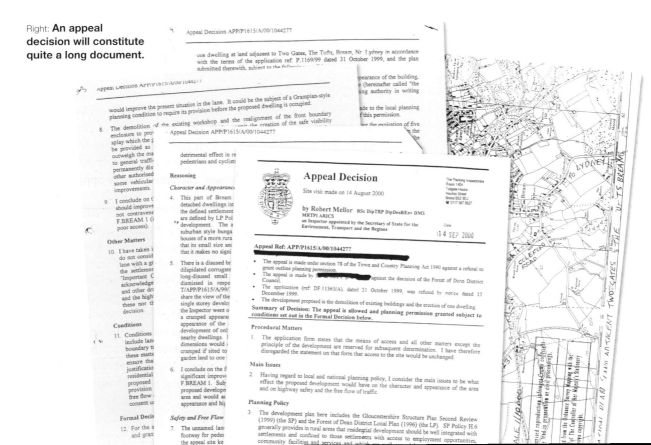

Right: **An appeal decision will constitute quite a long document.**

Above: **An imposing house on four levels, taking maximum advantage of the site.** © D&M

'village envelopes'. The inspector will be concerned that your proposal does not conflict with these adopted plans, or any plan which is being prepared, and will also be concerned to see that you have followed any published advice given out by your local planning authority. If you are appealing against a refusal for a scheme which conflicts with these policies or endeavours to create development in the Green Belt, then your chances of success are fairly slim.

If your site or property is within the village envelope or within an area zoned as residential and you can put together a reasonable case, with details of precedents, then your chances are greatly increased. Tour the area and look out for similar buildings in similar situations which have obviously recently been built. Ask about them, and get details from the local authority planning register relating to their approval and how they came by it. If they were granted on appeal then get a copy of the appeal documents to see if there is any argument in them that

Conducting a written planning appeal

A full description of how to conduct a written planning appeal is beyond the scope of this book, but the key points are as follows:

An appeal is against the reasons for refusal, and starts off with your written submission explaining why these reasons are inappropriate. You do not have to set out the reasons why your application should have been granted. You must deal only with the actual reasons for refusal listed on the refusal certificate, and explain that they are unreasonable. It will require a considerable mental discipline to restrict your submission to this simple formula, but anything else you write is irrelevant.

If a professional is putting this document together for you, you should ask him to let you have a look at it before it is sent off. If you are dealing with the appeal yourself, then somehow you should try to look at papers relating to other appeals. The grammar used is not important, nor is the quality of the typing or handwriting, but it is essential to avoid any extravagant language. Do not describe the council's decision on your application as a 'diabolical liberty'; use the correct phrase: it 'failed to take all the circumstances into account'!

A copy of your opening broadside is sent to the local planning authority, which then has eight weeks to reconsider the original application. If they consider that their original refusal should stand they then produce their own written reply. You will receive a copy of the council's written statement, and you have two weeks during which you can submit your replies. Following this exchange of statements there is a long pause, and then after some months you will receive a letter from the planning inspector saying that they propose to visit the site on such-and-such a date.

The site visit is important. The local authority will be represented, and of course you will go along yourself, accompanied by any professionals working for you. You will be told that at the visit the inspector will not allow either party to make any further submissions, nor will he discuss their written submissions with them. His purpose in visiting the site is simply to see the situation on the ground, and you and your agent, and the planning officer, are there simply to answer his questions. With some inspectors this will take the form of fairly perfunctory questions like 'Is this the brick wall you will be removing in order to create the visibility splays?' But with others the conversation can widen out to a quite detailed discussion of each aspect of the appeal that they identify. The important thing to do is to realise that the inspector is in the driving seat. If you try to browbeat him and launch into a detailed speech about your application and why you feel that he should support you, you will be doing little else other than harming your case. Respond to his questions quietly and get your points across within your replies. Stay close enough to the group as they walk around to be able to hear the answers given by the representative from the local authority so that, at an opportune moment, you can counter anything that you feel to be untrue. Avoid any display of enmity between yourself and any other representative and, at all costs, avoid any direct argument with any other party. If any other representative gets angry, remember that your very calmness contrasted with their anger will probably do your case a lot of good. Above all, let the inspector make the running in much the same way as you would a judge in court and defer at all times to his conducting of the appeal.

Finally, about a month after the site visit you will receive the inspector's findings, and these are final. If you have won, the findings act as your planning consent. If you have lost, you must realise that you have come to the end of the road with that application. Only if there is a major change in the local planning situation, or if a substantially different scheme is adopted, is any further planning application likely to be successful.

The whole of this process will probably take at least nine months and probably a year. You can do nothing to hurry it up. There is a provision in legislation for the inspector to give an Advanced Notice of Decision before he issues his official finding, but this is very unusual.

you could use on your own appeal. In every case I have been involved in, the inspector has always taken the trouble to visit these 'precedent' sites beforehand, and has referred to them both on site and in his eventual decision.

An appeal must be made within three months of the notice of refusal. The first thing you should do, therefore, upon receipt of a refusal, is to write to the appropriate office of the planning inspectorate and obtain, firstly, the necessary forms and, secondly, and most importantly, a copy of their excellent booklet entitled *A Guide to Planning Appeals*. From this you will discover that there are two sorts of appeal process, the written procedure and the inquiry procedure, the latter being subdivided into the informal hearing and the full-blown public inquiry. The booklet explains the differences between them and gives excellent general advice accompanied by flow charts showing how each type of appeal progresses.

At this point you have to decide whether you are going to handle the appeal yourself, or whether you are going to retain someone to deal with it for you. Many people do handle their own appeals, and the procedures are not difficult. The inspectors are not influenced one way or the other by finding they are dealing with the appellant rather than with a professional. However, the professional may be much better than you at marshalling and presenting the facts, and it is the facts on which the appeal will be determined. You should be very sure of yourself before you decide to handle your own planning appeal.

If you do ask someone to deal with it for you it should be someone with a great deal of relevant experience in handling appeals against refusals to allow individual houses to be built on individual sites in your local area, preferably with a track record of winning! It may be difficult to find the right person, but this is something that perhaps your solicitor or architect should be able to advise you on. Take your papers to the recommended person and ask them to quote you a fixed fee for handling everything for you. Be wary of anyone who says they want a fee just for reading your papers and appraising your situation. They are likely to be far too high-powered for your job, and probably more used to conducting planning appeals for supermarkets.

In most cases, I believe that the written appeal is the best course of action for an application concerning a single private dwelling house. Certainly the full public inquiry, with the need for expensive barristers, is beyond the scope of most individual self-builders. On the other hand, for those who feel that they would be better able to present their case verbally, rather than in writing, the informal hearing might well be their preferred choice. Anyone is free to pitch up and pitch in at such a hearing, including both supporters and objectors.

Unauthorised development and enforcement

If something is built without planning permission, and the planning authority does not challenge what you have done, then, after a period of four years, the unauthorised development becomes immune from enforcement procedures. Thereafter, the owner of the property can call for a Certificate of Lawful Use. It is mandatory for the local authority to issue this certificate. It confers all of the powers of a proper planning consent and it may have conditions attached to it in just the same way. The four-year rule also applies to a change of use where a building is brought into residential use. But for all other changes of use the breach must go unnoticed and unopposed by the planning authority for a period of ten years, in order for a Certificate of Lawful Use to be demanded. Breaches of conditions on a planning approval also fall under this ten-year rule. There is no time limit so far as unauthorised works to Listed buildings are concerned.

It was widely expected that in the 2004 Act the Government would move to limit or extinguish the authorisation of breaches of its planning laws. In the end they left things as they were. But it won't be long before they get back to these 'anarchic' rights and I can't see them existing for that much longer.

The principal way in which a planning authority will act against any breach of planning in its area is by the issuing of an Enforcement Notice. This notice details the nature of the breach and takes effect a minimum of one month after it is served, after which, if the breach of planning is not rectified, legal action may be taken. An Enforcement Notice is not served lightly. The enforcement officer will attempt to negotiate a settlement and/or rectification of the planning breach, and in certain circumstances, they may suggest a retrospective planning application to regularise the situation.

You can appeal against an Enforcement Notice within one month of its taking effect and the appeals process follows a similar pattern to that of other appeals. If the appeal is lost, the inspector will detail the time limit within which the breach must be rectified and failure to abide by this can lead to legal action. If someone is carrying out development that the planning authority feels will be extremely detrimental to a building, or is harmful to the locality, they can choose to issue a Stop Notice requiring that all work stops for up to 28 days. This requires that any activity is ceased immediately and failure to abide by this can lead to legal action being taken and an unlimited fine. Local authorities are loath to issue these except in exceptional circumstances, as, if the notice is withdrawn, the activity is authorised, or if the Stop Notice is deemed to have been legally incorrect, they may then be liable to pay compensation.

Scotland, Northern Ireland and the Republic of Ireland (Eire)

Just as with the legal systems, planning laws in Scotland, Northern Ireland and indeed in the Republic of Ireland (Eire) are branches of the same tree and in many respects, the procedures are very similar to those in England and Wales. Scotland is perhaps the most similar, with very little substantive difference in just how you go about the application and only a few minor changes in terminology.

In Northern Ireland, in the absence of devolution and with all executive powers being withdrawn to Westminster, the local authorities have a purely consultative role in the planning process and application is made to the Planning Service of the Department of the Environment, who then have a duty to consult with them. The Planning Service issues Planning Policy Statements, as now happens on the mainland, and any appeals are made to an Appeals Commission.

In the Republic of Ireland (Eire), a planning application is made to the local authority in very much the same way as it is in England and Wales. Importantly, you do have to have either a legal interest in the land or the consent of the owners to make the application. You are also required to advertise your intentions in the local press and display a site notice. It is usual to apply for a 'Permission', which is the same as Full planning permission in England and Wales, but you can also apply for an Outline permission, which has to be followed by an 'Approval'. This Approval basically fulfils the same role as an Approval of Reserved Matters in the United Kingdom, but with two very important differences: a consent lasts for five years, and the lifetime of the consent to build is determined by the Outline permission. You therefore need to apply for the Approval well in advance of its expiry in order to enable you to complete the works within its lifetime and this includes any necessary appeal to An Bord Pleanala (the appeals body). Additionally, there is not the strict division between planning and Building Regulations that exists in the United Kingdom. Applications for the detailed stages of a planning application must conform to the Building Regulations, and the enquiries that the planners make in connection with any proposal include those relating to the structure and integrity of the building work. The planning permission will include a clause that all work must conform to the regulations.

A decision to grant permission, with or without conditions, is notified to the applicant and anyone else who has expressed an interest in the application. This is in the form of a 'Notice of Intention to Grant Planning Permission'. For a period of one month following this notice, the applicant *or anyone else* may appeal to An Bord Pleanala. If no appeal is made, then one month after the original notice, the consent becomes operable and a 'Grant of Permission' is made. Where the planning authority decides to refuse an application, the applicant has one month to appeal and the appeals body usually aims to decide appeals within four months.

Chapter 9

BUILDING REGULATIONS/ STANDARDS, CONSTRUCTION DETAILS, WORKING DRAWINGS AND SPECIFICATIONS

Planning permission governs whether you build a new home at all and, if so, what it will look like. Building Regulations consent, on the other hand, is totally objective and confines itself to the structural aspects of the build by reference to the regulations themselves. An application for approval under the Building Regulations either conforms to those regulations and is approved, or else it fails to conform and is rejected, unless, in very peculiar circumstances, such as with a thatched roof, a relaxation can be negotiated.

The Building Regulations cover the structural and safety aspects of any construction and draw together a mass of other health and environmental issues. They are set out in denominated parts that deal with each aspect of building and it is the job of architects, designers and other professionals working within the industry to keep themselves up to date with those changes and to incorporate their requirements within any plans that they prepare or process. It is also their job, by inference, to make themselves as aware as possible of any impending changes to the legislation and warning is usually given about these in advance by way of published discussion papers and consultations.

The regulations are usually administered by the Building Control department of the local authority, who have a statutory obligation to enforce them and oversee their functions within their boundaries. However, the Government has also devolved the authority to inspect and certify compliance under the Building Regulations to other bodies, such as the NHBC, and in addition it is open for architects with the appropriate professional indemnity insurance to register to carry out this work. I have discussed the possible role of the NHBC in Chapter 1, so here I will confine my comments to the service and administration of the regulations by the local authority.

In most local authorities the Planning department and the Building Control department are situated in close proximity to each other and are usually lumped together as 'Technical Services'. Make no mistake. These are separate departments operating and receiving their powers through and from completely separate legislation from the various national parlia-

Right: **Building Regulations are only concerned with ensuring that the choice of materials complies with the regulations. On the other hand, some building societies do have reservations over timber cladding.**
© Nigel Rigden

It's as well to contact the Building Control department if you're in any doubt as to whether or not you need to apply for Building Regulations approval.

ments or assemblies. Although they can, and usually do, co-operate with each other, there is no certainty of this and it is possible to fall between conflicting legislation and interpretations. Planning says you *may* build something – it does not say that you *can* build something. If you get express planning permission for something or it is implied that you have planning consent for, say, Permitted Development, then it does not absolve you from having to seek Building Regulations approval for that development.

In like manner, if you get Building Regulations consent for a structure, it does not mean that you can build it without planning permission. A porch, for example, may well be exempt from the Building Regulations in some circumstances and, in many locations, its construction could well take place under the Permitted Development Rights laid down by the planning laws. In a Conservation Area those Permitted Development Rights could well be curtailed or removed and the fact that the porch could be built under a Building Regulations exemption would do nothing to change that situation.

It's as well to contact the Building Control department if you're in any doubt as to whether or not you need to apply for Building Regulations approval.

At the risk of being repetitive, I must stress that one may well still need planning permission for any of these works, so if you are at all unsure you should consult the Planning department of your local authority.

This is not a technical manual and it would not make sense simply to reproduce the Building Regulations here. If you want to read the regulations themselves then they are almost certainly available, probably with explanatory leaflets, on your local authority's website or on the Government websites www.odpm.gov.uk, www.sbsa.gov.uk and www.environ.ie. I would also recommend reading the NHBC 'Standards' manual and Zurich's *Technical Manual and*

Builders' Guidance Notes. These are not the Building Regulations but their expansion of them and the explanatory detail and drawings within them are extremely helpful. By the way, trees are probably the major reason for trenches having to go deeper, or for other foundation systems being adopted, and perhaps the best tables to determine the relationship between foundations and trees are to be found in these handbooks.

The regulations no longer contain tables of timber sizes and spans as these have been devolved to the Timber Research and Development Association (TRADA) and details can be viewed on their website, www.trada.co.uk. However, the NHBC and Zurich handbooks I've referred to do contain tables.

I have listed the various sections of the Building Regulations in a table overleaf and you can see from that the denotations that different parts of the realm and the Republic of Ireland (Eire) give to them.

The Scottish Building Standards (regulations) were completely altered in January 2005 and, although not identical, they now follow similar principles to the regulations currently in force in England and Wales, but with a few minor differences such as the requirement for sarking boarding and their currently more stringent requirement of a 'U' value of 0.30 for exposed external walling. Part 'P', although it has no direct equivalent, is mirrored to some extent by the inclusion of electrical safety and fixtures in Section 4.

It is hoped that these new standards will free up design north of the border, where the old regulations contained stringent and mandatory design guidance.

The Operation of the Building Regulations (or Standards in Scotland)

There are significant differences in the procedures available in the various parts of the realm and in Eire.

In England and Wales a Building Regulations application has to be accompanied by the necessary fees for the approval stages, after which the local authority has five weeks to process and determine the application. In practice, many applications cannot

In a nutshell...

Building Regulations approval is required if you intend to:

- erect a new building or extend an existing building (unless it is covered by the list of exemptions below and later)

- make structural alterations to a building, including underpinning

- (in certain cases) effect a change of use

- provide, extend or alter drainage facilities

- install a heat-producing appliance (with the exception of gas appliances installed by persons approved under the gas safety regulations)

- install cavity insulation

- install an unvented hot-water storage system

- carry out electrical works to domestic premises.

You do not need Building Regulations approval to:

- carry out certain very minor works to electric wiring

- replace a roof covering, so long as the same roof covering is used in the repair

- install new sanitaryware, so long as it doesn't involve new drainage or plumbing arrangements

- carry out repairs, as long as they are of a minor nature, and replace like for like.

In addition to the exclusions listed above there are common types of building work that are exempt from the regulations:

- the erection of a detached single-storey building with a floor area of less than 30 square metres, so long as it does not contain any sleeping accommodation, no part of it is less than 1 metre from any boundary and it is constructed of non-combustible material

- the erection of any detached building not exceeding 15 square metres, so long as there is no sleeping accommodation

- the extension of a building by a ground-floor extension of
    a) a conservatory, porch, covered yard or covered way, or,
    b) a carport open on at least two sides, so long as, in any of those cases, the floor area of the extension does not exceed 30 square metres.

- In the case of a conservatory or a wholly or partially glazed porch, the glazing has to satisfy the requirements of those parts of the Building Regulations dealing with glazing materials and protection.

be determined within the statutory period and it has become almost commonplace for applications to be rejected several times, with each fresh, and happily free, application dealing with different points raised. Such a system, which often seems almost incredible to the lay person, would not have evolved were it not for two important points. Firstly, the legislation is worded such that it is necessary to have *made* an application for Building Regulations approval or issued a Building Notice prior to commencement of works and, secondly, the fees for the necessary inspections stages are separated and, with a Full Plans

application, payable *after* the issuing of an approval.

This means that, as long as 48 hours' notice in writing is given of one's intention to start work on a site, following an application for Building Regulations approval or the issuing of a Building Notice, then there is nothing to stop you doing so. The building does, however, still have to be inspected and approved as it proceeds and the Building Inspectors will, therefore, come along and inspect at the relevant stages. If they approve the work, you may then carry on to the next stage in the normal way. If they do not approve or cannot sanction what you are doing,

Building Regulations/Standards documents

In England and Wales the various sections of the Building Regulations are as follows, with the important sections for Northern Ireland (blue), the Isle of Man (pink) and Eire (green) noted beside them. The Scottish regulations were revamped on 1 January 2005. Whilst they now follow the regulations in England and Wales quite closely in terms of their content, they have been renamed The 'Scottish Building Standards' and are listed in seven numbered documents, which do not directly compare with the English and Welsh lettered equivalents. I have therefore listed them separately.

Approved Document A – Structure **(D) (A)** (A,C,J)

Approved Document B – Fire safety **(E) (B)** (B)

Approved Document C – Site preparation and resistance to contamination and moisture **(C) (C)** (C)

Approved Document D – Toxic substances (D)

Approved Document E – Resistance to the passage of sound **(G) (E)** (B,E)

Approved Document F – Ventilation **(K) (F)** (C,F)

Approved Document G – Hygiene **(N,P) (G)** (G)

Approved Document H – Drainage and waste disposal **(N) (H)** (H)

Approved Document J – Combustion appliances and fuel storage systems **(M) (J)** (J)

Approved Document K – Protection from falling, collision and impact **(H) (K)** (K)

Approved Document L1 – Conservation of fuel and power **(F) (L)** (L)

Approved Document M – Access and facilities for disabled people **(R) (M)** (M)

Approved Document N – Glazing – safety in relation to impact, opening and cleaning **(V) (N)** (A)

Approved Document P – Electrical safety

There is also an Approved Document to support Regulation 7 – materials and workmanship (D)

The Scottish Building Standards documents are:

Section 0: General – Introduction, exemptions, changes of use, durability and workmanship, building standards and security of buildings

Section 1: Structure – Introduction, structure and disproportionate collapse

Section 2: Fire – Introduction, compartmentation and separation, structural protection, cavities, internal linings spread to neighbouring walls or buildings, means of escape, lighting and communication, fire service access, water supply and facilities

Section 3: Environment – Introduction, site preparation and protection, flooding, ground water and moisture, drainage, surface water and waste water, precipitation, sanitary facilities, heating, ventilation, condensation, natural lighting, combustion appliances, oil storage, solid waste storage

Section 4: Safety – Introduction, access, stairs and ramps, protective barriers, electrical safety and fixtures, danger from accidents and heat, lpg storage

Section 5: Noise – Introduction, resisting sound transmission to dwellings

Section 6: Energy – Introduction, policy, building insulation envelope, heating system, insulation of pipes, ducts and vessels, commissioning building services, written information

Appendix 'A' defines the terms.

Appendix 'B' lists the standards and other publications.

Appendix 'C' cross-references the new numbered regulations to the old lettered ones.

then you have to stop until either the approval is granted, or the necessary information is received that will allow them to agree to your continuing work.

Effectively, that means that although you will be advised that by working prior to the formal approval of the plans, you are proceeding at risk, so long as you do not go beyond that which the Building Inspector has agreed and approved on site, your position is really no different from that of someone who already has Building Regulations approval. The essential rule is that nothing is built that fails to conform to the regulations and, if therefore, the inspector feels that the work is contrary to the regulations then, whether or not you have a formal approval, he will stop you and he has legally enforceable powers to do so. I don't think it's bandied about too much but my guess is, on personal experience, that maybe as many as 60% of new self-build dwellings in England and Wales commence work without formal Building Regulations approval. Certainly, I have never waited for or had one when I started work.

In Scotland, the application for a warrant has to be accompanied by a fee that encompasses both the application and the subsequent inspections. A copy of the plans must also be coloured in architectural colours with green for concrete structures and block-work, red for brickwork, yellow for first-fix timber and carcass, brown for finishing and second-fix timber, blue for ventilation ducts, drainage, sanitaryware, and steel and red outlined for removals and downtakings.

Anyone wanting to build must obtain a warrant, which they get in one of two ways. They can show their designs to a verifier such as a local authority or private inspector who will confirm that the designs meet the new standards. Or they can produce verifier's certificates, which confirm that the property has been designed to conform to the new standards and has been checked by a certifier who is a competent third party. All certifiers must be approved and audited by the Scottish Building Standards Agency. At the moment there are two self-certification schemes in place. The Structural Engineering Registration Scheme

(SER) and one run by SELECT, the trade association for Scottish electrical contractors. The SER scheme issues a certificate for the design, which can be used instead of an inspection of the structural drawings by a verifier. The SELECT scheme certifies the construction and confirms that the electrical work has been safely carried out.

In Northern Ireland the procedures, fee structures and divisions are more or less the same as for England and Wales, save that the NHBC are not authorised to administer the regulations and this must be carried out by the local authority. In the Republic of Ireland (Eire) the detailed plans submitted to the planning authorities have to conform to the Building Regulations and there is not the strict division between planning and building regulations that exists in the United Kingdom.

In England and Wales, where the application and inspection fees are separated, you have to decide whether it's a good idea to make the application at the same time as the planning application. Obviously there is merit in the idea of having both approvals on the table as one commences work on site but there are some possible financial penalties involved. With

Right: **Check which local authority your site comes under.**

a planning application it is possible for plans to be radically or even completely altered, yet still remain under the auspices of the original application. No such sanction is given with a Building Regulations application. If the design changes then a completely fresh Building Regulations application will have to be made, attracting an equally fresh fee. As if the fee to the local authority weren't enough, you could also find yourself having to spend considerable monies on the preparation of new detailed plans, with any expensive calculations or engineer's details having to be repeated. You can see, therefore, that care needs to be taken and that a Building Regulations application should only be made when it is pretty certain that you know what you are going to be building.

There are two alternative procedures available to choose from in order to obtain Building Regulations approval – 'Deposit of Full Plans' or 'The Building Notice'.

Dealing with the last one first, if you choose this option then no detailed plans are generally required, as a far greater emphasis is placed on site inspection and supervision, although further details and/or plans may be requested during the course of the build. The fee is the combined total of the relevant application and commencement fees, so there is no saving to be made by this method as far as local authority fees go. This procedure is really only applicable to works of a completely straightforward nature where the party carrying out the works is totally conversant with the requirements of the regulations, as without plans there is no detailed check on the proposal before the work is carried out, and therefore no official decision notice is issued. The advantage is that there can be a saving in time and costs because there is no need to prepare and submit detailed plans. The disadvantages are that, firstly, there is no approved plan to work to and, whilst the inspector will try to anticipate problems, there can be delays and/or costly remedial works if any of the work fails to comply with the regulations. Secondly, building estimates may be inaccurate without the benefit of detailed plans to work to. In all the years I have been in the industry, I have no experience of any self-builder using this procedure. Whilst many proceed with the construction of their new homes without formal Building

Regulations approval having been issued, to do so without the benefit of detailed plans and full constructional details would seem to be singularly inadvisable.

A Full Plans application has to be accompanied by plans showing the full constructional details of the proposed work. Whether or not you managed to do the plans yourself for the planning application, I earnestly believe that these plans need to be prepared by a professional. If that's you, then fine. If not then you really need to examine your motives, swallow your 'go it alone' pride and engage a professional for this bit.

A Full Plans application should include:

1. The relevant application forms fully completed and with the appropriate fee.
2. Detailed drawings at 1:50 scale for floor plans, 1:100 for elevations and 1:500 for site plans. These should include floor plans, typical and particular sections, elevations and site details and boundaries.
3. A full written specification which can either be noted on the plans or provided separately and then cross-referenced.

The advantages of the Full Plans application procedures are that you will then be working to set plans along set guidelines and in strict accordance, at all times, with the regulations. Many of the lenders require that a Building Regulations application is made and some, but not all, will require a formal approval before commencement of work. The disadvantage is that time needs to be allowed for the preparation of the plans, prior to application and commencement of work. In the end, both that and the cost of the preparation of the plans are, perhaps, a constant factor and, as I've said, the thought of a self-builder trying to build their own home without the benefit of detailed plans gives me the jiggers.

When the plans are received by the Building Control department they are then checked out thoroughly. If the proposals are straightforward and the work shown on the plans complies in all respects with the regulations, then an approval will be issued as soon as possible and certainly within the five weeks deadline.

If, for any reason, your proposals do not satisfy the regulations or there are some unclear areas or points, then, if there is still time left on the application, the inspector will write to you inviting you to amend the plans in order to bring about compliance.

There may also be additional details and calculations that are required and in some cases it is possible for an approval to be issued conditional upon the subsequent receipt of this information. If you're building in timber frame then the details and calculations for the timber frame itself may not actually be prepared and available until the frame is in the process of being manufactured. In these cases, as with roof trusses and steel purlins, the consent will be issued as a conditional consent and work may well be allowed to continue up to and until these elements are reached. On the other hand, if the inspector has reason to suspect that there are conditions in the ground that will require a site/soil investigation and the design of special foundations, he will not allow work to commence until such time as all of the details have been formulated and approved.

The detailed plans will also have to be sent to your warranty company and in most cases if there is any suspicion of bad ground or a special foundation situation, they will require exactly the same information as the Building Inspector wants and may well require at least three weeks' notice of any intention to start work in those circumstances. If the NHBC are carrying out the role of inspecting and approving under the Building Regulations or if they are merely acting as your warranty company and you are building in timber frame, they will also require an HB353B certificate in England and Wales or an HB210S certificate in Scotland, to be supplied by the frame manufacturer or designer.

The Building Control department, in much the same way as the Planning department, have a statutory duty to consult with certain agencies and departments. If a proposal for a new building involves drainage and the discharge of effluent either into the subsoil or to a watercourse, then they have to consult with the Environment Agency. If the Environment Agency flag up a problem then the Building Control department will, in effect, act as their agent in enforcing their requirements and in making sure that your application is amended to take their recommendations into account. The Building Control department will also consult other agencies and departments including and especially those dealing with fire, highways and public health.

If all of these questions, amendments and additional information cannot be answered or provided within the five-week period following the application, then a rejection notice will be issued. If you're already building at this time, then a new application will have to be made as soon as possible, but if you have not started building then you cannot do so until, and unless, either a new application is submitted or a Building Notice is issued and the requisite 48 hours' notice is given. The principle of serial applications and rejections is, for many local authorities, an established fact and a normal way of proceeding. Others state, however, that they do not regard rejection as a particularly productive exercise and make strenuous efforts to approve Full Plans applications as quickly as possible. They are helped in that endeavour if the relevant information is provided at the application stage and if any anticipated requirements for calculations, soil and site investigations and foundation design details are available before, rather than after or approaching, their five-week deadline. Once again attendance at the school of forward planning will pay off.

If a formal approval has been issued it will usually be accompanied by a set of cards, each of which covers a particular stage in the construction of your new home. Even if you don't have these cards, or if you are proceeding with the construction prior to the issuing of a formal approval or under a Building Notice, you are required to notify the inspector at these stages. Obviously, for things like loft conversions the stages will be different but in general for new build they are:

• excavations for foundations
• foundation concrete
• oversite
• damp-proof course
• foul-water drains
• surface-water drains
• occupation prior to completion
• completion.

You will hear stories about not having to wait for the inspector beyond a certain period and of carrying on beyond these stages if the inspector fails to turn up. Ignore them please. The stages are carefully worked out so that no important work is irrevocably covered up before it has been adequately inspected and approved. If the Building Inspector feels that you have covered up something that is wrong or that you have carried out work that is in defiance of the regulations, they have the power to order its exposure and you will bear the cost.

In the end they have the legal right of enforcement and the power to issue what is known as a 'Stop Notice' that will bring your entire site to a grinding halt until such time as you have either rectified the incorrect work or satisfied them that the work is in order.

All of this serves to illustrate a radical difference between planning consent and Building Regulations approval and one that often confuses lay people. With planning permission, you have consent to build exactly what is shown on the plans and although the authorities do have some discretionary powers as already outlined, essentially you have consent to build *only* that which is on the approved drawings and referred to in the consent. With Building Regulations, the plans are approved as being in accordance with the regulations but then, after the consent is issued, the inspector has the power to vary the construction. It is no good pointing to your plans and saying that they were approved. The inspector's job in assessing your application was to make sure that what was *drawn* conformed to the regulations as far as was foreseeable. On the other hand, the inspector's job, when inspecting your building works, is to make sure that what is *built* conforms to the regulations. If they feel that, because of conditions experienced or evidenced on site, changes need to be made, then they have the powers to require those changes.

It's at this point that self-builders can become a trifle upset at this official who's insisting on changes, delaying the job and costing them a great deal more money. In some cases the inspector can almost be seen as being in cahoots with the warranty inspector, with both of them conspiring to push your project off budget. Nothing is further from the truth. If any of these officials or inspectors feel that it's necessary for changes to be made, then they are doing so in the interests of the stability and integrity of your new home and for no other reason. Their reasons and objectives, therefore, coincide quite nicely with your own and, if you've taken note of the preceding chapters, it's quite probable that you've already budgeted for the eventuality or allowed for its possibility within your contingency fund.

Most medieval cathedrals were built with the aid of fewer drawings than are now considered necessary for the construction of a public lavatory. Nevertheless, many of them suffered failures of some sort and in some cases these were catastrophic. In others the flying buttresses we now admire so much were added at a later date, or during the construction when it became apparent that the structure was about to fail. Today's regulations are designed to ensure that, as far as is possible, all that can be known, assessed or calculated to ensure the stability and structural integrity of your new home is known and appreciated *before* you start work.

The Completion Certificate

At the end of the job the Building Inspector will issue a 'Completion Certificate', which you should file away very carefully as it's quite likely that any subsequent purchaser will want to see it. Before issuing the certificate the Building Inspector will make a final inspection and will want to assure themselves that all the electrical works have been carried out by a competent person and that they have received signed copies of the electrical installation certificate conforming to BS7671 as detailed below. They will also want to know that the space and hot-water-producing appliances, together with their associated flues, have been commissioned, calibrated, tested and certified by a suitably qualified person, of which more later.

The SAP ratings, as referred to in Chapter 6, must be submitted for approval, within five days of completion, on all new-build homes or conversions that are intended for occupation as a dwelling. The Building Control department must have this in order to issue the certificate.

Building with the regulations

Of course nothing gets built without the regulations. Even if you choose to 'self-certify', using the NHBC or an architect, keeping clear of the local authority altogether, everything must be built to conform to the regulations. Even if what you are building is exempt from the need to apply for approval, everything that is built must also conform. It is an illegal act to build something that does not conform and it is a criminal rather than a civil offence. The local authority have the power to act within 12 months of a breach occurring but they and others have the right, almost in perpetuity, to take out an injunction to require a breach leading to a dangerous structure to be rectified.

It's not that difficult to conform. The regulations are really the Highway Code of building. Those who work in the industry know the way things should be done and in the end most of the rules boil down to a commonsense way of doing things.

Quite obviously, and as I've already discussed, many aspects of the building and design have to heed more than one of the Approved Documents. So perhaps the best way of illustrating their impact is to run through some headings relating to the building of a new house or extension, picking out the major points and requirements that the Building Regulations impose. Some of these observations may be referred to elsewhere in this book where they have particular relevance to, say, the operation of a trade. Some are embellished with the requirements of the NHBC.

Foundations

Normal strip foundations must be dug a minimum of 1 metre deep or below the influence of drains or surrounding trees. The trenches must be clean and square and the bottoms must be natural, undisturbed ground. Whatever it says on the plans, the Building Inspector, probably backed up by the warranty inspector, has the power to demand a variation. For example, if your plans show a 1-metre strip foundation and your Building Regulations approval was

Above: **Trenches awaiting concrete.**

Above right: **Concreted and loaded out with blocks.**

Left: **Consolidating the hardcore oversite.**

Right: **A beam-and-block floor.**

granted on that premise but, when it comes to digging the foundations, the ground is found to be unsuitable, then the inspector can, and will, require you to change tack. They may well require a soil investigation or a special foundation designed by an engineer and will require that you stop work until such time as everything is agreed. They can even demand that you switch to one of the special foundation types that I talked about in Chapter 3.

Strip foundations should have a minimum width of 600mm with the concrete in the bottom laid to a minimum thickness of 225mm. Trenchfill foundations can shrink the trench width into a minimum of 450mm but the concrete within them must have a minimum thickness of 500mm. The concrete mix should be ST2 or GEN1. Steps in foundation concrete must not exceed its thickness and should overlap by twice its thickness. In many areas two layers of C503 mesh reinforcement are required at the top and bottom of the concrete with 75mm cover.

Foundation walls should be built centrally on the concrete footing. Most foundation walls to a maximum depth of 1 metre are built using two skins of 100mm 7N blocks. If the foundation walls have to be any deeper then the blocks have to be 140mm thick, but in practice, most would bring the concrete up to that level as it's extremely difficult to lay blocks deeper in the ground than 1 metre with normal foundation widths. The cavity between the blocks must be infilled with lean-mix concrete to ground level or to within 225mm of the damp-proof course (dpc), whichever is the higher. The two skins of wall must be tied together with stainless-steel wall ties every 750mm horizontally and every 450mm vertically with a row at dpc to support any cavity insulation.

If you are building a second storey or converting a loft it will be necessary to ensure that the foundations and lower ground-floor walls are adequate to support the new loads. It may be necessary, at the discretion of the Building Inspector, to expose the existing walls and foundations and this may include opening up or excavating floors to check things. If they do not appear to be adequate then you will have to provide details of the proposed remedial works or alterations, including all necessary calculations and engineer's details.

Ground-bearing solid concrete floors

All topsoil and organic matter must be removed and the oversite filled with a minimum of 150mm and a maximum of 600mm of clean and compacted hardcore. This should then be sand-blinded before a 1,200-gauge continuous polythene damp-proof membrane is laid, linked to the dpc in the wall. Any joints in the membrane must be lapped and taped.

The concrete oversite must be a minimum of 100mm thick ST2 or GEN1 concrete with a trowelled smooth or tamped surface. In certain circumstances the inspectors may require that the oversite concrete has reinforcement mesh laid within it.

All ground floors must be insulated and the current requirements are that they should achieve a 'U' value of at least 0.25. Solid concrete oversites can be insulated with either 100mm Jablite/polystyrene, 70mm Celotex or Kingspan or 65mm Styrofoam laid below the concrete, above it or in a combination of the two. If it is exclusively beneath the concrete then there should be a 25mm upstand of insulation at the perimeter external walling to prevent cold bridging. If it is laid on top then it will support either the sand and cement final floor finish or else a floating floor. Any insulation should be stopped beneath non-load-bearing partitions built off the slab.

Suspended timber ground floors

Where a suspended timber floor is to be employed, sleeper walls are built to provide interim support. These can be founded on normal strip foundations but it is more usual for them to be built off the solid concrete slab or oversite that it is necessary to construct at a lower level. This is built on levelled-out and compacted ground using ST2 or GEN1 concrete trowelled smooth or tamped level. The concrete is thickened up beneath the sleeper walls, which are built in a honeycomb fashion to allow a free flow of air within the void. The external walls also have air-bricks built in to them at 1.5-metre centres around the perimeter of the building, sleeved through the cavity.

The timber joists, sized according to the span, are supported by means of metal joist hangers built into the blockwork. As an alternative, manufactured 'I' beams or engineered timber joists can be utilised. Insulation is obtained by the use of 120mm mineral wool insulation between the joists, supported by netting. Alternatively rigid foam types can be used, supported on battening nailed to the sides of the joists. However, it is notoriously difficult to get a snug fit.

If under-floor central heating is to be used then this will have to be installed before the decking is laid over the joists. Some systems employ metal baffle or spreader plates. Others use metal channel pipe runs fixed to the sides of the joists. In all cases the pipework must be above the insulation.

Suspended concrete ground floors (beam and block)

With a beam-and-block floor, inverted 'T'-shaped concrete beams span from wall to wall. These walls must be properly founded and cannot be built off a concrete oversite in the same way as for a suspended timber floor. In any event it is not usually necessary for there to be a concrete oversite as, as long as the subsoil is levelled out, with all vegetable matter removed, and there is a clear gap of 75mm between the subsoil and the bottom of the beams.

The size and spacing of the beams will be determined by the manufacturers. Most are infilled with normal building blocks, although there are proprietary systems for the infill, which provide greater insulation. Ventilation beneath the void is necessary but, as there is no concrete oversite, it is important that no light gets in. This is achieved by the use of 'cranked' ventilators built into the wall every 2 metres (1.5 metres in Scotland). Insulation is usually achieved by setting the insulation above the beam-and-block floor beneath either a screed or floating floor. The thicknesses are the same as for the solid floor above, according to the type of material used.

Garage floors

These can be solid concrete or beam and block. The construction details follow the same principles as for the rest of the house, except for the fact that the insulation is left out and, with a solid concrete floor, it is thickened at the door. A beam-and-block floor must receive a screed of at least 65mm with reinforcement mesh set within it.

The finished floor level in an attached garage where there is a connecting door to the house must be at least 100mm lower with an impervious masonry threshold.

Radon gas protection

In areas where there is radon gas the home has to be made airtight to the ground. This is achieved by taping the damp-proof radon membrane at all joints – this is required in any event – and sealing the membrane at junctions and service entry points with proprietary 'top hat' seals. The damp-proof radon membrane is taken through the wall and sealed to a cavity tray supported by the lean-mix cavity infill at ground level, with weep holes to the external skin.

In the Republic of Ireland (Eire), new houses outside high radon areas are required to have a radon sump with connecting pipework terminating and capped at suitable points outside the building. These terminals are to be marked to identify their purpose so that in the event of any future survey indicating the presence of radon, they can be activated, possibly by the installation of a fan.

External walling construction

The external leaf of a masonry construction cavity wall can be either flush jointed brickwork or 100mm dense concrete blockwork with two coats of sand and cement render. In high-exposure areas this render might need the addition of a waterproofing agent. The internal leaf should be a high-performance 2.8N 100mm insulation block with either a 13mm lightweight plaster finish or 12.5mm plasterboard skimmed drylining.

But if you swapped the high-performance block for a 100mm concrete block then you could still achieve the 'U' value by having an 85mm cavity, full-filled with 85mm Rockwool, Drytherm or Isowool batts or a 100mm cavity, full-filled with 100mm full-fill Jablite/EPS interlocking panels. And as I've said in the section on brick and block construction, a cavity wall with an external brick, a 100mm cavity, full-filled with mineral wool insulation and a 100mm lightweight high-performance block will have a 'U' value of no more than 0.30.

Two further points to note. In severe exposure areas these full-fill cavity options are not allowed. If

Cavity insulation regulations

In order to achieve the required 'U' value of no more than 0.35, the cavity width and insulation details must be as follows:

Clear cavity width required	Insulation type and thickness	Overall cavity width required	Internal block type
50mm	50mm Jablite/EPS	100mm	100mm high-performance insulation block
50mm	30mm Celotex, Kingspan or Xtratherm	80mm	Ditto
50mm	50mm Styrofoam Plus cavity board	100mm	Ditto
N/A	75mm Rockwool, Drytherm, Isowool full-fill batts	75mm	Ditto
N/A	75mm full-fill interlocking Jablite	75mm	Ditto

the house is a three-storey house, not including a loft conversion, then the lower-storey blockwork would have to be stronger, possibly 7N or more.

Whilst they talk a lot about masonry construction, the Building Regulations themselves and Approved Document 'A' are completely silent about timber frame. Timber sizes and specifications are referred back to TRADA, who publish the various tables to do with the use of timber in buildings. The NHBC are not at all silent. They have a whole chapter devoted to timber frame in their handbook and require that every timber frame should be checked by an NHBC listed certifier. In England, Wales, Northern Ireland and the Isle of Man this certifier is required to issue a 'Certificate for Timber Frame Dwellings HB353B'. In Scotland the name is the same but the number is HB210S.

The internal leaf of a timber-frame wall is the one that takes all the loading and provides most of the insulation by virtue of having the space between the studs packed with insulation. The cavity is always kept clear. Standard 89 x 39mm walling panels with high-performance mineral wool insulation have a 'U' value of around 0.35. Now that's good enough for England and Wales at the moment but it's not good enough for Scotland, where the 'U' value for an exposed external wall must be at least 0.30. This can be achieved in several ways. One is to change the insulation to a rigid foam type. But this is notoriously difficult to fit snuggly between the studs. Another is

to change the normal breather paper on the outside of the sheathing to an insulating breather paper. And perhaps the most popular is to increase the studs to 140mm with a consequent increase in insulation, taking the 'U' value down to 0.29.

Semi-exposed walls (walls to garages or unheated rooms)

Walls to a garage or unheated room must be constructed and insulated as if they were external walls. Alternatively they can be constructed using 200mm 2.8N solid high-performance insulation blocks, drylined and insulated with 12.5mm plasterboard and skim with a vapour barrier trapping a minimum thickness of 55mm Jablite/EPS or 50mm Celotex, Kingspan or Rockwool mineral wool, to achieve a 'U' value of 0.35.

Dpcs and cavity trays

Horizontal dpcs and dpc trays with stop ends and weep holes should be provided at least 150mm above finished ground level, continuous with the damp-proof membrane in the floor. Stepped or horizontal dpc/cavity trays are to be provided over all openings and roof abutments/projections, and over and between walls with different construction or materials. Vertical dpc or proprietary closers need to be provided to all closings, returns, abutments of cavity work and openings (see 'Cavity Closers' below).

Clearly this cavity tray, seen above left, has been incorrectly fitted as it does not meet up with the cover flashing. Any moisture coming down the cavity would therefore be conducted into the block, rather than harmlessly to the outside

Above right: **Specially shaped steel lintels might be required.**

Right: **Detail of a staircase trimmer.**

Horror pictures, courtesy of Forest of Dean District Council.
From left to right: **Loss of bond on the blockwork; walls out of vertical; walls not keyed in; joists out of level.**

Party wall construction

The regulations are concerned with party walls between dwellings and require that in masonry construction, there are two skins of dense concrete block, plastered to each side with a 50mm minimum cavity. The walls have to be tied to the internal leaf of the rest of the house with the junctions to the cavities, and all other horizontal and vertical cavities, fire stopped with a proprietary acoustic/insulated cavity closer.

Once again the Building Regulations are silent about timber frame and we have to turn to the NHBC handbook, where cavity barriers and firestops are required at the junction between a compartment wall that separates buildings and an external wall and at the junction between the separating walls with the roof.

Sound insulation to internal walls

The Building Regulations require that bedroom walls and rooms containing a WC should be provided with insulation. Once again the NHBC goes further, requiring that all partition walls between a room containing a WC and a living room, dining room, study or bedroom should have a weighted sound reduction index of not less than 38dB over the frequency range of 100-3150Hz. This does not apply when the room with the WC forms an en-suite to the bedroom it adjoins.

Blockwork walls where the blocks have a density of not less than 600kg/m3, i.e. they are not perforated or hollow, with plaster or drylining both sides will suffice. Timber frame or studwork partitions have to have either two sheets of plasterboard on each side or introduce 25mm of insulation into the void with one sheet of 12.5mm plasterboard on each side. Alternatively, if 9.5mm plasterboard is used, this must be skim-coat plastered rather than drylined.

Internal load-bearing partitions

Internal load-bearing walls must be built off foundations and must be at least as thick as the walls that they carry above. In a timber frame house the suppliers or designers will specify the make-up of the wall. In masonry construction the usual form is for the walls to be built of 100mm dense concrete blocks bonded or tied to the external or party walls with ties at each course and restrained by the ceiling joists or trusses. Ground-floor internal cross, spine or load-bearing walls in a three-storey house, or extending 1 metre or more below dpc level in a two-storey house, must be constructed in either 140mm 7N blockwork or 215mm 5N brickwork.

Internal masonry non-load-bearing partitions

Non-load-bearing walls can be built off a thickened slab or oversite rather than a foundation. They must be tied to the external or party walls at a minimum of 225 centres.

Internal non-load-bearing studwork partitions

Non-load-bearing studwork partitions should be constructed of 100 x 50mm softwood or 89 x 49mm CLS stress-graded timber with head and sole plates and intermediate noggings fixed at 600mm centres.

Wall abutments

The vertical join between a new wall and an old wall must be secured with a proprietary steel crocodile system with a continuous cavity and dpc, pointed with flexible mastic.

Lintels

Insulated lintels must be provided over all wall openings. Combined lintels, which form a cavity tray, do not need to have a damp-proof membrane built in over them. Inverted 'T'-shaped steel lintels and concrete external lintels must have a cavity tray built in over them. Weep holes must be provided at the ends of all lintels and along the cavity tray. Openings up to 1,200mm must provide for the lintel having a bearing at each end of at least 100mm. Above 1,200mm this bearing must be at least 150mm.

Cavity closers and closing around window and door openings

Proprietary acoustic/insulated fire stop cavity closers must be positioned to all cavity openings/closings, tops of walls and junctions with other properties. Checked rebates should be constructed to window or door reveals where the outer masonry skin projects across the inner skin by at least 25mm and the cavity is closed by an insulated closer, which acts as a vertical dpc, with the door or window sealed around with mastic. Alternatively a proprietary finned insulated cavity closer can be used.

All external door and window frames, as well as holes where services are taken through walls, floors and ceilings, should be sealed inside and out with proprietary waterproof mastic sealants, expanding foam or mineral wool and tape to ensure that they are airtight.

There is a strong possibility that a requirement for pressure testing for airtightness may be introduced in the new legislation. Most well-built homes do not leak significantly and there is, of course, a dilemma here in that other parts of the regulations call for adequate ventilation.

Expansion joints

In certain cases it is necessary to build in expansion joints in external walling. With clay brickwork these can be flexible cellular polyethylene, cellular polyethylene or even foam rubber. In blockwork or concrete brickwork they can be hemp, fibreboard or cork. All joints should be sealed externally with mastic. They are unsightly and if they are specified in your design it is best to site them behind a downpipe.

Strapping and restraint

All areas greater than 70 square metres must have lateral support in the form of internal partitions or cross walls. All walls must be restrained at intermediate floor level, at wallplate level and down the rake of each gable by the provision of 1,000 × 30 × 5mm lateral restraint straps, crossing at least three joists or rafters with noggings below, 38mm wide by three quarters of the depth of the main timber. These metal restraint straps can be notched into the joists where necessary to maintain a floor level.

Intermediate first floors

The floor can be constructed using sawn lumber joists to the sizes as specified in the TRADA tables referred to on page 302. Whilst not wanting to reproduce these tables here, I should explain that for most homes that means that if 47 × 147mm joists are used the maximum spans are 3.06m at 400mm centres, 2.94m at 450mm centres and 2.61m at 600mm centres. For 47 × 170mm joists these spans are 3.53m, 3.40m and 2.99m respectively and for 47 × 195mm, 4.04m, 3.89m and 3.39m.

Trimmers, which receive and bear the joists coming into a stairwell or open area within the floor, are usually 75mm wide and may have to be doubled up or bolted together in accordance with the designer's and engineer's specification.

Joists should be built into the wall with heavy-duty proprietary metal joist hangers. Where joists lie beneath and run in the same direction as internal partition walling and beneath baths, they should be doubled up and bolted together. The void between the joists should be insulated with a minimum thickness of 10kg/m3 of proprietary sound insulation quilt with 15mm plasterboard beneath and 20mm tongued-and-grooved softwood boarding or moisture-resistant chipboard decking to give at least 30 minutes' fire resistance. The joists should have solid blocking at each end between the hangers using timber at least 38mm wide by a minimum of three quarters of the joist depth. Spans of over 2.5m up to 4.5m should have midspan strutting, either solid block, timber herring bone or proprietary metal. Spans over 4.5 metres should have strutting at one third points.

Where joists are notched for pipework, the notches must be at the top of the joist, no deeper than 0.15 of the joist depth and positioned in a zone between 0.1 and 0.2 of the span. Holes in the joist must be in the centre of the joist depth, must not be more than 0.25 of the depth and must be in a zone between 0.25 and 0.4 of the span. There must be at least 100mm horizontally between any notches or holes.

Softwood or hardwood tongued-and-grooved flooring should be cramped up and either double or secret nailed to each joist. Nails should be two and a half times the thickness of the boarding and punched home. Chipboard should have the tongued-and-grooved edges glued together and be laid with the long sides at right angles to the run of the joists. They should also be glued to the joists. The boards should be nailed with ringshank nails two and a half times the thickness of the board or screwed at 200–300mm centres along the joists or beam-and-block floors. Boards must run to a joist on all sides or be supported by a beam-and-block floor with an expansion gap of at least 10mm left where the boards adjoin or butt up to a rigid upstand or wall.

Manufactured and engineered timber 'I' beams can be used in lieu of ordinary timber joists. They must be sized and installed in accordance with the manufacturer's instructions. 'I' beams are never notched. Instead, they are manufactured with punch holes, which can be taken out as appropriate. First and intermediate floors can also be created using a concrete beam-and-block system, which is often strong enough to support blockwork upper part partitioning. Once again the size, spacing and layout of the beams and blocks must be determined by the manufacturers.

New loft conversions can be formed by the use of proprietary prefabricated attic trusses, adequately braced with 15mm skim-finish plasterboard to the floor and 12.5mm minimum to the ceiling.

Exposed intermediate first floors (floors above integral garages)

Internal floors, which are over an unheated space such as a garage, a porch, walkways and canopies, are to be insulated to achieve a minimum 'U' value of 0.25 and boarded and skimmed to provide at least 30 minutes' fire resistance. In practice this is often achieved by two layers of plasterboard with the joints staggered and skim-coat plaster or Artex finish. Insulation can be achieved by the use of Jablite/EPS or Celotex to a thickness of 120mm, Kingspan to a thickness of 100mm, Xtratherm to a thickness of 125mm or mineral wool or fibreglass to a depth of 200mm.

Soil pipe boxing

The framing around a soil and vent pipe must be constructed as a continuous duct to within the roof space, from adequately sized softwood with two layers of 15mm plasterboard, skim coated with mineral wool sound insulation quilt packed into the void. If there is an air admittance valve then the vent pipe should be provided with grilles.

Pitched roof construction

The roof can be formed using kiln-dried stress-graded lumber with the sizes, spacings and fixings deter-mined by the designer/engineer. Cut single, hipped or gable roofs over 40 degrees must be braced to BS5268. Alternatively the roof may be formed by pre-fabricated manufactured trusses, erected and spaced in accordance with the manufacturer's specifications. Roofs may require built-in purlins or supports in either timber or steel. Steel purlins must be painted to resist rusting and supported on padstones or spreader beams built into the supporting blockwork.

Roofs must be braced diagonally beneath the rafters at 45 degrees from the wallplate end to the ridge using 47 x 22mm timber. Longitudinal bracing is also required at the ridge and at the ceiling node points where the bracing within the truss comes down to meet the ceiling joists. It may be omitted where the spacing between the brace nodes does not exceed 3.7 metres. It is also required at the rafter node points where the distance between them and the wallplate exceeds 4.2 metres. All roofs must be tied into the walls using lateral restraint straps across at least three timbers as mentioned above. Wallplates must be tied down to the blockwork/superstructure using proprietary 30 x 2.5mm straps at 2-metre centres.

The roof covering can consist of slate or tile plus associated capping, and verge/eaves details fixed in accordance with the manufacturer's details for pitch and exposure as detailed on the drawings. Tiles and slates are to be fixed to 50 x 25mm softwood battens fixed across the rafters above un{tearable roof felt underlay. In Scotland the roof timbers must be overlaid with rigid sarking boarding beneath the underlay and tile battening.

Ceilings to roof spaces must be finished using minimum 12.5mm foil-backed plasterboard with a skim coat or proprietary finish. In practice, as the NHBC require that where the timber support spacings exceed 450mm, all 12.5mm plasterboard joints are timber-nogged, it is often easier and quicker to use 15mm plasterboard.

Where new second storeys or loft conversions are being carried out it will be necessary to prove that the roof, ceiling structure and roof covering are adequate and capable of supporting any new loads. The Building Control surveyor can demand that any part of the roof is exposed and may require engineer's

Roof construction

DATA SHEET

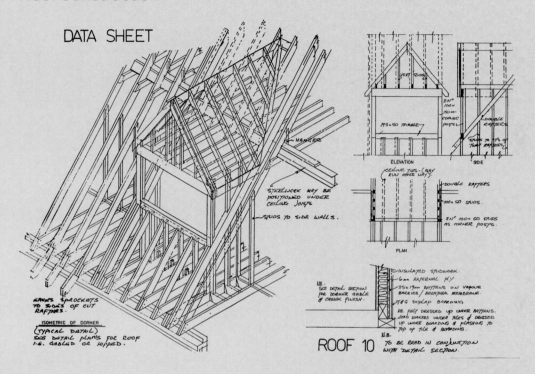

EAVES SPROCKETS
TO SIDES OF CUT
RAFTERS.

ISOMETRIC OF DORMER
(TYPICAL DETAIL)
SEE DETAIL PLANS FOR ROOF
I.E. GABLED OR HIPPED.

STEELWORK MAY BE
POSITIONED UNDER
CEILING JOISTS
STUDS TO SIDE WALLS.

HANGER

VENT STUDS

2No
100×
150×
CORNER
POST

175×50 TRIMMER

DOUBLE
RAFTERS

STRAP TO ⅓'S OF
JOINT RAFTERS

ELEVATION   SIDE

CEILING TIES - (MAY
RUN ONCE WAY)

DOUBLE RAFTERS

100×50 STUDS.

2No 100×50 STUDS
AS CORNER POSTS.

PLAN

INSULATED STUDWORK.
6mm EXTERNAL PLY
25×19mm BATTENS ON VAPOUR
BARRIER / BREATHER MEMBRANE.
T&G SHIPLAP BOARDING.
N.B. FELT DRESSED UP UNDER BATTENS.
LEAD SOAKERS UNDER TILES & DRESSED
UP UNDER BOARDING & FLASHING TO
TOP OF TILE & BOARDING.

N.B.

N.B.
SEE DETAIL SECTION
FOR DORMER GABLE
& CHEEK FINISH.

ROOF 10   TO BE READ IN CONJUNCTION
WITH DETAIL SECTION.

Dormer construction details

Above: **Setting out the trusses.**

Right: **Eaves details.**

ROOF 1c

Wallplate

overhang varies
with roof pitch.

N.B. MAYBE   STONE LINTELS OVER WINDOWS.
* N.B.:- ONLY ROOF VENTILATION WHEN TYVEK SUPRA TILE
ROOFING UNDERLAY IS USED.

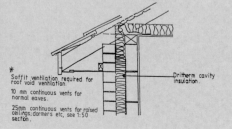

Dritherm cavity
insulation.

*
Soffit ventilation required for
roof void ventilation.

10 mm continuous vents for
normal eaves.

25mm continuous vents for raised
ceilings; dormers etc, see 1:50
section.

calculations and drawings to be submitted for approval.

Valleys and leadwork

Roof leadwork such as flashings, soakers, valleys and gutters, etc. should be formed from Code 4 lead sheet. Lead to valleys should be fully supported on valley boards and should be dressed at least 200mm beneath the tiles on each side. It should also be laid in lengths not exceeding 1.5 metres and each length should have a lap beneath the one preceding it of at least 150mm.

Roof insulation and ventilation

Flat ceilings to a roof void should receive 100mm of mineral wool insulation laid between the joist with a further 150mm laid across the joists, continuous with the wall insulation but stopped back at the eaves or at junctions to maintain a 50mm air gap. Cross-ventilation can be provided by proprietary eaves strips equivalent to a 25mm continuous gap at eaves level. If this cross-ventilation is not possible, as with a mono pitch, then it can be provided by means of proprietary ridge-level ventilation equivalent to a 5mm continuous gap in the form of vent tiles spaced in accordance with the manufacturer's instructions.

Sloping ceilings can be insulated using a combination of between and beneath rafter rigid foam insulation so as to provide an air gap immediately beneath the underlay of at least 50mm, namely: Celotex to a thickness of 120mm between the rafters and 25mm beneath, Kingspan to a thickness of 100mm between and 25mm below and Xtratherm to a thickness of 105mm with 25mm below.

Ventilation to the roof space can be omitted altogether if a breathing underlay or felt is used with a minimum 25mm thick treated counter batten beneath the tile battens with proprietary eaves carrier systems.

An alternative insulation method is to use a multi-foil insulation system, either above or below the rafters. These must have a clear gap of 25mm on each side in order to work. With the over rafter method the insulation is drawn across the top of the rafters and fixed down with 25mm horizontal battening. The roof is then overlaid with a breathable roofing underlay fixed down with vertical counter battens up the rafters, after which it is horizontally battened to receive the appropriate tiles or slates. The ceiling covering is created in the normal way using foil-backed minimum 12.5mm plasterboard.

With the under rafter method the insulation is tacked with non-corrosive fixings to the underside of the rafters, so as to maintain a clear air gap of 50mm between it and the underside of the roof underlay. Proprietary eaves ventilation equivalent to a 25mm continuous gap plus proprietary ridge ventilation equivalent to a continuous 5mm air gap must also be provided; 25mm battening is then fixed beneath the insulation to carry the minimum 12.5mm foil-backed plasterboard.

Loft hatches, doors and light wells to roof spaces

All openings into the roof void must have the same level of insulation as any other walls or ceilings and must be draught stripped and positively fixed.

Fire safety and detection

All storeys within the home must have mains-operated interconnected smoke alarms with battery back-up, separately wired up and fused back to the consumer unit, to all circulation areas and within 7.5 metres of all habitable rooms. Where the kitchen is not separated from the stairway or circulation area, compatible interconnected heat detection devices must be provided in addition to the smoke alarms. There are additional proposals in the pipeline that will require the installation of a smoke alarm in the main bedroom.

Walls between garages and the house must provide at least 30 minutes' fire resistance to roof or ceiling level and be fire-stopped with mineral wool. Garage floors must have a masonry cill between them and the house and the finished floor level must be at least 100mm lower. Doors between the house and garage must be half-hour fire doors with self-closing devices and intumescent strips around the perimeter.

All first-floor bedrooms and habitable rooms and all inner habitable rooms to the ground floor must be fitted with windows that allow escape in the event of fire. This means that they must not have locks and they must have minimum opening casement dimensions of 0.33m2 and 450mm, within 800mm to 1,100mm of the floor level and 1,700mm of the eaves.

New three-storey dwellings and second-storey loft conversions

If there are three floors or where a loft conversion or extension effectively turns the building into a three-storey dwelling, the new and existing staircases, landings and hallways, for all three storeys, must be protected and enclosed as a 30-minute fire-resisting construction. The protected stairway must have an external door or at least two FD20 fire doors opening into separate rooms that are of 30-minute fire-resisting construction, divided from each other by 30-minute fire-resisting construction, each having an external door.

Any new second storey must also be protected and separated from the remainder of the house by the existing floor being of 30-minute fire-resisting construction. Existing ceilings and studwork can be left untouched if they have 12.5mm skim-coated plasterboard. If they are to be renewed then 15mm plasterboard must be used. A loft conversion must have a new 20-minute fire door with intumescent strips and closers at either the bottom or the top of the new staircase leading up into it.

All rooms off the protected staircase, except bathrooms and toilets, must be fitted with FD20 fire doors, intumescent strips and self-closers where new doors are provided. Existing doors can be left but must be fitted with self-closers.

Means-of-escape windows or top-hung escape roof lights with clear minimum opening dimensions of 0.33m2 and 450mm within 800–1,100mm of floor level and 1,700mm of eaves level must be provided to all bedrooms and habitable rooms at the first- and second-storey levels and any new habitable rooms on the ground floor that are created by the works. The escape windows should be positioned so that they can be accessed from a ladder from ground level. Any glazing to new or existing doors or frames should be provided or replaced with 30-minute fire-resisting glazing.

Conversions of a bungalow to form a new first-floor storey

The conversion of a bungalow or single-storey building to form a new first floor does not require a protected hall, landing or fire doors. However, the supporting (ground) floor must still be provided with a 30-minute fire-resisting construction. The stair may be positioned in a ground-floor room such as a living room, as long as there is a door in that room that provides a direct escape to the outside.

All rooms and bedrooms on the new first floor, with the exception of bathrooms and toilets, must be directly accessible off the landing and provided with escape windows. Smoke detection, as described above, must be provided and, if the staircase is from a kitchen or open-plan area containing a kitchen, compatible interlinked heat detection devices must be installed.

Ventilation and windows

Window opening areas to habitable rooms must be a minimum of 5% of the floor area of the room they serve, typically 1.75 metres above floor level. Rooms such as kitchens, utility rooms, bathrooms and toilets should have opening windows or doors for rapid ventilation. Background or trickle ventilation must be provided to windows by means of hit-and-miss or two-stage catches unless a whole house mechanical ventilation system is employed. Mechanical ventilation is to be employed to the following rooms, directly ducted to the outside air and equivalent to the following rates:

Kitchen	over hob	30 litres per second or 60 litres elsewhere
Utility room		30 litres per second
Bathroom		15 litres per second
Toilet (without an openable window)		6 litres per second

Toilets and bathrooms with no openable windows must have the fan linked to the light switch with a 15-minute overrun and a 10mm gap beneath the door for air supply.

Doors and adjacent sidelights or windows within 1,500mm of the ground and floor level and 300mm of doors must be fitted with toughened safety glass to

BS6206. So too must windows where the cill level is less than 800mm of the ground/floor level. All other windows must be draught-stripped and glazed with a minimum of either double glazing with a 16mm air gap and 'soft' Low-E coating or double glazing with a 12mm air gap, argon filled with a 'soft' Low-E coating to provide a minimum 'U' value of 2.0. or, in the case of metal-framed windows, 2.2.

Sanitary appliances and waste pipes

All WCs should have a trapped toilet connected to a 100mm-diameter waste or vent pipe with a hand basin with hot and cold running water. Sanitaryware such as wash-hand basins, baths, showers, sinks, etc. must have a 50mm-diameter waste pipe, laid to a fall and with a 75mm-deep seal trap. If the waste run exceeds 4 metres then an air admittance valve must be fitted above the spill-over level of the appliance. The waste pipes must discharge into a trapped gully grating or directly into the soil and vent pipe via proprietary waste manifolds or bosses. Internally, all waste and drainage pipes should have rodding access eyes at changes of direction and be adequately supported using proprietary clips and provided with 30-minutes' fire protection where they pass through floors.

Foul- and storm-water drainage systems

Apart from the obvious example of foundations and below-ground work, there is one other aspect of routine inspection that is taken very seriously and that is drains. These need to be inspected before they are covered up and they then need to be tested, usually with pressure hoses and gauges. Now, you may feel that just leaving various sections or connections open will suffice, but you would be wrong and you will find that the inspector will want to see it all.

Both storm- and foul-water drainage systems should be laid using 100mm-diameter Pvc-u proprietary underground drainage laid at gradients of 1:40, surrounded in clean pea gravel. Where flows exceed 1.0L/second, 100mm pipe can go down to 1:80 and 150mm pipe to 1:150. The invert level of any drainage in ordinary ground should not be less than 400mm and, in drives and roads, not less than 900mm. Access must be provided at all changes of direction or at 45-metre spacings for drainage up to 1 metre deep. Drainage, with a pipe diameter of no more than 150mm, up to 600mm deep can be serviced by a rodding eye or an inspection chamber measuring 225 × 100mm. Beyond that depth and up to 1.2 metres deep inspection chambers must have minimum dimensions of 450 × 450mm or a diameter of 450mm. Beyond that depth and up to 1,500mm it becomes a manhole and must have internal dimensions of 760 × 675mm, or a diameter of 1,000mm. Greater than 1,500mm deep and the manhole size must be 1,200 × 1,000mm or 1,200mm in diameter and beyond 3 metres, 1,050 × 800mm with steps or 1,200 × 800mm with a ladder.

Unless a proprietary base is used, half round pipe will have to be laid within the manhole, properly benched up with mortar. Drainage runs entering the manhole from another branch should do so with a 'Y' connection or be 'slippered' in through the benching to drop gently into the main run. All gullies must be trapped and have rodding access where serving branches. Inspection chamber covers should be properly fixed and, in driveways and roads, suitable for vehicular loads. Those that are within the building should be suitably double sealed to be gas-tight and screwed down.

Foul water should discharge to a mains sewer or a suitable sewage treatment facility or plant. Storm water and water from the guttering and downpipes should be piped at least 5 metres away from buildings to be disposed of in a minimum 1 cubic metre clean, rubble-filled soakaway covered with polythene and topsoil. If a percolation test proves that this is not possible then alternative systems might have to be adopted such as the provision of deep perforated concrete ring chambers or proprietary interlinked plastic cages. In a very few cases, where there is no demonstrable alternative, some local authorities might let you connect to the foul drainage system – but don't count on it.

In areas where flooding is likely, with low-lying buildings or those with basements, it may be necessary to provide anti-flood protection in the form of one-way valves to prevent sewage from entering the building.

Above: **If the drainage is deeper than 1.2 metres manhole chambers must be constructed using concrete rather than preformed Pvc-u sections.**

The regulations are also concerned with the surface water drainage and with the pathways around the building. Paths and paved areas should have a non-slip finish with a cross fall of between 1:40 and 1:60 with a reverse gradient of at least 500mm away from any walls of the building. Surface water should be disposed of by natural soakaway or, if that is not possible, by an adequately sized and roddable drainage system connected to soakaways or another approved means.

Waste and recycling storage space

All dwellings must have a space of at least 1.2 square metres for the siting of dustbins and recycling bins. This must be within 30 metres of the collection point, without having to take the refuse through the house, unless it is a garage, porch or other non-habitable part of the dwelling. The route or path should not have a gradient of more than 1:12 or more than three steps.

Space and hot water heat-producing appliances

I have gone into the requirements and options for heating the water and space in your new home in Chapter 6. Suffice it to say here that in England and Wales new gas boilers must have an efficiency rating of at least 86%, and from April 2007 the same will apply to all new oil boilers. Most Building Control departments assume that this means that the boiler must of necessity be of the condensing type.

Any flue discharging from the boiler must do so at least 600mm away from any openings into the building and must be protected by a wire cage. The boiler must be provided with separate controls for heating and hot water with an interlock, timer and heat controls within the room such as a room thermostat or thermostatic radiator valves. Gas installations must be installed and comply with BS5440, BS5546, BS5864, BS5871, BS6172, BS6173 and BS6798, which means that the plumber, commissioner and calibrator must be CORGI registered. Oil installations must be installed and comply with BS5410 and BS5799, which means that the plumber, commissioner and calibrator must be OFTEC registered.

Hot-water vessels (tanks), also discussed in Chapter 6, must be insulated with 35mm of PU foam and both heating and hot-water pipes must be insulated with proprietary foam covers equal to their outside diameter within 1 metre of the vessel and in unheated areas.

Fuel storage tanks

The regulations governing the siting of an lpg tank are quite complicated but boil down to the fact that a 1.1-tonne-capacity tank must usually be sited at least 3 metres from the wall of a building or boundary. This is reduced to 2 metres if there is an intervening 30-minute firewall 1–1.5 metres from the tank, at least the height of the pressure relief valve and wide enough so that the shortest path from the tank to the building remains 3 metres. It can be further reduced to 1.5 metres if the wall of the building is constructed as a 60-minute firewall in an inverted 'T'. At the ground floor, and as high as the pressure relief valve, this wall should be wide enough that the distance from the end of the tank remains 3 metres with any openings a further 1 metre away. Above this level the firewall should extend at least 1 metre either side of the pressure relief valve with any openings a further 1 metre away. Lpg tanks are very unsightly. They can be put underground but this is quite a bit more expensive. Many of these requirements would pose difficulties where the site is a narrow or constricted one as the supply companies themselves also have restrictions on the distance the tank must be from the access road.

Oil tanks up to 3,500 litres must be positioned in the open air on a concrete base with a minimum thickness of 50mm at least 300mm wider than the tank. Certainly if the tank is within 10 metres of a watercourse, but preferably in any case, the tank should either be of the twin-walled type or provided with an impervious masonry bund wall capable of containing 110% of its capacity. They must also be provided with a proprietary fire-restraint pipe and valve system. They must be stood on a hard surface. However, if they are situated closer to the wall of a building than 1,800mm you must either provide a firewall or make certain that the affected wall has a 30-minute fire resistance. If they are sited less that 760mm from a boundary you will have to provide a 30-minute firewall at least 300mm higher and wider than the top and sides of the tank.

Propane or Calor gas cylinders must be sited at least 1 metre horizontally and 300mm vertically from a door, opening window or air brick, air intake or flue terminal and 2 metres from an untrapped drain or a cellar opening. The cylinders must be stood upright on a solid base, in a reasonably protected position and secured by straps or chains to the wall.

Right: **It's important that the details of flashings and tray DPCs are followed correctly.**

Solid-fuel fireplaces and chimneys

The walls of the fireplace must be built of a non-combustible material of at least 200mm thickness at the sides and rear. The hearth must be constructed so that it has a thickness of at least 125mm of non-combustible material and must extend at least 150mm to the sides of the side jambs of the fireplace and 500mm in front. The fireplace should be provided with a properly insulated fireback, throat and gathering components, although that does not mean that a fire recess to take a dog grate would not comply.

Clay or pumice flue liners to BS1181, having a minimum diameter of 225mm, should be laid vertically and continuously, socket up for fire recesses up to 500 x 500mm. Recesses bigger than that should have the internal dimensions of the flue measuring at

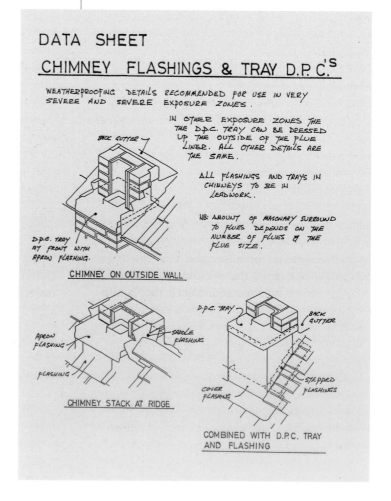

DATA SHEET
CHIMNEY FLASHINGS & TRAY D.P.C.'S

WEATHERPROOFING DETAILS RECOMMENDED FOR USE IN VERY SEVERE AND SEVERE EXPOSURE ZONES.

IN OTHER EXPOSURE ZONES THE THE D.P.C. TRAY CAN BE DRESSED UP THE OUTSIDE OF THE FLUE LINER. ALL OTHER DETAILS ARE THE SAME.

ALL FLASHINGS AND TRAYS IN CHIMNEYS TO BE IN LEADWORK.

NB: AMOUNT OF MASONARY SURROUND TO FLUES DEPENDS ON THE NUMBER OF FLUES & THE FLUE SIZE.

BACK GUTTER

D.P.C. TRAY AT FRONT WITH APRON FLASHING.

CHIMNEY ON OUTSIDE WALL

APRON FLASHING
SADDLE FLASHING
FLASHING

CHIMNEY STACK AT RIDGE

D.P.C. TRAY
BACK GUTTER
COVER FLASHING
STEPPED FLASHINGS

COMBINED WITH D.P.C. TRAY AND FLASHING

least 15% of the opening. Permanently open combustion air vents should be ducted to the outside in the same room as the fireplace with a free area equivalent to 50% of the appliance throat area.

The chimney wall thickness should be a minimum of 100mm with all combustible material, such as roof timbers, kept at least 50mm away from the walls. The chimney height must not exceed 4.5 times its narrowest thickness. If the terminal is at or within 600mm of the ridge then it must project above the ridge line by at least 600mm. If the chimney is on a roof slope or on a flat roof then the outlet must be at least 2,300mm horizontally from any roof, walls or tiles and at least 1,000mm above the highest point of intersection with the roof slope, or at least as high as the ridge. If the outlet is closer than 2,300mm to an openable roof light or dormer window then it must terminate at least 1,000mm above the top of the opening. If it is closer than 2,300mm to another building then it must terminate at least 600mm above the adjacent building.

All flues and chimneys should be tested at completion by a suitable qualified person and certificated with a plaque provided and displayed next to the flue detailing the type, size, category, installation date and use. Something I've never seen done.

Electrical installations

In January 2005 a new section was added to the Building Regulations for England and Wales, Northern Ireland and the Isle of Man concerning electrical safety bringing, for the first time, electrical works to domestic premises and their ancillary accommodation into the Building Regulations. Although there is no direct equivalent in the Scottish Building Standards, electrics are contained within the regulations and, more specifically in Section 4.5 (Electrical Safety) and Section 4.6 (Electrical Fixtures). However, these are pretty woolly in comparison and are confined to general exhortations to observe best practice and follow certain guidelines.

Part 'P' applies equally to buildings such as conservatories, porches, detached garages, sheds and greenhouses where the construction or alteration of such a building would be exempt under all other parts of the regulations. It also applies to electrics installed on land associated with dwellings, such as garden lighting, pond pumps and sewage treatment plants.

If the electrical works are being carried out in conjunction with a new build, extension, conversion, material alteration or change of use of a building where a Full Plans or Building Notice application has been made, then the works will be covered and dealt with within the principle application. But to ensure compliance with the regulations, a copy of an electrical installation certificate from a competent person (see below) must be provided to Building Control in order to obtain the Building Regulations Completion Certificate.

If works are only being carried out to the electrical system then as long as they are carried out by a competent person registered with an approved Part 'P' self-certification scheme, no separate Building Regulations application needs be made so long as the self-certification certificate is provided to the customer and a copy forwarded to the authorities within 30 days. If the works are carried out by an unregistered electrician, who must be a competent person as defined in ii) below then, as well as making a separate Building Regulations application, they must provide a written statement that the works have been designed, installed and tested to ensure that they comply with BS7671.

A competent person is defined as:

- a competent person registered under an electrical self-certification scheme, or
- a competent electrician who could be considered competent for the purposes of signing a BS7671 Electrical Installation Certificate, but is not registered with an electrical self-certification scheme.

These definitions create grey areas but would almost certainly exclude a DIY self-builder and most general builders. This puts the onus on the Building Control department to inspect and legitimise the work and, quite frankly, most Building Control departments do not have the time or expertise. Some accept established but unregistered contractors as competent. Others, in the absence of qualified inspecting staff, insist that only registered contractors are employed.

The various self-certification bodies and schemes are listed in the Further Information section at the back of this book (see page 456).

Bringing electrics into the regulations means that there is an interaction with other parts of the regulations and, in particular, Part'M'. New buildings must obviously comply with the requirements for positioning of sockets and switches within the 450–1,200mm zones above floor level. Extensions to dwellings built after July 1999 must also comply with part 'M'. Extensions to dwellings built before that date can either have the switches and sockets in conformation with Part 'M' or at the same heights as the existing, so long as access to them is not made worse. If an older house is being rewired without removing the plaster it is considered reasonable that the sockets and switches should be put back in the same place as they were before. If a complete renovation is being undertaken with plaster removed, then, in most circumstances the outlets should conform to the Part 'M' regulations.

For the frustrated DIY worker there are a very few electrical works that need *not* be notified to the

Below: **Get the leaflet and read the rules.**

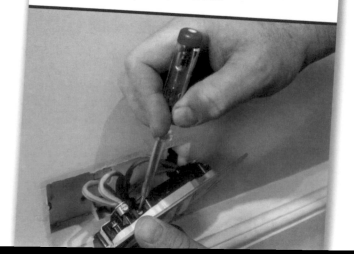

Building Control bodies, although the requirements of Part 'P' still apply and the installation must comply with BS7671. These are:

- replacing accessories such as socket outlets, control switches and ceiling roses
- replacing the cable for a single circuit only, where damaged, for example, by fire, rodents or impact
- re-fixing or replacing the enclosures of existing installation components
- providing mechanical protection to existing fixed installations
- adding lighting points (light fittings and switches) to an existing circuit, other than in a 'special location or installation'
- adding socket outlets and fused spurs to an existing ring or radial circuit, other than in a 'special location or installation'
- installing or upgrading main or supplementary equipotential bonding, other than in a 'special location or installation'.

A 'special location or installation' is defined as:

- a kitchen
- locations containing a bathtub or shower basin
- swimming and paddling pools
    - hot-air saunas
    - electric floor or ceiling heating systems
    - garden lighting or power installations
    - solar photovoltaic power supply systems
    - small-scale generators such as microchip units
    - extra-low voltage lighting installations, other than pre-assembled, CE marked lighting sets.

There are, in addition, certain conditions imposed on the works that can be carried out without notification:

1. Any replacement cable must have the same current carrying capacity, follow the same route and not service more than one sub-circuit through a distribution board.

2. The circuit's protective measures must be unaffected.

3. Any increased thermal insulation must not affect the circuit's protective measures and its current carrying capacity.

4. The existing circuit protective device must be suitable and provide protection for the modified circuit with all other relevant safety provisions being satisfactory.

5. All work must comply with other applicable legislation such as the gas Safety (Installation and Use) Regulations.

Much consternation has been expressed in the general media at the 'infringement' of rights that this new legislation entails. But in truth it was always going to happen. Even in newspapers where the objections to these new rules have been most vociferous, such as the *Daily Telegraph*, for which I write, it has always been policy never to encourage DIY electrics in recognition of the fact that if you get your plumbing wrong, you'll get wet but if you get the electrics wrong you'll kill yourself, or others. In the self-build world, most who expressed an intention to carry out one or more of the trades used to cite electrics as the one they would do. There was never any great saving and I often used to think that it was more for the sense of achievement than anything else.

The regulations also concern themselves with electrical energy efficiency, stipulating that energy-efficient light fittings must be provided to various rooms in accordance with the table below. The fittings must be dedicated to the use of low-energy bulbs, which have a greater efficiency of 40 lumens per circuit watts and must not accept screw or bayonet bulbs.

External lighting fittings must either automatically extinguish when there is enough daylight or when

Energy-efficient lighting requirements

Rooms created	Number of energy-efficient light fittings required
1–3	1
4–6	2
7–9	3
10–12	4

not required at night or else have sockets that only accept bulbs/fittings with an efficiency of 40 lumens per circuit watts.

Stairs, landings and changes in level of 600mm or more

Stairs must be constructed to BS5395 and must not have a pitch of more than 42 degrees. They must also have a minimum headroom of 2 metres at any point, measured vertically upwards from any step.

All steps on the staircase must have the same rise and going (tread) and must fall into the following classes:

1. Any rise between 155 and 220mm used with any going between 245 and 260mm, or

2. Any rise between 165 and 200mm used with any going between 223 and 300mm.

The rise of any tapered treads should be the same as that of the rest of the staircase and the going should be the same, measured from the centre line of the straight flights curving around the newel.

Handrails and balustrading must be provided at a height of 900mm (840mm in Scotland) and 1,000mm from the floor/nosing and must be continuous throughout their length. All balustrading must either be solid or of the vertical type, non-climbable and spaced so that a 100mm ball cannot pass through it. It must be able to resist a force of 0.36 Kn/M. Open treads are allowed so long as they have a bar and the staircase is built such that a 100mm ball cannot pass through any part of it.

Guarding to balconies, flat roofs and low-level window openings

Guarding to external openings, balconies and flat roofs where there is access must be at least 1,000mm high and provided with no climbable vertical balustrading, able to resist a force of 0.74Kg/m and, once again, constructed so as to not allow the passage of a 100mm ball through any part.

Opening windows to the upper storeys where the cill level is less that 800mm from the floor must be provided with similar containment or guarding. This must be removable (but not by a child) in the event of fire where it is provided to an escape window.

Part 'M' inclusive or disabled access

These regulations cover the need for inclusive access both within and outside the home, including external steps, ramps and access. I have already gone into these requirements in Chapter 6 (see pages 229–30) but they do bear repetition at this juncture.

The threshold of the entrance door, although it can be a secondary door, should be a level one with a retractable water bar, but in any event, there should not be a step of more than 150mm. This entrance door should also have a minimum opening width of at least 775mm. In addition there are tables that set down the minimum width of internal doors in relation to the width of the corridor, dependent on whether the approach to the door is head-on or not. These are designed to allow the free passage of wheelchairs.

The regulations require the provision of a toilet to the main-entrance storey with an outward opening door. Whilst it is recognised that it will not always be practicable for a wheelchair to be fully accommodated within the toilet compartment, thought must be given to making that access as easy as possible. The WC enclosure should provide for a clear space of at least 450mm on each side and 750mm in front of the pan to allow a wheelchair to approach to within 400mm of the pan from the front or within 250mm of the pan from the side. The washbasin must be positioned so that it does not impede access.

The regulations also stipulate that switches and plugs must be set at heights to assist those people whose reach is limited. In general, sockets must not be lower on the wall than 450mm measured from the finished floor height and switches must not be higher than 1,200mm above finished floor level. Accessible consumer units should be fitted with a childproof cover or installed in a lockable cupboard.

Access ramps for slopes of up to 1:15 should not be longer than 10 metres and those for gradients up to 1:10 no longer than 5 metres. Steeply sloping sites can, in the absence of a ramp, employ steps at least 900mm wide with a rise no greater than 150mm and a distance between landings of no more than 1,800mm. Additionally, if there are more than three risers, handrails must be provided to at least one side.

However, the regulations require 'reasonable provision for disabled people to gain access to a building' and if a steeply sloping site made this interpretation impossible and threatened to render a site incapable of being developed, a reasonable solution can often be negotiated.

Fees

It is not a level paying field and local authorities are free to set their own fees, which may vary considerably. I cannot, therefore, hope to tell you exactly what your fees will be and perhaps the best I can do is set down the fees that the local authority in my part of Gloucestershire are charging at the present time.

For new single dwellings of no more than 250 square metres the application charge is £102 plus VAT and the inspection charge is a further £312 plus VAT. For buildings over 250 square metres they have a sliding scale based on the cost of the works. For example, for a building with costs exceeding £100,000 but less than £1,000,000, the application charge is £291.46 plus VAT, plus £1.10 plus VAT for every £1,000 by which the cost exceeds £100,000. The inspection charge is £874.38 plus VAT, plus £4.35 plus VAT for every £1,000 by which the cost exceeds £100,000.

...a properly prepared set of drawings goes a very long way to making sure that there are as few queries as possible during the construction process.

Working and construction drawings

The working drawings play a big part in all of this and a properly prepared set of drawings goes a very long way to making sure that there are as few queries as possible during the construction process. In some cases, they are the same as for the Building

Extraneous charges

Regularisation applications to inspect retrospectively and approve work are charged at 120% of the normal charges. In addition there are other relevant charges for minor works, where they are not included in a full Deposit of Plans application of a Building Notice:

Installation, alteration or replacement of an oil-fired
  appliance/controlled heating system . . . .£50.00 plus VAT

Installation, alteration or replacement of a gas-fired
  appliance/controlled heating system . . . .£50.00 plus VAT

Installation, alteration or replacement of a solid fuel-fired
  appliance/controlled heating system . . . .£50.00 plus VAT

Installation of an oil or lpg tank . . . .£50.00 plus VAT

Installation of a chimney lining system . . . .£50.00 plus VAT

Trade replacement of external windows . . . .£50.00 plus VAT

Trade replacement of a single window or door . . . .£25.00 plus VAT

DIY replacement of external windows or doors . . . .£100.00 plus VAT

Installation of a lintel/beam into a load-bearing wall . . . .£100.00 plus VAT

Mains drainage connection . . . .£100.00 plus VAT

Installation, alteration or replacement works to the
  electrical system of a dwelling house or associated
  buildings or grounds . . . .£100.00 plus VAT

Regulations application. In others, they are elaborate sets of drawings, illustrating aspects of the build as far apart as the foundation design through to the intricate detailing on the corbelling. Either way these are important documents and their treatment on site does not always reflect that importance. Rolled up in a back pocket or stuffed into a bucket of tools at best and left out in the rain at worst, is it any wonder if details become smudged or obliterated and things get built wrongly? Properly pinned up in the site hut or, better still, laminated, they will remain in pristine condition and fulfil their purpose for the duration of the build.

Construction drawings are also used by sub-contractors to design their services. An electrician will require a drawing, which he will mark up with the wiring layout; the plumbing and heating engineer will want drawings for the same purpose. Others will be required when the kitchen is being planned. Central heating drawings are often provided free of charge by the fuel advisory agencies, and the kitchen layouts can be obtained from various bodies; but they all start with a print of the actual construction drawing.

All setting out of construction work should be done in the units used for the design, and the converted dimensions should be used with considerable caution as they are invariably 'rounded off' and, if added together, will give rise to significant errors. Remember that room sizes on construction drawings are masonry sizes and that the finished dimensions from plaster surface to plaster surface will be at least 25mm smaller. Carpet sizes will be a further 25mm smaller, allowing for the thickness of the skirting on two walls.

Revisions to drawings are normally made by altering the master drawing. When this is done the fact that the drawing has been altered should always be noted on it, and the date added. Prints of the outdated drawings should be carefully collected and destroyed to avoid confusion.

Drawings for complex and high-value projects are normally accompanied by a specification (written by an architect) and a bill of quantities (compiled by a quantity surveyor). Between them these highly technical documents describe and define every detail of the building. Many individual self-build projects confine the specification to the notations on the drawing, with or without a separate list. A full bill of quantities is sometimes relevant, but in many cases unnecessary as builders quoting will often take off their own quantities. If you are using a package-deal company or a timber frame manufacturer or supplier, then their specification will form part and parcel of the specification for your proposed new home.

Chapter 10

BUILDERS AND SUBCONTRACTORS – Finding, Contracting and Working with Them

Builders

In earlier chapters I discussed how the amount of time and money that are available for your project will influence how you build. Building with a builder who is going to take charge of the whole job and just give you a ring when it's all over can seem a very attractive option and, for those with a busy schedule, it is, more often than not, their first choice. Money, and the desired size of your new home, may well have dictated whether the project is feasible with a builder. Those who switch from this first choice to building, either with subcontractors or a combination of them and a builder, often do so in order to save money. But these are not hard and fast rules. Builders come in all sizes, from the large contracting companies with posh offices, fleets of vans and lorries, right through to the small local chap who undertakes one or more of the trades himself, drives a second-hand pick-up and, when he can't put it off any longer, does his paperwork on the kitchen table.

As you'd expect, the prices are equally varied. Whilst the posh builder is always going to be right at the top of the price scale, the small local guy might not be too far above, and in a few cases, below the prices one could expect for building with sub-contractors. Surely, therefore, if you can afford a builder, you're going to get so much more peace of mind and you're going to have to spend far less of your precious time on the project? Surely the bigger the builder, the less the hassle?

I wish it worked like that, but it doesn't. If you get the wrong builder, you can be involved with as much work, and sometimes more, than if you'd used subcontractors in the first place. If you get the right builder, then what you've got is an administrator, who'll rightly take responsibility for all of the co-ordination of labour, materials and services off your hands.

What isn't always appreciated is that in many cases, a builder is merely someone who organises subcontractors. Very few of the small to medium builders have many, if any, full-time employees other than themselves, on their books. Very few have their own major plant, tools or scaffolding. They hire in subcontract labour and things like diggers as they need them, and their price to you is really just the

Recommendation is the key here.

That and reputation.

Right: **Severe architectural lines can be softened by judicious planting and hard landscaping.** © Nigel Rigden

addition of all the tradesmen's prices plus the costs of the materials that they are going to buy and, of course, their mark-up. That's why I often preach the value of using a combination of a builder for the weathertight shell with subcontractors for the second fix and supply-and-fix following trades.

The difficult bit of any house is to get to the roofed-in and watertight stage. For this, five separate trades have to mesh in with each other to within the day and, sometimes, within the hour. The arrival of materials, too, has to be co-ordinated so that they do not clog up what is often a tight site, and building and warranty inspectors need to be pre-warned of impending stages. If ever there is thought of using a builder, rather than subcontractors, then these are the stages when one is most valuable. Once the weathertight shell is reached, then, although there is a sequence of events for the following or finishing trades, there is nothing like the imperative for them to mesh in together to quite the same degree. The plumber can go in next week. The electrician can be in there at the same time, or maybe he can go in the week after, or even the other way around.

And I question whether, in the end, the person choosing to build with a builder responsible for just the shell of the building always has extra work to do by employing tradesmen themselves for the later stages of the building. As I've said, most builders don't carry trades on their books, particularly plumbers, plasterers and electricians. If you've got a contract with a builder for the whole job, then it's a pound to a penny that the plumbing and electrical trades are covered by a 'prime cost sum' (see page 324). When the time comes for the plumber to be wanted on site, the builder will probably send him around to you, or arrange for you to meet him on site, so that you can tell him exactly what you want. After that, he'll get back to the builder with his actual price based on your specification and you could well find yourself at yet another meeting discussing ways in which the price could be brought down, or refinements of your specification. In all of this the builder is a bystander. Yet he is a bystander who is making a mark-up on the result of the negotiations. Maybe the plumber is already known to you. Maybe he has done work for you or a friend beforehand. Maybe he was or

is your principal source of information for the latest advances in plumbing technology. So just how much work have you had taken off your hands? Just how much money are you paying out to someone else, when you've all but taken over the management of this particular aspect of your project? I leave you to answer those questions.

Your architect or package-deal company is probably going to be either introducing you to, or helping you to find, a suitable builder. Recommendation is the key here. That and reputation. Subcontractors can move on with relative anonymity from a less than successful job but builders cannot leave their failings behind quite so easily. If you are on your own in the search for a builder then most of the sources of subcontractors and practically all of the recommendations made in the section that follows on the use of subcontractors apply with equal measure to the choice of a builder. In addition, even if you are going to use a builder and have the minimum of involvement with the various trades, I still think it is a good idea to be conversant with what goes on and, as far as is possible, the general sequence of events that flows through a building project.

Always ask to see a builder's previous work and always ask to be put in touch with a previous client. And then don't be afraid to go and see them. I can virtually guarantee that they will have a few moans. No job's going to absolutely perfect. But what you really need to find out is how they were during the job and particularly towards the end. At the beginning, when you're thinking of taking on a builder, you'll be amazed at how friendly they are. They may offer to help you with some minor but long-standing problems on your old house. You might be invited around to their house for a barbecue and you might begin to believe that you've really fallen on your feet. But what will they be like at the fag end of the job when there's no money left and when there are countless snags to sort out? Well, the only people who can tell you that are their previous clients.

And if you do identify shortcomings? Well, if they are serious enough then you will need to move on to the next name on your list. But if they are minor and you are tipped off about what to expect then you might still employ that builder, only with, perhaps, a few reservations to which you might like to draw their attention in writing. Alternatively, if you are told that such-and-such a builder is marvellous at most things but hopeless at one particular aspect of the build, you might like to consider removing that part of the work from his remit.

Always get a lump-sum price from a builder. Whilst measured rates might be applicable to subcontractors any builder worth their salt is, or should be, prepared to add up their costs and set it down in the form of a lump-sum price. You'll still need some idea of measured rates and even daywork rates for things like extras, but they should never be the basis for the contract. Avoid 'cost plus', where the builder agrees to build and you agree to pay his costs for labour and materials plus say 10%, like the plague. This gives them no incentive to finish on time, no incentive to keep the costs down, and little incentive to even bother about the quality of the work.

Qualities to look out for in a builder (or anyone else you employ, for that matter)

An ability to keep jobs running

Very few builders worth their salt can survive on just one job at a time. Very few tradesmen can expect to be continually employed on one site. The measure of a good man or company is their ability to keep continuity and progress on all sites. Watch other jobs that they are on before yours and check that work is always ongoing and that schedules are kept to.

Tidiness on site

It may seem pedantic, but it is a fact that a tidy site is one that runs smoothly and which normally comes in on time and on budget. Messy sites are where accidents happen, where materials are lost or spoiled, and where progress is slow and laborious.

An ability to relate to the self-builder

Self-builders are a peculiar bunch. They have deliberately set out to circumvent the normal channels to house ownership. They have chosen to become involved in things that are sometimes at the limit of their knowledge or which are at the start of a new learning curve. Yet at the same time they may have

fairly rigid opinions. It takes a very special sort of professional or builder to recognise these qualities and to accommodate them.

Forward thinking

The key to successful management on site is the ability to think ahead and anticipate requirements. Self-builders may miss some of the triggers, and a builder or tradesman who takes it upon themselves to prompt, in the interest of site continuity, is invaluable.

Helpfulness

You'd think this would go without saying. But it is an important and often overlooked quality. The best builder in the world who is unhelpful to the lay person self-building their own home is worse than many of lesser ability who are, at least, prepared to be helpful.

A willingness to pass on knowledge

Much of what happens on a building site may be new to the self-builder. A builder who is prepared to show how things are done and discuss alternative ways of doing things on site is invaluable for that site and for future projects.

A need to be 'up to speed' with modern innovations and new regulations

Many builders are so busy working that they have little or no time to investigate new innovations or to acquaint themselves with changes to regulations. Many self-builders, with just one project to consider, have the time and the inclination to investigate these things. Never use a builder or tradesperson who is not up to speed with modern innovations. If they cannot understand or have no knowledge of what you are proposing, then move on to someone else. It is not your job to be the teacher. On the other hand if they show a willingness to adapt to new technology and innovations and are clearly excited at the prospect, then you might take a different approach.

Contracts

Whenever you arrange for someone to do some building work for you, you make a contract with them. In it they undertake to do the job, and you undertake to pay them. You cannot escape it. Even if you simply say, 'Get this done, Ted, and I will see you right,' you have established a contract. However, you will want to make sure that the arrangements that you make to build a new home are a good deal more specific than that!

Now there are many textbooks on the law of contract, and they are heavy-going and omit to mention that very few people arranging to build their own homes establish contracts in the way that the textbooks advise, or indeed in the way that their solicitors would advise.

A contract is a way of expressing an arrangement, which both parties enter into without reservations, believing that they know exactly how everything is going to happen. When they make the contract they regard it simply as a convenient way of recording what they have agreed. If all goes well, everything is fine. If there are unforeseen circumstances or problems, they turn to the contract to see where they stand in the matter. If they should fall out, it is the contract that determines their legal position. The contract should therefore define exactly what the parties have agreed and, if there are problems, how they are to be resolved.

The best way of establishing a formal contract that deals with all of this involves solicitors, quantity surveyors and documents that are dozens of pages long. If you ask a solicitor the best way to arrange a contract or contracts to build a new house, they must recommend these involved procedures. However, most subcontractors will run a mile from a formal-looking contract and you'll scare off most small builders. The larger builders will be used to them but using them automatically puts you in a very special league – usually referred to as extremely expensive. For this reason only a very few of those building for themselves use them. The choice is yours. This book cannot advise you to ignore the best legal advice, but it can describe how most people arrange these affairs.

There are two very different ways of arranging for a builder to build a house for you – by using an architect to establish and supervise the contract, or arranging and supervising everything yourself. If you use an architect, he will invite tenders from builders,

advise you which one to accept and draw up a suitable formal contract, which he will supervise on your behalf. This is the Rolls Royce way of doing things. The architect will charge fees of around 10% of the value of the contract, and although he will be concerned that you get the best value for money, such architects do tend to operate at the top end of the market.

If you are making a contract with a builder it is important that you do not simply accept any arrangements that they suggest, and that you settle things in a way that you are happy with. Negotiating this in an amicable way may not be easy, but you should insist on what you want, whilst avoiding giving the impression that you are going to be a difficult customer who should be charged extra for being a potential nuisance! The standard forms of pre-printed contract that many of the bigger builders are used to dealing with are largely unintelligible to the layman and contain all sorts of clauses that you might not want even if you knew what they meant. Of far more use is the new short form of contract that has been produced by the Joint Contracts Tribunal (JCT), known as 'The Building Contract for a Home Owner/occupier'.

This clearly sets out the precise nature of the work to be done, the price, the terms and times of payment, the working hours and conditions, and all the details to do with insurances and guarantees. It also sets out just how any disputes that arise are to be settled and, most importantly, it covers things like changes to the work and specification or extras – those things that so often lead to arguments. It is written in plain English and at the time of this book going to press it costs around a tenner. It is just four pages long with different-coloured copies for each party and most of the items are simply covered by tick boxes!

With all of that so cheaply available one might wonder why someone would want to write their own specification. But the plain fact of the matter is that many do attempt to do so, spending hours poring over plans and books trying to list all the tasks for which they would want a builder to be responsible. A word of caution here. The tighter you attempt to draw up a contract, the more likely it is that something will be left out or overlooked. If your

relationship with the builder or contractor is a good one, it probably won't cause too much of a problem – after all, if everything goes right, any contract is merely a waste of paper. But if the relationship becomes strained, a builder could point to your list and claim that the point in question was never a part of his remit.

Many successful self-builders complete their projects with a builder on nothing more than a simple exchange of letters, referring to plans and specifications no more detailed or complicated than those prepared for the Building Regulations application,

Left: **Simple English, easy-to-follow contracts.**

Below: **Building in stone is always going to be more expensive.** © D&M

possibly with the specification from the timber frame or package-deal supplier attached.

Many specifications and quotations make extensive use of 'prime cost sums', otherwise known as 'PC sums'. At the stage when you are negotiating the contract you have probably not decided on the particular fixtures and fittings that you require, and so a prime cost sum is allowed for the items concerned. A prime cost sum of £3,000 for the kitchen units means that the builder must allow this much for the kitchen units. If you spend less then the contract price will be reduced. If you spend more then it will be raised by the difference. Does it, however, refer to the purchase price of the units, or does it also include the cost of fitting? These things need to be specified. You will need to establish just how much is allowed for the fixing element and you will also need to understand that if you buy kitchen units cheaper because they are flat packed, there may well be a corresponding increase in the fixing costs if you also want the builder to be responsible for their assembly. You may well also want the PC sums of certain items to reflect the huge discounts that are available and to reflect them in your favour.

Materials usually covered by a prime cost sum are kitchen units, bedroom furniture, sanitaryware, fireplaces, staircases and wall and floor tiling.

Somewhat confusingly, because the abbreviation is the same, provisional costs are sometimes used for trades such as the plumber and the electrician where the initial quotation from a builder, in the absence of detailed information, may include an amount that will reflect the bare minimum needed to provide a system to comply with the regulations and the minimum standards laid down by the NHBC.

In certain cases it may be as well to remove the items covered by the prime cost or provisional sum from the builder's remit. If you do, then you need to establish whether or not there was any profit element included in the total contract sum for these items. Should that too be removed or will the builder argue that part of it concerned the labour element or attendance upon labour? You might also like to consider whether by removing items from the builder's remit, you also remove them from his insurance liability and whether you then need to

make sure that they are covered by your own policies.

Another important matter is the cost of any alterations to the agreed work, or extras. This is a potential minefield. A simple request from you that something should be fixed the other way round can involve the builder in a great deal of expensive work, and, unless it is agreed in advance, the cost can be a source of dispute. This is all covered in the JCT building contract for a homeowner/occupier but, whether you're using that or not, the cost of all alterations and extras should be discussed and confirmed in writing before they are enacted, and the specification should detail the arrangements for their agreement.

Assignment of the work is also something to watch out for. If you take on a builder, because you have admired his work on another house, you probably want the same workmen to build your own new home, and you do not want him to assign the contract to another builder, or to use other workmen. If this is important to you, it should be set out in the contract or in the specification. However, whilst many builders will agree not to assign the whole contract, very few would be silly enough to commit themselves to the use of particular tradesmen or subcontractors, who might well be otherwise engaged or have gone out of business.

The stages at which payment is made, the arrangements for payment and retentions to be held for a maintenance period should also be clearly established and no payment should *ever* be made other than in accordance with these arrangements. Beware of requests for a payment in advance to enable materials to be purchased at a particularly advantageous price, or any other such story. If your builder needs money in advance then it is 100:1 that he is in financial difficulties, and it is not up to you to bail him out. This leads to the question of what your position is if the builder fails, or dies, or just does not get on with the work. It does happen and I've detailed the procedures to adopt in Chapter 13. On the builder's part, what do they do if you disappear or go bust? All of this has to be part of the contract.

Finally, when you have the best contract that you consider to be appropriate to the way in which you want to go about things, for goodness' sake stick to it. Be punctilious about making payments on time and generally fulfilling your part of the bargain. If you don't and the worst happens and you have to establish your contract in law, you could seriously weaken your position. If this is a frightening thought, console yourself with the fact that nearly all individual self-builders end up having their new home built without dispute, and retain good relationships with those who are building for them. Having the right contract is a very good beginning to this.

By the way, some thoughts on retention and penalty clauses. It may seem a great idea to have a retention clause whereby you'll retain, say, 5% of each stage for a period of six months or until an architect or surveyor has certified that everything is all right. The builder may agree to it. But many of the builders I've known would simply add in the 5% and discount it, assuming that they're probably not going to get it and accepting it as a bonus if they do. Penalty clauses as such are unenforceable in law unless they are worded as prearranged damages. You can't simply withhold an amount of money that you feel is fair compensation. You can have a clause that specifies the agreed amount of any penalty and the precise circumstances that would bring it into operation, but once again, most builders will simply add the likely cost to their price.

In the end a lot of the cost overruns on many sites are not the fault of the builder. Many are directly attributable to clients failing to make up their minds in time or changing their minds during the job. If you forget to order the kitchen units in time, it might be eight weeks before they are on site and the job will come to a grinding halt. If you change your mind on the electrical layout it might mean that the electrician has to spend another day at his job. That might cost you a bit more with him. But if it means that the builder has to put the plasterer off, then he might go on to another job and not be back for weeks. How many 'aggrieved' clients forget all of that when they're moaning about delays and cost overruns?

All of which leads me to say that all the contracts in the world are no substitute for choosing the right man or firm for the job and making sure that you are a good client and keep your end of the bargain.

Subcontractors

A self-builder who opts to build using subcontractors effectively becomes the builder, only with one big difference: there is no contract to fall back upon. When you build with subcontract labour the buck stops with you. It's up to you to manage and coordinate the various trades, materials, plant and services. Any unforeseen factors that affect the cost or the progress on site are your responsibility. It is you who will have to sort them out, and if there are any additional costs, then it is you who will have to bear them. There are great savings to be made by opting to build with subcontractors but the reverse side of this coin is that, in turn, you have to take on those responsibilities that would have been the builder's, and for which he would have charged.

Management is the key, of course, and that means attention to detail and forward planning. Subcontractors price for their specific trades only and any grey areas are the responsibility of the self-builder. A tidy site where all rubbish is collected to a given point, where all materials are placed and stored correctly with due regard to their accessibility and that of

When you build with subcontract labour the buck stops with you.

other materials, is likely to be far more successful than a site that resembles the aftermath of a bombing.

Of course there are degrees of management. I'm not suggesting for one moment that you stand behind each tradesman in a white coat, pointing to each broken brick or picking out the odd fallen leaf or pebble from within the mortar. Such overt interference would cause resentment and would very quickly lead to a breakdown in relations. What I'm suggesting is that in the evenings, when the workers have left site, you tidy up the old cement bags, pick up the bindings and rake the sand heap into a neat cone and cover it; that you discreetly pick up some of the better half-bricks from the ground and neatly stack them beside the other loaded-out bricks. There's no guarantee that they'll use these, and you still may

have to wince as yet another whole brick is deliberately cracked in half, but there is a chance.

I often tell the story of a couple called Peter and Enid who built a lovely bungalow in the Midlands. Peter took it upon himself to tidy up the site every day and then halfway through the job he suffered a hernia (nothing to do with the self-build) and was unable to continue his nightly duties. The subcontractors, impressed with working on such a tidy site, took it upon themselves to continue his nightly work until such time as he was better!

Perhaps what that serves to illustrate is that, not only does everyone appreciate a well-managed site, but also that the relationship between Peter and Enid and their subcontractors was particularly good. And that is another important factor to consider. These are self-employed people who, very much like the self-builder, have quite deliberately stepped outside the system. In so doing they have opted for the insecurities and uncertainties that go with their choice, in preference to the relative comfort of the factory floor. Confident in their respective and individual skills, they have removed themselves from regular employment to enter the world of hire and fire, or start and finish as it is called. In effect, each and every one of them, even the one-man band, is, therefore, the representative of their own company and needs to be treated as such, rather than as employees, or worse, servants. Like any small business they deserve to succeed or fail on the strength of their service and their product, and you, the self-builder, must ensure that as the one doing the paying, you get what you want.

Some subcontractors are completely disorganised in their approach to obtaining and quoting for work and they often prove just as disorganised in their attitude to the work itself. I would suggest that you take all possible steps to avoid these fellows. Others are splendidly efficient in dealing with enquiries, in giving out quotations and, as a result, in the work itself. I would suggest that these are the chaps you should seek to engage.

Left: **The lighting is as much of an architectural statement as any other element in this house.**
© Nigel Rigden

However you find your builders or subcontractors, you'll still need to make your own checks and in the end, the decision on whether to employ them is one for which you are going to have to take responsibility. That your decision has much to do with just how you go about finding and engaging builders or subcontractors is beyond doubt. The list of headings and tips that follows is by no means mutually exclusive and many are interchangeable. As stated previously, never forget to ask to see previous work, always check that it's actually their work, talk to previous clients and, if at all possible, try to get some sort of financial or professional references.

Finding subcontractors

By far the best way of identifying which subcontractors you should employ is by recommendation and many of the better ones don't need to advertise or look for work at all, preferring to rely on a constant stream of work that comes their way by word of mouth. Indeed many subcontractors seem almost reluctant to talk to potential new clients unless they approach them by or through some form of recommendation or third party.

Other ways of finding subcontractors, or indeed builders, are:

Other self-builders

Self-builders love to talk to other self-builders and self-build sites are a terrific source of recommendation for all sorts of things, not least labour. They'll be able to give you the names of the chaps they've used. They'll tell you how much they charged, whether they did the job properly and whether a particular tradesman is good at one section of his job but not so good at other aspects of it. A lot of what you'll get is, of course, often going to be about price but that's not all you should look for. 'Good' needs to mean more than just capable of doing a good job at the right price – it also has to mean helpful and reliable. It's no good having the best bricklayer in the world if he turns up one Monday morning and is absent by Tuesday with a promise to come back some day. You need to know that the people you engage will dedicate themselves, in the main, to your job and that they're as interested in continuity as you are.

Now, don't think that means that once on site, they should attend all day and every day until the job is done. There are times when subcontractors will be away from the site; all tradesmen have to go away at certain points in the construction, but the indicator of a reliable man is his ability to juggle the various jobs he's on, in order to maintain continuity on all of them. If a bricklayer has to leave your site because he's waiting for the roof construction to be completed, then he's not going just going home to sit and watch television. He will be going to go and do someone else's footings for a couple of days and then, whilst the groundworkers deal with the oversite on that one, he'll come back to your job in order to do the gable ends. All of this is perfectly reasonable.

Architects/designers and package-deal companies

One of the plus points with using a local architect or designer is that they'll be able to recommend builders and contractors who have done work for previous clients and with whom they have often formed a loose business alliance. On the minus side, however, if this relationship has gone on for too long and got a little too cosy, the prices might have crept up quite a bit. The same can of course be true of package-deal companies but here there is a limiting factor in that the company often only really makes money when and if the property is built. There is therefore a built-in imperative for prices to be sufficiently attractive in order to persuade or enable their clients to start work. In all cases, the recommendation or introduction will be designed to make the company's or practice's life easier and there is therefore an inherent convergence of interest, just so long as the prices are right.

Looking for boards

Any builder or subcontractor worth his salt will be more than willing to advertise his wares. If you're sitting at traffic lights or walking down the street, watch out for builders' vans and jot down their phone numbers. Drive around your chosen area looking for builders' boards outside new properties, or outside existing houses where they are, perhaps, building an extension. You'll have to look hard as the boards can

often be quite small and just propped against a hedge. Whilst you might not think that a builder doing extensions would be capable of constructing a whole house you'd probably be wrong. Extensions are a microcosm of all of the problems in house-building. When a builder first starts work he's often that wonderful chap who's going to build the new kitchen or bathroom. When he finishes he's often just the man who mucked up the lawn. The diplomatic and organisational skills acquired in this field of work make whole house building seem easy. Before contracting with the builder, however, do make sure that you get the chance to inspect their work and, above all, talk to the previous clients.

Walking on to other sites

Health and safety have to be borne in mind when entering a strange site and it doesn't do to go clambering around on scaffolding talking to guys who are trying to do their job. Instead, try to arrive during lunch or tea breaks and talk to the people in the site hut or rest room. If you're looking for a builder ask to speak to the site foreman, or the chap in charge, and then simply ask if they'd be interested in looking at your plans and giving you a quote. If you're particularly impressed with the standard of workmanship and the tidiness of the site then it's important to ask if that particular site foreman would be the one you'd get.

It's an amazing fact but of the people working on any site, a large proportion will have no clear idea of where they're going from there. If you're looking for subcontractors you can do no better than to ask those that impress you on the site whether they would be interested in giving you a quote. If they decline, then follow up by asking if they know of anybody who would be interested. However, do bear in mind the fact that it's often better to ask a tradesman for the names of disciplines working either side of them, rather than those from their own field. Tradesmen are hardly ever uncritical of others working in their own field, but a good tradesman will always want to follow another good one and they tend therefore to form loose groupings that consistently work together.

Builders' merchants and specialist merchants

A direct question at your local builders' merchants will get you names and recommendations. Remember that a builders' merchant's staff will know the chaps as well as the partnerships that form and re-form. They are also unlikely to recommend those who don't pay their bills or those who 'phoenix' leaving unpaid debts. Indirectly, hanging about in a merchant's yard could mean being able to speak to builders or to get their names from their vans. Remember too that you can sometimes judge the man or company by the van. Too scruffy or badly sign written means cheap and nasty whereas a very posh vehicle might well mean expensive. Aim at somewhere between the two.

Tool and plant hire merchants

These are very much like builders' merchants although, as well as the financial probity, they will be able to judge their clients by the way they return the tools and plant. They're hardly likely to recommend the chap who returns the mixer full of gone-off concrete. If you're looking for a smaller builder or subcontractor, then this is a good source because the larger ones will have their own plant and won't need to use hire companies.

Yellow Pages/classified adverts

In any area Yellow Pages and the classified advertisements in local newspapers are a good source of names. As the builders and tradesmen pay for these adverts, it is possible to make some sort of a judgement based on the size and scope of the advert itself. But this should never be the sole criterion. Yellow Pages is on-line at www.yell.com in association with various trade organisations. It has a Home Improvement section with an on-line source for locating, choosing and using a professional.

The Internet

The last few years have seen quite a few companies coming on to the market determined to take hold of the building industry by the scruff of its neck and shake out all of the cowboy builders. The theory was that they would carry lists of financially vetted and approved tradesmen and builders, all of whom had been inspected, passed some sort of qualifying interview and provided references from previous clients. All anyone would need to do would be to log on to be presented with the names of individuals and companies, listed by their discipline and postal code. It all sounded very promising. But it was doomed to fail and for the most part it has. The last survivor, HomePro.com, is now down to a rump of tradesmen, mainly concerned with the home improvement market.

What they didn't understand, and which I have to say I warned of at the time, was the fluidity of the building industry. John and Steve can come together and call themselves J&S Builders. They might be very good. But then they'll fall out or go their separate ways. John will team up with Richard to become J&R Builders. Steve might team up with Dave to become D&S Builders. Whatever it was that happened does not mean that they are bad builders. But it is impossible to track on a national basis partnerships that are made and broken all the time, rarely staying in business long enough to satisfy any worthwhile vetting procedures.

I expect that somebody will come along shortly who feels that they can get it right. It might even work for a short while but then it'll fail like all the rest. After all, even the Government tried to set up their own register and they failed even more miserably.

Trade associations/organisations

Scanning the membership of the trade associations, particularly those that provide some sort of insurance-backed guarantee or warranty, is a useful way of obtaining names of builders and tradesmen. The NHBC, perhaps the most widely known company working in this field, makes a small charge for information over the telephone but otherwise has its membership lists on the Internet, where you can browse for names in any given postal area or check whether a membership is current. They do not, however, list probationers. The Federation of Master Builders, who offer their 'Masterbond' insurance-backed warranty, also publishes lists of their members and this can be accessed on the Internet.

Various other trade organisations exist, mainly to do with the plumbing and electrical trades, but also for specialist trades such as roofing, decorating and thatching. Their lists can be accessed either directly or on the Internet. Although some do profess to vet members and require that they pass certain tests relating to competence and financial probity, in many cases the lists give nothing apart from the names and addresses of current members and they cannot be an indicator of reliability or any form of recommendation. There is a statutory requirement for plumbing and heating contractors installing or carrying out any work concerning gas or gas-fired systems to be CORGI (Council for Registered Gas Installers) registered. Electricians carrying out work to domestic premises must be registered with either the NICEIC (National Inspection Council for Electrical Installation Contractors) or a similar body and must be competent and capable of providing self-certification, as I have detailed in Chapter 9.

Building inspectors and warranty inspectors, Highways and Environment Agency employees

As you'd expect from local authority and statutory bodies, these officials are not actually allowed to recommend builders or contractors. However, the fact remains that, in their capacity as inspectors, they have the most intimate knowledge not only of the existence of companies but also of their performance. A question to one of them about reliable contractors will almost certainly be met with a statement to the effect that they cannot be seen to advise on this matter or to show favouritism in any way. However, further questioning will often persuade them to produce several names and it's normally possible to glean from expression or insinuation just those to whom they would give preference.

Below: **You'll find that the warranty provider's handbooks are extremely useful documents.**

Contracts, payment and competency

Detailed and legally enforceable contracts are rarely made with labour-only subcontractors, who often work simply on the basis of a verbal agreement. The best you can hope for is a quotation on a piece of headed paper. A quotation on a labour and materials basis may be quite detailed, but it will not deal with unforeseen contingencies in the way that a builder's contract does. As a result you have to rely on finding the right man, coming to an amicable agreement with him, making sure that he does the right job, paying him only for work done, and terminating the arrangement promptly and without rancour if things are not working out. The key word is amicable. Arguments between self-builders and subcontractors are rarely won by either party, as either the subcontractor will walk off the site, or else the work will proceed in an atmosphere that does not make for a good job.

It is virtually impossible to enforce an arrangement made with a subcontract workman in any legal way, and you have to handle problems on a give-and-take basis. Builders have experience of this; most self-builders have not. You may feel that, in order to prevent any disagreement over what exactly is included in the subcontractor's quotation to you, you should attempt to define and list the precise nature of his duties and obligations under the contract. Do be careful about this. If, for example, you receive a quotation from a carpenter that merely states, 'All labour for first fix, roof and second-fix carpentry for new house at 19 Acacia Avenue, Anytown' then it would be nigh on impossible for the carpenter to turn around subsequently and claim that the fixing of the facia board and soffit was not in his remit. On the other hand if you've attempted to list all of the carpenter's duties and for some reason omitted those items, then an unreasonable carpenter, or one whose relationship with you has become strained, could well argue that they were due some extra monies.

Fortunately there are ways in which you can take action to avoid misunderstandings and problems. Firstly, reinforce the arrangements made by giving the subcontractor a letter or a note which is either your acceptance of the written quotation if you received one, or, more usually, confirms a verbal arrangement which you have made. Secondly make sure that any acceptance is tied back to the plans and specification of the proposed building and that you have a note of the subcontractor having receiving them, together with a note of the plan numbers and any dated amendments.

The business of payment is important. Labour-only subcontractors expect to be paid promptly, and in cash. If you do not do this you are asking for trouble, and running the risk of your subcontractors going off to do other work. Although you should keep a record for your own accounts of whom you have paid and how much, you have no responsibility to notify the tax authorities of the payment, although a builder is obliged to do so. This is a complicated business and its very existence gives the self-builder an edge, in that the subcontractor who works for you, as opposed to the local developer, will, if he is paid the same rates, be approximately 20% better off. This is something that is only ever obliquely referred to in the industry but it is as well for you to be aware of it.

Those of you who've seen me talking at seminars will know that I advocate getting a lump sum price from all contractors and that I'm against the idea of daywork or even measured work for the lay person building their own home, although I do concede that in certain instances with difficult renovations or conversions those last two methods of pricing might have more validity.

Let me explain the differences. Every tradesman who gets up to work in the morning wants to earn a certain amount per day. If you paid them that amount to come and work on your site then you would be paying 'daywork' or 'timework'. But where's the incentive to get the job done? The longer they spend there the more they'll make and if they can spin it out, all the better for them. There is the argument that if they're not rushing things they can make a better job of it, and whilst I accept that in certain cases, with particular people that might well be true, I cannot accept or advocate it as way of proceeding in normal circumstances. An unscrupulous tradesman could knowingly do things badly in the knowledge that they were going to get paid to put things right.

'Measured work' is where the tradesman gives a price based on measured rates for each task. Bricklayers often work on this basis with a rate for every thousand bricks laid and another rate for each square metre of blockwork laid. The rates, of course, are designed to deliver the amount that the bricklayer wants to earn in a day and therefore reflect the speed at which they can lay the bricks. If you really know what you're doing this isn't a bad way of proceeding: it does indeed leave little room for argument and is very easily quantifiable. Builders will often employ tradesmen on this basis. But it does have its drawbacks for the uninitiated. Certain bits of a job can be done faster. The straight brickwork for example on the main body of a house can be laid to a string line and some bricklayers can easily lay 1,500 bricks a day. The gable ends, where each brick may have to be cut up the run of the rafters, may be much more time consuming and the same man, working just as diligently, might be able to lay only 400 in a day. If you've paid him on the basis of bricks laid, then, in the later stages of the build, the number of bricks still to be laid might bear little relevance to the amount of time needed to lay them. An honest man would acknowledge that fact. A rotten bricklayer might disappear to another site where he can earn more money per day and leave your gable ends undone.

A lump sum price is arrived at when the tradesman adds up the time that the job is going to take and the amount of work to be done and presents it as one large amount. I think that's the best way of proceeding. I've heard arguments that the contractor is going to increase the price because of the risk factor. That may be so. Prices can be higher or lower than expected for many different reasons. Maybe the guys don't really want the job, so they bump up the price and if you're mug enough to accept it then they're quids in. Or maybe they're desperate for the work and price the job so as to ensure that they get it. If it's too low and they're so desperate, are they any good?

So, you do need to check this price and the easiest way to do so is, having been given the lump sum price, to ask for the daywork and measured work rates too. Once you've got those you can use them to check that the lump sum price is right. You'll need them anyway. Some things, like your fireplace, made up from an amalgam of photographs from various magazines, or stopping to help unload lorries, must be priced on daywork. Other jobs, such as having to go deeper with the foundation blockwork, are best priced at measured rates.

Never pay upfront

It is a golden rule never to pay upfront or too far ahead. You are a self-builder, a renovator or a converter, but you are not a banker. Certainly with labour-only trades the aim should be to keep a tight rein on money going out and to try, as far as possible, to ensure that the payments schedule reflects the work done or, even better, keeps you well ahead, with an incentive left in at the end for the tradesman in question to finish.

On the other hand, if a plumber on a supply-and-fix contract, having done a pretty good job for you on the carcassing, comes to you and requests a down payment towards the purchase of an expensive boiler that you have chosen and which is not available from his usual supply sources, then it's a slightly different matter. Such a request should be calmly considered. If you're completely confident in the man, then, by all means, go ahead. However, I would suggest that a better way around such a problem would be for you to purchase the item yourself and then deduct either the cost, or the agreed prime cost sum, from the contract. That way title in the goods is always yours and if anything goes wrong, you're in a far stronger position. Never put yourself in the situation of effectively lending money to tradesmen, builders or anyone else for that matter, in order for them to work for you. That's the job of the banks and if they feel that they shouldn't be advancing money to someone, despite the attraction of his contract with you, then you can rest assured that they know a lot more about the fellow than you do and that they have perfectly good reasons for acting as they do.

Labour-only subcontractors will expect you to provide all the plant required for the job, and to have it there on time. If there is a difficulty with this, such as a mixer breaking down, they will expect you to solve the problem at once, otherwise they will want to be paid for their wasted time or will go off to another job. The same applies to delays in delivering materials, and to arrangements to replace materials stolen from a site.

Don't take chances

Although the subcontractors working for you will not be employees in the strict sense, you should ensure that you have employer's liability insurances. The tiler who falls off your roof will decide that he had a 'Deemed Contract of Employment' with you before he hits the ground, or if he does not remember this, his solicitor will! Dealing with a resulting claim will be expensive whatever the outcome, and it is best left to an insurance company. Appropriate cover is part of standard self-builders' insurance policies, as discussed in Chapter 1.

You'll be told by all and sundry that you've got to get at least three quotations from each trade and that anything less is laying yourself open to ruin. Balderdash is the word that springs to mind. Most builders and subcontractors in a local area are in almost constant touch with each other, either at work or in the pub. If you flood the local labour market with requests for prices then there's a chance that none of them will bother to do the necessary work to provide you with a quotation, thinking that the odds of them getting the job are too slim. Certainly get more than one quotation if you've got several names but, just as certainly, if a particular tradesman is recommended by, say, another self-builder, and his price comes within what you've budgeted for, why waste anybody else's time? More importantly, why risk missing the first chap's window of availability on a futile gesture?

Negotiation is a large part of management but do be very careful about trying to knock a price down. Certainly there is nothing to say that you can't tell somebody that you know very well that their price was a little high in comparison to that of others. They may be able to look at their sums again and they may well find that they have made a mistake or some wrong assumptions. On the other hand, do be aware that if they do come down in price reluctantly, they may well try to claw back the amount that they perceive to have been 'lost'. They may do this by finding extras or by skimping on the job itself. Either

way, you may find that it would have been better to have stuck with the original price or to have engaged somebody else. A golden rule is to get a clear idea of the general level of prices for a job like yours before discussing it with a potential subcontractor, and to make them aware of the fact that you do know about prices. This, again, is part of learning all that you can about self-build before you actually get involved on the site, and presumably why you are reading this book.

The last real issue to explore before I go on to consider each of the main trades in sequence is that of competency. Are they any good at what they do? Well, if you've arrived at the fellow by recommendation then you already have the answer to that one but, if you found him by some other method, what do you do? The answer is you do exactly the same, only in reverse – you ask around. Ask the tradesman himself for the names of the people he last worked for, then visit their site and ask them what they thought of him. Chances are that he would not give you the name of the last site he was ignominiously expelled from and chances are, therefore, that, if he's willing to give you the names in the first place, he's probably all right. Nevertheless do check it out. And when you're there, don't just listen to what you're being told but use your eyes to see for yourself. If it's a bricklayer you're investigating, you may feel that, as a lay person, you have no powers of judgement when it comes to such an important skill. Nonsense. Anybody can see if the bricks are all smudged with mortar, and if the general standard of work is untidy. Anybody can stand back and see if the perps (the vertical joints) are neatly in line, and anybody can see if the beds (the horizontal joints) are straight. If it's a carpenter then look for the joints on the skirtings and architraves. Are they finished well or are they gappy? Do the doors, and in particular pairs of doors, hang nicely with even spacing all around? The eyes in your head and the tongue in your mouth can find out a lot. Remember, a good tradesman is proud of what he does, and what you've got to realise is that you're entitled to find out as much as you can about someone who, after all, is going to be involved with you in what is probably the most important project of your life.

The trades

What follows is a brief description of the nature of each of the subcontract trades with which a self-builder is likely to be involved, together with a note of how prices are arrived at. If any of this touches on points I've made in other sections of the book, then I apologise. But I still think that it bears repetition in this context as I'm aware that many, rather than reading this book from cover to cover, will dip in and out for the sections they want. I have also included some warnings and specific things to look out for but would not want you to be left with the idea that all is doom and gloom. I bring these things to your attention in order to aid you in the management of your self-build site and not to put you off or to frighten you in any way. Indeed your very knowledge of these things will enhance your standing with any builders or tradesmen who work on your site and serve to assist them in doing a good job for you.

Groundworkers

This is the trade that is responsible for all of the work below ground including foundations, underpinning and drains. But it is also the trade that usually carries out work to driveways, pathways, hard landscaping and, to some extent, soft landscaping.

Just because their work is often dirty and most of what they do is eventually covered up, do not assume that the groundworker's job is in any way easy or that it lacks skill. Much of it, it is true, involves pure muscle. Much of it is simply a question of shifting muck one way and replacing it with concrete. But make no mistake, this is a skilled job and the measure of the men is the fact that their work is often difficult and dangerous. And yet they have to possess the knowledge and the ability to be able to react to situations quite fast. If trenches start caving in or bad ground is uncovered, it's no good just standing there looking at it – you have to be able to get in there to shore it up or stabilise the situation until the engineers have devised a different solution. And when that has been done, you have to understand the principles and the practicalities involved in carrying out that solution.

A measure of the importance of the ground-worker's job is the fact that of the eight stages of inspection that the Building Inspector normally requires, six of them concern this trade. Groundworkers also have to fit in with other trades, particularly the bricklayers, and the pattern of their work means that they have to be prepared to leave site on occasions whilst they wait for other trades to complete their respective tasks.

The trade can be labour only with all plant supplied by the client. It can be labour only but with the main plant, such as diggers, supplied by the contractor or it can be quoted on the basis of labour and materials. Those groundworking contractors who supply materials and plant tend to be more expensive.

Labour prices are assessed by working out how long the job is going to take and applying an hourly or daily rate. At the time of writing over much of England that happens to be around £120 per man day. However, in London workers would expect to earn a lot more than that, perhaps £150 per day and above. That's assuming that the worker is self-employed. If a firm is hiring out the men to you they may well want to charge them out at a minimum of £200 per day per man. A company pricing for the job will, therefore, assess how many man days are likely to be involved and total those up. If they are supplying materials these will usually be put in at list price with any discounts being to their advantage. Plant is then added in at an hourly rate for each item. The three elements will then be totalled up and a profit element of between 10 and 15% added in.

If you hire in the digger then it's probable that it'll be a one-man band where the digger and driver come for around £258 per day. Perhaps one of the biggest expenditures is going to lie in taking the muck away. It has to be taken to a proper landfill site and there's a tax on it at the dump. So in the country, with a long turnaround run, each 20-tonne lorry load is going to cost around £250. This makes it all the more important to consider whether or how spoil can be kept on site. It may mean having to hire a dumper at a cost of about £100 per week so that you can store it out of the way. But the most galling thing of all is to pay to have it all sent away and then, when you come to make up the levels and landscape the gardens,

The following are the groundworker's tasks on a typical job:

- Creating entry into and clearing site

- Laying hard base for access, deliveries and site storage

- Stripping topsoil and storing for re-use

- Setting out house to suitably positioned profiles (this may be carried out by a surveyor/architect)

- Marking out centre line of dig with lime or similar

- Excavating foundation trenches to indicated or required depth

- Loading spoil into dumpers for on-site storage/load spoil into tipper lorries for disposal off site

- Cleaning and bottoming out trenches

- Positioning level pegs to indicate top of concrete

- Pouring and laying footings concrete

- Laying foundation blockwork to dpc level, putting in cranked ventilators, all necessary drainage exit lintels and/or sleeving for services (this may be undertaken by bricklayers)

- Levelling out subsoil in oversite

- Backfilling trenches outside the building

- Filling cavities with lean-mix concrete

- Positioning floor beams on dpc

- Laying infill blocks in place

- Brushing grout floor
  or filling and consolidating hardcore to oversite

- Sand-blinding hardcore

- Laying damp-proof membrane

- Positioning below-slab insulation

- Laying further damp-proof membrane

- Laying oversite concrete

- Excavating trenches for foul- and surface-water drainage

- Laying drainage runs on pea shingle; bringing upstands to positions through oversite

- Haunching over all below-ground drainage in pea shingle

- Building all manholes

- Connecting foul drainage to foul sewer/the boundary for road connection by others; installing septic tank/cesspool/mini sewage treatment plant; installing and laying any weeper drainage or outlets

- Constructing soakaways and connecting surface water drains

- Backfilling all drainage trenches

- Excavating all service trenches and backfilling when supplies are laid

- Carrying out specified and agreed hard and soft land-scaping and fencing

- Laying driveways, pathways and patios to agreed specification

have to buy it all back again at considerably more expense.

Incidentally, if you send the spoil away to a landfill site then it is that site that possesses the necessary licences. If you keep the spoil on site then it hasn't been dumped. But if you dispose of the spoil on land that you own that isn't part of the site or other land then, under Section 35 of the Environmental Act 1990, it is an offence to deposit controlled waste on any land without the benefit of a waste management licence. However, there are exemptions for an individual acting in a private capacity, so long as the waste does not exceed 250 tonnes per hectare, demonstrates agricultural or ecological benefit, and does not cause a nuisance through noise or odours or adversely affect the countryside or places of special interest. And that's not easy, because the agricultural or ecological benefits have to be certified by an appropriately qualified person and the extent of the 'adverse' effects and the definition of 'places of special interest' are loosely defined. If you are going to dispose of spoil other than to a recognised and licensed tip you will need to check with the environment officer at the local authority. You can also find guidance and forms on www.environment-agency.gov.uk.

Foundations

The standard foundation over much of the country, and the one that in the absence of alternative information is the one that is normally quoted for, is the deep strip foundation. This involves a trench being dug under all external and load-bearing walls, usually to a depth of 1.2 metres 600mm wide. In the bottom, 225mm of concrete is then laid as a footing for the foundations, which are usually two skins of blockwork, the inside one of which is brought up to oversite or dpc level, whilst the outside one is left at just below the proposed external ground level. This is so that the chosen facing material can be laid at a later date without being damaged by any work to the oversite.

The blockwork foundations can be built by the groundworkers but are often undertaken by the bricklayers. The cavity below ground is filled with lean-mix concrete at least 225mm from dpc level, which itself must be a minimum of 150mm above external finished ground level. Where drains or other pipework pass through foundation walling the gap must be supported with suitable concrete lintels. Where they pass through concrete footings they should either be sleeved or any opening should be supported by a concrete lintel.

Trenchfill foundations are very similar to deep strip except that, in this type of foundation, the excavations are filled with concrete to within 200mm of the top of the trench. There are several reasons for going to this form of foundation, amongst which are instability of the trench walls due to loose soil, a high water table or simply the desire to be out of the ground as quickly as possible. In some cases, however, the trench may have to be dug deeper and

lined with compressible material and possibly a slip membrane. In the areas where this type of foundation is necessary or almost the norm, the groundworkers are quite used to working at greater depths. Obviously it needs the right machinery with the necessary reach and whoever is doing the job must be prepared for all eventualities with shoring, sheet piling and bracing available in short order as well as a water pump in the event of flooding.

The construction of a raft isn't that difficult as long as the plans and bending schedule are followed carefully. The wire cages and reinforcement are important and it's vital that they are positioned and wired up properly. But that shouldn't be beyond the capability of most experienced groundworkers.

Piled foundations are usually carried out by specialist companies, which takes the job out of the remit of the groundworker once the ground has been stripped of the topsoil. If the ringbeam or groundbeam spanning from pile to pile, upon which the walling is built, is also prefabricated, then that too comes outside the groundworker's responsibility. However, if the ringbeam is to be cast on site then the groundworkers must dig the necessary trenches, position the wire reinforcement cages and pour the concrete.

Oversites

The oversite or ground floor is the responsibility of the groundworker. Solid concrete oversites are still perhaps the most common method. The subsoil within the building must be levelled out and each bay filled with properly consolidated hardcore. This is then blinded with sand before a polythene damp-proof membrane is laid, dressed up at the edges to the dpc, upon which the concrete oversite is laid to a thickness of at least 100mm. The necessary flooring grade insulation can be laid beneath the concrete, above it or in a combination of the two. If it is exclusively below, it goes on top of the first layer of damp-proof membrane with a further membrane laid over it before the concrete is poured. In order to prevent cold bridging 25mm perimeter insulation is stood vertically between the concrete and external walling and held in place as the concrete comes up to it.

If the hardcore infill for an oversite slab is greater

than 600mm or if there is likely to be differential settlement, the slab may have to change to a suspended one with a concrete thickness of at least 150mm plus reinforcement. In so doing it will also have to be cast so that it is supported on the inside leaf of the external walls plus the partition walls. At this point many self-builders will decide that it is cheaper and easier to switch to a beam-and-block flooring system.

This utilises concrete flooring beams, in a sort of inverted 'T' shape, laid between the load-bearing walls. Blocks are then placed in the gaps between the beams and brush grouted to create a homogenous solid suspended floor. In most systems the insulation is laid on top of the floor beneath the screed or floating floor. But in some systems the necessary insulation is fixed below the floor or is created by the use of specialised insulating infill blocks. The oversite beneath the beam-and-block floor does not need to be covered in concrete and it is usually sufficient to leave a gap of a minimum of 75mm between the underside of the beams and the subsoil. Under-floor ventilation is important and this is provided by means of cranked ventilators, which allow the free passage of air but block light, and therefore any vegetative growth.

Drainage

The groundworkers are responsible for laying drains. Although straight plastic drainage pipe costs only around £7.50 per metre, the fittings and manholes, etc. are relatively expensive, the total material costs per metre run of drain, including the pea shingle surround, working out at just under £20. When you analyse the time spent excavating and laying each metre of drain, fitting the fittings, building the manholes and backfilling, then the cost of labour gets to around the same figure. Which means that drains can be roughly costed at £35–40 per linear metre, assuming a depth of around 1 metre.

Drains are usually laid at falls of 1:40, although in certain situations they can go as low as 1:80. The drains must be laid on 150mm of clean pea shingle and then haunched over with the same material to the same depth prior to backfilling. It is important that no backfilling takes place before the inspector from the

Building Control department and/or the warranty inspector has inspected the open trenches and arranged a water or air test on the pipework.

Most self-builders opt for plastic drainage systems, although clay might be needed in certain situations. The same applies to manholes, which can also be constructed in brick or in concrete rings or sections.

Contrary to many people's impressions, the connection to a foul sewer is not usually made at a manhole and instead is effected by means of a 'Y' or saddle connection into the run of the pipe. Only an Approved and Accredited Contractor can carry out works to or within the highway and therefore most subcontract groundworkers will stop at the boundary.

If a gravity connection is not possible it is sometimes necessary to employ a pumped system. The drains are laid in the normal way to a sump chamber within which there is a pump (often with a back-up) with a macerator, operated by a float switch. This pushes the effluent up a 50mm flexible pipe to a further chamber or manhole after which it continues to flow by gravity. An electrician will need to be in attendance on the groundworker during installation.

If mains drainage is not available there are several options including a septic tank, mini sewage treatment plant or cesspool, all of which I have discussed and described at length in Chapter 3, but which might bear repetition here. A septic tank is the cheapest of the off-mains foul drainage solutions. It collects the effluent, allows it to settle out and clarify and then passes partially treated discharge into the subsoil via weeper or percolation drains. There are many refinements on this process and some systems have been devised to pass a stream of air through the effluent to speed up the bacteriological process that takes place within the tank.

A mini treatment plant uses electrical power to refine the treatment of the effluent. Whereas most standard septic tanks utilise anaerobic bacteria that exist in water to break down and neutralise the sewage, a mini treatment plant uses both these and aerobic bacteria (those that exist in air), by alternatively exposing and immersing it as it passes through the chamber. The result is a relatively sterile effluent that can often be discharged directly into a watercourse.

Where neither of these alternatives is acceptable to the local authority or the Environment Agency a cesspool may be the answer. This is simply a holding chamber from which the effluent is pumped up by a tanker and taken away. It is the least popular option and the one that costs the most to maintain and run but in some cases it is the difference between building a house or not.

Most surface water is disposed of by means of simple soakaways, which are nothing more than rubble-filled holes. However, in areas where the ground has a high water table or is impermeable, this may not be possible and it might be necessary to employ more sophisticated soakaway systems utilising perforated concrete rings or plastic boxes plus filter beds.

Only Approved and Accredited contractors can carry out any works to the highway and, strictly speaking, that applies to any part of the highway whether metalled or otherwise. There are instances, however, where other contractors can sometimes be authorised to carry out works to the unsurfaced sections of the highway such as the grass verges, so long as they have the appropriate insurances, but I would stress that this is at the discretion of the highways authority. An Approved and Accredited contractor can be an individual who has passed the relevant tests and satisfied the stringent financial criteria, but it is more likely to be a firm, and the local authority will be able to supply you with a list of the names of suitable companies. A Section 50 licence, under the New Roads and Street Works Act 1991, is required to open up or carry out any work to the highway and this is issued by the highways authority, which is usually the County Council to whom the authority has been devolved. A new sewage connection, within the highway, will require not only this licence but also consent, given under Section 106 of the Water Industry Act 1991, to make a connection to the public sewer. There is a legal right to this connection which is issued by or on behalf of the water authority, although in many cases the local authority act as their agents and application to make the new connection has to be made through them. Some authorities insist on doing this work themselves.

In areas where it has been identified that the sewer is overloaded, the local authority may adopt a policy restricting further development or connection to the sewer. On the face of it this would seem to fly in the face of the legal right to connect that I have mentioned above, but the local authorities get around that one by operating and enforcing the policy through the planning procedures.

Any works to sewers, driveways or roadways, within the curtilage of your site, can be carried out by you and your normal contractors, even if it is intended that they will be adopted when completed. Of course, the works will have to be carried out to the specification and approval of the authorities and, in certain cases it will be necessary for a bond to be taken out. Once the works stray beyond your site and on to the metalled highway, including the creation of any bellmouth, then the work has to be put in the hands of an Approved or Accredited contractor. Many groundworkers will quote a self-builder for all works to the driveway and sewers within the site but make it clear that their responsibility stops at the boundary with the highway. This is all perfectly normal but it is important that the self-builder identifies the fact that there will be an additional contract, and not inconsiderable cost, for the works within the highway.

Basements are largely within the remit of the groundworkers although the bricklayers may also be heavily involved. Whilst the principles behind much basement construction are fairly standard, it is not a job that should be given to anyone without prior experience. Contractors who undertake basements must know what they're doing and must be familiar with the chosen method of construction. I have discussed the alternatives in Chapter 5. Building a basement is always going to involve a lot of spoil. Whilst you might be able to keep some on site the chances are that most will have to go and it's vital that whoever does the job identifies exactly where it's going and who's going to take it. Quick and easy access to plant and equipment is also important.

Renovations and conversions

The tasks of the groundworker on renovations or conversions are pretty much the same as for new

Above: **Foundation trenches do not always turn out as neatly as planned.**

Right: **Coming out of the ground.**

build except for the fact that new foundations may have to be dug through old foundations and new oversites built within existing rooms. Whilst that may be much more fiddly and may at times have to be done by hand, the requirements in terms of construction method and detail are the same as for new build.

One task that is peculiar to renovations and conversions is underpinning. Many groundworkers are quite capable of carrying out simple underpinning, although more complicated jobs might require specialist contractors. However, if you're having to carry

out underpinning as a result of a survey or at the insistence of a lender, then you might have to use a company that is able to issue you with an insurance-backed guarantee or warranty.

The standard way of carrying out underpinning is to dig down under the foundations and fill the void with reinforced concrete. Obviously this has to be done in sections and those sections are related to the pins or reinforcing rods, which are usually 1.2 metres long. Each section of 1 metre is therefore referred to as a pin and it is normally assumed that each section will go down 1.2 metres from ground level. Whilst that may not at first glance seem enough, the fact is that most houses experiencing subsidence problems have fairly shallow foundations, often of no more than 600mm, and to underpin to a depth of 1.2 metres is usually, therefore, sufficient.

Underpinning is not rocket science but it is difficult work, much of which has to be done by hand and, once again, the costs reflect the time that this takes. Each pin or metre section will therefore cost between £575 and £600 in most parts of the country. However, in London the cost can be greater because of congestion charges and the difficulty of tipping spoil.

Bricklayers, blocklayers and stonemasons

In many ways, because what they do is always on show, the bricklayers are often considered the most important of all of the trades and the prima donna attitude displayed by many of them is testament to this. They sweep on to site, stay only if everything is to their liking, and get on with their work in an almost mechanical rhythm amidst calls for more bricks or muck (mortar). Time is of the essence and time is money, so everything and everybody else on site races to keep up with them and keep them happy. The relationships that build as a consequence are often enduring and it is a fact that if one gets hold of a good tradesman within this discipline, most of the other trades will follow.

Choosing the right man for the job is important. It may seem tedious when you're thinking about giving a man the job, if he then turns around and starts asking a lot of questions about what bricks you're intending to use and what sort of mortar or sand you'll be getting. These, however, are the marks of a good tradesman and a conscientious worker. Bricks are all different. Some of the cheaper sand-faced Fletton bricks are entirely uniform in shape, have a high porosity and can be laid very quickly. More expensive wirecut or stock bricks have a much lower porosity and cannot be laid in as many courses per day. Even more expensive handmade bricks often have an irregular shape with creases (smiles) on the face. These have to be laid quite carefully and pointed

up with even more care and attention if they are not to get smudged with mortar. A tradesman considering pricing up a job would need to know these things before applying the right rate if he was aiming at consistency in his income.

The question of mortar and sand also exercises the mind of many tradesmen. Most have their own favourite sand, which they maintain gives a better consistency to the mix and/or flows more easily off the trowel. Of course, you should be the final arbiter of where the sand comes from. If you've determined that the mortar should have a specific colour or if you've got a restricted site, you may well feel that premixed mortar is the right answer. But if you've no strong views on the matter, why upset a perfectly good tradesman?

With this trade, over much of the country, costs usually equate to around £25 per hour per man. That's £200 per man day for the principal tradesmen and perhaps a little less, maybe £150 per man day, for the labourers (who'll then be paid around £120, with their 'boss' taking the difference). However, a competent gangmaster confident of his own abilities and the time it will take him to undertake a certain job should be able to express all of that in terms of a lump sum price.

Like most other trades, prices always, and in the end, relate back to time taken. But this trade, more than some others, is used to expressing its prices in terms of a price per measured square metre of walling or, in the case of bricks, a price per thousand. A gang of bricklayers, often a two and one gang (two bricklayers and one labourer), will therefore work out their prices at the going rate, which at the time of writing is around £300 per thousand bricks, although in London that could rise to over £400 and in parts of the south-east is more likely to be £350. If the gang lays around 1,800 bricks per day then each member will be earning his expected day rate.

The going rate for blockwork is about £8.50 per square metre rising to £10 per square metre and beyond in London and the south-east. The fitting of cavity insulation that has to be built in as work progresses is normally included in these prices. Frame fixing, the fitting of window formers and the bedding of lintels can sometimes be included but are

The following are the bricklayer's tasks on a typical job:

- Laying blockwork foundations to dpc level
- Building honeycomb sleeper walls (suspended timber floors only)
- Building in below-ground drainage exit lintels
- Building in cranked ventilators for beam-and-block floors, or building in airbricks and cavity sleeves
- Bedding dpc
- Bedding plates (timber suspended floors only)
- Positioning floor beams and laying infill blocks (if the groundworkers do not do this)
- Brushing grout flooring
- Building superstructure brickwork and blockwork
- Installing cavity insulation as work progresses
- Creating opening for windows and doors
- Installing cavity closers
- Fitting windows and door frames if appropriate

- Building in meter boxes
- Bedding lintels
- Laying padstones where appropriate
- Positioning steel joists and beams
- Laying first-floor beams and infill with blocks (if agreed)
- Brushing grout flooring
- Installing cavity trays where necessary
- Bedding wallplate
- Building up gable ends
- Building chimney through roof
- Building internal brick features and fireplaces
- Pointing up flashings and trays
- Filling putlog holes
- Building feature walling to garden

more often added in at a fairly nominal price.

Most bricklayers supply nothing but their tools and will require that you hire a mixer for their use at a cost of £20–30 per week. It may have to stay a lot longer than the 12 or so weeks that they'll require it so that it can be used by the plasterers and groundworkers, so it probably pays to think in terms of having one on site for most of the job. Most bricklayers will also want you to provide 'spotboards' – simple 600 x 600mm plywood or similar boards to take the mixed mortar.

A bricklayer pricing for the whole job would probably price on the gross amounts for bricks and blocks. On the other hand the gable, where bricks and blocks have to be cut up to the angle of the rafters, would take him more time. Most good bricklayers will take the rough with the smooth on this but if you are asking for work that only involves cutting work or fiddly brick details, then many brick-

layers would come away from the measured rate and revert instead to time work.

Although there are bricklayers who will raise and lower the scaffolding as they go, in general it is not a good idea. A hire-and-erect scaffolding company, who will undertake to provide a scaffold that complies with all of the necessary regulations, will want between £150 and £190 per week for a full scaffold for a normal house, assuming a minimum ten-week hire period. However, those building small extensions or carrying out repair works might well get away with the hiring of bandstands or tower scaffolding at a fraction of the cost, and with no minimum time requirement.

There are, as I've discussed earlier, many visible signs that point to whether a bricklayer is good or bad. But there are things that can be hidden and which the successful project manager or self-builder will learn to look for.

Wall ties

Cavity brickwork must have the two leafs of walling tied together. This gives the walling stability and is necessary whether you are building a home of traditional masonry construction or timber frame. Proprietary wall ties are available for all forms of construction. As a general rule there are about five for every square metre of walling but more specifically, they should be spaced at 450mm horizontally and vertically, increasing to 300mm vertically at the jambs of openings. They should be positioned in the bed so that they slope slightly downwards and outwards to prevent moisture from crossing the cavity, although many have spirals or twists built into them to prevent this.

Clean cavities

If the cavity is to be left clear it is important that it is clean and that there are no snots of mortar that either bridge the cavity or adhere to wall ties. If full-fill cavity insulation is being used it is tempting to think that its very presence will prevent the cavity from getting dirty. In fact, it is still very possible to see lines of mortar sitting on the top of each cavity batt of insulation, especially if the blockwork inner skin is being taken up faster than the outer leaf. It is therefore important that this is cleared off before the next insulation batt is laid if there is to be no breach of the cavity from both a moisture or a cold perspective. If partial-fill insulation is being employed it is vital that the cavity is kept clean. Watch out for lines of mortar adhering to the tops of each layer, preventing the top board from sitting down correctly and introducing a cold spot. Check that the correct ties have been used, that the restraining mechanism is in place to hold the insulation firmly back against the outside face of the inner leaf and that no snots of mortar are clinging to the ties.

Damp-proof courses (dpcs) and membranes (dpms)

It is important that these are positioned correctly and that they retain their integrity. The dpc at the junction with the substructure and the superstructure (dpc level) must be properly bedded with mortar. This constitutes an inspection stage by the Building Inspector.

Where floor beams are being utilised it is common to lay the beams dry on to the dpc and then bed the next courses of blocks on top. That's fine in that circumstance, just so long as the dpc is not torn or dislodged whilst the beams are being positioned. Many floor beams are not as tall as the blockwork course and it is often necessary to lay a course of split or proprietary blocks to bring the walling back to course. If this is the case it is often better to bed the dpc below this levelling course. This then allows the beams to sit directly on to the blockwork without harming the dpc.

Damp-proof membranes are usually employed on a solid slab oversite and it is therefore the responsibility of the groundworkers to see that they are properly looked after and blinded. Dpms are however sometimes employed beneath floor beams to prevent ponding or, in cases of radon gas, as a barrier, and it is important that they receive adequate protection.

Cavity trays

Wherever the cavity is breached, even by a door frame or window, it is necessary to have a cavity tray to prevent any moisture that does happen to find its way into the cavity reaching the inner leaf. Usually this is achieved by the simple expedient of building in a tray damp-proof membrane. Wide dpc or lead is built into the walling so that it bridges the cavity. The inside edge is higher than the outside (usually one block higher) and therefore any water coming down the cavity is caught by it and channelled outwards to weeper holes left in the external leaf. Proprietary cavity trays in plastic and lead can also be built in. Some of these are made so that they simply rest against the outside face of the inside leaf of walling rather than being built in. Where a pitched roof abuts a wall it is necessary to employ stepped cavity trays down each side. These are made in both hands and are designed to catch the moisture safely, passing it down to the next tray and eventually arriving at a stopped end tray, where it is passed harmlessly to the outside via a weeper hole.

It is important to check that they are in at the right level. Their job is to catch water and channel it either to the outside or harmlessly into the cavity,

Above: **This structure is getting quite close to wallplate level and the trusses should have been ordered.**

Below: **It is important not to smudge the bricks with mortar.**

where it can go to ground. If they are set too low then all they will do is collect the moisture and conduct it into the building. If cavity trays are created on site from lead or dpc it is important to check that they lead right through the external leaf of the wall and that they dress over any cover flashings below them.

Certain lintels are shaped so as to form a cavity tray. Others need a cavity tray built in above them. All need the weeper holes positioned correctly and kept clear of any obstruction or mortar.

Chimneys

Where a chimney comes through a roof it is necessary to employ a tray to prevent the waterlogged masonry from conducting damp to within the home. This should be built right through the chimney above the highest level of the flashings. Usually it is made from lead and it should be big enough to dress down over the stepped chimney flashings. Where chimneys are on the end gable wall it is important to maintain the cavity.

Stone and flint

Do not expect that stone will cost anything like bricks to lay – it is going to be much more expensive. Brickwork labour at £300 per thousand equates to around £18 per square metre. Stonemasons will often want three times that amount in areas where stone is prevalent and perhaps four times more in places where stone is no longer the norm and there is a skill shortage. On top of that the stone itself costs more – £250 per thousand for bricks means material costs of £15 per square metre whereas stone starts at £27 per square metre and can go up to around £100. Some quarries sell it by the tonne, which can be confusing as one variety of stone might be considerably heavier than another. On average, though, 1 tonne of stone will provide between 4 and 6 square metres of walling.

With many types of stone it's necessary to have a backing block, which is effectively a third leaf of walling. This costs the same to lay as any other leaf of blockwork and is therefore a direct extra. And as if all that's not enough, with three leafs and a cavity, the lintels have to be considerably wider and therefore cost more.

Flint walling is becoming popular again in those areas where it was traditionally used. But the modern methods of laying it are considerably different in that it too requires a backing block in most circumstances. Knapped flint, either ex chalk, which tends to be bluish, or ex gravel, which tends to be browner, costs £288 per tonne. Even a simple heaped wheel-barrowful of rough dug and therefore unknapped flint will set you back £70. One tonne of knapped flint will provide around 4 square metres of walling, so it's every bit as expensive as the dearest stone. But it's very different to lay and similarly when it comes to labour costs, for if you lay it with a sand and cement mortar you cannot really go any higher than 300mm per day. With nil porosity the mortar simply doesn't go off and the flints will 'float' on the bed. So it's probably better to think in terms of laying it with a lime mortar. All of this puts you in a different category altogether and one that may well be outside the knowledge of most bricklayers. If you can find the right person for the job they'll probably want to revert to daywork and the labour cost will end up at around £100 per square metre.

Whatever you do steer clear of the flint-faced blocks. They look awful. The finished ones are the worst. If you must use them, use the type where the flints are proud of the block and where the pointing can flow from block to block with some semblance of reality.

By the way, I have not dwelt too much on recon-stituted stone, which to all intents and purposes is really just a form of concrete brickwork. Some types have 'T' blocks and fit together like a jigsaw puzzle. Others are simply various sizes of lookalike concrete stones laid to a chosen pattern to emulate the stonework of various districts. If the bricklayers are pricing on measured rates they will switch to a price per square metre of walling, which is quite likely to be around double the price it would be for brick-work at around £36.

Working with other trades

Being in a pivotal trade means that bricklayers have to work in with many other trades. Some ground-workers will undertake the foundation blockwork but many will expect that the bricklayers will carry out this task and build in the cranked ventilators. However, it is not the bricklayer's job to fill the below-ground cavities.

According to new regulations, if timber joists or 'I' beams are being used the old relationship between carpenters and bricklayers regarding building in of the joists is now broken and, instead, the joists are hung on metal joist hangers. These need to be built in level if the joists and resulting floor are to be even.

If a beam-and-block first floor is to be used then it is often undertaken by the bricklayers. Sometimes, however, a crane is needed, and sometimes the groundworkers will come back and lay this floor when the bricklayers have got to the right level.

The carpenter cuts and scarfs the wallplate. But it is the bricklayer who beds it.

Timber joinery is often built in by the bricklayers as they go. Pvc-u, metal or some hardwood joinery is put in afterwards. It is therefore important that the bricklayers leave the correct-sized openings and that the cavity closers are built in.

If there are gable ends the bricklayers will require that the end trusses or rafters are reared by the car-penters as a template for their brickwork.

Any flashings are usually, but not always, the responsibility of the plumbers. The bricklayers will build in trays and dpcs but they won't make them. When they build the chimney or any brickwork that protrudes above the roof they will rake out the joints for the flashings. But they won't usually fit them, although they may well undertake their pointing in. They need to work quite closely, therefore, with the plumbers and/or roofers.

If there are to be fireplaces or any fancy or decorative brickwork within the home then the bricklayers will have to build these before the plasterers do their job. They will also have to make sure that the work is protected, usually by the simple expedient of building in a cover flap of polythene membrane.

Lastly, the bricklayers team up with the groundworkers again to build any external patio or boundary walls.

Renovations and conversions

With renovations there may be times when things are just the same as for new build or extensions, but in most cases the pace is a little slower and it is as important as ever to choose the right man for the job. A modern bricklayer will just pick up the next brick on the stack and lay it. With renovations it is often necessary for the bricklayer to examine the brick he has just picked up and decide whether it is the right one for the immediate job in hand or whether he should look for one with a slightly different camber or colour.

It is also important that tradesmen working on renovations should have some idea of the history of building and, whilst I've covered this in the Chapter 7, I do think that it perhaps bears repetition here for those who are not reading cover to cover.

Many older properties were built with solid walls with no damp-proof membranes and no damp-proof courses. Natural moisture within the ground would from time to time find its way into the structure. External rain would, to a large extent, run off the outside face harmlessly to the ground and, most importantly, the roof covering would prevent the ingress of water into the top of the walling. The important thing was that a natural balance was established whereby any moisture that did find its way into the walling would be allowed to evaporate – the walls are able to breathe.

The most important factor in creating this ability to breathe was the use of lime mortars, renderings and plasters. Lime-based mediums never really fully set. They develop a more or less hard exterior veneer but always remain pliable behind the face and present no barrier to the wall's ability to breathe.

If modern materials and methods are applied to these older buildings then the act of restoration or renovation can create long-term problems that could

Even the best bricklayers may not be that hot on laying stone and the art of doing so is often best left to someone who describes themselves as a stonemason.

eventually lead to the virtual destruction of some buildings. The application of a cement-based render to the outside, especially one with a waterproofing additive, can, I agree, prevent wind-driven water from penetrating a wall. But if the natural balance is disturbed and the natural moisture within the walling is unable to escape, problems can ensue. Most of the evaporation from solid walling is to the outside, where passing wind naturally dries off the wall and draws the damp outwards. If this avenue of escape is withdrawn then the only alternative can be that the moisture expresses itself on the internal face of the wall with resulting dampness within the home. If its progress internally is also impeded by the use of cementatious renders or modern hard plasters then there can be a build-up of moisture and the salts that crystallise as a consequence. The result will be patches of plaster coming lose from the substrate. Often an indication of this being the cause of the problem is where previously damp patches at the bottom of the wall are cleared, only for new patches to appear further up.

But the single greatest cause of destruction occurs when lime mortars to old brickwork or stone are replaced with cement-based mortars. Most stone used in building, with the exception of the granites, is a relatively soft material, often limestone. Many of the bricks used in older buildings are also soft in comparison to new bricks; for which harder firing methods have been devised. The lime sand mortar with which these traditional materials were laid was always weaker than the principal walling material. It was designed to be sacrificial. Any moisture that got into the wall would express itself through the mortar and any damage caused by salts or frost would affect the mortar and not the walling material itself. From time to time it would be necessary to re-point the walling; but that was accepted and acceptable.

When this kind of walling is re-pointed using hard and virtually impermeable cement-based mortars, the moisture within the wall cannot find its way out through the joints and instead is forced to express itself through the softer brick or stone. The result is what we call 'spalling', where through the action of natural pressures and frost, the face of the brick or stone is literally delaminated or split off. Alternatively the sulphates within the mortar can literally attack some stones or bricks so that they look as if they have been worn away by acid. In extreme cases the bricks or stone will 'die back', leaving the new mortar proud of the face of the walling. Now that I've

Above: **It took all the strength of these seven men to lift this frame into position.**

Left: **Topping out – chimney pot on!**

brought the problem to your attention, I bet that you will, unfortunately, find examples of this exact phenomenon in the streets around you.

Make yourself aware of these problems and ask bricklayers or builders if they are competent at building with lime. If they answer 'Yes', you must ensure that they mean the proper use of non-hydraulic lime putty and sand rather than the idea of simply adding bagged lime to an ordinary sand and cement mix. Lime is often added to cementatious mortars or renders for the purposes of colouring or in order to make the mix smoother. That has nothing whatsoever to do with the preparation and use of a proper lime mortar or render.

Incidentally, it is normally quite all right to re-point modern brickwork with a sand and cement mortar as that's what it was probably laid with in the first place. As a general rule, however, never make the mortar stronger than the brick.

You can expect, as an average, that one man can rake out and re-point 2 square metres of brickwork per day. If he is expecting to earn £200 per day then each metre of re-pointing is, therefore, going to cost, for the labour only, around £100. It could be cheaper if he puts his labourer on it but do check that he is competent.

I have already mentioned that the re-pointing material must be sympathetic to the walling medium and why this is so important. It is also important that any re-pointing should look right. Strap pointing, where the pointing is square edged and proud of the joint, might make the person doing it feel good and allow them to stamp their mark on stonework or brickwork. But it certainly won't do much good to the wall, where it will serve to channel moisture within the joints. The same goes for ribbon pointing, where the mortar resembles an ugly ridge-backed snake wandering through the stones.

Most stone walls look best with the pointing slightly recessed. Most brick walls look best with the pointing flush with the face of the brickwork, square and flat or slightly recessed in a shallow curve, produced by an iron. Weatherstruck pointing, where the pointing is pushed back at an angle, should always have the pointing recessed at the top only,

coming flush with the top edge of the brick below, if it is not to channel water into the walling material.

In certain areas, particularly inner cities, the traditional pointing is 'tuck' pointing. This is a complicated procedure involving, first of all, raking back the bedding mortar and then pointing flush with a mortar mix that closely resembles the brick in colour. When this pointing has started to go off a 'V'-shaped groove is cut into it using a straight edge before a white lime-based mixture is tucked into the slot and finished, in straight square lines, proud of the brickwork. Such a long and involved process obviously takes time and one would expect that the costs would reflect that and be at least double that for ordinary forms of pointing.

As with new build, the business of building walls often gets lumped together under the general heading

Some 'bricklayers' are only really good at laying blocks, which is not to say that such a person might not be perfectly useful in a renovation project...

of 'bricklaying'. This does not mean, however, that all bricklayers are good at laying both bricks and stone. Some 'bricklayers' are only really good at laying blocks, which is not to say that such a person might not be perfectly useful in a renovation project, as much of what needs to be done involves the construction of block walls or the creation of new openings within internal walls. What it does mean is that such a person should not be let loose on the cosmetic part of the walling.

Even the best bricklayers may not be that hot on laying stone and the art of doing so is often best left to someone who describes themselves as a stonemason. In many areas where stone is no longer the norm in building practice, the art of laying stone has been almost completely lost. In other areas where stone exists alongside brick, some bricklayers will boast that they can lay stone as well. Many may well be right but others, those with no grounding in building history, will make a pig's ear out of it. Each area has its own way of laying stone, which has more or less evolved from the nature of the stone itself. In some areas, stones of equal size are laid in courses, almost as if they're large blocks. In other areas the stone is laid in random courses where, although the horizontal emphasis is maintained, jumpers, or larger stones, are set within them to break up the strict coursing. Many modern bricklayers, however, when laying stone, choose to build the wall in random rubble where there is no particular coursing and where the stones are just laid as they come. This method, which was employed in a very few areas, is the easiest to do. But nothing looks as incongruous as an extension or repair to a wall where the stone is not laid as the original.

Part of the problem can be with the stone itself. The art of dressing the stone, or shaping it on site, has been largely lost in many areas and stonemasons have come to rely on the stone being delivered to a cut size and, in particular, a cut size to the bed or width. This often has to be laid, in modern construction, with a backing block. Stone laid without the backing block tends to sag on the bed, making the maintenance of a cavity difficult. In the old days when the walls were solid, this problem was overcome by building the wall as two skins and then filling the centre with a rubble and mortar mix as they came up, to stabilise both leafs.

That indeed is how most flint was laid in a solid wall. There is, however, another method, still used in garden walling. Here, the flints are laid on beds of mortar between two upright boards, which are struck when the mortar has practically gone off and raised to continue the next section once the joints have been raked out and the flints brushed up to reveal their face.

Renovation of walls may well involve taking down old and unstable sections and rebuilding them. It may also mean re-pointing, the creation of new openings and the installation of new lintels or beams. This requires muscle as much as skill and jobs such as this can often only be priced on the basis of time. But that does not mean that, just as with new build, a competent tradesman confident of his own abilities and the time it will take him to undertake a certain job should not be able to express all of that in terms of a lump sum price.

One other form of walling needs mentioning and that is cob – basically a mixture of clay or chalk, straw and/or animal hair and dung. It is created by plank formers that are lifted as each successive layer is rammed home and allowed to dry. Once dry it is rock solid, just so long as it is kept dry. If water is allowed to get into it, particularly from the top if the roof fails, then it will very quickly revert to its constituent parts. A variation on this theme is wattle and daub, where the walls were created by the use of open timber wattles or woven panels of lathing between the main upright timbers, into which a daub of mud, clay, animal hair and dung was pushed and then smoothed off to create a wall surface. There are very few exponents of these arts today and those that there are can virtually name their own price for new work.

Where the repair of such walling has to be undertaken, it is best done by analysing the mixture, creating as near a match to it as is possible and literally daubing it into any cracks or holes. If the external rendering breaks down then it should be attended to quite quickly, preferably by the use of a lime render strengthened by animal hair that allows the wall to breathe. On the other hand, as I hinted at before, I have to admit that in many properties I have seen in the West Country, the use of a cementatious waterproof render on the external face, coupled with a breathing roughcast or lime plaster on the inside, seems to work quite well. Perhaps this is because the excessive damp in these areas seems to produce some sort of equilibrium in the natural moisture necessary within the walling. These plastering methods and costs are discussed under the heading of plasterers.

Carpenters and joiners

This is the trade that is responsible for all the woodwork in your new home, including both structural timbers, which are largely hidden from day-to-day view and finishing joinery, and which can set the whole tone and the lasting impression of its worth. In some parts of the realm, mainly in the north of England, the tradesmen are referred to as 'joiners' rather than 'carpenters', whereas in the south, that term is usually reserved for cabinet makers.

Some publications would have you believe that this trade is priced on measured rates – at given prices for each square or linear metre of the task. In fact, for most one- or two-man carpenters, that simply isn't the way they go about things. It is possible to work prices backwards and extrapolate costs and at times these figures can give a guide. But beware of taking them as gospel. If a rectangular floor, with no corners or cuts, takes two days to lay, that does not mean that a floor half the size with odd shapes, where the cut from each end cannot be carried forward to the next run, will take half as long. It may take just the same time and therefore cost just as much.

Most carpenters cost a job by assessing how long each task will take and how many men will be required. They then add up the number of 'man days' or hours and multiply by the rate per day or per hour they wish to make. At the moment over much of the country that rate is £20 per hour or £160 per day for a fully qualified carpenter (much more in London and major cities). Certain tasks need two men and it's not unusual for a single carpenter to have a mate who is employed from time to time. They won't receive as much but you will, nevertheless, be charged at the full rate.

The carpenter's price is usually broken into three phases, 'first fix', 'roof' and 'second fix'. The problem is that, distinct as these stages are, the timing within them is not consistent and many tasks included, say, within the heading first fix cannot be carried out until after the roof is done. These facts are well known and understood by those who regularly work on site either alongside or in conjunction with carpenters. It is, however, important that the self-builder is aware of the sequences involved because some of the timings are critical to within the day if continuity is to be maintained.

It is normal for this trade to be labour only with the main contractor or self-builder responsible for the provision of all timber, nails, screws and fixings, including glues. Most competent carpenters will have all their own tools but there may sometimes be instances where you might need to hire a generator. If the carpenter is going to be responsible for the fitting of the kitchen units and worktops it might also be necessary to hire in a mitre cutter.

In most self-builds, the first time that the carpenter will appear on site is to cut and lay the first-floor joists. Sometimes the bricklayers will offer to carry out this work. If they are really competent then that's fine but otherwise it's far better left to a carpenter. First-floor joists have to be properly levelled if you are not to experience squeaking at a later date. The Building Regulations require that the ends of joists running into external walls are supported by joist hangers, rather than being built in. This may mean that the bricklayers build the joist hangers into the relevant course and then carry on. It may equally mean that when the carpenter comes to lay the joists he will have to pack up or cut out in certain places in order to achieve a level top surface for the eventual decking. This is done by fixing the joists at each end of the bay and then stringing a line over a batten nailed on top of each one. All intermediate joists are then levelled to this line and held in place by counter battens tacked across the run.

Where the unsupported span exceeds 2.5 metres it is necessary to provide midspan strutting to prevent deflection or twisting. In spans over 4.5 metres there is a requirement for strutting at two equally spaced points. This is achieved by herringbone struts of batten or metal fixed in a cross pattern from the top of one joist to the bottom of its neighbour. It is also necessary to build in lateral restraint straps to tie the walls and upper floors together. If the joists run parallel to the wall, these must be placed at 2-metre intervals to cross at least three joists with packing noggings beneath. If the joists run counter to the wall and the joist hangers are not the type that provides restraint then, once again, the straps must be built into the wall and fixed to the sides of the joists at minimum intervals of 2 metres. Solid blocking between the joists is required where the joists run into a wall and these can then double up as perimeter noggings for the plasterboard.

Where there are open spaces within the floor zone such as for staircases, the joists running into the void need to be supported. This is usually achieved by the use of thicker joists or beams known as 'trimmers'. The joists running into this trimmer are supported on joist hangers.

The following are the carpenter's tasks on a typical job:

First fix

- Cutting, laying and levelling of suspended ground-floor joists (mainly in Scotland)

- Fixing of decking (flooring) to suspended ground-floor joists (if appropriate)

- Cutting, laying and levelling of first-floor (chamber) joists and trimmers

- Fixing door linings (casings) to openings in ground-floor blockwork

- Laying first-floor decking

- Making up and installing first-floor studwork partitioning, including door linings

- Fixing window boards

- Fixing staircase flight

- Making up and fixing garage door frames

- Nogging out for plasterboard

- Hanging temporary external doors, where appropriate for security

- Making up tank stands in the loft (only if a vented plumbing system is being used)

- Boxing out pipework (usually done at second-fix stage)

Roof

- Erecting and completing roof using prefabricated trusses or cutting and pitching a roof made on site from sawn lumber. To include gable ladders, valleys, hips, dormers or roof lights as well as any porch or bay window roofs.

- Laying sarking boarding (Scotland only)

- Fixing facias and soffits, including, where required, any soffit or eaves ventilation

- Fixing bargeboards where required

Second fix

- Laying insulation and decking to floating ground or first floors

- Assembling and fitting staircase newels, ballustrading, aprons and handrailing

- Hanging all internal doors

- Fixing all skirting, architrave and decorative timber mouldings

- Assembling and fitting timber French doors

- Hanging timber external doors

- Fitting garage doors including personnel doors

- Hanging doors to fitted wardrobes and cupboards and fitting out, including slatted shelving to airing cupboard

- Fitting or fixing loft traps

In addition there are several other tasks, which the carpenters may or may not be called upon to carry out. These include:

- Making up and fixing templates for window and door openings

- Placing insulation within the floor or ceiling zone

- Putting insulation within the studwork

- Boarding out the loft

- Fixing loft ladders

Right: **Joists levelled and ready for the brick-layers to carry on.**

Below: **Wallplate half jointed, or scarfed, and bedded.**

Prefabricated timber flooring is becoming increasingly popular; the fact that they are manufactured under controlled conditions using ply materials means that they eliminate shrinkage and can be proven for spans of up to 6 metres. They are usually referred to as 'I' beams due to their profile. The top and bottom sections must not be cut or notched, so the web contains punch holes for services to pass through.

Most carpenters will leave site once the first-floor joists are fixed and will not return until the house has reached roof height. When they do come back their first job is to cut the wallplates and scarf (half lap) any joints. These are then bedded on mortar by the bricklayer and when this is dry, the plates are tied down to the blockwork by metal holding straps set at 2-metre intervals. If the roof is to be a hipped

roof then the carpenter can continue with its construction. If it is a gabled roof then it is usual for the carpenter to 'rear' the end trusses, so that the bricklayers can use them as templates, and then leave site whilst they complete the gable ends.

Most roofs are built using prefabricated trusses delivered to site and erected according to a schedule prepared by the manufacturers. A trussed roof is undoubtedly quicker, easier and therefore cheaper to erect than a roof that is constructed on site using sawn lumber. Trusses come in various forms. The standard truss, with a web of cross bracing between the rafter and ceiling tie sections, often in the shape of a 'W', does not allow occupation of the roof void other than for light storage purposes. An 'attic' truss is designed, using thicker timbers with vertical supports and ceiling ties, so that the roof section can be occupied. They are very heavy and it may even be necessary to hire a crane to get them up into the plate and into position. Trusses can also be designed for more complicated roofs. Girder trusses, often made by bolting multiple trusses together, are able to support other trusses coming in at right angles, allowing clear span 'L-shaped sections of roof. Hip trusses, often flat-topped and in reducing sizes, allow the creation of a hipped end to a roof and mono trusses can be used for 'lean-to' roofing situations.

Roof trusses must be spaced at maximum 600mm centres and fixed to the wallplate with proprietary truss clips. As they are being set, battens are used to hold them upright on a temporary basis before being replaced with 100 x 25mm diagonal bracing running underneath the rafters from wallplate to ridge and back down again at an angle of 45 degrees. Additional stability is provided by timber binding at the ceiling, rafter and ridge node points, abutted tightly to the blockwork. Finally, metal restraint straps are built in at 2-metre centres up the gable and at ceiling level, to cross at least three trusses with noggings beneath.

Although most roofs use prefabricated trusses, it is not uncommon for those in more complex houses and bungalows to be made up on site from sawn lumber. These roofs, known as either 'cut and pitch' or 'purlin and spar', have to be very carefully designed with a cutting list detailing the size of timber that is to be used for each component part.

Moving the manufacture of the roof from a factory-controlled environment to the site obviously means that the labour costs, if not the material costs, are going to be considerably increased. Whilst prefabricated trusses for a standard roof may take two men no more than three days to complete, roofs of this sort might extend that to ten days or more.

The secret is careful planning. A roof of this type means that an enormous amount of timber will be delivered to site and it is not unusual for the first day to be taken up entirely with the sorting of this lumber into the various lengths and cross sections, before ever a cut is made.

Except for the smallest of buildings most cut roofs require the rafters to have some support along their length between the wallplate and the ridge board. This is achieved by the use of purlins, which are built into the end walls and run along beneath the rafters or spars. If the purlins are timber then the carpenters will cut and position them to be built in by the bricklayers. If the purlins are steel, then the bricklayers will position them and build them in on padstones at the correct level, with the carpenters cutting and bolting any timber plates, if required.

Triangulation is achieved at ceiling or floor level by ceiling ties or floor joists whilst additional support is often achieved at a higher level by collar ties.

The skill of the carpenter is employed with the construction of the hip or valley trees or blades where 'jack' rafters in reducing sizes span from the wallplate to the hip or valley rafters. Additional bracing, to prevent spreading, may be achieved at the corners by the use of 'dragon ties', or beams, between the wallplates. Whilst the existence of hips or valleys might well have been the original reason for opting for a cut roof rather than a prefabricated one, it has to be said that many trussed roofs revert to sawn lumber for these sections. It is also the carpenter's responsibility to build the 'lay boards' up the valley, and to construct any dormers and fix roof lights.

When the main timbers for the roof are finished, the carpenter will move on to complete the facias and soffit, together with any associated ventilation. In some cases where there is an overhang at the verge, the carpenter may have to construct or fit gable ladders and bargeboards. In Scotland it is the carpenter who fits the sarking boarding across the top of the roof timbers.

Once the roof is complete, the carpenters leave site to give way to the roofers and will not return until at least the underlay and battens are fixed and the property is 'in the dry'. When they come back they will do so in company with the plumbers and electricians. With the plumbers working from the top, notching the joists, and the electricians working from below, drilling through them, the carpenters will busy themselves with the fitting of window boards and door linings to openings within the blockwork partitioning. These will have been left oversized to allow the carpenters to pack out the lining to achieve square and vertical in all planes.

Once the plumbers have finished, the carpenters can move on to the laying of the first-floor decking. These days this is usually made from tongued-and-grooved chipboard sheets, laid with the long edges at right angles to the joists and nailed at 200–300mm centres along the joists and intermediate supports. The short edges should always run to a joist or nogging. All grooved joints must be glued and the boards should also be glued to the joists to prevent squeaking.

With the first floor down, the carpenter can move on to the cutting and assembly of any studwork partitioning, including the fixing of door linings. The electrician may well be in attendance at this time in order to thread wires through the studwork and fix back boxes to the noggings. Sometimes the carpenters will agree to install the insulation as they go but at other times this task may fall to the self-builder or the tackers.

The three trades of plumber, electrician and carpenter are all now working towards finishing their first-fix jobs in preparation for the arrival of the tackers and plasterers. All of which, illustrates that, although I and others, for the sake of convenience, write about all these trades in isolation, the reality is that they have to work as a team. With the first floor in, the staircase flight can be assembled and fixed with the main newels and any aproning, although the balustrading and handrails will probably be left until later. Before the plasterers come in, it is a good idea to get the carpenter to cut and tack pieces of ply or hardboard to the treads to protect them from damage.

Any floating floors also need to go in at this stage with the chipboard laid on to flooring-grade insulation over a damp-proof membrane. It is important to make sure that all the tongued-and-grooved edges are properly glued and that the boards stop short of the wall by at least 12mm (a gap that will be masked by any skirting), to prevent humping up later.

If any pipes, vent pipes or service ducting need boxing in the carpenter will probably do them at this stage, together with the fixing of any loft traps. They can then either leave the site to the tackers and plasterers or drop on to the garage where they can fix the garage door frame and hang the doors, including any personnel doors.

With the plasterers finished many trades can come back with the carpenters, who will probably get on with the fixing of skirtings, architraves and the hanging of internal and external timber doors. At this time they will also finish off any mouldings, fit the balustrading and handrails to the staircase, cut and fit the slats to the airing cupboard, and finish off the loft traps and any ladders. Any built-in bedroom or bathroom furniture will also be tackled at this point.

Whether they then go on to fit the kitchen units depends upon the suppliers. Many kitchen specialists include fitting within their remit. Others work on a supply only basis. The self-builder might be tempted by the lower prices of a flat-pack kitchen. Beware. It can take up to three days to assemble the units for an average kitchen and at a day rate of £160 per day that might well mean that the ready-assembled units become more attractive. It is essential to make sure that you have the correct fixings on site, particularly for the hanging of wall units. The plumbers and electricians will also need to be on hand to co-ordinate the fitting of sink units and wet appliances and, as mentioned, you might need to hire a mitre cutter for the worktops.

Renovations and conversions

For renovators or converters the pricing is a little more complicated. A man quoting for such a job may be tempted to do so on the basis of an hourly or daily rate for the whole job and in some cases, there may well be no alternative. But wherever possible try to get the estimate of time converted into a lump sum price.

Everyone knows what a carpenter does but very few seem to know the sequence in which they do it. This may because, as I've said above, the trade is often split into three distinct stages, yet the timing of many of the tasks within those phases is not consistent. For the renovator these stages are often academic and only come into play when the prices are given. Of much more importance is the choice of tradesman. A carpenter who is good at structural timber may not necessarily be good at the finishing part of the trade. Just because a man is fast, efficient and competent in dealing with new work doesn't mean that he'll have the skills needed for refurbishment: the patience and the knowledge required to hang old doors rather than new. Perhaps what marks out the best carpenter from the rest is their love of the material they work with. A carpenter who professes a love and a knowledge of wood – and you can literally see the affection with which they stroke and smell the timber as they work it – will often turn out the very best work.

With renovation there is frequently the complication of having to lift old boarding before either putting it back down again or replacing it on joists which may well have to be packed up or strengthened.

Left: **A modern home designed to emulate a barn conversion.**

Below: **Roof on, ready for tiling.**

Where pipe runs have caused the joists to be notched out, new boarding might have to be spaced so that the joints span the gap and, if that's not possible, packing or firring pieces might have to be fixed to the sides of the joists.

If the internal doors are second-hand reclaimed doors then the price for hanging each one will double. If the skirting is of a complicated section that required scribing at all internal corners then the time taken to do the job will increase and so will the price. A good carpenter will, as I have said, be prepared to add such figures up and take the rough with the smooth. If one of the items, such as the roof, takes a little longer then he might be prepared to 'stop over' and work a longer day. And if one of the items, say the skirting, takes less time then that will probably pay him for the time lost.

With a renovation project if the roof has to be completely replaced, then the costing process, as far as the carpenter is concerned, is relatively easy. So long as the walls are sound and a new plate can be bedded level, the work on the roof is not really any different from that in a new construction and its costing will follow similar lines. If, however, the roof is to be largely retained then it is a completely different matter. Scarfing in new bits of timber to old,

replacing other bits completely and making up new using the existing as a template may sound fine on the ground. But when you're up there things begin to change and the probability is that a carpenter will want to revert back to daywork.

With older roofs it is important that the carpenter understands the principles behind their construc-

Above, below and right: **Second fix can include doors, kitchens and flooring.**

tion. This book is not meant to be a building manual but it does behove the serious renovator or converter to make themselves aware of just how older roofs were built. In most modern roof construction we are used to the fact that the rafters – provided either as part of the prefabricated truss or as separate timbers spanning from wallplate to ridge, supported by purlins on the way – are the sole support for the roofing battens that cross them.

Many of the older forms of roof construction work on the basis of 'principal' trusses, spaced along the building supporting purlins that are also built into the end walls. These principal trusses are often of a fairly standard configuration with ceiling and collar ties and either diagonal or vertical bracing. But they can be of the 'scissor' type, where crossed members span from the wallplate to the centre point of the opposing rafter. Another variation is sometimes referred to as a 'cruck' roof. In this type of roof the main support is given by curved cruck blades that

Various roof truss configurations

Typical modern truss

A RAFTER
B CEILING JOIST (TIE)
C STRUT
D TIE
E BRACE
F WALL PLATE

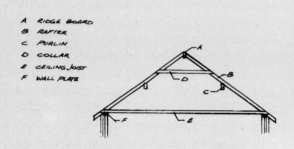

Attic truss

A KING POST
B RAFTER
C QUEEN POST
D STRAINING BEAM
E STRUT
F CEILING JOIST (TIE)
G BRACE
H WALL PLATE

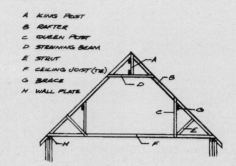

Modern purlin and spar roof

A RIDGE BOARD
B RAFTER
C PURLIN
D COLLAR
E CEILING JOIST
F WALL PLATE

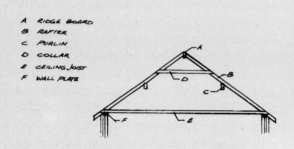

Typical double roof

A COMMON RAFTER
B PRINCIPAL RAFTER
C COLLAR
D TRENCHED PURLIN
E RIDGE PURLIN
F WALL PLATE

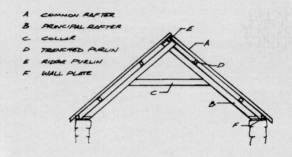

Cruck roof

A COMMON RAFTER
B CRUCK BLADE
C PURLIN
D RIDGE PURLIN
E YOKE
F CRANKED COLLAR
G COLLAR BEAM
H PLATE

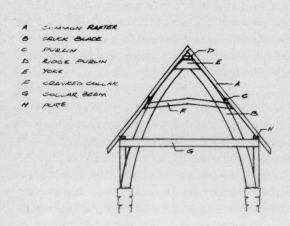

Scissor truss roof

A COMMON RAFTER
B PRINCIPAL RAFTER (TOP CHORD)
C RIDGE PURLIN
D PURLIN
E BOTTOM CHORD
F WALLPLATE

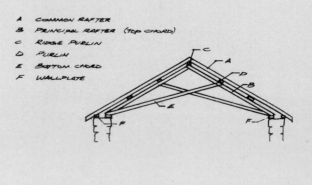

Mansard roof

A   COMMON RAFTER
B   KING POST
C   QUEEN POST
D   PURLIN
E   RIDGE PURLIN
F   BRACE
G   STRUT
H   TIE BEAM
J   PRINCIPAL RAFTER

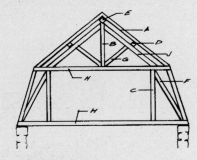

Component parts of older type roofs
(not necessarily used together)

A   COMMON RAFTER
B   PRINCIPAL RAFTER
C   PURLIN
D   RIDGE BEAM
E   KING POST
F   CROWN POST
G   QUEEN POST
H   STRUT
I   COLLAR TIE
J   TIE BEAM
K   WALLPLATE

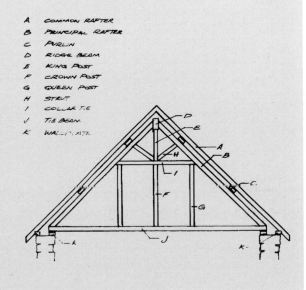

are built into the wall below the wallplate level and curve up to meet at the ridge pole or purlin. All of these types ingeniously transpose the loadings into a downward rather than an outward force with the principal trusses, spaced along the building, supporting 'common' rafters. These common rafters, spanning from the wallplate to the ridge beam, supported by purlins on the way, in turn support the tile or slate battening and the roof covering.

Principal rafters, crucks and purlins are usually made from heavy oak, elm or chestnut beams. The common rafters were often made of thinner pieces of the same material or even of softwood. When a roof 'goes' it is often these 'common' elements that deteriorate and in many cases the principal timbers remain sound.

'Never cut a prefabricated truss'– certainly not without the say-so of the manufacturers or a qualified timber engineer – is a golden rule. Likewise, never cut away any principal supporting timbers without first consulting your engineer or architect. It may be that in past years others have cut away things like collar ties, which became 'inconvenient'. The lateral or outward thrusts that this creates can lead to the roof failing or the walls being pushed out. You may have to replace such beams by either splicing in new ones or introducing new restraints using steel beams, plates or straps.

Mansard roofs enjoyed a brief period of popularity as a means of getting more space in the roof. They rely on a square being formed, supported on the wallplates with queen struts, bracings and king posts. Extending the roof down at a near-vertical angle to the wallplate was always ugly and this type of roof largely fell out of favour, with its place and function being taken up by the attic truss.

Although there are purpose-made and prefabricated dormers available on the market they are not often successful with older buildings and the likelihood is that any dormer windows will have to be constructed on site. A carpenter would normally price a dormer at five man days. This would include the doubling up of the rafters on each side, the construction of the dormer and its roof together with the crippling of any rafters, the making up of the cheeks and apexes, and the fitting of the window itself.

Roofers – tiling, slating, thatching and flat roofing

The roof tiler or slater will come in as soon as the main roof timbers are finished and braced and once the gable end walls are completed. Although they work alone they do need to fit in with the carpenters, plumbers and bricklayers, all of whom may need to be on the roof at the same time.

The trade can be labour only with the sub-contractors supplying their own hand tools, or it can be supply and fix. Labour-only roof tilers normally work their prices out on the basis of how long the job is going to take, with a rate of £160 per man day being the average. Supply-and-fix companies work on a price per square metre, with concrete interlocking tiles working out at somewhere around £25

per square metre and slate coming in at around £50 for natural Spanish and £60 for Welsh. These prices are surprisingly competitive and when you add up the cost of the tiles and ancillary items and the labour, you can be left wondering just how they make their money. The answer undoubtedly is that they screw the labour rates right down and, as specialists, they are able to command huge discounts from the manufacturers.

Tiles and slates are normally quoted on the basis of a price per thousand and the uninitiated can often assume that a tile with a lower cost per thousand is cheaper than one at a higher price. Their assumption might, however, be completely wrong, as the coverage rate for all tiles is vastly different. Some of the larger interlocking tiles, usually concrete, have a coverage rate of ten to the square metre. Some of the smaller concrete or clay plain tiles have a coverage of 60 to the square metre. But the fact that so many are needed means that the material cost for the tiles alone with no allowance made for ancillary items is well over double that for the interlocking.

The labour costs are, similarly, also going to be very different. One man must assume that, including ancillary bits and pieces involved, he can lay 30 concrete interlocking tiles in one hour. That's 3 square metres. Now if you switch to plain tiles, although a competent tradesman could expect to lay far more – say 80 – tiles in one hour, this only covers 1.33 square metres, so laying plain tiles is more than double the time and, therefore, the cost.

As you can see interlocking concrete tiles, which come in a variety of profiles, are undoubtedly the most cost-effective roof covering. The cost for the tiles varies, but in general it is between £600 and £925 per thousand. Supply-and-fix rates work out at between £25 and £30 per square metre. They are laid with a single lap, side by side, with the grooves on the underside at the edge of one tile resting within those on the upper side of the edge of the preceding tile.

Plain tiles come in both concrete and clay forms with most costing around £300 per

The following are the roofer's tasks on a typical job:

- Covering in roof with underlay and rough batten

- Fixing GRP (glass reinforced plastic) valleys or attending plumber fixing lead valleys

- Bedding or fixing undercloak to verges

- Fixing counter battens if necessary

- Gauging and fixing tiling battens to suit tiles or slates

- Loading out tiles/slates

- Laying roof tiles/slates, nailing as appropriate

- Laying valley tiles if appropriate

- Fixing verge tiles/slates

- Interleaving upstand and cover flashings to chimney

- Interleaving lead soakers

- Attending to and interleaving vent pipe skirts

- Fixing or bedding ridge and hip tiles

- Pointing up space between underside of tiles/slates and undercloak

Left: **New slates on the left can be gauged across a level roof. An old misshapen roof** (above) **needs much more thought.**

thousand to buy, although the most expensive handmade clay tiles can get up to around £700 per thousand. Supply-and-fix rates vary between £40 and £75 per square metre. The tiles are usually laid treble-lapped, each tile having parts of two other tiles beneath it, bringing about a consequent increase in the amount of battening required. They also weigh about twice as much as interlocking tiles, and as clay tiles are even heavier when wet, measures might need to be taken to beef up the roof structure. Although the clay tiles, and in particular the handmade varieties, cost more to buy that the concrete ones, the labour costs should not be appreciably more.

Pantiles are traditionally made from clay, although there are modern concrete varieties, which roughly equate in cost to the top end, price wise, of the interlocking tiles even though the coverage rate per tile is slightly less at 12–15 to the metre. They are laid single-lapped with the downward roll of each tile rolling over the upward roll of the tile below.

Slates vary from region to region but a typical size is 500 x 250mm with a coverage rate of 20 to the square metre and supply-and-fix rates of around £45 per square metre. The further north you go, the smaller the slates become. Traditional slates are cut from metamorphic rock and they are imported from as far afield as China, Spain and Brazil, although many purists will maintain that the Welsh slates are the best. Sadly they're not really available new, although there is a thriving market in reclaimed. They're more expensive at £70 per square metre as they're fiddly to lay and might need re-drilling. Metamorphic slates are laid treble-lapped with each slate nailed at least once to the batten. Man-made alternatives are available in either cement fibre or made from a mixture of glass fibre resin and slate dust. These are laid in precisely the same way as the traditional. Certain companies have, however, devised hybrids, which combine the technology of the inter-locking tile to create a slate-effect, single-lapped roof. They are, nevertheless, more expensive to lay than ordinary interlocking tiles, with a coverage rate of around 13.5 to the square metre. Each slate also has to have one, sometimes two, clips nailed to the batten, which is time consuming.

Perhaps the most expensive mainstream roofing option is to use stone slates at prices approaching and even surpassing £100 per square metre. These can be natural stone, cut to size and shape, or they can be man-made. There are variations from region to region. In many parts they are laid in reducing courses as they work towards the ridge and in some parts, the stones are limited to the eaves level with pantiles or plain tiles on the upper sections. Stone slates, whether man-made or natural, are extremely heavy, difficult to lay and, therefore, expensive.

The tiler's first job on arriving on site is to lay the underlay and batten the roof. The choice of tile or slate, plus the gauge or lap, will determine the spacings of the battening. In England and Wales the underlay is usually drawn across the tops of the rafters and the roof battening fixed down through it. In Scotland there is a requirement for 'sarking' boarding on top of the rafters and the underlay is laid on top of this with counter battens down the roof to support the roofing battens.

If the roof is to be ventilated the necessary eaves ventilators will be fixed with the soffits or facia by the carpenter. If a breathable membrane is being employed then 25mm counter battens must be fixed down the lay of the rafters, above the underlay, and beneath the roofing battens in order to create a breathing space.

If the verges have a gable ladder or are to be boxed, the carpenter may well have fixed the undercloak to support the mortar pointing that the tiler will place beneath the verge tiles. If not, then it's really the tiler's job. If the verge is clipped then the tiler will have to first bed the undercloak on to the bricks. If a dry verge system is being used then the undercloak is not necessary.

The carpenter will need to fix lay boards of plywood or tongued-and-grooved softwood in and up the val-leys. If the roof covering is slate then it is usual for the

valley to be leaded, this job being done by either the plumber or the tiler. Profiled tiles often employ a glass reinforced plastic (GRP) valley. Plain tiled valleys usu-ally use valley tiles. Costs for work to the valleys usually come out at around £20 per metre run.

Fixings to the tiles and slates are important. With slates, each slate should be nailed at least once. With interlocking tiles the nailing schedule devised by the manufacturers should be adhered to, and with plain tiles it is common for at least every third course to be nailed. Check that this is done and that proprietary verge and ridge tile fixings are used where appropri-ate. To check, stand on the scaffold and push the tiles up slightly with a batten. If they're nailed they won't move. Slate and plain-tiled roofs will need larger tiles called 'tile and a halves' for the verges and interlock-ing tiles will need left- and right-hand verge tiles. Eaves tiles are laid beneath the last tile at the bottom of the roof and 'top slates' are laid over the last tile at the top, beneath the ridge.

Ridges can be dry laid with proprietary ridge tiles, often incorporating ventilation. More often, however, ridge tiles, costing just under £2 each, are bedded on mortar. Hips follow the same principles except that with plain tiles, bonnet tiles can be employed. The end hip tile should be held in place using a hip iron. Slate or plain-tiled hips that would be too intru-sive using tiles as the cover can be cut close on the mitre with lead soakers beneath, or employ a broom pole ridge where the lead is rolled over a wooden pole and dressed down each roof plane.

Leadwork to the roof area needs a mention simply because there is often confusion about just which trade's responsibility it is. In the past only a plumber would work with lead and the joke was that that was why all plumbers were mad! Be that as it may, it is the plumber's job to make up the flashings, skirts and trays on site from loose rolls or sheets of lead that are cut out and soldered together. To an extent that still holds true, and on many sites the plumber makes up the leadwork and hands it to the roofer, who then installs it as part and parcel of his overall roofing price. The advent of purpose-made skirts to fit around vent pipes and proprietary cavity trays has reduced the involvement of the plumber to the point where many roofers now simply cut out and fit their own flashings as they go, whilst the bricklayers take sole responsibility for the installation of cavity trays and their associated weepers and flashings.

For bigger or more complicated jobs it is sometimes necessary to hire in a hoist to raise the tiles to the top lift of the scaffold, after which the men will walk them up on to the roof.

Renovations and conversions

Many who are renovating will be faced not with a new roof situation but the refurbishment of an existing roof. Patching a roof is not easy – it is time consuming and difficult and it does not always achieve the desired results. It is relatively easy to replace a tile if the rows above and beside are not nailed. If they are, and the nails are tight then, on a plain-tiled roof, lifting the necessary two rows of tiles immediately above the tile sufficiently to enable the nib of the new one to lip over the batten might be difficult. The temptation, of course, is to rip the nails. But how does one then replace them?

On top of that, the chances are that a roof that is suffering is probably failing simply because the battens are rotting or there is no underfelt. In such a case it often pays to strip the roof and re-lay the tiles, augmenting any broken ones with purchases of the nearest thing from the local demolition or reclamation yard. Removing the old tiles to the scaffolding is a slow job that has to be done carefully if you're not to end up with just a pile of broken tiles and the only way of costing it is on a man day basis. As always, that does not mean that you cannot seek a lump sum price for the job from a reputable tradesman who is prepared to quantify his likely work but who won't then rush the job.

Repairing or replacing slates is slightly easier, despite the fact that most slate roofs have every slate nailed twice to the batten. A special tool called a slate rip can be slid up under the slate to remove the nails. It is not possible, however, to nail the replacement, and the traditional way of re-fixing is to loop a thin strip of lead over the top of the tile beneath and then bring it out at the bottom end of the replacement slate, bending it up in a hook to hold it in place. Another method, which might alarm purists but which I've found works perfectly, is to use one of the tube glues. Once again this kind of work has to be priced on a daywork basis and if large areas have to be replaced and there is no underfelt, it is often better to strip the roof and start again.

The other things to watch out for are whether the tradesmen gauge for square and level the battens. Many older buildings are out of square and if the tiler or slater doesn't take that into account when he gauges the tiles or slates across the roof you will be left with an unsightly verge row at one end. The rafters in many older buildings were far from straight and true and indeed many are simply rough-hewn timber. If the tiling battens are laid on these without being levelled and packed up where necessary, it will introduce unsightly undulations in the roof plane.

A few years ago many people thought that thatch was a dying trade and that it would only be relevant to a declining number of properties, many of which would eventually abandon it and switch instead to tiles or slates. In fact there has been a huge revival in popularity and in parts of the West Country, particularly in Wiltshire, it is becoming quite common to see it used on brand-new houses. Nevertheless, be prepared for waiting times of up to a year for the best of the thatchers and be prepared to have to pay at least £100 per square metre for the work on a supply-and-fix basis.

Flat roofs, which are thankfully largely inapplicable to new properties, are often seen as a necessary evil and a potential source of problems – mainly because they are. Architecturally they fall into two genres – those that look good, such as the flat-roofed extension to a Georgian house, possibly with a parapet and possibly also serving as a balcony to an upper room, and those that are simply cheap bolt-ons to a 1960s or '70s house or bungalow. The latter are often best eliminated altogether by the creation of a mono pitched roof against the house, but in certain cases that's not always possible. All flat roofs have a relatively limited life and all will eventually need attention or completely re-doing. I venture to suggest that most of the temporary repairs or solutions that are marketed will last, at best, only a short while, and, at worst, look extremely ugly. Far better, I think in most cases, to bite the bullet and completely renew.

Flat roofs are either 'cold' or 'warm'. A cold roof,

which is illegal in Scotland for new work and frowned upon in England and Wales, has the insulation at the bottom of the roof structure against and immediately above the plasterboard ceiling. It must have a void above the insulation between it and the bottom of the decking of at least 50mm and there must be adequate ventilation of this void. A warm roof has the insulation on top of the decking, with the weatherproofing either on top of or below it. The space below, between the joists and above the plasterboard ceiling, does not have to be ventilated.

Lead, zinc or copper roofing can be attractive and long lasting but does work out frightfully expensive at up to £150 per square metre. Additionally, it often can't be walked upon. The most common form of flat roofing is made up from rolls of reinforced bituminous felt in two to three layers, each of which is bonded down to the one below by hot or cold bitumen. Hot-rolled is best with the top sheet covered in stone chippings and any exposed sections or upstands in mineral felt to protect them from the sun. Costs vary between £15 and £20 per square metre (depending upon the quality of the felt and the number of layers) and many contractors will give a five- to ten-year guarantee. If you want to walk on this kind of roof you will have to employ a lightweight fibre cement tile, bonded to the topcoat of felt.

Mastic asphalt roofs are created by melting the bitumen in a cauldron and spreading it in a layer 18–50mm deep over a sheathing felt. It is hard-wearing, can be walked on, with or without the addition of tiles, and presents an impervious barrier to the weather. You can't just lay it willy nilly, however. The roof has to be of the right construction and profile with the necessary upstands and lips. Costs on a supply-and-fix basis are around £50 per square metre. Another form of roofing that has become popular is the single-ply butyl membrane. This is made to order and fixed over an underfelt using secret fixings and flaps to protect it. Costs vary but one should normally allow about £70 per square metre with a 20-year guarantee.

A modern and long-lasting alternative is the GRP resin bonded type of roof. With these roofs the installers usually replace the top decking with their own proprietary insulated boarding before spreading various layers of fibre matting and polyester resin which, with the addition of a hardener, set to a durable surface. Costs work out at roughly £50 per square metre on the prepared boarding with a 30-year guarantee. They can be walked on but I have heard tell that they can also be noisy in heavy rain – something that the softer butyl and felt surfaces don't suffer from quite as much.

Plumbers and heating engineers

The trade is often supply and fix, although most plumbers working within the self-build industry accept that the self-builder may want to supply much of the principal equipment including under-floor central heating, the boiler, cylinders and so on.

Prices are reached by reference to the materials and the number of days involved in installing the system, with 15–20 man days perhaps being the average for most self-build homes. Throughout much of the UK the labour rate is £200 per man day, but considerably more in London and inner cities. In most homes with normal domestic hot and cold plumbing and a standard radiator system, the materials and labour will be roughly equal.

Although the bulk of the plumber's work will not take place until the new home is well and truly under way, it is a good idea to have identified one before work commences. Almost the first service that you require in order to build a house is a supply of water, so a plumber will be needed to install a stopcock with a non-return valve in a lockable position, protected from frost. In addition, when the groundworkers dig the foundations, it is not unusual for them to come across previously unknown water pipes and it's handy to have a willing plumber on call just in case the digger inadvertently cuts a supply.

In most instances the person carrying out work to the hot and cold domestic plumbing is also responsible for the installation of the central heating, although it is possible for the latter to be carried out by a heating engineer. If it is decided to split these responsibilities it is all the more important that

The disciplines of plumbing and central heating have seen more changes over the past few years than any other trade, with new materials, equipment and systems constantly coming on to the market.

The following are the plumber's tasks on a typical job:

- Installing standpipe for building supply

- Laying first-fix carcassing pipework

- Placing tanks in the roof (where applicable)

- Running any gas pipework to boiler and outlets

- Making up any lead flashings or soakers to the roof

- Fixing guttering and downpipes

- Fixing vent pipes to drainage upstands, then taking them through the roof

- Fixing skirts to vent pipes

- Fitting hot-water cylinder

- Fixing radiators to the wall and connecting

- Laying under-floor central heating pipework

- Connecting under-floor heating loops to the manifold

- Fitting boiler and connecting to system

- Attending to flues and chimney liners

- Connecting boiler to oil or lpg tank (if applicable)

- Fitting sanitaryware

- Connecting sanitaryware to domestic plumbing and wastes

- Plumbing in kitchen and utility sink units, washing machines, dishwashers and so on

- Lagging all exposed pipework

- Firing up boiler and testing system

- Balancing and commissioning system

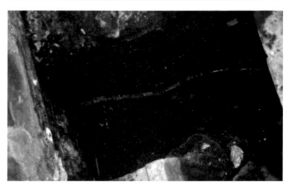

Above: **Finding a water main in the footings means that you will need a plumber on call from the off.**

Below: **Plastic push fit plumbing.**

whoever is managing the site makes sure that they liaise with each other and with the surrounding trades, particularly the electrician.

To a large extent, I have covered many of the available options within the plumbing and central heating trade in Chapter 6, but the table overleaf provides an overview of some of the available options and their pros and cons.

The disciplines of plumbing and central heating have seen more changes over the past few years than any other trade, with new materials, equipment and systems constantly coming on to the market. Many of these are enthusiastically taken up and gain acceptance in the self-build market. However, when making your choices, check that whoever is going to carry out the work for you does understand what you are

Plumbing and heating choices

Boilers	Pros	Cons
Standard	Tried and tested. Cheap to buy.	Relatively inefficient. May not come up to 2006 requirement for 86% efficiency.
Condensing	Up to 97% efficient. Flue gases so cool that plastic pipe can be used.	Relatively expensive. Does produce a white plume when condensing. Needs a drain-off for the mildly acidic condensate.
Combination	No need for water cylinders. Can be conventional or condensing.	May not always be capable of handling high hot-water demand. High-output types have to be floor mounted. Needs mains pressure of at least 1.2 bar.

Fuel source	Pros	Cons
Gas	The most acceptable in the market. Wide variety of boilers to choose from. Few add-on costs. Environmentally, the cleanest of the fossil fuels. Cheapest to run.	
Oil	The acceptable alternative when gas is not available. The next cheapest to run.	Needs an oil storage tank which in many situations needs to be bunded (twin walled). Can be smelly.
Lpg	Indistinguishable from gas in use. Can also be used for cooking	Needs a storage tank. The most expensive fuel choice to run but acceptable in the market.
Electricity	Relatively low capital costs. Brings household fuel requirements into one camp. Dry heat source. Flexible.	Expensive to run (but not as expensive as lpg). Market perception is bad – hard to sell on. Useful for warming up under tiles rather than as the central heating itself.
Solid fuel	Great for those who like stoking fires and using ash in the garden. Good when used as a feature fireplace giving back-up heat or in a wood-burning or multi-fuel stove.	Medieval and not really suited to a modern programmable home. Smelly and dirty. Needs storage facilities.

Heat emitters	Pros	Cons
Radiators	Relatively cheap to install. Efficient with TRVs. Good response times. Useful for drying things on.	Take up wall space.
Under-floor heat	Creates a warm ambience in the home. Makes tiled floors warm. Takes up no wall space. Becoming trendy in the general market.	Slow response times. Greater installation costs. Not suitable for intermittent or occasional occupation. Works best with solid floors.
Warm air	Very fast response time.	Dusty. Noisy. Not good for asthmatics.

System	Pros	Cons
Vented	Understood by the general public.	Needs tanks in the loft. Delivers hot water to the tap at low pressure, especially in bungalows.
Sealed	No need for roof tanks. Delivers hot water at mains pressure. No need for expensive power showers.	May need explaining to a potential purchaser.

trying to achieve and is familiar with the selections you have made. If you're planning to use plastic push-fit-type plumbing and the plumber you had hoped to employ tells you that he's never used it before and doesn't hold with these new-fangled things, then choose a different plumber or change back to copper. It's not your job to become the teacher; if they try to learn on your job it'll cost you in time and money.

The first time most plumbers will call on site to carry out substantive work is once the roof is closed in, at least to the felt and batten stage and 'in the dry', when they will commence what is known as 'first fix' or 'carcassing'.

At the risk of being repetitive, since it is very important, where timber first-floor joists are used, any pipe runs taken through notches in the top of the joists must have the notch no deeper than 0.15 of the joist, positioned in a zone between 0.1 and 0.2 of the span. This has to be done before the decking is laid. If plastic plumbing is used, and this is one of the best things in its favour, then, because it doesn't have to go in straight runs, it need not go through notches in the top of the beams. Instead, it can be drilled though the centre of the joists in exactly the same way as the electrical cables.

'I' beams or engineered timber floor joists have pre-formed holes in the web and the plumber can, therefore, work from below after the decking is laid. Where beam-and-block floors are used, the plumber will not lay the carcassing plumbing on top until the screed or floating floor is about to be laid and may well, therefore, not start carcassing until after the main walls are plastered.

The carcassing effectively concerns all or most of the pipework that will eventually be hidden in the floor zones or behind sheathing in the plasterwork. The plumber will leave upstands for radiators, sanitaryware and sink units.

With a suspended timber floor and decking, the under-floor central heating loops will have to go down before the decking is laid. Under-floor central heating in screeded floors will not usually go down until the plasterer is ready to screed. With a timber floating floor it will not go down until the carpenter is ready to lay it.

First fix for the plumber will also include work to

the vent pipes, together with the making up of any leadwork and flashings to the roof in concert with the roof tiler. If a vented system is being used, then the plumber will fix the tanks in the loft space prior to the ceilings being tacked and will need to liaise with the carpenter for the making up of tank stands. The plumber will often agree to fix the guttering and downpipes before the scaffolding comes down.

Second fix involves fitting the boiler and any hot-water cylinders, fixing the radiators to the walls or connecting the under-floor heating loops to the manifolds. The supply of kitchen units usually includes white goods such as the sink and any wastes, built-in dishwashers and washing machines and the hob and oven. It is the carpenter's job to fit these into the cupboards and the worktops but it is the plumber's job to plumb them in to the domestic hot- and cold-water systems, to join up any wastes and to connect them to the gas. It is also the plumber's job, in concert with the electrician, to plumb in any waste-disposal units or water softeners. The plumber is responsible for fitting the sanitaryware and connecting it to the hot and cold supplies and wastes, and whilst the fitting of purpose-made shower units and bath panels comes within the remit of the plumber, the carpenter may be responsible for boxing out and fitting purpose-made or decorative panels. Finally the plumber will be responsible, in tandem with the electrician, for firing up, testing and commissioning the system.

Plumbers should be qualified. Either OFTEC (Oil Firing Technical Association) members for oil-fired systems or CORGI- (Council for Registered Gas Installers) registered for any work to gas appliances or boilers.

Renovations and conversions

Installing a new kitchen, creating a new bathroom or upgrading existing sanitaryware are important ingredients for the successful renovation. Renewing, replacing or providing central heating and improving the domestic hot- and cold-water systems may well be essential or advisable.

Some older houses may have a direct hot-water cylinder. With this the hot water comes directly from the boiler into the bottom of the cylinder and then is drawn off at the top to the taps with a 'T' to a vent pipe, which discharges into the tank in the loft. Using the primary heating circuit as the source of domestic hot water in this way is obviously not very satisfactory, and means that it is not at all easy to introduce inhibiting agents to counteract limescale and the sludge that can build up in any hot-water system. Most of these cylinders will be fairly old and therefore pretty inefficient. They should be replaced as a matter of course with a modern indirect cylinder.

Most older homes will also have a vented hot-water system. Unless you're going to be ripping out the whole lot and completely re-plumbing, it's best to leave things as they are as it's quite likely that the joints and pipework won't stand up to hot water at mains pressure.

All boilers have a finite life and one of the most important things that a potential renovator should consider is whether or not the existing one is coming to the end and should be replaced. Hammering when the system is running might indicate that the boiler is 'kettling' and that the heat exchanger is wearing thin. Explosive rumbles or bangs when the boiler comes on might indicate that the boiler is allowing too much gas to get into the firing chamber before igniting. You can sometimes get a little extra life out of an old boiler by flushing out the whole system with a chemical restorer and then re-filling with a concentrate silencer and system protector, but in many cases, the best course of action is to change the boiler. In which

case, as I've already discussed in the Chapter 6, the boiler must now conform to the latest stringent requirements for efficiency. If you're installing a completely new system in a property where previously there wasn't one, the space-saving attributes of a combi boiler might well make it an attractive choice.

If gas is available then I guess most renovators and converters would choose this as the fuel option. If not, the next best choice for most will be oil. But don't discount electricity, especially if you're trying to balance capital outlay with resale values. It does suffer from some unpopularity due to perceived high running costs. But they're not as high as, for instance, lpg. And in older properties it is much more acceptable in market terms than it is in newer homes. You don't have to use the usual night storage or convector radiators; a wet system of conventional radiators fired by an electric boiler such as the Trianco 'Aztec Gold' can be used. So it can be the right choice and its low capital installation costs make it attractive in certain situations.

Most homes in the UK employ radiators as the method of delivering the heat to the home, often with the addition of thermostatic radiator valves. These are very efficient and are inherently responsive, but they provide heat in a localised form. For the renovator they represent what the market is expecting and they are undoubtedly the cheapest and most tried form of heat delivery. A drawback in certain renovations can be that getting pipework through walls and between and through joists can cause considerable disruption, which can mean that other ways of heating the home might come into the running.

Under-floor central heating and warm-air ducting are other alternatives but once again, the disruption caused to the structure has to be taken into account. Nevertheless if you are completely gutting a property, or if there are substantial new extensions, either of these forms of heating can be attractive.

Although the plumber working in a renovation or conversion is going to want to earn the same amount per day as they would if they were working in a new home, it's often going to take a lot more time and therefore the simplified equation of 50% labour and 50% materials might get tilted a little towards the labour costs. In a new build it's fairly easy to assess how much time will be taken. But in a renovation

VAT

You will recall that in Chapter 1, I talked about VAT and how those building new homes or converting a property into a dwelling could recover VAT paid out on the job. You will recall with some sadness, I'm sure, that renovators or those building an extension do not have that facility. So why mention this here? Well, most subcontractors are not registered for VAT. But plumbers and electricians, being largely supply-and-fix trades, are quite likely to be. In which case, I'm afraid, the renovator or those having an extension built will be charged VAT but will not be able to recover the VAT that they have to add to their bill.

project there may be carpets and furniture to be moved and it may be necessary to lift boards and fiddle pipework though walls and floors. In a new home a plumber could maybe hang and connect up to seven radiators in a day. Putting just one radiator into an older house or moving one along a wall could take the same amount of time. On the other hand, jobs such as hanging and fitting a new boiler on the wall will take the same time – about a day – in either project. Each situation is going to be different but the principle remains the same – time taken or allowed for the job is converted into the final price.

Electricians

This is one of the major supply-and-fix trades, with the price being arrived at by reference to the cost of the materials plus the cost of the labour to fit them. An electrician will want to earn at least £165 per day in most parts of the UK and, on average, most new homes will involve a total labour input of between eight and ten days. Material costs on a fairly standard job will be just a little bit less or the same as the labour costs. Some tradesmen will add a profit margin. Some, as this is a very competitive trade, will

The following are the electrician's tasks on a typical job:

- Fitting temporary consumer unit to building supply
- Installing and connecting earth rod
- Laying and fixing all carcassing wiring
- Drilling joists where necessary
- Fixing backplates to outlets and controls
- Fixing proprietary sheathing over wires in walls
- Fixing and wiring up faceplates to outlets
- Fixing and wiring up light pendants
- Fitting and wiring up ceiling and wall lights
- Fitting and wiring up all external and security lighting
- Fitting and wiring up extractor fans and cooker hoods
- Cross-bonding and earthing all pipework and sanitary-ware
- Fitting and wiring up consumer unit
- Wiring up thermostats and programmers
- Attending with plumber for firing up and testing boiler and central heating
- Testing system

Left: **Getting the wiring through steel joists can be problematic.**

NHBC minimum standards for electrical service

Room	Power points	Lighting	Remarks
Kitchen/utility room	6	1 per room	If the rooms are separate then the kitchen should have 4 power points with 2 to the utility room and at least 3 free for general use rather than being taken up with appliances. Plus extractor fans to each room.
Dining room	2	1	
Living room	4 1 TV aerial point	1	At least one double outlet should be near the TV aerial outlet
Main bedroom	3	1	
Other bedrooms	2	1	
Hall	1	1	
Landing	1	1	2-way switching to staircase
Bathrooms and toilets	1		Plus extractor fan

simply price on the addition of the two and make their money on the labour and the discounts that are available to them from specialist suppliers.

If a detailed electrical plan has not been formulated, the electrician may quote on the basis of the minimum NHBC standard with itemised prices for extra lights, power points, spurs and switches. This is a very basic specification and most self-builders wouldn't dream of sticking to it. However, it can be very useful in helping you to determine just which tradesman you are eventually going to deal with because it ensures that they are all quoting on a like-for-like basis.

Once you have identified who you would like to engage to carry out the work, you will need to firm up on exactly what you want so that you can obtain a definitive price. Do not be surprised if this comes out at two or even three times the original quotation. This is one trade where it is very easy to go over the top and over-specify. Always, once you have agreed a price, get figures for extra power points or light switches.

Take a plan and devise symbols for each light, power point, switch, spur and wall light. Mark up the plan with your requirements, thinking very carefully about each one, whether you will need it and where in each room it will be in relation to furniture and opening doors. Don't forget things like cupboard lights, loft lights, 5-amp ring mains for table lamps, TV aerial points, telephone points and doors bells. If you want an immersion heater make a note on the plans. Make a note also that you are expecting the electrician to be responsible, working alongside the plumber or heating engineer, for the electrical components involved in the domestic hot water and central heating. If you want the electrician to deal with computer or any other wiring, make this clear. Keep a copy of this plan so that you can refer to it in the future if necessary.

Before the electrician starts on site, walk around, in a quiet period, and mark up the walls with the position of everything you have chosen. It will seem different in real life from how it was on the plans. Close your eyes and imagine the room furnished. You may well find that you wish to change things a little. If you do so at this stage, it won't cost anything. Moving things at a later date will be very expensive.

Around half of the electrician's time is spent on

the first-fix or carcassing stage. This involves drilling the joists and threading the loops of wires, which will eventually become the ring mains and spurs for the lighting and power circuits, taking them down the walls into the back boxes and covering them with sheathing conduit. This may involve cutting out or chasing the walls. Wherever possible wiring should run vertically to or from the outlet. For the ground floor of a house, or a bungalow, the power and switch cables come down from the ceiling. In a house the power cables on the upper floors come up from the floor and the switch wiring comes down from the ceiling.

In most cases the electrician won't come back until after the plasterer has finished. Second-fix concerns fixing and wiring up the faceplates to switches and plugs, fitting and wiring the light pendants, external and security lighting and the wall lights. If you have purchased your own light fittings, the electrician will usually fit these, but don't expect a refund on the unused pendants. This stage also includes wiring up the immersion heater and any extractor fans or cooker hoods. If any special wiring or cabling for things like speakers, intercoms or computers and the like has been included in the price it will be attended to at this time and it is usual for the electrician to supply and fit the TV aerial points and telephone points. The co-ax cable is usually left coiled up in the loft and the telephone wiring is taken to a convenient point for the service suppliers. All pipework, radiators, sanitaryware and sink units must be cross-bonded and earthed and all room thermostats, heating controls and programmers wired up.

The temporary consumer unit will be discarded and the new one wired up. Modern consumer units split the power and lighting into a series of separate circuits. The lighting, central heating and smoke detector circuits are protected by MCBs (miniature circuit breakers) that detect any short circuit and cut off the power. The power circuits are protected by RCDs (residual circuit devices) that detect the slightest earth leakage and cut off the power immediately.

The final stage of the electrician's job is to test each circuit before finally turning on the power. The plumber will want to fire up the boiler and test run the domestic hot water and central heating and the electrician should be in attendance at this time.

As noted in Chapter 9, recent legislation requires that with the exception of the most minor jobs, this trade must now be carried out by a suitably qualified or competent person. This rules out work by the self-builder or even a general builder and you are best advised to use an electrician who is registered with an approved Part 'P' self-certification scheme.

Renovations and conversions

The advice given in Chapter 7 holds good, in that unless the wiring is relatively modern and has been thoroughly tested, consideration should always be given to complete re-wiring. If you are stripping a building right out, putting in new floorboards, ceilings and plaster, then the job of the electrician is really no different from that on a new house. If you're trying to re-wire beneath existing floorboards, however, or to existing positions in lathe and plaster ceilings, then the job is very tricky and time consuming. And for 'time consuming' read expensive. Maybe wires can be pulled through with draw strings. Just as maybe, you'll find that you have to contemplate the removal of certain boards. As an alternative consider surface-mounted wiring run and protected by galvanised metal sheathing. This need not be intrusive, especially if thought is given to hiding it behind curtains, in corners or within plumbing boxing.

Whatever you do (or don't do) to the rest of the electrics, wherever possible you should change the old fuse box to a modern consumer unit with RCD and MCB protection.

Plasterers

Plasterers belong to, perhaps, one of the most sought-after trades. In any one town you might only be able to count the number of plasterers on the fingers of one hand. They are, therefore, expensive, often wanting to earn between £200 and £300 per day per plasterer, plus £100–120 per day for the labourer. Their prices are usually worked out by reference to measured rates but often expressed as a lump sum figure. These days most plasterers work on a labour-only basis. There are supply-and-fix contractors around but they tend to be even more expensive.

The following are the plasterer's jobs on a typical job:

- Tacking ceilings with plasterboard or gypsum fibreboard
- Fixing all beading and lathing
- Floating and setting all masonry walls
- Dry lining walls with plasterboard or gypsum fibreboard
- Taping and jointing plasterboard walls, or skim coating all dry lined walls
- Taping and jointing ceiling boards
- Skim coating or Artexing ceilings
- Fixing mouldings and coving
- Rendering external walls
- Screed floors

Right: **Tacking the ceiling.**

Most plasterers will have their own trestles and spotboards. They will also have their own buckets and drums in which they mix plaster using an electric drill with a large egg whisk attachment. If they need a mixer for render or screed then this is usually supplied by the main contractor or self-builder. But as I said in the section of bricklayers, in all probability the same mixer hired in for them will stay on site for use by other trades and, therefore, it's best to cost it at £30 per week for the duration of the job.

Once the first-floor decking is down and the plumbers and electricians have finished their carcassing or first fix, then the ceilings can be tacked with plasterboard. Sometimes this is done by the plasterer, but increasingly it is done by the carpenters. A reasonable rate for this, on a labour-only basis, is around £3.50 per square metre. One reason why this is often done by the carpenter is the amount and complexity of timber noggins that are required. If

9.5mm plasterboard is used, costing £4.05 per 2,400 x 1,200mm sheet, and the ceiling timber spacing exceeds 400mm, then noggings are needed to all intermediate joints, and at the perimeter. If 12.5mm plasterboard, costing around £4.30 per sheet, is used, then at 600mm timber spacings, intermediate and perimeter noggings are also necessary. This is very time consuming and it might be best to switch to 15mm plasterboard, at a cost of around £6.28 per sheet, where no noggings are required. Fixing is often by nailing (tacking) with galvanised 40mm plasterboard nails at 150mm centres to the joists and noggings. However, a neater and better job can be done using self-loading screw guns with 36mm zinc electroplated or black phosphate screws at 230mm centres. These avoid battered edges and loss of integrity to the plasterboard by careless hammer blows.

Although there is no set pattern, and some tradesmen might prefer to do it first, it is usual for the ceiling finish to be left until after the walls have been plastered. Timber-frame houses are dry lined with the plasterboard tacked to the upright studs and cross noggings over a vapour barrier, once the insulation has been put in place. Internal studwork walls to both timber-frame and masonry-construction houses are also tacked on both sides with plasterboard. Nail fixings should be at 150mm centres but screws can be at 300mm centres The labour cost for this work is usually around £3.25 per square metre. If dry lining is to be used with a masonry form of construction then the usual form of fixing is by plaster dabs at 300mm centres, horizontally and vertically with a continuous ribbon at the perimeter to external walls and openings. Expect to pay a little more at something like £3.70 per square metre on the labour for this job. Dry lining may be carried out by the plasterer but it is often carried out by specialist dry liners who are very quick at what they do.

If the plasterboard is to be finished by taping and jointing then it is often easier to use a tapered edge board. The joint is filled with jointing compound and a paper tape is pressed into it. When the filler has stiffened, more compound is applied and smoothed off at the edges with a trowel or damp sponge. Internal angles are similarly taped but external angles can use a very thin embedded metal bead, with the jointing compound once more smoothed off at the edges. To my mind, however, a better finish is achieved by a 3mm skim coat of plaster to the whole wall, and the labour-only rate for this is around £4.25 per square metre. The finish plaster or Thistle will cost around £3.86 per bag and one bag will cover about 10 square metres.

Masonry walls can be 'hard' plastered directly on to the blockwork. The usual practice is to use a sand and cement render, mixed at one part cement to eight parts plastering sand, perhaps with the addition of lime or a plasticizer, as a 'scratch' coat, finished with plaster. Sometimes it is necessary to 'dub' out the walls with a base coat and then, when that has gone off, apply the scratch coat. Lightweight aggregate blocks have a very high suction and it is necessary to take precautions against the render drying out too quickly. In warm weather the wall should be hosed

Above: **Sand and cement render first coat for hard plaster.**

Below: **Skim coating dry lining.**

down the night before and then sprayed again the following morning. A canny plasterer will then wait for the right moment, when the glisten has gone off, before applying the render. External angles have metal lath and beading embedded in the render.

The topcoat plaster is applied to the render to a minimum thickness of 3mm. If this is done too soon, before the render has gone off, then when and if the render shrinks it will lead to crazing or, at the extreme, failure of the plaster to adhere to the render. If it is left too late, when the render is too dry, then it must be hosed down to prevent the plaster from going off too quickly. If the plastering is to run across two different backgrounds, such as plasterboard and hard-plastered walls, make sure that a proper glass fibre reinforcement tape or scrim is embedded at the junction. Plasterers often plaster nearly down to the floor and then leave a gap, which they presume will be masked by the skirting. All too often this gap is too high or the plaster gobs create an uneven surface for the skirtings to fix to. An alternative is to either insist on the plaster going right to the floor or else to fix a batten at the bottom to which the plaster is run. This can then be removed or better still, if it is fixed firmly and flush with the wall finish, used to screw the skirtings to. Floating and setting a wall on a labour-only basis is usually about £7.50 per square metre. One tonne of sand, costing around £32 per tonne, will cover around 72 square metres of wall and require between seven and ten bags of cement at £2.79 each plus around £30 worth of additives, beadings and bits and pieces. Thistle will cost around £3.86 per bag and each bag will cover around 10 square metres.

Ceilings to be Artexed are paper-taped at the joints before the Artex is applied from the floor and finished in the required pattern. Any decorative mouldings or coving are fixed beforehand. Costs vary but are usually between £3.00 and £4.50 per square metre on a supply-and-fix basis. Ceilings to be 'set' or plastered are taped at the joints with a fabric scrim tape and plastered, as with the walls, usually from a board scaffold. Mouldings and coving are put up afterwards. If no coving is wanted, make sure that the joint between wall and ceiling is reinforced with scrim tape. Labour-only costs work out at about £4.50 per square metre.

If a solid screed floor is utilised then this does not go down until the walls and ceilings are finished and all pipework and under-floor central heating has been laid and filled to avoid damage. Floors to be screeded usually use a sand cement mix (one part cement to three parts sharp sand) laid to a minimum thickness of 65mm over insulation and damp-proof membrane, or 50mm where it is bonded to the oversite. Floors in garages must have metal reinforcement mesh within them. Screed mixes can be bought in ready mixed for consistency and, if the area to be screeded is large, make sure that there are expansion joints at either the perimeter or within doorways, especially if used with under-floor central heating. Screed is laid working out from the room and should not be walked on directly until it has gone off after two days. The labour charge will obviously depend on the thickness but should be between £6.30 and £7.30 per square metre. A 1-tonne bag of sand should cover 14 square metres of floor but will require 14 bags of cement for each tonne.

External rendering is also within the remit of the plasterer. The usual method is to utilise a two-, sometimes three-coat, sand and cement render. The base coat for solid concrete blocks is normally mixed one part cement to four parts plastering sand, perhaps with the addition of lime or a plasticizer and applied to a thickness of 10mm. External angles receive an embedded metal lath and bead, and where the render comes down to a plinth or the head of a window, a metal stop bead or bellmouth lath is embedded. The base coat is scratched to receive a topcoat, mixed one part cement to six parts sand, usually with the addition of a retarder and waterproofer, applied to a thickness of about 6mm. Labour rates for external render should be between £9 and £11 per square metre. Timber frames might need to be battened out to provide a minimum 25mm gap and wired with expanded metal lathing or proprietary insulated laths to receive the base coat, after which the topcoat is the same as for masonry. If a smooth finish is required this final coat is rubbed over with a wooden float. If a pebbledash finish is required, the topcoat is thickened and then pebbles are 'dashed' into the wet render and pushed home with a trowel. For a 'Tyrolean' finish, a mixture of render and stones is dashed on to a dry, unscratched undercoat render.

Mention should be made of alternative products. Plasterboard comes in many guises and can include thermal insulation board in various thicknesses as well as vapour check board. Gypsum fibreboard, of which the best known is Fermacel, is much stronger than ordinary plasterboard and can be fixed up and finished with proprietary jointing compounds to replace plasterboard altogether and give better sound insulation. Single-coat plasters are available. Carlite refers to a range of plasters for use with various substrates. 'Browning' is used for average suction situations such as blockwork, 'tough-coat' is used on expanded metal lathing, and 'bonding' is used for low-suction applications such as engineering bricks and solid concrete blocks. One bag will cover between 3.5 and 4 square metres at 12mm thickness. Plaster of Paris is used for decorative mouldings.

Renovations and conversions

I've already talked about the need to use lime plasters and renders with older solid-walled buildings where the walls need to breathe. Working with these materials is a skill on its own. Hydrating lime creates an almost explosive heat and the material is caustic to the skin. Not all tradesmen are prepared to work with it. Almost all modern plasterers habitually add lime to a sand and cement render. But the lime they use is pre-slaked hydraulic lime, which lends smoothness to the mixture. It is not the same and you need to be careful that when somebody tells you that they are used to working with lime mortars or renders, they are actually talking about traditional materials.

Your tradesmen don't have to work with raw lime. Lime putty and sand are available in ready-mixed 20-litre tubs, either fine (for internal plasterwork) or coarse (for mortars or external renders). Animal hair – usually goats' – is also available for mixing with the render to give it strength.

Walls and ceilings may be plastered on lathes. These are split willow or chestnut nailed to the joists or studs with the render or plaster forced between them and then smoothed over to give the internal finish. The 'key', which holds the render in place, is the gob of plaster that swells out behind the lathe. If the lathes get wet and rot, then the ceiling or wall

finish will come away. Obviously before any renovation of the surface is planned the root cause of the damp must be addressed. Once that is done many renovators or converters will decide that it is better to remove the existing lathe and plaster and replace it with plasterboard. Others will want to retain the original. This is perfectly viable.

New lathes can be purchased. Repairs can be effected by screwing the sagging plasterwork back to the walls or ceiling using plate washers etched into the plaster. Alternatively ceilings can be left with their 'acquired character' and stabilised by the addition of hessian sheeting and plaster of Paris, either draped over the joists or fixed to battens screwed to the sides. Holes can be filled in walls or ceilings using plaster together with chicken wire or hessian.

If you choose to retain the original look and materials then try to impress on the plasterer that a modern absolutely glass-smooth finish might not be appropriate. If you decide to replace with plasterboard, then by all means go for a perfect surface. If you're using plasterboard on solid walls then use a foil-backed type and fix it either with a batten to create a cavity or with dabs that hold it away from the wall to allow it to breathe. But don't apply it to walls that are persistently damp. Cure that problem first; don't just try to hide it.

Decorators and ceramic tilers

Although this is the 'Cinderella' trade and the operatives doing it are paid a lot less money per day than any of the other tradesmen, it is one of the most important. It is the decorator's job to 'snag' or make good the walls and timber from the preceding trades. If the carpenter makes a bad job of joining up the architrave or if there is a gap between the skirting and the wall then it is the decorator's job to fill it. If the electricians and plumbers leave untidy holes in the walling it is the decorator's job to make good.

The trade is almost always labour only with either a lump sum quoted for the job or, occasionally, a daywork rate agreed. In most parts a painter and decorator can be employed for as little as £65 per day with 14 days on average being required for most standard homes. It is usual for the decorator to supply

The following are the decorator's tasks on a typical job:

- Snagging and rubbing down all walls

- Filling all holes

- Rubbing down and filling all joinery

- Knotting all timber to be painted

- Priming or undercoating all internal and external joinery and second-fix timber

- Gloss coating or staining all internal and external joinery

- Painting all walls with one mist coat and, usually, one topcoat

- Painting all ceilings with two-coat emulsion

- Painting all external render with two coats proprietary finish

their own brushes but they will expect you to supply the paints and stains plus fillers, sand papers, cleaning materials and solvents. On the average house these can add up to around £350 but if special colours or textures are required or if brand names are insisted upon, these costs can rise quite dramatically. If ladders or scaffolding are required then they are usually provided by the client.

It is not the decorator's job to tidy up and clean the house out. Yet if they attempt to carry out work in a house where there are piles of rubbish or where other trades are still working, clearly their work will suffer. It is no good just sweeping things to the middle of the floor; it will only walk or blow back. Each room should be cleaned out and dusted by the main contractor or cleaners, often in the guise of the self-builder, before any work is started.

Preparation is two thirds of the decorator's job.

Below and both right: **Good decoration is the key to a properly finished home as it truly sets off all the other trades.** © Potton

Rubbing down and filling walls, knotting, priming, sanding and filling timber all need to be done before any paint is applied. If paint is applied to badly prepared surfaces no amount of careful work with brush or roller will make up for the deficiency. Knotting, which seals and prevents the natural oils from coming out of the wood, is particularly important where timber is to be painted. Timber skirtings, architraves and mouldings should also be painted, primed or stained on the backside before fixing.

Care needs to be taken where different substrates adjoin. At the meeting of the plasterboard ceiling and the plastered walls, unless you're coving, it is better to use a flexible caulk rather than a filler, which may be liable to crack at a later date. Where timber is planted on to plasterwork, the joint should either be masked by an architrave or filled with a flexible sealant.

All external timber joinery should be primed or stained on what will be the hidden sides, before fixing, and then given at least one coat to the visible surfaces as soon as possible. External timber to be painted should be dry and it may be necessary to wait for the right weather for finishing coats. The use of microporous or breathing paints and stains is strongly recommended.

Internal walls to be painted usually receive one watered down or 'mist' coat plus a topcoat for dry lining with an additional coat for hard-plastered walls. Set ceilings are usually two-coat painted with a roller, whilst Artex ceilings are usually painted with a brush. It is important to wait until the surfaces have dried out naturally before decorating commences. Any attempt to speed up the drying out process will result in cracking.

External render is usually painted with an emulsion-based paint and will obviously have to await good weather. However, these paints are usually fairly quick drying.

The ceramic tiler

The trade of the ceramic tiler falls neatly into walls and floors. It is usually quoted on a labour-only basis with the client providing all tiles, adhesives, grouts, trimmings and spacers. The labour price will most often be quoted at a meterage rate of around £14 for

The following are the ceramic tiler's tasks on a typical job:

- Laying all floor tiles with the correct adhesive
- Grouting all tiles
- Fixing all wall tiles using spacers
- Grouting all wall tiles

walls and £15 for floors but may occasionally be converted to a lump sum price. Tiles can cost as little as £5 or as much as £100 per square metre. In my own house the kitchen wall tiles cost £29 per square metre, but only 4–5 metres are needed on the average kitchen, so you can push the boat out here. The floor tiles cost around £16 per square metre and the wall tiles in the bathrooms cost £6 per square metre. These last tiles were then cheered up with relatively expensive dado tiles.

The setting out of floor tiles is important. Contrary to what you might think, it is not normally correct to start along one wall. Instead, a single room is usually centred by measuring halfway along each wall and then drawing these points to a cross in the centre from which the tiling commences. This ensures that the spacing of cut tiles around the edges of the room is even and compensates for any lack of square in the room. If more than one room is to be tiled then the line of sight through any openings, centred on each of the rooms, is the starting point. If a kitchen is to be tiled and the tiles are not to run under the units, then the room is centred as if the front face of the units is the edge of the room. Tiles laid on a timber floor must be fixed using a flexible adhesive and grout. Those laid on a cement screed or oversite may be fixed with a cementatious adhesive. However, where the screed is new, laid over insulation or with under-floor central heating, it is advisable to use the more expensive flexible adhesive to prevent movement in the floor from cracking the tiles.

Wall tiling never starts from a corner or the foot of the wall either. Instead a batten should be fixed to the wall at less than one tile's height from the floor and the tiling started from this. The cuts, which go below this line when it is removed, therefore take up any unevenness in the floor. The vertical line up of the wall tiles is started from a plumb line in either the centre of the wall or the centre of any window or opening in the wall. This compensates for any lack of plumb or square in the walling and, at the reveal, leaves equal-sized cuts down each side. It is important to use spacers when fixing wall tiles.

Grouting for both wall and floor tiles should be the correct mixture for the type of tile. It should be pushed home thoroughly using a rubber float and ironed smooth by finger or a damp cloth. Once set, the tiles should be wiped over several times with a clean, damp cloth. Certain floor tiles and stone slabs may need feeding and sealing with proprietary compounds.

Renovations and conversions

The decorator's tasks and required skills for older buildings are pretty much the same as for a new build, save that there may be an element of having to strip off old paintwork. This can be done by burning and scraping but is often best achieved with a chemical stripper. There are companies who specialise in analysing paint samples and providing the correct compound for its safe removal. If you've gone to all the trouble of making sure that the renders and plasters are of a breathable lime mix, then it makes no sense to stop that all up with impervious modern paints. Investigate limewashes, which are available in many beautiful natural colours.

Flooring that is to be re-stained should always be sanded down by machine beforehand. It is a dirty and dusty job but if you want the proper results it is well worthwhile.

Wallpaper is more likely to be encountered on older houses. Its removal can cause problems, and indeed can damage the substrate if it is not carried out correctly. Modern steam removers may work but in the end most removals come down to elbow grease and plenty of warm soapy water. Vinyl wallpaper is hellishly difficult to remove down to the plaster as the top surface peels off, leaving the backing paper firmly fixed to the wall. However, if this is sound, you can often paper over it or, if it is only slightly tatty, consider lining the wall with lining paper before decorating.

Golden rules for engaging and working with builders and subcontractors

- Always take up references or talk to previous clients.

- Wherever possible go by recommendation.

- Check that memberships of organisations or trade bodies are current.

- Get as many quotes as you can – but don't miss the chap you really want.

- Don't push too hard to get them to work for you – if they don't seem interested, then they're not. They probably won't do a good job and you should move on to someone else.

- Wherever possible insist on a warranty or insurance-backed guarantee.

- Don't become the teacher – if they don't understand what you're trying to achieve, move on to the next tradesman.

- Make sure all site insurances are in place.

- Tie up contracts as much as possible or feasible, either by using standard forms of contract or by confirmation in writing with reference to plans and specification.

- Negotiate prices for extras before they are enacted.

- Don't be afraid to put your own interests first.

Above and right: **Both of these very different kitchens employ the idea of having an eating area.** ©Potton above D&M right

Many older homes have encaustic or geometric quarry tiles on the floors. Many will want to retain these and if you scout around your local architectural salvage yard, you may well find replacements if necessary. If you need to clean the tiles off or if they have been splashed or stained with mortar try a mild acid solution such as that used to clean up brickwork. Test it first on a small patch or a loose tile, though, to make sure it doesn't damage the surface, and wash the tiles off thoroughly afterwards.

Walls to older buildings might not be true enough for wall tiles and their use can exaggerate imperfections that would otherwise just lend character. In these cases, consider more traditional panelling or limited use of tiled splashbacks. Another alternative, but one that definitely makes the room more modern and might, therefore, not always be appropriate, is to use one of the waterproof wallboards, which come in various finishes and colours.

Building Control and warranty inspections

I've already mentioned these in previous chapters but it does bear repetition here just to remind you that the Building Inspectors and the inspectors from whichever warranty company you've chosen to use will need adequate notice that you have reached the various stages in the build. If there are cards then someone needs to be responsible for them being sent in and you need to make sure that no work is progressed further than any satisfactory inspection. Remember, these inspectors, and especially the Building Inspectors, can be very good friends or very bad enemies. On all my sites I prefer to think of them being on my side, helping me to get the best out of the builders or subcontractors and making sure that my new home is sound and trouble free.

Deliveries

Many people combine building their own home with holding down a nine-to-five job. Deliveries of materials such as blocks and bricks are often quoted by the day, with no particular time of arrival specified. The common solution to this problem, when it's known that the site will be empty, is to leave instructions posted on a board. But boards can blow over, children can remove them and the lorry could arrive at an unearthly hour of the morning. Whilst not directly accusing lorry drivers of insensitivity, I have known them to just put materials down at what seems to be the most convenient place for them, with no thought being given to the fact that they might be blocking off the site entirely. I have even known of loads of bricks and blocks simply being left on the pavement or highway and can recall many an evening when I had to frantically remove vast piles of materials before my prospective neighbours lost all remaining

patience with me and my undertaking.

Wherever possible, either arrange to be on site yourself, or, if necessary, pay someone to be there on your behalf – preferably a tradesman who can be getting on with something whilst they wait.

Site foremen

The idea of employing someone to specifically look after and manage a site on a day-to-day basis is a very attractive one but it's more often thought of than actually executed. Nevertheless, from time to time one does come across a self-builder who has engaged a site manager or working foreman for the day-to-day supervision. Invariably this is a retired professional, and I am told that they usually welcome the job to liven up an otherwise dull retirement. This has always seemed a very sensible thing to do, and if you find the right man who has spent a lifetime working for a builder or developer, he should be able to save you enough to cover the cost of employing him, particularly if he is paid on an informal basis.

Do be careful to pick the right person for this job and beware the 'white coat' syndrome. If you've found someone who's retired from the building industry then all should be well, but if it's someone who used to be a factory foreman, where everyone clocked on and off, then you could find yourself with an empty site.

Some of the package-deal companies operate schemes whereby they introduce you to builders who either undertake the construction as builders or 'project manage' your new home. In effect they look out for and engage the various tradesmen and purchase their materials, whilst you pay the bills plus an agreed fee for this service. Be slightly careful of the situation where the representative of the company is then prepared, for an extra fee, to become your project manager. There could be, and usually is, a conflict of interest here. If there's a problem with the delivery or with the proper manufacture and erection of the package, whose side is he going to be on? Yours, you might think, as you are paying him a not inconsiderable sum. Wrong! Almost certainly he'll side, in fact if not by admission, with the people who'll be supplying him with all of his future work.

Health and safety

There are various statutory requirements for those who run building sites, most of which are studiously ignored by self-builders and subcontractors alike. Provision of latrine facilities, a hut for meals, protective clothing, a first-aid box and an accident register are required by the factories inspector, who is extremely unlikely to visit your site. However, the provisions and requirements still stand and, particularly if you are employing more than five people on your site at any one time, you could find yourself running foul of what is essentially criminal rather than civil law. The Management of Health and Safety at Work Regulations 1992 apply to everyone at work, regardless of the type of work, and they require that adequate risk assessments take place regarding every aspect of work. Employers and the self-employed must identify any hazards involved with their work, the likelihood of any harm arising and the precautions that they feel are necessary. In particular the self-employed must safeguard, so far as is reasonably practicable, their own health and safety and that of other workers or members of the public. There are various methods and suggestions contained in the regulations, which can be obtained from the Health

Site safety is just as important an aspect of site management as any other, and a well-managed and tidy site is often the one with the best safety record.

and Safety Executive (HSE), but they all really boil down to a commonsense attitude to safety at work.

One thing that is glaringly absent on most self-build sites is the wearing of hard hats. Keep a few handy in your site hut and insist that all workers on site wear them. Chances are that whenever your back is turned or you're away from site, they still won't wear them, but at the very least, when a tile falls off the top lift of the scaffold, if the man whose head it enters isn't wearing one, it'll be down to him. More importantly, if your instructions regarding wearing the hats are backed up in writing or by a notice, prominently displayed in the site hut, your insurance won't be invalidated.

The building industry has a worse safety record than coal mining. Consider what will happen if you are injured and cannot deal with the work on your self-build site. Add to this the fact that amateurs are always more likely to be injured in any situation than professionals. Perhaps this will convince you that positive safety procedures should be part of your project planning.

Employees whose misfortunes are covered by the 'employer's liability' section of the insurance are defined as:

- direct employees
- labour-only subcontractors, whether working directly for you or working for someone to whom you have given a subcontract
- persons hired or borrowed from another employer.

This does not include members of your family who are working for you without any charge for their services, nor does it include friends who are giving you a hand. It is a nice legal point that it does not include other self-builders who are helping you in exchange for you helping them on their own job. However, these others who may be hurt on the site are covered under the public liability section of your policy, and this includes those who are on the site in connection with some sort of business arrangement made with you (the architect making a routine inspection), those invited to the site by you (your friends and family) and trespassers on your site (the child who climbs your scaffolding whilst you are not there).

If you have children you should think very carefully about the extent to which you are going to let them visit the site. Having your kids help by clearing rubbish is happy family togetherness, and a good thing. The moment one of them is hurt it becomes an irresponsible disregard of safety legislation. There is no doubt at all about this. In law they should not be there. New European safety legislation emphasises this. Unfortunately, in most family situations your children are likely to become involved with what you are doing, so you will have to make your own careful decisions, decide what the rules are going to be and see that everyone sticks to them. If you are living on the site in a caravan you should fence off the caravan and family area from the building site. Remember that besides more obvious hazards, children are at risk from toxic materials on a building site. The worst of these, and certainly the one that gives most trouble, is cement. Cement dust, mixed concrete and wet mortar are very corrosive and lead to concrete burns.

As far as you are personally concerned, a self-build site insurance policy gives you no help at all if you are injured. For this you have to take out personal accident, death and permanent injury insurances if you do not already have this cover in some other way.

Valuable as these insurances are, they should not encourage you to ignore commonsense precautions. Not only is the food in a hospital unlikely to be up to the standard that you normally enjoy, but your inability to manage the job whilst you are recovering from your injuries is going to be very expensive, and this loss is not covered by any sort of insurance. Most of the precautions you should take are commonsense matters but please do take serious note of all of this and use the checklist 'Self-build site safety' on pages 382–3. Site safety is just as important an aspect of site management as any other, and a well-managed and tidy site is often the one with the best safety record.

Scaffolding needs careful thought. It is possible to hire scaffold for erection on site and indeed there may be instances where, at the end of the job, it's necessary to hire in something like a tower scaffold for a particular task. I do not believe, however, that it's a good idea for the self-builder to attempt to provide a full scaffold for on-site erection by either himself or one of the other tradesmen. Bricklayers will often volunteer to erect the scaffold as they go and, in the past, I have to admit that this is what I have often done. But in today's climate of awareness about health and safety in general, and the new legislation in particular, I really believe that this is not good practice. Bricklayers may well erect a scaffold that gets them

through their trade but may not really care about how the tiler is going to get on or how the plumber will get to do his flashings around the chimney, knowing that by the time those chaps are up on it, they'll be long gone. And if the scaffolding's dangerous or illegal and one of your tradesmen or a member of your family falls off or through it, I'll give you one guess who's going to be liable. Yes, it's you.

Reputable hire-and-erect scaffolding firms who will come along to site and erect a proper and legal scaffold are the answer. Most of them are fairly reliable and will usually come with just 24 hours' notice to raise, lower or extend the scaffold, working in with the other tradesmen as they go. To cover yourself even further, make sure that when you engage a company you state, in writing, that their scaffold should conform to all of the Health and Safety legislation and to best practice. Hire is usually quoted for a minimum period, often ten weeks, with a weekly rate thereafter, and it is normally quoted by reference to the plans. Foot scaffolds, for uneven ground or, board scaffolds, for internal plastering of ceilings etc., are not usually included, and if you need these then you'll have to ask for a separate price.

One thing that you should especially watch out for is the treatment of the scaffolding by other tradesmen:

- Do not ever let them alter the scaffold by themselves, for that could invalidate any liabilities of the main hire-and-erection company and any warranties they will have given you.
- Keep an eye out for tradesmen cutting up scaffold boards or using the angle grinder you've hired in for another job to cut off the end of a putlock. It's you who will be charged for these at the end of the job, as indeed you will for the pile of fittings and clips that gets buried, simply because nobody bothered to move them.

Finally, electrical tools should always be connected through an RCD contact breaker. The hire companies have suitable plug-in units available, but they do not provide them unless you ask for them because most hirers plan to do jobs at houses that have contact breakers in the fuse box. If your temporary site supply is not RCD protected, hire a plug-in unit.

Self-build site safety

● Get into the habit of wearing a hard hat on site. Make sure that there are spare hats in the site hut and a notice on the wall stating that they should be worn at all times. When accepting quotations from subcontractors, slip a little paragraph in about expecting them to wear theirs on site.

● Wear protective footwear. Wellies and boots with steel toecaps are readily available – look under 'Safety' in Yellow Pages.

● Buy two or three pairs of plastic goggles and always use them when cutting or grinding tools etc. Encourage others on site to wear them when appropriate by hanging the spare sets up, next to the hard hats, with a suitable notice.

● Use specialist and bona fide scaffolding contractors only and make sure that when you accept their quotation, you confirm that the scaffold is to be erected and maintained in accordance with Health and Safety legislation and by reference to best possible practice. If scaffold boards are, quite rightly, turned back at night by the bricklayers, make sure that they are properly replaced each day and that no 'traps' are formed by the boards failing to run to a putlock.

● With conventional scaffolding the short lengths of scaffolding that carry the boards are called putlocks. They project beyond the scaffolding at lead level and building professionals know that they are there, almost by instinct. Self-builders, however, bump into them on a regular basis. Tape some empty plastic bottles over the ends – it looks funny but is very effective.

● Whenever you hire equipment from a hire firm, ask if instruction leaflets and safety manuals are available. You may feel rather self-conscious about doing this but most hire firms will welcome your enquiry and will probably be pleased to give you the benefit of their experience. They will all have stories of the wife returning the tool that put the husband in hospital.

● Keep petrol for mixers in a locked hut, preferably in the type of can that is approved for carrying petrol in the boot of a motor car. Do not let anyone smoke in the hut where you keep the petrol. Better still use diesel equipment.

● Professional electric power tools from a plant-hire company will normally be 110 volts and equipped with the appropriate safety cut-outs etc. If you are using 230-volt DIY power tools or any other 230-volt equipment, including lighting, take the supply through an RCD contact breaker.

● If trenches for services or your foundation trenches are more than a metre deep, treat them with respect, and go by the book with shoring. If they show any tendency to collapse, deal with them from above, in company with another person. Never work in a deep trench alone.

● Packs of bricks and blocks that are crane off-loaded, with or without pallets, must always be stacked on stable ground and never piled more than two high. Take great care when cutting the bands and re-stack them by hand if packs are in any way unstable. Stop children from climbing on them and sheet them up if at all possible.

● Concrete burns are a self-build speciality. Bad ones can leave the bone visible and require skin grafts. Never handle concrete or mortar with your bare hands and in particular, do not let it get down your wellies or in your shoes. If it does, then wash out the offending footwear or clothing immediately. Remember, cement burns do not hurt until after the damage is done. If you get cement dust in your eyes, flood your face with water immediately. Do not let children or animals play with or walk through wet concrete.

● Do not get involved with work on roofs unless you are used to and confident with heights. Do not take risks and never go on to a roof without the appropriate scaffolding.

● Self-builders regularly fall down stairwells. If they do not then their visitors do. Use rough timber to form a temporary balustrade until you fix the real one.

● Do not use old-fashioned wooden ladders. Always tie the ladder on at the top and if there is any danger of the feet slipping, fix a cross board at the bottom.

● Be obsessive about clearing away loose boards or noggings with a nail sticking out of them; and, in case you miss one, never wear thin-soled shoes on site.

● Put together a first-aid kit containing plasters and antiseptic and fasten it on to the site hut wall. You will suffer your fair share of cuts and abrasions and a poisoned finger is a nuisance.

● Watch your back when unloading heavy items or if you are handling more weight that you are used to. This also applies to digging work. The risk of straining yourself is very real. The most scrawny-looking professional builders can handle heavy weights without any risk of injury. If you try doing so, you could put yourself out of action for a week or more.

● Watch out for machinery moving about on site and be aware that the driver might not be able to see everything behind.

● Always be careful when walking on joists. Many inexperienced people fall through these either because they are considerably less skilful at balancing than they supposed or because the joists weren't fixed. Use scaffold boards laid across the joists and make sure that the joists are either built in firmly or held in place by battening, nailed across and to each one.

● Cover up old or new drainage manholes and pay particular attention to the backfilling or covering over of disused septic tanks and the like. If dumpers or other site vehicles are likely to go near these, then hire a metal plate rather than trusting to a sheet of ply.

Project planners

The successful management of any building project relies on the ability to anticipate requirements for both labour and materials. In order to do that it is essential that you make yourself aware of the sequences involved. What follows are two schedules for the main methods of building: brick and block (masonry) and timber frame (brick and timber). They span the same time frame; events on site might alter this but the general progression of events will remain the same.

Project Planner for **traditional masonry construction**

	6 Weeks Before Start on-site Preliminaries 1–2 days	Week 1 Clear and Set Out Site 1–2 days	Week 1 Strip Topsoil and Dig Foundations 2–3 day	Week 2 Pour Concrete Foundations 1 day	Week 2 Build Up to Damp-proof Course level 2–4 days	Week 2 Construct Oversite 2–4 days	
Project Management/ Self-builder's Tasks	Obtain quotations from service suppliers. Arrange a water supply. This can take up to six weeks unless you can make an arrangement with a neighbour. Arrange a temporary electricity supply. Provide site WC facilities and storage. Arrange site insurance and warranty. Line up groundworkers and notify all trades of expected schedule.	Send in commencement of work card to Building Inspector and advise warranty inspectors that you are starting on site. Provide first-aid kit, accident book, hard hats and goggles. If setting out is being done by a surveyor rather than the groundworkers you will need to pre-book them.	If you are sending soil away you will have to identify where it is going and at what cost. You will also need to establish turnaround times and, if necessary, arrange for more than one tipper lorry. When foundations are dug, notify Building and warranty inspectors to inspect trenches.	Ready-mixed concrete suppliers will have to be notified and often paid in advance. Decide how you are going to place the concrete. If you are pumping you will need to organise the pump and notify the concrete suppliers of your intention. Once poured, arrange for building and warranty inspection.	Building the foundations can be done by the groundworkers but the bricklayers often make a better job of it. On completion arrange for Building and warranty inspectors to check damp-proof course. Pick up meter boxes and ducting from gas and electricity suppliers.	This can be carried out by either the groundworkers or the bricklayers. If the floor beams are long and heavy or access to the oversite is difficult you might need to organise the hire of a crane or use a telescopic lift. On completion, arrange for the Building and warranty inspectors to inspect oversite.	
Trade, Materials and Tools Needed on Site	Check lead-in times for long delivery items and place advance orders.	Groundworkers: digger and dumper. Timber stakes and batten for the profile boards together with string lines. A level (Cowley, Laser or similar). A bag of lime for marking out.	Groundworkers: digger, dumper, tipper lorries. Level. Pump. Level pegs.	Groundworkers: wheelbarrows. Scaffold boards. Concrete pump (optional). Concrete. Steel reinforcement bars or cages, clayboard and slip membranes if required. Leave access openings for services.	Bricklayers: foundation blocks, wall ties, plasticiser, sand and cement. Drainage/service exit lintels. Cranked ventilators, mixer, spotboards, foot scaffold for bad or sloping ground. All in ballast or cement. Damp-proof course.	Bricklayers: floor beams. Coursing bricks, infill blocks. Sand and cement. Damp-proof course. Groundworkers: NB drainage pipe and pea gravel.	
Groundworks/ Landscaping	Fence off and secure the site around its boundaries. Secure any trees that must be protected. Possibly plant hedgerows and other boundaries.	Create temporary site access. Clear site of any existing debris. Strip topsoil and stack for reuse later. Set out building. Secure site with lockable gates.	Excavate foundation trenches (and service trenches, if practical) to satisfaction of Building and warranty inspectors.	Oversee pour of concrete. Tamp and level concrete. Position clayboards, membranes or reinforcement as directed by engineer or building surveyor.		Position internal drainage pipes through foundation walls and oversite.	
Bricklaying					Build foundation blockwork. Fill cavities level with outside ground level. Install cranked ventilators. Lay damp-proof course.	Position floor beams to ground floor, infill with blocks and brush grout.	
Carpentry							
Roof Tiling and Leadwork							
Glazing							
Plumbing	Lay in temporary water supply using minimum 22mm blue plastic piping and fix standpipe. Above-ground pipework must be insulated to prevent freezing.						
Electrics	Fix lockable meter box for temporary electricity supply to site.						
Plastering and Artexing							
Decorating and Ceramic Tiling							

NOTES: Project planner checklist for a two-storey house constructed in brick and block with a beam-and-block ground and first floor, gable roof with one valley and clipped verges. Labour-only subcontractors with the exception of plumbers, electricians and plasterers which are supply-and-fix trades. All general/personal tools supplied by labour. Materials and plant provided by the project manager (this might be a builder or the self-builder managing their own project).

Part one: weeks 1–13

Weeks 3–5 **Build Up to First -Floor Structure** 7–14 days	Week 5 **Build First-Floor Structure** 1–2 days	Weeks 6–7 **Build Structure to Wall Plate** 7–14 days	Week 7 **Build Up Gables and Chimneys** 3–5 days	Weeks 8–9 **Complete Roof Structure** 4–7 days	Weeks 9–11 **Felt, Batten and Tile Roof** 5–10 days	Weeks 11–12 **Fix Rainwater Goods; Glaze** 5–10 days
Hire-and-erect scaffolding to be called in for progressive lifts up to and including roof and gables. Check what notice is required for each new lift. The scaffolding will need to stay up until after roof tiling in order for the plumber, glazier and decorator to work off it.	There is no definite trade responsible for this. The bricklayers may well agree to do it or else the groundworkers will have to come back. For a timber first floor the bricklayer may position floor joists or it may be left to the carpenter.	If using a building warranty arrange for the warranty inspector to inspect up to plate height.	Decide who is to be responsible for leadwork. This is traditionally the plumber but may now be a lead specialist.	If using a building warranty arrange for warranty inspector to inspect roof. Arrange for plumber to install any large tanks in the attic before the trusses are finally spaced (whilst there is still access space).	This may be a supply-and-fix trade. Alternatively specialist suppliers will quantify a quote for all roofing materials.	Start to choose second-fix items such as internal doors that may be on long delivery lead-in times. Place kitchen units on order and any other special joinery items.
Bricklayers: bricks, blocks, wall ties, wall insulation, door and window frames, cavity closers and fixings. Lintels, fireplace lintels, starter block and flue liners. Meter boxes. Sand and cement.	Bricklayers: floor beams, infill blocks, sand and cement. Plasterboard. Batten Clips. Coursing bricks. Plant: this usually requires a crane on site.	Bricklayers: bricks, blocks, wall ties, lintels, wall insulation, window frames, cavity closers and fixings. Carpenter: wallplate and straps.	Carpenter: roof trusses. Truss clips. Battening. Bricklayers: bricks including any special bricks, blocks, sand and cement. Flue liners, chimney pots, bricks including any specials, lead tray.	Carpenter: balance of roof trusses and pre-fabricated roof including and valley lay boards. Nails, bolts, truss clips and gable straps. Fibreglass valleys or lead laid *in situ* unless valley is to be tiled. Plumber: roof tanks.	Roofers: felt, batten roof tiles, roof and eaves vents, undercloaking, nails and fixings. Coloured mortar if required. Plumber: lead, vent pipes, including lead skirts. Bricklayer: sand and cement.	Glazier: glazing units and ancillary glazing materials. Decorator: decoration materials. Plumber: rainwater goods. Plasterers: sand, cement, lime for render.
Build superstructure to first-floor level.	Position first-floor concrete beams, infill blocks and brush grout. Fix batten clips for ceilings.	Build superstructure to wallplate. Bricklayer to bed wallplate.	Build and cut up gable ends. Build chimney through roof.		Point in flashings to chimney and install any cover or stepped flashings.	
	If a timber first floor is being used the joists may be cut and fitted by the carpenter.	Carpenter to scarf wallplate. Tie down with wallplate straps.	Raise end trusses as templates for gable end brickwork and blockwork.	Carpenters to fix remaining trusses and finish roof, including fascias and soffits. Cut in dormer windows or roof lights. Build timber porch and any other structures, e.g. bay window roofs.		
					Felt, batten and tile roof. Bed ridge, point verges and valleys. Fix flashings around chimney, abutting walls, dormers etc.	
						Glaziers to glaze all windows and doors.
			Provide lead trays for bricklayers to build in.	Place tanks in loft. Fix soil vent pipes.	Position vent pipe skirts. Make up lead flashings and skirts.	Plumbers to fix guttering and downpipes.
						Undertake any external rendering.
					Decorators to paint/finish fascias and soffits.	Paint rainwater goods if necessary and complete external decoration before scaffold comes down.

Project Planner for **traditional masonry construction**

	Weeks 12–14 First-fix Carpentry 10–15 days	Weeks 13–14 First-fix Plumbing and Electrics 5–10 days	Week 14 Connect Drains 5 days	Week 14 Backfill Drains and Complete Access 5 days	Weeks 14–15 Tack Ceilings and Lay Floors 5 days	Weeks 15–16 Plaster Out and Screed Floors 5–10 days
Project Management/ Self-build Tasks	Once all external render and decorating is complete, arrange for scaffold to come down.	Finalise position of all power points, switches, light fittings, TV and telephone points, boiler, extractor fans, cooker, fridge and other white goods. Finalise plans for any security alarms, hard-wired smoke detectors, outdoor lighting and sockets. Final chance for central vacuum, home network, speaker cables, etc.	Drainage and service trenches can be dug at the same time as the foundations but it is often better to leave them until the scaffolding is down even if this means bringing back the digger. Arrange for Building and warranty inspectors to inspect drains and test.	Oversee final fireplace design details.		If it is decided to have screeded floors in lieu of floating then these require sharp sand and cement. Garage floors are screeded with mesh reinforcement. Artexers will often put any coving up as well on a supply-and-fix basis and they work from the floor rather than from a scaffold. Arrange for warranty inspector to sign off first fix complete.
Trade Materials and Tools Needed on Site	Carpenter: door linings, window boards, tank stands, loft trap, external doors and patio doors. Plasterboard ceiling battens. First-floor noggings. Garage door and frame. Nails, screws and fixings. Staircase.	Plumbing and electrical goods for first fix are usually on a supply-and-fix basis. Alarm installation may be subcontracted, as may under-floor heating installation, whole-house ventilation, central vacuum and home networks.	Groundworker: drainage materials including pipe, fittings and gullies, inspection manholes and covers and pea shingle. Ducting.	Digger and possibly dumper. Pea shingle. Excavated soil. Bricks, stone or other fireplace surround and materials. Lintels and bressumer beams etc. Groundworker: sand and aggregate.	Plasterboard, plasterboard nails. Trestles and boards. Deadmen props. Flooring-grade insulation, vapour barrier, moisture-resistant T&G chipboard flooring. Wood glue.	Plasterboard and fixings for dry lining, taped and jointed or skim coated. If using wet plaster, bagged and ancillary materials. Board scaffold or trestles.
Groundworks/ Landscaping	Bricklayers to fill in putlock holes left by removal of scaffold.		Dig trenches for drains from house to inspection chamber and arrange pressure test.	Backfill drains and service trenches. With machine on site complete landscaping, build final access to road and finish off driveway.		
Bricklaying			Start work on any external brickwork such as garden walls, and landscaping.	Bricklayers to build in fireplaces and any decorative internal brickwork.	Complete any garden walls and landscaping brickwork.	
Carpentry	Fix door linings, window boards, external doors, carcassing for partition walls, bath stands, fitted furniture. Fix first-floor noggings, battens for plasterboard to ceilings, loft trap, cylinder stands and staircase.		Box in any services left exposed by first-fix plumbing and electrics, ready for plasterers to tack out.		Lay all floating floors.	
Roof Tiling and Leadwork						
Glazing						
Plumbing	Confirm position of cylinder and any header tanks. Install any cylinders/header tanks in attic before final ceiling joists are fitted.	Install tanks and cylinders. Fix all piping and ducting for radiators, heated towel rails (under-floor heating if appropriate), install hot and cold supply to all outlets. Fit all vents.	Oversee connection of mains water and gas. Check cross-bonding and earthing.			
Electrics		Install wiring for all lights, power points, switches, cookers, fridges, boilers, immersion heater, heating elements, shaver sockets, extractor fans, smoke detectors, etc. Install telephone, TV aerial, alarm, speaker cables, home network, etc.	Oversee connection of mains electricity. Check cross-bonding and earthing.			
Plastering and Artexing					Tack plasterboard to all ceilings and to any stud walls and boxing. Fix scrim to any steel lintels ready for plastering. Fix all beading ready for plastering.	Plaster out all walls and apply skim to all ceilings and walls. Tape and joint any feather dry lining. Artex ceilings if appropriate. Screed floors if required.
Decorating and Ceramic Tiling	Complete any external decoration. Make good and finish exterior of all window frames and window cills.					

Part two: weeks 13–25

Weeks 16–18 Second-fix Carpentry 10–15 days	Weeks 17–18 Install Kitchen and Fitted Furniture 10–15 days	Weeks 18–20 Second-fix Plumbing and Electrics 5–10 days	Week 20 Commission Boiler 1–2 days	Weeks 21–23 Decorating and Ceramic Tiling 10–15 days	Weeks 23–24 Snagging and Landscaping 5–10 days	Week 25 Final Inspections and Moving in 1–2 days
	Keep a special vigilance as high-value items are delivered to site.	Arrange for carpenter to return to complete work to bath panels and any other outstanding work. Arrange for telephone connection and second fix of alarm system. TV aerial and/or satellite dish will usually need to be installed by a specialist.	Arrange for plumber and electrician to both be present to commission boiler and test heating system. Roof insulation may be fitted by carpenter or a general labourer.	Clean house thoroughly reading for decoration.	Basic landscaping will be undertaken by groundworkers. Approved Contractors only to drop kerbs or carry out work within the highway. Turf laying is usually handled by specialist contractors. All tradesmen to return to fix snags/problems prior to final inspection. Decorators to make good.	Arrange for Building and warranty inspectors' final inspections. Make good any requirement for issuing of final Completion Certificate and warranty. Clean through and arrange for householder's insurance to take over from self-build insurances. Arrange house move.
Internal doors and furniture, skirtings, architraves, bottom tread of stairs, balustrading, airing cupboard slatting.	Kitchen and utility-room units and furniture by specialist suppliers or carpenters. Fitted bedroom furniture by specialist suppliers or carpenters. Plumber: boiler and flues.	Plumber: sinks, baths, basins, WCs, cisterns, taps, valves etc, radiators, heat emitters, shower doors. Electrician: sockets, switches, light fittings, consumer unit, heating controls, etc. Others: alarm fittings.	Carpenter: roof insulation, mask and protective clothing if required.	Decorator: filler, undercoat and paints, sealants, stains, varnishes. Filling tools, sand paper, brushes, rollers etc. Tiler: ceramic tiles; tile adhesives, grout. Tile cutter; etc.	Turf: paving materials, sand and cement. Driveway materials.	
					Complete landscaping and turf or seed lawn areas.	
Hang all internal doors and fit door furniture. Fix skirtings and architraves. Fit bottom tread and balustrading to stairs and landings. Fix airing cupboard slatting. Complete any boxing in. Lay any wooden floors.	Fit kitchen. Install any fitted bathroom furniture/vanity units. Install any fitted furniture, wardrobes, cupboards, etc.	Complete bath panels, boxing in of concealed cisterns, etc.	Install roof insulation.		Return to complete any unfinished items or repair any defects.	
	Site and install boiler and flues.	Fit all baths, basins, WCs and cisterns, taps, showers. Plumb in fridges, dishwasher, washing machines, etc. Fit radiators, flush out heating system. Ready for final connection of mains supply to house.	Flush out primary system and refill. Test boiler. Balance system.		Return to complete any unfinished items or repair any defects.	
		Connect consumer unit. Fix all light fittings, switches and sockets. Connect cooker hood. Fit smoke detectors. Test ready for connection of mains to the house.	Be present for testing of heating system and all controls. Programme boiler/ thermostats.		Return to complete any unfinished items or repair any defects.	
Decorators or flooring contractors to fix any stone flooring, ceramic flooring.				Prepare all surfaces for decoration. Seal and undercoat. Paint all interior ceilings, walls and woodwork. Fix all ceramic tiling to bathrooms, kitchen and utility room.	Complete interior decoration and make good any final repairs. Carpet fitters/flooring contractors to fit all carpets and floor finishes.	

Project Planner for **timber-frame construction**

	6 Weeks Before Start on-site Preliminaries 1–2 days	Week 1 Clear and Set Out Site 1–2 days	Week 1 Strip Topsoil and Dig Foundations 2–3 days	Week 2 Pour Concrete Foundations 1 day	Week 2 Build Up to Damp-proof Course level 2–4 days	Week 2 Construct Oversite 2–4 days	
Project Management/ Self-builder's Tasks	Obtain quotations from service suppliers. Arrange a water supply to the site. This can take up to six weeks unless you can make an arrangement with a neighbour. Arrange a temporary electricity supply. Provide site WC facilities and storage. Arrange site insurance and a self-build warranty. Line up groundworkers and notify all tradesmen of expected schedule.	Send in commencement of work card to Building Inspector and advise warranty inspectors that you are starting on site. Provide first-aid kit, accident book, hard hats and goggles. If setting out is being done by a surveyor rather than the groundworkers you will need to pre-book them.	If you are sending soil away you will have to identify where it is going and at what cost. You will also need to establish turnaround times and, if necessary, arrange for more than one tipper lorry. When foundations are dug, notify Building and warranty inspectors to inspect excavations.	Ready-mixed concrete suppliers will have to be notified and often paid in advance. Decide how you are going to place the concrete. If you are pumping you will need to organise the pump and notify the concrete suppliers of your intention. Once poured arrange for Building and warranty inspection.	Building the foundations can be done by the groundworkers but the bricklayers often make a better job of it. On completion arrange for Building and warranty inspectors to inspect damp-proof course. Pick up meter boxes and ducting from gas and electricity suppliers.	This can be carried out by either the groundworkers or the bricklayers. If the floor beams are long and heavy or access to the oversite is difficult you might need to organise the hire of a crane or telescopic lift. On completion arrange for the Building and warranty inspectors to inspect oversite.	
Trade, Materials and Tools Needed on Site	Check lead-in times for timber frame and other long delivery items, and place orders. Frame lead-in times can be several months.	Groundworkers: digger and possibly dumper. Set out building. Stakes and battening for the profiles together with string lines. A level (Cowley, laser, or similar). A bag of lime for marking out.	Groundworkers: digger, dumper, tipper lorries. Level. Pump. Level pegs.	Groundworkers: wheel-barrows. Scaffold boards. Concrete pump (optional). Concrete. Steel reinforcement bars or cages if required. Clayboard or slip membrane if required.	Bricklayers: foundation blocks, wall ties, plasticiser, sand and cement. Drainage exit lintels. Cranked ventilators. Mixer. Spotboards. Foot scaffold for sloping or bad ground. All in ballast and cement. Damp-proof course.	Bricklayers: floor beams. Coursing bricks. Infill blocks. Sand and cement. Damp-proof course. Groundworkers: drainage pipe and pea gravel.	
Groundworks/ Landscaping	Fence off and secure the site around its boundaries. Secure any trees that must be protected. Possibly plant hedgerows and other boundaries.	Create temporary site access. Clear site of any existing debris. Strip topsoil and stack for future use. Set out building. Secure site with lockable gates.	Excavate foundation trenches (and service trenches, if practical) to satisfaction of the Building and warranty inspectors.	Oversee pour of concrete. Tamp and level concrete. Position clayboards, slip membrane or reinforcement as directed by engineer/surveyor.		Position drainage pipes through foundation walls and oversite.	
Bricklaying					Build foundation blockwork. Fill cavities level with outside ground level. Install cranked ventilators. Lay damp-proof course.	Position floor beams to ground floor, infill with blocks and brush grout.	
Carpentry							
Roof Tiling and Leadwork							
Glazing							
Plumbing	Lay in temporary water supply using minimum 22mm blue plastic piping and fix standpipe. Above-ground pipework must be insulated to prevent freezing.						
Electrics	Fix lockable meter box for temporary electricity supply to site.						
Plastering and Artexing							
Decorating and Ceramic Tiling							

NOTES: Project planner for a two-storey house constructed in open-panel brick and timber with a beam-and-block ground floor, gable roof with one valley and clipped verges. Timber frame erected by suppliers. Labour-only subcontractors with the exception of plumbers, electricians and plasterers which are usually supply-and-fix trades. All general/personal tools supplied by labour.

Part one: weeks 1–10

Weeks 3–4 Erect Timber Frame 7–14 days	Week 5 Build Chimneys Through Roof 1–2 days	Weeks 5–6 Felt, Batten and Tile Roof 5–10 days	Weeks 7–8 Glaze to Make Weathertight 5–10 days	Week 8 Begin External Brick Cladding 15–20 days	Weeks 8–9 First fix Plumbing and Electrics 5–10 days	Weeks 9–10 Insulation and Vapour Barrier 5 days
Hire and erect scaffolding as an independent scaffold, open ended to allow panels to be carried/craned in. The scaffolding and boards will need to be raised as work commences. Check what notice is required. It will also need to stay up until after roof tiling in order for the plumber, glazier, decorator and bricklayers to work off it.	Warranty inspector to inspect timber frame erected.	Decide who is to be responsible for leadwork. This is traditionally the plumber but may now be a lead specialist. Roofing materials are often supply-and-fix. Alternatively specialist suppliers will quantify a quote for all roofing materials.	Warranty inspector to inspect finished roof.	The brickwork outer cladding can be going on at the same time as the other trades are working inside. Alternatively it can be left until later. Scaffolding boards need to be lowered and then raised as work commences.	Finalise position of all power points, switches, light fittings, TV and telephone points, boiler, extractor fans, cooker, fridge and other white goods. Finalise plans for any security alarm, hard-wired smoke detectors, outdoor lighting and sockets. Final chance for central vacuum, home network, speaker cables, etc.	Finalise who is to be responsible for installing insulation and vapour barrier. This will usually be the carpenter or a general builder/labourer.
Erectors: erecting the timber frame usually requires a crane on site.	Materials: bricks/blocks including any specials, wall flue liners, sand and cement, chimney pot, lead trays. Plumber: vent pipes, lead.	Roofers: felt, batten roof tiles, roof and eaves vents, undercloaking, nails and fixings, coloured mortar if required. Plumber: lead, vent pipes, including lead skirts. Bricklayer: sand and cement.	Glazier: glazing units and ancillary glazing materials.	Bricklayers: bricks, ties, sand and cement. Scaffolding boards need to be lowered and then raised as work commences.	Plumbing and electrical goods for first fix are usually on a supply-and-fix basis. Alarm installation may be subcontracted, as may under-floor heating, whole-house ventilation, central vacuum and home networks.	Insulation material, vapour barrier and fixings. Roof insulation. Protective masks and clothing if required.
	Build chimney/s through roof.	Point in flashings around chimney, step and cover flashings.		Bricklayers to build external brick skin.	Bricklayers to build external brick skin.	Bricklayers to build external brick skin.
Erection of timber frame including first-floor joists and decking and complete roof including any valley or lay boards, fascias and soffits. Fix window and door frames.						Install insulation between studwork and fix vapour barrier to timber frame external walls. Insulate roof space.
		Fix flashings around chimney, dormers, etc. Felt, batten, tile roof. Bed ridge, point verges and valleys.				
			Glaze all joinery.			
	Provide lead trays for bricklayers to build in.	Fix vent pipes. Position vent pipe skirts. Make up all lead flashings and skirts.			Install tanks and cylinders. Fix all piping and ducting for radiators and heated towel rails (under-floor heating if appropriate). Install hot and cold supply to all outlets. Fit all vents.	
					Install wiring for all lights, power points, switches, cookers, fridges, boilers, immersion heater, heating elements, shaver sockets, extractor fans, smoke detectors, etc. Install telephone, TV, alarms, speaker cable, home network, etc.	

Project Planner for **timber-frame construction**

	Weeks 10–12 First-fix Carpentry 10–15 days	Weeks 12–13 Tack Ceilings and Lay Floors 5–10 days	Weeks 12–15 Fix Guttering and Downpipes 2 days	Weeks 12–15 Tape and Joint or Skim Plasterboard 5–10 days	Week 15 Connect Drains 5 days	Week 16 Backfill Drains and Complete Access 5 days
Project Management/ Self-build Tasks	Start to choose second-fix items such as interior doors that may be on long delivery. Place kitchen units on order.	Arrange for warranty inspector to inspect brick elevations. If it is decided to have screeded floors to the ground floor in lieu of floating then these require sharp sand and cement as well as the appropriate insulation and vapour barrier. Garage floors are screeded with mesh reinforcement.	Fix guttering and downpipes before the scaffold comes down. Scaffold to come down.	If it is decided to have Artex ceilings then this is often a different tradesman. They will usually put any coving up as well on a supply-and-fix basis and they work from the floor rather than from a scaffold.	Drainage and service trenches can be dug at the same time as the foundations but it is often better to leave them until the scaffolding is down even if this means bringing back the digger. Arrange for Building and warranty inspectors to inspect drains and test.	
Trade Materials and Tools Needed on Site	Carpenter: door linings, window boards, material for any tank stands, loft trap, external doors and patio doors. Garage door and frame. Nails, screws and fixings. Staircase. Plasterers: sand, cement, lime for render.	Plasterers: plasterboard and nails. Trestles, boards and props. Carpenter: flooring, grade insulation, vapour barrier, moisture-resistant T&G chipboard flooring. Wood glue. Bricklayers: sand, cement and fireplace materials.	Plumber: rainwater goods.	Plasterers: bagged and ancillary materials. Plasterboard and fixings. Board scaffold or trestles. Decorator: decoration materials.	Drainage materials including pipe, fittings and gullies, inspection manholes and covers and pea shingle. Ducting.	Digger and possibly dumper. Pea shingle. Excavated soil. Lintels and bressummer beams. Groundworker: sand and aggregate. Bricklayers: lintels and bressummer beams.
Groundworks/ Landscaping					Dig trenches for drains from house to inspection chamber and arrange pressure test.	Backfill drains and service trenches. With machine on site complete landscaping and build final access to road and finish off driveway.
Bricklaying	Complete external brick cladding.	Bricklayers to build in fireplaces.	Start work on any external brickwork such as garden walls and landscaping.			Bricklayers to build fireplaces and any internal decorative brickwork.
Carpentry	Fix door linings, window boards, external doors, carcassing for partition walls, bath stands, fitted furniture. Fix first-floor noggings, battens for plasterboard to ceilings, loft trap, cylinder stands and staircase.	Lay floating floors.			Box in of any services left exposed by first-fix plumbing and electrics.	
Roof Tiling and Leadwork						
Glazing						
Plumbing			Plumbers to fix guttering and downpipes.		Oversee connection of mains water and gas. Check cross-bonding and earthing.	
Electrics					Oversee connection of mains electricity. Check cross-bonding and earthing.	
Plastering and Artexing	Carry out any external rendering as required.	Tack out all walls and ceilings with dry lining.		Tape joints or skim coat plasterboard. Artex ceilings if appropriate.		
Decorating and Ceramic Tiling		Decorators to paint/finish fascias and soffits.	Paint rainwater goods if necessary and complete external decoration before scaffold comes down.	Complete any external decoration. Make good and finish exterior of all window frames and window cills.		

Part two: weeks 10–25

Weeks 16–18 Second-fix Carpentry 10–15 days	Weeks 17–18 Install Kitchen and Fitted Furniture 5–10 days	Weeks 18–20 Second-fix Plumbing and Electrics 5–10 days	Week 20 Commission Boiler 1–2 days	Weeks 21–23 Decorating and Ceramic Tiling 10–15 days	Weeks 23–24 Snagging and Landscaping 5–10 days	Week 25 Final Inspections and Moving in 1–2 days
	Store units in a secure place following delivery as thieves watch out for high-volume deliveries.	Arrange for carpenter to return to complete work to bath panels and any other outstanding work. Arrange for telephone connection and second fix of alarm system. TV aerial and/or satellite dish will usually need to be installed by a specialist.	Arrange for plumber and electrician to both be present to commission boiler and test heating system.	Clean house thoroughly ready for decoration.	Basic landscaping will be undertaken by groundworkers who will also be able to complete the access/drop kerb. Turf laying is usually handled by specialist contractors All tradesmen to return to fix snags/problems prior to final inspection. Decorators to make good.	Arrange for Building and warranty inspectors' final inspections. Make good any requirement for issuing of final Completion Certificate and warranty. Clean through and arrange for householder's insurance to take over from self-build insurances. Arrange house move.
Internal doors and furniture, skirtings, architraves, bottom tread of stairs, balustrading, airing cupboard slatting.	Kitchen and utility-room units and furniture by specialist suppliers or carpenters. Fitted bedroom furniture by specialist suppliers or carpenters. Plumber: boiler and flues.	Plumber: sinks, baths, basins, WCs, cisterns, taps, valves etc, radiators, heating emitters, shower doors. Electrician: sockets, switches, light fittings, consumer unit, heating controls, etc. Others: alarm fittings.	Tiler: ceramic tiles, tile adhesive, grout, tile cutter, etc.	Decorator: filler, undercoat and paints, sealants, stains, varnishes. Filling tools, sand paper, brushes, rollers, etc.	Turf. Paving materials, sand and cement. Driveway materials.	
					Complete landscaping and turf or seed lawn areas. Contractors to lay driveways and pathways.	
Hang all internal doors and fit door furniture. Fix skirtings and architraves. Fit bottom tread and balustrading to stairs and landings. Fix airing cupboard slatting. Complete any boxing in. Lay any wooden floors.	Fit kitchen. Install any fitted bathroom furniture/vanity units. Install any fitted furniture, wardrobes, cupboards, etc.	Complete bath panels, boxing in of concealed cisterns, etc.			Return to complete any unfinished items or repair any defects.	
	Site and install boiler and flues.	Fit all baths, basins, WCs and cisterns, taps, showers. Plumb in fridges, dishwasher, washing machine, etc. Fit radiators, flush out heating system. Wire in appliances and test ready for final connection of mains supply to house.	Flush out primary system and refill. Test boiler. Balance system.		Return to complete any unfinished items or repair any defects.	
		Connect consumer unit. Fix all light fittings, switches and sockets. Connect cooker hood. Fit smoke detectors. Test ready for connection of mains to the house.	Be present for testing of heating system and all controls. Programme boiler and thermostats.		Return to complete any unfinished items or repair any defects.	
Decorators or flooring contractors to fix any stone flooring or ceramic flooring.			Fix all ceramic tiling to bathrooms, kitchen and utility room.	Clean house thoroughly ready for decoration. Prepare all surfaces for decoration. Seal and undercoat. Paint all interior ceilings, walls and woodwork.	Complete interior decoration and make good any final repairs. Carpet fitters/flooring contractors to fit all carpets and floor finishes.	

Chapter 11

BUYING THE MATERIALS AND DEALING WITH SUPPLIERS

If you attend any of the self-build exhibitions or read the self-build magazines you will realise pretty quickly that there are a lot of companies out there fighting for your business. Because you are big business. You might think that you're alone out there but there are upwards of 20,000 just like you and the market you create has greater potential than that of any of the major house-builders.

I can't and don't want to argue the pros and cons between this brick and that, this boiler and that. I'm going to have to leave you to make up your own mind on the actual makes and models that you purchase. But I can exhort you to shop around. Listen to the sales spiel but don't get carried away with it. Never lose sight of the fact that the salesperson in front of you is not impartial. Take away what they say or give you and evaluate it in the calm of your own surroundings. Don't allow yourself to be hassled. If you need more time to make up your mind, then take it. They may try to convince you that if you don't commit immediately, you'll lose that discount – it's probably not true and even if it is, the chances are that if you make your purchase conditional upon you

receiving it anyway, most companies would agree.

I've discussed the costs of many of the prime items as I've gone through this book. I've also discussed how many of the choices for external materials are, to a large extent, taken out of your hands by the dictates of the planners. That still leaves an awful lot to choose and this is going to be one of the biggest shopping trips of your life. You'll have sample tiles down all over the place so that you can see them in different lights. You'll have bricks and stones in the garden to see how they look when they're wet, rather than pristine in the showroom. You'll agonise over this tap or that sink.

Enjoy it! It is important, and the way your new home ends up will depend upon your choices. But it's not life or death. Keep it all in proportion and remember that if you do make a mistake, in most cases you may be able to change things a little later on, or else just decide to live with it until you build your next home.

Often builders' merchants will take in your plans, free of charge, and provide a quantity take off and costings. Some of them are pretty accurate, whilst others are wildly inaccurate and the sheets can only really be used for comparative purposes. Some, but not all, have dedicated staff to deal with the self-building client, and most will actively assist you in the selection, evaluation

Never lose sight of the fact that the salesperson in front of you is not impartial. Take away what they say or give you and evaluate it in the calm of your own surroundings.

and costing of materials. Whether you use a package-deal company or not, at some stage you will also need to buy the materials that are not included in the package and it's important to establish just where you're going to go shopping for those, before you start work. The selection of the builders' merchant, or merchants, you will use should be based on the same criteria as the selection of any other company or professional you are thinking of using. Make sure that you feel comfortable with them, make sure that they appreciate just what it is you're trying to achieve and, above all, make sure that they offer the user-friendly service that you will need to rely on.

Many suppliers are quite prepared to put their facilities at the prospective buyer's disposal but be aware that this may be the sprat to catch the mackerel. It does, however, make complete sense to make use of kitchen and sanitaryware suppliers who are prepared to undertake a design service. Specialist suppliers of plumbing and heating equipment will often provide a full take-off not only of their own, but also of ancillary supply. Ask all suppliers about after-sales back-up. Check on lead-in and delivery times. Read the suppliers' literature carefully and study the performance figures given in their published literature, comparing them wherever possible with their competitors.

Getting the best prices

BuildStore have tied up with Jewson and Wolseley UK to get self-builders a better deal with their BuildStore Self-build Trade Card. As one of, if not *the* biggest providers and facilitators of finance for self-builders, renovators and converters alike, they knew just how many of their clients were going on to build and would need materials. They realised that the combined spend of all their clients would amount to more than that of most of the major house-builders and reasoned that they should, therefore, enjoy the same kind of discounts that large developers enjoyed. Happily Jewson, along with Graham, agreed and later on Wolseley UK, encompassing Build Center, Hire Center, and Plumb Center, came on board as partners.

Now the centralised account equates to a turnover of more than £1m a month and that allows substantially better prices for their clients. It also, and this is

important, gives these single clients the clout and the respect that the larger clients had. A builders' merchant's counter can be a daunting place for the lay person not quite sure of what they want or need. You may have £50,000 or more to spend but in many merchants the staff might ignore you in favour of a regular small-builder client whose annual spend is less than £5,000. But with the little credit-card-sized Trade Card, available free of charge, you are identified as important. It also helps with credit limits. Most merchants will only entertain a credit limit for a new customer of between £3,000 and £5,000. Now you could breach those limits in the first week. Trade Card customers usually get a credit limit of £15,000 and, if they're getting their finance through BuildStore, it's upped to £25,000.

Certain builders' merchants on the continent, such as Leroy Merlin and Lapeyre (from St Gobain, the same group as Jewson), have long recognised that at the weekend over half their customers hail from this side of the channel and have hired English-speaking staff to cope with the demand. Prices on some items can be astounding, with tiles costing around a third of the price charged for exactly the same thing in the UK, and sanitaryware at almost half the price but with far more flair. Next time you're early for the ferry and stop at the hypermarket to stock up on booze, see for yourself. You might think that it's worthwhile going back for a day trip with a hired van. It's probably the second-fix or finishing items that are the best bargains, although having said that, many British merchants source bricks and tiles from abroad and, as I've already mentioned, most natural slates come from other countries.

The cost of getting there and subsequent delivery of materials can, of course, negate any supposed savings and most people taking advantage of this 'bonanza' will be from the south coast of England or live close to a port. You also need to check on your guarantee position. Although in-store guarantees may be offered, they will be of little use to you if you have to add on the additional cost of travel. Many foreign companies set up business in this country to sell their wares, but these British subsidiaries might well refuse to recognise their main company's manufacturer's guarantee. Always check compatibility with UK materials and compliance with local or statutory regulations. Having said that, it's not as much of a problem as some would want you to think. Many of the 'smarter' sanitary-ware suppliers who set up shop around the country get their supplies from abroad. So the taps that you buy in England may well be French and the English supplier will include any adapters necessary. You may, of course, be paying three times as much as you would have had you bought them yourself in France.

By the way, as I mentioned in Chapter 1, if the VAT is recoverable for a new build or conversion, then VAT paid out in the European Union is also recoverable at the rate paid. If VAT is paid for purchases made outside the Union at the port of entry, then this is also recoverable.

Many materials have long lead-in times that need to be worked into your build programme. Failure to anticipate these often leads to work falling behind schedule, leading, in turn, to the 'stop-start' that is symptomatic of a badly managed site. This will almost certainly mean that the windows of availability for many important tradesmen are missed.

Even in the best of times frame companies will

A builders' merchant's counter can be a daunting place for the lay person not quite sure of what they want or need.

Above: **The size of a credit card and the key to savings.**

often quote 8–12 weeks from order to delivery. If you are hoping to start soon after receipt of planning permission then, unless you are prepared to take a flyer on the order, and in many cases the payment, you might reach oversite and have to wait. Some of the more expensive and handmade bricks and tiles are always on long delivery. Specially shaped bricks and tiles from mainstream manufacturers are only ever made to order. With second-fix and specialist items it might be as well to have alternatives in mind in case the delivery times become extended. Use the Project Planners on pages 384–91 to work out when you're going to need certain materials and then track back to the date when you should be ordering them.

The words 'purpose made' have many connotations, the principal ones being, special, costly and not easy to replace. If you are having purpose-made items then the lead-in times are likely to be greater and you will need to make allowances for this. Make sure that whatever is being made for you complies with all the necessary regulations and requirements of your warranty undertaker and Building Control. If you are likely to want additional matching items then it's a good idea to make the manufacturers aware of this when ordering so that they can keep any necessary templates, and it goes without saying that wherever possible you should buy from established companies who are likely to be around later to honour any guarantees.

In law you cannot pass on the burden of a contract. If your purpose-made windows are supplied through your builder and he goes out of business, you may not have recourse to the suppliers. Check the worth of any guarantee and if necessary insist on some form of collateral contract. Follow the instructions given with any purchase. Incorrect usage or installation could very well invalidate any guarantee. Structural warranties do not always cover such items as boilers and radiators that are fundamentally important to the enjoyment of a home, and although warranty companies require that materials supplied have the necessary agreement certificate, if they do not notice a failing during the inspection period, they might deny liability.

In the small print of many agreements there is a right for the manufacturer to change the specifica-

Above: **A well-stocked local builders' merchant is essential for most of the day-to-day materials.**
© Seccombe & Sons

Left: **Many high-quality second-fix items are imported. Why not go and get them yourself and save money?**

tion without notice. This might happen where, for example, the manufacturer finds that there is a fault on the original design. They won't want to admit to the fault because that could leave them open to action by those who've already bought the same item. What you want is the goods you have ordered, and perhaps paid for, but what you don't want is faulty goods. You might have to be pragmatic here and either accept the up-rated design or, if it isn't suitable or doesn't fit, ask for your money back. Of course if you change the specification following your order, you will effectively be moving your delivery to the bottom of their list. So make sure that you've specified exactly what you want in the first place.

Paying suppliers

Most specialist suppliers will require some sort of deposit, particularly before commencing manufacture of purpose-made items. Wherever possible keep the amounts to the minimum and if at all possible insist that the deposit is returnable in the event of the supply being delayed through no fault of your own. Package-deal and timber frame suppliers will more often than not require large stage payments in advance of deliveries. Make sure that these monies are only paid into a properly dedicated client's account and make certain that the trustees of that account are only authorised to pay the monies across to the main company account when the staged contract has been fulfilled. Wherever possible, try to ensure that the stage payments accord with the value of the materials supplied.

If a supplier goes bust before the goods are delivered then you effectively become an unsecured creditor for any monies you have paid. Given the length of time that it can take to sort out the financial affairs of a bankrupt company you will probably have no alternative but to write off the cost and look elsewhere for the materials. If a supplier goes bust after the goods have been delivered then you need to move quickly to make sure that they are secure from the attentions of creditors who might feel they have the right to enter your site and repossess the goods. Technically if they are fixed then they are yours but this is a grey area. If you have paid for them in full then title will have passed to you. If not, then you are probably better off making your own arrangements with the Official Receiver.

Reputable suppliers will generally try to give at least 24 hours' notice of delivery, if only to ensure that there is someone there to assist in or direct offloading. If you fail to turn up then the driver may well make his own decisions about where to put goods. Make suppliers aware of the immediate road conditions. If you are on a narrow lane or a site with restricted access, large or articulated lorries may not be able to get in. Sometimes a dumper or fork-lift truck may be needed to bring goods in. At other times you might need to arrange additional labour. If a lorry damages your property or the property of a third party then it's important to make a note of the driver's name and the vehicle number. Be aware that waiting time may be added if you delay a delivery.

Once delivery is made and items are paid for, your importance with the suppliers is considerably lessened, as by then they're on to their next customer. Check all deliveries. Even when faced with an impatient lorry driver, check all items for scratches or damage and make a note on the delivery ticket. If you are unable to check everything there and then, write 'goods unchecked' on the ticket. This isn't ideal but it may give you some comeback. If you find that any goods that are incorrect or damaged, put them back on the lorry. Legal action should only ever be a last resort when all other avenues have been exhausted. Try to sort the matter out face to face with the suppliers and try to deal with people as near to the top as you can.

Whilst there is often a charge for returns, this will be greatly outweighed by the costs involved in making up shortfalls and most self-builders would rather have something left over than have the site held up for the sake of, say, a few bricks. It is well worth buying more tiles, particularly floor tiles, than you need. If any are broken or damaged and you have to replace them you might find that tiles from a new batch will be a different shade or even a different size. Reclaimed materials have a higher wastage factor than new ones and you might need to over-order by up to 20% on some second-hand bricks and tiles against the normal 5% for new ones. Remember that materials such as second-hand bricks and tiles will be sourced by the suppliers from a particular demolition site and that any subsequent deliveries might be significantly different. Quality is often and of necessity almost on a 'buyer beware' basis so check that the items being supplied are fit for your purpose and that they comply with the necessary regulations.

It's an unfortunate fact that many items go missing just after delivery. Whether this is because thieves keep a look-out for high-value and easily disposable deliveries or whether there is a tip-off arrangement is debatable. Loss of certain goods at critical times can severely disrupt your programme, so when receiving goods make certain either that they are secure or that you unpack and fit them as soon as possible to make it difficult for a thief to sell them on. Site insurance is a must for all self-builders but this can never compensate for the loss of momentum to your project. If goods are damaged on delivery take this up with the supplier. If they are subsequently damaged on site then, unless the value is greater than the insurance excess, you might have to take it on the chin.

Although specialist suppliers working within the self-build market have increased the ability of the individual to purchase their own materials, many trades remain principally supply and fix. Roof tiling is one where a supply-and-fix contract can often work out cheaper and the electrical trade is another. This is principally because large discounts are available for bulk purchase of both prime and ancillary items. Plumbing is also largely supply and fix for the more mundane items. However, the self-builder is often able to supply specific items for fixing within the main contract.

'Prime cost' figures relate to the supply of materials. Do not confuse them with 'provisional sums', which are usually related to specific trades and are used when the actual specification is yet to be established. If there are prime cost sums for items to be supplied then you will need to establish whether they are the list price or whether they take into account any discounts. In the case of the former you might consider deducting the sum from the contract and purchasing these items yourself. But beware: some contracts specify that the builder is still entitled to the profit element. Try to establish that provisional sums truly reflect the supply-and-fix cost of the relevant trade to the Board electricity, gas and water and NHBC requirements.

Dealing with service providers for things like electricity, gas and water can be a time-consuming business and it's best to seek a quotation as soon as you've got some reasonable plans of your proposals.

Once they've quoted they won't do anything until you've paid any necessary fees and most of them have long lead-in times of six to eight weeks or more. Don't delay dealing with these things. No work can start on site until water is available. If you can't get the standpipe in on time it might be necessary to arrange for a hose from next door's outside tap or else a bowser. Electricity is not as critical and in any event many tradesmen use a generator. The supply of electricity is going to cost around £500 for a typical home in a normal suburban street, gas is going to cost £300, and the water and sewage connection charge is going

Dealing with service providers for things like electricity, gas and water can be a time-consuming business and it's best to seek a quotation as soon as you've got some reasonable plans of your proposals.

to be around £1,200. Most of the undertakers will bring the supply to the boundary and then expect you to take it from there and into the meter or connection point. Some will supply the ducting and meter boxes, whilst others will expect you to buy these yourself. None will allow the final connection and the turning on of the supply until the work has been carried out and certified by a registered, qualified or approved contractor. Note that any service and drainage connections involving work to the highway may only be carried out by Approved Contractors. You can obtain a list of these from the local authority. But be aware also that they are expensive and in great demand.

What follows is a list of the key materials, plant and equipment needed within the various sections or stages of the build. I have deliberately repeated certain materials and plant where their need is duplicated. It's not meant to be a full bill of quantities: there are so many variations and choices that that would be almost impossible. But it should provide a useful guide.

Preparation and up to ground/dpc level

Materials/plant	Range	Typical sizes	Notes
Security fencing	Galvanised steel mesh with concrete or rubber feet	2.5m x 3.5m	Panels should be GS7 anti-climb to meet HandS regulations. Can be bought or hired to include gates, pedestrian barriers and stabilisers
Signage			A good idea to put signs up for deliveries, letting people know where you can be contacted in an emergency
Lockable storage	Walk-in containers. Site box or tool safe	3-, 6-and 12-metre containers various	Containers may require a hardstanding
Profile and setting out timber		50mm x 50mm stakes plus 75mm x 38mm heads	Available in sets or bundles
Laser level, dumpy or Cowley			Some groundworkers have them. They can be hired and surveyors will have their own
Tipper lorries		10-, 15- and 20-tonne	Identify these early on and find out where they will be tipping
Diggers/ excavators	Typical JCB types or tracked 360-degree machines	700mm, 600mm, 450mm and 300mm buckets required	Usually hired with a driver
Dumpers	2- and 4-wheel drive	1–4-tonne	Necessary if storing spoil on site
Toilets			Hired and emptied weekly by contractors
Water bowser		500–1,130-litre with washer	May be necessary if standpipe not yet in
Water butt and hose		180 litre. Butts or drums	Position at the mixing point close to the sand
Generator	Static or mobile. Diesel or petrol	550w upwards	
Transformer			Converts supply to 110 volts for site tools
Skip	Fully enclosed or with drop end	1.5cu. m–2.5 tonnes 3cu. m–5 tonnes 6.2cu. m–7.8 tonnes	Hired on a weekly basis. Ramps available as extras.
Shute	Corrugated tube or slides		For use in renovations and conversions, stripping and demolition
Adjustable steel props			Plus bearing boards and pins. To support masonry, floors, etc.
Boarding	Plywood, OSB or Stirling board	2,400mm x 1,200mm x 12.5mm	For boarding up windows. Making spotboards. To put in front of the mixer
Tarpaulin	Pvc-coated polyester	9m x 6m	To cover materials or protect buildings from the weather. Can be hired or purchased. Make sure you have sufficient rope.
Mixer	Electric or petrol	3.5 and 5cu. m	Hired by the week
Crane hire			Could be required for floor beams or attic trusses
Hoist and elevators	Range from 5–4m		May be necessary for sloping sites and demolition. Identify hire point for roof tiling
Scaffolding	Hire and erect	Putlock or independent	Hired by the week usually on a 10-week minimum
Type 1 stone		10-, 15- and 20-tonne loads	For access and hardstandings
Vibrating plates		400mm x 370mm 540mm x 290mm	For compacting roadstone and hardcore infills
Rollers		560mm x 750mm widths	Hired by the day

Materials/plant	Range	Typical sizes	Notes
Power floats	Petrol or compressed air driven	6m	Achieves a good finish to concrete oversites
Polythene	Low-grade medium or heavy duty		For covering materials or closing up unglazed windows
Tools	Full range of hand tools		Most trades have their own. Make sure they know yours are yours!
Traffic cones	Standard or flashing		Necessary for works on the highway
Concrete	Ready mixed in 4-, 5- and 6-cu. m loads. Site mixed		GEN 1 for foundations
Concrete pump	30–100m range		Gets the concrete to the right spot without fuss. Hired by the day
Reinforcement mesh bar	C503, A142 and A252	4800mm x 2400mm 10mm and 12mm in 6m lengths	May need wiring together. May need to be in two layers 50mm from top and bottom of concrete
Wire cages	To engineer's bending schedule		For use in groundbeams or rafts. Prefabricated
Preformed spacers			To stand mesh, bar and cages at the correct position in the concrete
Cement	Standard, masonry, rapid hardening, sulphate resistant, coloured	25-kg bags	Store in the dry
Plastisiser		1–250 litres	Follow dosages and instructions
Sand	Sharp or soft	1-tonne non-returnable bags. 10-, 15- and 20-tonne full loads	Use the same sand to maintain the mortar colour
Ballast	'All in' – mixture of sand and stones	1-tonne bags 10-, 15- and 20-tonne full loads	For use in site-mixed concrete and for filling oversites
Geotextile		10m x 4.5m rolls	Spreads loads. Used to protect ground or beneath Type 1 stone
Damp-proof membrane	High-grade polythene. 300 or 250MU	4m x 25m rolls	Use as slip membrane. Use as dpm laid over blinded hardcore beneath concrete. Laid over concrete beneath and above insulation
Compressible material Blocks	Fibre board or expanded polystyrene Solid concrete, aerated concrete, lightweight. 2.8N to 25N strength	50mm–150mm in 2,400mm x 1,200mm sheets 215mm x 440mm 215mm x 620mm 75–450mm thick	Divorces structure from moving or heaving ground Buy in direct loads. Use the right blocks for each situation as specified
Bricks	Commons in clay or concrete, Class B and A Engineering, handmade, wirecut or stock, sand-faced Flettons	63mm x 220mm standard	Different materials for different situations. Use the right ones as specified
Drainage exit lintels	Pre-stressed concrete	125mm x 450mm, 600mm 900mm and 1,200mm	To support brick/blockwork over drainage and service exits
Wall ties	Wide variety of sizes and shapes. All to DD140 in stainless steel	200mm, 225mm and 250mm	
Air bricks	Fireclay, terracottta and plastic	225mm x 75mm and 150mm	To vent beneath voids
Cavity liners	Fireclay, terracotta and plastic	225mm x 75mm and 225mm x 150mm	Provides clear space air bridge in the cavity
Cranked ventilators	Plastic	Extendable	Vents beneath floor beams without letting light in
Lean mix concrete	Weak mix 1:12	Usually site-mixed	Mixed with ballast and cement to fill cavities below ground

Materials/plant	Range	Typical sizes	Notes
Damp-proof course	Polythene and pitch polymer	100–600mm (polythene in 30m rolls. Pitch polymer in 20m rolls)	Prevents damp rising into main structure. Must be properly bedded on mortar
Suspended timber joists and trimmers	Wallplate Joists	100mm x 50mm and 75mm 50–150mm x 150–225mm in various lengths	Plain sawn lumber
Bolts and plates	Various types	Various sizes	To bolt joists and trimmers together with dog plates
Prefabricated timber joists	'I' beams	Various lengths and profiles	
Joist hangers	Galvanised steel	Various sizes from 50–150mm. Various configurations	Carry joists to all external walls
Decking	Moisture-resistant chipboard Tongued-and-grooved timber	2,400mm x 600mm x 18mm and 22mm 150–175mm x 19mm or 28mm in random lengths	Fix with ringshank nails or screws. Glue all edges and to board. Screwfix for quietness
Noggings	Sawn lumber random lengths	50–100mm x 50–150mm in to support decking	For use between joists and at perimeters
Concrete floor beams	Various lengths and profiles	175mm and 225mm	Lay in accordance with manufacturer's instructions and layout
Infill blocks	Solid or aerated concrete Polystyrene purpose made	Standard block sizes	Must be brush grouted when laid
Consolidation	Type 1 roadstone, all in ballast, or hardcore		No stones bigger than 100mm. Must be properly consolidated
Concrete	Ready mixed in 4-, 5- and 6-cu. m loads. Site-mixed	GEN 3 for oversites	May need to be pumped
Insulation	Rigid polystyrene sheeting Rigid polyurethane sheeting Glass, mineral and acoustic wool	2,400mm x 1,200mm sheets 25–100mm thick 200mm thick x 4.5m rolls	Can be laid under oversite concrete, over or in combination Must be supported by netting beneath ground floors
Support netting		300m x 2m 100m x 2m	
Nails/screws	Plain, galvanised, zinc electro plated and black phosphate	Various lengths widths and profiles	Cheaper to buy in boxes
Lateral restraint straps	Galvanised steel – pre-drilled	1,200mm	Built in every 2m to cross 3 joists
Glues	Wood glues	5-litre containers	Use on all tongue-and-groved edges and between boards and joists

Drainage

Materials/plant	Range	Typical sizes	Notes
Pvc-u drainage pipes	Socketed or plain end. Perforated	100mm and 150mm internal diameter in 3-m and 6-m lengths	Will need proprietary lubricants to fit collars
Pvc-u fittings	Huge range of gullies, traps, rodding eyes and flexible joints		One manufacturer's products may not fit another's
Clay pipe		100mm and 150mm in 1.6m and 1.75m lengths	Needs collars. Heavy and difficult to stand to test
Clay pipe fittings	Collars, connectors, bends, branches, etc.		

Materials/plant	Range	Typical sizes	Notes
Inspection chambers	Rodding eyes, pre-formed plastic, pre-formed concrete rings or sections. *In situ* built in Engineering brick	225mm x 100mm, 450mm x 450mm, 450mm diameter, 760mm 675mm, 1,000mm diameter and upwards	Performed inspection chambers save time and money but can only be used up to 1-m deep. After that it may be necessary to use concrete sections or rings
Soakaway sections	Perforated concrete rings Perforated plastic interlocking cages	450mm–2m diameter Various sizes to fit together	For use when a rubble-filled hole won't do
Manhole covers	Cast iron, Ductile iron, galvanised steel or plastic	100mm diameter to 600mm x 450mm	Use the correct strength for each situation. Covers on roads or drives must be cast iron
Pea gravel	Clean washed stone	10mm	All pipes must be bedded and surrounded in 150mm of pea gravel
Plastic ducting		50–150mm in 25m coils or 6m lengths	Used to bring services into the property

Superstructure to wallplate plus gable ends

Damp-proof course	Pitch polymer or polythene	100–600mm widths 10–30 rolls	High-load dpcs may be needed for some situations
Blocks	Solid concrete, aerated concrete, lightweight. 2.8N to 25N strength	215mm x 440mm 215mm x 620mm 75–450mm thick	Buy in direct loads. Use the right blocks for each situation as specified
Bricks	Commons in clay or concrete, Class B and A Engineering, handmade, wirecut or stock, sand-faced Flettons. Reclaimed bricks	63mm x 220mm standard 75mm x 225mm second-hand/reclaimed. Various shapes and sizes such as squints and plinth bricks	Different materials for different situations. Use the right ones as specified. Reclaimed bricks may have high wastage
Reformed stone	Smooth, pitched or moulded. Various colours	Various sizes and mixes	Can be laid by bricklayers. May be in sections
Natural stone	From local quarries	Cut to 100–150mm on bed or random as dug	May need a backing block
Flint	As dug or knapped. Blue–brown	Often sold by the oil drum or by the tonne	May need a backing block
Hessian		1,370mm x 46m rolls	Used to protect new masonry from frost
Wall starter	Stainless steel	75–200mm widths	To tie new brickwork to old
Scaffolding	Hire and erect	Putlock or independent	Hired by the week usually on a 10-week minimum. Use a putlog scaffold for brickwork facia and an independent for rendered finish or timber frame. Erect an open-ended scaffold with timber fame and close it around the completed structure
Water butt and hose		180-litre butts or drums	Position at the mixing point close to the sand
Mixer	Electric or petrol	3.5 and 5cu. m	Hired by the week
Cement	Standard, masonry, rapid hardening, sulphate resistant, coloured	25kg bags	Store in the dry
Plasticiser		1–250 litres	Follow dosages and instructions
Sand	Sharp or soft	1-tonne non-returnable bags. 10-, 15- and 20-tonne full loads	Use the same sand to maintain the mortar colour
Ready-mix mortars	Various colours	0.25cu. m tubs in 1cu. m mini-loads	Tubs can be refilled. Retarders added
Non-hydraulic lime	Mature, course and fine	20-litre tubs	Pre-mixed ready to use

Materials/plant	Range	Typical sizes	Notes
Hydraulic lime		25kg and 30kg bags	Added to mortar for colour and smoothness
Architectural masonry	To form heads, cills, lintels, mullions, transoms, surrounds, arches, quoins, columns, ballustrades, etc.	Standards sizes or purpose-made	May be on long delivery. Reformed stone or natural
Flue liners	Clay or pumice	150–300mm and over	Must be laid socket up
Starter block or throat	Fire-proof concrete	Various sizes	Used instead of corbelling to narrow off the fireplace opening to the flue
Firebacks	Fire-proof concrete	Various sizes	
Chimney pots	Open roll top, cowled, vented, fan assisted, decorative, etc.		Usually clay. Reclaimed ones can look good
Meter boxes	GRP white or brown		May be supplied by boards. Otherwise available from merchants. Hockey-stick connection needed with electricity box
Wall ties	Wide variety of sizes and shapes. All to DD140 in stainless steel	200mm, 225mm and 250mm	Plus plastic clips to secure insulation if using partial fill
Expanded metal		65mm, 115mm, 175mm, 225mm and 305mm x 20m rolls	To reinforce brickwork
Lintels	'T' lintels, combined lintels. Steel, galvanised and insulated	Full range of profiles and shapes to suit each situation, 600–4,800mm	Use combined insulated wherever possible
Weeper vents	Plastic in red or black	65mm x 15mm x 75mm	To allow moisture to vent harmlessly to the outside at lintels and cavity trays. To vent cavity in timber frame
Air bricks	Fireclay, terracottta and plastic	225mm x 75mm and 150mm	To vent beneath voids
Cavity liners	Fireclay, terracotta and plastic	225mm x 75mm and 225mm x 150mm	Provides clear space air bridge in the cavity
Cavity wall insulation	Glass fibre or mineral wool batts.	455mm x 1,200mm x 40mm–150mm	Used as full-fill cavity insulation
	Rigid foam sheets	450mm x 1,200mm x 17mm–100mm	Used as partial-fill insulation
Weatherboarding	Shiplap, feather-edged or wany-edged	8–15mm x 191mm–225mm in random lengths	Must be tanalised or pressure-treated
Expansion jointing	Fibreboard	10–15mm x 2,400mm x 100mm	For use with large areas of blockwork and with concrete bricks
Mastics and sealants	Sand mastic – trowel applied Tube mastics	3.5kg tubs 310ml tubes	For sealing gaps around external frames and over expansion joints
Expanding foam	Aerosol tubes		To fill gaps in brickwork and blockwork or seal around exits
Cavity closers	Pvc-u, expanded polystyrene and rock fibre	2.1–6m lengths to suit various cavity widths	Closes the cavity at reveals and openings whilst preventing cold bridging
Steel purlins, RSJs, laminated beams, oak beams	Available in various sections Can be used in decorative situations	Size and profile to engineer's specification	Steel beams must be painted in red metal primer before being placed
Padstones and spreader beams	Cast in situ. concrete Pre-stressed lintels	Size determined by engineer	Padstones prevent point loading and crushing. Spreader beams spread the point load across a wider wall area
Cavity trays	Built-in lead or polythene. Proprietary stepped and stop-ended plastic with lead skirting		Must be used where a lower roof abuts a wall

Materials/plant	Range	Typical sizes	Notes
Lead	Code 4	150–600mm rolls	Used as chimney trays, skirts, flashings, cavity trays, soakers, etc.
Timber joists and trimmers		150–225mm x 50–150mm in various lengths	Plain sawn lumber
Bolts and plates	Various types	Various sizes	Used to bolt timber together with dog plates or to bolt RSJs together with washers
Prefabricated timber joists	'I' beams	Various lengths and profiles	
Joist hangers	Galvanised steel	Various sizes 50–150mm Various configurations	Carry joists to all external walls
Lateral restraint straps	Galvanised steel – pre-drilled	1,200mm	Built in every 2m to cross 3 joists. To strengthen joints
Framing anchors	Various profiles		
Decking	Moisture-resistant chipboard Tongued-and-grooved timber	2,400mm x 600mm x 18mm and 22mm 150–175mm x 19mm or 28mm in random lengths	Fix with ringshank nails or screws. Glue all edges and to board Screwfix for quietness
Glues	Wood glues	5-litre containers	Use on all tongued-and-grooved edges and between boards and joists
Board clips Concrete floor beams	Standard or acoustic Various lengths and profiles	Various profiles 175mm and 225mm	To fix battens to screed or concrete. Lay in accordance with manufacturer's instructions and layout
Infill blocks	Solid or aerated concrete Polystyrene purpose made	Standard block sizes	Must be brush-grouted when laid
Insulation	Rigid polyurathane sheeting Glass, mineral and acoustic wool	400mm, 450mm, 600mm and 1,200mm x 2,440 sheets – 25–100mm thick 200mm thick x 4.5m rolls	Used between joists and within internal and external studwork
Timber frame panels	Supplied and erected as part of the timber-frame package	As designed by manufacturer	Check what is included in the package, i.e. trusses and external joinery
Vapour barrier	300MU	4m x 25m rolls	For use with open-panel timber frames
Noggings	Sawn lumber in random lengths	50–100mm x 50–150mm	For use between joists to support decking, at perimeters to support plasterboard and within studwork to brace and support fittings
Nails/screws	Plain, galvanised, zinc electro-plated and black phosphate	Various lengths, widths and profiles	Cheaper to buy in boxes
Studwork internal partitioning	CLS timber Sawn lumber	47mm x 89mm x 2.7m 75mm and 100mm x 50mm nominal in various lengths	Smooth-planed finish Rough-sawn
Door linings	Softwood and hardwood	115mm and 138mm widths in sets to suit 2'3", 2'6" and 2'9" doors	Supplied in sets of two legs plus a head, plus stops. Doors sold in imperial
External joinery – windows	Pvc-u, steel, softwood, hardwood and aluminium. Casement, sash, tilt and turn. Plus purpose-made, arched bay, bow and porthole	Standard widths 400mm, 450mm and 600mm modules. Standard heights 600mm, 900mm, 1,050mm, 1,200mm, 1,350mm and 1,500mm. Plus purpose-made	Can be built in as the building progresses or left to be fitted later within profiles or clear openings
External joinery – door frames	Standard door frames Plus sidelights French doors	Single mobility 933mm x 2,100mm. Single standard 900mm x 2,100mm.	Hardwood, softwood, Pvc-u, aluminium. Standard cills, level or retractable thresholds

Materials/plant	Range	Typical sizes	Notes
Patio doors		Standard or purpose made 1,200mm, 1,500mm 1,800mm, 2,400mm	
Garage door frames		Usually 75mm x 75mm softwood but can be hardwood or steel. Size to suit opening and garage door	
Thresholds	Various profiles to provide a level threshold	775mm upwards	Aluminium with retractable rubber water bar
Staircase flights	Softwood, hardwood or combinations. Steel, cast iron. Straight flights. Quarter and half landings. Turned flights. Spiral.	To suit ceiling heights rising and going	Cover treads to prevent damage
Wallplate	Sawn lumber	75mm and 100mm x 100mm and 150mm in random lengths	Must be scarfed and bedded. Ties plate down to superstructure
Wallplate straps	Galvanised pre-drilled	900mm	

Roof construction

Materials/plant	Range	Typical sizes	Notes
Pre-fabricated roof trusse	Standard and attic trusses .	To manufacturer's design and specification	Must be assembled in accordance with instructions. Never cut a truss unless authorised by manufacturer and supplier
Truss clips	Various widths to suit rafters		Fixes trusses to plate
Sawn lumber	Rafters, purlins, hips, valleys, ceiling and collar ties, etc.	Various sections and lengths determined by designer	For constructing a cut and pitch roof on site.
Nails/screws	Bright and galvanised	Various lengths, diameters and profiles	Cheaper to buy in boxes
Bindings and bracings	Sawn lumber	100mm x 25mm in random lengths	Trusses and rafters must be braced longitudinally at the node points and diagonally from plate to ridge
Batten	Sawn lumber	50mm x 25mm in random lengths	For temporary bracing
Plywood	9.5–20mm exterior quality	2,400 x 1,200 sheets	Used to construct valley lay boards, dormer cheeks and back gullies
Facia board	Planed all round softwood or hardwood. Pvc-u. Grooved or plain	175–225mm x 25mm in various lengths	Masks ends of rafters and carries guttering
Soffit board	Plywood, fibreboard or Pvc-u	2,400 x 1,200 sheets or various widths	Masks underside of rafters beyond the walling
Soffit ventilator	Plastic in various colours	3m lengths	For use with ventilated or 'cold' roofs
Roof lights	Opening or fixed	300–1,200mm wide by various depths	Rafters may need crippling and doubling or trebling up on each side
Insulation	Mineral wool or glass fibre Rigid foam	100–200mm thick rolls or batts 17–100mm in 2,400mm x 1,200mm sheets	Laid between ceiling joists and between rafters with an air gap. Can be laid over, under or between rafters

Roof covering

Materials/plant	Range	Typical sizes	Notes
Hoist and elevators	Range 5–34m		For loading out the roof tiles
Sarking boarding	OSB, moisture-resistant chipboard or exterior-quality plywood. Sawn timber	2,400mm x 1,200mm x 18mm sheets 150mm x 15mm in random lengths	Used mainly in Scotland

Materials/plant	Range	Typical sizes	Notes
Underslating/ sarking felt	Reinforced bitumen felt, polythene-based or breathable membrane	1m x 15m and 20m rolls	Use of a breathable membrane may negate need for ventilation
Counter and tile battens	Sawn treated lumber	50 x 25mm in random lengths	
Nails	Galvanised	Preferably 2.5 times batten thickness	
Concrete inter-locking roof tiles	Flat or profiled. Plus verge tiles and top slates. Dry verge available with some types	9 –11 to the square metre	Nailing in accordance with manufacturer's instructions and weather rating
Clay pantiles	Single or double roll Plus verge tiles and top slates	16 to the square metre	
Plain tiles	Clay handmade or machine-made or concrete. Plus tile and a half, eaves and valley tiles	268mm x 165mm – 60 to the square metre	Handmade clay are the most expensive. Normally nailed every 3rd course
Natural slate	Welsh (expensive), reclaimed, Spanish, Chinese, Brazilian and Canadian	Various sizes but typically 500mm x 250mm – 20 to the square metre	Each slate must be nailed at least once
Simulated slate	Single lap interlocking Treble lap standard	13 to the square metre 20 to the square metre	Needs proprietary clips and nails
Slating nails	Hot galvanised steel, copper or aluminium	30mm, 40mm and 65mm	
Fixtures and fittings	Tile clips, vents, soffit strips		
Undercloak	Fibreboard	300mm x 2.4m	Bedded to top brickwork at gable ends or nailed to gable ladders beneath verge tiles
Mortar	Natural or coloured Available in ready-mixed 5-litre tubs	Sand and cement usually available from other trades' use	For pointing up at the verges and bedding ridge tiles
Ventilation	Continuous dry ridge	3m lengths	Fixes ridge tiles without the need for mortar bedding
Ridge tiles	Clay or concrete in various colours and profiles	350mm, 375mm and 450mm	Angled in various pitches or half round
Hip tiles	Clay or concrete in various colours and profiles	350mm, 375mm and 450mm	One third round or angled in various pitches
Hip irons	Galvanised steel	Various sizes and profiles	To hold the hip tiles in place
Valleys	Formed in situ. in lead Preformed GRP Valley tiles	Various pitches and lengths	Must be dressed over the batten at the edge of the layboard beneath the tiles/slates. Used with plain tiles
Lead	Code 4	150–600mm rolls	Used for valleys, chimney trays, skirts, flashings and soakers

Domestic hot- and cold-water plumbing and central heating

Roof plumbing components	Guttering, downpipe and fittings. Plastic, square, half round and ogee. Copper, aluminium and cast iron	Standard 110mm with 65mm downpipe	Use high capacity in Scotland and severe-weather-rated areas
Screws	Black phosphate, brass or zinc	25–40mm	
Supply piping	MDPE pipe	25mm diameter in 25m and 50m rolls	

Materials/plant	Range	Typical sizes	Notes
Copper pipe		15mm, 22mm and 28mm diameter in 3m and 6m lengths	Various fittings available including capillary, soldered joints and compression
Polybutylene pipe		15mm, 22mm and 28mm diameter in 3m and 6m lengths or rolls	Push fit and compression
Microbore pipe	Copper	6mm, 8mm and 10mm in rolls	
Insulation sheathing	Foam polyethylene	9 –25mm internal diameter	
Fittings	Straight connectors, tap connectors, valves, bends, blank ends, stopcocks, branches, drain offs, reducers, washers, gate valves, etc.	Available in copper, brass and plastic to suit pipe chosen. Full range of sizes and uses	Match the plumber with the chosen pipe system. Don't force a plumber to use a system with which they are unfamiliar
Pipe clips	Plastic, brass or copper	To suit tube	Allow space for pipe insulation
Waste water system	Pushfit or solvent weld plastic	32mm, 40mm and 50mm plus 100mm ventpipes and bosses	Vent pipes directly connect to underground drainage at the oversite
Overflow		22mm plastic piping, usually white	
Header tanks	Black plastic	4-, 25-, 50-, 60-, 70- and 100-gallon	Will need tanks stands building in roof. Still quoted in imperial
Cold water jackets		40mm to suit various sized tanks	
Warm water jackets	80mm thickness to suit most tanks		Think carefully about replacing older uninsulated tanks
Indirect cylinders	Copper with applied insulation	117 litres, 140 litres and 162 litres	
Direct cylinder	Copper with applied insulation	117 litres, 140 litres and 162 litres	
Mains-pressure hot-water cylinder	Steel with applied insulation and casing	150–500 litres	Most homes have 250–300-litre size
Gas piping	Yellow-coated copper tube	15mm and 22mm in 3m and 6m lengths	
Oil piping		10mm x 25m rolls	
Oil tank	Single or twin-walled GRP	900–5000 litres	1,200 litres is the most common
Fire valve			Fitted at the boiler to cut off supply in case of fire
LPG tank	Overground or underground	Various sizes	Usually provided on contract from lpg supply company
Boilers	Gas, oil or lpg system, condensing and combination	40,000–120,000 Btu	Use boilers with an efficiency of at least 86% from SEDBUK ratings 'A' and 'B'
Electric boilers	For wet systems	2–5Kw	Suitable for small flats or houses, garages, conservatories and outbuildings
Heat pumps		Various capacities and outputs	There may be a grant towards the use of this technology
Photovoltaic cells	Various types. Some more obtrusive than others	Array of sizes to suit requirement	There may be a grant towards the use of this technology. Converters and battery storage may be necessary
Solar panels	Various types	Array of sizes to suit requirement	Best used for hot water rather than space heating requirements
Cooker boilers	Gas-, oil- or solid-fuel-fired	Various sizes and colours	Very heavy. Make sure the floor can take it. Some heat the hot water. Some can run radiators. Some just cook
Radiators	Round-top, seamed-top or compact. Special design types available. Towel rail radiators	Huge range – single or double	

Materials/plant	Range	Typical sizes	Notes
Thermostatic radiator valves	Various brands	15mm	
Under-floor central heating pipework	PEX or polybutylene	Various sizes but nominally 15mm	System, fittings, manifold and controls designed by suppliers and manufacturers
Motorised valves and pumps	To suit system		Control the system – operated by the timer or programmer
Programmer		Huge range from 24-hour to 28 days	Some can be remotely controlled
Room thermostat	Various types		May be supplied by system installer
Warm air heating	Various types		Ducting needs to be thought of at groundwork stage
Heat recovery and mechanical ventilation	Various models		Can include air conditioning
Air conditioning	Various models		Can be combined with heat recovery and whole-house ventilation systems

Electrics

Materials/plant	Range	Typical sizes	Notes
Cables and wires	Various. Two core and earth, three core and earth, single core, steel wire armoured, bonding cable etc. TV co-ax cable. CCTV. Telephone wire. 2- and 3-core bell wire	5–30 amp	Your electrician will decide what goes where
Cable clips	White plastic with obo nails	Various sizes	All cable should be securely clipped to joists and studs
Earth sleeving	Green and yellow		To sleeve earth wires
Earth clamps			Grade depends on loading
Earth rod	Various		Used with overhead supply and on mobile homes
Back boxes	Galvanised steel	Various sizes and depths to suit plaster and plasterboard substrates	
Sheathing and conduit	Pvc-u or galvanised metal	Various lengths and widths	All wiring to be buried in plaster or behind plasterboard must be adequately sheathed. Surface wiring must be run through conduits
Switches, sockets and pendants	White or coloured plastic, brass, brass and timber. Fused spurred outlets. Dimmer switches. Cooker panels. Plain or moulded ceiling roses	Single, double	Changing from standard white can greatly increase the costs
Connectors and distributors	White plastic	Various opening numbers that can be punched out	
TV points	White plastic, brass, etc.		
Telephone jack points	White plastic		Service providers may supply jack points, digital access boxes and broadband units
Lighting	Chandelier, standard pendant, wall lights, main voltage halogen, low-voltage downlighters, strip lighting, external lighting, security lighting with PIR, emergency lighting, etc.	Various	Electricians will quote for standard light fittings but will fit fancy fitments free of charge. Do not expect a refund on the standard, which will pay for the extra hassle
Transformers		20–300W	For use with low-voltage lighting

Materials/plant	Range	Typical sizes	Notes
Extractor fans	Through wall, in-line, low-voltage centrifugal	Kitchen over hob 30 litres per sec. Elsewhere 60 litres per sec. Bathrooms 15 litres per sec. Utility rooms 30 litres per sec. Toilets 6 litres per sec.	In bathrooms and toilets the fan should come on with the light and have a 15-minute overrun
Power showers	Various models	7–10Kw	High load
Consumer unit	Various		Split lighting and power. Lighting and central heating protected by MCBs (miniature circuit breakers) to detect short circuit and cut power. Power circuits protected by RCDs (residual current breaker devices) that cut power at slightest earth leakage. Alarms on separate circuit
Smoke alarms and heat detectors	Mains-operated with battery back-up		Smoke alarms within 7m of any habitable rooms on each floor. Heat detectors for kitchens
Shaving point			Can incorporate strip light
Pelmet and strip lighting		Various lengths	

Plastering and rendering

Plasterboard	Square or tapered edge. Moisture-resistant. Foil-backed. Fire-retardant. Acoustic	9.5mm, 12.5mm and 15mm and plank @19mm	No need to nog joints in ceiling if 15mm used
Thermally bonded plasterboard	Polystyrene, urethane or pheolic-bonded	2,400mm x 1,200mm x various thickness	For use on external walls, walls to unheated spaces and on ceilings to Insulated lathing board improves insulation. Used in place of expanded metal to provide extra insulation
Joint filler	Numerous products	10kg and 12kg bags. 12-litre and 22kg ready-mixed	
Gypsum fibreboard		2,400mm x 1,200mm x various thicknesses	Good for carrying weights and sound insulation
Scrim tape	Plain or GRP-reinforced. Self-adhesive. Paper or 'silk'	90–150m rolls	Used at all board joints and at junctions with another substrate plus ceilings to walls
Beadings	Stop, bellmouth, angle, embedded, etc.	2.4m and 3m lengths plus 33m rolls	Expanded mesh type for renders and hard plasters. Embedded for skim and top coat
Expanded metal	Rolls or sheets	600mm x 1,200mm 305mm x 20m rolls	Fixed to battening to take render. Used to strengthen junction of different substrates
Plaster	Thistle, hardwall, tough coat, renovating, bonding browning, one coat. Plaster of Paris	25kg bags	Finishing 3mm coats and one coat Used for mouldings and to repair lathe and plaster ceilings
Hessian		1,370mm x 46m rolls	Used with plaster of Paris to repair lathe and plaster ceilings
Mixer	Electric or petrol	3.5 and 5cu. m	Probably the same one as used by the bricklayers and roofers
Cement	Standard, masonry, rapid hardening, sulphate resistant, coloured	25kg bags	Store in the dry
Plasticiser		1–250 litres	Follow dosages and instructions

Materials/plant	Range	Typical sizes	Notes
Sand	Sharp or soft	1-tonne non-returnable bags. 10-, 15- and 20-tonne full loads	Use the same sand to maintain the mortar colour
Ready-mixed screeds	1:3 sharp sand and cement	1-cu. m min. loads	Retarders added
Ready-mixed renders	Various mixes with retarders, waterproofers and colouring added	12-cu. m min. loads	
Non-hydraulic lime	Mature, coarse and fine	20-litre tubs	Pre-mixed, ready to use
Hydraulic lime		25kg and 30kg bags	Added to mortar for colour and smoothness
Fine fillers		7kg tubs	
Animal hair	Usually goats'	Bundles	Added to lime mortar when rendering or plastering
Split lathes	Chestnut or oak	3', 3'6" and 4'	Lathes sold in imperial
Coving and mouldings	Plaster of Paris or polystyrene. Coving, dado rails, ceiling mouldings, cornices, picture rails, niches and columns, etc	Various sizes and styles	
Adhesive	Proprietary from mouldings makers or PVA	5kg and 12kg bags	
Artex		15kg and 25kg bags	
Damp-proof membrane	250 and 300MU	4m x 25m rolls	Used as vapour barrier and as membrane beneath screeds and insulation

Second fix, fitting out and decoration

Internal doors	Hardwood, softwood. Fully or part glazed. Pre-finished or for staining or painting. Moulded, panel, ledged and braced, framed ledged and braced, etc.	2'3", 2'6" and 2'9" x 6'6"	Doors sold in imperial sizes. Frames in metric. See tables in Part 'M' regulations for required widths
Fire doors	Available in most of the sizes and styles of standard doors. FD30 denotes 30 minutes' fire resistance	FD30 = 44mm FD60 = 54mm	May have the intumescent strip built into the door or frame Must be self-closing
External doors	Pvc-u, steel, hardwood, softwood. Moulded, panelled, fully and partly glazed, framed ledged and braced, etc.	807mm x 2,000mm standard 2'9" x 6'6"	Take care not to hang too early in case of damage. Consider temporary doors. Doors sold in imperial
Patio doors and French doors	Huge range. Pvc-u, hardwood, softwood and aluminium	Usually 1,200mm, 1,500mm 1,800mm and 2,400mm	
Garage doors	Huge range. GRP, steel, hardwood and softwood. Up and over, rolling, side opening, etc.	Various sizes available. Standard 2,139mm x 1,980 high and 2,130mm x 2,130 high	Remember that side-opening doors may further restrict the opening width. Automatic garage door opening is available for most types. Can be pre-finished
Window boards	Hardwood, softwood, Pvc-u or MDF. Usually bullnosed and rebated	200–300mm x 32mm by various lengths	Usually fixed at first-fix stage before plastering
Staircase newels, balustrading, aprons, hand rails, etc.	Huge range of styles. Steel, cast iron, glass, perspex, hardwood and softwood		A 100mm ball must not be able to pass through any part of the staircase
Loft access covers	Timber or GRP. Hinged or loose	Various sizes	With or without ladders

Materials/plant	Range	Typical sizes	Notes
Timber mouldings	Skirtings, architraves, dado rails, picture rails, cornices, etc.	Various sizes and mouldings such as Torus, ogee, bullnosed, chamfered, etc.	Prime, stain or undercoat back before fixing
Glues	Wood glues Contact adhesives	5-litre containers 310ml tubes	Use on all tongue-and-grooved edges between boards and joists
Mastics and sealants	Tube mastics	310ml tubes	For sealing gaps around frames
Expanding foam	Aerosol tubes		To fill gaps in brickwork and blockwork or seal around exits
Nails/screws/fixings/fastenings	Plain, galvanised, zinc electro-plated and black phosphate	Various lengths, widths and profiles	Cheaper to buy in boxes
Plywood	9.5–20mm	2,400 x 1,200 sheets	Final boxing in and framing
Ironmongery and door furniture	Huge range of styles. Brass, anodised aluminium, satin and bright chrome, black cast iron and black painted	Often sold in pre-packed sets	Use five-lever mortice locks to all external doors, plus barrel locks. Security and espanolette locking available
Shelving	Melamine, timber, steel, etc.		
Fitted wardrobe tracking	Timber, Pvc-u and aluminium		Huge range of floor- and ceiling-mounted sliding tracks
Sanitaryware	Huge range	Huge range	Remember, flair and imagination count for more than just money
Kitchen/utility room/fitted bedroom units	Huge range	Flat pack or pre-assembled	Remember: flair and imagination count for more than just money. Flat pack may be cheaper but labour costs will be higher. Many suppliers include appliances
Heater or de-humidifier		Various types	Hired by the week. Take care not to force a house dry – it'll cause cracking
Paints, stains and varnishes	Undercoat, primer, gloss and emulsion. Microporous stains. Matt, vinyl, satin and gloss. Non-drip or standard. Solvent or water-based. Exterior paints in smooth or textured. Metal paints and rust-protective coatings. Huge range of colours	0.5 –20-litre cans and tubs	Use trade emulsion for first decoration of hard-plastered walls
Knotting		0.5–5-litre cans	Essential if painting timber
Tools	Brushes, palette knives, scrapers, etc.	Various sizes and qualities	
Sandpaper	Various grades	S2, F2, M2, etc.	
Fillers	Wood fillers. All-purpose fillers	1.8kg boxes. 2.5 and 5-litre tubs	Readymix or powder
Floor and wall tiles	Huge range. Ceramic, stove, slate, earthenware, clay, terracotta, marble, etc.	Huge range of sizes, shapes and thicknesses	Use the correct adhesive and grout for each situation and in accordance with the supplier's instructions. Consider flexible adhesive and grout for most flooring situations. Make sure grouting in bathrooms etc. is waterproof

External hard and soft landscaping

Laser level, dumpy or Cowley			Some groundworkers have them. They can be hired and surveyors will have their own
Tipper lorries		10-,15- and 20-tonne	Identify these early on and find out where they will be tipping

Materials/plant	Range	Typical sizes	Notes
Diggers/ excavators	Typical JCB types or tracked 360-degree machines required	700mm, 600mm and 450mm buckets	Usually hired with a driver
Dumpers	2- and 4-wheel drive	1–4-tonne	Necessary if storing spoil on site
Concrete	Ready-mixed in 4, 5 and 6cu. m loads	GEN 1 for foundations	Site mixed
Mixer	Electric or petrol	3.5 and 5cu. m	Hired by the week
Water butt and hose	180-litre. Butts or drums		Position at the mixing point close to the sand
Reinforcement mesh bar	C503, A142 or A252	4,800mm x 2,400mm 10mm and 12mm in 6m lengths	May need wiring together. May need to be in two layers 50mm from top and bottom of concrete
Type 1 stone		10-, 15- and 20-tonne loads	For access and hardstandings
Vibrating plates		400mm x 370mm 540mm x 290mm	For compacting roadstone and hardcore infills
Rollers		560mm or 750mm widths	Hired by the day
Blocks	Solid concrete, aerated concrete, lightweight. 2.8N to 25N strength	215mm x 440mm 215mm x 620mm 75–450mm thick	Buy in direct loads. Use the right blocks for each situation as specified
Bricks	Commons in clay or concrete, Class B and A Engineering, handmade, wirecut or stock, sand-faced Flettons	63mm x 220mm standard	Different materials for different situations. Use the right ones as specified
Reformed stone	Smooth, pitched or moulded. Various colours	Various sizes and mixes	Can be laid by bricklayers. May be in sections
Natural stone	From local quarries	Cut to 100–150mm on bed or random as dug	May need a backing block
Flint	As dug or knapped. Blue–brown	Often sold by the oil drum or by the tonne	May need a backing block
Wall ties	Wide variety of sizes and shapes	All to DD140 in stainless steel	200mm, 225mm and 250mm
Fencing	Panel fencing in various types. Close-boarded fencing. Feather-edge boarding and arris railing. Posts and rails. Hit and miss. Ranch style. Paling. Posts can be treated timber, softwood, oak or concrete. Gravel boards can be in timber or concrete	All sizes 100mm x 100–150mm x 100mm and 150mm timber in 2m and 2.4m lengths. 100mm x 80mm concrete in 2m and 2.4m lengths	Make sure all timber is treated
Timber decking	Hardwood, cedar or softwood. Ribbed or smooth	20mm x 94mm, 27mm x 118mm or 33mm, 118mm in various lengths	
Timber joists and trimmers		150–225mm x 50–150mm in various lengths	Plain-sawn lumber. Timber posts as for fencing
Joist hangers	Galvanised steel	Various sizes from 50–150mm. Various configurations	
Decorative aggregates	Pebbles and stones	25kg bags 1-tonne bags Full 10–15-tonne loads	
Turf	Various grades available, which all end up the same if not treated	Sold by the square yard	Must be watered every day when laid
Top soil	10–20-tonne loads		Watch the small ads in your local paper. Keep spoil on site as far as is possible
Hedging and trees	Native is best		Bare-rooted is cheaper in the autumn

Chapter 12

THE EXAMPLE HOUSE

Throughout this book I have made reference to 'the example house'. Well, here it is, together with the costings on which many of the assertions within this book are based. Interestingly, although they are put together using costs for labour and materials in the last two homes I have built, the costings actually work out at considerably less. Why should this happen?

As I said earlier, if you work the figures out on strict measurement and without adding in contingencies they are bound to come out less. Without contingencies added in the house works out at £515 per square metre, which is a lot lower than the figures in the *Homebuilding & Renovating (H&R)* table. However, if you add in a 10% contingency that brings

it up to £566 per square metre, and at that figure it begins to accord with the 'standard' specification for houses of this type built in the south-west of England. Are these figures impossible? Well no, actually. I have recently met and written a story about a couple who built for exactly £500 per square metre.

All of the labour and material prices are exclusive of VAT and renovators will have to add this to their prices. Plant is inclusive of VAT as, even with new build, this is not recoverable.

In order to be able to compare this hypothetical house with the real thing it is necessary to add in some figures for the preliminaries, service and professional charges. For these I have drawn largely on the experiences of the first of the two self-builds in Chapter 14, as in terms of accommodation, it is very similar to the example house. What I haven't included are solicitors' and agents' costs.

Similarly, at the end, I've largely assumed external hard landscaping and gardening costs that are broadly in line.

One thing that is absent in cost terms is carpeting, although I have included some areas of floor tiling. Perhaps that is an oversight, especially as I have included them in the expenditure for my own self-builds. But on the other hand, many developers selling a house of this type would not include carpets. The magazines also tend to exclude them in their costings.

Pre-start costs	
Drawings (architectural technician), say	£1,500
Structural engineer's fees	£100
Planning & Building Regulations applications and fees	£642
Supply of electricity, say	£500
Supply of gas, say	£300
Supply of water and sewage connection charge, say	£1,200
Warranty provider	£1,200
Site insurance	£660
Total	**£6,102**

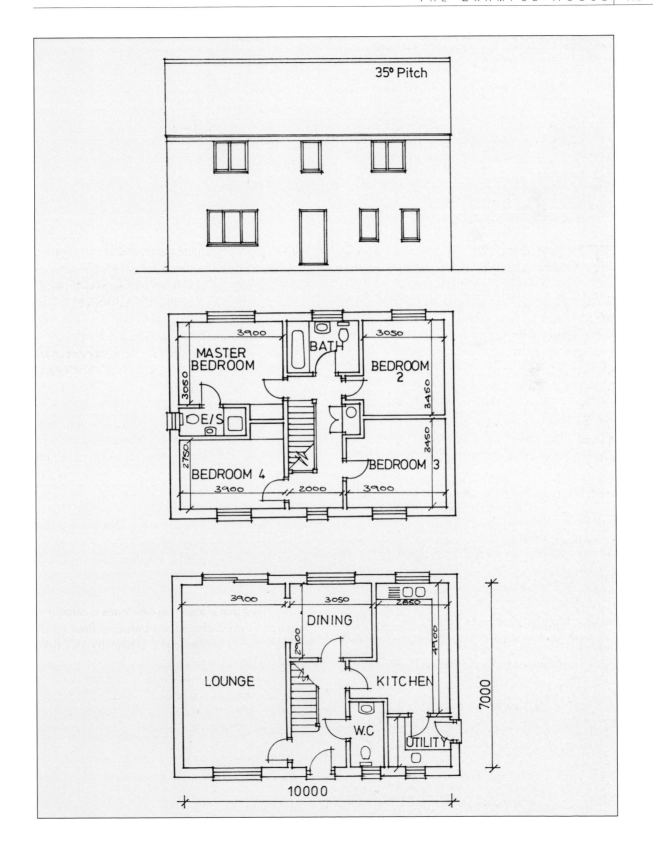

35° Pitch

MASTER BEDROOM
3900
3050
BATH
BEDROOM 2
3050
3460
E/S
2750
BEDROOM 4
3900
2000
BEDROOM 3
3900
3450

DINING
3900
3050
2850
2900
4100
LOUNGE
KITCHEN
W.C
UTILITY
7000
10000

Groundworks

Operation	Materials (ex VAT)		Plant		Labour		Total
Stripersite and set out	Pegs	£15	Digger hire, 1 day	£258	2 man days	£240	£513
Dig foundations	Level pins	£30	Digger hire, 3 days	£775	6 man days	£720	£1,525
Muck away			5 lorries @ £250 each	£1,250			£1,250
Concrete foundations (trenchfill)	36cu. m concrete @ per cu. m (6 loads) = £2,160	£60	Pump hire	£382	2 man days	£240	£2,782
Build footings in 100sq. m blockwork (3 courses internal and 2 courses external)	blocks Mortar Dpm/dpc Wall ties Lintels	£500 £72 £110 £50 £30 £762	Mixer hire	£70	90sq. m @ £8.50 = £765		£1,597
Consolidate and fill oversite	Hardcore (20cu.m) Sand blinding Membrane Insulation	£250 £75 £65 £98 £488	Wacker plate	£18	4 man days	£480	£986
Concrete oversite	6cu. m @ £60	£360			2 man days	£240	£ 600
Drains	Say 30 L.metres (including manholes)	£600	Digger hire, 3 days	£775	6 man days	£720	£2,095
						Total	£11,348

Bricklayers

Build blockwork inner skin and partition walls	160sq. m insulation blocks @ £7.30 per m = £1,168 50sq. m partition blocks @ £4.20 per m = £210 £1,378		10 weeks' mixer hire @ £30 per wk + VAT = £350 10 weeks' scaffold hire @ £190 per wk + VAT = £2,235 £2,585	210sq. m blockwork @ £8.50 per sq. m	= £1,785	£5,748
Build brickwork outer skin in conjunction with above	11,000 bricks (inc. wastage) @ £260 per 1,000 = £2,860			10,000 bricks @ £300 per 1,000 = £3,000		£5,860
Frames. Pvc-u. Front door, patio door, back door and casement windows	PC sum	£4,000		Fixing	£500	£4,500
Ancillary materials	Sand Cement Plasticiser Wall insulation Cavity closers Wall ties Lintels Steel joist Lateral restraint & plate straps Dpc	£256 £224 £8 £400 £200 £55 £400 £156 £30 £20 £1,749		£420		£2,169
					Total	£18,277

Carpenter
FIRST FIX

Operation	Materials		Labour		Total
Cut and lay first-floor joists	Joists 168.3m @ £2.28 per m	= £384			
	Trimmers 5.7m @ £3.55 per m	= £20			
	Strutting	= £66			
	Joist hangers	= £28	3 man days @ £160	= £480	
	Nails	= £19			
	Batten	= £7			
	Lateral restraint straps	= £64			
		£588			£1,068
Door linings to ground floor	5 sets @ £11.71 per set	= £591	man day	= £160	
	Fixings	= £12			
		£71			£231
First floor decking	55 sheets @ £8.98	= £494	2 man days	= £320	
	Nails & glue	= £74			
		£568			£888
Studwork	292m @ 87p	= £254	3 man days	= £480	
	7 linings @ £11.71	= £82			
	Nails & fixings	= £19			
		£355			£835
Window boards	12 metres	= £43			
Staircase flight		= £102			
Plasterboard noggings		= £35			
Pipe boxing (done later)		= £105	3 man days	= £560	
First-floor zone insulation (done later)		= £263			
Studwork insulation (done later)		= £273			
		£821			£1,381
				Total	**£4,403**

Roof

Operation	Materials		Labour		Total
Erect and finish prefabricated roof using standard 'fink' trusses	17 trusses @ £36.22 each	= £616			
	Bindings 140m @ 69p per m	= £97			
	Truss clips and fixings	= £24			
	Wallplate 25m @ £1.78 per m	= £45			
	Plate straps	= £35			
	Facia board 22m @ £3.97 per m	= £88	7 man days	= £1,120	
	Soffit 22m @ £1.95 per m	= £43			
	Nails & fixings	= £19			
	Soffit ventilators	= £13			
		£980			£2,100
				Total	**£2,100**

SECOND FIX

Operation	Materials		Labour		Total
Lay floating floor to ground floor	55 sheets @ £8.98	= £ 494			
	Insulation 25 sheets 75mm	= £296	2 man days	= £320	
	Membrane (1 roll)	= £39			
	Glue	= £65			
		£894			£1,214
Assemble and fit staircase ballustrading, newels and handrails	Components	= £ 295	2 man days	= £320	
	Glue	= £13			
		£308			£628
Hang internal doors	13 no. @ £21.56 each	= £ 280	3 man days	= £480	
	Furniture @ £5.22 per set	= £68			
		£348			£828
Skirting & architrave	23 sets architrave	= £129			
	150m skirting	= £170	2 man days	= £320	
	Glue & nails	= £22			
		£321			£641
Airing cupboard slatting & loft trap	Slats	= £9			
	Offcuts + ply + insulation	= £10	¹/₂ man day	= £80	
		£19			£99
Kitchen units (flat pack)	PC sum	say £2,500	5 man days	= £800	£3,300

Total £6,710

Roof tiler

Materials		Labour		Total
Battens 530m @. 22 per m	= £117			
Nails 25kg + 2.5kg	= £ 53			
Breathable membrane 2 rolls	= £240	4 man days @ £160	= £480	
Undercloak 4mm x 3.9mm x 300mm	= £ 36			
Sand & cement & colouring, say	= £25			
	£471			£951
1,012 tiles 74 eaves tiles 80 toperslates } @ £790 per 1000 30 l/h verge tiles 30 r/h verge tiles	=£972	7 man days	= £1,120	
22 ridge tiles @ £1.85 each	= £41			
	=£1,013			£2,133

Total £3,084

Plumbing and central heating

Operation	Materials		Labour		Total
Hot & cold domestic plumbing	12 radiators, 10 with				
Boiler & tanks	TRVs	=£756			
Central heating	Controls	£174			
Fixing sanitaryware	Mains pressure cylinder	£570			
Guttering & downpipe	Boiler	£708	15 days @ £200 per man day		
	Pipe & fittings	£753			
	Gutter & downpipe	£213		= £3,000.00	
	Sanitaryware PC sum	£800			
		£3,974			£6,974

Total £6,974

Electrical

Operation	Materials	Labour	Total
First-fix electrical carcassing	Cable, channel, earth rods, back boxes, etc. £220.00	4 days @ £165 per man day = £660	£880
Second-fix electrical including faceplates to switches and sockets, extractor fans, light pendants, consumer unit and fitting of light fittings. Cross & earth bonding to pipework & sanitaryware. Wiring of boiler, thermostats and controls. Attendance with plumber for firing up and testing	Faceplates, fans, light pendants £377.00 Consumer unit £ 40.00 TV aerial (supply & fix) £140.00 Light fittings PC sum £300.00 £857.00	4 days @ £165 per man day =£660	£1,517

Total **£2,397**

Plasterer

Tack ceilings	50 sheets 15mm plasterboard @ £6.28 each £314.00 Fixings £28.00 £342.00	140sq. m @ £3.50 = £490	£832
Set ceilings	14 bags thistle @ £3.86 each £54.00 Scrim tape £25.00 £79.00	140sq. m @ £4.50 = £630	£709
Float & set walls	Mixer hire 2 weeks £60.00 3 bags sand @ £32 each £96.00 21 bags cement @ £2.79 each £58.59 2 bags lime @ £12.82 17 bags Thistle @ £3.86 each £65.00 Additives £12.00 Beading £34.00 £338.41	205sq. m (inc. openings) @ £7.50 =£1,538	£1,876
Tack studwork	30 sheets 12.5mm plasterboard @ £4.30 each £129.00 Fixings £20.00 £149.00	77sq. m @ £3.25 £250	£399
Skimcoat studwork	Tape & filler £27.00 Beadings £25.00 8 bags Thistle @ £3.86 each £31.00 £83.00 £166.00	77sq. m @ £4.25 £327	£493

Total **£4,309**

Decorator

Operation	Materials		Labour	Total
Snagging. Walls – mist plus I emulsion. Timber – undercoat plus Satinwood. Ceilings – 2 coats emulsion	72 litres emulsion	£172.62		
	10 litres undercoat	£42.76		
	10 litres Satinwood	£55.68	14 days @ £65 per man day	
	Fillers, solvents & cleaners		= £910.00	
		£46.58		
	Brushes/sandpaper	£23.23		
		£340.87		£1,250.00

Total £1,250

The ceramic tiler

Tile floors	30sq. m tiles @ £12	= £360.00	30sq. m @ £15	= £450.00	
	Adhesive	£126.30			
	Grout	£23.08			
	Additive	£14.42			
		£523.80			£974

Tiles walls	23sq. m tiles @ £5	= £115.00	23 sq. metres @ £14 = £322.00	
	7 x 10 litres adhesive @ £15.10 each	= £105.70		
	Spacers	£3.58		
	Grout 5kg	£6.62		
		£230.90		£552

Total £1,527

External works

Operation	Materials		Labour		Total
40sq. m tarmac driveway	Slabs 120 @ £2 each	= £420.00	Supply & fix	£740.00	
Fencing – say 55m	Ballast	£29.00	Supply & fix	£720.00	
Pathways & patios – 42sq. m	Cement 10 bags @ £2.79		5 man days @ £120	£600.00	
		= £28.00			
Turf	272sq. m	£459.68	2 man days	£ 240.00	
		£936.68			
				£2,300.00	£2,147

Total £3,237

Total build cost £72,000

140sq. metre = £515 per sq. metre
Plus 10% contingency = £79,200 = £566 per sq. metre

With land ever scarcer and plots becoming smaller and smaller, building a basement can be a great way of increasing the floor area without increasing the footprint. But it's not easy and it doesn't come for free.

POSSIBLE EXTRAS – ALL SUBJECT TO A 10% CONTINGENCY:

We could cheer this house design up considerably without altering the floor plan, simply by adding a gable projection to the roof, laying back on the main roof. It would cost more but it might add value, and at only just over £8 per square metre extra it might be well worthwhile.

Gable projection to roof line – 5-metre span

Operation	Materials		Labour		Total
Gable end	10 sq. m blocks	£42.10	10sq.m blockwork		
	500 bricks	£150.00		£ 85.00	
	Mortar & ties	£50.00	500 bricks	£150.00	
		£242.10		£235.00	£477
Extra roof work	Trusses	£86.00	1 man day	£160.00	
	Plywood	£18.00			
		£104.00			£264
Roof tiling	Undercloak	£18.00			
	Lead valley	£75.00			
	Underlay	£120.00			
	Batten	£10.00	1 man day	£160.00	
	Toperslates	£25.00			
	Ridge tiles	£12.00			
		£260.00			£420

Total £1,161

The house is drawn and costed for face brickwork. But if you decided to have a rendered finish, then although the bricklaying costs would go down, the plastering costs would go up:

Possible plastering extras

External 2-coat render	3 bags sand @ £32 each= £96.00			
	21 bags cement @ £2.79 each			
	= £58.59	185sq. m (inclusive of openings)		
	Retarder & waterproofer	@ £9.00 = £1,665.00		
	£11.22			
	Beading & stops £62.35			
	£228.16			£1,893
Screed ground floor to 65mm depth	5 bags sand @ £32 each £160.00			
	70 bags cement @ £2.79 each	70sq. m @ £6.30		
	= £195.30	= £441.00		
	£355.30			£796

Total £2,689

In addition, you would have to have an independent scaffold and it would have to stay up longer for the painter. All in all this would probably cost another £4 per square metre of walling over and above the costs we've got in for a normal brickwork finish.

Screeding the floor instead of using a floating floor represents a minor saving on paper. But it's a wet trade at the later stages of the build and could contribute to longer drying-out times. The insulation and membrane, by the way, remain a constant factor, as we've decided in this example to put 25mm beneath the oversite with 75mm above it in both cases.

Many people think that a basement is always a good idea. And so it can be. With land ever scarcer and plots becoming smaller and smaller, building a basement can be great way of increasing the floor area without increasing the footprint. But it's not easy and it doesn't come for free. I've done it myself and it was always terrifying: a huge hole, which at times threatened to swallow up the neighbouring houses and which, when it rained, filled with water and started to slide inexorably in. Tanking, however hard you try, is always suspect. One pinprick and the whole structure would be compromised. What follows is the best case, but be aware that in bad ground these costs would inflate horribly.

Full basement

Operation	Materials		Plant		Labour		Total
Stripersite & set out	Pegs	£15	Digger hire, 1 day	£258	2 man days @ £120 = £240		£513
Excavations			Digger hire, 11 days	£2,838			
			Water pump	£60			
				£2,898	20 man days	£2,440	£5,338
Muck away – 325cu. m.	17 loads @ £250						
	= £4,250					£4250	
Concrete foundations	36cu.m @ £60 = £2160		Concrete pumper	£382	2 man days	£240	£2782
Build walls	102sq.m 100mm blocks				187 sq. m. @ £8.50		
	@ £4.21 = £430					= £1,590	
	85sq. m Hollow blocks		Mixer hire				
	@ £6.90 = £578		3 weeks @ £30 = £90		85 sq. m. @ £12		
	Mortar £200					= £1,044	
	Ties £50					£2,634	
	Reinforcement bar						
	105 x 6m @ £2.81 = £296						
	£1,554						£4,278
Consolidate & fill oversite	Hardcore (20cu. m) £250		Wacker plate	£18	4 man days	£480	£748
Concrete oversite	11cu. m @ £60 = £660		Concrete pumper	£382	2 man days	£240	
	Reinforcement mesh £181						
	£841						£1,463
Concrete infill	3 cu. m. handmixed						
	leanmix £60				2 man days	£240	£300
Tanking	External waterproofer						
	£100				6 man days	£720	
	Bituthene 16 rolls						
	@ £136 each = £2,176						
	£2,276						£2,996
Protective floor screed	6cu. m.@ £60 = £360				70sq. m @ £6.30 = £441		
	Insulation £360						
	Membrane £65						
	£785						£1,226
External ballast and land drainage	3 loads clean stone £300		2 days' digger hire		2 man days	£240	
	Land drains, say £100			£516			
	£400						£1,156
						Total	£25,000

So what does that mean? The cost of the basement shell is £25,000. But the shell is also the foundations for the original house. So if we assume the drainage costs remain constant, the actual extra cost is around £15,000. Therefore, we've gained 70 square metres for just £215 per square metre, which is good value. But I would remind you again that we have taken best case, and we have yet to fit out this shell. Still, on these figures this space could come in at around £85 per square metre cheaper than the rest of the house, less, of course, the contingencies, which in a structure of this complexity should be slightly more than for the rest of the house.

However, before you plan to build a basement, ask yourself one question. Why is it that in Germany basements are so popular, and yet they are virtually unheard of in much of Holland? The answer, of course, is ground conditions and water tables. Likewise, in heavy clay areas of this country or low-lying areas with high water tables there are exactly the same factors as those that mitigate against basements in Holland. It's not impossible – nothing is – but it should not be undertaken lightly and it's definitely not for amateurs. Certainly every self-builder I've ever warned about the dangers and complexities of building a basement has come back to me and told me I was quite right. I think if ever I was going to build a basement again, I'd choose to do it using the prefabricated concrete type from a company such as Thermonex. Whilst, on paper, and at the beginning, they might appear to be slightly more expensive, the fact that it's 'job done' when they've finished means that far less can go wrong and there's a lot less heartache involved.

Of course not everyone wants a full basement and in many cases it's simply the lie of the land that dictates that part of the building is going to find itself below ground.

Partial digging in – extra groundwork costs

Operation	Materials		Plant		Labour		Total
Extra excavations			Digger hire 2 days	£516	4 man days	£480	£996
Extra soil away	3 loads @ £250	= £750					£750
Extra hollow blocks	15 sq. m. @ £8.30 = £125 Mortar £50 Reinforcement bar £39	£214	Mixer hire 1 week	£70	Bricklayers – daywork	£300	£584
Infill blocks	1cu. m lean mix	£40			2 man days	£240	£280
Tanking	6 rolls bituthene @ £136 per roll = £816	£1,056			2 man days	£240	
External ballast & land drainage	1 load stone £100 Land drains £64	£164	Digger 1 day	£258	2 man days	£240	£662

Total £4,328

That works out at £31 per square metre extra plus contingencies.

Another way of dealing with this sloping ground would be to dig in and build a retaining garden wall to hold the land back and avoid having to tank the house. This would only really be cost effective if the wall is less than 1.2 metres high and the slope of the land means that it can be set approximately a metre back from the house. Once you get over 1.2 metres you're involved with engineers and a major construction project. But you might consider whether you could terrace the land back in increments of 1 metre.

Retaining wall

Operation	Materials		Plant		Labour		Total
Dig foundation	Concrete 3cu. m	£180.00	Digger hire 1 day	£258.00	2 man days	£240.00	£678.00
Soil away			3 loads @ £750				£750.00
Build retaining wall	Blocks 23m @ £4.21 = £97.00 Bricks 1000 @ £200.00 Mortar & ties £75.00	£372.00	Mixer hire	£30.00	23m @ £8.50 = £195.50 £300.00	£495.50	£897.50
Backfill	Stone 1 tonne	£39.00			2 man days	£240.00	£279.50

Total £2,604.50

And, amortised over the area of the house, that works out at an addition of just £19 per square metre. Plus, of course, the contingencies.

Chapter 13

TROUBLESHOOTING AND PROBLEM AVOIDANCE

I am not that guy in the pub telling tales of woe that invariably happened to somebody twice removed. Nor do I want to be Job's comforter. However, I firmly believe that knowledge is power: if you have a map of the minefield then you're far less likely to get blown up.

The avoidance of problems should be at the forefront of every self-builder's mind. Careful project planning, scrupulous attention to detail and strict criteria in the choice of both labour and materials should mean that most are indeed avoided.

But sometimes things do go wrong and when this happens it may mean a change of course or having to make a different choice. For the most part, a problem can be replaced with a solution. There are times, however, when it can be difficult to see the answer, and a major problem can appear to threaten the viability of the whole project. Even then, however, it's unlikely that all is lost. There are usually warning signs. There may have to be some compromises and maybe some hard swallowing of pride. But usually there is a way forward.

Making the right choices in the first place

The selection of anybody who is going to work on your site should follow certain strict rules. However good the price, however friendly the prospective builder or tradesman seems to be before they get the job, you need to find out what they are going to be like at the fag end of the project. Are they still going to be as affable when all of the little niggling details and snags need sorting out and very little money is left on the job?

The first rule is to investigate their track record. That means inspecting their previous work and talking to previous clients. It's the only way you're really going to find out what they are like and it's the best insurance policy that you can take out. The same goes for suppliers. Talk to their clients. Find out how their equipment performed and what their after-sales service was like. Don't just accept the claims in their advertising brochure or their sales patter.

Site problems

Discovering that there is a ransom strip preventing access to the site, a main drain that is not where you believed it to be, or visibility splays that cannot be achieved is bad enough at the best of times. If you discover these problems when you are thinking of buying a site then you might decide to walk away. What you don't want is to find these things out after you've bought the site. Vendors hide things like this or conveniently forget about them. But if there's a ransom to be paid then it's the vendors who should pay it, not you, either directly or by a reduction in the price. If the planners are only going to allow a two-bedroom cottage and the site is valued for a four-bedroom house, then you need to know before

Right: **If you depart from the norm you are more likely to encounter problems, but it is nearly always worth it.** © Nigel Rigden

you buy. And if the price does not reflect this or any other immutable problems then you might, once again, have to pull out.

Sometimes, in spite of your having taken all the precautions, and despite soil investigations and surveys, the excavation of foundation trenches may turn up ground conditions which you had not anticipated and which require a change of foundation design. Above ground, most building is a simple matter of a huge jigsaw coming together and extras are normally either completely foreseeable or elective. Below ground, the only survey that is 100% accurate

The avoidance of problems should be at the forefront of every self-builder's mind.

is the one that you effect when you construct your house. Always have a contingency sum. As I've said, it's highly unlikely that it'll all be used up for one eventuality. But if it's there at the beginning it can be used to cover problems in the ground and if it's not required, then it can be rolled forward to meet other choices. Either way it'll get used up, I promise you.

If your excavations do turn up unexpected ground conditions then the thing to do is to remain calm and to seek the very best professional advice as soon as possible. Start with the Building Inspector and/or your architect and get them to put you in touch with a suitable engineer who will come out to site whilst the excavations are still open. Give them time to do their tests and to come up with a solution. Once that's prepared, make sure that you get approval for what they propose from the Building Control department of the local authority and from your warranty company before you recommence work. If necessary, pay your contractors or subcontractors for the abortive work and agree a new price for the revised specification, almost as a completely new contract. They'll be as keen as you are to get restarted and their price will often reflect the fact that they're on site already and all geared up to go. Don't let them jump the gun, though, and make sure that when things do start again, everything is approved and that all and any of the revised materials required have been

properly sourced; otherwise your site will just come to another halt.

Selling the existing home

Having the facility to build without having to sell your existing house is great, but it's not problem-free. If you reach the end of the build and find yourself saddled with two homes you may have to think things out very carefully. If you're going to occupy them both until such time as one of them sells then you will have to think in terms of two Council Tax commitments and the lighting, heating, insurance and running costs of two homes. If you're going to leave one empty then you will have to think in terms of insurance for the unoccupied dwelling, and if the empty one is the one you're trying to sell, remember that empty houses never have the sales appeal of a lived-in home. If this goes on for longer than two years, a Capital Gains Tax liability will arise. You need to add up the figures and make a decision, long before it's 'stale on the market', as to what your cut-off or break-even price is. If necessary, and if it's the wrong time of year to sell houses, you might want to consider cutting your losses by means of a shorthold letting for six months. Don't forget that you'll have to pay tax on the income from the tenancy and probably also management fees to a letting agency.

Accidents

The building industry has a bad accident record and self-builders are even more at risk than professionals. There is a real chance that you will suffer an accident whilst you are building. Guard against this by learning what all the potential hazards are and taking commonsense precautions. In particular beware of cement burns – I write this as someone who still bears the scars of my inexperience, decades ago.

Coping with death

If you walk under a bus whilst you are building the new house, your estate will still have the building finance available to get the job finished. However, in order to arrange for this your executors will probably want £20–30,000 of additional money to be able to employ the best builder in town to finish it quickly, perhaps so that it can be sold. If something happens to you, will this money be available in your estate? The prudent person should always take out an appropriate short-term life insurance policy, which is unlikely to cost very much at all.

Domestic problems

One of the most common reasons why work comes to a stop on a self-build site is that the couple who are building have split up. This has a disastrous effect on both the finances of the project and the enthusiasm to get the job done. If your relationship is going through a sticky patch, avoid self-build until things are better. Many is the time a self-build project has been seen, usually by one party, as the means by which, striving with common purpose, a couple can bring a shaky marriage back into line. The reality is far different and the stresses and strains that inevitably occur in any building project can be the reefs upon which the marriage eventually founders.

Problems with the authorities

Dealing with authority can sometimes be likened to charging, head first, at a brick wall without a hard hat on. Nevertheless it is a skill that each and every self-builder should acquire, and there are times when you need to be able to stand back, cool off and think carefully about your objectives. Most authority is there to perform a function and one that is not usually clouded by too much sentiment. Employees of authorities and statutory undertakers do not, for the most part, have very much freedom of expression in the carrying out of their duties and are bound to follow strict guidelines and procedures, laid down and to be adhered to with just as much zeal as that required by tablets of stone from on high. What you need to do is to find the words to state your objectives in a way that conforms to these regulations and procedures and to do that you may, sometimes, have to put yourself in the shoes of the other person and try to look at things from their perspective.

Planning departments

For some self-builders, problems with planning departments will commence at the Outline stage of planning permission and for quite a few of them, those problems will remain insurmountable. In Chapter 8, I discussed ways of maximising the chances of an Outline application being successful. But as I also said, there are times when it pays to recognise when the end of the road has been reached and that it is perhaps better to move on to another plot.

For those dealing with the planning authorities at the Detailed stages there are a whole raft of other problems, most of which I've already covered, but all of which may require that you stand back and look at the bigger picture. Planning officers do have some leeway. But not enough to allow you to form the vanguard of precedent that will remove or destroy their authority's whole planning ethos. In any negotiation for Detailed consent a balance has to be reached between your desire for individuality and the planning officer's duty to maintain conformity within the Local Development Framework and design guidelines. Keeping the emphasis on the achievement of every one of your desires, however at odds they are with the local vernacular, can only lead to conflict and a loss of momentum to your whole self-build project. The golden rule has to be to steer clear of contention wherever possible or to present potentially contentious issues in as non-contentious a manner as possible. If you've got the time and the money to turn your new home into a crusade, then by all means take things to the limit but, for the

The golden rule has to be to steer clear of contention wherever possible or to present potentially contentious issues in as non-contentious a manner as possible.

average self-builder, time and money are in short supply and a reasonable compromise is the order of the day.

Planning consents are fairly concise documents written in plain English on very bad-quality paper. The words used are specific and precise, and they are meant to be read, understood and complied with. This seems straightforward, but it is surprising how many self-builders choose to ignore the conditions of their planning consent. Those who do this may decide that there is no need to bother with what they consider to be unnecessary formalities; they will then find that they are involved in a dispute with the authority that will take a long time to resolve, and may delay all work on site until it is settled.

Building Control departments

It is not at all unusual for an application for Building Regulations approval in England and Wales to be rejected several times. It doesn't mean that there is necessarily something wrong with your plans. In all probability it has much more to do with the fact that the authorities have a set time limit within which they must determine the application and if they haven't managed to clear up all of the points, they simply reject it. They and your architect or designer know that serial applications are commonplace and that, in any event, re-applications are free. They also know that it's not even necessary to have a Building Regulations approval before starting work and that you can either start on a Building Notice or by giving 48 hours' notice in writing of your intention, once a fresh application is made. In Scotland, the warrant must be issued before work commences on site.

Bad tradesmen will often portray the Building Inspector as some sort of an ogre. However, as a self-builder, you should always keep in mind that the inspector has precisely the same objectives as you in that both of you are trying to ensure that your new home is built properly and in compliance with the regulations. It is true that some of the older and wiser Building Inspectors can appear to be more lenient, whilst some of the younger and more eager ones may seem to be 'going by the book'. In reality appearances are almost always wrong, in that the objectives of all of them are the same. If the older inspector

suspects bad ground, they may throw up the query at the early stages of an application and when they come on site, they may be able to suggest a course of action or remedy. The younger one, without the background knowledge will, nevertheless, come to precisely the same conclusion, just as soon as they see the excavations, and the end result is almost certain to be the same. Remember that the Building Inspector is on your side, looking out for your interests.

The Highways and Environmental Agencies

To a large degree the requirements of both of these agencies will be dealt with by the Planning and Building Control departments. Remember that before any work can be carried out involving the highway, including creating a new access or connecting to a public sewer in the highway, a licence will be required from the highways authorities, consent will be needed to make a connection to the sewer and periods of notice will be required before the works may take place. Remember also that only Accredited or Approved contractors can carry out works that involve digging up or disturbing the metalled sections of the highway, including the footpath.

Where any of the agencies are involved, try to ensure that, as far as is possible, their requirements are anticipated and conformed to and try to ensure that, when making your applications, you make the Planning and/or Building Control departments aware that you have taken these factors into consideration. If you do find yourself stuck in the middle of what will be to them an interesting conflict of interests, then try to arrange a meeting between the sides and go to that meeting, with your professionals, in the capacity of arbitrators seeking a solution, rather than as an injured party.

Electricity, gas, water and telephone companies

For me these have always been the hardest brick walls into which I have charged. All of the inflexibilities of both personnel and procedure seem to coagulate within and under their vast monolithic umbrellas. Procedure is the thing, that and timescales which, despite the dictates of your site, have to be adhered

Above: **All lights blazing. Now you see why the Government wants us to use energy-efficient lighting.** © Potton

to. Make sure that you obtain the necessary quotations for supply in good time, and make doubly sure that you send off any payment or order for that supply within the time frame laid down in the documentation. If the water board want six weeks' notice of your requirement for a building supply, the chances are that you will have to wait for at least the requisite period no matter how long and loudly you shout that you need it the following day,

On the other hand, if you accidentally cut a main, you'll be amazed at how quick the response will be and how positive the action taken is, right down to the bill for damages that will inevitably follow. If you have a suspicion that a main crosses your land, ask the relevant board to provide you with a plan and to pinpoint the exact position. That way, if they're wrong, at least you will have a counter-claim against them.

One problem that many self-builders come across is meter boxes. Some boards provide these together with the hockey sticks and ducting pipes. Others do not. Those that do require you to collect the materials from a depot by reference to an order which, yes you've guessed it, has to be processed within certain timescales. Make sure that you've got the boxes on site before your bricklayer gets to the point of needing them to build in. Although they can be cut in and fixed at a later date it's never as good a job. And most builders' merchants do now stock them.

Problems with builders

Careful investigation can tell you if a builder has been reliable in the past and that should, in theory, be a pretty good guide as to how they will perform in the future. However, every builder is only as good as their last job and there are many things that can bring about a fundamental change in their performance: marriage problems, ill health or money problems can all affect the quality of their work. You are a self-builder – you are not a marriage guidance counsellor, nor are you a doctor, and you are certainly not a banker.

Warning signs are long periods during which nothing is happening. Follow-on trades fail to arrive, or plumbers and electricians fail to turn up to carry out the second fix. If a builder's personal problems are to blame then the problem may be an organisational one, in which case you can step in and help by making judicious calls to subcontractors and/or suppliers. Don't expect a reduction from the builder. In helping him you are helping yourself and that should be reward enough.

If it is a money problem, however, you may need to do some very careful thinking. A warning sign for this may be a request for money ahead of schedule. This will often be accompanied by a story that so-and-so hasn't paid up on the previous job, leaving them with a bit of a cashflow problem. Resist this at all costs. It may come to the point where you have to, with his agreement, make direct payments to subcontractors or suppliers or both, but for now take time to take stock of things.

Most builders have cashflow problems. Many have overdrafts that are considerably bigger than your eventual mortgage and they learn to live with them and to juggle the money from one job to pay for another. Usually it works, but occasionally they over-stretch themselves, the result being that one job or another has to stop. It doesn't necessarily mean that they are heading for bankruptcy.

You need to find out what the situation is. Talk to the subcontractors, but be very careful not to inflame the situation. What you don't want is to create rumours that become a self-fulfilling prophecy. Be

Immediate action to take if your builder goes bust

- **Get to site and secure all gates and fencing**
- **Post a notice denying access to any person not directly authorised by you**
- **Change the locks on the house**
- **Camp out or engage a watchman**
- **Inform the police**
- **Contact your warranty provider**
- **Contact your insurers**
- **Make an appointment with your solicitor**

circumspect in your questioning. 'Is everything all right between you and Bloggs Builders?' is a better question than 'Is Bloggs going bust?"

If materials are failing to arrive you may simply be told that there's been a mix-up somewhere. Equally, they may not have been ordered or the builder's account might be on stop at the builders' merchants, and you need to know what the problem is. Strictly speaking the merchants are not at liberty to discuss their client's account details with you. So the question to ask at the merchants is 'What's the situation on those materials that Bloggs Builders have ordered for my site?' The answer might be that they're not yet ordered, or it might hint at some trouble with the account. Bear in mind that Bloggs Builders might have told them that one reason he can't pay his bills is that you haven't paid him.

Think and act calmly. The last thing you want is to have to switch contractors; whilst technically possible it is fraught with legal and organisational difficulties. If you've paid for half the job and half the job has been done, a new builder will want much more than the remaining 50% to finish another's, perhaps inferior, work.

So, on a practical level, if you find that your builder is experiencing a cashflow problem, you might decide to do one of three things. You can:

• move to sever the contract on a quantum merit

basis, in which case you'll be faced with finding a new builder or dealing directly with the sub-contractors and effectively becoming the builder yourself

- agree to pay on a weekly basis according to an agreed schedule of work that ensures that you are never paying for more than you're getting
- agree that the builder continues to manage the project and that you will pay directly for all materials and labour.

Warning signs to watch out for
● **Long delays on site**
● **Tradesmen not arriving to complete their jobs**
● **Materials not arriving**
● **Requests for payments upfront or in advance of an agreed stage completion**

If you are one of the very few that entered into a written contract before the work commenced then that document will almost certainly detail the arrangements by which a dispute or the severance of the contract is settled. But for most self-builders the solutions will have to come from within their own resources.

If your builder goes bust

If your builder does go bust you need to be the first to hear of it and you need to act fast. Builders' merchants will arrive at the site and pick up everything and anything that they can. They will assure you that they have the right to do this, as legal title does not pass in the goods until they are paid. And they will be right in many respects. Except that the goods are on your land and they have no legal right of entry.

You need to prevent them from gaining access. You must inform them that the goods were supplied to you by the builder and that their problem should be addressed to the liquidator. Strictly speaking, you may at some stage have to negotiate with them before you can actually use any of the materials but your first task is to keep them on site. Buy strong chains and padlocks and secure the site security fencing. Change all of the locks on the house and if necessary arrange to camp out there or maintain a presence.

The other danger is subcontractors, some of whom, highly aggrieved, will want to storm on site and rip out everything of value. Once again they have no legal right of entry and they have no right to cause damage to your property. If goods are fixed they have become part of your property. That does not mean that they do not have to be paid for and that the title

in them does not continue to rest with others. It does mean, however, that their removal will be detrimental to your property and an infringement of your rights, and as such will have to be negotiated. Goods such as a boiler supplied by a plumber but not yet fixed might legitimately be considered the property of the subcontractor. So that may prove, but for now it is in your interests to keep such goods on site and prevent them from being removed, even if that means that you have to promise to negotiate for them when the dust has settled a little.

As long as you can keep these people off your site you have the upper hand. If you have stuck to the payments schedule with the builder you will either be well in front in monetary terms or at the very worst you will have paid up only to the preceding stage.

Things can get pretty unpleasant. Some subcontractors may be facing ruin and they may be determined to assert their rights or at the very least to exact revenge. You need to make them understand that you are not the problem and that you might indeed be the solution.

As a precaution you should also inform the police. They won't be concerned about the nature of the contract or the dispute but they will be concerned to prevent a breach of the peace and if things get out of hand you might need them fairly quickly.

If the builder's insurance policy was the principal cover on site then you will need to make alternative arrangements quickly. In any event a self-build insurance policy is always a good bet as many of the items at risk on your site may not have been purchased by the builders. Self-builders do a lot of their own shopping and a builder's policy won't cover goods that he didn't buy.

Several parties may be involved in this scenario. They include the warranty providers, the liquidator, the builder, and the subcontractors. It's important to understand each of their roles and to act accordingly:

The warranty providers

You will need to inform the warranty providers of your situation and eventually you may have to come to an arrangement with them to vary the policy or change the name of the providers.

Most of the warranty companies will offer little but sympathy. The exception is the NHBC, which offers quite considerable help in that they will:

- pay you the amount needed to complete the home substantially in accordance with their requirements, together with the cost of putting right any defects or damage, or

- reimburse you any amount you have paid to the builder for the home under a legal obligation but cannot recover from him, or

- at their own option, arrange for the works to be carried out.

The maximum liability of the NHBC is 10% of the original purchase price (house value) up to a maximum of £100,000.

The NHBC will only be liable for what was in the original contract. They will not be concerned with extras. If you have retained any part of the original contract price this will be deducted from the sum that they pay out and if they arrange for the work you will be required to pay them the amount still owing on the original contract.

The liquidator

Whatever you do, you have to be aware that it will come under the scrutiny of the liquidator, whose job it is to make as much as possible from the builder's assets and distribute it fairly to all of the creditors.

If you have not already come to an arrangement with suppliers, it might be necessary for you to make the liquidator an offer for materials on your site. This

offer may well be less than the face value as the goods will have been unwrapped and will therefore be 'second hand'.

If you owe money to the builder under your contract then the liquidator will want to know why you should not pay it. It's no good saying that he was a dirty rotten scoundrel for letting you down. You'll have to address the situation properly by preparing a counter-claim. This will detail the expenses you have incurred – the amount it has cost you to rectify the situation, including payments to other builders and subcontractors. It can also include an amount for the distress and wasted time that you have been put to.

The builder

The builder may want to come to a private arrangement with you. If you owe him money under the contract he may well try to get you to pay this. Don't. That money, if it is payable, should go to the liquidator. In similar vein the builder may try to get you to employ him under a different guise. It's not always a good idea. It could put you in the wrong with the liquidator and it could lead to friction with other workers on site who have lost out as a result of his misfortune.

The subcontractors

The subcontractors who worked for the bankrupt builder are a different matter. After their initial anger has subsided they may well seek to come to an arrangement with you. If that means you paying them directly for any future work then that is all right.

Whilst, strictly speaking, you have no legal responsibility to pay them for work that they did for the builder, if you are a stage in hand with the builder then you haven't yet paid for their services.

Your goal is for your new home to be built. If that means that you have to negotiate a figure with them to finish the job, that does not leave you out of pocket, then surely that's the best option.

Problems with subcontractors

Prevention is always better than cure and if you've followed all the earlier advice about choosing a subcontractor and about talking to previous clients, then it's unlikely that you've engaged a bad one. This is where the skill of management comes into play. By self-managing your project you stand to make considerable savings compared to the fellow who went and employed a builder. But that means that you have to be prepared to take on the management role of the builder. Sometimes that will mean having to dispense with the services of a tradesman altogether or refusing to pay unless and until work is put right. All of this may seem daunting but it is part and parcel of what you have taken on, and if you feel that you may not be capable of dealing with these situations, you need to question your chosen method of building.

Although bad workmanship by one subcontractor might set your project back a little whilst you either have the work put right or seek other tradesmen, it is unlikely that it would scupper your whole venture, horrendous though it may seem at the time. Keep a close watch on workmanship and make sure that it's up to the standard you picked the man for. If you're in any doubt, consult with your architect or the Building Inspector and get them to let you know whether everything's all right. If, despite your very best endeavours, you and your advisors feel that the chap isn't any good after all, then move quickly to terminate your arrangement with him and, having decided on this course of action, never change your mind. Do not concern yourself with the other chap's feelings: a bad subcontractor will have been let go many times before. Pay him in full for the work that he has done, and do not deduct the cost of putting right any defective work; your choice of subcontractor or lack of supervision was at fault, and you will have to pay for your mistake. This is what the contingency figure in the budget is for.

If a subcontractor goes bust on your site this is unlikely to jeopardise the project. In all likelihood, payments to a subcontractor will be on the basis of work done and there is, therefore, little chance that their going broke will leave you at a disadvantage.

Problems with suppliers

Firstly, don't pay for goods in advance unless you are absolutely sure of the source. If there is an element of bespoke manufacture then try to pay into a dedicated client's account or to a stakeholder who will release the money when the goods arrive.

From time to time even the best of suppliers will let you down and you will find that many of them have a *force majeure* clause in their terms and conditions of sale, absolving them from any responsibility for knock-on problems.

If what you've ordered does not arrive you have two alternatives. Either you continue waiting or you buy elsewhere. However, that's not as straightforward as it sounds, especially if you've paid a deposit. And even if you can source an alternative, the lead-in delivery time may be even longer than the time in which the original suppliers are now promising to deliver.

Sometimes it's better to walk away from a deposit. There are always alternatives. They may mean some level of compromise on your part but if a company is unreliable at this stage, what on earth is it going to be like on after-sales service?

Goods should always be checked immediately on delivery. Even if the driver is impatient to be away you need to check that the goods are undamaged. If he won't wait you should mark the ticket 'Goods received unchecked'. If damage is subsequently found you will have a much stronger case for replacement. If goods prove to be unsatisfactory then you have the same rights as anybody buying from a shop in that the goods should be 'of merchantable quality and fit for the purpose'.

Getting replacements from some firms is like getting blood out of a stone. On the other hand the major builders' merchants and most of the better-known suppliers working within the self-build industry know that their reputation is important and almost all will change faulty goods without demur. And you should have found that out in your initial enquiries with their previous clients.

Difficulties with professionals

Never lose sight of the fact that the person with the string of letters behind their name is, nevertheless, just one of the people *you* are going to employ to assist in the building of *your* new home. They may well be very august people in their own right but, as far as the building of your new home is concerned, they are just one of many whose input you will use and it is you who is in the driving seat. Do not let yourself be intimidated into agreeing to or going along with something with which you are not comfortable. If you are not completely happy, stop and think carefully before going on and, if necessary, and as long as you are not legally committed, pull away and seek another avenue.

Of course if you have tied yourself into a legal contract with a professional, then you must, at some stage, have been happy with their services or you wouldn't have made the commitment. But what do you do if it all starts to go wrong part of the way through the project? A bricklayer who is dismissed will, especially if he's paid up to date, just shrug his shoulders and go, albeit leaving a few choice words ringing in your ears. A professional who has failed to live up to your expectations or even to his own promises may not be so easy to get rid of. Any attempt at dismissal may well result in a very large bill for abortive work and a writ if you do not pay it promptly. If it's a package-deal company that is failing to perform, then there may well be an element of manufacture and supply to which you are undoubtedly committed. Unless, therefore, you are very sure of your ground, you may well end up with a very large bill for damages, breach of contract and/or loss of profit. All of this makes it essential that you satisfy yourself well before the commitment stage that you are dealing with the right people.

So if you do get into difficulties with your professional make sure that you do things by the book. First of all try arranging a meeting with the company or professional with whom you are in dispute and, at that meeting, try to resolve the problem to your mutual benefit. Do not cut your nose off to spite your face. Do not imagine that your differences are irreconcilable or, at least, do not approach such a meeting in this frame of mind. Set down your grievances in writing, clearly and without resort to intemperate language. Commit to paper your earnest desire to

Never start work on site without adequate self-build insurance and always listen to advice from solicitors and others about single-premium indemnity policies where they are deemed necessary.

find a suitable way forward and, if one can be found, take it.

And if, despite all of your endeavours, you feel that you have no option but to sever your relations? Well, if you do have to terminate a contract with a professional, only do so after careful consideration and in consultation with and on the advice of a solicitor who has been given the opportunity to examine carefully all of the facts and, in particular, the contract or terms of engagement.

Forgetting about insurance and warranties

How could you possibly do this after all of the exhortations and hints I've dropped throughout the text? Yet the fact is that people still do forget, or even, at times, feel that they can get away without insurance. Maybe some do but it only takes one gale or one errant child to make a mockery of a whole self-build project, sufficient to blight a lifetime. Never start work on site without adequate self-build insurance and always listen to advice from solicitors and others about single-premium indemnity policies where they are deemed necessary.

Warranties need to be put in place long before work actually commences on site and certainly long before trenches are opened. If there are trees present or if bad ground is suspected, then the lead-in period of notice of commencement of works may well be extended and you will need to take this into account in your programme. I've known of self-builders building without a warranty. But I've also known of times when all of the bravado disappears in the realisation that a mistake has been made. It's not impossible to sell a house without a warranty and retrospective guarantees are available. But it's certainly very difficult and it involves expensive and extensive structural surveys and complicated policies.

One last thing on the subject of insurances. Don't be afraid to ask any of the people you engage for details of their insurance and indemnity policies. Ask your builders for a copy of their insurance policies even if you're playing safe by arranging one of your own. If they're going to be digging up the Queen's highway then you need to know that they're adequately covered. And if they're not you need to insist that either they increase their cover or you engage another party to carry out that work. Ask any of the professionals for details of their indemnity policies and make sure that the amount of cover provided equals or exceeds the rebuilding costs of your project.

Problems with neighbours

Almost all neighbours of a plot will have objected to its being granted planning permission in the first place and, even if they're the vendors, they'll be happy to take your money but less than happy at the prospect of you actually building on the land. Try your best to get the neighbours on your side. You may not always manage to do so but in the end you, and hopefully they, will have to realise that you're all going have to live near each other.

Deliveries are the one thing that upsets neighbours and, I'm afraid, quite rightly so. Firstly, if the plot is on a narrow lane and the block lorry arrives in the morning, then the driver will put his feet down and proceed with unloading, seemingly oblivious to the queue of angry commuters who are going to miss their train. If you're not there or the space to put the blocks is not obvious or clearly marked out, or if there's not room on the site, he'll have no compunction about stacking them on the road or the footpath and you'll have to spend the rest of the day, when you do arrive on site, moving them.

I recall one case where the lorry driver arrived on site and decided that the best place to put the blocks was on the side of the plot in front of the garage doors. And not only that but that the best way of getting them there was to park on the next-door neighbour's drive! The problem was that the neighbour's drive hadn't actually been designed or constructed to take the weight of a fully laden block lorry and it collapsed.

Try, as far as is possible, to ascertain just when deliveries are going to be made and make sure that, if you can't be on site, somebody else certainly is. If you know that work or deliveries are going to block off the road at a certain time then take the trouble to inform your neighbours and to warn them that they may need to park their cars up the street. They'll never be too happy about it but at least you will have done your best.

If the complaints are about noise or smoke, then do something about it. Maybe a diesel mixer could be swapped for an electric one. Maybe the radios could be turned down a little or at the very least tuned in, and maybe fires could either be stopped altogether or limited to reasonable hours with the old tyres sent to the tip instead of turning the whole sky black.

Remember, above all, that this is not just any old building site, it's the site of your new home and, as such, the neighbours are going to be an important factor in your enjoyment of it. A short letter to each one apologising in advance for any inconvenience, a visit to those most affected and, perhaps, a few bunches of flowers won't go amiss at all.

Pragmatism

Once you have started to build a new house it is important to get it finished on time; otherwise the interest charges on the building finance will get out of hand. If you do become involved in a dispute with others, settle it quickly so that the whole project is not held up. This may involve making a pragmatic decision to let others get away with things, even though you are convinced they are wrong. Agreeing to a neighbour's view of where a boundary post should be put, or paying a few pounds more than agreed for materials or services, can be the right decision if it saves time and keeps up the momentum of the whole job. Don't be a soft touch but, in equal measure, don't cut off your nose to spite your face.

Right: **Good design complements the landscape as well as taking advantage of it.** © Nigel Rigden

Final checklist

- Start off with the budget

- Tailor the project to your financial abilities and not the other way around

- Take out the right insurances and warranties

- Read all you can. Get the magazines and study the articles and, in particular, the advertisements

- Cost out any proposals fully

- Explore every avenue to find the right project

- Always have a contingency fund

- Follow the Site details checklist on page 130 and don't leave anything out, hoping for the best

- Choose the right solicitors

- If at all possible have a professional mentor or friend

- Design your new home to fit the plot or the project, and not the other way around

- Always keep a check on things on the ground

- Evaluate every aspect of your lifestyle when arriving at your design wish list

- Make sure that the brief you give your architect and designer includes that wish list

- Make sure that your architect or designer is aware of your budget and that what they produce is designed to accord with it

- Never hear what you want to hear

- Carefully consider all your options. If you're not completely happy then stop, draw breath and think things through again

- Consider whether there are more cost-effective options available that will not detract from your enjoyment of your new home

- If you feel you're going down the wrong route, stop and change tack

- Learn about planning and understand that it is all about compromise

- Learn the sequences and timings of the building process

- Talk to other self-builders. They will be able to give advice on land, professionals, local authority attitudes, labour and materials

- Never lose sight of your goal – to build a new home – even if that means that you have to trim some of your ideas

- Keep on working out the finances and stay on budget

- Never pay for work in advance

- If you pay a deposit for materials, make sure that you have a record of your payment

- Wherever possible, pay monies into a dedicated client's account or establish the existence of an insurance-backed bond

- Be aware that most extras in self-build projects are elective

- Balance extra expenditure against savings in other areas in order to stay on budget

- Never jump the gun. Get all consents and authorisations in place before commencing work

- Don't underestimate the costs of services

- Judge the effect on your family's and your own life before taking on any self-build, renovation or conversion project

- Carefully consider your living arrangements whilst you are building. The more comfortable you can make them, the less stressful the project will be

- Don't let your job or career suffer because of your project – that's what's paying for it!

- Keep the neighbours on side as far as is possible

- Never bite off more than you can chew. Know your own limitations

- Avoid false economies

- Agree all changes or extras in writing

- Never leave old or superseded drawings around. Collect them up and destroy them

- Never put too much trust in individuals with whom you have only a fleeting relationship

- Always be prepared to admit that you have made the wrong choice and, if you have, move decisively to put things right

- Plan for all eventualities

- Aim to finish within budget

- Enjoy it! … You'll be back!

Final checklist

Chapter 14

THE STORY OF TWO SELF-BUILDS

et me tell you about our last two self-builds; respectively the ninth and tenth since Mrs Snell and I were married 34 years ago. Does that seem a lot? Well, spread over the whole period it works out at only one every three and half years, which somehow seems more reasonable. What it maybe doesn't tell you is that in order to achieve that, we have had to move home a total of 27 times!

In previous books and in other writings, I've avoided giving away any detail relating to my personal experiences of self-building, thinking that this was private. I've cheerfully chronicled the self-build stories of others, aware, as I did so, that perhaps there was a better cross-section and currency in the monthly magazine's case histories. But the truth of the matter is that everything I write and talk about is predicated upon my own experiences of self-building. And anybody who has seen me talking at seminars and lecturing at residential self-build courses, or who has read pieces by me and about me in the magazines, knows that I don't hide the fact that my life hasn't been a bed of roses. I've been up and I've been very, very down. We've had to start again from scratch twice in our married life and in both cases, self-building was what finally put me firmly back on the ladder.

I want to tell the stories of these last two self-builds to illustrate just how one comes across land, how even the best of us can make mistakes and, above all, how self-building can change your life. It's not easy; nothing really worthwhile ever is. But I can tell you, and others have said the same to me, that you'll never feel quite so alive as when you're self-building. And when it's all over, you'll have a good rest for a while and then maybe, just maybe, you'll hanker after the excitement and that same sense of self-worth all over again. You'll want to reduce the mortgage and you'll realise that it wasn't so bad after all. And you'll do it all again. I know I will.

The story of house no. 1

In the summer of 2000 I had to go into hospital for an operation and whilst I was in there I met a chap who I got on awfully well with. It turned out that he lived barely 300 metres from where we were living at the time in a semi-detached house that we'd bought in 1998 to climb back on to the property ladder after a disastrous company failure.

When we were both out of hospital and had recovered I would often nip round to his house in the afternoon for a few gin and tonics in the conservatory. The house he and his wife lived in was a small cottage set on a plot that had a road frontage of around 20 metres and a depth of about 50 metres. The cottage was positioned to one side of the plot with a garage to the other side, a large lawn behind that and a huge vegetable garden.

One day they rang up and asked if I

I can tell you, and others have said the same to me, that you'll never feel quite so alive as when you're self-building.

could go round and give them some advice. It turned out that they were fed up with mowing the lawn and managing this huge garden and they wanted to know whether I thought it would be worthwhile trying to get planning permission for a 9-metre-wide plot, the full depth of the land. Well, it was definitely an infill plot but both the cottage next door and their own had fairly low roof lines. The land sloped a little from side to side, which would mitigate the effect on their home, but next door was bound to kick up a fuss.

The planning stages

The planners indicated that, whilst they were not averse to the idea of the plot being developed in principle, there were some reservations about the design. Although they would accept an Outline application it would have to be accompanied by drawings showing the type of house proposed and its positioning on the site. My friend Beverley Pemberton, chief designer for Design & Materials Limited, drew me out some sketches for a four-bedroom house. Because of the narrowness of the plot and the need for a garage and parking, this, of necessity, had to be fairly long on the plot and, as expected, when I put in the plans there were howls of protest from the immediate neighbours on the left.

We reluctantly changed the plans to shrink the overall length at least to the upper floors. This meant that part of the lounge and dining area protruded as a single-storey section at the back with a lean-to roof. It also, disappointingly, meant that, if it was to remain a four-bedroom house, we would have to lose the en-suite. The width of the plot had already dictated the necessity for a lean-to roof over part of the garage. You can take a single-storey structure almost up to the boundary, but a two-storey section has to be at least 1 metre away. We needed a path down the left-hand side for access to the rear garden and to bring the house away from the objecting cottage. We also needed to have the garage hard up against the right-hand boundary. The solution was to design the garage as half in and half out of the main house with a lean-to roof that set the upper part a metre from the boundary. This meant that the first-floor walls on this side would have to be supported on steels, and that caused quite a few problems later on when it came to building the house.

The application went to a site meeting of the sub-committee at which the neighbour's representatives registered their continuing objections. We were able to put forward our point of view, in that we had moved to reflect all of the reservations expressed by the officers in our revised drawings and that, in any event, this had always been a plot as the street numbering reflected. We then had to sit back and wait.

The approval came through in the summer of 2001. There were many conditions on it, including a withdrawal of Permitted Development Rights and a condition that the house should be positioned on the plot in line with the frontage of the adjoining cottage. I didn't take much notice of this at first as I really had no intention of buying the plot. We were financially stable after several years of upheaval and I was busy finishing the 17th edition of this book.

So my friends put the plot on the market. All the local estate agents valued the plot at £50,000 and one was given the task of selling it. All went quiet for a while and then an offer came in at £37,500. It was from a local builder and the agent recommended that my friends accept it, which they did. Then it all went quiet again until my friends received a notice from the planners telling them that an application had been received for Full planning permission and would they like to drop in to the council offices to inspect them. This they did and were horrified to see that the builder was proposing a much bigger house that would have a deleterious effect on their own property.

The planners indicated that they were resolved to refuse this application and it became quite clear that the builder was dragging his feet in buying the land in the hope that he could get Full planning for something much larger before he had to shell out any money.

It was, by now, the spring of 2002. The book was now finished and on hearing these developments from our friends, Mrs Snell and I decided to take the plunge: I went back to my friends and offered to buy the land. They insisted that I only paid the same as the builder had offered and I agreed to build to the plan for which I'd originally got Outline planning permission. I then went to meet a new bank manager at HSBC to whom I'd been introduced, and happily, he thought it was a great idea. By now, with the rise in property values, we'd got a healthy equity in our home, more than enough to cover the value of the land, so he simply opened a business account with an overdraft limit enabling us to buy the land without selling our house.

With past experiences in mind we wanted to proceed with caution. The property market can go down as well as up and we decided that, whilst we were happy to secure the land, as plots always keep their value, we would not start building until we'd released the equity in our home. So we put the house on the market and, after the usual trials and tribulations of selling homes, we moved into rented accommodation with the land all paid for and money in the bank.

In the meantime we'd gone back to the planners with an application for Approval of Reserved Matters. Even though the plans were exactly as before, the same objections were raised by the same neighbour. The planners paid lip service to their complaints, now articulated by a local councillor, and it all dragged on with more site meetings. But in the end we got the consent.

Getting the project under way

I'd seen a couple of guys building an extension just down the road and I made a habit of stopping off to talk to them. It was apparent that they hadn't built a whole house before, and from the state of their van it appeared that they were not that clued up financially either. But as I would be supplying the materials and only wanted labour prices, I felt they might be up to the job. In any event, builders who build extensions have to be pretty good at most things.

June/July 2002

The price for labour only to the weathertight shell stage was £16,216 and work started in June 2002. The first thing to do was to fence the site off (as required by the contract for the purchase of the land) and they did this under a separate supply-and-fix contract. It was July before work really started in earnest. As it was a narrow site we were always going to have a problem with storage of materials. The land to the front of the house would be needed for the sand and the mixing station and that left little or no room for anything else. So we skinned off all the topsoil and stored it at the back. Then the whole area of what would eventually be the patio to the rear of the house was stoned to a depth of around 300mm, allowing us to get all of the foundation and many of the superstructure blocks stacked out within the site before we started digging.

I set it out and realised that if we were to maintain the same building line as the cottage next door, as required by the planning, we wouldn't have room for a car to park in front of the garage. Could I move it back a metre? The planners didn't mind as long as I could get a letter from the neighbour saying that they were in agreement. Luckily the objector had upped sticks and moved away in a huff and the new lady who'd bought the cottage didn't mind at all.

The dig started and it was immediately apparent that things weren't going to go precisely to plan. The drawings showed neat lines for the foundations 600mm wide and approximately 1.2 metres deep. On paper that works out at just over four lorry loads of muck away and around 8 cubic metres of concrete. The digger driver was quite 'enthusiastic'. At times he went too deep but to be fair, with the size of the boulders that he was pulling up, the trenches just got wider and wider. In the end it resembled the Battle of the Somme with trenches that were supposed to be separate combined and others over 3 metres wide. It took 54 cubic metres of concrete to fill them, using a pump to get it in.

Watching the guys handling this pump made me realise that they'd never done anything like this before. They were clinging to the end of the tube, balancing on the edge of the trenches and making a hell of a mess. When I showed them how to loop a rope around the trunk and have two men directing the nozzle remotely, they were grateful and the job went smoothly.

The amount of spoil had been huge and on top of this we had to find somewhere to store the full loads of thermal blocks for the superstructure that were about to arrive. At the end of the road the football club wanted to create a bank of earth to one side of the pitch. They agreed to take the spoil and to let me store the blocks on their car park in return for a new set of nets. So the neighbours had to endure an endless succession of dumpers going up and down the lane. This, and other things that occurred, cost me several bunches of flowers.

The guys stated that they'd arranged for brickies to come in as this would be quicker and a three-and-one gang duly arrived and got the property out of the ground in a couple of evenings. It worried me slightly as I realised that they were moonlighting. But what worried me more was the height that the proposed oversite was going to be out of the ground on the lower side and the degree of overlooking that this would entail to the cottage next door. If we put floor beams on the blockwork, as planned, it would be even higher.

I'd already bought the cranked ventilators and ordered the beams but a sleepless night brought me to the conclusion that I had to change tack and switch to a solid oversite. Furthermore, we would have to take off one course of blockwork. All of this produced some mumbling and, together with the spoil and the block storage, resulted in a bill for an extra £2,794 plus £217 for the football nets.

August/September 2002

The oversite went down fine and the brickies started on the superstructure and got to around first lift all the way around. Then it all came to a grinding halt. The brickies decided that they didn't want to be working in their spare time and the main man of the two-man partnership that I'd employed for the job went on holiday. Virtually nothing happened in August but in September he returned and vowed to take hold of the project, which meant that he and his mates started laying the blocks themselves.

By now we needed the steels. These were enormous. The ones at the back had to run the entire width of the rear wall, supported on 21N pillars of concrete blocks with padstones, bolted together and with a steel pillar, within the spine wall, down to foundation. The ones supporting the upper part at the side had a bearing at the rear of the garage but, at the front, they bore on what were effectively the lintel steels above the garage door. The engineer was worried about the stability of the outside pillar and at the last moment proposed that we had a vertical steel pillar within it down to foundation. This was steel upon steel upon steel, and it all had to be bolted and

Above: **The infill plot.**

Below: **Pumping in the oversite concrete.**

then welded together. He kept changing his mind. Almost every morning a new set of calculations and requirements was faxed over. Steels had to be changed and supporting pillars strengthened. In the end I said that enough was enough. We were building it as he had by then proposed and no further changes would be accepted. Nevertheless, it had involved me in quite a few extras.

The brickwork was going ever so slowly and the guys eventually brought in two local bricklayers to speed the work up. Things looked good and as we came off the steels with the inner leaf of blockwork I was pleased to see that the cavity trays were in to the right height to conduct any moisture harmlessly to the outside.

By now I'd taken on a consultancy with BuildStore and I was away in Edinburgh quite a lot. When I got back one Tuesday the outer leaf of blockwork was up on the steels over the garage and the cover flashings were hanging down, ready to be dressed, eventually, over the tiles of the lean-to roof. I stood and looked at them. They seemed too long for the width of lead that I'd bought. I fished around one on the weepers and pulled it out so that I could get my finger in. There was a gap of around 50mm between it and the cavity tray. If any water got into the cavity it would be conducted within the block and express itself in the ceiling of the garage below!

Sharp words were exchanged and I considered 'sending someone down the road'; in the end I opted for pragmatism. We were late on schedule. My lease was going to run out at Christmas and if we had to find new labour, then it would drag on indefinitely. However, from now on I was going to be keeping a sharp eye on everything.

The lead-up to Christmas 2002

With the roof tiled in September/October, I agreed with the guys a price for the labour for the second fix of £9,146. This excluded the electrician, the plumber and the decorator as I'd made separate contracts with them. It was also to exclude the kitchen fitting, various extras such as cupboards, plus the ceramic tiling and the garden. Crucially it included the tackers and the plasterer.

Work proceeded. The tackers swept in, moaned

Left: **Steel on steel to facilitate the design.** Below left: **Nearly ready.**

Below: **The finished house.**

like hell and swept out. The plasterer got on inside and when he was finished the carpenter, electrician and plumber started their second fix. The floor tiler laid the tiles to the kitchen, dining area, cloakroom/shower room and bathroom floors, and by Christmas 2002 the sanitaryware and kitchen units had arrived. That's when we decided that the downstairs cloakroom/shower room wasn't really big enough and, in any event, our need for some sort of a utility room was greater. So back went the shower tray and cubicle; instead, we put in a butler sink and built a cupboard in the corner to house the washing machine.

January 2003

It all dragged on in horrid weather until after Christmas. Our landlords had agreed to extend our lease by just one month so we had to crack the whip. The staircase seemed to take for ever and the decorator laboured manfully, doing his best to press on whilst other tradesmen mucked up his work, often meaning he had to do it again. I thought about asking him to lay off and wait but he wanted to carry on as he was working within a window of availability. In the end I got somebody else to do the outside as he was otherwise engaged. Fitted carpets went down the day before we moved in at the end of January 2003 and the external works to the front drive and the garden, which I contracted separately, happened in the weeks that followed.

Cost of the project

The total cost of the building work and ancillary costs was £87,000 or just over £705 per square metre. Added to the land cost of £37,500 that makes a grand total of £124,500 to set against the eventual value and resale of £197,000. Yes, that's a gain in equity of £72,500 or, to put it another way, close on 60%. Granted, when we came to sell, there were estate agent's and solicitor's fees to come out of that and I've included them as part of the next project. I also haven't included my finance costs or the cost of renting. But whichever way you cut it, it was very worthwhile.

COSTS RELATING TO HOUSE NO. 1 (as they were spent)

March 2002

Solicitor and ancillary costs	£517.13
Architectural technician. Plans	£250.00
Planning fees	£190.00
Building Regulations application fees	£117.50
	£1,075

June 2002

Water supply	£1,221.00
Gas supply	£282.00
Electricity supply	£823.11
Building Regulations inspection fees	£305.00
NHBC warranty	£920.00
Supply & fix fencing	£1,685.00
Architectural technician. Plans	£250.00
Structural engineer. Calculations	£90.00
Standpipe	£17.24
Setting out pegs	£12.00
Concrete blocks. Foundation & superstructure	
227m @ £4.21 + pallets	£1,064.84
	£6,670

July 2002

Architectural technician. Plans	£100.00
Scalpings 34.44 tonnes @ £7.00 per tonne	£241.07
Footings concrete 54 cu. metres @ £56.74	£3,063.96
Concrete pump hire	£240.00
Steel fabricators. Joists & posts	£1,017.00
Labour. Original contract for shell	£4,580.00
Labour. Extras. Transportation, storage and removal of spoil. Hire of forklift. Extra foundation depth/concrete + alterations to oversite and blockwork	£2,794.00
Mortar. 80 bags cement @ £2.28 each	
6 bags sand @ £28.23 each	£351.78
Reinforcement bar & mesh	£181.36
Concrete pump hire	£240.00
Oversite concrete 9.5m @ £56.74	£539.03
Flooring insulation	£166.96
Membrane. 2 rolls	£77.80
Thermal blocks. 189m @ £7.29 per m	£1377.81
Pallets	£50.00
Commons/engineering bricks	£124.56
Cavity closers	£548.47
Wall ties, clips & plasticiser	£82.67
Wall insulation slabs. 360 sheets @ £1.40 each	£504.00

Payment to football club for storage (new nets)	£217.38
	£16,552

August 2002

Building sand. 2 bags @ £28.23 each	£56.40
Sink taps & fittings. Purchased in France	£49.00
Padstones (pre-stressed concrete lintels)	£95.57
Steel Catnic lintels	£388.92
	£590

September 2002

Labour. Original contract for shell	£5,950.00
Mortar. 36 bags cement @ £2.28 each	
6 bags sand @ £28.23 each	£251.46
Nails & fixings	£44.59
Lateral & vertical restraint straps	£20.76
Damp-proof membrane	£13.48
Joist hangers	£6.18
Pre-stressed concrete lintels	£71.11
Steel bracing. Welding	£342.00
Cavity trays & weepers	£390.51
Lead flashing	£58.29
Common bricks	£16.09
Sawn carcassing timber	£84.11
Joists & trimmers	£340.10
Trusses	£483.23
	£8,072

October 2002

Cash payment to brickies. Extra dentil brickwork	£360.00
Digger/dumper and 2 men to clear rear land	£550.00
Labour. Original contract for shell	£1,936.00
Labour. First-fix electrician	£600.00
Electrical carcassing materials	£218.10
Scaffold hire & erect	£1,940.00
Common bricks	£6.91
Lead flashing	£37.73
Velux roof lights. 2 No. plus flashings	£252.28
Door lining sets. 6 No. @ £10.10 each	£60.60
Staircase flight	£101.81
Sawn lumber	£321.66
Water pipe	£13.88
Mortar. 22 bags cement @ £2.28 each	
5 bags sand @ £28.23 each	£216.31
Common/Engineering bricks	£131.53
Concrete blocks. 28.8m @ £6.61 per m	£190.36

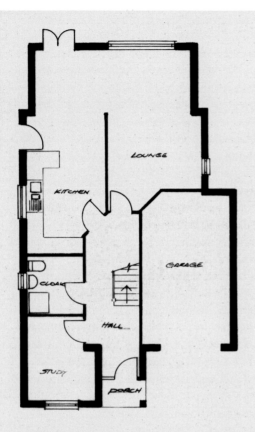

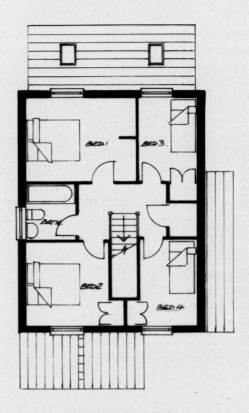

Lead flashing £18.48

Roof tiles. 1,045 tiles. 109 eaves tiles. 115 top slates
    62 verge tiles. @ £790 per 1,000.
    22 ridge tiles. Secret GRP gutter. Nails & fixings £1,166.04

Roofing underlay. 2 rolls @ £120 each £240.00

Eaves vents & soffit strip. £56.37

Lateral restraint straps £46.31

Nails, fixings & glue £94.83

Damp-proof course £10.49

Airbricks & cavity liners. £47.94

Chipboard flooring. 36 sheets 2,400 x 600 x 22
    @ £8.98 per sheet. £323.28

Stirling board. 5 sheets for loft 2,440 x 1,220 x 11
    @ £13.10 per sheet. £65.50

Plasterboard. 31 sheets 900 x 1,800 x 12.5 @ £3.71 per sheet
56 sheets 1,200 x 2,400 x 12.5 @ £3.68 per sheet £321.09

Additional steel pillar £401.85

Labour. Extra. Additional blockwork support to steels £626.00

Mixer hire £360.00

                                                                  £10,701

November 2002

Labour. Original contract for shell £3,750.00

Pvc-u windows £2,475.00

Labour for fitting windows. £450.00

Engineering bricks. 1 pallet. £92.00

Concrete blocks. 7.2m @ £6.21 per m £44.06

Soffit strip £24.68

Mastercrete cement. 2 bags @ £2.84 each £5.68

Mortar. 14 bags cement @ £2.51 each £35.14

2 bags sand @ £28.23 each £56.46

Lead flashing £23.10

Plasterboard. 8 sheets 1,200 x 2,400 x 12.5
    @ £3.35 per sheet. £26.80

Dry lining/plastering materials. Tape. Angle bead.
Adhesive. 12 bags Thistle @ £3.25 each £131.76

Labour. Second-fix contract £3,646.00

Nails, fixings & adhesives £120.53

Guttering & downpipe. £389.47

Door lining sets. 3 No. @ £10.10 each £30.30

Internal doors.13 No. @ £21.56 each £280.28

Furniture & hinges £91.64

Skirting & architrave £298.65

Sawn lumber £187.75

Drainage materials £59.06

Prepared timber £17.51

£12,236

December 2002

Labour. Second-fix contract £2,500.00

Electrical Second-fix materials £396.08

Door lining sets. 4 No. @ £14.00 . . . . £70.00

Floor tiles 28 sq. m @ £12 per sq. m £336.00

Floor tiler £14 per sq. m + adhesive and grouting £764.72

Light fittings £322.55

Lintels. 2 No. £55.85

Chipboard. 45 sheets 2,400 x 600 x 22 @ £8.98 per sheet £404.10

Flooring insulation. 24 No. 2,400 x 1,200 x 75
@ £12.19 per sheet
24 No. 2,400 x 1,200 x 25 @ £3.92 per sheet £386.64

Membrane £64.06

Fixings £53.95

Kitchen units & appliances £2,334.71

Insulation board. 10 sheets 2,400 x 1,200 x 59
@ £29.06 per sheet £290.60

Plasterboard. 85 sheets 1,200 x 2,400 x 12.5
@ £3.68 per sheet £312.80

Dri-wall adhesive. 15 bags @ £4.85 each £72.75

Thistle. 21 bags @ £3.25 each £68.25

Tape, beading, etc. £58.19

Sawn timber & ply £46.78

Mineral wool insulation. 1 roll £14.75

Soffit strip. 3 No. 2, 400 x 300 @ £4.28 each £12.84

Garage door £276.00

Mastercrete cement. 4 bags @ 2.84 each £11.36

Ordinary Portland cement. 5 bags @ £2.51 each £12.55

Common bricks £4.14

Drainage materials £288.80

£9,158

January 2003

Labour. Second-fix contract £1,000.00

Kitchen fitter £825.00

Additional carpentry. Understair and storage cupboards £200.00

Plumber. First-fix payment £3,000.00

Internal decorator £650.00

Plastering/rendering materials

Sand, thistle, board finish, plasticiser and beading £107.23

Plasterboard. 6 sheets 1,200 x 2,400 x 12.5
@ £3.83 per sheet £76.60

Thermal-bonded plasterboard. 6 sheets
1,200 x 2,400 x 30 @ £18.57 each £111.42

Electrical items £17.95

Lights £53.09

Additional kitchen unit £313.17

Sanitaryware £764.98

Staircase. Balustrades, newels, handrails, caps, etc. £322.49

Drainage materials £281.54

Ballast, sand & cement £123.79

Mineral wool insulation. 13 rolls @ £17.05 each £217.65

Nails, glue & fixings £52.51

Paint & decorators' materials £306.92

Sawn carcassing timber £9.74

Skirting, architrave, prepared timber £179.70

Guttering & downpipes £104.83

£8,719

February 2003

Labour. Second-fix contract £2,000.00

Internal decorator £200.00

Electrician £600.00

Plumber. Balance of supply-&-fix contract £2,975.00

Landscaping. Labour-only garden, paths, patios, fencing . . £2,500.00

Driveway supply-&-fix tarmac
75m @ £17.50 per sq. m £1,132.50

External decorator. Supply & fix £1,268.00

Fitted carpets £989.00

Electrical materials £29.72

Supply-and-fix aerial £140.00

Plasterers sand & cement £21.98

Paving. 63 No. 600 x 600, 49 No. 600 x 300, 52 No. 300 x 300
59 No. 450 x 450, 2 No. 450 x 300, 13 No. 600 x 450 . . £1,024.08

Sand, ballast & cement £144.73

Fencing materials £123.49

Fixings, screws, nails £21.51

Decorator's materials £38.72

Skirting, architrave & prepared timber £34.24

£13,243

Total **£87,055**

123.32 sq. m = £706 per sq. m

Above: **The design emulates an old schoolhouse. I love the light tower.** ©Nigel Ridgen

And that was supposed to be that for a while, until…

The story of house no. 2

… in the summer of 2003, barely six months after we'd moved in to our new home, I was sitting in the lounge when I heard the clatter of the letter box. I got up to retrieve the local classified newspaper and sat down to read it. On the back page there was a photograph of a plot described in the blurb as measuring about 600 square metres and for sale for £100,000.

Ten minutes later we were on the plot. It was walled on one side with an old pent-roofed brick and stone building to one front corner near the entrance gate. At the back right-hand corner there were some old pigsties. All the other boundaries were a mixture of native and coniferous hedging and there was a large cobnut tree to one side, partially obscuring the

next-door bungalow. It was in a small hamlet on a lane barely 3 metres wide and although next door's garden curled around the back of it, there were views to open countryside and the forest. I reckoned it was quite a lot bigger than the 600 square metres quoted in the paper.

Another ten minutes later and the agent had arrived. We told him we'd have it at the full asking price. Ten minutes after that, I telephoned my bank manager at HSBC and told him what we'd done. He was cool. There and then on the telephone he told me to write what cheques I needed to and he would cover them. And this time, he added, there would be no need to sell up and move into rented accommodation. We could stay in the house whilst we built.

Ten minutes after that I telephoned my solicitor and told him all about it. He contacted the agent and set the ball rolling. We weren't going to hang about on this one and I was going to do my absolute best to make sure nobody else got it. The board on the plot mysteriously disappeared and the agent, whom I knew quite well, allowed me to change the 'For sale' on the one at the end of the lane to 'Sold subject to contract'.

The planning stages

There seemed to have been quite a long planning history, with an application for two dwellings having been refused and then the subsequent one for just one bungalow also having been refused, then granted on appeal. In his report the inspector stated that he saw no reason why this site couldn't take a modest bungalow, situated to one side of the site to preserve the open character of the area. Only I didn't want modest here. This was a lovely site and, unlike the previous house, which had been on an infill plot and really didn't deserve to have the boat pushed out architecturally, I felt this one did. I took some rough measurements of the site and then sat down and did some sketches, which I sent up to my dear friend Beverley.

What I wanted was a bungalow that fitted into one end of the plot with the garage at the rear right-hand corner where the pigsties were. I toyed with the idea of putting it facing into the plot and showed that on my sketches. I also wrote a 'wish list'. I have a thing about bungalows not looking like railway carriages and I wanted the design to emulate an old schoolhouse. I wanted cathedral ceilings in at least the lounge and I felt that a full-height window in one gable would reflect the character of such a schoolhouse. I also hate bungalow designs that mix up the living and sleeping accommodation and I wanted there to be a clear distinction between the two with an outer entrance hall and an inner hall separated from it, giving access to the bedrooms. What worried me was that this inner hall might be like the black hole of Calcutta.

When the drawings came back from Beverley I was dumbstruck. They were great. They were everything I'd dreamed of and more. The front elevation looked just like an old schoolhouse and, with the inner hall, she'd got around the problem by putting a light tower through the roof to emulate a bell tower.

The only problem was that as it looked so good, I felt that it should present its face to the lane rather than into the plot and so I cut and pasted the sketches to turn it around by 90 degrees and sent them back to Beverley to alter. I also asked her to delete the reference to bedroom four and replace it with the word 'office'. As a writer working from home I needed an office and surely three bedrooms was modest?

Before I went to the planners I commissioned a full survey, which did in fact reveal that the site measured 806 square metres. Interestingly enough, whilst I was on the site with the surveyor, a couple walked by and called over the hedge to ask if this was the plot that was for sale. 'No,' I replied. 'I've bought it.' I hadn't. Contracts hadn't yet exchanged but I went down to the solicitor and hurried things along. In fact, we then had a worrying few weeks as contracts did not exchange until the end of the first week in September, with completion delayed until late September as the vendors wanted time to clear their things off the land.

In the meantime, I made an appointment to see the planner, who turned out to be a very nice lady. She looked at the plans and her immediate reaction was, 'Oh, this looks good.' She then turned up the file and read the notes and the appeal document. 'But it's a bit big,' she continued. I explained that the site was 200 square metres bigger than the original applicants had estimated. I also pointed out that the inspector, in granting the appeal, had not withdrawn Permitted Development Rights. If she ruled that I would have to make it smaller, I would extend it and neither of us would really end up with what we wanted. She agreed.

A big problem was the fact that the consent was about to expire. Condition number two stipulated that application must be made for Approval of Reserved Matters before three years expired. I had until 14 September to beat that deadline. The planning officer assured me that it didn't really matter. They had conceded the fact that this plot could be developed and they would accept a new Full application.

Unfortunately, that wasn't good enough for me. The inspector had not restricted the Permitted Development Rights on the Outline consent. To attempt to place such a condition on any Approval of Reserved Matters would almost certainly result in me appealing the condition in view of the fact that the inspector hadn't seen fit to impair these rights. However, if the current Outline consent was allowed to expire, then a subsequent Full approval could contain such a condition and I would have great difficulty in overturning it.

Beverley hadn't finished the revised drawings but she sent me down some blank copies of a very boring bungalow plan and I made an application on 12 September for Approval of Reserved Matters, pursuant to the original Outline consent. This was a purely sacrificial application and I telephoned the planning officer to explain what I'd done and to tell her that I would be substituting this for revised plans in the very near future. In the meantime she had to process the application and both she and I were quite amused when the Parish Council came back and said they liked the plans. When they received the proper plans, they didn't like them at all!

But the planner did and, in the final analysis, it's the planners who hold the whip hand. So too with the objections of the Highways Agency, who reported that they'd prefer to see the access in the centre of the frontage with a passing place at the front right-hand corner. This passing place was, by the way, another of the conditions on the original Outline consent. 'Do you really want the stone bank and natural hedge ripped out along this lane?' I asked the planning officer. 'Not on your nelly' was the gist of the reply!

In the end she accepted and approved the entrance bellmouth and the passing place as being combined on the right of the frontage. Most importantly, as I pointed out, this meant that the very minimum of hedging would have to be removed and that the passing place could not now be utilised by neighbours as a parking place. We had our consent by the end of October.

Getting the project under way

I was very busy in the early part of 2004 and decided that I really didn't have time to manage subcontractors for at least the shell part of the build. During the previous self-build I'd got chatting with a local

builder, Les Hatton, who had commiserated with me during the time that nothing was happening on the house and said that next time, he would see me right. I duly contacted him and he gave me a price of £76,814 to build the shell of the bungalow and garage on a supply-and-fix basis. There were a couple of exclusions: I was to buy the plinth stone or, as it later became, the plinth bricks and also the external windows and doors.

I'd met a chap in the village, Mark Mathews, who is a master joiner. He works from a small garage in his back garden and he gave me prices for the cathedral window, the entrance door, the garage doors and, later on, the gates to be made in oak. I was also in touch with the makers and installers of the Pvc-u windows that I'd had on the previous house and it turned out that they were quite used to working with the joiner regarding the glazing.

There were quite a few things decided on the specification at this stage, although as the job evolved, things inevitably changed. For a start we had decided on rendered white painted walling above the brickwork plinth and we'd also plumped for a natural slate roof. The garage reflected strong views of mine. I hate square boxes with roofs and garage doors. So Beverley had drawn a single garage with an open carport to give it more of a cart barn feel.

February 2004

Work started on site in the first week of February 2004 and it went just swimmingly. The fencing (under a separate contract) went up first, once we'd taken down the high cypress hedge to the rear and gained around 2 metres in so doing. Then the site was cleared and the topsoil stacked in an enormous mound against the front hedge. This was enlarged still more at one end by the spoil that came out of the footings and, in fact, we sent nothing away this time, which really paid off at the end of the job. The footings were concreted with little or no fuss, the blockwork came up to dpc, and the floor beams went on with about a fortnight's delay (due, I think, to the fact that the builder had forgotten to confirm the measurements – I never really got to the bottom of that one).

Above: **The main bedroom** right: **the en-suite** left: **looking up into the light tower** far right: **the vast kitchen/dining/living room.** © Nigel Rigden

May 2004

By May the shell was weathertight and the builder and I agreed a price for the second-fix part of the contract on a labour-only basis with me supplying all subsequent materials. In reality that meant that he and one other were authorised to buy on my account and this worked quite well. I think that I found just £112 of stuff that wasn't for my site on the account and even that was credited immediately.

June/July 2004

It went a bit quiet in June as they'd taken on another job as well and for a time, I was left wondering if I was going to end up in the same situation as I'd been in before. But by July they were cracking on again with a promise to finish by the end of the month. That was driven by the fact that I'd sold the first house and the purchasers were insisting on a completion date of 31 July.

The garage roof was the last bit of the shell contract and the arrival of the trusses occasioned yet another change. They came with the rafters extended, ready to be cut off to suit. When they were up, it occurred to us that it would look quite nice to leave them and to extend the roof on one side as a sort of lean-to, supported by chamfered oak posts.

It also occurred to us that it made no sense to take up one of the bedrooms as an office and that I could use the carport section of the garage instead. Mark, the joiner, had already made the garage doors. They were oak, hinged on each side to open like proper doors. Now I needed to fill in the front of what would have been the carport. The side would be blocked in and there would be two Pvc-u top opening windows, almost hidden from view under the overhang. But the front was important. Too many garage conversions look like just what they are. And I wanted this to look right and not like an oversight.

I sketched out a stable front. To the left there would be a stable door and to the right, panelled timber with vertical bars above, between which we would fit double-glazing units. It looked good on paper, and when Mark had finished making it, it looked even better.

Of course we weren't finished by 31 July. Most of the hard landscaping was done. The retaining walls were in and the vast mound at the front was used to backfill behind them with the topsoil reserved for the three distinct areas of lawn. The turf was paid for and awaited. The patio slabs were all down. But the kitchen and some of the decorating weren't finished. In the case of the kitchen it was because the granite worktops hadn't yet arrived. The decoration was just taking longer because the vaulted and cathedral ceilings plus the light tower needed scaffolding and towers to reach them.

We did not want to risk failing to complete. We

also had a wedding to go to in France, so on Thursday 29 July we moved out into storage and went to Kent to stay with our daughter before taking a ferry to France on the Monday. Whilst we were in France we kept in daily contact with the site. The worktops arrived. However, as the suppliers and installers carried them in they dropped one and broke some of the Portuguese floor tiles. More seriously, they cracked a large chip out of the back of one of the longer sections. Les, the builder, phoned me. Apparently the contractors had offered to fill the crack in with black filler but he reckoned it would still show. He recommended that we refuse to accept this and when he relayed that to them, they agreed to supply granite upstands free of charge, which mask the chip completely.

August 2004

We arrived back in England on 3 August and the project was still not finished. An army of blokes and their wives were painting, cleaning and sweeping. We were told it would be ready for the carpet layers by the Monday. And it was. We had to stay in a hotel for four nights but we moved in on Wednesday 18 August, just 18 days late. Not bad for the building industry.

Cost of the project

It had taken six and a half months to build what was a complicated design with a top-notch specification. We'd done nothing by halves this time but, having said that, we stuck to our usual trick of mixing and matching expensive with cheap to achieve what we wanted at a reasonable cost. Most of the living floor area is tiled with Portuguese ceramic tiles at a cost of £16 per square metre. The kitchen units, on the other hand, are relatively cheap ones from Jewson's range, cheered up with Chinese granite worktops. The total cost of those, including appliances, came to a smidgen over £8,500. The oak windows, doors garage doors and office front came to nearly £5,600 plus the cost of the glazing, which is included in the supply-and-fix cost of the Pvc-u windows and doors. But they are well worth it and add considerably to the 'wow' factor.

The under-floor central heating at £2,590 supply only, plus the boiler and the mains pressure cylinder, probably cost me a bit more than if we'd opted for a conventional radiator-type system. But in the previous house, where we'd had radiators, we'd had tiled floors to the kitchen and dining area, which were very cold underfoot on entering in the morning. With such a large expanse of tiling in this house, under-floor heating was, and is, the only sensible option. I think it costs more to run: I've spent £1,250 on oil for a full year. I think that many companies' brochures are slightly misleading in that they talk of temperatures way below what I would consider comfortable, and even below the minimums set down by the NHBC. I think that the condensing boilers do work better at lower temperatures and I know that, after a cold night, it can take the system over three hours to bring the lounge up by just 2 degrees to the daytime setting. Of course one end of the room is a cathedral window, there are ceilings approaching 5.5 metres high, and there is a huge bay window. The house is also carpeted, which undoubtedly slows down the transfer of heat to the room, and, up to now, it hasn't had curtains because I don't like them. Mrs Snell has, however, insisted on changing that and we'll see (if we stay long enough) whether or not that will improve things.

Does this mean that I'm against under-floor central heating? Not a bit of it. I love it. I love the ambience within the home; the fact that each cubic metre of air space is at the same temperature as any other in the room. But it's not suitable for all situations or for all lifestyles. We occupy the home 24/7, as they say. The heating is actually never turned off. It has a night-time set-back of 2°C and it stays on throughout the year. Why not? You can have cold snaps in the summer as well as warm periods in the winter. With thermostats in every room, our home, with the exception of that problem lounge, remains at an almost constant temperature. And even the lounge isn't that much of a problem because we tend to occupy it in the evenings, by which time it's as warm as toast.

The build costs for this bungalow were always going to be greater than those for the previous house. It was a complicated design and I'd chosen to build with a much more hands-off approach.

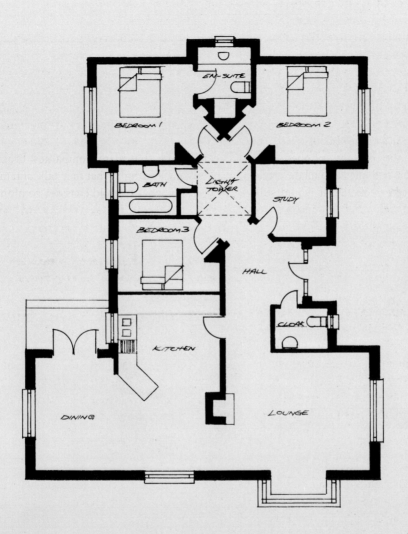

COSTS RELATING TO HOUSE NO 2. (as they were spent)

September 2003

Planning fees	£220.00
Land survey	£352.50
Solicitor's fees, disbursements and Stamp Duty	£1,577.88
	£2,151

January 2004

Building Regulations application	£117.50
Site security gates etc.	£594.00
Water supply	£1,169.01
NHBC warranty	£1,000.00
	£2,881

February 2004

Site insurance	£660.00
Architectural technician. Plans	£485.00
Structural engineer	£125.00
Buildings Regulations inspection fees	£358.38
Supply-&-fix shell contract	£20,000.00
Electricity supply	£425.42
	£22,054

March 2004

Supply-&-fix shell contract	£15,000.00
Supply-&-fix fencing	£2,000.00

Labour. Sewer connection £2,500.00

Labour. Lay service trenches. Clear trees £500.00

£20,000

April 2004

Supply-&-fix shell contract £20,000.00

Plinth bricks. 4,944 @ £267 per 1,000

Squint bricks. 504 @ £173 each £2,301.98

Architectural technician. Extra drawings £45.00

. . . . £22,347

May 2004

Supply-&-fix shell contract £10,000.00

Under-floor heating £2,590.00

Steel joists £225.00

£12,815

June 2004

Supply-&-fix shell contract £11,814.00

Labour. Finishing contract £12,814.00

Schoolhouse window £2,128.00

Timber stain £33.00

Guttering & downpipe £590.94

Supply-&-fix Pvc-u windows & doors £4,678.09

Light fittings £389.91

Fixings/screws £44.53

Decorator's materials £139.23

Lead flashing £8.99

Plumber's materials £22.61

Insulation board. 32 sheets 2,400 x 1,200 x 100
  @ £28.40 each £908.80

Portland cement. 16 bags @ £2.79 each £44.64

Thistle. 20 bags @ £3.86 each £77.20

Plastering materials. Angle & stop beads. Scrim tape £164.13

Plasterboard. 64 sheets 1,200 x 2,400 x 15 @ £6.28 each £401.92

Plasterboard. 32 sheets 1,200 x 2,400 x 12.5 @ £4.30 each £137.60

Thermal-bonded plasterboard.

  13 sheets 1,200 x 2,400 x 30 @ £14.30 each £185.90

Sawn lumber £71.63

Slate ventilators. 2 No. £36.00

Membrane. 2 rolls £65.00

Flooring insulation. 152.64 sq. m @ £5.74 per sq. m £876.15

£35,632

July 2004

Labour. Finishing contract £22,000.00

Ceramic tiles. 79 sq. m @ £16. 4 sq. m @ £28.86

35 m @ £6.14. Borders. 56 @ £2.50 each
  40 @ £1.00 each £1,957.94

Ceramic tile adhesive, grout & trims £625.91

Bricks. Retaining walls/landscaping. 4,120
  @ £267 per 1,000 . . . . £1,100.04

Stone. Front wall. 32 sq. m £750.00

Plumbing materials £459.43

Mains-pressure hot-water cylinder £570.00

Condensing boiler £1,132.00

Front door & frame £740.00

Boiler house door £51.26

Oil tank £486.00

Turf. 330 sq. m £556.09

Internal doors. 9 @ £34.99. 1 @ £18.99.

2 pairs @ £139.99 per pair. 1 @ £59.99 . . . . £673.87

Kitchen unit & appliances £5,806.51

Granite worktops £2,695.00

Sanitaryware £2,709.15

Plastering materials. Incl. 4 bags sand @ £32 each

42 bags Thistle @ £3.86 each
2 bags bonding @ £5.33 each, Beading etc £450.08

Thermal-bonded plasterboard.

  8 sheets 1,200 x 2,400 x 30 @ £14.30 each £114.40

Cement. 122 bags @ £2.79 each £340.38

Mortar ancillaries.

Plasticiser. Reinforcement. Colouring £42.31

Ballast. 1 bag @ £29.00 . . . . £29.00

Readymix concrete.

12 cu. me @ £55.41 per cu. m £664.92

Paving slabs. 103 No. 600 x 300 @ £4.68 each

243 No. 600 x 600 @ £9.04 each. 38 No. 300 x 300
  @ £2.62 each £2,778.32

Concrete blocks. 43.2 m @ £6.76 per m £292.03

Mineral wool insulation. 27 rolls @ £19.18 each £517.86

Decorator's materials £204.27

Nails, fixings, screws & adhesives £99.35

Drainage materials. Including 3m pipe @ £8.00 each.
Manholes & covers. Fittings £743.46

Roofing underlay. 1 roll £120.00

Damp-proof course. 3 No. 30m rolls @ £2.59 each £7.77

Window board. 6 No. 3m lengths @ £9.45 per m £170.10

Door linings. 10 sets @ £12.47 each. 1 set @ £10.48.

Two sets @ £15.40 each £165.98

Sawn lumber £73.32

Meter box £41.50

Soffit vent strip. 24 m £48.60

Agent's fees to sell previous house £2,955.00

Solicitor's fees and disbursements to sell previous house . . . £442.75

£52,615

August 2004

Labour. Finishing contract £10,000.00

House nameplate £50.54

Scalpings for driveway. 10 tonnes £150.00

Cotswold stone for driveway. 5 tonnes £115.00

Plumbing materials £532.68

Aluminium level threshold £10.49

Window boards £52.36

2 No. aerials £300.00

Stone cappings for front wall. £200.00

Carpets. £2,863.00

Plastering materials. Incl. 2 bags sand @ £32 each . . . .

13 bags Thistle @ £3.86 each. 2 bags bonding @ £5.33 each

2 bags lime @ £6.41 each. Beading. Tape. £171.30

Plasterboard. 2 sheets 1,200 x 2,400 x 15 @ £9.06 each . . . £18.12

Plasterboard fixing £7.69

Thermal-bonded plasterboard. 12 sheets @ £21.45 each . . £257.40

Cement. 30 bags @ £2.79 each £83.70

Ballast. 1 bag £29.00

Building sand. 4 bags @ £32 each £128.00

Exmet, plasticiser £63.03

Ceramic tiles. 9 sq. m @ £4.71 per m £42.39

Ceramic tile adhesive, grout and spacers. £147.86

Decorator's materials. Incl. fillers, brushes. Sealants. Silicones.
Removers, etc.

(10 litres emulsion £24.66 per litre) £352.91

Guttering & downpipe. £204.86

Paving slabs. 16 No. 600 x 600 @ £9.04 each £144.64

Timber £93.50

Plywood. 2 sheets 2,440 x 1,220 x 12 @ £25.57 each.

1 sheet 2,440 x 1,220 x 5.5 @ £12.95 . . . . £64.09

Drainage materials/fittings £251.81

Lead flashing £12.74

£16,347

September 2004

Labour. Finishing contract. £6,000.00

Supply & fix tarmac £1,000.00

Scalpings. £40.00

Office/stable door £1,000.00

Garage doors £850.00

Gates £850.00

Purpose-made cupboard doors £110.00

Electrician. Additional time clocks/frost thermostats £92.10

Boiler commissioning £147.91

Flooring chipboard. 16 sheets @ £6.55 each £104.72

Flooring insulation. 5 sheets 2,400 x 1,200 x 100
@ £19.95 per sheet. £99.75

Plumbing fittings £27.00

Plastering/rendering materials. £91.68

Building sand. 2 bags @ £32 each £64.00

Cement. 14 bags @ £2.79 each £39.06

Decorator's materials

Paint. Filler. Brushes. Remover. Silicone

(10 litres Sandtex emulsion = £44.07) £316.37

Door furniture £31.44

Timber. £18.52

Plywood. 3 sheets 2,440 x 1,220 x 9 @ £17.46 each £52.38

£10,935

Total. **£197,777**

186 sq. m = £1,063 per sq. m

So, at £198,000 plus the land costs of £100,000 the bungalow cost me £298,000 to build. Shortly after we moved in an estate agent came round and valued it at £390,000, so we've made £92,000 on it, less the agent's fees when we sell. Not too shabby!

I love this bungalow. It is everything I've ever wanted in a home. It's warm in the winter, cool in the summer. Light floods down and into every room. No seasonally affected disorders here! But will we stay? No. We're already looking for the next plot. And it does give me something to write about, after all.

FURTHER INFORMATION

Books

The New Home Plans Book by David Snell and Murray Armor, Ebury Press

Renovating for Profit by Michael Holmes, Ebury Press

The Housebuilder's Bible by Mark Brinkley, Ovolo Publishing

The Planning Game by Ken Dijksman, Ovolo Publishing

Self Build – Design & Build Your Own Home by Julian Owen, RIBA Enterprises

Practical Housebuilding by Bob Matthews, Blackberry Books

All About Self Building by Bob Matthews, Blackberry Books

How to Find a Building Plot by Speer & Dade, Stonepound Books

How To Get Planning Permission by Speer & Dade, Stonepound Books

How to Finance Building and Converting Your Own Home by Speer & Dade, Stonepound Books

Magazines

Homebuilding & Renovating Tel: 01527 834400 www.homebuilding.co.uk

Build It Tel: 020 7837 8727 www.self-build.co.uk

Self Build & Design 01283 742950

Planning inspectorates and appeal boards

England – The Planning Inspectorate Tel: 0117 372 8754

Wales – The Planning Inspectorate Tel: 02920 825007

Scotland – The Scottish Executive Inquiry Reporters Unit Tel: 0131 244 5649

Northern Ireland – The Planning Appeals Commission Tel: 02890 244710

The Republic of Ireland (Eire) – An Bord Pleanala Tel: 00 353 1872 8001

Architectural, design and engineering associations and societies

Royal Institute of British Architects (RIBA) www.architecture.com Tel: 020 7580 5533

Royal Incorporation of Architects in Scotland (RIAS) www.rias.org.uk Tel: 0131 229 7205

Royal Society of Architects in Wales www.architecture-wales.com Tel: 02920 874753

Royal Society of Ulster Architects www.rsua.org.uk Tel: 028 9032 3760

Royal Institute of Architects in Ireland (RIAI) Tel: 00 353 1676 1703 www.riai.ie

Associated Self-Build Architects (ASBA) Tel: 0800 387310 www.asba-architects.org

Architects Registration Board (ARB) Tel: 020 7278 2206 www.arb.org.uk

Royal Town Planning Institute Tel: 020 7636 9107 www.rtpi.org.uk

The British Institute of Architectural Technologists Tel: 020 7278 2206 www.biat.org.uk

Architectural Designers Association Tel: 0118 941 6571

Institute of Civil Engineers Tel: 020 7222 7722

Building trades associations

British Interior Design Association Tel: 020 7349 0800 www.bida.org

Federation of Master Builders Tel: 020 7242 7583 www.fmb.org.uk

HomePro/Fair Trades Ltd. Tel: 0870 738 4858 www.HomePro.com

Association of Plumbing & Heating Contractors Tel: 02476 470626 www.aphc.co.uk

Institute of Plumbing & Heating Engineering Tel: 01708 472791

Council for Registered Gas Installers (CORGI) Tel: 01256 372200 www.corgi-gas.com

National Inspection Council for Electrical Installation Contractors Tel: 020 7582 7746 www.niceic.org.uk

The Construction Federation Tel: 020 7608 5080

National Federation of Roofing Contractors Tel: 020 7436 0387 www.nfrc.co.uk

Guild of Master Craftsmen Tel: 01273 478449

The Painting & Decorating Association Tel: 02476 353 776 www.paintingdecoratingassociation.co.uk

The Thatching Advisory Service Tel: 01256 880828

Joint Contracts Tribunal (JCT) Tel: 0121 722 8200 www.buildingcontract.co.uk

Yellow Pages Tel: 0118 959 2111 www.yell.com

Government agencies and establishments

Office of the Deputy Prime Minister www.odpm.gov.uk

The Scottish Building Standards Agency www.sbsa.gov.uk

Department of the Environment, Heritage & Local Government (Eire) www.environ.ie

Department of Finance and Personnel (NI) www.dfpni.gov.uk

The Building Research Establishment (and BRECSU) Tel: 01923 664000

National Radiological Protection Board Tel: 01235 831600

Radiological Protection Institute of Ireland www.rpii.ie

HM Land Registry Tel: 020 7917 8888 www.landreg.gov.uk

Floodline Tel: 0845 988 1188

The National Federation of Housing Associations Tel: 020 7278 6571

The Housing Corporation Tel: 020 7393 2000

HM Customs and Excise helpline Tel: 08450 109000 www.hmce.gov.uk

VAT self-build claims Tel: 0121 697 4000

SEDBUK boiler ratings www.boilers.org.uk

Self-certification schemes or bodies

BRE Certification Ltd. Tel: 01923 664100 www.brecertification.co.uk

British Standards Institution Tel: 01442 278607 www.kitemartoday.com

ELECSA Tel: 020 7864 9913 www.elecsa.org.uk

NAPIT Tel: 0870 444 1392 www.napit.org.uk

NICEIC Certification Services Ltd. Tel: 08000 130900 www.niceic.org.uk

The Structural Engineering Registration Scheme (SER) www.ser ltd.com

The Scottish Building Standards Registration Scheme (SELECT) www.select.org.uk

Special-interest groups or associations

The Association of Self-builders Tel: 0704 154 4126

The Traditional Housing Bureau Tel: 01344 725757

Timber Research & Development Association (TRADA) Tel: 01494 569600 (England and Wales), 01259 272143 (Scotland) www.trada.co.uk

The British Woodworking Federation Tel: 0870 458 6951 www.bwf.org.uk

The Basement Development Group Tel: 01344 725737

The Glass & Glazing Federation Tel: 0870 042 4255

The Disabled Living Foundation Tel: 020 7289 6111

The Disability Alliance Tel: 020 7247 8776

The Society for the Protection of Ancient Buildings (SPAB) Tel: 020 7377 1644 www.spab.org.uk

English Heritage Tel: 020 7973 3000 www.english-heritage.org.uk

Council for the Protection of Rural England (CPRE) Tel: 020 7253 0300

Historic Scotland Tel: 0131 668 8600 www.historic-scotland.gov.uk

Cadw Tel: 02920 500200 www.cadw.wales.gov.uk

The Environmental & Heritage Service (Ulster) Tel: 028 9023 5000

The Council for British Archaeology Tel: 01904 671417

The Ancient Monuments Society Tel: 020 7236 3934

The Georgian Group Tel: 020 7387 1720

The Victorian Society Tel: 020 8994 1019

The Community Self-Build Association Tel: 020 7415 7092

The Young Builders' Trust Tel: 01730 266766

The Walter Segal Trust Tel: 020 7388 9582

The Bat Conservation Trust Tel: 020 7627 8827

Royal Society for the Protection of Birds Tel: 01767 680551

National Conservatory Advisory Centre Tel: 0800 608 5050

Architectural and design practices featured in this book

The Border Design Centre Tel: 01578 740218

Julian Owen Associates Tel: 0115 922 9831

Renovation and reclamation specialists

The Lime Centre Tel: 01962 713636

Strippers of Sudbury Tel: 01787 371524

Professional VAT reclaim assistance

Michael J. Flint Tel: 01435 813360 www.mjfvat.btinternet.co.uk

Plumbing & Heating Consultant

Terry Troth Tel: 01784 450213/07881 667656 terry.troth@terrytroth.me.uk

Photography

Nigel Rigden Tel: 01349 877329
E-mail: nigel@nigrig.com
www.nigrig.com

Companies and agencies assisting in land finding

Plotfinder – 24-hour hotline Tel: 0906 557 5400
Faxback Service Tel: 01527 834428 www.plotfinder.net
Plotsearch Tel: 0870 870 9994
www.buildstore.co.uk/plotsearch
English Partnerships Tel: 01908 692692
www.englishpartnerships.co.uk

Exhibitions and shows

The *International Homebuilding & Renovating Show* – early spring at the NEC, late spring at Glasgow SECC, summer at East of England Showground Peterborough, early autumn at ExCeL London Docklands, late autumn at Harrogate Exhibition and Conference Centre and winter at Bath & West Showground, Tel: 01527 834400
www.homebuildingshow.co.uk
Ideal Homes Exhibition – every spring at Earls Court, London
Grand Designs Exhibition – summer at ExcCeL, London Docklands

Self-build & renovation centres

National Self-Build & Renovation Centre – Swindon
Tel: 0870 870 9991 www.buildstore.co.uk
Scottish Self-Build & Renovation Centre – Livingston
Tel: 0870 870 9991 www.buildstore.co.uk

Self-build courses

Developing Skills (in association with *H&R* magazine) – four-day, and two-day residential courses
Tel: 01480 893833 www.selfbuildcourses.co.uk
Constructive Individuals – weekend and three-week hands-on courses Tel: 020 7515 9299
www.constructiveindividuals.com
The Centre for Alternative Technology (CAT) – various courses Tel: 01654 705981 www.cat.org.uk
The Lime Centre – one-day courses, monthly in the summer Tel: 01962 713636 www.thelimecentre.co.uk
The Society for the Protection of Ancient Buildings (SPAB) Tel: 020 7377 1644 www.spab.org.uk

Self-build insurances

DMS Services Ltd. – for all self-build insurances
Tel: 01909 591652
Project Builder Tel: 020 7716 5050
Self-Builder Tel: 0800 018 7660 www.self-builder.com
Self-Build Zone Tel: 0845 230 9874
www.selfbuildzone.com
St Paul Travellers' Insurance Co. (Eire)
Tel: 00 353 1609 5731
Capital Insurance Brokers (Eire) Tel: 00 353 1496 6268
Autoline Insurance Group (Eire & Ulster)
Tel: 028 3026 6333
Brophy & Co. (Eire) Tel: 00 353 5028 2130
www.brophys.ie

Warranties

NHBC – 'Buildmark' and 'Solo' Tel: 01494 434477
Zurich Self-Build Building Guarantee
Tel: 0870 241 8050
Premier Guarantee Tel: 0151 650 4343
Project Builder Tel: 020 7716 5050
NHBG – 'Homebond' Tel: 00 353 1491 0210
Coyle Hamilton (Eire) Tel: 00 353 1661 6211

Specialist self-build companies, package-deal companies and timber-frame manufacturers

Border Oak Design & Construction Ltd. Tel: 01568 708752 www.borderoak.com
Buildstore Ltd. Tel: 0870 870 9991
www.buildstore.co.uk
Custom Homes Ltd. Tel: 01293 822898
www.customhomes.co.uk
T.J. Crump Oakrights Tel: 01432 353353
www.oakrights.co.uk
Design & Materials Ltd. Tel: 01909 540123
www.designandmaterials.uk.com
Fleming Homes Ltd. Tel: 01361 883785
Frame Homes (South West) Ltd. Tel: 01872 572882
www.framehomes.co.uk
Guardian Homes Tel: 01772 614243
Maple Timber Frame Tel: 01772 683370
Potton Ltd. Tel: 01480 401401 www.potton.co.uk
Scandia-Hus Tel: 01342 327977
Southern Timber Frame Tel: 02380 293062
Scotframe Timber Engineering Ltd. Tel: 01467 624440
Taylor Lane Timber Frame Ltd. Tel: 01432 271912
www.taylor-lane.co.uk

GLOSSARY

Here is a list of words that may be unfamiliar, or which have specific meanings and uses peculiar to the building industry:

Apron – Decorative timber around a staircase opening

Architrave – Timber moulding masking the joint between the door frame and the plaster

Arris – Timber with a triangular section

Apex – The triangular section above the window in a dormer

Ballustrade/balustrading – The bars and handrails around a staircase

Bat – A half brick

Batt – Slabs of fibre insulation

Batter – To slope

Bed – The horizontal joint in masonry

Bed – To lay something on mortar

Bellmouth – The splayed junction of a drive where it enters the highway

Bellstop – An angled-out section of render above a window or opening

Bressumer – The visible beam over a fireplace

Binders – Timber fixed longitudinally to provide stability

Blind/blinding – Use of a sand layer to prevent membranes being punctured

Box sash – Windows which slide up and down independently

Bracing – Timber fixed diagonally to provide stability

Butt – A water barrel

Butt – A hinge

Butt – To join

Cantilever – An oversailing upper section

Carcassing – To put in the basic infrastructure

Cesspit – A tank for holding untreated effluent

Chamfer – Slope off

Chase – Cut out

Cill – The external bottom lip of a window or opening

Collar – A usually horizontal tie between rafters at ceiling or floor level

Collar – The fitting joining two lengths of pipe

Compo – Slang for mortar

Coping – The covering or weathering to the top of a wall

Corbell/corbelled – Stepped-out masonry

Coveing – Rounded-off section between wall and ceiling

Cruck – A curved rafter or roof member

Curtilage – The boundary of land or the limit of buildings

Dado – Waist high on the wall. May have a decorative moulding

Dashing – The act of applying one material to another by throwing it

Daywork – Price given by the hour or day

Deep strip – Foundation trenches with concrete in the bottom

Dead man – A 'T'-shaped prop used to hold up plasterboard

Dragon beam – Timber support and tie across the corners of a roof

Dressing – Flattening one material over another

Dog leg – A right-angled bend

Dog plate – Toothed metal plate placed between timber to strengthen the joint

Dormer – A window protruding above the roof plane with its own roof section

Dubbing – Filling in and smoothing out depressions

Dwang – (Scottish) Interim support between structural members

Dpc – Damp-proof course

Dpm – Damp-proof membrane

Drip – A groove or overhang to prevent water running back into the wall

Dust – Cement

Eaves – The lower end of a roof where it meets the walling

Espagnolette – Multi-point locking

Facia – Board that masks the bottom end of the rafters and carries the guttering

Flaunch – To smooth over with mortar

Filigree – Intricately carved and shaped timber

Fill – packing

Firrings – Tapered timber fixed to joists to provide a roof slope

Firrings – Sections of timber fixed to the side of other timber to provide extra strength

Fishplate – Toothed plate used to join timber

Flashing – Creating a weathertight seal or upstand using lead

Float – To smooth over

Floating – Bricks or stone remaining loose when mortar doesn't go off

Floating floor – Timber flooring laid on insulation

Flue – Chimney pipe

Frog – Indentation in a brick

Furniture – Ironmongery

Gable – The end of a building beneath a pitched roof

Gauge – To measure either by volume or by distance

Gluelam beam – A structural beam made from laminated timber sections

Green – Mortar, brickwork or stonework that has not yet 'gone off' or set

Going – The horizontal distance of a tread or staircase

Hanger – A metal device to support the ends of beams

Haunch – To cover over

Hawk – Implement to carry mortar or plaster

Head – The top horizontal section of a door frame or window

Header – A brick showing its shorter face

Hip – The sloping junction between the outside angles of two roof planes

Hipped roof – A roof that slopes back on to another roof plane

Infill – Usually consolidated hardcore beneath a load-bearing floor

In situ – Made or cast on site

Intumescent – Designed to expand and seal gaps during fire

Jet – A ladle with a long handle

Kingpost – A single vertical roof member

Lean-mix – Weak concrete

Lining – Frame

Measured rates – Pricing work by reference to the itemised or measured amount

Muck – Waste or unwanted soil

Muck – Slang for mortar

Mullion – The vertical section or division strip in a window

Newel – The upright support posts on a staircase

Nogging – Interim support between structural members

Nosing – A projecting timber or the part of a stair tread projecting beyond the riser

Oversite – The levelled-out subsoil beneath a floor or the concrete floor itself

Ogee – A moulding shape

Ovolo – A moulding shape

Pargetting – Moulded decorative plasterwork or render

Pendant – A hanging light

Perp/perpends – The vertical joint in brickwork

Pig – An uneven section in brickwork

Piled/piling – Concrete or steel sections driven or bored to lower levels for support

Plate – A timber on top of, within or fixed to a wall used to support or fix other elements

Plinth – A brick or stone section at the base of a wall

Plumb – To carry out the plumbing

Plumb – To make upright

Pricework – Work quoted as a lump sum

Proud – Standing or lying above or beyond the surrounding material

Point/pointing – The face of the mortar joint in masonry

Purlin – Timber support built into the walling and beneath joists or rafters

Putlock – The short scaffold pole built into the walling to support the boards

Queen – Three-quarter-length brick

Queen post – A paired vertical roof member

Quoin – Corner stones or bricks

Raft – A reinforced concrete slab

Rafter – The top or sloping roof member supporting the roof covering

Rebate – A stepped recess in timber or masonry

Reveal – The visible part of the walling inside an opening

Ridge – The apex of a roof

Rise – The height of a tread or staircase

Roof light – A window lying within the roof plane

RSJ – Rolled steel joist

Saddle – A sewer connection made on top of the pipe run

Sarking boarding – Timber boards laid over the roof members to provide structural stability

Sarking felt – Roofing underlay, laid beneath the tiles

Sash – The glazed section of a window

Septic tank – A tank for storing and partially purifying effluent

Scarf/scarfing – Joining timber using a halved joint

Screed – A smooth layer of sand and cement flooring

Skillion ceiling – A sloping ceiling beneath the roof

Skim/skim coat – A thin coat of plaster

Slipper – Two open channel sections of pipe joining at a gentle angle

Soakers – Lead sheets interleaved between tiles or slates and then dressed up the wall

Soffit – Area beneath the rafters at the eaves

Soldier – Bricks laid upright

Soleplate – The timber upon which a timber frame is erected/the bottom rail of a timber frame

Solum – The ground or concrete beneath the floor

Spar – A rafter or top member of a roof

Sparks – An electrician

Sparking – Carrying out the electrical works

Spoil – Waste or unwanted material or subsoil

Spread – A plasterer

Stretcher – A brick showing its longer face

Studding/studwork – Walling made from vertical sections of timber

Spreading – The act of plastering

Square – All angles and planes at 90 degrees

Stile – The vertical section of a door frame

Strap – Metal used to fix two items together

Stringer – The covering timber section up the run of staircase flights

Tabled verge – Where the gable wall is taken above the roof level and capped

Tack/tacking – To fix plasterboard

Tamp – Smoothing off concrete using a length of timber

Tanking – The act of making waterproof

Template – Pattern

Transom – The horizontal section or division within a window

Trenchfill – Filling the foundation trenches almost to the top with concrete

Torching – Lime mortar pointing or bedding to tiles or slates

Torus – A moulding shape

Tosh – To nail at an angle

Trimmer – A joist that receives and supports other joists

Truss – A sectional roof component

Underpin – To reinforce foundations by digging out beneath them and filling the void with concrete

Valley – The sloping junction between the internal angles of two roof planes

Universal beam – An 'I'-shaped steel joist

Verge – The edge of the roof at the gable

Wallplate – Longitudinal timber fixed to the top of a wall to take joists or trusses

Weepers – Perforated land drains

Weepholes – Holes left in walling to allow the egress of moisture

INDEX